Spitalfields

The History of a Nation in a Handful of Streets

DAN CRUICKSHANK

WINDMILL BOOKS

1 3 5 7 9 10 8 6 4 2

Windmill Books
20 Vauxhall Bridge Road
London SW1V 2SA

Windmill Books is part of the Penguin Random House group of companies
whose addresses can be found at global.penguinrandomhouse.com

Penguin
Random House
UK

First published in Great Britain by Random House Books in 2016
First published in paperback by Windmill Books in 2017

www.penguin.co.uk

A CIP catalogue record for this book is available from the British Library.

ISBN 9780099559092

Typeset in 9.49/12.54 pt ACaslon by Jouve (UK), Milton Keynes
Printed and bound in Great Britain by Clays Ltd, St Ives Plc

CONTENTS

PREFACE

This book has been many years in its conception and nearly a decade in its execution. I first got to know Spitalfields well in the early 1970s, when I started to explore its then generally desolate and abandoned streets, and to photograph its decaying historic buildings that, it seemed at the time, stood very little chance of survival. In the mid 1970s a group of friends and I became involved in a campaign to attempt to stop what seemed its inevitable obliteration, forming the still-thriving Spitalfields Historic Buildings Trust in 1976. The idea to write this book emerged gradually, partly as a result of research undertaken during many, often desperate and hard-fought conservation campaigns, and partly as a result of buying an early-eighteenth-century Spitalfields house nearly forty years ago, and then repairing and living in it. Also, strange as it might seem, my desire – indeed obsession – to explore in detail the history on my own doorstep has been stimulated by years of writing about architecture around the world. It's easy to be entranced by remote and distant places, but it gradually dawned on me that the architectural, social and cultural history of Spitalfields is as rich and as extraordinary as that found in more apparently exotic locations.

There have been many detailed and very useful books written on the buildings of Spitalfields. But I still feel there is room for another, particularly one that seeks to tell the area's extraordinary story in the wider context of the nation's history. And relating that story seems especially urgent now, since Spitalfields is on the cusp of dramatic and speedy change that could result in its special character being erased and our ability to imagine its past vastly reduced.

I have been fortunate, over the years, to have met many remarkable, sometimes unlikely, people with Spitalfields stories to tell. I have also received generous assistance from a wide range of historians, archaeologists, librarians and London chroniclers who have proved endlessly willing to share their insights and discoveries. My friends and neighbours, too, have helped me, invariably indulging my curiosity by making their historic homes available – on an almost regular basis – for minute scrutiny.

I'd like to thank the following – some, sadly, no longer living – without whom this book would not have been possible in its published form. First there is the team from Museum of London Archaeology (MOLA) – notably Chiz Harwood, Nigel Jeffries and Chris Thomas – whom I first met during the 1990s when they were excavating the site of the north precinct of the former Spitalfields Priory and the Old Artillery Ground and to whom I am most grateful for their generosity in sharing and explaining their discoveries. Their 2015 publication, *The Spitalfields Suburb, 1539–c.1880*, is a truly outstanding publication that, along with the 1957 *Survey of London* volume dealing with 'Spitalfields and Mile End New Town', has proved to be one of my 'Bibles' during the process of researching and writing this book. I also want to give special acknowledgement to the support and insights over the decades that I have received from my colleagues on the Spitalfields Trust, notably Colin Amery, Douglas Blain, Andrew Byrne, Francis Carnwath, John Chesshyre, Mark Girouard, Charles Gledhill, Gareth Harris, Marianna Kennedy (whom I'd also like to thank for her generosity in allowing me to reproduce Marshall Sisson's 1920s photographs of long-lost houses on the Old Artillery Ground), Barra Little, Ian Lumley, Richard MacCormac, Elizabeth and Peter McKay, William Palin, Caroline Roughton, Patrick Streeter, Tim Whittaker and Oliver Leigh-Wood.

Special thanks also to Stefan Dickers at the Bishopsgate Institute for the help he has given me with my research; Sandra Esqulant for her tireless enthusiasm and generosity of spirit; Marenka Gabeler for her photographs and selfless support through the years; the 'Gentle Author', creator of the informative *Spitalfields Life* website, who has shared information with me in a most generous manner and guided me to fruitful areas of research; Gilbert and George – long-term residents of Fournier Street who have repaired two houses in exemplary manner and allowed me to benefit from their discoveries; Peter Guillery for his pioneering work on the humble Georgian buildings of Spitalfields and Bethnal Green; Robin Gwynn for information about Huguenot Spitalfields; James Howett, who has made – and shared – many remarkable discoveries about the history and buildings of Spitalfields; Phillip Lucas for information about the eighteenth-century home and its fittings; Jerry White, an old Spitalfields friend, whose extensive and scholarly writing on eighteenth- and nineteenth-century London – and on the Rothschild Buildings in particular – have provided me with insights and essential information; Sarah Wise to whom I am indebted for her pioneering work on life in the nineteenth-century East End; and Bella and Alexander Cruickshank who have given me the determination to complete what seemed, at times, a most daunting project.

Thanks also to: Ben Adler, Geoffrey Archer, Nick Barratt, Mary Bayliss, Jenny and Oliver Black, Neil Burton, Dave Chesterton, Kevan Collins, Basil Comely, Adam Dant, Paul Gazerwitz, Mariga Guinness, Julian Harrap, Nick Hedges, Julian Humphries, Jocasta Innes, Eleanor Jones, Theo Jones, Santokh Kaulder, Tarik Khan, Martin Lane, Chris Legg, Pat Llewellyn, David Milne, John Nicholson, Heloise Palin, Olga Pavlova, Marco Pensa, Hugh Petter, Lisa Reardon, Raphael Samuel, Dennis Severs, Susie Symes, Taylor Thomson, Christine Waite, Charlie de Wet, Jeanette Winterson, Donna de Wit, Peter Wyld, and Simon Young.

Finally I thank my agents Charles Walker and Christian Ogunbanjo, and my publisher Nigel Wilcockson for his unwavering and cheerful support and skilled transformation of a vast and unruly manuscript into a finished book, a task in which he has been ably assisted by Rowan Borchers and Lynn Curtis.

Dan Cruickshank
Elder Street, Spitalfields
September 2016

The history of Spitalfields is a direct and dramatic echo of the history of London, even of England. Great and pivotal events and characters that have shaped the nation during the last 2,000 years have left their mark here, while the area's strategic location next to one of the great roads – Roman in origin or earlier – which helped connect London to the rest of the country, ensured that it played a constant part in the history of the nation as a whole. Known as Ermine Street, the road passed along the route of what is now Bishopsgate to Lincoln and then York.

Spitalfields has witnessed such tumultuous events as the Reformation of the 1530s, the Civil War of the 1640s and the waves of immigration from the late seventeenth century onwards that transformed London's character and its patterns of life, trade and manufacturing. Virtually everything of significance that happened in London in the centuries after 1530 had a profound influence upon life and architecture in Spitalfields – in some cases, indeed, these epoch-making events had their origin in the area.

Spitalfields possesses an extraordinary vitality. It is continually transforming and evolving. Walking its streets can be spellbinding – there is continuity but also change and ever present are the shades of the past. This means the streets of Spitalfields are full of ghosts – of houses, of people, of events – almost visible and tangible once you know their histories. Spitalfields is a place so poignant and evocative that even its least promising byways or alleys can prove unexpectedly moving, with the forms of long-lost buildings and those who worked and dwelt in them rearing up in the shadows of the imagination.

An astonishing number of people who played a key role in the development of British culture, and who helped to hone the nation's distinct character, lived, worked or frolicked in or near Spitalfields. These include playwrights and actors such as William Shakespeare, Christopher

Marlowe, Richard Burbage and Edward Alleyn; writers Sir Francis Bacon and Mary Wollstonecraft; herbalist and astrologer Nicholas Culpeper; architects and developers Nicholas Hawksmoor and Nicholas Barbon; diarist Samuel Pepys; aristocrats including the 2nd Earl of Devonshire and the 3rd Earl of Bolingbroke; and the brewers Joseph and Benjamin Truman.

And then, as well as these familiar names, there were the industrious Huguenot business entrepreneurs and families – the Ogiers, Dalbiacs and Bourdons – who from the early 1680s started to make Spitalfields a thriving merchants' quarter; the Irish journeymen who from the 1720s made Spitalfields their home; and the Jewish and Asian migrants who followed in their footsteps. In addition there were the less desirable denizens of Spitalfields, who made their names through dark and criminal activities, the early-eighteenth-century housebreaker Jack Sheppard and the late-nineteenth-century serial killer Jack the Ripper among them. Observing and chronicling so many of these people were a host of philanthropists, social reformers and novelists, who included among their number Daniel Defoe, Charles Dickens, Charles Booth, Israel Zangwill and Jack London.

Spitalfields also saw the early stirrings of movements that have done much to shape modern Britain. In the 1760s the journeymen weavers of Spitalfields, Bethnal Green and Shoreditch organised themselves in well-disciplined 'combinations' to protect – in most militant manner – their employment and livelihoods. The protest movement related to trade and industry rather than to politics directly, but in its scale, management, determination, aims and Luddite tendencies, it was radical and potentially revolutionary. It can also be seen as an early prototype of the trade union movement.

Later, as Spitalfields slid into grinding poverty, philanthropists took the stage, helping those struggling at the bottom of the heap with such enterprises as the Quaker-organised Spitalfields Soup Society of 1797, and also establishing the principles by which concerned private individuals could, in the absence of adequate or appropriate parish or public aid, organise and fund 'relief' for the poor.

As well as sustenance for the body there was also, locally, a concern for sustaining the mind. Learned institutions – such as mathematical and ornithological societies – flourished among the weaving community throughout the eighteenth century and, in their encouragement of self-improvement through study, provided a model for the Mechanics' Institute

movement of the early decades of the following century. They also anticipated the arguments of Samuel Smiles – the great mid-nineteenth-century
champion of 'self-help' – who said:

> Knowledge is of itself one of the highest enjoyments. The ignorant man
> passes through the world dead to all pleasures, save those of the senses . . .
> Every human being has a great mission to perform, noble faculties to cul-
> tivate, a vast destiny to accomplish. He should have the means of education,
> and of exerting freely all the powers of his godlike nature.[1]

Today Spitalfields is not just a rich repository of memory and an epitome
of London history, it is also a crucible within which a vision of the city of
the future is being forged. As I write this book the fate of the area hangs
in the balance. Despite its popular status as an historic quarter, with
streets of houses listed as being of historic or architectural interest and
large Conservation Areas, Spitalfields is now also viewed as a prime development opportunity. A series of large schemes are either proposed or else
already under construction for sites within Spitalfields or on its fringes,
and these will fundamentally transform its appearance and its ways of life,
ushering in high-rise living and large slabs of commercial space. I set out
to document a fascinating area, with a 2,000-year history that is, in a
sense, characterised by change. But the scale and nature of the changes
now proposed mean that Spitalfields could soon be transformed beyond
recognition. This book, which I started nearly ten years ago as a celebration of Spitalfields, may well turn out to be its valediction.

WHERE AND WHAT IS SPITALFIELDS?

The physical boundaries of the area are strangely hard to define. Spitalfields was the name that by the mid sixteenth century had been bestowed
on former monastic lands or fields on the north-east edge of London, near
Bishopgate-without-the-wall. The area belonged from around 1197 until
the Reformation of the 1530s to the Augustinian Priory or 'Hospital' of St
Mary that marks, by tradition, the heart of Spitalfields. It is this that is
designated 'The Spitel' on London's earliest surviving map – the so-called
'Copperplate' map of c.1553 – and 'The Spitel Fyeld' on the 'Agas' map of
c.1562, and 'The Spitel Fields' on Braun and Hogenberg's map of 1572. And

so, in colloquial manner, the fields around St Mary's Hospital became known as Spital Fields.

In the late sixteenth century most of Spitalfields was in the huge parish of St Dunstan's Stepney, but with key portions being administered by two small, self-governing Liberties. These, the Liberty of the Old Artillery Ground and the Liberty of Norton Folgate, seem – broadly – to have been formed after the Reformation to govern the former monastic land of St Mary's Hospital that had been extra-parochial, that is to say outside the ecclesiastical parish system. Small, peripheral portions of Spitalfields also fell within the parishes bordering St Dunstan's and the Liberties, with parts of north Spitalfields being in the parish of St Leonard's Shoreditch, and portions of south Spitalfields in the parishes of St Botolph's Bishopsgate, St Botolph's Aldgate and St Mary Matfelon, Whitechapel. What's clear is that, historically, Spitalfields was more a state of mind, an idea or perception, than a geographic locality. Its borders were permeable – expanding and contracting at different times – with further complexity added when in 1690 Mile End New Town was constituted a separate and largely self-governing hamlet of 'handicraft tradesmen' within the parish of St Dunstan's. Daniel Defoe makes it clear that, at times, Spitalfields was the generic name for East London's weaving and artisan quarter. In his *Journal of the Plague Year* of 1722 he writes of the 'parishes of Shoreditch, Stepney, Whitechapel and Bishopsgate . . . that is to say . . . Spitalfields'.[2] Following this, in 1729 the parish of Christ Church Spitalfields and in 1743 the parish of St Matthew's Bethnal Green were carved out of St Dunstan's.[3] Mile End New Town is the part of Spitalfields that stretches east from Brick Lane to Vallance Road and from Buxton Street in the north to Old Montague Street in the south. Its ancient heart was the High Street, now part of Greatorex Street.[4] It is the stories of these districts, Liberties and parishes that form the heart of this book.

George Dodd, who in the 1850s worked with Charles Dickens on the weekly journal *Household Words*, confirmed the difficulty of defining the physical boundaries of Spitalfields and suggested its identity was, for most Londoners of his time, linked to the traditionally dominant trade of the area – silk weaving. As he put it in the 1842 book *London*, on which he collaborated with Charles Knight:

> Spitalfields . . . parish contains a small portion only of the silk-weavers and
> it is probably that . . . most persons apply the term Spitalfields to the whole

district where the weavers reside [and] in this enlarged acceptation, we will
lay down something like a boundary in the following manner – begin at
Shoreditch Church and proceed along the Hackney Rd till it is intersected
by Regent's Canal, follow the course of the canal to Mile End Rd and then
proceed westward through Whitechapel to Aldgate, through Houndsditch
to Bishopsgate, and thence northward to where the tour commenced . . .
the entire district is frequently called Spitalfields . . . .[5]

Dodd admitted that this conception of Spitalfields included 'large portions of Bethnal Green, Shoreditch, Whitechapel and Mile End New
Town'. He also emphasised a fact that would have seemed strange to many
Londoners in the 1840s. Despite the district's then notorious overcrowding, poverty and squalor, 'the larger portion of this extensive district was
open fields until comparatively modern times. Bethnal Green was really a
green and Spitalfields was covered with grassy sward in the last century.'

For most people today, Spitalfields is defined by Bishopsgate to the
west, Bethnal Green Road to the north and Wentworth Street/Old Montague Street to the south, while to the east it has no firmly defined
boundary but merges gradually with Bethnal Green and Whitechapel in
the small streets and open spaces between Brick Lane and Vallance Road.
I have taken a generous view of its precise extent, allowing myself on occasion to look beyond these somewhat arbitrary limits.

A close reading of the book will reveal the topographical complexities
that can potentially lead to confusion on occasion. Over the centuries
street names have changed – often more than once – and their spelling has
frequently been fluid. White Lyon Yard, for example, became the west
end of White Lyon Street, then became White Lyon Street and is now
Folgate Street. The streets themselves have altered their physical form,
many over time being entirely or almost entirely obliterated, others emerging quite late. And house numbers, which only came into use from the
very late eighteenth century, were radically revised in the late nineteenth
century. My policy has been to give both old and new versions of street
names and house numbers when relevant, and to put old names and the
names of streets that no longer exist in inverted commas.

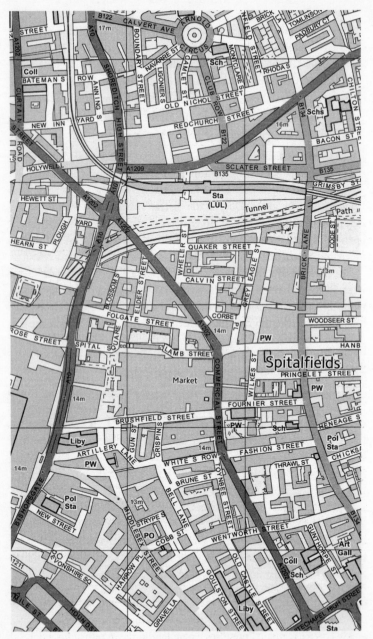

Spitalfields in 2014.

THE GOLDEN HEART OF SPITALFIELDS

The Golden Heart stands on the corner of Hanbury Street and Commercial Street, not too far from the mighty Christ Church, designed by Nicholas Hawksmoor and completed in 1729 as the new parish church. The Golden Heart marks the physical heart of Spitalfields, but for many of the people who now live and work in the area it also marks something more difficult to define than the area's boundaries. It is – like many pubs – a place where people's lives overlap and where, on occasion, they mesh together in unexpected ways.

There has been a pub on this site since the portion of Commercial Street on which it stands was cut through Spitalfields between 1849 and 1857. But there could have been a tavern or pub here for centuries – or at least very nearby – because Commercial Street, when it was constructed, sliced through an already populated area, while Hanbury Street, known earlier as 'Browns Lane', is one of the most ancient streets in the East End.[1] At any rate, by 1821 an establishment known as the Golden Harp stood very near the site of the existing pub. It was presumably so named to attract the area's Irish-born population. A few years later, in 1837, the Golden Harp became the Golden Heart.

Given the popularity since medieval times of the inn name the White Hart (after Richard II's emblem), it's not clear why this particular pub should have become the Golden Heart rather than the Golden Hart. Nor is it entirely clear why a change of name should have been decided upon in the first place. It is possible, though, that the renaming had something to do with the passing of the Beerhouse Act of 1830. Designed to improve the quality of beer through competition, and to reduce public drunkenness in the street or at disreputable, unlicensed drinking dens, the act introduced a new type of regulated premises where landlords, in return for a one-off payment of two guineas, could brew and sell beer and cider, both of which were regarded at that time as relatively harmless drinks – safer than water and less lethal than spirits such as gin (low-alcohol 'small beer' was thought suitable for children). Perhaps the then landlord of the Golden Harp, aiming for an air of respectability amid this new legislation, thought it best to move away from a name that, to many, might have suggested a premises full of carousing and boisterous Irish journeymen or market porters. The Golden Heart sounded safe, reassuring and welcoming.

By 1860 a new pub had been constructed on the recently created Commercial Street, set back a little from its predecessor and occupying what was now a prominent corner site. This building is recorded in old photographs. It was handsome, with a shallow quadrant front following the line of the street, with three closely spaced windows on the first and second floors and a ground floor with three doors – presumably leading to three separate bars – and two windows. The 1861 census reveals that the 'victualler' of this new 'Golden Heart' was sixty-year-old Joseph Jacobs, who occupied the pub with his wife, four children and a servant.

The Golden Heart that exists today was constructed by Truman, Hanbury and Buxton in 1934–6, almost adjacent to its Brick Lane-based Black Eagle Brewery. It was one of a new generation of 'reformed' pubs intended to be not just liquor saloons but convivial retreats that would attract a greater number and a wider mix of customers, including middle-class drinkers, families, and even respectable female customers unaccompanied by men. Such venues generally included restaurants, function rooms and – wherever possible – gardens. But the niceties of the class structure were also preserved. So these 'reformed' pubs continued to incorporate the fundamental division between the public bar, intended for working men, and the saloon bar where the bosses would drink and in which beer and spirits would be a few pence more expensive.

The preferred architectural styles for this new breed of pub were neo-Tudor and neo-Georgian, which of course expressed solid, old-world values; and the Golden Heart, despite its cramped urban site where a garden was simply not an option, epitomises the social and artistic aspirations of the 'reformed', inter-war public house. It was designed by Arthur Edward Sewell, Truman's principal architect and surveyor throughout the inter-war period, in a somewhat idiosyncratic, but distinguished, neo-Georgian style. The importance of the pub, on a key and very visible site just across the road from the brewery, is made immediately apparent by its well-considered design and by the materials used in its construction.

The frontage – slightly wider than its 1860s predecessor's – has an unusual and striking form. Its entrances and architectural features are set within a bevelled tripartite elevation, which is a spirited response to the curving or wedge-shaped site. The central portion of the elevation is clad with expensive Portland stone and with a pediment at first-floor level. All very imposing. Above the stone elevation is an early – perhaps original – neon sign proclaiming 'Truman's', in splendid contrast to the stone-wrought classicism over which it presides. But the neon is not the elevation's only Art Deco flourish. There is also faience tiling, originally cream-coloured but now over-painted, that incorporates typical Art Deco geometric fluting framing the doors. The pair of elevations flanking the stone centre are each faced with fine red brick, and in their details – such as keystones – are evidently a considered response by Sewell to the early-eighteenth-century silk merchants' houses that, in the late 1930s, stood near the Golden Heart in Hanbury Street and Spital Square. Now most of these early buildings have gone, leaving the pub somewhat marooned in a sea of banal architecture and ever more intense traffic.

Inside the Golden Heart there are now currently two bars. The one entered from Hanbury Street is the more intimate. Still retaining its panelling and some original benches, it was the most exclusive of the pub's original five rooms – the realm of the area's leading citizens. Beyond it – separated by a now long-lost screen – was the saloon dining room or lounge, where families perhaps could have taken Sunday lunch or women could have relaxed in discreet and respectable isolation. This room would have been very small, and somewhat dark – the only natural light would have come through a roof lantern – and sitting within it could never have been very peaceful for the ladies' and gentlemen's lavatories are accessed from it. But it would have been genteel in appearance, with panelled walls and a large – and thankfully surviving – Arts and Crafts-style arched brick fireplace. Food cooked in the kitchen above was delivered via a dumb waiter. The saloon bar and dining room were united many years ago, but the room as it is now constituted feels like the heart of the Heart. On its walls hang photographs of people who live or work in Spitalfields, many of them artists of international repute – Gilbert and George, Tracey Emin, Michael Landy, Gillian Wearing.

The door on Commercial Street leads into what was the public bar. This room retains dado-rail-height panelling and advertising slogans extolling some of Truman's more popular tipples in the 1930s – 'Eagle Ale' and 'Eagle Stout'. Beyond it there would once have been the 'tap' or off-licence and the dining room for the pub's less choosy customers. The door in the centre of the pub's elevation – now blocked – led to a small 'private bar' or snug that, screened from the public bar by a baffle, would most likely have been used by women wanting a quiet half-pint of stout and a cigarette. All these spaces have now been subsumed into one, their former existence marked by three brick-made fireplaces (a couple of which are embellished with carvings of Truman's Black Eagle emblem) – one for each room.[2]

I moved into my house in Spitalfields in 1977, the same year that Sandra and Dennis Esqulant took over the Golden Heart, and we soon became friends. Sadly Dennis died in 2009, but Sandra continues to run the Golden Heart with tremendous energy and enthusiasm. She is naturally generous, with a genuine belief in the beneficial power of friendship, and we sometimes sit in the heart of the Golden Heart, talking of Spitalfields past and present, of the living and the dead, of things that have been, that are and that might be.

We talk, for example, of the strange array of characters who occupied the area before the great watershed of 1991 when the ancient fruit, vegetable and flower retail market closed. While it was going strong the market transformed night into day, with pubs – granted special licences – and cafés thriving in the small hours, serving drinks and vast dinners to lorry drivers and market workers while wholesalers and shop owners arrived to buy their daily stocks. The Golden Heart was then a market pub and, like most market-related establishments, attracted not just local workers and visitors to the area but also society's outsiders, who were drawn to the nocturnal life of Spitalfields and the sense of liberty that pervades all great markets. I remember the prostitutes who eased the lives of the hard-driving hauliers transporting fruit from Spain, flowers from the Netherlands or vegetables from the north. They gathered on the corners of streets leading to the market – at Fournier Street next to Christ Church, along Commercial Street – chatting to the lorry drivers with good humour, occasionally asking me, as I made my way home in the early hours of the morning, if I 'wanted business, darlin''. And I remember the piles of debris created by the market on a daily basis: the heaps of timber pallets, the abandoned crates of fruit and vegetables that seemed, to my inexpert eye, without blemish. I collected and burnt the pallets, which kept me warm as I repaired my house in Elder Street, and I ate the fruit and vegetables and took pleasure from bunches of discarded flowers. And I was not the only one.

The market helped to support a truly remarkable community of men and women. Once they would have been called 'tramps' (but most of them tramped nowhere) or 'down and outs' – certainly more accurate – or derelicts. I have no idea what they should be called – but I know their like no longer exists. Many were ragged, grimy, aged, eccentric, fiercely individual and independent – people who must have seen and suffered things beyond the comprehension or imagination of most. They gathered on corners at night, warming themselves in the early-morning light with huge fires, kindled from pallets, papers and any other available combustible debris. I remember they particularly favoured the corner of Brushfield Street and what had been Steward Street, in the heart of the market area, where they lingered against a backdrop of long-decayed or derelict late-eighteenth-century houses, like animations from the drawings of Hogarth. Such vivid images of outcast London were spellbinding and brought the mean streets of the past to life with an intensity and authenticity that it is now hard to imagine and impossible to see in the new, brittle, commercial and consumer-orientated Spitalfields, with its array of chain stores and ersatz 'Victorian-style' lamps and bollards. Much of the fabric and paraphernalia of life in the area is now fake, many of its historic houses ruthlessly 'made-over' and modernised. But – forty or so years ago – things were very different.

As far as I can remember Spitalfields' destitute street characters never begged for money. Possibly they were too proud, or perhaps they just took the basics they needed – food and wood from the street, companionship from each other. Sandra too remembers many of these transient characters. Some would occasionally sneak into the pub for refuge, to watch television – she recalls the BBC's current affairs programme *Panorama* was a favourite – and she of course would end up buying drinks for these penniless people. Sandra confirms that they never begged for money, but she recalls they would occasionally borrow £5 and then scrupulously pay it back, usually from the proceeds of erecting stalls in Petticoat Lane market. Some would offer to help out at the pub in lieu of repayment, collecting glasses and ashtrays, but unused to the niceties of civilised life they would as often as not cast the ash upon the floor and create more chaos than order.

There was 'Big Jean' who was – Sandra insists – given to drinking Esso Blue (something that seems hardly possible given that more than a few mouthfuls of this deadly paraffin would kill most people, or, at least, turn them blind). 'Big Jean' must have been made of heroic stuff. She was regularly purged by the Catholic nuns in the mid-nineteenth-century shelter in Crispin Street, a place that has seen many desperate cases through the years, and would just as regularly return to her inebriated and unpredictable ways. Then there was 'Cat Woman', a mesmerising prostitute, and Elaine, who ran the all-night food van outside Christ Church and who was famed for her massive bacon and egg rolls known as – no one can now say why – 'cowboys'.

And Sandra remembers – as do I – the lost peoples of East End life. We recall, for example, the families of Irish tinkers who arrived in due season to sell Christmas trees in the market. They would gather in large and extended family groups in the Golden Heart – women in one bar and men in the other – and drink through the long hours of the night and early morning, enjoying the pub's liberal market licence. We also cast our minds back to the last days of Spitalfields' Jewish community that as recently as the 1930s had occupied nearly all the streets and courts around Wentworth Street and Old Montague Street. By the late 1970s almost all of them had gone, leaving the odd bakery or hardware shop in Brick Lane, a delicatessen in Petticoat Lane and Bloom's Restaurant in Aldgate. Just two of Spitalfields' once numerous synagogues – those in Fournier Street and in Sandys Row – remained open. Now only the Sandys Row synagogue continues in operation as a living reminder of a once vibrant community.

Sandra and I also consider the future, and try to imagine a neighbourhood that may soon be as remote from the Spitalfields of today as contemporary Spitalfields is from the East London of the Huguenot weavers. Spitalfields has always been a place of change, but in recent years the changes have been so great and rapid that it seems little of the old locality will be left: just a handful of early-Georgian buildings clustered around Christ Church and the junction of Folgate Street and Elder Street, and memories that are fast fading. Even as I write a block of eighteenth-, nineteenth- and twentieth-century buildings between Blossom Street and the section of Ermine Street named Norton Folgate is threatened with demolition. If this happens yet one more portion of Spitalfields will have gone, and a rich mix of buildings – small-scale and on a site on which Londoners have lived and worked for at least 2,000 years – will have given way to corporate-style schemes, incorporating open-plan commercial space and rising as high as fourteen storeys behind some pathetic fragments of retained brick façades and a few interiors.

This book – among other things – celebrates lost and disappearing worlds.

PART ONE

A WORLD OF OUTSIDERS

From Roman Times to the Great Fire of London

THE LAND OF THE DEAD

Roman and Medieval Spitalfields

Nearly 2,000 years ago the area that became known as Spitalfields lay immediately to the north-east of Londinium, just outside the city wall and east of Ermine Street. Londinium had been founded, some time soon after AD 43, on high land rising just above the unpromising marsh-land bordering the wide and meandering Thames. The site was well suited to the ambitions of its Roman settlers – it lay next to a navigable river that formed a trade and military connection to the wider world at a place where that river could be bridged. It thus lay astride a waterway and a road that linked the useful harbour of Dover in the south to Roman settlements north of the Thames.

By the beginning of the first century AD, Londinium had become not just a trading and administrative settlement but the capital of the Roman province of Britannia, and by AD 250 or so the boundary that was to define the heart of London for the coming millennia had been drawn. The Roman wall – masonry built and moated magnificently – stretched from a hill in the east, later to be known as Tower Hill, to Ludgate Hill and the River Fleet in the west, and from the banks of the Thames inland for three-quarters of a kilometre or so. There was a substantial suburb south of the Thames, along the Dover Road, and some small scatterings of buildings on the north bank beyond the wall. The River Walbrook flowed through the heart of the city, from the north to the Thames, with the Temple of Mithras, built in the mid third century, and the Governor's Palace on its east bank. To the west of the Walbrook was the early-second-century amphitheatre, a bath complex and the large Cripplegate Fort. Between the River Walbrook and Tower Hill there was the predictable orthogonal grid of streets – with the second-century forum and its vast basilica at their centre – which connected ultimately to the city's six gates including one, later known as Bishopsgate, that stood astride Ermine Street.

Roman law prohibited the burial of bodies or funerary urns within towns and cities so the fields and roadsides outside the wall of Londinium became the land of the dead. Here remains could be interred decently and hygienically and the dead honoured through appropriate memorials. Roman London had four main cemeteries that remained in use until Rome abandoned Britain in AD 410: first, from the late first century AD, to the west (just beyond Newgate next to the road to Silchester); to the south in Southwark (next to the Dover road); to the east in Aldgate (next to what is now the Minories); and finally, from the mid third century AD, just beyond Londinium's main north-east gate. This great north cemetery occupied fields to either side of Ermine Street, but with most burials being to the east of the road, perhaps because of associations with sunrise and rebirth. (Before this large cemetery was begun burial on the north edge of the city took place on the banks of the Walbrook from the late first century AD, on the site of what is now Finsbury Circus.)

As the north cemetery came into use Londinium was occupied by fewer people than 150 or so years previously, when the population of the rough and ready frontier trading town was probably as high as 50,000. By the end of the second century AD the population could have been as low as 20,000, but the residents were more cultured and wealthier.[1] The elevated status of the residents of second- and third-century Londinium is revealed by excavations of burials from the period.

Roman funerary monuments, like those that still survive beside the Via Appia outside Rome and along the roads leading from Pompeii, served to ensure that the names of the lofty dead would greet, inspire, and linger in the memories of the living as they thronged the great roads of the Empire. Londinium, too, would have had its fine funerary edifices, as is suggested by the 2013 discovery on the site of the eastern cemetery of a sixty-five-centimetre imperial eagle, carved out of Cotswold limestone in about AD 200, depicted clutching a serpent in its beak to symbolise immortality and power – clearly part of a large memorial to a once mighty man. Such exuberant funerary monuments must have lined Ermine Street, too, marking the final resting place for cremated ashes in urns or bodies placed in coffins and stone sarcophagi accompanied with grave-goods for use in the journey to the Underworld and afterlife.[2] Inhumation tended to become more common from the late first century, possibly in response to an increasing belief in an afterlife achieved through the resurrection of the body, inspired by Middle Eastern religions such as the Persian Mithraic mystery cult and then from the fourth century onward by Christianity. At the same time, inhumation offered an opportunity to honour the dead through rich offerings and, perhaps, burial ritual and the insulation of the body in sanctified earth was seen as a way to prevent the dead from haunting the living.

The landscape around Ermine Street was, it seems, sacred to the late Romans and Romano-British just as later it would be to Anglo-Norman Christians. Its location just outside the city wall made it a legitimate and convenient place for burial. But was there another reason why this was designated holy ground? There is evidence of local springs. Perhaps a small tributary of the Walbrook meandered through the fields around Ermine Street. This could have been enough to transform the terrain, in Roman imagination, into the marshy hinterland of the emblematic Acheron – the 'River of Woe' and source of the Styx – across which the newly dead were supposedly ferried by Charon to enter the Underworld.

During excavations in the late 1990s of part of the north cemetery, on the western edge of Spitalfields, around 150 Roman graves and two cremation urns were found. For the most part these were not particularly well preserved, and most contained people of humble status. But there was one notable exception that reveals the grandeur of late-Roman London. In a lead coffin set within a limestone sarcophagus – and perhaps once marked by a striking stone monument – was found the body of a wealthy young woman, whose burial shrouds included fabrics made of silk and gold thread. Artefacts found within the sarcophagus suggest that she died around AD 400, and she appears not to have been a Christian. Recent research has revealed lead content in her bones characteristic of a native of Rome. We know little else about her, but it is intriguing to think that only a decade or so before Roman legions were withdrawn from Britannia, Rome-born citizens of high birth were still coming to Londinium, perhaps to visit or oversee the estates that remained in their possession even as the empire receded. Or perhaps they were even still settling in the city. It suggests that the end – when it came – was dramatic and largely unexpected.

Tantalising brief and partial evocations of the Spitalfields Roman dead are offered by fragmentary memorials that have, over the decades, been found on the site of the cemetery. These give names, ages and sometimes occupations, but little else. For example in 1922 a slab measuring 34 x 26.5 centimetres was found off Bishopsgate. It commemorated 'Sempronius

Sempronianus, centurion of the [erased] Legion, aged fifty-one, and his brothers Sempronius . . . and Sempronius Secundus.' The memorial, now in the Museum of London, was erected by Sempronius Sempronianus's freedmen to honour their 'well-deserving patrons'.

A more vivid portrait of the ritual and artefacts of Roman death is offered by John Stow, who described the first large-scale excavation, admittedly inadvertent and most brutal, of the great north cemetery. Stow, who was born in about 1525 in Cornhill in the City, was a merchant tailor but later kept a shop near Aldgate pump. An amateur topographer with a love of London – its customs, traditions and history – he was also a pioneering antiquarian who looked not just at documents, tombs, paintings, churches and great buildings but at everyday, humble, even mouldering objects. For him these were things of wonder and full of interest. He seemed to like nothing better than to visit demolition sites or excavations in and around London, to see what might turn up and to document what he saw. Even in the 1570s London was still small enough for one man, with energy and commitment, to walk all its streets and get to know them well, and that's just what Stow did. His walks, explorations and discoveries formed the basis of his *Survey of London*, published first in 1598 and soon reissued in 1603. In the late 1570s his wanderings took him to Spitalfields where ancient and curious objects were being unearthed. To the east of the former priory churchyard, he noted in his *Survey*:

> . . . lieth a large field, of the olde time called Lolesworth, now Spittle field; which about the year 1576 was broken vp for Clay to make Bricke; in the digging whereof many earthen pots, called Vrnae, were found full of Ashes, and burnt bones of men, to wit, of the Romanes that inhabited here.

He observed that:

> . . . euerie [one] of these pots has in them with the Ashes of the dead, one peece of Copper mony, with the inscription of the Emperour then raigning: some of them were of Claudius, some of Vespasian, some of Nero, of Anthoninus Pius, of Traianus, and others: besides those Vrnas, many other pots were there found, made of a white earth with long neck, and handels, like to our stone Iugges: these were emptie, but seemed to be buried ful of some liquid matter long since consumed and soaked through: for there were found diuerse vials and other fashioned Glasses . . . [some of which] had Oyle in the verie thicke, and earthie in sauour, some were supposed to

haue balm in them, but has lost the vertue: many of those pots and glasses were broken in cutting of the clay, so that few were taken vp whole.

Interestingly, if Stow is correct about the coins, and if they date the burials with which they were associated, then they reveal that the north cemetery was in use from the mid first century AD – like the other city cemeteries – and well before the time suggested by more recent archaeological evidence. Stow also listed among the finds made in 1576:

> . . . diuerse dishes and cups of a fine red coloured earth, which shewed outwardly such a shining smoothnesse, as is they had beene of Curall, those had in the bottomes Romane letters printed, there were also lampes of white earth and red, artificially wrought with diuerse antiques about them, some three or foure Images made of white earth, about a span long each of them: one I remember was of Pallas, the rest I haue forgotten.

He also revealed his collector's instinct:

> I my selfe haue reserued amongst diuerse of those antiquities there, one Vrna, with the Ashes and bones, and one pot of white earth very small, not exceeding the quaintitie of a quarter of a wine pint, made in shape of a Hare, squatted vpon her legs, and betweene her eares is the mouth of the pot.

Stow came to the conclusion that not all the burials dated from Roman times:

> There hath also beene found in the same field diuers coffins of stone, containing the bones of men: these I suppose to bee the burials of some especiall persons, in time of the Brytons or Saxons, after the Romanes had left to gouerne here. Moreouer there were also found the sculls and bones of men without coffins, or rather whose coffins (being of great timber) were consumed. Diuerse great nailes of Iron were there found, such as are vsed in the wheeles of shod Carts, being each of them as bigge as a mans finger, and a quarter of a yard long, the heades two inches ouer, those nayles were more wondred at then the rest of thinges there found, and many opinions of men were there vttred of them, namely that the men there buried were murdered by driuing those nayles into their heads, a thing vnlikely, for a smaller naile would more aptly serue to so bad a purpose, and more secret place would lightly be imployed for their buriall. But to set downe what I haue obserued concerning this matter, I there behelde the bones of a man

lying (as I noted) the heade North, the feete South, and round about him, as thwarted his head, along both his sides, and swart his feete, such nailes were found, wherefore I coniectured them to be the nailes of his coffin, which had beene a trough cut out of some great thicknesse, fastned with such nayles, and therefore I caused some of the nayles to bee reached vp to mee, and found vnder the broad heades of them, the olde wood, skant turned into earth, but still retaining both the graine, and proper colour: of these nayles with the wood vnder the head thereof, I reserued one, as also, the nether iaw bone of the man, the teeth being great, sound and fixed, which amongst other many monuments there found, I haue yet to shew, but the nayle lying drie, is by scaling greatly wasted.[3]

Sadly Stow's collection of antiquities – which must have been extensive and exceedingly interesting – has been lost without trace. His assumption that the cemetery continued to be used into the early Anglo-Saxon period, though, was probably correct. The north–south orientation of the buried would seem to suggest these were the bodies of non-Christians (this orientation was common in Roman burial grounds though; so too was an east–west orientation). Had Stow found remains with the head placed at the west end of the grave and looking east – towards sunrise, Jerusalem and Christ coming at the End of Days – then it would almost certainly have suggested the body was that of a Christian.

The history of Spitalfields after Rome withdrew its protection from Britain in AD 410 is frustratingly vague, and the next 600 years or so are shrouded in obscurity. It would seem that the Roman city was gradually and largely abandoned with, naturally, the great north cemetery rapidly falling into disuse and its graves and monuments left to decay or to the predations of robbers.

It is possible that the western part of the city might have contained administrative and religious areas: St Paul's Cathedral is generally believed to have been established on or near its current site in AD 604 by St Mellitus, a missionary – and later Archbishop of Canterbury – who was sent from Rome to Britain by Pope Gregory I to help St Augustine re-establish Christianity among the pagan Anglo-Saxons. But it also now seems clear that by this point, in the early seventh century, the preferred settlement area for Londoners was to the west of the ruins of the Roman city, on the

Thames near what is now Covent Garden and Aldwych. This area became the Anglo-Saxon trading settlement of Lundenwic – meaning 'London trading town' – that used the River Fleet, over which St Paul's presided, as its protected anchorage.

The Anglo-Saxon attitude to the ancient and brooding remains of Roman Londinium is suggested by an eighth-century poem now known as 'The Ruin'. Generally thought to refer to the heroic remnants of Roman Bath, it offers an insight into the way the vast, well-wrought and solemn – indeed haunting – ruins of Londinium, with its awe-inspiring fortifications, must have struck the superstitious people now settled nearby. The fragments of walls and buildings must have seemed the very image of human transience, and of hubris – mighty works, wrought by seemingly supreme or supernatural beings, laid low by some catastrophe and ravaged by time.

> Wondrous is this stone wall, wrecked by fate;
> The city-buildings crumble, the works of the giants decay.
> Roofs have caved in, towers collapsed,
> Barred gates are broken . . . houses are gaping, tottering and fallen,
> Undermined by age . . . A hundred generations
> Have passed away since then . . .
> The city still moulders, gashed by storms . . .
> . . . fate the mighty altered it. Slaughtered men
> Fell far and wide, the plague-days came,
> Death removed every brave man.
> Their ramparts became abandoned places,
> The city decayed . . .
> The place falls to ruin, shattered
> Into mounds of stone . . .[4]

Much of the fabric of the abandoned Roman city of Londinium nevertheless endured – notably the stone- and brick-built city walls and gates – and this in the late ninth century formed the basis for Alfred the Great's resettlement and refortification of London (now known as Lundenburh) in 886. A strategically and economically vital bridge was almost certainly constructed on the site of the Roman London Bridge. And over time Lundenwic was in turn largely abandoned in favour of the revived city.

One of the key reasons for Alfred's repossession of the ruins of Roman London was to deny them to hostile forces. The strategic importance of the ruins as a military position – due to the scale and preservation of the Roman fortifications and the riverside location – made the old city an attractive target for invaders. In 871 Viking forces had used the city as a fortified camp from which to launch raids into the surrounding area, so it had become clear that whoever held the ancient walled city of London controlled the Thames – a prime highway of invasion – and the region over which London presided. The significance of the city after Alfred's time is confirmed by the unsuccessful attacks mounted on it in 1013 by Sweyn Forkbeard, King of Denmark, who claimed the throne of England (and held it for just forty days), and by the fact that when his son Cnut the Great gained control of London in 1016 he also gained firm and lasting control of all England.

The role of Spitalfields in these stirring and martial events in the history of England is unclear. But located just outside the Roman city wall and next to Ermine Street, it must have a fascinating, if now lost, early-medieval history. Viking raiding parties and invading armies would have tramped through it, and no doubt structures – of ephemeral timber, plaster, and mud – would have lined sections of Ermine Street. But of these no significant physical record has been found. And again the area must have been transformed when, soon after the successful Norman invasion of England in 1066, the conquerors started to build the huge and daunting White Tower, next to the Thames and the Roman city wall and little more than a kilometre to the south of Spitalfields. Such stone-built castles were unknown to the natives of London so the Tower was an intentionally intimidating structure expressing power, permanence and control. It proclaimed that a new order had arrived and that – whether the natives liked it or not – this new order intended to stay.

Spitalfields' own first known – and well recorded – major medieval structure, or rather complex of structures, was built over a century later. The Augustinian Priory of the Blessed Virgin Mary was founded around 1197 by Walter and Roisia Brune or Brown on fields to the east of Ermine Street and just outside the city's Bishopsgate. The land had once been the northern portion of the Roman north cemetery. The Priory of St Mary, as it was commonly known, was for Augustinian canons and lay sisters, and soon established itself as a vital London institution, looking after the sick and distressed, and serving – in particular – as a lying-in hospital for women just before and after they gave birth. The priory and its function as a hospital soon gave a name and identity to the area – its location became known as Spitalfields, meaning the Hospital in the Fields. In the Middle Ages the term hospital – usually abbreviated to 'spitele' – was applied to institutions, almost invariably under religious control, for the reception of the indigent, the ill or of those in need, or which operated as charitable foundations to care for the aged or the incurably diseased, such as lepers.

Walter and his wife Roisia were eminent Londoners – Walter was a City Sheriff – and their foundation constituted an act of both altruism and self-interest: the medieval view was that charitable works on earth ensured the laying up of treasure in heaven, helping the souls of the benefactors after death to speed through purgatory to paradise. The land the Brunes chose for their venture, outside the walls and consequently relatively cheap, had the additional advantage that it had – in part – already been consecrated, for in the 1120s large numbers of bodies had been buried in Spitalfields following an unknown catastrophe, perhaps a famine.[5] This earlier use of land as a post-disaster cemetery was logical. It was largely open and lay just outside the city wall and, of course, continued the Roman tradition of burial in the area, which might well have been evident from decayed memorials or because bodies were from time to time unearthed.

The Augustinian Order, named after St Augustine of Hippo who died in 430, became well established in medieval London. Canons and nuns of the order lived a semi-monastic life and were dedicated to the pastoral care of the communities in which they lived. In practice this often involved taking responsibility for the poor and sick, and a priory set just outside the city, next to a great road, must have been literally a God-send for many a weary or infirm traveller. The order also had a high regard for the spiritual benefits of beauty – experienced through architecture, painting and music – that delighted the senses. For Augustinians beauty was next to godliness. St Augustine wrote of God's 'beauty so ancient and so new', and in praise of music claimed that 'to sing once is to pray twice'.[6] Such beliefs must have influenced the architecture and the furnishing of the church and priory buildings of St Mary's.

The overall appearance of St Mary's Priory in Spitalfields – as it evolved during the 340 years or so from its foundation until its dissolution – has been meticulously documented and reconstructed in recent times by teams of archaeologists. They have traced the gradual growth of the priory – from modest beginnings – and confirmed that the priory church grew into a most impressive building. The initial and relatively humble late-twelfth-century form of the priory has been described by Museum of London archaeologist Chris Thomas as probably comprising 'a small hall for the sick, which would have looked like the nave of a church with a chapel at one end'. The capacity of this would have been limited. Such establishments, notes Thomas, 'were often for twelve or thirteen sick people, reflecting the numbers of Christ and his disciples'. But although it could not house many of the infirm, the hospital was far-reaching in the care it offered and the responsibility it took for its patients. Surviving documents reveal that as well as looking after the aged and sick and women after childbirth, the hospital, in Thomas's words: 'also . . . cared for their children up to the age of seven, if the women died during childbirth but the children survived.'[7] During these seven years the children in the hospital's care – presumably orphans since their fathers had either absconded or were also dead – would no doubt have received a rudimentary education as well as religious instruction, making it possible for them to enter and function within the monastic system as monks or nuns, with some of the boys receiving additional education and training fitting them to become priests or government clerks or administrators.

The ambitions of the hospital grew, presumably due to the success of its endeavours, and in 1235 its founding body issued a new charter, which reveals that additional land had been acquired. Now the hospital covered about five hectares or thirteen acres – essentially the area that would eventually become the Liberties of Norton Folgate and the Old Artillery Ground.

In addition the priory's water supply – an essential commodity – was guaranteed in 1277 by the Bishop of London, who granted it the use of the 'Snekockeswelle' – also known as 'Snecocke's well' or 'Simcocks'. As far as can now be deduced the conduit head of the well or spring was located just to the east of modern Brick Lane, near what is now number 88 Cheshire Street. The water was piped west towards Shoreditch High Street and then south, roughly along the site of the later Blossom Street, to the priory, presumably feeding the pond that stood approximately at the junction of the current Folgate Street and Spital Square.[8] Recent water divining on the priory site has come up with additional, speculative, information – notably that a well or spring was located below the altar at the east end of the priory church.[9] If so then this must have been a holy well, although there appears to be no documentary reference to its existence. The site of the altar – and the possible holy well – is now marked in the road by a large manhole and watercock, both inscribed 'Thames Water'.[10]

As enlarged and improved the priory consisted of a range of buildings – mostly and largely stone-built – integrated in complex form around a series of small open spaces or courts including a cloister. The outline of some of its buildings, boundaries and courts is now commemorated – in a rough and ready way – by the road forming the west–east arm of Spital Square, which marks the nave of the church; by Spital Yard, which follows the west elevation of the church's south transept; and by a narrow passage off the north side of Spital Square, which relates to the church's north transept and perhaps commemorates a path to the infirmary garden. Folgate Street echoes a subsidiary route into the priory that connected Bishopsgate, via a gate, to its service yard, pond and orchard.

The heart of the priory was, of course, its church: its largest and most important building. This was T-shaped in plan, like a medieval Oxford or Cambridge college chapel, with a chancel-like nave and, to its west, large transepts – all furnished with parallel rows of columns to create basilica-style spaces. The absence of a nave west of the transepts – as was conventional in parish churches of the time – was simply a reflection of the fact that this was no parish church. As with college chapels, the priory church was not organised to house a large lay congregation but was intended to accommodate all its users within the chancel-like nave at its sacred east end. The transepts originally served as infirmary accommodation, with one transept or ward allocated to men and one to women. There was a small separate infirmary but this was converted into a chapel in 1235 after which a new two-storey infirmary was built. When this happened the transepts were converted into chapels.

As Chris Thomas explains: 'The eastern side of the north transept contained a series of chantry chapels, which in the medieval church were an important source of revenue, which I suspect was the motivation for converting the infirmaries.'[11] Typically the founder of a chantry chapel would give money to the church for the construction of the chapel and an endowment that paid for prayers to be said for his soul in perpetuity. The founder's object was to attain grace after death in the belief that the living could, through prayer, intercede for the dead and reduce the time a soul had to spend in purgatory. The new and greatly enlarged infirmary consisted of two wings, each operating as an open ward with thirty beds, again with men and women segregated. The main entrance to the infirmary was probably through the west porch to the church. With later enlargements the infirmary was, by the early 1530s, capable of accommodating 180 patients, making it the largest hospital in London and one of the largest in the land.[12]

The entrance area of the church was located where the north and south transepts met the western end of the nave. The 'chancel' portion of the nave and High Altar was to the east, no doubt within a screen topped by a rood loft. Patients would have gathered to worship in the nave, while the canons and clerics would have worshipped in the chancel. Above the crossing – where nave and transepts met – was a tall and stout square-plan crossing tower. This is shown – as a large and impressive feature on the London skyline – in Anton van den Wyngaerde's London panorama of 1543. By this time the tower, each face of which had two tall lancet windows (at one time it was thought there were three) recessed within a pointed arch, had a pyramidal roof. It must have been a key visual guide for travellers approaching London along Ermine Street, proclaiming the imminence of the city.

Other priory structures included a main gatehouse located on Ermine Street that led into a court and to the porch leading into the nave of the church. On the north side of this court was the original infirmary building. Leading south was an L-shaped passage skirting the south transept – the north–south portion of its route now probably marked by Spital Yard – leading to the cemetery, the combined charnel house and chapel, and the pulpit or Spital Cross to the south-east of the church. Lining this passage would have been tenements for families employed by the priory and various service buildings.

North of the infirmary and north transept were lodgings and gardens for the lay sisters who looked after the infirm, and the latrines. North of the chancel/nave was a cloister for the canons, with their refectory located off its north side and their dormitory and square-plan chapter house to the east. The location of dormitory and chapter house are now marked approximately by the west side of the north–south arm of Spital Square. Arranged around informal courts to the north of the north transept and church were the sisters' garden and infirmary garden, with the kitchen garden next to the kitchen and immediately north of the refectory. Within

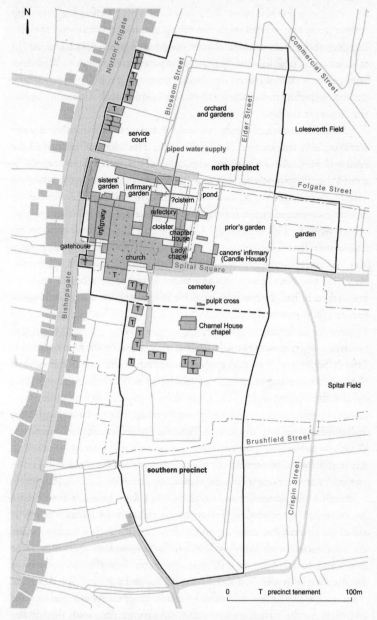

St Mary's Priory at the time of its dissolution in 1539, with the modern street pattern shown. Older roads are shown in solid grey. (MOLA)

the kitchen garden was probably a cistern, receiving water piped from the 'Snekockeswelle' and from which a supply was dispersed around the priory. East of the church's chancel/nave was a handsome Lady chapel, added in about 1400, in which the Virgin – the priory's protectoress – would have been venerated with especial devotion. The site of the Lady chapel is now marked by the junction of the east–west and north–south arms of L-shaped Spital Square.

To the east of the Lady chapel were the detached buildings of the canons' infirmary, also referred to as the candle house. And immediately east of the infirmary were the prior's garden with, to its north, where Elder Street now stands, the priory's orchard. To the west of these orchards, on the land now lying north of Folgate Street and between Blossom Street and Ermine Street/Norton Folgate, was the priory's service court, incorporating brewhouse and bakery with – in all probability – lightweight, timber-frame rather than masonry structures, facing on to Ermine Street. St Mary's Priory in its prime must have been like a small, self-contained town on the outskirts of London. As Chris Thomas observes: 'Whilst we might imagine monasteries to be quiet, calm places, St Mary would have been a bustling place with many hundreds of people living in it.'[13]

The one medieval structure within the precinct of St Mary's to survive today to any great extent is now located well below modern ground level. This is the charnel house that was constructed, in fine style, in the 1320s. It was a freestanding building – of robust masonry construction – with a stone-vaulted ground-floor room (its floor level set just below the then external ground level) and chapel above, reached via an external staircase, dedicated to St Mary Magdalene. When it was excavated in the 1990s, it was found to have external buttresses – originally three on each of its long north and south elevations – to resist the thrust of the stone ribs of the ground-floor vault, each buttress clad externally with ornamental panels of knapped flint set within stone frames. There could have been an earlier structure on the site because the vault incorporated a rib embellished with a chevron pattern and evidently reused from a late-twelfth-century building. John Stow, in his *Survey of London* of 1598, includes a short account of the charnel house, describing the 'chernell and Chappell of Saint Edmond the Bishop and Marie Magdalen, which chappell was founded about the yeare 1391 [sic] by William Euesham Citizen and Peperer of London, who was there buried'. He also notes that set against the north side of the charnel house was:

one faire builded house in two stories in height of the Maior, and other honourable persons, with the Aldermen and Shiriffes to sit in, there to heare the Sermons preached in the Easter holydayes. In the loft ouer them stood the Bishop of London, and other Prelates, now the ladies, and Aldermens wiues doe there stand at a fayre window, or sit at their pleasure.

Just to the north-east of the charnel house once stood the Spital Cross, a pulpit topped by a cross (it's clearly shown in the 'Copperplate' map of c.1553), and the venue for the famous Spital Sermon. Stow describes it in the following terms:

And here is to be noted, that time out of minde, it hath beene a laudable custome, that on good Friday in the after noone, some especiall learned man, by appointment of the Prelates, hath preached a Sermon at Paules crosse, treating of Christ's passion: and vpon the next Easter holydayes, Monday, Tuesday, and Wednesday, the like learned men, by the like appointment, haue vsed to preach on the forenoones at the sayde Spittle, to perswade the Article of Christs resurrection . . . At these sermons so seuerally preached, the Maior, with his brethren the Aldermen were accustomed to bee present in their Violets at Paules in good Fyrday, and in their Scarlets at the Spittle in the holidays, except Wednesday in violet . . .

Stow also suggests how the custom arose:

Touching the antiquitie of this custome, I finde that in the yeare 1398, king Richard hauing procured from Rome, confirmation of such statutes, and ordinances, as were made in the Parliament, begun at Westminster, and ended at Shrewsburie, hee caused the confirmation to be read and pronounced at Pauls Crosse, and at Saint Marie Spittle in the sermons before all the people. Philip Malpas one of the Shiriffes in the yeare 1439 gaue 20 shillings by the yeare to the three preachers at the Spittle: Stephen Froster Maior, in the yeare 1454 gaue fortie pounds to the afore said house, wherein the Maior and Aldermen do sit at the Spittle, was builded for that purpose of the goods, & by the Executors of Richard Rawson Alderman, & Isabell his wife, in the yeare 1488.[14]

The sermon delivered by Royal Decree at the Spital Cross was, from the fourteenth century, one of the great public events in the life of London – sacred, ceremonial and, no doubt, also commercial – with hucksters present in great numbers. It must have made the priory precinct a place of great prestige and pageantry, confirming St Mary's as one of the most significant institutions in the medieval city. By tradition the sermon was preached by a bishop, with the city's Lord Mayor and Aldermen in attendance, and with the aim of raising alms for the hospital. The practice continued after the Reformation and the Civil War (as recorded by Samuel Pepys – see page III) but in the 1680s the sermon was relocated to St Bride's Fleet Street, and then Christ Church Newgate Street. Today the sermon is delivered in St Lawrence Jewry, next to the Guildhall.

During the archaeological dig on part of the priory site in the late 1990s the skeletal remains of around 10,500 bodies were found within the priory's burial ground – mostly around the charnel house. With the exception of a few Roman remains, these had been interred between c.1120 and c.1530 – just over half of the total of 18,000 bodies that it is estimated were interred in the cemetery. Evidently Spitalfields was a popular place of burial in medieval and early-Tudor London. The disposition of the remains and the very existence of the charnel house tell us much about burial practices of the period.

In the High Middle Ages skeletons would be regularly disturbed in large cemeteries in constant use because burials and plots were generally not marked or recorded. However, when bones were lifted from consecrated ground it was the custom to preserve the main ones and to place them, neatly and by bone type rather than as the discrete skeletal remains of individuals, in blessed and sanctified ground or lodgings. For the Christians of the time it was essential to protect the body from evil after death within consecrated grounds or buildings and to preserve it more or less intact – if dispersed – so that, at the 'End of Days', it could undergo resurrection and once again house the soul in readiness to face the Last Judgement. It was believed that without a body there could be no last judgement for the soul, and without judgement the soul could not be justified and so enjoy eternal life. However, at some point it had also been decided that a body could be represented by its major bones – skull, thigh, forearm – and that these could be stored by type in sanctified places like charnel houses, leaving it to God in His wisdom to reassemble all in the correct manner, with minor missing parts supplied, at the time of judgement. And so charnel houses like that in Spitalfields evolved.

St Mary's Priory did not stand, or grow, in isolation. The east and northeast of the city was girdled by sacred ground and monastic houses – mostly founded during the twelfth century. These reflect the fact that London perceived itself as a sacred city, much like Jerusalem. The evidence for this is generally tangential or circumstantial but compelling nonetheless. It is touched on by John Stow in the late sixteenth century, who certainly appeared to see London as a sacred place – 'divided from East to West and from North to South', like Jerusalem with its four quarters.[15] And Stow noted that it was subdivided into wards, 'even as Rome', with sheriffs instead of consuls and aldermen instead of senators. Stow observed that the number of these wards was, originally – or at least in the reign of Henry III – 'twenty-four in all', a number that was, for the medieval Christian mind, highly charged: the *Book of Revelation* states that around Christ's throne were 'four and twenty elders sitting'.[16] The analogy is clear. The City Aldermen – each representing a ward – perceived themselves as operating in a divine universe, as supporters or advisers of the Lord Mayor, who himself owed 'fealty' to the divinely appointed monarch. And since the Lord Mayor was also an Alderman, an amendment of 1393, whereby the number of wards was increased to twenty-five, happily perfected the biblical model, yielding a Lord Mayor sitting 'in judgement' advised by his twenty-four Aldermen. So it is perhaps not too far-fetched to suggest that the city's structure of government was inspired by this biblical model, much as the initial organisation of the infirmary in St Mary's Priory was inspired by the biblical account of Christ and his twelve disciples.

To the south of Spitalfields, immediately to the east of the Tower of London and just outside the city wall, was St Katharine's by the Tower, founded in 1147 by Queen Matilda, wife of King Stephen, in memory of two of her children who had died in infancy. It functioned as a small religious community, caring for the poor and infirm, with the status 'Royal Peculiar', which meant it was extra-parochial and so exempt from the jurisdiction of the Diocese of London and subject to the direct jurisdiction of the monarch. Nearby, just a few hundred metres to the north, was the great Cistercian Abbey of St Mary Graces – founded in 1350 by Edward III, it was at the time of its suppression in 1538 the third-richest Cistercian abbey in Britain – and just to the north of that, near Aldgate, was the house of the Grace of the Blessed Mary, or Abbey of the Minoresses of the Order of St Clare – an order of enclosed nuns – that became a favoured place of patronage, donation and refuge for the elite of the land (widow of the Earl of Warwick, Margaret

Beauchamp, for example, was given papal dispensation to reside there after the death of her husband). Of all these foundations, suppressed at the Reformation, nothing now remains above ground – though the buildings and precinct of St Katharine's survived until the 1820s when they were destroyed to make way for St Katharine's Dock. Other ecclesiastical establishments in the area included in Aldgate the mighty and majestic Priory of Holy Trinity, just within the city wall (Mitre Square now marks the site of the priory's cloister), which in the late twelfth century was a renowned centre of learning with a significant library; Holywell Priory in Shoreditch High Street, founded c.1150 for Augustinian canonesses and a most significant establishment; and, next to the church of St Botolph's Bishopsgate, the Priory of the New Order of St Mary of Bethlem – or Bethlehem – better known as Bedlam, which by the late fourteenth century had became a hospital for the insane.

The fact that so many of these foundations – not least St Mary's Priory – were dedicated to the Virgin was no coincidence. By the mid fourteenth century she was regarded not only as the priory's but the country's 'protectoress', who interceded in heaven on behalf of the English and with St George was the nation's patron saint. Indeed, in a sermon of 1350 a mendicant preacher stated that 'it is commonly said that the land of England is the Virgin's dowry.'[17]

The life of the lay community living around, and working within, the priory is not well documented. Recent archaeological finds, however, have revealed that there was a row of 'precinct tenements' along Norton Folgate, north of the priory church and backing onto the service court, and a scattering of freestanding or paired tenement buildings south of the church.[18] These would have been relatively ephemeral structures – timber-framed with wattle and daub panels. Until the late fifteenth century most of the houses would have consisted of a small double-height hall – open to the roof timbers – that would have been the main living and entertaining space. It would have contained a centrally placed open-hearth fire that heated the room and was used for cooking, and a high-table at which the head of the house – the lord in his own home - presided over his family and guests. In addition there would probably have been an adjoining chamber and pantry. During the sixteenth century most of the houses would have been made more comfortable and convenient by the addition of a chamber in the upper portion of the hall – probably to serve as a private bedroom – and masonry-built chimney breasts that would have

A detail from Anton van den Wyngaerde's London panorama of 1543, showing the tower and church of St Mary's Priory in the 'Spital' dominating the view to the north-east of the City. A row of gabled buildings along Bishopsgate links the church and priory buildings to the city.

ensured that smoke no longer eddied about the interior. By this period
most of the tenements would have become two storeys high, perhaps some
with a third garret storey set within a gabled roof, topped off with tall
chimney stacks.[19]

Life in Spitalfields during the thirteenth and early fourteenth centuries
appears to have been relatively stable and further development there minimal. But there were isolated, dramatic disruptions. One such was revealed
when the bones from the unearthed charnel house and surrounding burials were scientifically examined after their recovery in the 1990s. Analysis
revealed that many came from the bodies of people who had perished
during some mid-thirteenth-century catastrophe, perhaps as the result of
sudden climate change sparked by a vast volcanic eruption in Central
America or Indonesia. It has been estimated that maybe as many as 15,000
of London's population of 40–50,000 died as a result of this natural
disaster, Museum of London archaeologists speculating in 2012 that the
sulphurous gases released by a huge and catastrophic eruption would have
released a stratospheric aerosol veil or dry fog that blocked out sunlight,
altered atmospheric circulation patterns and cooled the earth's surface,
causing crops to wither and heralding a period of famine and pestilence.

Barely a century later, another catastrophic disaster arrived in the
form of the Black Death of 1348. Known in the Middle Ages as 'The
Great Pestilence', bubonic plague is thought to have killed 30–40,000
Londoners – perhaps as many as half the population of the city – and
about 1.5 million Britons, roughly a third of the population of the
British Isles. Burial of the dead was a desperate business – urgent and
hazardous – as a huge number of cadavers had to be disposed of at speed
by a population that was decreasing rapidly in numbers, while trauma
and terror – and horror – must have been increasing even more rapidly.
The large, conveniently located and time-honoured burial ground of St
Mary's Spitalfields must have been heavily used. But recent excavations,
involving the recovery of 10,500 skeletons, revealed no signs of great panic.
Many well-ordered communal graves were found, but no mass graves into
which bodies had been tumbled in haphazard manner. It seems the people
of mid-fourteenth-century Spitalfields, even if grieving and terrified at
what seemed to be the coming of the Apocalyptic End of Days, did not
lose their nerve or the sense of obligation they felt to their family, friends

and neighbours to bury their bodies in as respectful and Christian way as possible. Presumably the officiating monks and those acting as gravediggers or sextons knew full well that within a few days they were more likely than not to be the corpses being buried, so they did as they would be done by, and as they thought necessary to achieve the chance of resurrection.

The next major disruption in Spitalfields' life was of a very different character. In 1471 the inhabitants of the area found themselves embroiled in most direct manner, if only briefly, in the prolonged dynastic struggle known as the Wars of the Roses. In that year an extraordinary character – Thomas Neville, the illegitimate son of the Earl of Kent and known to history as the Bastard of Fauconberg – led an assault on London that involved street fighting in Spitalfields as well as an attack on the city wall and on the Bishopsgate itself.

In his youth the Bastard had won acclaim as a sea captain for his success in clearing pirates from the Channel and in 1454 was granted the freedom of the City of London. When the Wars of the Roses broke out, he initially supported the House of Lancaster, but in 1460, along with his cousin, Warwick the Kingmaker, switched allegiance to the House of York and played a significant role in putting the Yorkist claimant on the throne in 1461 as Edward IV. Growing tensions with the new king, however, caused Warwick to reverse his new allegiance and in 1470 he helped restore the Lancastrian Henry VI. Edward IV fought back, and the following year ousted Henry and imprisoned him in the Tower.

This set the scene for the Bastard's bizarre and audacious adventure. By 1471 he had followed Warwick back to the Lancastrian cause. Then in April came a terrible blow for the supporters of Henry VI: Warwick was slain in the Battle of Barnet whilst leading Lancastrian forces against Edward IV and the Duke of Gloucester. The Bastard, however, was undeterred. In May, while Henry VI's wife Margaret of Anjou raised troops in the West Country to restore her husband to the throne, he launched an invasion from France, landing at Sandwich with a force consisting of many French and foreign soldiers. He then marched through Kent while his ships moored in the Thames Estuary, to act if necessary as an amphibious force in the assault on London. He took Canterbury and marched on to Southwark, halting at the fortified southern end of London Bridge. But this speedy early success was suddenly cast into doubt. Margaret's forces were defeated on 4 May at the Battle of Tewkesbury and dispersed. The Bastard therefore had no choice but to fight on alone to take London – and quickly before opposition forces could be rallied against him in overwhelming force.

It was a desperate gamble. He demanded entry into London and was refused. With London Bridge barred to him, he used his ships to cross to the north bank of the Thames and on 14 May launched a surprise attack from the east – on the manor of Norton Folgate, Spitalfields and Bishopsgate. Simultaneously his forces attacked Aldgate and London Bridge. Lancastrian soldiers – French and English – stormed through Spitalfields, up to the city wall, but after some initial success were beaten back. For the Bastard the game was up. He retreated to his ships at Blackwall, causing damage as he went, but most of his forces were eventually seized at Sandwich, while the Bastard himself was captured in Southampton, imprisoned and beheaded in September. The dethroned Henry VI had died in the Tower on 21 May 1471, presumably on the orders of Edward IV. The House of York held the throne until 1485 when Richard III was defeated at Bosworth by the Earl of Richmond, a Lancastrian protégé who, as Henry VII, became the first of the Tudor kings.

The story of the Bastard's ultimately reckless assault on the City of London has an intriguing possible literary consequence. Whilst the attack was being readied Sir Thomas Malory was in, or had just been released from, Newgate prison. The reasons for his imprisonment and indeed release are not now clear, but it appears he had been a Yorkist who had changed sides and entered into the Duke of Warwick's conspiracy to overthrow Edward IV. Whether or not this Sir Thomas Malory is one and the same as the 'Sir Thomas Malory' who wrote *Le Morte d'Arthur* remains hotly debated, but it seems likely, and, if so, the dynastic conflict that came to a head in 1471, and with which Malory was so intimately involved, might well have informed this work of Arthurian romance, even though Malory's death, which probably occurred in March 1471, came too early for the Bastard's attack on London to be a direct inspiration. It is easy to see how the spectacle of struggling royal lines, of battle and betrayal, of seemingly divinely appointed monarchs warring with seeming usurpers, fighting queens and turncoat knights, could find appropriate analogies in King Arthur, Sir Gawain, Sir Lancelot, Mordred, Merlin and Morgan le Fay.

Imagery derived from Arthur's court and other references to this ancient exemplary king were regularly used by English kings in their bid to legitimise or sustain their own hold on the throne. Edward III did this in dramatic fashion in the mid fourteenth century with the foundation of the Arthurian Order of the Garter. Henry VII and the Tudors likewise sought to align themselves with the heroic ancient monarch – indeed Henry's first and short-lived son was even called Arthur. So Malory's tale of the ancient court of King Arthur – seemingly written while in Newgate although not published until the 1480s – had, in tumultuous late-fifteenth- and early-sixteenth-century England, great political and contemporary resonance. Little wonder then if Malory took inspiration from the complex conflict – which was for him ultimately calamitous – that included the brief, potentially epoch-making, but now largely forgotten Battle of Spitalfields.

Whatever damage and destruction had taken place in the Manor of Norton Folgate, Shoreditch and Bishopsgate during the violence of 1471, the Augustinian priories were not seriously harmed and certainly not reduced in circumstances. Indeed when the Holywell Priory closed just over sixty years later during the Reformation it was the ninth-richest nunnery in England and a place of some prestige. From the reign of Henry III onward it had been under the patronage of the Manners family, Earls of Rutland, whose property it was, and as late as 3 July 1536 – even as the implications of Henry VIII's break from Rome were becoming alarmingly clear – the priory saw the double marriage of the 16th Earl of Oxford to his first wife Dorothy Neville, while Henry Manners, 2nd Earl of Rutland, married Dorothy's sister Margaret. Oxford was the father (although Dorothy not the mother) of the 17th Earl of Oxford, who was to live in Fisher's Folly on Bishopsgate. The 16th Earl was from 1555 to become patron of 'Oxford's Men' – a theatrical troupe he supported until his death in 1562. Rutland was a successful soldier and courtier, eventually becoming Lord Lieutenant of Nottinghamshire and Rutland and President of the North.

The presence of the Earls of Rutland and Oxford in and around Bishopsgate and Ermine Street hints at the events the sixteenth century held in store for Spitalfields. In its first decades the great monastic houses of the area endured, even if they did not thrive as in former times, and trade continued to rumble productively to and from the city along the ancient Ermine Street. This highway must have sustained further life along its route, with inns, waggoners and blacksmiths, and presumably establishments for drovers bringing cattle and sheep into the city, gathered around the village of Shoreditch and along the stretch of Ermine Street that had become Shoreditch High Street.

But when the priories were dissolved in the late 1530s old patterns of land ownership and use changed, and these fuelled the astonishing transformation that overtook London in the decades after the Dissolution. The capital started the century as essentially a medieval city and so it remained in 1530. But, a hundred years later, it was in many ways a modern Renaissance city, with elegant and courtly north Italian-style classical architecture in Whitehall and far-flung Greenwich and planned for Covent Garden. The industrial and economic might of the city was also transformed. The population in 1530 was probably little more than 70,000. By 1630 it had grown to a massive 250,000. Life in the expanded city was, of course, to a large degree defined by new building – greatly spurred by the disposal of monastic land after the Reformation, by political and religious intrigue, by revolutionary propositions about the nature and true purpose of kingship and government, and by an explosion of interest in – and expression of – the arts. All these emblems of the new city and the new age found dramatic and tangible expression in Spitalfields, which, between 1530 and 1630, expanded from a scattering of buildings beyond the city wall into a substantial and significant suburb.

TWO

REFORMATION AND REBIRTH

Tudor and Early-Stuart Spitalfields

The change that engulfed Spitalfields after 1530 was extraordinary not just in its scale but in its speed. For someone like John Stow, born in Cornhill in around 1525, the Spitalfields he would have known as a middle-aged man would scarcely have been recognisable as the area he'd visited as a child.

In 1530 Spitalfields was, essentially, St Mary's Priory – or more particularly the northern or inner precinct of the priory in which the main monastic buildings were grouped. These would have been dominated by the priory church, and it's important to remember that this was not just significant in the semi-rural setting of Spitalfields but in the context of London as a whole. In the first place, it was one of the biggest churches in the capital. Its nave, chancel and Lady chapel combined measured, from west to east, nearly seventy-five metres (the length of the nave and western transepts of Canterbury Cathedral – arguably England's premier church), and its tall tower made it, visually, one of London's great landmarks. Moreover, the priory played an important role in the life of the capital. It had become London's largest hospital, caring for the sick and for women in childbirth, and its precinct was the setting for the delivery, by royal decree, of the prestigious Spital Sermon.

But by 1560 the tower of the great church had gone, its interior had been dismantled and replaced by gardens and courts, and only parts of its south wall and transept walls survived. The numerous priory buildings that surrounded the church had been reduced and converted to serve secular uses – mostly as houses and tenements of varied status.[1] A world that had been sacred for nearly 350 years, and which had served a public good, had within only a few years become profane, and given over to the quest by speculators for private profit or domestic pleasure.

Such a radical and rapid physical and functional transformation is a reminder of the extraordinary impact that Henry VIII's decision to dissolve the monasteries – in the wake of his quarrel with Rome over his divorce from Catherine of Aragon – had on early-Tudor England. Over 800 religious communities in England, Wales and Ireland were wound up between 1536 and 1541. In 1540 alone closures ran at about fifty a month. The consequence was the destruction and mutilation of buildings of age and beauty; the slighting of sacred art on a colossal scale; the destruction of libraries; the brutal severing of age-old traditions, rituals and relationships; the termination of many charitable and beneficial practices; and the casting out upon the world of around 12,000 monks, canons, friars and nuns, together with no doubt substantially more lay people, many of whom had little or no experience of life beyond their monastic walls and few immediately productive skills.[2] The Dissolution changed the social and economic framework of England, as well as its religious loyalties and its urban and rural landscape. Old certainties and customs were swept away.

The vacuum was rapidly filled by the opportunistic and ambitious 'new men' of Henry VIII's regime who were, naturally, the greedy beneficiaries of the wholesale confiscation and reallocation of the ownership of land and buildings that was such a key aspect of the Reformation. They tended to be well-connected members of the royal court or government administration, ideally placed to buy former monastic property on the cheap or else acquire it in other ways. Their actions sometimes seem little more than brigandage aided and abetted by the Crown. Some shameless officials simply assigned former monastic property to themselves and then indulged in asset stripping and crude private profiteering, often reducing fine ancient buildings to no more than materials for sale or for use in self-aggrandising construction projects. Thus Thomas Mildmay, or Mildemaye, auditor of the Court of Augmentations, which was the body responsible for administering and disposing of confiscated former monastic land and buildings, acquired his landholding in the city. The Court's treasurer – Sir Thomas Pope – managed to get his hands on the huge Bermondsey Priory, which had initially been passed to a fellow Court of Augmentations member, Sir Robert Southwell, who made a fortune speculating in former monastic land. Pope was evidently a skilled operator in the art of mopping up former church property because he also acquired the Benedictine Durham College in Oxford, which he re-founded in 1555 as Trinity College. One suspects that he took this action for the good of his soul and perhaps to soothe a guilty conscience, since the students of that admirable institution were required to take Holy Orders and to pray for the soul of their college's founder.

Nowhere was this rapid and often brutal reconfiguration of England's life and landscape more apparent than in Spitalfields, where St Mary's Priory was finally surrendered to the Crown in January 1539. The demise of one of London's 'greater religious houses' was accompanied by 'the frenetic sale and resale of leases around the former precinct . . . as courtiers tried to consolidate their holdings.'[3] Within the northern or inner precinct, where the priory's major buildings were grouped, buildings were demolished, reduced in size or remodelled to meet the requirements of new owners, occupiers and functions. The substantial remains of one of these adapted monastic structures can still be seen. The early-fourteenth-century charnel house, located on the south edge of the inner precinct, was at some point in the 1540s converted, at least in part, into a dwelling house, complete with fireplace and chimney. And, as excavations in the 1990s revealed, a number of new, often freestanding buildings were constructed within the former priory site. For the next hundred years or so, the inhabitants of the area would have lived in surroundings that were semi-ruined – some buildings patched up and inhabited, others left open to the elements – constant reminders of a lost religious world, much as the modern inhabitants of Bury St Edmunds in Suffolk or Walsingham in Norfolk still live with the ruins of the mighty and majestic monastic past.

The southern, or outer precinct, which represented nearly half the priory site, and which at the time of the Dissolution was largely open ground with only a scattering of buildings, met a rather different fate. In 1537/8, just before the priory was formally dissolved and taken into Crown ownership, much of it – then referred to as the 'Tesell Grounde' – was leased out by the prior for military exercises and the testing of ordnance.[4] The timing of the lease suggests that the last prior, William Major, anticipated the consequence of the impending Dissolution and was trying to take the initiative by turning priory property assets into ready and portable cash. He had shown similar financial foresight a few years earlier in 1531 when he is recorded as being in negotiation with the Prior of Charterhouse over the receipt of rents for properties in the parish of St Margaret Bridge Street,[5] and again in 1536 when he leased priory buildings – notably one called the 'posterne' in the cemetery and the 'Candle House' – to William Wyld, a 'citizen' and Merchant Taylor. Other priory buildings leased out between 1531 and 1538 included 'le oldehalle' and 'a garden platte [plot]' to

Joan Rosse, 'widow'; a tenement and garden to John Aport, 'gentleman'; a tenement over the priory's west gate and a garden, which were acquired in March 1537/8 by Patrick White, 'a gentleman', and a mansion called 'le brick house' within the cemetery of the priory that was leased to John Halles, 'gentleman'.[6]

This was shrewd work on Prior William's part – presumably undertaken for the good of his religious order rather than for personal gain. It was also a common enough tactic at the time. In 1532, for example, the Prioress of the Holywell Priory in Shoreditch leased land fronting on to Shoreditch High Street to Thomas Towle for the construction of three 'messuages', or dwellings. These survive, although in rebuilt form, and include the fine early-eighteenth-century 190 Shoreditch High Street.[7]

On 23 June 1534 Prior William and eleven others at the priory acknowledged the spiritual supremacy of Henry VIII, rather than that of the Pope. It was an act of subservience that allowed the prior and the key men around him to remain in post – at least for a little while – and the chance to realise, or dispose of, the priory's assets. When it was eventually surrendered to the Crown in January 1539 Prior William accepted a generous pension of £80 per annum. This, paid at Christmas 1539/40, was in crude terms his reward for failing to make a fuss. Six canons received only between £8 and £4 each while two lay sisters received forty shillings each.[8]

Others were less passively accepting of the Dissolution. St Mary Spital, after all, housed London's largest hospital. It was a useful and beneficial establishment. Lord Mayor Sir Richard Gresham therefore petitioned the king in 1540, begging that the priory might continue its charitable work under the rule of the city. Gresham also pleaded, in similar vein, for St Bartholomew's Augustinian priory in Smithfield and St Thomas's in Southwark – also an Augustinian priory that was dissolved in 1539.[9] In the case of these latter two institutions Gresham proved persuasive, as was the case slightly later when Sir John Gresham intervened on behalf of St Mary of Bethlem off Bishopsgate. St Bartholomew's was re-founded by the king in 1546 as a hospital, as was St Thomas's in 1551, under the control of the City Corporation. But in the case of St Mary Spital the king remained unmoved. The only concession made was that the poor and infirm already in occupation could remain there. No new inmates, however, were to be admitted.

The recipient of the 1537/8 lease from Prior William for the southern precinct – or 'Tesell Grounde' – was the 'Fraternyte or Guylde of Artyllary of longbows, Crossebowes and handegonnes', which was probably affiliated to the Guild of St George, and from which the Honourable Artillery Company (HAC) would seem to derive.[10] The 'Fraternyte's' occupation of the precinct was confirmed when it became Crown property in 1538. The land had been walled in before being let, and the 'fraternyte' proceeded to construct various buildings within the enclosure, using its southern portion to practise military manoeuvres, to exercise with firelocks, pike and bows, and to test and demonstrate artillery. The land was additionally used by the 'Gunners of the Tower' – who disputed the 'fraternyte's' sole title to it – and was also occupied by various small cottage industries. A clue to their nature is given by the name this part of the southern precinct acquired at some point in the early sixteenth century: 'Tesell Grounde'. Teasels are prickly plants with spiny flower heads, which were used to brush up the 'nap', or raised hairs, on woollen cloth. Grown within the southern precinct, they played an important role in the area's wool industry, which had become significant enough at the time of the Dissolution to merit commemoration on the very first map of Spitalfields: the 'Copperplate' map of c.1553. This shows washed or dyed woollen cloth staked out with 'tenter hooks' to prevent it warping or shrinking as it dries on 'tenter grounds' shown behind buildings on the west side of Bishopsgate (opposite the south end of the 'Tesell Grounde'), and also a little further to the west in Moor Field.

Stow, in his *Survey of London* of 1598, offers a succinct portrait of the 'Tesell Grounde' and suggests a chronology of its use. North of Petticoat Lane there was, he records:

> . . . a large close called Tasell close sometime, for that there were Tasels planted for the vse of Clothworkers: since letten to the Crosse-bow-makers, wherein they vsed to shoote for games at the Popingey: now the same being inclosed with a bricke wall, serueth to be an Artillerieyard, wherevnto the Gunners of the Tower doe weekly repaire, namely euerie Thursday, and there leuelling certaine Brasse peeces of great Artillerie against a But of earth, made for that purpose, they discharge them for their exercise.[11]

The 'fraternyte' used at least part of the 'outer precinct' for around 120 years, by which time it seems to have become synonymous with the HAC that moved in 1658 to establish itself at nearby Bunhill Fields, Finsbury.

Pepys visited the 'Gunners' from the Tower at the ground on 20 April 1669 and recorded in his diary: 'In the afternoon we walked to the old Artillery-Ground near the Spitalfields . . . by Captain Deane's invitation . . . to see his new gun tryed, this being the place where the Officers of the Ordnance do try all their great guns.'[12] In 1682 the military and ordnance use of the ground finally ceased, and it was sold by the Crown to a consortium of builders for the construction of a network of new streets lined with speculatively built houses.

The disposal, dismantling, adaptation and reoccupation after 1539 of the main priory buildings in the northern precinct was a complex business. This was particularly so, initially at least, because of the widely scattered nature of the leasehold interests in the precinct. As we have seen, the prior entered into a number of leasehold agreements between 1531 and 1538. Then, over the next couple of years, the Crown leased 'le Priours lodge-yng', the 'kytchen garden', and all the church, cloister and 'le Frater' (the refectory), with all 'buildings, barns and stables', to Nicholas Bristowe, a 'gentleman' of London. Bristowe held a position at court – which he no doubt used to acquire the lion's share of the available priory buildings – being a 'clerk of the wardrobe of robes and beds'. Most of the remaining buildings and land east of the priory church were leased by the Crown in April 1540 to Richard Morysyn or Moryson.[13] Morysyn's acquisitions included the infirmary, dorter – or dormitory – and the buildings beneath it, the hospice, 'le Pryours gardyn', 'le Covent garden' stables and tenements, as well as large amounts of land between the buildings.

What Bristowe and Morysyn did not get, of course, were the buildings in which the sick were housed, since the king had decreed they could remain there for the terms of their lives. Nor were they able to lay their hands on the lead from the priory roofs. This, all twenty-five tons of it, had been held on to by the Crown and used to repair the 'westminster hall Rouff'.[14]

In November 1542 the future of the leasehold possession of the buildings and land of the former northern precinct was radically simplified when the Crown granted Stephen Vaughan the reversion of leases that had been agreed by the prior in 1531 and 1538 and the king in 1540. Vaughan was well placed – he was described at the time as the 'King's servant', being under-treasurer of the mint and a clerk for the Court of Augmentations – and so was in a position to ensure that the reversions were as beneficial and speedy as possible.[15] But, even so, not all the leasehold buildings he acquired control of came with vacant possession, nor did all pass smoothly from their initial lessees. William Wyld, for example, retained tenements he had leased from the prior in 1536 – notably the 'posterne' in the cemetery and the 'Candle House'. His adaptations of these former monastic buildings not only helped to ensure a certain architectural continuity between pre- and post-Dissolution Spitalfields, but also meant that the monastic routes on which these buildings stood became enshrined in the later urban grain of the area.

Patrick White, similarly, decided to keep a firm grip on the buildings and grounds that had been leased to him, and so entered into prolonged dispute with Stephen Vaughan, which remained unresolved at Vaughan's death in December 1549. As for Vaughan himself, he made his home within the canons' former refectory and dormitory – which were set along the north and east sides of the cloister – and within the chapter house and Lady chapel to the east of the nave and chancel of the church. The walls of the Lady chapel seem to have been retained but its roof removed to allow it to serve as a court or yard.[16] While Vaughan incorporated parts of the priory structure into his home, he demolished the north and west walls of the church for their building materials and created a large garden on the site of the chancel end of the nave and cloister garth.[17] In his will he left a portion of the income from his property in the former priory to the king – seemingly to repay a debt to the Crown – for the period of his son Stephen's minority, and 'my mansion howse at St Mary Spittell with the gardeyn and orchard thereunto belonging' to his wife for nine years and then to his son.[18]

A fascinating amount of information about the fabric within the northern portion of the precinct and the nature of its inhabitants is revealed in a lease of 1580 granted by Stephen Vaughan the Younger to Robert Hare.[19] The main property discussed in the lease is the 'principal tenement or messuage . . . sumtyme in the tenure and occupacion of Edward Isaake . . . gentleman, deceased.' This 'Principal Tenement', as it was called, was not the Vaughan family house, but a large house they had built immediately to the west of their home and which incorporated some of the fabric of the former church and buildings of the priory. The consideration for which the lease was granted was to include 'the greate coste and chardge' which Hare had 'heretofore . . . bestowed and hereafter intendeth to bestow in building repayringe and amending . . . the principle tenement or messuage' of the precinct.

The site of the north precinct of the former St Mary's Priory in c.1600, showing surviving
The nave of the church has given way to courts and gardens, although its south wall

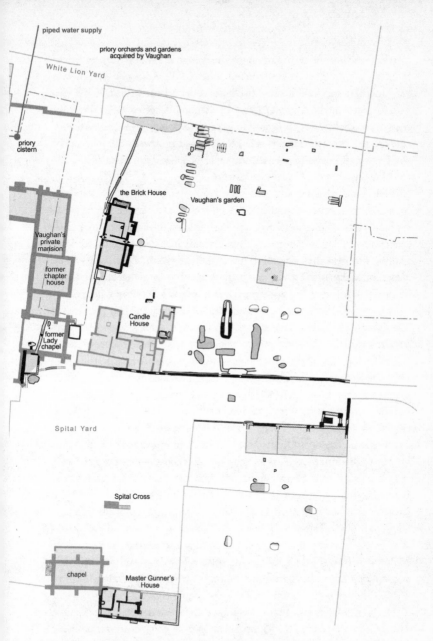

portions of priory buildings, adaptations, and additions that include the Brick House. survives. Walls shown in black are post-Reformation structures. (MOLA)

Also, on the southern portion of the Vaughan property a new brick-built tenement had been constructed 'wherein Sir Edmonde Huddilston [or Huddlestone] knight now dwelleth'. This was described in the 1580 lease as 'lately buylded and repayred' by Stephen Vaughan the Younger for his own use but let out. This building, at some point in the later sixteenth or early seventeenth century, was incorporated into what became one of the largest and most important houses in pre-Georgian Spitalfields, latterly known as Spital House (see page 56).[20]

The Principal Tenement had been constructed by Stephen Vaughan Senior out of the former prior's lodgings, the west side of the former cloister, and parts of the north transept and aisle of the priory church. The tenement was organised around a court and included a first-floor long gallery. This was the largest and most ambitious of the houses created by Vaughan within the former precinct. According to archaeologist Chris Thomas, 'it was clearly a fairly grand town house of its time' whose occupiers were 'keen to flaunt their wealth for all to see'.[21] In their publication *The Spitalfields Suburb*, Museum of London archaeologists speculate why Stephen Vaughan the Elder did not choose to live in this impressive house himself but in the smaller house he created to its east: 'Perhaps', they suggest, 'he originally intended to live in the principal tenement but later decided to rent it out . . . for reasons of financial expediency'.[22]

The grandeur of the Principal Tenement ensured that it attracted some important tenants. Sir Thomas Wyatt, who was executed in 1554 for raising a rebellion against Queen Mary, lived there in 1550, or in a tenement within or adjoining the surviving priory gatehouse on Bishopsgate (see page 67). In 1567 the French ambassador Charles de Foix moved into the tenement. If an enigmatic engraving of the north side of Norton Folgate (made c.1870 but copied from an earlier print or drawing) does indeed show part of the Principal Tenement, as Museum of London archaeologists have suggested, then it appears to have been a substantial four-storey building with tall gables containing attic rooms.[23] It can also be made out – along with Vaughan's own house – on the 'Copperplate' map of c.1553, although both are rendered in very simplified form.

William Wyld's two main buildings – 'le Posterne' and the 'Candle House' – also appear on the 'Copperplate' map. 'Le Posterne' was probably adjoining, or an extension of, a tenement in the cemetery that had been occupied by the priory's bailiff and 'collector' for all the priory lands in London. It is described as standing 'over and against' the pulpit cross and

Norton Folgate, perhaps in c.1600, from a nineteenth-century rendering of an earlier view. The winding path in the foreground would appear to be Hog Lane, now Worship Street. It is probable that the gabled building – set back and centre right – represents the Principal Tenement.

near the charnel house.[24] On the 'Copperplate' map one can make out
such a building to the east of the Spital Cross and to the south of a narrow
lane connecting the site of the lost priory church to 'The Spitel' field to the
east. At some point it seems to have become known as the Brick
House – something of a generic name in late-sixteenth-century Spitalfields, since another Brick House was built c.1599–1600 on Spital Yard, just
south of 'White Lion Yard', and a third Brick House was constructed on
the west side of the cemetery.[25] This would seem to suggest that brick was
an unusual building material in the area in the mid to late sixteenth century. Most of the former priory buildings were wrought of stone or
timber-frame, while the majority of domestic or commercial buildings in
Spitalfields were made of timber and lath-and-plaster. A brick-built building, therefore, clearly stood out.

As for the Candle House, this was not only the most important building controlled by Wyld but also one that – in enlarged and altered
form – played a significant role in the social and architectural history of
Spitalfields throughout the seventeenth century, and probably survived
until the early 1730s.[26] It stood immediately to the east of the Lady chapel
of the priory church and was – before the Reformation – the canons'
infirmary.[27] The building is shown on the 'Copperplate' map as a gabled
structure to the north of the charnel house, standing on land that became
part of the east portion of the L-shaped Spital Square and of Lamb Street.

Archaeological exploration undertaken by Museum of London archaeologists during the 1990s, combined with documentary research, shows
that by the time of the Dissolution, the canons' infirmary had grown into
a large and complex single-storey timber-frame structure rising from a
masonry dwarf wall 'with several wings' that 'had evolved over more than
two centuries'. The original fourteenth-century core of the building, the
archaeologists noted, 'consisted of a north hall with a central hearth and a
louver in the open roof, with a subdivided wing to the south.' The eastern
rooms had been added in the late fourteenth and fifteenth centuries when
'the building was enlarged by the addition of an entrance lobby and two
narrow rooms . . . There was also a narrow, fifteenth-century north-east
wing with an external chimney at the south end and a large hearth at the
north (it is possible that this wing was the monastic candle workshop and
gave the building its name).'[28]

The 'Copperplate' map that shows these various buildings also gives a very good impression of the speed at which – as well as the extent to which – Spitalfields was being transformed. Produced in impressive detail by an anonymous cartographer probably around 1553, but perhaps as late as 1559 – in other words, within a couple of decades of the suppression of St Mary Spital – it originally consisted of fifteen sheets, printed from engraved copper plates, of which only three have so far been found. The Spitalfields plate shows an area that stretches from Norton Folgate and the beginning of Shoreditch High Street in the north to the city wall and 'Busshoppes Gate', the 'Papye' and Moor Gate in the south, with 'Busshoppes gate Strete' almost in the centre and Moor Field and 'Fynnesburie Field' to the west and 'The Spitel' to the east. It is, in a manner typical of the time, a hybrid between a flat plan (a new idea) and the more traditional bird's eye view. This means that the street pattern is clearly shown in plan but buildings rendered in slight perspective, with roofs revealed and elevations hinted at. The map is enlivened with images of people – drawn to a larger scale than the buildings they are meant to inhabit – pursuing activities that reveal their trades, occupations or status.

The map shows a deep ditch immediately north of the city wall that runs east and west off 'Busshoppes Gate'. The northern edge of this ditch is lined with a long row of tenements. This row – facing onto the ditch – stands on a narrow road named 'Unsdiche' – now Houndsditch. At the western end, on the corner with 'Busshoppes gate Strete', is a long, low and uniform building with three doors. This is, or is the site of, the Pye Inn, later called the Dolphin, which in the 1580s was owned by the Alleyn family, one of whom – Edward Alleyn – was to become such a major figure in the world of Elizabethan theatre (see page 81). At the end of the century John Stow described it as:

a large Inne for receipt of trauellers, and is called the Dolphin of such a signe. In the yeare 1513 Margaret Ricroft widow, gaue this house, with the Gardens, and appurtenaunces, vnto William Gam, R. Clye, their wiues, her daughters, and to their heyres, with condition, they yearly to giue to the warden or gouernour of the grey friers Church within Newgate fortie shillings, to find a student of Diuinitie in the Uniuersitie for euer.[29]

To the north of this large building – separated by two smaller buildings – is a large complex, incorporating a courtyard with a pair of walled gardens to its east. A little later in the century this building – or perhaps one that replaced it, given Stow's description – would became home to a rich and socially aspiring goldsmith called Jasper Fisher. John Stow in his *Survey* describes the Folly as a:

> large and beautiful house with Gardens of pleasure, bowling Alleys, and such like, builded by Iasper Fisher, free of the Goldsmiths, late one of the six Clarks of the Chaunceries, and a Iustice of Peace . . . This house being so large and sumptuously builded by a man of no greater calling, possessions or wealth, (for he was indebted to many) was mockingly called Fishers folly . . . It hath since for a time beene the Earle of Oxfords place. The Queenes Maiestie Elizabeth hath lodged here.

The 'Earle of Oxford' referred to was Edward de Vere, patron of the arts, spendthrift, lyric poet, and since the 1920s widely promoted as the concealed author of the works of Shakespeare.

South of the Pye Inn, and just within the city wall east of 'Busshoppes Gate', is the 'Papye', a substantial building that before the Dissolution had been St Augustine's Church. It stands in the centre of a collection of buildings that served principally as a refuge for the poor (hence 'Papye' as in pauper) and for indigent priests. Just south of the 'Papye' – so not shown on the map – stood the majestic Crosby Hall on Bishopsgate. Built in 1466 by a rich wool merchant called John Crosby, the hall became the city court of the Duke of Gloucester before he grabbed the crown to reign as Richard III. The spectacular fifteenth-century great hall survived obliteration in the late nineteenth century by being dismantled for re-erection on Chelsea Embankment – where it survives, now part of a grandiose neo-Tudor private house.

'Busshoppes gate Strete', which runs past Fisher's Folly, and which incorporates a well or conduit head within its width, is shown lined with buildings, all of which have extensive walled enclosures or gardens behind. To the east of the gardens serving houses on the east side of the street are large walled yards, pastures, paddocks or fields – one with cattle grazing and another to its north named 'The Spitel'. This paddock was also known as Lolesworth Field, and here the map shows armed men exercising – some with longbows (they are, presumably, members of the 'Fraternyte or Guylde of Artyllary of longbows, Crossebowes and handegonnes'). To the west of this field – towards 'Busshoppes gate Strete' – is a smaller walled enclosure with a pair of men ('Gunners of the Tower') discharging firelocks towards a butt. And at the north end of the ground is a group of houses or tenements including the one known as 'le Posterne'.

Running south-east from the artillery ground is a meandering lane that connects to 'Busshoppes gate Strete' by means of a straight alley, seemingly marking the site of what became Petticoat Lane (now Middlesex Street) and Widegate Street – a name which presumably commemorates the substantial gate that once closed this alley to prevent livestock wandering from the fields onto the street. The meandering lane is not built up, but is flanked by trees after it abruptly swings east towards Aldgate. The western portion of the lane was known as 'Hog Lane'. The eastern portion leading to Aldgate was Wentworth Street or Lane. Stow, in his *Survey* of 1598, states that the name of the byway was 'Berwards lane, of olde time so called, but now Hogge lane, because it meeteth with Hogge lane, which cometh from the Barres without Aldgate.' By Stow's time it was 'a continuall building of tenements, with Alleys of Cottages, pestered, &c.'[30]

To the north and west of the Artillery Ground and reaching west to 'Busshoppes gate Strete' are the substantial remains of the main priory buildings with, to their east, a large court planted with trees. This is named as 'S. Ma. Spittel'. On the southern edge of this court is a freestanding structure – five windows long, with buttresses – with a smaller, vertical structure to its east, topped with a gable and a cross. These are the early-fourteenth-century charnel house and the Spital Cross. The buildings to the west of the court, on the site of, or incorporating portions of, the main priory buildings, include the Principal Tenement. This is shown as a multi-gabled structure, with ranges organised around a central court, which dominates the group. To its north-east is the house of the Vaughan family. And running east from the court containing the charnel house and Spital Cross is a narrow lane that in time was to become part of Spital Square and Lamb Street. What is almost certainly the Candle House stands on the north side of 'S. Ma Spittel' court, opposite the charnel house.

To the north and east of the court, the Principal Tenement and the Vaughans' house are orchards and walled, formally planted gardens. These would formerly have been the prior's orchards and gardens – places not just for the production of fruits for consumption and plants and herbs for medicine, but for contemplation, too. The view of the orchard is terminated by the edge of the map, just at the point where 'Busshoppes gate

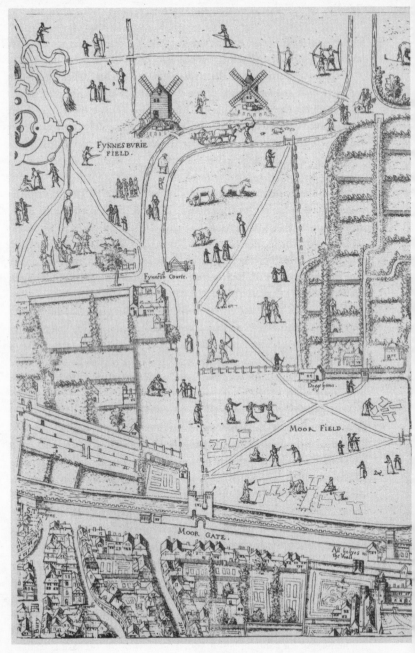

The 'Copperplate' map of c.1553–9 showing Bishopsgate

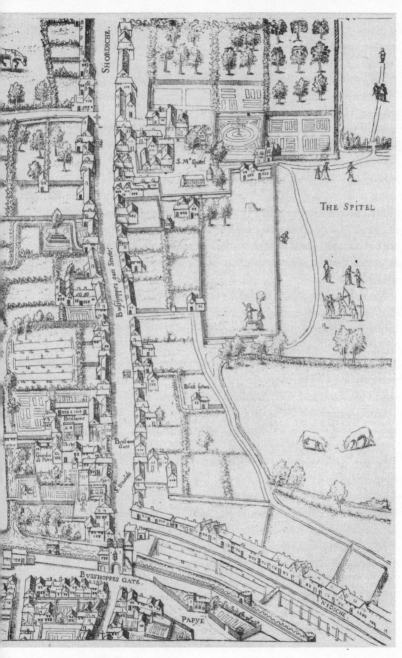

and, to its right, Spitalfields.

Strete' is named 'Shordiche'. This is the portion of road known as Norton Folgate.

The west side of 'Busshoppes gate Strete' is shown as more densely developed than the east, with a number of large, institutional buildings and a series of gardens – framed by walls, fences or hedges – that stretch far west from the street. The larger buildings include 'Bedlame' – the Bethlem Hospital – with a gate on 'Busshoppes gate Strete', and 'S. Bwttols' church – St Botolph's. The gardens behind the buildings are fascinating. One contains a stepped pyramid topped by a flat plateau on which is planted a single tree – a typical Elizabethan garden feature that allowed people to enjoy views over the surrounding gardens and country. The house it served must have been of some grandeur – perhaps it was the large structure, possibly with ranges organised around a large court, shown on the map immediately to the south of the pyramid garden feature.

Another garden reveals one of the major trades of the area and hints at what helped sustain the local economy. In it lengths of cloth appear to be fixed to upright poles: presumably wool drying in the sun after being dyed. A similar scene can be seen on Moor Fields to the south. Here lengths of cloth and cut garments are shown lying on the ground, some fixed by tenter hooks. Elsewhere, on the northern portion of Moor Field, once named Mallow Field, men practise with longbows, people walk and cattle and horses graze. To the west of this field is a wide lane, marked as 'Fynnesb. courte', now Chiswell Street. And north of this is the rural Bunhill Field, named 'Fynnesburie Field'.

To the north of Moor Field/Mallow Field is a wide lane that separates it from a field yet further to the north. This lane – almost entirely devoid of building – is 'Hog Lane' (one of two roads in the area with that name, the other being part of the road that is now Middlesex Street), now Worship Street. In the fields to the north are windmills. These, it seems, were a feature of Norton Folgate notable enough to attract Stow's attention, who recorded that in 'the High Field ... commonly called Finsbury Field ... three Windmills stand, abutting upon the high way that leadeth unto Norton-Folgate ... the high way that leadeth to Hollywell, and the lands belonging to the Earle of Rutland.' The reason the windmills were there is hinted at by the name of the field. This was, presumably, relatively if only slightly high land where windmills could be sited to advantage to catch the wind. Around the windmills men – yet again – practise with longbows. Henry VIII had encouraged expertise with the longbow – he saw it as an expression of manhood, English traditions and military prowess. Seemingly Henry's advice was taken most seriously by the martial men of Spitalfields and Finsbury.

Finally, at the junction of 'Hog Lane' with 'Shorditch' is a large cross, possibly marking a sacred site, or serving as a reminder to travellers arriving from the north to assume a pious and reverend state of mind when crossing this threshold. After all the land to the south was, in a sense, holy ground: it was the great City of London, 'founded' by Brutus and a favoured domain of the Virgin, St George and St Paul.[31]

Just a few years after the 'Copperplate' map was completed, the first surviving map to show all of London appeared. It dates from between 1561 and 1570, and is generally known as the 'Agas' map – although it should be said that the name is something of a misnomer, since the surveyor Ralph Agas was not born until 1545 and this map is in any case very different in style from the ones he is known to have produced.[32] It's very dependent on the 'Copperplate' map – indeed its rendering of Spitalfields and Shoreditch is in many respects an exact copy, although far cruder, as is to be expected of a map printed from woodblocks rather than from finely engraved copper plates. Bishopsgate Street looks much the same, if less detailed. The men still discharge their firelocks in the Artillery Ground. To the east of Bishopsgate Street fabric still dries on 'Moor Fyeld', cattle graze and men – although fewer in number – continue to practise with their bows. But it's intriguing in two respects.

Firstly, of course, it shows much more of the area. To the east of Bishopsgate Street and 'The Spitel Fyeld' it depicts open pasture, where cattle graze, as far as Brick Lane – shown unbuilt – with to the east of this more fields, grazing cattle, bowmen, and people and dogs walking along country paths. It's known that Brick Lane existed under its current name as early as 1550 when a survey of the Manor of Stepney mentions tile 'garths' – places where clay was dug to make bricks or tiles – on the east side of the lane.[33] To the north of the precinct of the former St Mary Spital and 'Shordich' High Street is shown the village of Shoreditch clustered around the medieval St Leonard's Church. Beyond that, and shown in foreshortened perspective, is open country with, in the distance, the hill of Stoke Newington. To the east of Bishopsgate Street, beyond 'More Fyeld' and Chiswell Street, is 'Olde Street', the Barbican, and then Charterhouse and 'Clarken Well' – with their buildings marking the northern edge of London and set among large gardens and flanked by fields.

The other reason why the 'Agas' map makes such a fascinating complement to the 'Copperplate' map is because it shows the development that has occurred. As one might expect – given St Mary Spital's fate – no obvious architectural remains are shown of the once mighty Holywell Priory (not, of course, included on the 'Copperplate' map), although a long, tall wall with a large gate on the north side of 'Hog Lane' might be a reference to the monastic use of this land. (Similarly scanty remains are shown on the slightly later Braun and Hogenberg map of 1572, although we know that the priory possessed a great barn that survived into the seventeenth century at least, and priory buildings – including its church – were arranged around a square, which survives today as New Inn Yard and King John Court, just north of Holywell Lane.) There's one feature, however, shown on the 'Copperplate' map – the cross at the junction of 'Hog Lane' and 'Shordiche' – that does not appear at all on the 'Agas' map. And there's one feature – the Spital Cross structure – that has seemingly changed: in the 'Agas' map it is shown without its crowning cross. Do these omissions or disappearances have significance? Was the 'Agas' map perhaps a more puritanical production in which crosses were eschewed because they hinted at a Roman Catholic past, or could it mean that the crosses had actually been pulled down? It is impossible to be sure.[34]

Late-Elizabethan Spitalfields and Bishopsgate – and the suburbs on the north-east edge of the city more generally – were favoured locations for the mansions of grand and ancient families and for the urban palaces of the capital's nouveau riche. John Stow, writing about the site of St Mary's Spital in the late 1590s, recorded that 'in place of this Hospitall, and nere adjoining, are now many faire houses builded, for receipt and lodging of worshipful persons.'[35] He also noted that Fisher's Folly, just to the south, 'now belongeth to Sir Roger Manars'. As already noted the Manners family, which included the Earls of Rutland, owned the site of the Holywell Priory in the sixteenth century and, indeed, had been the former priory's patrons since the thirteenth.

Stow's reference is probably to the Roger Manners who became 5th Earl of Rutland in 1588 and who died in June 1612. He was a significant figure in contemporary court circles, participating in the Earl of Essex's futile rebellion in 1601 against Queen Elizabeth (for which he escaped with his life but was fined £30,000 and jailed) and then, like many of his co-conspirators, finding favour with James I after his accession to the throne in 1603; presumably the conspirators regarded James as the 'strong man' they wished to see on the throne in place of the aged and ailing queen, and, in time, were rewarded for this view. Intriguingly, Manners is another of the putative pretenders to the works of Shakespeare – having been nominated in the early twentieth century by the German academic Karl Bleibtreu – which means that Fisher's Folly was occupied or owned in the late sixteenth century by two men who have been credited with authorship of Shake-speare's plays (the other, of course, being Edward de Vere). John Strype, in his 1720 revision of Stow's *Survey of London*, records that, in his day, the house remained an 'airy and creditable place, where the Countess of Devon-shire, in my memory, dwelt in great repute for her hospitality.' The site is now commemorated by Devonshire Square and Cavendish Court.

In the former precincts of St Mary Spital, meanwhile, the old priory continued to be demolished, adapted and added to. And by the end of the sixteenth or early seventeenth century it sported a number of substantial houses, including the Candle House – essentially the priory's old infirm-ary, the Brick House (built in around 1599–1600 just to the north of the Candle House), and the properties owned by the Vaughans. And it was the Vaughans who were ultimately responsible for what became, perhaps, the grandest of all the houses of Elizabethan and Jacobean Spitalfields: Spittle (or Spital) House.

In his will of 1588/9 (proved in 1605/6) Stephen Vaughan the Younger left his property, including his 'mancion house wherein I now dwell', to his third son Rowland Vaughan because his eldest son Stephen had 'fallen into a kind of phransie or lunacye' and his second son Henry had 'gone I know nott whither'.[36] When the then Sir Rowland died in 1641, his Spital-fields properties passed to his daughter Elizabeth, the widow of Sir Paulet St John, second son of the 1st Earl of Bolingbroke (a Royalist who, by the time the Civil War broke out in 1642, had turned Parliamentarian; he died in 1646). This marriage had, of course, united the St John and the Vaughan families with – for a while – Elizabeth, Lady St John perhaps the matriarch. As far as can now be known, Lady St John occupied – or at least retained – her old Vaughan family home in the precinct that had, apparently, by the early seventeenth century been let to the Venetian ambassador. But at some point between 1641 and 1685 the St John/Bolingbroke family decided finally to move from this old, smaller house into the one that back in 1580 had been described as 'lately' built for Sir Edmonde Huddilston (Huddlestone or Hodlestone).

This Huddilston home appears to have been incorporated within a larger mansion in the later sixteenth or early seventeenth century, and subsequently let out. In 1632, just a few years before Lady St John inherited it, the house had been leased to no less a figure than Richard Weston, diplomat, Chancellor of the Exchequer, Lord Treasurer, suspected Catholic and loyal supporter of Charles I, who helped the king find funds independent of Parliament's support. He was created Earl of Portland for his pains in 1633, but died just two years later.[37] It is not now clear if the St John/Bolingbroke family occupied the existing Spittle House after Weston's time there, or if they immediately rebuilt it in a grander fashion. The former is more likely since the family rebuilt the house in around 1700 – when it was known as Spital House – in a stylish and grand manner when Spital Square was starting to take shape.

The archaeologists who explored the remains of Spital House during excavations in the late 1990s describe the house as the most architecturally ambitious in seventeenth-century Spitalfields. It was a 'large brick building, apparently four storeys in height and seven bays wide . . . the main, southern, façade was 18.4 m long' with its various ranges grouped around a small court. A rudimentary elevation of the house appears on Ogilby and Morgan's map of 1681–2 (it does not appear on the earlier edition of 1676). This elevation suggests the house was an impressive and elegant affair. The *Survey of London* describes it thus: 'an Elizabethan or Jacobean house of considerable size, four storeys high and seven bays wide. The second and sixth bays projected for two storeys, and the middle one for three, all being finished with crested balconies.' No such house is shown on the admittedly imprecise Faithorne and Newcourt map of 1658 but as the *Survey* records, the Hearth Tax assessments for 1662–4 include a 'house in "Spittle Yard" occupied by Lady Elizabeth St John assessed for eight hearths'.[38] (The Hearth Tax was a property tax imposed in England from 1662 with duty based on the number of hearths, or fireplaces, a house contained. It was abolished in 1689.)

But, as the 'Copperplate' map shows so graphically, not all of the Spitalfields area was being given over to fine houses for the well-to-do, and in the years after it was made other structures arose to serve very different purposes, reflecting Spitalfields' 'frontier' role on the built-up edge of the city and its long tradition of being sacred ground. Thus, for example, a new building was erected in 1594 immediately to the east of the Spital Cross, for the use of the governors, masters and children of Christ's Hospital (located near St Paul's Cathedral) when the Spital Sermons were being delivered. A mixture of brick and timber-frame, it was presumably conceived as a pavilion with an open arcade to the west to allow a good view of the Cross. It was, however, evidently not of good quality because only a few years after its completion John Stow noted that it was 'decaying and like to have fallen' had not the City repaired it at great cost. Nevertheless it shows that, although the Priory of St Mary Spital had gone, the sermons associated with it continued to flourish.

Meanwhile, on the north edge of the Old Artillery Ground, abutting the early-fourteenth-century charnel house, a very different type of building was going up. The Master Gunner's House – for use by the 'Master Gunner of England' – was, according to archaeological evidence gleaned in the late 1990s, probably built in 1581. It was of two to three storeys, with its lower portion constructed of brick, its upper storey perhaps timber-frame. Divided into two halves by a large central chimney stack, it had its hall on the east side and its kitchen and service rooms on the west, with the kitchen sharing the central stack with the far larger hall. Some ground-floor rooms were ornamented with tiles reused from priory buildings. Records survive of the works carried out on the house in 1623 for Master Gunner William Hammond. These offer information about its form and fittings, so we know that on the ground floor there was a hall with a porch and the kitchen, while on the first floor was a dining chamber with two deal partitions.[39]

The house serves as a reminder of just how important the Artillery Ground was in later Tudor and early-Stuart England. The Master Gunner, who not only had the house as his official residence but also worked here, was the Crown's key technical adviser on all aspects of artillery, including shot and gunpowder. He kept a register of all certified gunners in the country and organised their training, as well as maintaining a list of all guns in the realm – in ships as well as forts and elsewhere – which also included a note of their condition. In addition, he had responsibility for testing guns and gunpowder, and these proving tests took place in the artillery ground over which the house presided. The house must, at times, have been a hive of activity, with great military leaders coming and going, conferring and dining with the nation's leading expert and record keeper on all things to do with ordnance.

The Master Gunner was one of the most important people in the defence of the nation and also one of the best judges of its offensive and defensive potential at any given moment and so, at crucial moments in the nation's history, this now lost and almost forgotten building in Spitalfields would have been at the centre of military planning.[40] It's easy to imagine, as the Spanish Armada approached the English coast in August 1588, how frantic the activity must have been in and around the newly completed Master Gunner's House. It was, in a sense, the nerve centre – certainly from the technical point of view – of the embattled realm

When it was excavated in 1999, the house was found to have possessed a cellar at its north-west corner (where it adjoined the charnel house), which was presumably reached by a ladder from the room above. It must have been the wine cellar – at least in the house's later years – because within it were found fragments of a large number of wine bottles, most dating from the later seventeenth century. Two, of onion form and dating from c.1680, were actually complete when found and retained their original contents, sealed with corks. Analysis showed these to be Iberian dry Madeira – and still drinkable. They perhaps belonged to Captain Valentine Pyne, a Royalist Civil War veteran who had been Master Gunner since 1666 and in 1668 was granted a pension of £71 per annum for his war service. Pyne died in 1677 and was probably the last Master Gunner to occupy the house just before the whole area was transformed in the wake of the Great Fire of London (see chapter 5).[41] That complete bottles of wine should have been left in the cellar suggests the house was abandoned in some haste, or at least carelessly, between 1682, when the Crown sold the land, and 1685 when it was finally demolished. Within a few years a whole new range of buildings arose in the area, built on fire debris from the ruined city. The Master Gunner's House and the charnel house thus became submerged as the ground level around them rose by around two metres to form the level upon which new streets were constructed, the foundations of the Master Gunner's house eventually being overlaid by Fort Street.

Possibly connected with the Master Gunner's House is one of the most mysterious structures of historic Spitalfields to have been unearthed in recent years: the Star Fort. It is not shown on contemporary maps of the area, nor is it specifically mentioned in contemporary documents (although that might simply be to do with the fact that the Artillery Company's records before the 1650s were destroyed in the aftermath of the Civil War).[42] Museum of London archaeologists, however, have shown that it stood immediately to the west of the Master Gunner's House and south-west of the charnel house, that it was formed with earthen ramparts rising above a ditch and that it would essentially have taken the form of a three-pointed bastion, measuring about forty-five metres from west to east. Curiously the fort appears to have faced south – towards the City – with an open back that faced north, towards the surrounding fields and so the more likely direction of attack.

Current thinking, supported largely by archaeological evidence, is that the fort was constructed in the 1630s, but Chris Thomas, the leading Museum of London archaeologist, suggested in 2004 that it might well have been constructed – or at least significantly altered – in the 1640s.[43] This slight difference in the dating is highly significant. Although there is no obvious reason why a fort would have been built here in the 1630s, by the early 1640s England was gripped by Civil War and it is likely that, in some way, this fort, adjoining land that from 1641 came under control of the Parliamentarian St John family, was part of Parliament's London defences. Even so, this still does not explain its strange orientation and form unless, for reasons now impossible to explain, the far less critical southern half of the fort was built first and the north portion was never built at all. Or, stranger still, for a brief period it was feared that an assault on the city's defences would come from within, mounted presumably by a Royalist 'Fifth Column' or by disgruntled citizens. It is intriguing that the Venetian ambassador[44] – whose residence in the 1640s was perhaps in Spitalfields or in Sir Paul Pindar's former mansion on Bishopsgate – observed in 1642 of the city's forts that 'the shape they take betrays that they are not only for defence against the royal armies, but also against tumults of the citizens and, to ensure a prompt obedience on all occasions'.[45]

Less dramatic explanations for the fort's orientation are that it was cre-ated as an exercise in preparation for the construction of larger defensive works or as a means of training troops to assault such works. Certainly surviving physical evidence suggests that the fort – with its earth-built ramparts and approximate star form - was of exemplary design, well illus-trating the military theories of the time.

It holds one further mystery. During excavations, archaeologists made a perplexing discovery. In the western ditch two graves were found, evidently dug after the construction of the fort, that were orientated north–south.[46] This is, of course, most unusual for Christian burials, although Dissenters occasionally chose to be buried in this way.[47] Were they Dissenter burials, then, or do they offer evidence of a hasty and careless interment – possibly of enemies caught up in the turmoil of the Civil War? We simply don't know.

If the Star Fort was built in the peaceful years of the 1630s for purely training purposes, its erection was nevertheless prophetic. For within a decade Spitalfields and Shoreditch were transformed in appearance by mighty forts, bastions, ramparts and ditches that were built in deadly earnest. When the Civil War started in 1642 Spitalfields and Shoreditch rapidly became a fortress zone and a key part of Parliament's system of defence – its so-called 'lines of communication' – to protect London from Royalist attack.

By the time the Civil War started in 1642 London had grown vastly beyond the medieval masonry walls and gates that even then still mostly survived. This expanded city therefore needed new fortifications that could be constructed at speed and that would be practical in the new age of gunpowder warfare. In other words – as with the Star Fort – it needed ramparts constructed of earth, thick enough in section to absorb the shock of gunfire, low enough in profile to offer a minimal target, and defended by wide ditches to prevent infantry penetration. From the offensive point of view the forts and ramparts of the city defences had to be fitted with platforms suitable for the mounting of artillery, and in a form and configuration to allow for effective long-range and enfilading fire.

Construction of such a ring of fortifications around London, on both sides of the Thames, was promoted to the City's Court of Common Council in February 1642 by Alderman and Colonel Randall Mainwaring. It was executed the following year by Sergeant-Major-General Phillip Skippon, probably using Dutch engineers for the detailed design. Over the course of two or three months up to 20,000 Londoners laboured, at speed, on the construction of the largely earth-built defensive system.

A plan of London 'as fortified by Order of Parliament in the years 1642 and 1643' was produced many years later, in 1738, by George Vertue. It

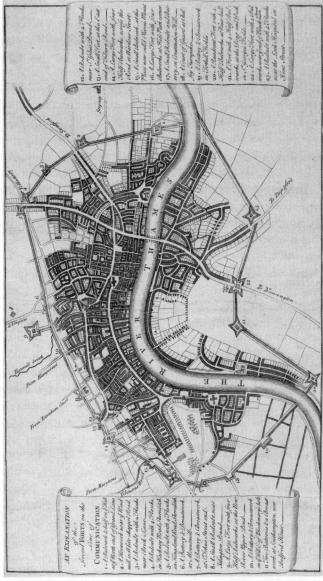

A plan of the fortifications constructed around London in 1642–3 by Parliamentary forces at the start of the Civil War. The plan was produced in 1738 by George Vertue. The pair of 'redoubts' at Shoreditch are numbered 4 and 5, and to the south-east of these is a 'redoubt . . . near Brick Lane'.

shows the city girded by a rampart that was strengthened by artillery forts and redoubts. In the Spitalfields area, on each side of Kingsland Road, just north of Shoreditch High Street and Shoreditch church, at the junction with Hackney Road, was 'a Redoubt with 4 Flanks' – in effect a pair of star forts, each with four points, or flanks, guarding the road into London from the north-east. Just south of this formidable work, and connected to it by a rampart, was 'a Redoubt with 3 Flanks near Brick Lane'. This appears to have stood to the east – roughly where Heneage Street is today – with Brick Lane itself determining the line of the rampart and acting as the wall walk.

The plan does not show the star fort within the Artillery Ground, although the ground itself, framed by its brick wall, is made clear, with the open space of the Spital Field to its east. Nor does it give more than a rudimentary impression of Spitalfields' buildings. It does, however, contain one detail that serves as a useful reminder that even maps don't always tell the truth. It shows a row of houses running north from the priory precinct – presumably buildings that formed Wheler Street. However, the Wheler Estate only started construction in or soon after 1649, a fact forgotten by the time Vertue drew up his plan.

The construction techniques and scale of these Civil War fortifications were described at the time by William Lithgow, a renowned traveller, aged sixty in 1642, who had been imprisoned as a spy in 1621 by the Spanish, had travelled on foot through much of central Europe, the Middle East and North Africa, and who walked the walls of London during the war and described them. They were, noted Lithgow, 'erected of turffe, sand, wattles & earthen works'.[48] The ramparts were generally 2.2 metres wide at their base, 5.5 metres high and were protected by a ditch, which in places was flooded to act as a defensive moat. Stone and brick were used to face gates and perhaps redoubts, and timber palisades stood on the top of the ramparts. Main roads were defended by chains, posts, ditches and drawbridges set between gates.

The dramatic manipulation of the landscape around the edge of London – through the construction of ditches and the heaping up of earth – must have had a significant if subtle influence on local topography. Land levels must have been altered around the site of the fortifications with roads like Brick Lane terraced, and surrounding land raised, as the vast earth ramparts were quickly dispersed with only a portion of their bulk being used to fill the parallel works of ditches and moats.

But by the time Ogilby and Morgan produced their great post-Civil War London map in 1676, the fortifications were no longer a feature worth recording because they had already been almost entirely removed. The redoubt on the Whitechapel Road, however, lingered for years, and actually increased in size because it became a favoured location for dumping ash. In the eighteenth century it was known as the Mount. In the early nineteenth Mount Terrace took its place. It still survives – just to the south of the London Hospital – a faint reminder of the great, lost walls of Civil War London.

THREE

ON THE FRINGES OF SOCIETY
Catholics, Outsiders and Actors

Throughout the Middle Ages and well beyond, Spitalfields was border territory: a place where parochial and administrative boundaries met – an edgeland and, by tradition, a place of refuge and liberty, congenial to those living outside the religious or social norm. Bishopsgate was the closest Ward (that is, a City district represented by an Alderman and Common Councilmen on the Court of Common Council). It was divided into Bishopsgate-within-the-wall and Bishopsgate-without-the-wall, and that extramural portion covered the area of Bishopsgate Street beyond the gate as far as the north side of the charnel house, marking approximately the boundary of the southern and northern precincts of the former St Mary's Priory. But most of Spitalfields, notably the area to the east of the northern precinct of the former priory, including Lolesworth Field, lay outside the Ward and so beyond the control of the City of London. In the sixteenth century the City's Aldermen, and particularly the Lord Mayor, were at a local level very powerful indeed. The Lord Mayor was no mere ceremonial figurehead. He was an authority politically, legally (he was the chief magistrate of the City), and militarily as captain of the City's trained bands or militias. He was in a sense a petty prince with considerable autonomy in his Square Mile domain. But his power did not extend as far as Spitalfields.

Further administrative anomalies contributed to the area's relative independence. Not only did the core of Spitalfields – notably much of the land of the former priory – lie beyond the City's control, it also lay between the four ancient parishes of St Dunstan's Stepney (from which the parish of Christ Church Spitalfields was extracted in 1729 when the new parish church was completed), St Mary's Whitechapel, St Botolph's Bishopsgate, and St Leonard's Shoreditch. It was not therefore under the control of one local unified religious authority. What's more, at the Dissolution, Spitalfields' former monastic land transferred to the possession of the Crown was not absorbed into adjoining parishes but was constituted as two Liberties. The former northern precinct of the priory became the Liberty of Norton Folgate and much of the land of the southern precinct became the Liberty of the Old Artillery Ground.[1] These Liberties were extra-parochial areas in which the usual system of parish government did not apply and where rights traditionally reserved to the king or the lords of the manor were devolved into private hands (hence, for example, the 'Regalian Right' – that of a monarch to receive income from a dismantled or moribund monastic estate – was revoked). The detachment of the Liberties from conventional parochial and regal control did not mean that they were allowed to operate outside the laws of the land, but it did mean that the execution of those laws and the conventions of parochial authority tended to be more relaxed.

So Spitalfields was conveniently near the City yet relatively free from its control, and also relatively free from the restrictions conventionally imposed for much of the sixteenth and seventeenth centuries by Anglican clergy and Protestant authorities. In consequence, Spitalfields within the Liberties became popular with those seeking freedom – political, artistic or religious. A similar atmosphere distinguished life in the late sixteenth century in the adjoining Holywell Liberty that had also been created from former monastic land. All three Liberties – particularly that of Norton Folgate – became the domain of a wide, and sometimes exotic, range of outsiders.

Among the first was William Rugg (or Reppes), who according to Stephen Vaughan's will of 1549 (see page 41) was at that time in the 'holding' or possession of the 'Brick House' (one of perhaps two buildings in mid-sixteenth-century Spitalfields known by that name and probably the one that was also known as 'le Posterne'). Rugg was a Benedictine, who became Abbot of St Benet's Abbey, Norfolk in 1530 and then Bishop of Norwich when St Benet's was unified with the Bishopric of Norwich at the Dissolution. Evidently he felt able to take the Oath of Supremacy, repudiating the Pope and accepting Henry VIII as 'the only supreme head on Earth of the church in England'. But he nevertheless disputed publicly with evangelical Protestants and fought to retain key aspects of his conservative and Catholic faith within the emerging Anglican doctrines and theology. He was one of the forty-six clerics who in 1537, under Thomas Cranmer, compiled *The Bishops' Book* that instituted the doctrinal reforms necessary to separate the newly established Church of England from the Roman Catholic Church. His traditional leanings were, however, betrayed during the debates surrounding the compilation of this book by his (unsuccessful) attempts to retain the age-old practice of pilgrimage to holy sites as a means of gaining spiritual grace. To puritanical Protestants such actions were no more than Roman Catholic idolatry and idle superstition.

Rugg was clearly walking a tightrope and in 1549 he lost his balance. That year – the third of Edward VI's reign – saw the outbreak of Kett's Rebellion, a popular uprising in Norfolk provoked by official indifference to, or sanction of, the enclosure of common land by rich and powerful landowners for their own profit, use or pleasure. The common people, already hard-pressed to make a living through agriculture, saw this as no more than theft and an unchristian abuse of power that made the rich richer and the poor poorer. The uprising started at Wymondham, Norfolk where a yeoman farmer called Robert Kett took the peasants' part and led them to Norwich in violent protest. They took the city but in August were defeated in battle by the forces of the Earl of Warwick.

The uprising had not been specifically pro-Catholic, but it is significant that its followers had celebrated the feast of St Thomas Becket (a Catholic saint removed by Henry VIII from the church calendar) and had shown particular animosity to Sir John Flowerdew, not only a rich landowner who had enclosed land but someone who had also overseen much of the destruction of Wymondham Abbey. His exploitation of a place that had once fulfilled both a spiritual and a social role was clearly resented – in their list of grievances the protesters included a demand that the power of the new 'gentry' should be limited and the over-exploitation of communal resources prevented. Ultimately the rising was bloodily suppressed with nearly 3,000 protesters killed. As for Robert Kett himself, he was hanged from Norwich Castle. His brother William was hanged from the west tower of Wymondham Abbey.

As the rebellion unfolded, it was noted that Rugg did not oppose it with any enthusiasm. Indeed he was open to the accusation that he actually supported the protesters when they arrived in Norwich. This provoked royal anger, inflamed no doubt by the influence of Thomas Cranmer who, as a leading Protestant reformer, had long found Rugg an irritant. So immediately after the suppression of Kett's rebellion Rugg was obliged to resign the diocese and remove himself. The refuge he chose was the Liberty of Norton Folgate. He was to enjoy this pleasant semi-rural retreat for only a few months before he died in 1550.

While those suspected of Catholic sympathies came under suspicion during Edward VI's short reign, after his death in 1553 the religious mood of the country swung violently the other way when his staunchly Roman Catholic half-sister Mary defeated an attempt to put the Protestant Lady Jane Grey on the throne and seized it for herself. Her reign was to be marked by bloody retribution against unrepentant and 'treasonable' Protestants: thirteen were burnt at the stake in a single day in June 1556 at Stratford, only a few miles east of Spitalfields. And Spitalfields itself, which just a few years before had provided a refuge for a pro-Catholic bishop, now became a retreat for a rebellious Protestant aristocrat.

Among the individuals mentioned in Stephen Vaughan's will of October 1549 is Sir Thomas Wyatt the Younger (the son of the poet), who is recorded by Vaughan as occupying 'one tenement within the gate of Saint mary Spittell'. This statement is ambiguous. It could mean a tenement literally within the gatehouse or a tenement – such as the stately Principal Tenement – located within the precinct served by the gate.[2] Wyatt was absent from London in the wars in France from 1544 to 1550 so he had little time to occupy his Norton Folgate 'tenement' in person, but it seems likely that on his return he used it as a power base from where in 1554, provoked by Queen Mary's betrothal to the Catholic Philip of Spain, he could plan a Protestant rebellion against her. His close proximity to the City seems to have paid off in the short term: when he marched on London some of the City's trained bands (or trainbands) sent against him deserted their command or even joined him, suggesting that Wyatt had used his Spitalfields base as part of a strategy to win the support of these City forces.

Ironically, the trained bands were led by Wyatt's own godfather, the eighty-year-old Roman Catholic grandee the 3rd Duke of Norfolk, who had been saved from execution himself in 1547 by the death of Henry VIII and who had been recently reinstated in power and titles when the new queen made him her Earl Marshal. Wyatt's initial successes, however, failed to secure final victory and he was eventually lured into an ambush and captured. Mary's reaction was vicious. Lady Jane Grey, who had initially been spared and had nothing to do with Wyatt, paid for this Protestant uprising with her head and was executed at the Tower in February 1554. Wyatt followed her two months later, with his body quartered and his limbs displayed around the country to discourage further rebellion.

With Elizabeth I's ascent to the throne in 1558 and the re-establishing of the Protestant faith as the state religion, Roman Catholics once more became a persecuted minority. And their position now was more desperate than it had been in the years before Mary's reign. Mary's persecution of Protestants meant there were scores to settle. Moreover her marriage to King Philip II of Spain – the nation emerging as England's main competitor for world trade, possessions and power – cemented an association in the popular mind between national enemies, such as Spain and France, who were Roman Catholic, and Roman Catholics in general. It was but a small step – easily and often taken – to believe that all Catholics were in league with the enemy and to see them as actual or potential traitors. The consequence of these fears was the imposition of penalties on Catholics in England that over time involved the loss of civil rights and the enforcement of prohibitions that prevented public worship, that made private worship dangerous and that barred Catholics from all forms of public office, military service and the law. Catholics were also forbidden to matriculate at the universities.

Clearly for London-based Catholics, facing ever-greater scrutiny and suspicion in the years after 1558, the attraction of finding somewhere to live that was relatively free from official control but also right next to the capital was compelling.[3] Those few acres around Spitalfields' former priory building must therefore have offered a real sense of security in a largely hostile world, as is made clear by a government list of the numerous eminent Catholics living in Spitalfields in 1578.[4] By 1567 the French ambassador had moved there. He was followed by the Flemish ambassador, who from 1581 was ultimately a spokesman for Spanish interests in what became known as the Spanish Netherlands, and in the early seventeenth century, if not before, by the Catholic Venetian ambassador. The Flemish and Venetian ambassadors were probably tenants of the Vaughan family, the Venetian ambassador probably occupying the Vaughan family house after the Vaughan/St Johns had moved to nearby 'Spittle House' (see pages 55–6) and the Flemish ambassador taking up residence in the Principal Tenement. Not only did they clearly feel comfortable there, but their presence in Spitalfields must have greatly increased the sense of security of other resident Catholics. These foreign diplomats were, after all, privileged, protected and allowed to maintain Catholic chapels that could, informally at least, be used by non-embassy worshippers. And, if the worst came to the worst, the embassies could offer refuge to fellow believers in their secure enclaves.[5]

Among English Catholics in Spitalfields was Lord Chidiock Paulet, listed in the 1578 State Papers as a Catholic living 'In the Spittle, Without Bishopsgate' (at the end of the century John Stow recorded that at the south end of Bishopsgate, immediately to the north of the Dolphin Inn, was 'a faire house of late builded' by the 'Powlet family').[6] Lord Chidiock came from eminent stock, for he was the third son of William Paulet, one of the most prominent statesmen of mid-sixteenth-century England, who had been created Baron St John in 1539, Earl of Wiltshire in 1550, Lord High Treasurer in 1550, and Marquess of Winchester in 1551. Lord Chidiock himself was rather less distinguished, though he attended Inner Temple in 1535 and held – thanks to his father's patronage – a series of public offices, mostly of a minor nature and none with any notable distinction. Part of his failure to rise was no doubt due to his Roman Catholicism. His father was pragmatic about his faith but Lord Chidiock seems to have been more defiant, refusing, for example, to sign the Act of Uniformity that, through various manifestations in the 1540s and 50s, attempted to impose religious orthodoxy on church services by enforcing the use of an increasingly Protestant Book of Common Prayer. He also seems to have been the focus of a circle of Catholics, for the State Papers' list of Catholics in the Liberty in the late 1560s and 1570s includes Rob. Hare and Saunders of the Inner Temple, who 'repair to Lord Paulet'. Robert Hare had previously been in the service of Paulet's father, the Marquess of Winchester, so clearly his link with Paulet was not simply their shared involvement with the Inner Temple. And it was Hare, the second son of Sir Nicholas Hare, Master of the Rolls and a Roman Catholic antiquary, who in 1580 leased land in St Mary's precinct, including the Principal Tenement from Stephen Vaughan the Younger. He may have been the occupant of the tenement immediately before the Flemish ambassador. Indeed, given his Catholic credentials, he may have taken the tenement on the ambassador's behalf.

There is no evidence to suggest that Paulet or anyone in his circle ever sought to challenge the Protestant establishment. Two other prominent Catholics, however, the 13th Earl of Arundel and the senior Jesuit Henry Garnet – both of whom had interests in Spitalfields – very certainly did. Philip Howard, Earl of Arundel, became involved with a property in Spitalfields in secret and desperate circumstances. Born in 1557 during the reign of the Catholic Queen Mary, Howard had as his godfather Philip II

The Braun and Hogenberg map of London of 1572. 'The Spitel fields' is top right.
indicated. To the south of the Thames on Bankside are circular arenas for

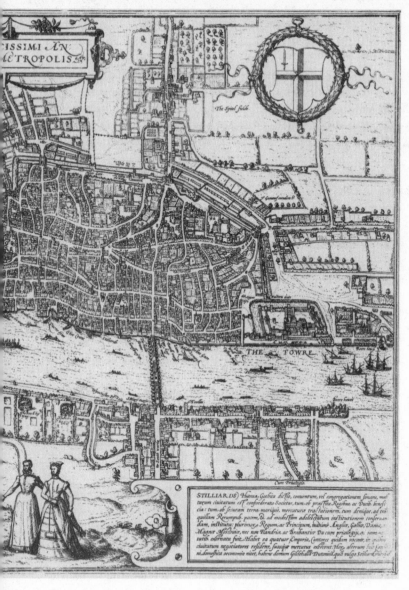

The following text labels appear within the map image:

The Spitel fields

Gravel conduit

Posterns Gate

THE TOWER

Tower Hill

STILLIARDS Hansa, Gothica dicto, conuentum, vel congregationem sonans, mul-
tarum ciuitatum est confœderata Societas, tum, ob præstita Regibus, ac Ducib. bensi-
cia: tum, ob securam terra mariq́ue, mercatura traslationem. tum deniqúe, ad tro-
quillam Rerumpub. pacem, & ad modessim adolescentum institutionem conseruan-
dam, instituta: plurimæ, Regum, ac Principum, nuxuni Angliæ, Galliæ, Daniæ,
Magna Moscouiæ, nec non Flandriæ, ac Brabantiæ Ducum priuilegijs, in summa re-
tutib. ornatæ fuit. Habet ea quatuor Emporia, (interore quidam vocant, in probri
ciuitatum negotiatores resident, suæqúe mercatus osserent. Hoc, alterum hoc est
ni domestica œconomia nitet, habent domum Gildhalla Teutonica quæ vulgo Stiluardumvoce

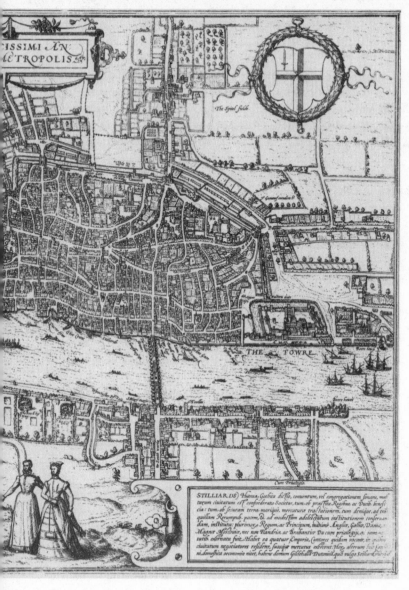

*The map stops just south of Shoreditch but no significant remains of Holywell Priory are
bull and bear 'baytyng'. After Shoreditch this was to become London's theatreland.*

of Spain, the queen's husband. But it was only in 1581, after hearing a debate in the Tower of London between the Jesuit missionary Edmund Campion and his Protestant jailers, that Howard's Catholic faith became the dominant force in his life. At about the same time his strong-willed wife Anne became a most determined supporter of the Catholic faith. In 1585, unable any longer to hide his religious conviction, Howard attempted to flee to France but was arrested as his ship left port. He was placed in the Tower, charged with high treason and eventually tried in 1589, found guilty and sentenced to death. At some point soon after her husband's arrest the countess acquired a house in Spitalfields, no doubt so as to be close to London's beleaguered aristocratic Catholic community and to her husband in the Tower.[7]

At the time of her husband's trial the countess appointed the Jesuit – and future saint – Robert Southwell as her domestic chaplain. He probably used the Spitalfields house before his eventual arrest, torture, trial and execution in 1595. Meanwhile her husband languished in the Tower, condemned but unexecuted. This was a fine exercise in mental torture since he would have known that on any day he might be put to death in an agonising manner. As an added refinement, he was told that he would be released and his possessions restored if he attended one Protestant service – something his jailers knew full well he could not in conscience do. And so the earl died, still imprisoned in the Tower, in the same year as Southwell, allegedly from dysentery. On his death he was proclaimed a Catholic martyr and eventually canonised by the Pope in 1970.

Quite where the Howards' Spitalfields house was is unknown. The family's connection with Jesuit missionary (and martyr) Edmund Campion, however, opens up an area for speculation that is also Spitalfields-related. We know that in the late 1530s a Christopher Campion had been involved in the dismantling of the priory's monastic buildings and in the acquisition of former priory land, and that he had bought the roof timbers of the priory church's 'south choir'.[8] In 1540 he built a mansion between Bishopsgate and the northern portion of the newly created Artillery Ground, presumably utilising these roof timbers in the new building. Was he related to Edmund Campion, born in 1540 to a bookseller in Paternoster Row in the City? And if Christopher, like Edmund, was a fervent Catholic, was his property dealing partly motivated by a desire to preserve sacred objects, materials and land by purchasing them from the Crown or demolition gangs? The purchases would, of course, have had to appear to be for secular use but perhaps they represented an effort, if only in a small way, to keep elements of the old faith alive or in sacred or reverential use. Presumably a house with a roof from a consecrated Catholic church would have had much meaning for, and have offered much comfort to, a Catholic family, although this cannot be proved.

Father Henry Garnet's relationship with Spitalfields is better documented than the Earl and Countess of Arundel's and appears to have been more intimate. In 1599 he is known to have been living in a house 'in a place called Spital',' perhaps in the Spittle House that from the 1580s had been occupied by the Huddlestone, Hodlestone or Huddilston family. The Huddlestones were almost certainly the same eminent Roman Catholic family that built Sawston Hall, near Cambridge, between the late 1550s and early 1580s, now famed for the large number of ingenious 'priest holes' – for hiding illicit Catholic clergy – that were created within its fabric. The Huddlestones leased their Spitalfields land from the Vaughans, which – given the Vaughans' dealings with other known Catholics – makes one wonder whether they themselves were also, secretly, Catholic. If so it would be intriguing to know how they treated the former priory buildings in order to turn them into a home; archaeological evidence suggests that the demolition of the walls of the church was far from hasty, even though its roof timbers and lead were soon removed and the fate of its monuments and fittings remains unknown.[10] At any rate, the known Catholic sympathies of this small enclave made it a natural bolthole for a man such as Henry Garnet.

In 1597 another Jesuit priest, John Gerard, made a spectacular escape from the Tower and stayed briefly in Spitalfields – probably in the Huddlestones' house – before riding away from London.[11] And then in late 1605 Garnet himself achieved national notoriety when he became embroiled with the Roman Catholic intriguers who were held to be responsible for the 'Gunpowder Plot' that aimed to blow up James I while he was in the House of Lords at the state opening of Parliament. Eight of the plotters were tried and executed in January 1606. Garnet, who was aware of the plot but had warned against it, was hunted down. When arrested he was described as being of 'a middling Stature, full Faced . . . of Complexion faire . . . of Age betweene fiftie and threescore . . . his Gate upright [but] comely for a Fatte man.' Sadly this would soon change in ghastly fashion. Garnet was horribly tortured – as was habitual with Jesuit prisoners, in order to extract information and also to mock them and break their defiant spirit. He was then tried, convicted, hanged, drawn and quartered in May 1606.

Garnet's trial and death have an intriguing literary dimension to them. In the same year Garnet faced his grisly end William Shakespeare wrote his *Tragedy of Macbeth*. It has long been argued that several of the play's major themes – treason, betrayal, the murder of a king, a monarch's legitimacy to rule – may have been a response to the Gunpowder Plot. But one particular recurrent theme – that of 'equivocation' – seems very specifically linked to Garnet himself. It was alleged that he had been told about the plan to murder the king by one of the plotters during Confession but had felt bound to silence by the Catholic concept of the 'seal of Confession'. At his trial this internal moral conflict continued, and was expressed by an agonising and ultimately fatal use of words or phrases with multiple or ambiguous meanings that were calculated to protect him from the sin of telling a lie while also allowing him to avoid admitting a perhaps fatal truth.

Such equivocation – for which Jesuits were notorious – did not save him and seems to have been met by the public with a mix of derision and frustration. Indeed, to judge from Shakespeare's response, equivocation became synonymous with treason and with evil in general. The witches and apparitions in *Macbeth* indulge in a farrago of equivocation, suggesting one thing but meaning another. Thus, for example, they assure Macbeth that he will not be vanquished 'until Great Birnam Wood to high Dunsinane Hill shall come against him', but that seemingly impossible event does indeed come to pass, prompting Macbeth 'to doubt th'equivocation of the fiend /That lies like truth' (Act 5, Scene 5). In a more direct reference to Garnet's equivocating performance at his treason trial, the porter of the castle where King Duncan is murdered hears a knocking at the gate and, fantasising that he is in charge of 'hell-gate', wonders who might be trying to gain access: 'Who's there . . . Faith, here's an equivocator that could swear in both the scales against either scale; who committed treason enough for God's sake, yet could not equivocate to heaven: O, come in, equivocator' (Act 2, Scene 3). Shakespeare lived for a while in nearby Shoreditch. Garnet was perhaps frequenting Spitalfields by 1598. Is it possible the two men met?

Not all of Spitalfields' outsiders, it should be said, were rendered so by their religious beliefs. Some were common-or-garden crooks or at least people whose lives would not stand up to close examination by the authorities. According to some accounts, for example, St Leonard's Church in Shoreditch became the final resting place for Sir Thomas Manners, son of Eleanor Manners, Countess of Rutland. The Countess – a staunch Roman Catholic – was lady-in-waiting to four of Henry VIII's wives: Anne Boleyn, Jane Seymour, Anne of Cleves and Catherine Howard. She died in the Manners house in Shoreditch and may have been buried in Shoreditch church (although there is a monument to her in the Rutland chapel in St Mary's Church Bottesford, Leicestershire). Her life was exemplary but that of her son was not. Although an eminent soldier, he died in disgrace in 1591, 'outlawed' and with his goods forfeited, as a serial offender for debt. Thomas was, it seems, yet one more 'outsider' who found a final resting place near Spitalfields, in Shoreditch church.

And then there were the men of the theatre.

Until the mid sixteenth century England's dominant theatrical tradition was that of 'Mystery' or 'Miracle' plays – drama that presented moral and improving stories from the Bible and that was generally performed by troupes of amateur actors or members of guilds, in churches or on temporary scaffolded stages. With the Reformation, however, such plays fell from favour. Protestants – particularly Puritans – viewed them as an expression of Catholic superstition and mysticism. In their place, secular productions therefore came to the fore, performed by 'professional' strolling players, generally in the courts or yards of galleried inns. But these in turn had their critics. While Miracle plays could be viewed as blasphemous by unfavourably minded Protestants, secular plays could often be viewed as licentious, obscene, rabble-rousing, even treasonable or seditious. London's Elizabethan City fathers certainly disliked them. In 1572, in an attempt to prevent the spread of plague, they banned the production of plays, and in 1575 they expelled players from the City altogether. The general view of those in authority was that public theatre was more trouble than it was worth, at the very least distracting apprentice boys from their work.[12] Better to have plays performed out of sight and out of mind – or, at least, only in front of courtiers. The new legislation obliged players to move outside the City, to Newington Butts south of the Thames, for example, and to Whitechapel, Shoreditch and Finsbury.

One of the victims of this clampdown was the actor, joiner and theatre manager James Burbage. Up until then he and his theatre companies – initially Lord Leicester's Men, then Lord Howard's (soon known as the Admiral's) Men – had attempted to function in the court of the Bull Tavern, on Bishopsgate, opposite St Helen's Place, and so within the wall and City authority. Now Burbage needed to look elsewhere. And the site he chose was in the Liberty of Holywell – immediately to the north of the Liberty of Norton Folgate – once owned after the Dissolution by Henry VIII's porter and now by entrepreneur Giles Allen, by repute a greedy man with no interest in the theatre, only in the profits such an activity could generate. Here in 1576, within the remains of the Holywell nunnery and next to the surviving great barn, James Burbage constructed what was arguably London's first permanent, purpose-designed and -built structure since Roman times dedicated solely to theatre. Known simply as the Theatre, it made Shoreditch and Norton Folgate, if only briefly, London's first serious theatreland.

We know tantalisingly little about the Theatre. It was constructed too late to be included in the three early maps of Spitalfields and Shoreditch described earlier (see pages 47–54), and did not last long enough to be included on later maps. There appear to be no certain views of it and only one – a vague and anonymous sketch of the environs of London produced in about 1598 – that might possibly give us a rough idea of what it looked like. This sketch shows the eastern edge of the City of London from the north and is evidently not very accurate for it suggests that the city sat on a plain flanked by high hills – even mountains – to the south. It shows, in the area of Shoreditch and Holywell, a tall, broad, tower-like structure, perhaps polygonal in form, from which a flag is flying, and to the right of it, some way off, a lower building, rectangular in shape, with a pitched roof and also flying a flag. The first building could be the Theatre – though this is far from certain – and the second the Curtain Theatre, opened in 1577, possibly by one Henry Lanman or Lenman, who clearly sought to capitalise on the instant success enjoyed by the Theatre, just 190 metres away. The flying flags depicted in the drawing suggest that both these structures were indeed theatres, with performances underway.

A seven-year agreement between Lanman and Burbage was signed in 1585, which stipulated that the Curtain was to function as a 'supplementary' venue for Burbage's company of players – which in 1594 became known as the Lord Chamberlain's Men – and that the two signatories were to 'pool' their profits, an arrangement suggesting that in the mid 1580s at least the Curtain must have been as successful and profitable as the

Theatre. The Curtain, incidentally, was not so-named because of any feature it contained – the curtained proscenium did not exist in the Eliza-bethan theatre – but because it was built in Curtain Close.

James Burbage financed, constructed and probably designed the Theatre in collaboration with his wealthy brother-in-law and partner John Brayne – who was a member of the Grocers' Company and who in 1567 had created the temporary Red Lion Theatre in Whitechapel. The Theatre was built quickly: a timber-frame construction resting on a masonry plinth. (Initial archaeological discoveries made in June 2012 suggest that the Cur-tain, too, was largely timber-framed, with three tiers of galleries on three sides, a stage on the fourth, and open to the elements.) In the case of the Theatre, the archaeological evidence, although slight, suggests it was round or polygonal in plan, probably with an open court, galleries, a partly weather-protected stage on one side with a 'tiring house' – a room behind the stage into which actors would retire during a performance – and perhaps a bal-cony above the stage. If so it established – at a stroke – the essential form of the majority of London's permanent theatres for the next fifty or so years. Shakespeare's famous reference in the prologue of *Henry V* to the 'wooden O' in which his play was being performed would seem to confirm the design of the Theatre and suggest that this play was intended to premiere in this striking location.

It's perhaps worth noting, though, that in the event, the first perform-ance of *Henry V* was probably given not in the Theatre but in the Curtain. Assuming the play's premiere took place in 1598 or 1599, as is generally agreed, it was during a period when outbreaks of bubonic plague were regularly closing London theatres or causing chaos with productions and when the Chamberlain's Men seem to have temporarily left the Theatre for the Curtain (probably between 1597 and 1599). This might seem a mere foot-note in literary history, except for the fact that, judging from what archaeological excavation tells us about the form of the Curtain, this particu-lar building did not approximate a 'wooden O' like the Theatre, but was more rectangular in shape. If that is indeed the case, then the famous promise made by the Chorus in *Henry V* to evoke the 'vasty fields of France . . . within this wooden O', must have caused a degree of puzzle-ment to the play's first audience. One pictures them looking around the rectilinear interior in bewilderment and wondering what on earth the actors were talking about.

As to why the pioneering Theatre, at least, should have been circular or

A detail of an enigmatic London perspective from 1598 looking south–west to Shoreditch and Holywell. It appears to show the polygonal form of the Theatre, built in 1576 and London's first purpose–built permanent theatre since Roman times. The flying flag suggests a performance is under way. To the right is a rectangular, gabled building, also with a flag flying. This could be the Curtain, built in 1577.

polygonal in plan, it seems most likely that it and most of its progeny were designed to echo what was known of the shape of ancient Roman theatres (whose forms would have been familiar from the mid-sixteenth-century publication of Sebastiano Serlio's *Tutte l'opere d'architettura* and from Andrea Palladio's *I quattro libri dell'architettura* of 1570, both of which include reconstructions of Roman amphitheatres). At the same time, it is clear that circular forms also held symbolic meaning. A theatre with a round, oval or polygonal plan could be seen to encompass the world in miniature, within which all emotions could be evoked; a place of magic; a place of transformation in which the imagination was stimulated, through poetry and story-telling, so that passing shadows assumed substance and meaning. As William Shakespeare explained in his prologue to *Henry V*, the playwright's task was to '[o]n your imaginary forces work'.

Our best guess as to the internal appearance of the Theatre comes from a sketch by a Dutch visitor named Johannes de Witt made of the Swan Theatre, erected in 1595 in Southwark (contemporary maps and perspectives show the Swan to have been tall and polygonal in plan with an open court surrounded by tiers of galleries and a small tower rising above the stage). The sketch, which survives in a copy made by his friend Arend van Buchel, shows the polygonal inner court with galleries and a stage, set between a pair of columns, thrusting forward into the courtyard. These two columns suggest a biblical reference to the Temple of Solomon, where the Holy of Holies – the location of the Ark of the Covenant and the divine fount of all knowledge, all beauty – was approached by passing between a pair of guardian columns, Jachin and Boaz.[13] These columns later became a key image in Freemasonry but in the Swan (and presumably in its fellow theatres) were no doubt intended to signify the magic that took place on-stage through words and acting, where worlds were conjured up, all human emotions plumbed, and – through art – a written play was transformed before the eyes of the audience into a living thing that touched upon universal truths. Certainly, Shakespeare cast spells with his poetry – as Frances Yates puts it: 'Though Shakespeare never wielded a wand, nor thought of himself as a magus, he *is* a magician, master of the spell-binding use of words, of poetry as magic.' And a play such as *The Tempest* is 'infused through and through with spiritual alchemy and . . . transformation.'[14]

De Witt's sketch confirms the Roman amphitheatre-like appearance of the interior, with tiers of galleries rising above the courtyard into which the stage (served by two doors as in classical theatres) thrusts to occupy at least a quarter of its area. This relationship is no doubt an expression of primary geometry where the circle that defines the plan of the building contains a square delineating the stage. The combination of the circle and the square was a traditional part of sacred geometry, the circle representing the spiritual world and the square the material one, with its four sides and corners symbolising the four elements and the four seasons – even the four evangelists who, in a sense, through the Gospels gave Christ's sublime teachings, or 'Good News', to the wider world. No doubt the designers of these theatres contrived to include other sacred numbers in the geometry of their constructions – notably the number twelve representing the signs of the zodiac and the planets through which, by tradition, the gods of old ordered the lives of men. Sacred geometry would have been viewed as appropriate because theatres were – in a broad sense – sacred or alchemical places where base material was transformed into gold every time a band of players managed to transfix, enthral or inspire its audience.

Johannes de Witt apparently bound his sketch into the journal (now lost) recording his London visit. With the drawing was a written description, a copy of which survives, and what it has to say is most informative. It records that:

> There are four amphitheatres in London so beautiful that they are worth a visit, which are given different names from their different signs. In these theatres, a different play is offered to the public every day. The two more excellent of these are situated on the other side of the Thames, towards the South, and they are called the Rose and the Swan from their signboards. There are two other theatres outside the city towards the North, on the road that leads through the Episcopal Gate called Bishopsgate in the vernacular [these, of course, were the Theatre and the Curtain]. The most outstanding of all the theatres, however, and the largest, is that whose sign is the Swan . . . as it seats 3,000 people. It is built out of flint stones stacked on top of each other (of which there is great store in Britain), supported by wooden pillars which, by their painted marble colour, can deceive even the most acute observers . . . its form seems to bear the appearance of a Roman work . . .

The Lord Chamberlain's Men went on to build the first Globe Theatre in Bankside in 1599 (it burnt down and was rebuilt in 1614) and its six shareholders included Richard and Cuthbert Burbage (sons of James, who had died in 1597) and William Shakespeare. The first Globe seems to have been similar in size to the Swan, as presumably was the Theatre. Records suggest that the Globe was three storeys high, had a diameter of approximately one hundred feet, with a stage forty-three feet wide and twenty-eight feet deep, and could hold 3,000 people. And if the Theatre was also similar to the Swan in proportion, detail and appearance then something very extraordinary had been erected in Shoreditch in 1576: a building that was not only to provide a model for future theatres but which, in its form, was seen as a representation of the world at large, and a place in which theatrical performance could touch the soul.

The troupe of actors who performed at the Theatre was impressive, and included Burbage's son Richard as well as Shakespeare, who worked initially as an actor in the 1580s before becoming part-owner of the company. Richard Burbage lived in Holywell Lane, just south of the Theatre, and it is thought that Shakespeare lodged in 'Hog Lane' (now Worship Street), 'six doors from Norton Folgate' and Shoreditch High Street.[15] Indeed the area became quite a magnet for people from the world of the theatre: John Webster (c.1580–c.1625), who wrote *The White Devil* and *The Duchess of Malfi*, like Richard Burbage took up lodgings in Holywell Lane. The famed Pye Inn, shown on the 'Copperplate' map (see page 50-1) and slightly ominously named after the magpie, a bird of questionable omen, was owned in the 1580s by the Alleyn family, who counted among their number the actor and impresario Edward Alleyn.

Baptised in St Botolph's Bishopsgate in 1566, Alleyn played, early in his career, the title roles in Christopher Marlowe's *Tamburlaine the Great* (c.1588), *Doctor Faustus* (c.1592) and Barabas in *The Jew of Malta* (1589), and went on to become the great rival of Richard Burbage and partner of Philip Henslowe, with whom he owned the Rose on Bankside and the Fortune (built 1600) in Finsbury Fields. Later in life Alleyn founded Dulwich College.

The company seems to have worshipped at nearby St Leonard's Shoreditch, and this was where James Burbage was buried in February 1597. Indeed St Leonard's became a necropolis for London's early theatre community for here were interred, along with Richard Burbage, William Sly and Richard Cowley, who acted in some of Shakespeare's plays.

Ben Jonson was also an habitué of Spitalfields and its environs. The fact that his seven-year-old son, who died from bubonic plague in 1603, should have been buried in St Botolph's Bishopsgate suggests that Jonson and his family were at the time living in or near Spitalfields. Jonson was heartbroken by his loss and expressed his grief, and his reaction to such an unseasonable death, in verse:

> Farewell, thou child of my right hand, and joy;
> My sinne was too much hope of thee, lov'd boy . . .
> Rest in soft peace, and, ask'd, say, 'Here doth lye
> Ben. Jonson his best piece of poetrie . . .'

If the City fathers had a low opinion of theatrical people, then the conduct of one or two of their number must have served as confirmation and made the authorities grateful that the dramatic community had decamped beyond the City walls. Ben Jonson himself was clearly no angel. In September 1598, possibly following a drinking bout near the Curtain, he quarrelled with and then killed his erstwhile friend, drinking companion and fellow actor Gabriel Spencer, near the site of present-day Hoxton Square. Another playwright based in Spitalfields, Christopher Marlowe, enjoyed an even worse reputation. Indeed much that we know about him is gleaned from the court records peppered with his name.

Marlowe appears to have lodged in Norton Folgate with his fellow playwright Thomas Kyd. His first brush with the law came in September 1589 when he got into a brawl in 'Hog Lane' (probably Worship Street, off Norton Folgate) with William Bradley, said to have been the son of a local innkeeper. Ostensibly the quarrel was over an unpaid debt. Thomas Watson, a Cambridge friend and poet, who also lodged in Norton Folgate, came to Marlowe's rescue and in the ensuing melee Watson stabbed and killed Bradley. Marlowe fled, and a warrant for 'Thomas Watson of Norton Folgate in Middlesex County, gentleman, and Christopher Marlowe of the same, yeoman . . .' was issued for their arrest. They were apprehended on 18 September by Stephen Wylde, 'Constable' of the Liberty of Norton Folgate, on suspicion of murder, and both were imprisoned in Newgate. At their trial on 3 December 1589, however, Watson's claim of self-defence was accepted and both were discharged and warned to keep the peace.

Marlowe, though, seems to have been incapable of keeping out of trouble, for just three years later, in 1592, he was summoned to appear at the Middlesex sessions for assaulting two constables in Holywell Street, just off Shoreditch High Street. This time there is no evidence that he ever stood trial for the offence. The reason for this is not clear but it may have something to do with the rather peculiar status Marlowe seems to have enjoyed. There is a strong possibility that he was involved during the 1580s in the Elizabethan intelligence service, operated by the wily Sir Francis Walsingham, Secretary of State and Queen Elizabeth's 'spymaster', and engaged in subtle plots of counter-espionage.[16] In point of fact, the two men lived very close to one another, Marlowe in Norton Folgate, Walsingham, until his death in 1590, in the house known as the Papye (see page 47), at the south end of Bishopsgate and just within the city wall. One wonders whether the two men might have used the nearby Pye Inn as a convenient and perhaps relatively neutral and anonymous place in which to meet. One wonders, too, whether Marlowe's services to the state rendered him immune, to an extent, to the processes of the law.

Whether Marlowe's clandestine life spilled over into his work is a moot point, but some have suggested that in some of his plays – notably *The Tragical History of the Life and Death of Doctor Faustus* of c.1592 – he was arguably fulfilling a political role by seeking to undermine the mysticism and occult 'superstition' that Protestants saw within the ever-present and threatening Roman Catholic Church of such state enemies as Spain. *Faustus* can be read as anti-mystical propaganda of a beguiling and sophisticated sort, or indeed as an attack upon the occult interests of the Elizabethan Renaissance – personified by such figures as the mathematician and astrologer John Dee – that greatly troubled Puritanical Protestants.[17] *Faustus* can also, in its association between magic, occult learning and demonic possession, be seen as a forerunner of the anti-witch craze and witch hunts of the early seventeenth century – an obsession reflected in the future King James I's *Daemonologie* of 1597 in which he approved witch hunting and the punishment of 'these detestable slaves of the Devil'. Of course, it's also quite possible that Marlowe was simply capturing – or anticipating – the mood of the moment.

The playwright's violent death in 1593 seems of a piece with his life and is equally mysterious. On the evening of Wednesday 30 May, he was stabbed to death by one Ingram Frizer at Eleanor Bull's rooming house in Deptford, apparently in an argument over a bill. Frizer, termed a 'gentleman' at the time and some sort of property speculator or commodity broker, appears to have been one of Walsingham's inner circle, being the agent and financial adviser to a close relative, Thomas Walsingham. Also present on that fatal evening was another of Walsingham's men, Robert Poley, a double-agent, *agent provocateur* and evil genius of the Elizabethan espionage underworld, who had played a key role in exposing the Babington Plot against Elizabeth I in 1586. He is thought to have lived in a tenement in Houndsditch, just east of the Pye Inn towards Aldgate and just beyond the City wall, north of the Papye. Needless to say, these were men one did not want to mess with. But, in some way, Marlowe did. It's also possible that he was the victim of an assassination ordered by these men's bosses and controllers within the Elizabethan intelligence service. At the time of his death Marlowe was under arrest, for reasons unknown, and due to appear before the Privy Council, for which – among his many 'intelligence' jobs – Poley was an agent. What on earth did these men imagine Marlowe was about to do, or what dark secret did they think he knew? After the killing Frizer was found to have acted in self-defence and was granted a royal pardon.

By the early 1580s the Theatre – as well as the Curtain – was well established, and it seems likely that a number of Shakespeare's early plays were premiered there, even if it is now impossible to say which: as already noted, outbreaks of the plague, notably in 1592–4, 1597 and 1599 (and between 1603 and 1608), caused huge disruption to and the temporary closure of various theatrical venues. It seems entirely feasible that *Richard III*, probably written in 1591/3 (perhaps because Shakespeare had time on his hands due to the plague), could have been first performed in 1593/4 at the Theatre. So could *Romeo and Juliet* in 1594 or 1596. Others were probably premiered at the Curtain. Marlowe's plays were probably never staged in Shoreditch; Southwark seems a more likely venue. As for Ben Jonson's works, we know that in 1598 the Lord Chamberlain's Men gave the premiere of his second-known play, *Every Man in His Humour*, at the Curtain, with Shakespeare acting a leading role. The reference in the play to old clothes dealers from Houndsditch suggests that the Petticoat Lane area's reputation as a market stretches back a long way.

But by the time *Every Man in His Humour* saw the light of day the Theatre was already history.

After James Burbage's death in 1597 his share of the business was taken on by his sons – Richard, the actor, and Cuthbert, who operated as theatre manager. By now the Lord Chamberlain's Men were flourishing and clearly eager for bigger things. They therefore made the decision to move from the Theatre to a venue that was larger, more prestigious and potentially more profitable, and to this end purchased the Upper Frater Hall in Blackfriars – another ex-monastic and marginal area, this time to the west, that lay outside the strict control of the City authorities – converting the hall to theatrical use. Unfortunately, they had misjudged their new neighbours. Some were rather grand and clearly disliked the thought of what a bunch of actors might do to the tone of the area. They complained to the Privy Council. Sharing the City Aldermen's less than admiring view of the theatre, the councillors in turn made clear their own concerns. This was more serious than the tussle with the Aldermen. The Privy Council was part of the apparatus of state, a great power in the land, and that power could be exercised ruthlessly. The company therefore bowed to the inevitable and in the autumn of 1598 Cuthbert Burbage went to Giles Allen to discuss renewing the lease on the Holywell site.

The negotiations did not go well. It might be that Allen, who lived near the Theatre, had tired of the noisy theatre-going crowds that gathered so near to his house. It seems more likely, though, that he was determined to squeeze as much money from the company as possible and knew that with a potential new site denied to them their bargaining position was weak. At any rate Allen informed Burbage that as their old lease had expired, their former landlord now owned the Theatre and was of a mind to tear it down and put its timbers to 'better use'. For its part, the company decided not to play Allen's game. Rather than upping their offer for a new lease they hatched a plot. Their original lease contained a clause stipulating that the company had the right to dismantle the building. Since the lease had expired, the status of this provision was unclear, but it seemed to give the company at least a shadow of legitimacy for the act they were about to commit – the removal from Allen's control of the materials of the Theatre. Clearly the company's legal position was that while Allen owned the land, they owned the building and had the right, by the terms of the now defunct lease, to dismantle their own building even if it meant trespassing on Allen's land to do so.

The company waited until Christmas, when Allen left his Holywell house for the country and a long holiday. Then on the night of 28 December 1598 the Burbage brothers, their carpenter Peter Street and a body of workmen descended upon the Theatre. It must have been an extraordinary sight as the men removed the fittings and fixtures and dismantled – speedily but carefully – the roof structure and heavy timber-frame forming the Theatre's robust structure. The materials were immediately transported across the Thames to Bankside – another marginal area with a riotous reputation and home to brothels and bull- and bear-baiting rings – and from 1587 London's new and favoured location for theatres. The Rose was opened by Philip Henslowe in that year, followed in 1595 by Francis Langley's Swan Theatre. And so, alongside these polygonal or cylindrical theatrical structures – seemingly inspired by the Theatre – the Burbages, Shakespeare and their partners constructed the Globe Theatre, its polygonal form determined by the nature of the salvaged timbers re-used from the Theatre. The choice of name for this new theatre – the Globe – revealed very directly the all-encompassing aspirations of the Elizabethan theatre. The first play performed within this new 'cockpit' – in late 1599 – was probably Shakespeare's *Tragedy of Julius Caesar*.

The sudden removal of the Theatre, in such dramatic circumstances, seems to have expunged it from memory, with even meticulous map-makers failing to revise existing maps to document its existence and appearance. No one seems even to have recorded its extraordinary and speedy disappearing act during the quiet days of a Christmas holiday. All that is certain is that Giles Allen, when he returned home to Holywell after Christmas, was far from amused by the trick that the actors had pulled.

First he let it be known that he would sue the Burbages' carpenter Peter Street for the £800 Allen calculated he had lost by the 'theft' of the building. Street was, presumably, the only individual Allen believed he could prove had been involved in the dismantling. An action was duly heard but the court found against Allen, who did not pursue the case further.

As for the Curtain, it remained a working theatre until 1622 and was part of Shoreditch's struggle to remain London's theatreland in the face of the Burbage defection to the opposition represented by the newly erected theatre at Bankside. Strangely, this fight-back was fuelled by two of the pioneers of Bankside's theatreland – Philip Henslowe and the Bishopsgate-born Edward Alleyn, who was Henslowe's son-in-law – and their company the Admiral's Men, with which the Burbages had once been involved and who had used the Theatre. When faced by the competition offered by the newly arrived Burbage team with their Globe, Henslowe and Alleyn decided to expand and diversify their operations by opening a new theatre in the area that the Burbages has just deserted. It was a bold but also a canny move – to fill the gap left by the Lord Chamberlain's Men and become the main company in London's oldest theatreland, where many businesses must have felt exposed by the sudden desertion of the Burbages. The site Henslowe and Alleyn chose was about a quarter of a mile to the west of Holywell, but still outside the jurisdiction of the City authorities. It was at Golden Lane, just north of the Barbican, and here in 1600 they built the Fortune Playhouse. Soon after this, in about 1603, the company from the Rose on Bankside – Queen Anne's Men (named in honour of James I's queen) – moved to the Curtain and so no doubt reinforced the renaissance of Shoreditch theatreland.

Intriguingly, the carpenter Henslowe and Alleyn chose to build the Fortune was Peter Street, who had recently built the Globe for the Burbages using the Theatre's timbers. But the theatre built at Golden Lane bore little physical resemblance to the round or polygonal theatres on Bankside. It was rectangular or square in plan – perhaps similar in appearance to the nearby Curtain. Was this resemblance to affirm some point that is now not clear? And who was the designer of the Fortune? As with the Theatre, the Globe and the others we do not know for sure. Presumably theatre owners and the more learned actors or playwrights took a leading role, working with masons or master carpenters like Peter Street and using published sources.

Despite Henslowe and Alleyn's investment in the Fortune and Queen Anne's Men's in the Curtain and the Red Bull in Clerkenwell, the Shoreditch–Golden Lane–Clerkenwell arts nexus did not grow to compete with Bankside. When the Globe was built south of the river it made the area unassailable as London's premier place of dramatic entertainment. After the Curtain closed in 1622 the Fortune continued – indeed was even rebuilt after a serious fire in 1621. It didn't close until 1642, by which time the newly established Puritan authorities in London, strengthened by the outbreak of the Civil War, were also busily closing and then destroying the theatres on Bankside.

FOUR

PEOPLE OF SPITALFIELDS

Doña Luisa de Carvajal y Mendoza and Sir Francis Bacon

During the late 1990s, archaeologists from the Museum of London carrying out excavations in the former northern precinct of St Mary's Priory, on the site of part of Spital Square, unearthed the remains of a large house constructed in about 1600. Documentary research suggested that it had been known as the Brick House – the latest and largest of three structures in the area to go by that name. Built on what had been a virgin site, it straddled land belonging to the Candle House to the south (which had been owned by Vincent Goddard since 1582, having passed to him from William Wyld via the Wilkinson family), and land to the north owned by the Vaughan family. It's possible that the construction of the Brick House was a joint venture, and it is no doubt significant, as the archaeologists point out, 'that the central corridor of the building – alley or possibly a covered (ground-floor) passage . . . is on the line of the property boundary and divides the house into northern and southern rooms'.[1]

The excavation showed that the house was indeed, as its name suggested, brick-built. It was four windows and two rooms wide and one room deep. It had two doors in its main, west, elevation – one leading to the central entrance passage or alley and another leading directly into the ground-floor room to the south. This was without a fireplace and so was perhaps intended to house a shop or workshop, or adapted to do so in the late seventeenth or eighteenth century. The ground-floor room to the north contained a kitchen and scullery with a large chimney breast, incorporating an oven, set against the east side of the room, and a more or less intact if undulating brick floor. On the east side of the south room was a separate long, thin structure serving as a 'garderobe' – or lavatory set above a cesspit – and incorporating chimney flues and supporting a stack. On the north side of the house was an oblong staircase tower leading to a series of upper rooms.

A reconstruction of the west elevation of the house, on what was originally

Spital Yard and then Spital Square, has been undertaken by the archaeologists and suggests the house was probably four storeys high, including garrets with small windows set within three gables on the west and east elevations.[2] The two first-floor windows to the north were fitted with larger mullioned and transomed bays, probably lighting a main chamber or hall. In the view of the archaeologists the stairs 'probably led up to a large first-floor hall extending over both the northern and southern rooms, with a fireplace along the east wall and a privy chamber with a large garderobe further south along the wall . . . There would have been an upper, second, floor of chambers above the first-floor hall, perhaps with smaller servants' chambers in the garret above that. The garderobe stack might also conceivably have functioned as a chimney stack at the upper levels, allowing the chamber or chambers in the south side of the house to have been heated.'[3]

To the east of the house was a large garden, containing a well and a detached privy over a cesspit shared by another dwelling. To the south was a yard, shared with the neighbouring Candle House, which contained another detached privy.

The Brick House was clearly well appointed and commodious. And in 1611 it became home to one of the most unlikely residents of Spitalfields, indeed of Jacobean London: Doña Luisa de Carvajal y Mendoza.

Doña Luisa was born in 1566, the daughter of wealthy, noble Spanish parents, but was orphaned at the age of five and grew up with a maternal uncle, who had close links with the Jesuits. Meetings with exiled English Catholic priests in Madrid seem to have inspired her in 1605 to travel to London as an independent Catholic missionary. This was a dangerous undertaking. The Treaty of London of 1604 made the trip possible because it ended nearly twenty years of war between England and Spain, but political relations remained strained, Spaniards were viewed with deep suspicion in England and Catholic worship was proscribed and could have fatal consequences.

The reason Doña Luisa came to London was probably the same reason that the English College in Douai in Flanders – run by Spanish Jesuits and eventually supported by a Papal subsidy – trained and smuggled English Catholic priests into their home country during the late sixteenth and early seventeenth centuries, to almost certain, and painful, death. The Jesuits of Douai wanted to preserve and 'augment' the faith of the Catholics in

England and keep the country within the Catholic community of nations. So Luisa's mission was simple although seemingly impossibly ambitious – to help convert 'England's capital city to what she looked on as the one true faith and the only means to salvation.'[4]

The English Protestant authorities viewed the secret arrival and ministrations of Jesuits and Catholic missionaries in a very hostile light. These were not spiritual emissaries in the view of the Protestants, but agents of temporal and potential or actual enemy powers – notably Spain – sent to cause mayhem and strife, to encourage sedition and rebellion amongst English Catholics, and to gather information helpful for military invasion. This suspicion was lent vivid substance by the Papal Bull of 25 February 1570, issued by Pope Pius V, that excommunicated Elizabeth I, 'the pretended Queen of England', and released her subjects from allegiance to her, and charged all not to obey her, her mandates or laws, in fear of 'like sentence of excommunication'. It was a blatant encouragement to English Catholics to disobey Elizabeth and her government. Moreover, it granted the 'legal' and ethical right and religious authority to her subjects, in certain limited circumstances, to topple or even kill their queen. Naturally this state of affairs encouraged the Protestant authorities to view the Catholics in their midst 'as a body of potential rebels, who only waited for foreign invasion to declare themselves'.[5]

One consequence of the atmosphere of alarm this Bull created was to increase persecution of Catholics in England. From 1570 it was high treason and thus potentially a capital crime to bring into the country any 'instrument' obtained from the 'Bishop in Rome', to attempt to 'reconcile' any of the queen's subjects with the instruments of the Bishop of Rome or to be 'reconciled'. In addition, to bring into the country or receive any object of devotion, 'tokens, crosses, pictures, beads or such like vain things from the Bishop of Rome', was punishable by the confiscation of property.[6] The anti-Catholic feelings generated, and the fact that being a Catholic was increasingly synonymous with political and national disloyalty, meant that Jesuits and Catholics who were arrested after 1570 were rarely charged or executed for their faith alone but dealt with as instigators of civil unrest, as traitors and as agents of foreign enemies. And in consequence their deaths were painful – many were tortured on the rack as a routine procedure after capture and before execution, to extract information about their contacts and for propaganda purposes. If a Jesuit broke down under torture he could be accused of displaying little 'patience' or fortitude, of being untrue to his religious convictions, and his weakness would be celebrated by his Protestant tormentors and publicised.

Anti-Catholic legislation in England gradually increased. An Act passed in 1581 'to retain the Queen Majesty's subjects in due obedience' imposed an increased scale of fines. For hearing Mass the penalty was 100 marks and a year's imprisonment. This was the first time that the Mass had been specifically proscribed in England.[7] The same Act also provided that the penalty for not attending Anglican church services should be £20 per month, per head for those over the age of sixteen. This was cunning legislation. Many Catholics felt it blasphemous and a dishonour to their religion and beliefs to attend Protestant church services. By this legislation, therefore, principled Catholics were forced to reveal themselves to the authorities and, at the same time, pay huge sums that would swell the coffers of their persecutors while at the same time impoverishing themselves.

According to one twentieth-century Catholic chronicler of these events: 'The object of this legislation was to outlaw and ruin the Catholic community' in England,[8] the immediate result being to drive it underground, into a world of fear, with Masses whispered in secret, priests travelling in disguise, sacred vessels kept in hidden cupboards and strangers viewed with deep suspicion. Another consequence was to create a network of Protestant spies, informers and *agents provocateurs*, inflamed not so much by religious zeal or patriotism as by profit. Rewards were great, not least because a third of the value of fines exacted from people revealed to be Catholic went to the informers. Blackmail became a profitable profession because the potential punishments for Catholics were so dreadful – poverty, imprisonment, torture and execution – that buying silence could be an attractive alternative. Perhaps worse still – certainly most unsettling – was the fact that the laws were not only harsh but often enforced in a most arbitrary and wilful way.

One provision was that any person who twice refused to take the Oath of Supremacy – which was re-introduced in 1559 and acknowledged Elizabeth as the legitimate queen and supreme governor of the Church of England – was guilty of high treason and thus liable to be executed. The Act of Uniformity – also of 1559 – finalised the liturgical form of the Church of England and made much Catholic doctrine illegal. These were devastating threats to Catholics that could be applied at any moment if a particular magistrate had a mind to apply the thumbscrews to the local recusant, or Roman Catholic, population.

This compositionally curious print depicts a tribunal – seemingly gathered within an idealised Renaissance city – contemplating Edmund Campion being racked as an excruciating prelude to execution. Torture was not intended primarily as a means of extracting information but as a form of humiliation that, the Protestant jailers hoped, would lead to the physical, emotional and spiritual collapse of their Jesuit prisoners.

Some families and influential individuals known to be Catholics were left in peace, such as the well-connected family of Sir William Petre based at Ingatestone Hall, Essex. Sir William had been a Secretary of State to Henry VIII, Mary and Elizabeth, and was evidently pragmatic about his religion, but his son John was a committed Catholic, although this did not prevent him from being raised to the peerage in 1603 as Baron Petre. And Ben Jonson was generally known to have converted to Catholicism in 1598 though was still employed by the court of James I to write masques before his public return to the Anglican faith in 1610. But others, if they raised their profile too high or were caught hiding Jesuit priests, faced destruction. As Evelyn Waugh observes, 'raids for proscribed objects – rosaries, religious pictures, crucifixes, etc. – took place capriciously . . . everything depended on local goodwill and the activity of the professional informers.'[9]

In the context of these events and legislation it is clear that in early-seventeenth-century London, to be Spanish, openly Catholic and to display proselytising zeal, was to court disaster and invite accusations of espionage and incitement to treason or insurrection. But Doña Luisa was clearly undaunted – and she had a precise operational plan. Her aim in London was to succour persecuted Catholics, both native-born and foreign, to give support to those under arrest, to help Catholic women in their worship, to secure the body parts of martyred English Catholics so they could serve as inspirational relics of spiritual power, and – in essence – to do what she could to save the souls of the benighted Protestant English from eternal damnation by guiding them back to the true faith.

Doña Luisa travelled to England with her confessor and spiritual adviser, the English Jesuit Michael Walpole (1570–1624), a member of an ancient Norfolk family that was eventually to produce Sir Robert Walpole, Britain's first prime minister. For the purposes of the journey, Walpole disguised himself as Doña Luisa's servant. They arrived on Easter Saturday 1605 and once in London soon contrived to live beyond the eyes of the law: visiting imprisoned Catholic priests, hiding fugitives, undertaking conversions to Catholicism (Doña Luisa had a special mission amongst the city's prostitutes) and arranging baptisms into the Catholic Church – all highly dangerous activities. For a long time they went undetected but finally, in 1610, Walpole was arrested while attending Luisa. He was imprisoned, and although pressure from the then Spanish ambassador, Antonio de Valesco, led to his release, Walpole was compelled to leave England. He did not return until 1613, when he accompanied the incoming Spanish ambassador, Don Diego Sarmiento de Acuña, Lord of Gondomar, as he took up his new post.

During this early period of her stay in London Doña Luisa lived as part of the household of the Spanish ambassador at that time, Pedro de Zúñiga, in the embassy, just outside the city walls in Aldersgate Street, Barbican.[10] The house, with chapel and walled garden, was later known as Bridgewater House and the site was latterly marked by Bridgewater Place. Luisa also stayed with local Catholic families where she tried to learn to live as an Englishwoman. But then in late 1611, having survived approximately six years of underground religious activity, she took the gamble of becoming fully independent and establishing her own 'mission' or secret nunnery. And the location she chose for this risky enterprise was the Liberty of Norton Folgate, Spitalfields, where she rented the Brick House from its official tenant, a Mrs Threele.[11]

Thanks to Doña Luisa's Spitalfields papers, along with over 170 of her letters and poems that survive in Spanish archives, we know quite a lot about her '*conventito*' in 'Spetele'.[12] 'The house made of bricks, with the little round tower',[13] as she described it in the summer of 1612 to her brother, who was planning to come and visit her, was located 'just where the countryside begins, [it] is the last house in this part of London, spacious and full of light, and with cleaner air than anywhere else in London.'[14] Situated next to fields and among orchards, gardens and the open spaces around Spital Yard, it must have come as a wonderful contrast to the congested and noisy Barbican where Doña Luisa had previously lodged, with the fresh country breezes particularly welcome in an age when it was generally assumed that diseases spread through noxious air. Moreover, Doña Luisa was living among people she could trust – fellow Roman Catholics. In her letters she describes her convent as adjoining the garden and house of Antonio Foscarini, the Venetian ambassador, which itself lay next to the house of the Flemish ambassador – a representative of a territory then under Spanish control – whose wife had, by strange coincidence, once been little Luisa's maid.[15]

Among the 'recusant' Catholic community present in the Liberty when Doña Luisa arrived – or at least with an interest in the area – was Anne Vaux, a wealthy and aristocratic Catholic lady whose main contribution to the promotion of her religion was to rent houses in which Catholic priests could shelter. She was well known to the authorities but her high and good connections kept her relatively unscathed. At the end of Queen Elizabeth's reign Vaux is known to have kept a 'safe house' in Spitalfields that for many years provided a base for Henry Garnet, the leading Jesuit figure and her particular friend. It is not known for certain where this house was but it could have been Spittle House, or a house on its land owned by the Huddlestones, who were almost certainly a Catholic family from Cambridge (see page 44). Garnet had met Luisa on her arrival in England in 1605.

The presence of this Catholic community, including protected dignitaries such as the ambassadors, was evidently a key, practical reason for establishing the nunnery in Spitalfields, even if Doña Luisa was taking a huge risk in placing herself beyond the pale of the Spanish ambassador's direct diplomatic protection. But another factor might well have appealed to her as well. The land on which her Spitalfields house stood had once been sacred, monastic ground, home to a priory dedicated to the Virgin Mary, and hallowed by over 300 years of Roman Catholic worship. For anyone of Doña Luisa's mystical sensibility, this link with the past must have exerted a powerful attraction.

Her letters offer some details about life in what she called her 'miniature nunnery'.[16] The small religious order secreted within the Brick House was called by Luisa the 'Society of the Sovereign Virgin', and according to Museum of London archaeologists, using Glyn Redworth's translation of Doña Luisa's letters, 'The unofficial order included de Carvajal and perhaps a dozen companions, including a French servant, the disguised Jesuit Michael Walpole [who had come to live with Doña Luisa on his return to England] and other priests in hiding, and Englishwomen en route for Continental nunneries.'[17] Four English Catholic girls seem to have stayed with Luisa, as her assistants and companions, in the Barbican and in Spitalfields. Ann Garnet – related to the Jesuit Henry Garnet – Juanna, Susana and Faith. It is not clear why these girls, all seemingly in their early twenties, preferred to stay within an embryonic and illegal convent in London rather than go abroad.[18] But they provided Luisa with invaluable help, particularly Ann Garnet. Luisa offered 'testimonial to her cooking, her skill at making communion wafers and . . . her willingness and ability to resort to fisticuffs.'[19] As Doña Luisa wrote on 29 June 1608, 'One day I was coming out from Mass in Don Pedro's house [the Spanish ambassador] . . . with my rosary in my hand, and one of the passers-by, a heretic, came over to take it away from me and she immediately attacked him and punched him hard several times, saying "wretched man! So you want the rosary?" . . . in matters of religion, she is like a lion . . .'[20]

In 1611 Doña Luisa's idyllically located Spitalfields house cost her £10 a year in rent – a not inconsiderable sum – and financial pressures mounted as the size of its Catholic community grew. Soon a house in the Barbican, where Luisa had earlier lodged, had also to be kept in commission.[21] Doña Luisa's main, if not only, regular income to support these two houses and her community was the pension she received directly from the Spanish king that amounted to 200 reales per month (increased in 1613 to 500 reales or £12). This was paid through the Spanish Embassy.[22]

Security within the Brick House was an abiding concern. 'Innumerable locks were fitted' and Luisa 'drilled her companions in how to repel unwanted visitors'.[23] The house was fitted with a series of double-doors, not only to offer defence but to delay access to its inner parts if an incursion took place; the front door had a grille so bread could be passed through without the door being opened and with the face of the person inside the house being obscured; water was channelled into the house directly from the garden which, to aid self-sufficiency, was used to grow lettuce, onions, beans and cabbage. The chapel was on an upper floor – almost certainly the first floor – 'so hidden from everyone that only those who searched very carefully were able to discover it.'[24] Luisa liked to think of the house as 'our Oran' – referring to Spain's strong fortress on the North African coast.

One of Luisa's companions later wrote about the fortress mentality that prevailed in the house:

She was very careful and watchful over the house, preventing still the dangers that might happen by these bad folks the pursuivants [meaning a junior officer 'of arms', presumably serving the Lord Mayor or Bishop of London] and other such like, as she had heard that in the Catholics' houses sometimes they would break in at the windows and walls of the house and when the doors had been opened to thrust themselves into the house by force; but she with her wisdom and sharp understanding did prevent their devilish desires . . . As for the doors, she was always careful to choose one of the house most careful, obedient, and punctual that would follow her directions in all things for to be the porter and to keep the keys of all the doors. When anyone had knocked at the door she must look out of the window to see whom it was, then to tell her [Luisa] that such a one was there; and this she would have always done . . . because if anything should happen she would be one of the first that should know of it. Luisa also instructed the porter never to open the front door without getting one of the maids to 'shut the second door before she opens the first'.[25]

Although the nunnery was intended primarily as a staging post for Englishwomen who wanted to go overseas to become Catholic nuns, it also had another, more mystic function. Luisa made it a repository of Catholic relics. In early-seventeenth-century London these were in ready supply because executions were frequent and the body of every executed Catholic martyr instantly became a sacred relic. The gathering of the body parts of martyrs – who had usually been hanged, drawn and quartered – was dangerous and more than a little physically demanding, if also – for a Catholic – spiritually thrilling. One gruesome story is typical of many. On 30 May 1612 a monk named William Scott – whom Luisa had known – was executed along with a Catholic priest named Richard Newport, their quartered bodies thrown into a deep grave near the place of execution and then covered with the unquartered bodies of sixteen common criminals. Luisa organised a rescue mission. She recruited a dozen men – mostly from the Spanish Embassy where Scott had acted as a confessor – who were 'armed in case they were spotted by the guards who were posted there by the authorities'.[26] One of the embassy men later remembered a particularly distressing moment. When he lifted one of the criminal's bodies it fell back on him, spraying his face with decaying detritus. But the much-tried relic-hunter took comfort from the fact that it was a noble thing that Luisa had asked him to do and that 'the smell coming off had not been bad but good'.[27]

The body parts of Scott and Newport were eventually collected, placed in pouches made from Luisa's sheets and, for reasons of secrecy and security, taken to Spitalfields at dead of night in an anonymous-looking hired coach. The scene is described by Glyn Redworth using Luisa's letters. The house in Spitalfields was 'brimming with flowers' given to Luisa by well-wishers. The pouches containing the body parts were carried in sombre, candle-lit procession to the chapel, across a floor strewn with flowers and floral wreaths. The bodies were placed 'on the carpet in front of the altar, and covered with a large piece of red material that was new, with lots of sweet-smelling flowers on top. On bended knee, we offered up a prayer.'[28]

During the following twenty-four hours Luisa cleaned the body parts, using dry cloth and spittle, before coating them in spicy unguents and sealing them in properly labelled lead boxes.

Why precisely did she go to all this trouble? Redworth explains: 'Catholic teaching held that holy relics created an environment akin to religious "hot spots", being places where heaven and earth intersected. Miracles could happen . . . and prayers that were offered up in their vicinity were far more likely to be heeded.'[29] In addition, the Council of Trent – held between 1545 and 1563 – had stated that altars could be sanctified by incorporating the remains of those who had suffered for their faith. So, at one level, Luisa was giving her house and chapel a mighty spiritual charge.

Carluccio's restaurant now stands on the site of the Brick House but, because the land has risen by about two metres in the last 350 years, the current ground level marks almost exactly the first-floor level of Doña Luisa's house. And it is perhaps worth noting, for those with a feel for such things, that the serving counter where smoked and cured meats are now displayed marks the location and level of Doña Luisa's first-floor chapel altar where the body parts of Catholic martyrs were placed.

The martyrs' relics did not, however, remain long in Spitalfields. Members of the Spanish Embassy seem to have taken them when they returned to Spain, and parts of Scott and Newport probably ended up in the village of Gondomar in Galicia.

There can be little doubt that the authorities had their suspicions about what was taking place in the Brick House – not least because nuns and novices were hooded and veiled while inside and bells were rung for services. But for a while an attitude of tolerance prevailed, perhaps because of Doña Luisa's close connections with the Spanish Embassy, perhaps because her behaviour was generally pretty discreet. Certainly James I, made aware of this strange little Catholic nest on the north-east edge of London, chose to do nothing. But in the autumn of 1613 his laissez-faire attitude changed.

That year had seen the publication of a book entitled *A Defence of the Catholic and Apostolic Faith against the Errors of Anglicanism* by a Jesuit living in Portugal named Francisco Suarez. Tackling one of the cornerstones of James's kingship head-on, it dismissed his long-held view that kings were appointed directly by God, ruled in His name, and so – ruling by Divine Right – were above the machinations of ordinary mortals. Indeed, for James, kings were almost gods. Suarez put the contrary argument: 'No king or monarch has or had the power to rule immediately from God or by divine institution, but only by the will and investiture of the people.'[30] He also argued that there were circumstances that justified people rising up and dethroning a tyrannical or godless king. James was furious. Here was yet more evidence of the Jesuits' deep-laid plan to undermine his right to rule. He claimed that Suarez' book 'would rob kings and princes of the loyalty of their subjects'[31] and he authorised action against known Catholic houses, especially those associated with Jesuit or missionary activity.

On 18 October 1613 (Margaret Rees says 28 October) the Sheriff and Recorder of the City raided Luisa's house in Spitalfields. The raiders were ostensibly acting on the 'request' of the Archbishop of Canterbury, George Abbott, who had long harboured a particularly strong antipathy towards Catholics, but it had been the king himself who had instigated the raid. The Sheriff and Recorder were evidently keen to terrorise for they were accompanied by 'sixty halbardiers, with both infantrymen and cavalry back-up troops'.[32] These armed men surrounded the house, used ladders to scale the garden wall and then broke down all the doors – a process that, given Luisa's precautions, took half an hour.[33] Once inside this armed multitude found nothing more than an ailing and slight middle-aged matron, living in poverty with a few young women. Such was the astonishment of the armed throng – who evidently expected something very different – that they did not search the house properly and failed to enter the chapel, where they would have discovered some of the Catholic regalia they had expected to see throughout the house.

But if the raid was an anticlimax it was also, in some respects, dramatic. One of the maids in the house – 'a gentleman's daughter of good worship' named Ann – died within a few hours of the raid, according to Jesuit Richard Blunt, presumably from shock. Happily this was not the pugnacious Ann Garnet, who was to outlive Doña Luisa. Seemingly a second member of the household – suffering from smallpox – died the next day.[34] During the raid the Flemish ambassador, Ferdinand de Boisschot, came to Luisa's aid and through his quick thinking managed to extricate Walpole from the house by pretending that he was a meddling servant. De Boisschot was made a Knight of the Order of Santiago just over a year later by King Philip III of Spain – perhaps partly as a reward for this admirable action that almost certainly saved Walpole's life.

The Spanish ambassador – Gondomar – arrived while the raid was still under way, alerted by an alarm bell fixed on the house. He tried to arrange for Doña Luisa to be released into his custody but since the king himself had ordered her detention this civilised solution was not possible. Instead Luisa and her companions were arrested and carried to the Archbishop of Canterbury's residence at Lambeth Palace. There she was accused by the archbishop of being a 'Jesuitess', along with all her 'disciples', and he demanded to know how many were in the nunnery and what rule did they follow? Doña Luisa calmly told the archbishop that he was not her judge.

Doña Luisa and her companions were held for three days in the palace's Gatehouse Prison, where they were voluntarily accompanied by the stalwart wives of the Spanish and Flemish ambassadors. For his part Gondomar launched a spirited defence of Doña Luisa, arguing (with Philip III's direct support) that she was part of his household and therefore had diplomatic immunity, and that she had only been visiting the house in Spitalfields at the time – a seemingly plausible claim given that while negotiations were going on, he managed to organise the removal of Doña Luisa's chalice and religious ornaments, compromising papers and incriminating evidence from the Brick House. Gondomar was a man of influence at the English court, not least because when he arrived in 1613 he brought with him a proposal that the Infanta Maria Anna of Spain, the daughter of Philip III, should marry James I's son Prince Charles – a proposal not without its appeal to James I, who stood to gain (among other things) a handsome 'dowry' from Spain that would spare him from having to go to Parliament for cash. The negotiations ultimately came to nothing, but they gave Gondomar useful influence during the Doña Luisa case, and he was thus able to save her from imprisonment and execution. However, his attempt to achieve her release back into London society failed. Doña Luisa and her companions were given over to his custody on condition that she should leave England as soon as she was well enough to travel.[35]

Doña Luisa returned to her former house in the Barbican. But here she made it clear she did not want to leave London. She believed she had been chosen by God for the mission of restoring Catholicism to England and declared that she wanted to save the souls through conversion of those damned by their Protestant error of faith. She was therefore imprisoned and questioned again, if only for a few days. Her health, though, was failing fast, and she died in London on 22 December 1613, acknowledged by her fellow Catholics as a martyr for her faith. Her funeral was held at the

chapel of the Spanish ambassador's residence (which by this time was perhaps already in Ely Palace, Ely Place, Holborn, where the surviving
late-thirteenth-century St Etheldreda's Church served as the chapel),
attended by the leading Catholics in the city. Doña Luisa's body – now
itself a precious relic – was sealed in a lead coffin within a wooden casket
and in the late summer of 1615 was shipped to Spain. Here a squabble
erupted about possession of the relic, which was resolved when Philip III
ordered that it should be deposited in the Royal Nunnery of the Incarnation in Madrid. And that is where the casket remains, in the reliquary
room, with Luisa's body still unburied. An earlier move to have Doña
Luisa recognised as a saint petered out, was revived in the early twentieth
century and remains in abeyance. But there might yet be a Catholic Saint
Luisa of Spitalfields.[36]

The Brick House seems to have stood until around 1725, although how
its survival can be reconciled with the general rise in ground level in the
area that took place from the early 1680s remains a puzzle. Certainly the
site on which it stood is shown occupied by a building or buildings on
Ogilby and Morgan's map of 1676, and this looks in plan much like the
Brick House – an alley is shown where the house's internal passage would
have been.

A map of the area prepared in 1712–13 in connection with the proposed
building of one of the 'Fifty New Churches' shows an 'Old Building'
marked near the site of what was soon to become number 22 Spital Square.
According to the *Survey of London* the house is shown 'approached by a
flight of steps and traversed by a winding passage'.[37] This almost certainly
records the Brick House. If so, it was not destined to endure much longer.
By the late 1720s the site had been cleared and raised for a new development, and by the early 1730s numbers 19–21 Spital Square stood over the
remains of the Brick House, with their basement levels set just above the
ground level of the old house. Excavations in the late 1990s confirmed that
the ground floor of the Brick House was around two metres lower than
the early-eighteenth-century street level.

The early-Georgian houses were, in their turn, demolished in the
early and mid twentieth century and today a curious mixture of modern
buildings – constructed from the late 1990s – stand on the site of the
Brick House. The construction of these modern buildings led to the
destruction of the physical remains of the Georgian terrace and the Brick
House, although not before they were fully documented by Museum of

London archaeologists and with key archaeological items documented, conserved or retained. But curiously one long-lost element of the Brick House has – by chance – been recreated in the modern development. The Brick House's large garden, which stood to its east and was largely built over after 1730, has been cleared and is now occupied by the western portion of the newly created Elder Gardens. These stand a couple of metres above the early-seventeenth-century ground level but now, once again, people stroll and sit where Doña Luisa grew her vegetables and where her nuns would have taken the healthy country air.

At the time that Doña Luisa lived in the Brick House the building next door to the south, the Candle House, was in the tenancy of a Lady 'Millmaye', possibly the diarist Lady Grace Mildmay, one of England's earliest, if largely self-taught, female medical practitioners and wife of the MP Sir Anthony Mildmay, whose own claims to fame included that he was Sir Francis Walsingham's nephew and that he served for a while as the English ambassador in France. In 1616, three years after Doña Luisa's arrest and death, the Candle House was occupied by scientist, philosopher, lawyer and statesman Sir Francis Bacon.[38]

Assuming that Lady Millmaye was indeed Lady Mildmay it's understandable why someone who was so independent-minded and unconventional in their tastes, belief and manner of life might have gravitated to Spitalfields. In Sir Francis Bacon's case, though, the appeal of the area may seem less immediately obvious – after all, in 1616 he was still one of the most publicly successful and powerful men in Britain. But Bacon had a secret life that, if exposed, could have led to accusations of heresy and sexual deviancy, and Spitalfields offered him a relatively safe place in which to pursue his somewhat risky interests.

Bacon's rise had been rapid but not without the dangers that any ambitious man of his time had to contend with. He had been the 2nd Earl of Essex's friend and adviser since 1591, but when the Earl moved towards open rebellion in 1601 Bacon faced a dilemma: should he support or denounce his friend? In the event he chose to distance himself from Essex and make clear his support for Queen Elizabeth; and at Essex's subsequent trial Bacon, in his role as an eminent lawyer, was part of the team – led by Attorney General Sir Edward Coke – prosecuting his former friend and benefactor, and after the trial had run its course and Essex was condemned to death Bacon was ordered by the queen to write an official and justificatory account of the procedure, which was published as *A Declaration of the Practices and Treasons attempted and committed by Robert, late Earle of Essex and his Complices, against her Majestie and her Kingdoms*. At the time his stance must have seemed an entirely prudent one, but when, just two years later, James I succeeded Elizabeth I its wisdom might have seemed more questionable: for Essex had been rebelling to remove a 'weak' and aged woman from the throne and replace her with a strong prince – and the prince he'd had in mind was the man who had just assumed the English throne. James's accession, then, could have seen Bacon's rising star toppled and his ambitions crushed.

Bacon, however, moved fast, and in 1604 published his *Apologie concerning the late Earl of Essex* for his role in the fall of his friend. It could very easily have been a hopeless and grovelling exercise that led to charges of hypocrisy and his ultimate humiliation. But Bacon's brilliance was such that he was able to pull it off, even if his principal defence – that he had frequently proclaimed Essex's good character to the queen and attempted to intervene to stave off disaster – seems, to us, at least, a very weak one. James at any rate was impressed. He also admired Bacon's subtle and enquiring mind, and shared his interest in magic, esoteric studies and experimental science. Bacon was knighted, in 1607 he was made Solicitor-General and in 1608 was in addition made clerk to the Star Chamber.

Despite these profitable and powerful public positions his debts started to pile up. He therefore sought yet more offices, selling his soul to the king to secure them, and so becoming party to royal policies that were often wild, wilful and arbitrary. He also used – indeed abused – his offices to farm 'gifts' from those he was increasingly in a position to help. At first he managed to survive difficult times with admirable aplomb, and to secure ever more prestige: he became Attorney-General in 1613. But by 1614 there were signs that the tide might start to turn against him. In April of that year a number of Members of Parliament objected to Bacon's presence amongst them, arguing that although he held the seat for Cambridge, his close connections to the king were incompatible with the independence required of an MP. He weathered that storm, and retained his seat, but Parliament responded by passing a law forbidding Attorneys General to sit in Parliament.

Even so, in 1616 – the year Bacon took the Candle House in

Spitalfields – his ascendancy in public life seemed assured and he became prominent in one of the most extraordinary and mysterious legal cases of seventeenth-century England: the prosecution of Lord Somerset and his wife Frances Howard for murder. Somerset – as Robert Carr – had been one of the great favourites at the court of James I, who had a notorious liking for handsome young men. The king had showered gifts and honours upon him. Those honours included being created the 1st Earl of Somerset in November 1613 and Treasurer of Scotland in December. The gifts included Frances Howard, with whom Somerset seems to have been infatuated. Inconveniently she was already married to the 3rd Earl of Essex, son of the 2nd Earl who had been executed in 1601 and of Frances Walsingham, the daughter of Sir Francis Walsingham. The Essexes had been barely in their teens when they were married in 1604 and had been obliged to live apart. The marriage was not happy, was not consummated and was finally annulled in September 1613, thanks to the intervention of the king, and on Boxing Day of the same year Somerset and Howard were married.

Somerset's close (perhaps intimate) friend and mentor Sir Thomas Overbury distrusted Howard (or more likely was jealous of her) and had tried to prevent the marriage. In revenge Howard managed to have Overbury removed from court for being disrespectful to the queen and then persuaded the king to make Overbury an offer she knew he would not accept. Overbury was appointed ambassador to the court in Moscow, which was tantamount to banishment. He refused the post, which Howard was able to present as an act of treason that resulted in his being sent to the Tower in April 1613, where he died five months later.

After Overbury's mysterious death Somerset's career continued to soar and in 1614 he was made Lord Chamberlain. But then, typical of the wilful and arbitrary court of James I, things rapidly started to go wrong for him and for Howard. In 1615 Somerset and the king fell out, perhaps because James was starting to focus his attention on a new favourite, the young George Villiers, later Duke of Buckingham. Now it was Somerset and Howard's turn to find themselves the victims of manipulative and hostile forces. In September 1615 it was announced that Overbury had been poisoned while in the Tower and Somerset, Howard and a number of their minions were accused of the crime. Sir Francis Bacon, working once again with Sir Edward Coke, was directed to discover the truth of the matter. He was, of course, hardly neutral given his controversial relationship with Howard's first father-in-law – the 2nd Earl of Essex.

Howard soon confessed her role in the murder, while Somerset protested his innocence. Certainly, there was no hard evidence against him, and there were also great fears that he might be indiscreet if the case came to trial, and reveal details of his relationship with the king. Eventually Howard and Somerset were found guilty, but while their agents were executed, their lives were spared. Although they did not face execution, husband and wife were imprisoned in the Tower. Howard was soon pardoned but, strangely, Somerset was not. Clearly negotiations were afoot. The guilty pair wanted to secure their lives and eventually their freedom; the king seemingly didn't want to take their lives but did want to secure their silence. In all the toings and froings Bacon was the central, and no doubt brilliant, negotiator. Eventually in 1622 Howard and Somerset were freed and Somerset was then pardoned two years later in 1624, after which he lived a life of relative obscurity, dying in 1645. Nothing was made public about the king's role in the life of this unappealing couple. That presumably was Bacon's triumph.

It's tempting to believe that Bacon took the Candle House as a suitable and private place, within a short distance of the Tower, in which to conduct discreet interviews while this long case rumbled on. But there may have been another reason, too, connected to his private life. John Aubrey, in the biographical notes he compiled in the late seventeenth century that were eventually published as *Brief Lives*, asserted that 'Bacon was a *paiderastos*' and that 'his Ganymedes and Favourites tooke bribes'.[39]

To be a pederast in the London of James I was not necessarily a problem, if it meant no more than admiring – in a softly erotic way – young and comely members of one's own sex. After all this is what the king did repeatedly with such as Carr and Villiers. But if this admiration got out of hand and resulted in physical activity, then not only would convention be flouted but the law broken. And if this physical action involved penetration then one's very life was in danger. Buggery was a capital offence and those who indulged in it and were caught, brought to trial and found guilty, faced public humiliation and execution.

The possibility that Bacon did take his pederasty to the extreme is most strongly argued by Sir Simonds D'Ewes, a character of some interest as being a typical product of a troubled and turbulent age. D'Ewes, born in 1602, was a Suffolk gentleman of Puritanical leanings and antiquarian tastes, who trained as a lawyer, became a politician, was knighted by Charles I in 1626 but who supported Parliament – in an undemonstrative manner – when the Civil War came. He was also a diarist and in an entry for 3 May 1621 records of Bacon:

> His most abominable and darling sinne I should rather burie in silence, then mencion it, were it not a most admirable instance, how men are enslaved by wickedness & held captive by the devil. For . . . would he not relinquish the practice of his most horrible & secret sinne of sodomie, keeping still one Godrick, a verie effeminate faced youth, to bee his catamite.

This, stated D'Ewes, was a habit Bacon 'had practiced manie yeares, deserting the bedd of his Ladie [Bacon was married], which he accounted, as the Italians and Turkes do, a poore & meane pleasure in respect of the other.' D'Ewes suggests the danger Bacon was running when he indulged his nature:

> . . . it was thought by some, that hee should have been tried at the barre of justice . . . & have satisfied the law most severe against that horrible villanie with the price of his blood; which caused some bold and forward man to write these verses . . . & to cast it down in some part of York house in the Strand, where [Bacon] yet lay [York House was Bacon's family home, where he was born, and was known as one of his more favoured residences]:

> > Within this sty a hogg doth ly,
> > That must be hang'd for Sodomy.

If Bacon was indeed a pederast and a sodomite, then he might well have thought that the Candle House in remote and marginal Spitalfields was the safest place in which to indulge his dangerous interests. At the same time, a place on the edge of society might have suited a man who was also fascinated by the occult and keen to indulge in speculations that many at the time could have regarded as heresy, or at least incompatible with conventional Christian doctrine. As he himself noted in one of his own maxims: 'an habit of secrecy is both politic and moral.'[40] He may, for example, possibly have been a member of the Brotherhood of the Rosy Cross (the Rosicrucians), a secretive Christian order dedicated to the discovery and application of ancient esoteric knowledge, including alchemy and the Hebrew and Christian Cabbalas, and fascinated by legends that had, or seemed to have, profound spiritual meanings – such as the quest for the Holy Grail by King Arthur and his knights of the Round Table. It's a claim that remains unproved but Frances Yates suggests that his allegorical book *New Atlantis*, published posthumously in 1627, portrays a utopian religious and scientific society moulded by Rosicrucian beliefs and ideals.[41]

In 1617 Bacon was appointed Regent of England. It was a post that lasted only a month, but for that brief period the Candle House could have served as the centre of his own court – the 'extensive' seventeenth-century alterations to the fabric of the building, noted by Museum of London archaeologists, could be evidence of improvements Bacon himself undertook around this time.[42] The following year he was created Lord Chancellor and Baron Verulam, elevated in 1621 to Viscount St Albans.

But from this date Bacon's public career plummeted speedily downwards towards dismal disgrace, as the powerful enemies he had inevitably made during his glittering ascent circled him and then attacked. In 1621 he was investigated by a Parliamentary Committee and charged with twenty-three separate counts of corruption (his erstwhile legal colleague Sir Edward Coke prepared the charges). Rather than fight these, though, Bacon admitted them, while arguing that the gifts he had received had never influenced his legal judgements. Puzzled by such a response Parliament sent a deputation to check with Bacon that the confession it had received was indeed his. Bacon confirmed that it was: 'My lords, it is my act, my hand, and my heart; I beseech your lordships to be merciful to a broken reed.' That he had been corrupt is unquestionable: as Attorney General and Lord Chancellor he had freely accepted 'gifts' to free himself from crippling debts. Why he should have confessed so speedily, however, is much less clear. One can't help wondering whether he was being blackmailed because of his homosexuality by those seeking his fall, and had decided to confess to a corruption charge that was unlikely to bring with it the death sentence, rather than one of buggery that – if proved – almost certainly would.

In the event Bacon was fined £40,000 and committed to the Tower at the king's pleasure, and although James stepped in to remit the fine, and Bacon was released within days and retained what money he had and even his titles of nobility, his public humiliation was complete. Stripped of his offices and declared by Parliament to be unfit to hold any public position in the future, his career was at an end. Even so, if Sir Simonds D'Ewes is representative, there remained a vindictive and vengeful body of people who continued to wish Bacon ill. Writing in his diary just after Bacon's fall D'Ewes approved the fact that 'upon his censure at this time his ambition was moderated, his pride humbled, and the meanes of his former injustice and corruption removed', but regretted that Bacon 'never came to anye publicke triall for his crime; nor did ever, that I could heare, forbeare his old custome of making his servants his bedfellows . . .'[43]

So, in these bleak circumstances and hostile environment, Bacon had no alternative but to devote himself to his philosophical and theological studies, to his scientific speculations and experiments, to his writing – and perhaps to his private passions.

The length of Bacon's sojourn in Spitalfields is not known, but he died less than five years after his fall, after contracting pneumonia during an experiment to discover if meat could be preserved by freezing.

It is possible that Bacon's choice of Spitalfields as a refuge attracted other like-minded men who, inspired by interests that were esoteric and could be viewed as heretical, even diabolical, sought refuge on this obscure edge of the city. For example in the 1640s Nicholas Culpeper – a herbalist but also an astrologer – chose 'Red Lyon Street' (later part of Commercial Street), located in the part of Spitalfields most distant from the City, to live and work.[44] After Culpeper's death in 1654 John Heydon – astrologist, seer, alchemist and occultist – took lodgings in Culpeper's house with his widow whom he married in 1656. Heydon – author of *The Angelical Guide* – managed to be imprisoned for his convictions by both the Commonwealth and the restored monarchy and, among other things, seems to have been a Rosicrucian in the Baconian pattern (about which he published much) and a Cabbalist.

As for 'Red Lyon Street', this seems to have become something of a centre for unconventional thinkers because, apart from Culpeper and Heydon, it also attracted John Holwell – astrologer, mathematician, visionary and author of the prophetic 1682 book *Catastrophe Mundi: or, Europe's many Mutations until the year 1701*. And by Holwell's time Spitalfields was attracting a whole new population of religious outsiders. If, at the beginning of the century, it had provided refuge to Catholics like Doña Luisa, by the latter decades it was proving attractive to Protestant Dissenters and Quakers, not least the radical Presbyterian Samuel Annesley (grandfather of two of the founders of Methodism, John and Charles Wesley) who lived near Spital Yard (see page 186). Licensed in Spitalfields in 1672, Annesley preached there until his death, sometimes up to three times a day. He also found time, according to the antiquarian and gossip Anthony Wood, to father 'a quarter of a hundred children'.[45]

PART TWO

A LAND OF SILK

Late-Stuart and Georgian Spitalfields

FIVE

BUILDING ON RUBBLE

The Rise of the New Spitalfields

On 2 April 1662 Samuel Pepys went to Spitalfields to hear the Spital Sermon. He arrived in time to see 'my Lord Mayor and the blewe coat boys' processing in pomp to the Spital Cross, immediately north-east of the charnel house;[1] and then he and his friend Mr Moore 'got places' to hear the sermon itself, probably in the gallery erected in the 1590s on the orders of the Lord Mayor against the north wall of the charnel house, or in the grandstand erected to the north-west and facing towards the Spital Cross.[2]

The landscape he surveyed would have been one familiar to a pre-Civil War visitor: the charnel house still standing amid scattered remains of the former monastic precincts, notably the Candle House, and a number of late-sixteenth or early-seventeenth-century buildings, including the Brick House and the Master Gunner's House. But within a few decades everything was to change. The charnel house was to be demolished and its remnants – along with those of the adjoining Master Gunner's House – buried under two metres of rubble. Gradually the last visible remnants of the priory were to disappear, and completely new buildings were to spring up. By the late 1720s, medieval Spitalfields was no more and the birth of a new Spitalfields – different in architectural and social composition – was well under way.

Some significant new developments had actually taken place in the years before Pepys came to hear the Spital Sermon. These were the initiative of the Whelers, who in many respects were the key force in the development of seventeenth-century Spitalfields. They were a country family and their involvement in the area seems to have been the outcome of an advantageous marriage. In 1594 the freehold of the forty-three acres of Lolesworth Field (also called 'Spittlehope') – the land immediately to the east of the former priory precincts, stretching as far as Brick Lane – was

acquired by Richard Hanbury, a City goldsmith. The transfer of the freehold of Lolesworth to the Wheler family took place when Hanbury's
daughter Elizabeth married Sir Edmund Wheler who, through the marriage, also acquired property in Datchet, Buckinghamshire. Thereafter
various Whelers became involved in the possession of Lolesworth in a
series of arrangements of almost Byzantine complexity and involving various branches of the family.[3]

The Whelers were also responsible for one of the most significant religious buildings in seventeenth- and eighteenth-century Spitalfields. In
1693 the Reverend Sir George Wheler built St Mary's Spital on the spot
where the Liberty of Norton Folgate met the Parish of St Dunstan's Stepney: on 'Church' (now known as Nantes) Passage running south of 'White
Lion Street' (now Folgate Street).[4] It was intended to serve as a chapel-of-
ease for the Wheler Estate tenants – relieving them of the need to travel
to distant parish churches – and until the completion of Christ Church in
1729 it was the only Anglican church within the heart of Spitalfields.
Rebuilt in 1755, and subsequently much altered, it was finally demolished
in 1911 when the site was sold to the City Corporation and eventually used
for the expansion of the Spitalfields flower market.[5]

The estate acquired by the Wheler family was bounded on the south by
the line of what became White's Row and Fashion Street, on the east by
Brick Lane, on the north by Swan Field and on the west by the precincts
of the former Priory of St Mary, later the Liberties of Norton Folgate and
the Old Artillery Ground. It was divided roughly into north and south
parts by the west–east line that became Lamb Street and 'Browns Lane'/
Hanbury Street.

The western edge of the Wheler Estate came as far as the garden wall
of the Brick House, occupied until 1613 by Doña Luisa de Carvajal (see
pages 89–102). This meant that, in addition to Lolesworth Field, the
Whelers also acquired land that had in the mid sixteenth century been
part of Stephen Vaughan's garden, and before Vaughan's time part of the
priory garden. By the early seventeenth century this land was known as
the Old Brick Orchard;[6] and it seems the family extended, in gradual and
piecemeal fashion, its estate to the west of this. Evidently in 1645 a house
called the Brick House (almost certainly that once occupied by Doña
Luisa) was owned by William Wheler, as he at that time confirmed the
charitable annuity paid out of it. It seems that the house was at this time
occupied by Mrs Wheler.[7]

In 1648/9 one of the Whelers – William Wheler of Datchet – conveyed the portion of the estate south of Lamb Street and 'Browns Lane' in trust to Edward Nicholas and George Cooke, for the benefit of himself, of his wife Jane for her life, and then to raise 'portions' for their seven daughters. The estate north of Lamb Street and 'Browns Lane' passed by 1654 to William Wheler of Westbury. According to the *Survey of London*, 'in the 1640s Lolesworth Field remained entirely undeveloped' but it 'was by this William Wheler that the northern part of Spitalfields was first laid out in streets . . . north of the line of Lamb Street and Brown's Lane . . . in the 1650's and 1660's'.[8] For example, in April 1656 a ninety-nine-year lease of ground 'probably near Vine Court was granted to Andrew Bond, tyler and Bricklayer. Thomas Wildgoose, a carpenter, was also granted a lease on this part of the estate.'[9]

The stimulus to build was at least in part due to the relaxation in the early 1660s of the prohibitions against house construction on new foundations that had characterised life in London over the previous four decades – prohibitions that had resulted from a fear that an ungoverned growth of the city would suck people in from essential and productive activity in the country to uncertain futures in the capital, and thus help create a rabble inclined to discontent and insurrection. Charles I had issued a proclamation to ban new development in May 1626, and others had followed during the Commonwealth period in the 1650s. In a statute of August 1661 the Restoration government had forbidden any building on 'new foundations within two miles of any gate of London or Westminster' unless on a site of four acres or more (it had also stipulated that where building was permitted, brick and stone rather than timber should be employed). There had always been ways round this ban, either by paying 'fines' to the Crown, gaining an Act of Parliament to permit building, or by simply taking a chance and going ahead (an option that was risky because proclamations repeatedly recommended that illegal buildings should be demolished, and undesirable because illegal builders tended to skimp on construction costs and secrete new buildings in cramped alleys and courts).[10]

But prohibitions against growth were, in themselves, rapidly becoming unsustainable by the time of the Restoration. As Norman Brett-James points out, there is little doubt that London in the early 1660s 'needed cleansing and remodelling, and [that] the actual effect of the rules against building had been, in so far as they were obeyed, to produce still greater overcrowding in the narrow streets of the City and the existing suburbs, and to render the sanitary conditions still worse.'[11] And the Great Fire of 1666 changed attitudes profoundly, from a desire to hinder to a desire actively to encourage new building. For these reasons, and given the remorseless growth of London's population, prohibitive legislation fell into disuse and during the 1660s consent for construction was more easily obtained, as in the case of the Wheler family and its Spitalfields estate.

A portrait of Spitalfields just before 1660 is offered by William Faithorne and Richard Newcourt's London map, published in 1658. The Artillery Ground, occupying most of the southern precinct of the former priory and defined by its brick wall with buildings along its south boundary, is shown clearly. To its east is a large field containing what appear to be three long rows of fabric drying in the sun – presumably dyed wool. This field – the 'Tenters' ground – is separated from the still undeveloped Spitalfields to the north by a straight road or lane, built along only at its west end. This became White's Row/Fashion Street. To the south is Wentworth Street, fully lined with buildings as far as its junction with Brick Lane.

The northern precinct of the former priory is shown as a large oblong court surrounded by a compacted huddle of gabled buildings. These buildings probably represent the charnel house, with the Master Gunner's House on its south side and the Principal Tenement complex of buildings and the Vaughan/St John house to the north. The east side of the court presumably represents the Candle House, to the north of which is the gable end of the Brick House. North of the Brick House is a west–east lane that was 'White Lion Yard' and is now Folgate Street. The west end of this lane, where it joins Bishopsgate/Norton Folgate, appears to be closed by a large structure. This could be a representation of the remains of the gatehouse that gave access to the northern portion of the priory and its service yard.

To the east is Brick Lane – curving gently on a line from the north-west to the south-east. There is no indication of the Civil War rampart, ditches or redoubt, but there is a continuous group of buildings along its east side, approximately as far as 'Browns Lane', all furnished with large and partly communal gardens or pastures.

Just a few years later Wenceslaus Hollar's maps, produced in 1666 and 1667, immediately before and after the Great Fire, show an extraordinary transformation. By the mid 1660s the western and southern portions of Spitalfields were being absorbed into the ever-growing body of the City; and by 1667 Wheler Street – long, relatively wide and straight – running

north through the open space of 'Spittle Fields', had been established as
the principal new street of the area. Hollar shows it lined with continuous
terraces and tenements, presumably built largely of brick as current building proclamations specified and ornamented with robust and charming
vernacular classical details. A notable feature of the street is that most of
its buildings have gardens of generous size. To the west of Wheler Street
is a large open garden and orchards (seemingly undisturbed since the time
they formed part of the priory's orchard) that stretch as far west as the
buildings along Norton Folgate. To the east of Wheler Street, 'Vine
Street' has emerged, parallel to Wheler Street and also running north off
'Spittle Fields'. The open space of 'Spittle Fields' is now framed on three
sides by closely packed buildings with only its west side still open to the
walled Artillery Ground. To the south of the 'Spittle Fields', towards
Petticoat Lane, all has become urbanised as gardens dwindle to make way
for tenements. To the east the prospect remains more open, with fields as
far as Brick Lane, and country beyond.

Spitalfields' transformation from being essentially rural – a place of fields
and scattered free-standing buildings – to essentially urban was given
added momentum by the events that took place in the City between 2 and
5 September 1666. London's Great Fire had no immediate physical impact
on the area – the fire was stopped within the City walls before it reached
Bishopsgate-without – but as the subsequent rebuilding of the fire-ravaged
portion of the City neared completion, speculative house builders – flushed
with financial success – turned their attention to City fringe areas like
Spitalfields.

The new demand for housing would have been sufficient to transform
Spitalfields, but the aftermath of the Great Fire was another major influence. From the later 1660s onwards the various owners of land in
Spitalfields – notably the Wheler family and the owners of the former priory precincts, including the Bolingbroke/St John family (in whose hands
much of the land of the Liberty of Norton Folgate had been since the late
1630s or early 1640s) – seem to have come to a collective decision: that the
best way to profit from the building boom and to transform the former
monastic precincts and neighbouring fields into coherent streets of terraced
buildings, was to raise and level the land – both to facilitate drainage and
as a convenient way to avoid the cost of having to remove existing walls

and ruins. It is probable that the Wheler family introduced this practice on a limited scale even before the Great Fire with the construction of Wheler Street in the late 1650s. But it gathered pace with the first really large-scale raising and levelling – that of the Old Artillery Ground in the early 1680s – and in so doing drew on a new and seemingly inexhaustible source of raw material for levelling in the form of waste and rubble from the fire-damaged City. It was a brilliantly simple approach. It was also lucrative: landowners probably charged for rubble to be deposited on their land, and so were not only able to level it very easily, but also got paid for doing so.

Nevertheless, for all its common-sense nature, the changing ground level of Spitalfields still remains something of a puzzle. When exactly did this raising and levelling start? How quickly and in which directions did it progress? How were the ground floors and basements of existing buildings reconciled with neighbouring new buildings that might rise from a new ground level up to two metres higher than the old? And how were the 'edges' of this landfill reconciled with surrounding areas? The nature of the latter conundrum is well illustrated by two buildings. Sir Paul Pindar's house was built in about 1599 and stood on the west side of Bishopsgate, virtually opposite Widegate Street. It was demolished in 1890 for the extension of Liverpool Street Station but a portion of its remarkable main façade, made of timber and articulated by an array of bay and oriel windows, survives in the Victoria and Albert Museum.

Photographs of the house, taken just before its demolition, make it clear that the ground level of Bishopsgate when the house was constructed was much the same as it is today. The ground level of the partially surviving early-fourteenth-century charnel house, just to the east of Bishopsgate, however, is about two metres below the level of Bishopsgate. This suggests that significant changes of level between Bishopsgate and central Spitalfields existed from at least 1600. Presumably buildings along Bishopsgate had long been elevated on a terrace, created perhaps as a result of the road being raised, paved or levelled. Or perhaps the former priory precincts were always below Bishopsgate, which had, since Roman times, been something of a causeway created above the marshy grounds surrounding the River Walbrook and its small tributaries. Whatever the case, the people of Spitalfields, and the part of the city to its south, must have long been used to living with, and navigating around, an undulating landscape. It is, of course, possible that the change of level between Bishopsgate and Spitalfields to its east could largely have been accommodated within the buildings lining the street. As with many late-eighteenth-century London developments, where roads were built up or 'terraced', the descent from street level to lower garden level could be achieved within buildings in easy stages by the use of short sections of stairs and landings.

The archaeologists who investigated western portions of Spitalfields during the late 1990s described an interesting situation: 'for thirty-odd years [from the early 1680s]', they suggested, 'the ground levels immediately around the Brick House (of c.1600) and the candle house (of priory origin) *must* have been lower . . . as strange to us as that might seem.' It was only in the late 1720s, when the landlords developed the northern arm of Spital Square, demolishing the Brick House and raising and levelling off the land above its remains, that the last vestiges of undulating ground levels finally disappeared. Elsewhere – on the land to the north of Spital Square – this levelling off must have occurred slightly earlier, because the development of Elder Street, dating from the early 1720s, was at the new, raised, ground level. And the same is true of the land to the east, being developed by the Wheler family from the mid seventeenth century. As one of the archaeologists involved in the 1990s excavations, Chiz Harward, has pointed out, the ground floors of existing buildings now became basements, or half-basements, with 'some slopes down to original ground level at the edge of developments, at least on the roads'.

In some places, raising ground levels seems to have been a continuous process over quite an extended period of time, involving not just debris from the Great Fire (as with the Old Artillery Ground) but from subsequent decades as waste from the City was regularly 'brought out by cart, sifted and screened, and then sold on'.[12] Not all, incidentally, went to landfill. Some was recycled. A portion of a fine large-scale eaves cornice – incorporating sections of deeply carved acanthus leaves – was found in 20 Princelet Street serving as a humble joist. At 36 Elder Street, the oak-made door and frame connecting the yard with the street appears to be of seventeenth-century origin. Both, presumably, had been rescued from local mounds of waste.

The fate of the charnel house reveals how this key building from Spitalfields' medieval past finally succumbed to seventeenth-century re-development. At what point the land around it was raised is unclear. Certainly, when Pepys returned to the precinct on 13 April 1669 to hear a sermon at the Spital Cross he made no reference in his diary to any changes in ground level or to the submerging of ancient buildings beneath a wave of spoil, noting only that he thought the sermon 'dull' but that he had stayed to watch the departure of the civic dignitaries and their wives, a 'sight' that 'was mighty pleasing'.[13] (That said, nor does any other contemporary record appear to mention the depositing of rubbish from the fire-ravaged City.) That the charnel house survived into the 1680s seems evident from the fact that it's still shown on Ogilby and Morgan's maps of 1676 and 1681–2. But shortly afterwards, as archaeological excavations in the late 1990s revealed, its upper floor was removed and its ground floor (and the ribs of its collapsed vault) buried beneath waste and seemingly quickly forgotten – so quickly, in fact, that when new buildings were constructed over its remains no attempt was made to use its stout walls as any kind of footing. It was as though it had never existed.

When the remains of the charnel house finally saw the light of day again in the late twentieth century, the foundations of the nearby Spital Cross and of many other structures were also unearthed. These included numerous cesspits, their walls formed by steers' horns with their valuable horn-rim removed ('horncore' was a very cheap building material in the early seventeenth century, gleaned from nearby slaughterhouses). Discoveries included the ground floors of sixteenth- or early-seventeenth-century structures ornamented with tiles reused from the medieval monastic buildings. The material heaped on the former ground level was extraordinary: dark black, full of decomposing minerals and packed with tile and pot shards, fragments of bone and other debris – clearly spoil from a calamity. When I walked through the excavation trenches I found myself surrounded by shattered fragments of domestic life: slipware, spongeware, slivers of glazed Delft earthenware plates and tiles, some chips of Chinese imported porcelain, bits of glass, bones, oyster shells, pieces of clay pipe and wig curlers and – most interesting – a large number of blue-glazed earthenware bowls for the preparation of medicines. Many of these items had, it seems, been lost or destroyed during the Great Fire and subsequently dumped in Spitalfields. Most have been retained by the Museum of London but others were dispersed and only the ruins of the charnel house have been preserved in situ within a glass-roofed pit. The foundations of the Spital Cross, the cesspits, the tiled floors of the free-standing houses and even the extensive remains of the Tudor artillery ground, standing well over a metre high and furnished with recesses – perhaps for beehives – were dismantled after documentation.

By the time Ogilby and Morgan produced their first London map in 1676 (with a revised version in 1681–2 showing a far larger area of London but in less detail), the new process of urbanisation in Spitalfields was well under way – if still not quite complete. Many of the older buildings survived. To the south of 'Spittle Yard', formerly at the heart of what had once been the northern precinct of the priory, Ogilby and Morgan clearly show the charnel house, with the Master Gunner's House breaking slightly forward from its south-east corner. On the east side of the yard is the Christ's Hospital stand (probably of the 1580s) and on the north side are the Candle House and the Brick House - perhaps somewhat rebuilt, divided and extended, and certainly engulfed to a degree by later, seventeenth-century buildings. To the north-west of the charnel house can be made out – again embedded among later structures – Spittle House, and the remains of the Principal Tenement and what was the Vaughan family's private mansion.[14] Elsewhere, though, what had been country lanes and partly developed streets just a few years before have become more fully developed, and a large number of new streets, courts and alleys appear.

By 1676 'White Lion Yard' (elsewhere known as 'White Lion Street' and now Folgate Street), running north of Spital Yard, is wide, straight and lined with buildings on both sides, though with a large court off its south side that forms a northern extension to Spital Yard, and a large open space to its north (shown as garden and orchard on Hollar's map of 1666/7 but now a blank and seemingly characterless area named 'Porter's Close'). The 1681–2 version of the map shows the north end of Wheler Street joining 'Ankor Street' with, to its east, the large oblong area of Swan Field or 'Swan Close', still open ground, as are large areas east of 'Spittle Field' towards Brick Lane. So, too, is the Artillery Ground, though that situation would change rapidly in the 1680s.

'Browns Lane' (now Hanbury Street) – one of the most ancient thoroughfares in Spitalfields, possibly even of Roman origin, and by now the main west–east route on the Wheler Estate – is clearly shown with its south side only partly built but its north side fully lined with buildings as far as Brick Lane.[15] At this time, according to the *Survey of London*, one of its prominent tenants was William Browne, possibly a weaver by trade, who 'held, in succession to Jeffrey Browne, three houses, a yard, two sheds, a cowhouse and a garden and orchard, at the western end of the lane, probably on its south side.'[16] Browne also leased 'all that open field called Spitalfields' that was then a pasturage and that later in the seventeenth

Part of Ogilby and Morgan's map of 1676. The north-east boundary of the map
Although Spitalfields had expanded significantly since the Great Fire of 1666, there

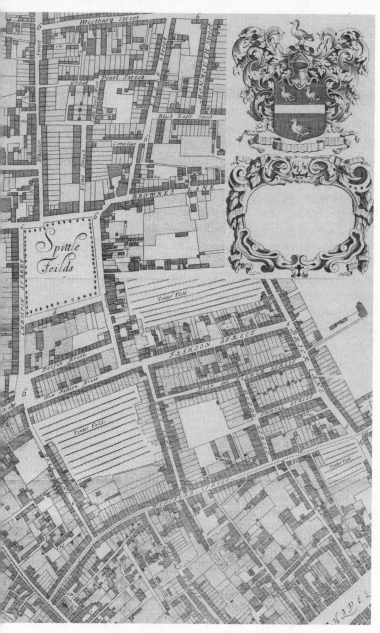

is marked by Westbury Street, now Quaker Street.
were still numerous and large open areas available for would-be house builders.

century was to become the site of the fruit and vegetable market. In all he paid £22 per annum rent. He held a further lease from the Wheler family for three acres of pasture to the north of 'Browns Lane' on which, from 1656, he laid out Quaker Street, initially known as 'Westbury Street', after the Wheler Estate in Wiltshire. He may possibly have given his name to the lane, although it could also have been named in memory of the Braun family who had founded the priory, to which the lane led, in 1197.

Running west from 'Browns Lane' to Spital Yard, Ogilby and Morgan show (but do not name) Lamb Street, which forms the northern edge of the large, roughly square, open space that on the 1676 version is named as 'Spittle Feilds'. The buildings the map depicts running north from Lamb Street and 'Browns Lane' are, from the west, Wheler Street (by 1676 lined by virtually continuous terraces nearly as far as Shoreditch) and 'Vine Street'. This street extends only a little to the north before giving way to a grid of smaller streets and alleys – including 'Little Pearl Street' and 'Great Pearl Street' (both shown as just Pearl Street on the 1681–2 edition), built from the late 1650s to the mid 1670s. This pattern of more informal development continues with the streets north of 'Browns Lane' and east of 'Vine Street', including Corbets Court and Black Eagle Street, but there are also two wider and evidently finer streets running north–south: 'Eagle Street' (later named Grey Eagle Street) and to its east 'Monmouth Street', connecting with the west–east 'Westbury Street'.

The 1681–2 edition of Ogilby and Morgan's map includes the area north of 'Westbury Street': 'Phenix Street', then above it 'King Street' and, to its north, 'Swan Close'. North of the close is 'Cock Lane' (which eventually became part of what is now Redchurch Street and Bethnal Green Road). To the east of the 'Spittle Field' – according to the maps of 1676 and 1681–2 – an almost continuous row of buildings defines the east side of what was 'Red Lyon Street' (absorbed into Commercial Street in the mid nineteenth century). Running east from here towards Brick Lane are a number of alleys or courts, with buildings, gardens and tenter grounds. The most sustained of these alley developments, no doubt informal in its architectural character, runs along what in the early eighteenth century was to become the north side of 'Church Street' (now Fournier Street). This row of buildings extends east almost as far as Brick Lane.

As for the west side of the 'Spittle Field', both the 1676 and the 1681–2 maps show this as being formed by Crispin Street, which was developed from 1668–70 on land owned by the Wheler Estate, while the southern edge of the 'Field' was 'Paternoster Row' (roughly the site of the eastern portion of the existing Brushfield Street). To the south, and parallel, is 'Dorset Street'. Both 'Paternoster Row' and 'Dorset Street' were laid out and lined with buildings between 1672 and about 1675. South of 'Dorset Street' was a more ancient thoroughfare named 'New Fashion Street' and now called White's Row.

I've dwelt on this frenzied spate of development in some detail because virtually all that now remains of it are scattered and truncated elements of the street layout. Many of the early streets were destroyed by the westward expansion of Truman's Brick Lane Brewery in the mid and late eighteenth century; by the construction of the railway from the 1830s and the expansion of the Bishopsgate Goodsyard; by the construction of Commercial Street in the mid nineteenth century; and by gradual erosion resulting from the area's decline into slums from the early nineteenth century onwards. What we're left with are fragments, such as the south end of Crispin Street, the north end of Wheler Street, Folgate Street and Hanbury Street. Dorset Street survived in ghostly manner until 2015 when, despite great opposition, it was obliterated (see page 632). As for those buildings that still survive from the period – for example, a pair of houses on the west side of Crispin Street (now numbered 45 and 46 and much altered externally and internally) – their almost minuscule size suggests that everything was done in a pretty modest manner. Certainly, in terms of scale, they do not begin to compete with the houses that were to be built in the area in the following century.

Although buildings and streets have gone, surviving documents reveal much about these lost Spitalfields buildings. Most, it seems, were not solidly built. Landlords and speculative builders cut corners in attempts to maximise profits by increasing density and skimping on materials, and judging from some of the disputes that arose, not all of them were particularly scrupulous. The 'Bricklayer' John Pike of Stepney, for example, who (along with William Savill 'citizen and carpenter') was involved in the construction of Crispin Street, got into trouble with the Crown in March 1668/9 for excavating brick earth too near the Old Artillery Ground wall, and so presumably threatening to undermine it. Pike was forbidden to fire bricks on the site, but because he had 'contracted for a great quantity of bricks' was allowed to extract brick earth – although evidently away from the wall – providing he fired the bricks elsewhere.[17] We know from John Stow's account that brick clay was being dug in Spitalfields in the late sixteenth century and it's interesting to see that the practice continued a century later. Whether the clay was good enough to make facing bricks, or was only adequate for more inferior, and usually concealed, 'place' bricks, is uncertain.

Behaviour of a seemingly even more questionable nature was displayed during the development of the south side of the 'Spittle Field'. Here in June 1672 Edward Nicholas and George Cooke – trustees acting for the landowner William Wheler and his seven daughters – petitioned the Privy Council to build on the southern portion of the 'Field'. The petition was necessary because there was still a lingering official presumption against the uncontrolled expansion of the City. Part of the developers' argument was that the site had been 'a noysome place and offensive to the Inhabitants through its Low Situation till by the Petitioners great charge it was filled up and Levelled'. Having carried out this land-raising levelling work Nicholas and Cooke argued that the improved land was 'very commodious for more Buildings to be erected whereon some Foundations are already laid and neere finished', and they assured the Privy Council that, after development, there would be 'a large Space of Ground that will be left unbuilt for ayre and sweetnes to the place'.[18]

But not everyone was happy. An Order in Council dated 5 March 1669 shows that even before Nicholas and Cooke got to work, some locals were worried about moves to develop large swathes of the 'Spittle Field' and to dig and burn brick earth. They argued that such activities would make the area 'very noisome' and 'prejudice the cloathes which are usually dryed in two large grounds adjoining, and the rich stuffs of divers colours which are made in the same place, by altering and changing their colours'.[19] In August 1672 the Lord Mayor and Sir Christopher Wren were consulted about Nicholas and Cooke's proposed development, and both, while expressing their concern about the speedy and large-scale eastward expansion of London, eventually concluded that the scheme would not add greatly to the size of the City and that the proposed levelling operation was to be welcomed: 'the Feild will remaine Square and open and the wettnesse of the lower parts remedied.'[20] But some locals still opposed development – and these now included the seven Wheler daughters in whose interests Nicholas and Cooke were meant to be acting. In May 1672, after the death of William Wheler and his wife, the seven daughters had brought a petition in Chancery against Nicholas and Cooke, claiming that the trustees had conspired with Thomas Joyce of London, merchant, to deprive them of the benefit of their property; the eastern portion of which – defined by 'Red Lyon Street' on the west, Brick Lane on the east, 'Browns Lane' on the north and Fashion Street on the south – became known as 'Joyce's Garden'. In response Joyce claimed leasehold rights, granted by William Wheler to John Dashwood in around 1648/9 and then to Joyce in February 1660/1 for £270. Although the outcome of the 1672 suit is uncertain, Joyce appears to have remained in possession under the lease-hold tenure, which expired c.1701.[21]

Nicholas and Cooke must have been persuasive and forceful fellows because, despite the daughters' resistance, the development of the south-west portion of their estate – namely the south end of the 'Spittle Field' – went ahead. By early 1673 'Dorset Street' and 'Paternoster Row' had been laid out and eighty-year building leases granted to various specu-lative builders for the construction of houses along both sides of 'Dorset Street', along the south side of 'Paternoster Row' and the north side of the already existing White's Row or 'New Fashion Street'.

But even then things do not seem to have gone smoothly because in the summer of 1675 Wren reported a complaint to the Privy Council against Nicholas and Cooke's building works. The complaint was made by Nath-aniel and John Tilly, who owned existing buildings on the south side of White's Row. As one might imagine, raising the ground level for the benefit of new buildings could well prove difficult to reconcile with the rights and privileges of existing buildings nearby. And so it proved, but a difficult situation was made far worse by what seems a blatant disregard by Nicholas and Cooke for most of the constraints and conditions that had been agreed. Wren reminded the Privy Council that when permission to build had been granted in November 1673 it was 'directed' that a '24 foot Street' was 'to be layd out and left open before the houses of Mr. Tilly'. He then reported that instead of making a street open to the north and to the width stipulated, Nicholas and Cooke had 'begun to build another row of houses fronting ye houses of ye said Mr. Tilly' that was far narrower than agreed and appropriated much of the reduced street as yards for the new houses, leaving open a passage only ten feet wide in front of the existing buildings. In addition the developers had not only failed to provide sewers as required in their patent but their raising of the ground level obstructed and made damp the ground floors of the Tillys' houses.[22]

Ogilby and Morgan's map of 1681–2 covers a larger area than their map of just a few years earlier, but in a little less detail, although the elevation of Spittle House, on Spital Yard (the future Spital Square), is shown. Building was just about to start on the Old Artillery Ground.

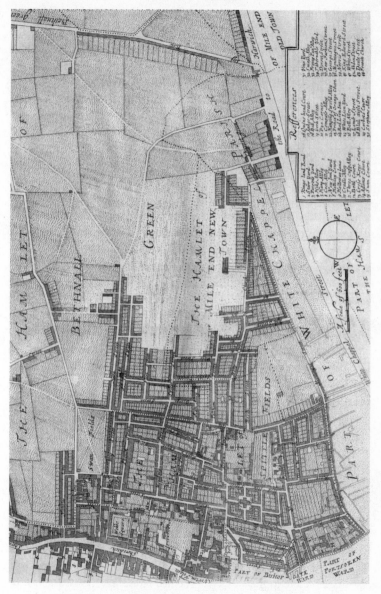

*Spitalfields in 1720 in John Strype's Survey of London and Westminster.
The Old Artillery Ground is shown as developed – the curving street to its north
is Fort Street. The depiction of Spital Yard is confusing. The terrace of 1700 defining
the north side of the new Spital Square is not shown.*

Nicholas and Cooke's behaviour was arrogant and generally outrageous. They did not deny the charge but claimed that since the granting of the patent they had conveyed their interest in the land to the Wheler daughters, who had made a partition of the land with the contested portion now under the control of Alice Wheler. So, Messrs Nicholas and Cooke suggested, the problem was now nothing to do with them but must be resolved by Alice and her husband John Whitehall. And, for good measure, they observed that the Tillys' houses abutted the Wheler Estate and were not part of it so had no right of access from Wheler land and suggested that the Tillys were lucky to have been granted a passage of ten feet! A wider passage could be constructed, stated Nicholas and Cooke, 'for a valuable consideration' as was 'reasonable' if the Tillys wanted use of another's land. Wren rejected this defence on the simple grounds that it contradicted the conditions of the patent that all parties had agreed and suggested that, if Nicholas and Cooke did not amend their scheme, the parties should be left to 'try their Rights by due course of Law'. As the *Survey of London* explains, the precise outcome of the dispute is not known,[23] but the evidence of late-seventeenth-century maps – notably Ogilby and Morgan's of 1676 and 1681–2 – and the existing form of White's Row make it clear that Nicholas and Cooke backed down and followed the terms of the patent, at least as far as road width was concerned.

Given the dubious and contested nature of the development, and the ruthless business practices of Nicholas and Cooke, it is not surprising to learn that completion of the new houses was delayed, that they were not generally well built, and that they were neither large nor ambitious in scale (most of them had frontages of about sixteen feet). It seems that the speculative builders who chose to realise the development picked up the desperate nature of the enterprise and cut corners more than was usual, to save money and reduce risk. The Tylers' and Bricklayers' Company made a 'search' of the construction site and subsequently fined various builders for the use 'of badd and black mortar . . . work not jointed [and] bad mortar and bad bricks'.[24] However works appear to have been completed by 1676 when Ogilby and Morgan's map shows 'Dorset Street' and the south side of 'Paternoster Row' fully built up.

An even more ruthlessly money-minded figure was involved in one of Spitalfields' most significant developments: the transformation of the Old Artillery Ground into an architecturally coherent City suburb. Ogilby and Morgan's map of 1681–2 shows that at that time, despite encroachment and increasing urbanisation, the 'Old Artillery Garden' remained open space. Building operations along its west and south edges had, however, become intense, with Artillery Lane, leading east off Bishopsgate, fully developed, along with 'Whitegate Alley' (now Widegate Street), which also ran east off Bishopsgate. Widegate Street continued east, to define the southern tip of the Artillery Ground, and terminated as 'Smock Ally' – now Artillery Passage. (This east end of Artillery Passage was later known as 'Raven Row' and is now part of Artillery Lane). South of Widegate Street and 'Smock Ally' was a network of alleys and courts, including the very narrow Frying Pan Alley.

And now Dr Nicholas Barbon stepped in. He was something of a pioneer in the creation of the post-Fire City. Roger North (a lawyer, amateur architect and associate of Sir Christopher Wren) described him as the 'inventor' of the 'new method' of speculative house building that speeded up the rebuilding of the City and led to the rapid urbanisation of semi-rural areas – like Spitalfields – on its fringes. Barbon also, in 1680, came up with the idea of insuring houses against loss due to fire. The Fire Insurance Office – England's first fire insurance business – was a joint stock company and like all Barbon's enterprises stimulated by the prospects of heady profits.

In February 1682 the five acres and one rood of the Artillery Ground was sold by the Crown to two of Barbon's agents, George Bradbury and Edward Noell, for £5,700.[25] And what followed was typical of Barbon's actions elsewhere in London, a 'new method' of building that was characterised by North as 'casting . . . Ground into streets and small houses, and to augment their number with as little front as possible, and selling the ground to workmen by so much per foot front, and what he could not sell build himself.'[26]

In 1682 Barbon leased the land to an associate and then mortgaged the lease when only the foundations and basements of the houses were built. Presumably by this time the number and position of the principal streets to be created on the Old Artillery Ground, and the size and location of individual house plots, had been agreed. The street plan was economical and basic, calculated to create – as North observed – the highest number of house plots of reasonable size and value, with little ground wasted on circulation and none on urban ornamentation or flourishes. Three streets ran north – roughly parallel to each other although fanning out very slightly – off the existing Artillery Lane. These were, from west to east,

Duke Street, Steward Street and Gun Street. Parallel to Gun Street was the existing Crispin Street. The widest street – with slightly deeper house plots – was Steward Street. The three streets were linked at their north ends by Fort Street (presumably named after the star fort of the 1630s or 40s that had been situated here), which ran east–west but curved up to the north-east, no doubt influenced by the site rather than the presence of the early-seventeenth-century Master Gunner's House that, according to Museum of London archaeologists, was demolished in 1685. Barbon also rebuilt houses on 'Smock Alley', now Artillery Passage, and in neighbouring Frying Pan Alley.

By the time the streets had been laid out by late 1682, the land level had been raised. As Museum of London archaeologists put it: '. . .the new houses were to have full lower-ground floors and Barbon's developers used an interesting technique to achieve this. Rather than digging deep foundations for the new lower floors, they simply built the houses up from the existing ground level and raised the road level by up to 1.9 metres in between the rows of houses. The black, ashy material used to "make up" the road levels (and, to a lesser extent the rear yards) was probably debris from the giant clear-up and rebuilding operation that followed the Great Fire of 1666. [S]ome of this material cleared out of the burnt City had probably been dumped in the Artillery Ground in the 1670s,' they speculated, 'and it seems likely that Barbon was ingeniously getting rid of an unwanted spoil heap *and* saving construction costs and time.'[27]

In December 1683 Barbon settled the freehold of the land on the Fire Insurance Office that he had set up.[28] The complex transfer of control of the Old Artillery Ground was, it seems, part of the manner in which he raised money for the development of the land. And by the time the development of the Old Artillery Ground was completed in the late 1680s around 185 houses had been built, most of modest size with frontages no more than sixteen feet (4.9 metres) wide – although a few were twenty feet (6.1 metres) wide – and most with elevations only three storeys above ground. Seventeen different speculative builders had been involved in the construction of the houses during the 1680s – typically obtaining building leases from Barbon and his associates, then investing their own time and money in construction, in the hope of making a profit when selling on the lease and completed house. Their work, as Museum of London archaeologists observed, was 'probably not of high quality'. In June 1682 Ralph Harwood, who was building on the Artillery Ground, was fined by the

The junction of Artillery Lane/ 'Raven Row' (left) and Artillery Passage/ 'Smock Alley' in 1912. The three–window–wide house in the passage dated from the 1680s and was typical of the more modest houses built under Barbon's control on the adjoining Old Artillery Ground. The splendid shopfront on the left dates from the mid 1750s.

Tylers' and Bricklayers' Company for using broken bricks.[29] His corner-cutting was, presumably, not untypical.

The process of speculative construction pursued by Barbon and his colleagues on the Old Artillery Ground and in their other London projects was broadly typical of the speculative house-building system that, with great speed, if not with great solidity, helped the City to be restored after the Great Fire and ultimately enabled the great expansion of Georgian London. Speculators believed they had a ready market because demand for housing in London was high, and seemed set to remain so. Barbon argued in his pamphlet *An Apology for the Builder*, published in 1685, that with an average of ten to twelve occupants the typical London house was overcrowded. This analysis made it clear to him that a large number of new houses were required and that their speculative construction could not fail to be profitable if undertaken in an appropriately economical manner. For Barbon, it was not about beauty or architectural excellence. The fact that ruthless speculative building often achieved sophisticated levels of urban design, and houses exemplary in their fusion of function and ornament, was something of a coincidence, not the original intention. These were, in a sense, accidental works of art.

An unusual feature of the manner in which the Old Artillery Ground was developed is the fact that the main 'undertaker' or instigator of the speculative building – Barbon – had acquired the freehold of the land. More usually the system involved three clearly defined interests, belonging to the landlord, the speculative builder and the first occupier of the house. In broad and simple terms each stood to gain by the system if the market was reasonably healthy. The occupant acquired satisfactory accommodation at a relatively low cost (until the mid eighteenth century, the usual approach followed by the builder was to let a house when it was little more than a shell, allowing the future occupant to finish it in a style that suited his taste and pocket). The speculative builder turned a quick profit, unless, for whatever reason – economic, social or political – demand slumped, the bubble burst, and the bottom fell out of the market, in which case the speculator was likely to terminate his career in debtors' gaol. For his part, the landlord got his estate 'improved' by building for little or no financial outlay on his part. That said, he did have to take a long view: typically getting only low ground rents and not acquiring ownership of the houses built on his land until the first leases terminated, which by the late seventeenth/early eighteenth century in London were usually granted for between sixty-one and ninety-nine years. Obviously it was ultimately in the landlord's interest for the houses on his estate to be well built and relatively long-lasting. Only that way could he be confident that his estate was gaining a valuable asset for the benefit of his heirs or on which he could raise money.

And therein lay a significant potential flaw in the speculative system. The estate's interest was generally long-term. The builder's, on the other hand, was almost invariably short-term. He wanted to build as quickly and cheaply as possible, get a satisfactory return on his investment, and move on. It was tempting for builders to opt for economy, which could easily result in corners being cut – as the Tylers' and Bricklayers' Company observed in the Artillery Ground in 1682. The one saving grace of the system was that the speculative product had – in order to appeal to the market – to display at least superficial elements of style and solidity. So facing bricks were usually of good quality – if only a veneer over structurally vital but concealed poor-quality bricks – and key details such as brick window arches, doorcases and staircases were generally beautifully designed and wrought, even in modest houses.

To help ensure a reasonable quality of design and construction, it was not unknown for some estates to incorporate building specifications in their lease agreements. These, as a rule, mirrored current building legislation. In the wake of the Great Fire, various acts were passed to try to ensure a more ordered approach to planning in the capital than had been the case in the past. And since their particular intention was to avoid replicating the insanitary and congested conditions and timber-built architecture that had been partly responsible for the plague of 1665 and then the Great Fire itself, they included quite detailed stipulations about construction. The first major post-Fire Building Act, passed in 1667, sought to minimise fire risk and secure the building of sound and incombustible houses by promoting the use of brick and stone, restricting the use of external timber, and relating the thickness of a wall to its height. (In this regard it simply gave added force to building proclamations that since 1607 had encouraged masonry rather than timber construction.)[30] It also sought to relate height of building to width of street (to avoid tall houses being rebuilt on narrow alleys or courts) and, as part of this control, introduced the idea of four 'rates' or 'sorts' of houses, each determined by the scale and expense of construction. This promotion of a small number of standard house types encouraged a new uniformity of design in London architecture. Because easy-to-carve external timber was now limited, it also encouraged simplicity rather than exuberance at a time when simplicity was, in any case, starting to become fashionable. So carved bay windows went and all external ornamental timber-work with the exception of timber doorcases and – initially – timber eaves cornices.

Since, however, the 1667 Act applied only to the City of London, and its jurisdiction was not extended until the first decade of the eighteenth century, it is almost certain that in marginal areas like Spitalfields speculative landlords and builders remained essentially unregulated. The London Building Acts of 1707 and 1709 – which applied to the City of Westminster as well as the City of London – added further building controls, notably the abandoning of timber eaves cornices in favour of masonry-built parapets, and the requirement that timber window sash boxes be set back one brick-width, or four inches, from the face of the building. Both these stipulations were, of course, to help prevent the spread of fire. The fact that in virtually all surviving Spitalfields houses of the 1720s timber sash boxes are still set flush with the elevations confirms forcefully – and in a most practical manner – that the writ of the early Acts was not observed in early-Georgian Spitalfields.

One of the key problems with these early Acts – even in areas where they were in theory applied – was that enforcement was difficult, depending almost entirely on 'informers', whose motives could be dubious and expertise negligible. It was only with the passing of the 1774 Building Act that proper supervision of new building projects was brought to bear. From then on district surveyors, appointed by magistrates, were charged with the task of inspecting new buildings in their designated area and enforcing building legislation. At the same time, the principles of 'rates' of building were reinforced with a scientific exactitude that led to increased standardisation, simplicity and uniformity of design. A yet higher degree of incombustibility was achieved by legislating that sash boxes be not only set back but also recessed behind masonry.

Water supply, drainage and sewage removal were also of great concern in expanding late-seventeenth-century London. Barbon provided sewers, but these were generally for street drainage; bodily wastes were discharged into cesspits, usually located in rear yards but sometimes in cellars, and these had to be regularly cleared out. Samuel Pepys records why regular maintenance of cesspits was essential: 'Going down into my cellar . . .', noted Pepys, 'I put my foot into a great heap of turds . . . by which I find that [my neighbour] Mr Turner's house of office is full and comes into my cellar, which doth trouble me.'[31] Water was supplied by private companies, via elm pipes and at limited times so had to be stored within the house in lead cisterns for future use.

———

However questionable the quality of some of these new houses may have been, they were all clearly intended for the fairly well-to-do. But that shouldn't be taken to imply that the area as a whole suddenly became a uniformly genteel and prosperous enclave. As in previous generations, late-seventeenth-century Spitalfields was home to the poor as well as to the affluent. Within walking distance of the houses of successful businessmen and merchants, in the handsome suburb Barbon created on the Old Artillery Ground, were the far more humble dwellings of labourers and artisans. In his documentary novel of 1722, *A Journal of the Plague Year*, Daniel Defoe's narrator – who lives 'without Aldgate' and so on the edge of Spitalfields – suggests that in a representation to 'my Lord Mayor' of the 'condition of the poor', it was reckoned that there were 'no less than an hundred thousand riband-weavers in and about the city, the chiefest number of whom lived then in the parishes of Shoreditch, Stepney, Whitechappel, and Bishopsgate . . . namely, about Spitalfields.' The figure is almost certainly an exaggeration, but it underscores the reality that Spitalfields had a large, impoverished population.

Predictably, the plague of 1665 hit such overcrowded and unhygienic poor areas particularly hard. Looking at the mortality figures for 8–15 August 1665, Defoe noted that 'it was observed the [high] numbers mentioned in Stepney parish at that time were generally all on that side where Stepney parish joined to Shoreditch, which we now call Spittlefields, where the parish of Stepney comes up to the very wall of Shoreditch Churchyard, and [where] the plague at this time . . . raged most violently.'[32]

The many deaths in and around Spitalfields meant that a large number of ad hoc burial grounds had to be speedily created: 'many if not all the out-parishes', Defoe wrote in *A Journal of the Plague Year*, 'were obliged to make new burying-grounds . . . some of which were continued, and remain in use to this day. But others were left off, and (which I confess I mention with some reflection) being converted into other uses or built upon afterwards, the dead bodies were disturbed, abused, dug up again, some even before the flesh of them was perished from the bones, and removed like dung or rubbish to other places.' He recalled, in particular, 'the upper end of 'Hand Alley', in Bishopsgate Street, which was then a green field, and was taken in particularly for Bishopsgate parish'. He also vividly remembered what happened in the years after 1665:

> the ground was let out to build on . . . on the very same ground where the poor people were buried, and the bodies, on opening the ground for the foundations, were dug up, some of them remaining so plain to be seen that the women's skulls were distinguished by their long hair, and of others the flesh was not quite perished; so that the people began to exclaim loudly against it, and some suggested that it might endanger a return of the contagion; after which the bones and bodies, as fast as they came at them, were carried to another part of the same ground and thrown all together into a deep pit . . . which . . . is not built on.

Other burial sites included one on 'the very edge of Shoreditch Church-yard' and 'two other burying-places in Spittlefields, one where since a chapel or tabernacle [presumably the one built by Sir George Wheler] has been built for ease to this great parish, and another in Petticoat Lane.'[33]

The names of those who died are almost all lost to us. And, indeed, for the most part we know very little about the identities and lives of the poor of seventeenth-century Spitalfields. But contemporary documents do occasionally shed a little light. One such is a somewhat sensationally titled pamphlet from 1674: *A True and Perfect Relation of the Execrable and Horrid Fact committed in White-Lion Yard, in Nortonfolgate, near the Spittle, by some Malicious, Diabolical-sperited Persons* – which deals with a mass poisoning that took place at the house of a victualler named Mr Emson in 'White-Lion Yard' (now occupied by the western part of Folgate Street). Mr Emson appears to have run a kind of eatery-cum-takeaway where, as the pamphlet tells us, 'many poor Weavers and Throsters did buy Broath for their Breakfast'. Apparently, at nine o'clock one morning, 'there came several to the house to eat their Messes of Broath, according to their usual manner; and many others that had Families did send at the same time for Broath, both for themselves and Household.' However, those who ate the broth 'fell immediately Vomitting, others flung themselves on the ground . . . horribly crying out and roaring, by reason of a most sudden torture and pain in their Bowels and Stomacks . . .' An immediate search of Emson's premises revealed yellow arsenic in his 'boyling Furnance' upon 'a piece of Beef', but Emson was apparently not the culprit because he and his household – including his wife and children – were in the same desperate condition, along 'with a number of other poor Ladds that Lodg there with other Weavers there-abouts'.

A 'Great Inquiry' was held to identify the 'Accursed Monster of Mankind' who 'like the Devil would practice his hatred' and 'Murder a multitude at once'. But, as was to be the case over 200 years later in these same streets during the Jack the Ripper murders, no perpetrator was apprehended, or even identified. The pamphleteer had to satisfy himself instead with a moral message: '. . . see how dangerous a Creature Man is, when left to the leadings of the Devil, who was a Murderer from the beginning.'[34]

What's interesting here is that the victims are described as 'Weavers and Throsters'. These could have been people involved in the wool industry that had existed in the area for generations. They are much more likely, though, to have worked in the silk trade because the term 'Throster' is usually applied to a person who twists silk into yarn. So these were some of the 'hundred thousand riband-weavers' referred to by Defoe, and this snapshot view of what was clearly an appalling incident helps to confirm that some years before the silk trade for which Spitalfields would become so famous was fully established, there were silk weavers living in the area, probably exclusively producing silk ribbons. We know that the English silk industry was significant enough to give employment to 40,000 workers in 1661, with some contemporary observers agreeing with Defoe and claiming that, in London alone by the mid 1670s, there were as many as 100,000 silk ribbon weavers.[35] We also know that in 1675 weavers of silk ribbons rioted for four days in Shoreditch, Whitechapel and Stepney against the introduction of engine-looms with which, it was argued at the time, 'one man can do as much . . . as near twenty without them'.[36]

The Spitalfields poisoning shows weavers as victims. A riot of 1675, however, shows them in a guise that was to become rather more familiar over the following decades: as agitators and demonstrators. In 1675 the object of their anger was new technology. Five years earlier, it had been foreign competition. Just before May Day 1670 a group of London apprentices and journeymen gathered at the Red Cow (perhaps a tavern near the Red Cow Farm on the corner of Brick Lane and what is now Bethnal Green Road or else the farm itself) to discuss their grievances. And following their deliberations they issued a pamphlet entitled 'Feare God' and addressed to 'all Gentlemen Apprentices and Journimen inhabitants of

London and suburbs'. Their aim, they said, was 'to acquaint you that by forraigne nations wee are impoverished by them tradinge within our Nation espetially by the French'. They argued that London tradesmen should be 'fearful' not only for their livelihoods but also for their very lives because 'forraigne nations' were riven by 'Rebellion' and were responsible for the Great Fire of 1666. What was needed, they suggested, was force:

> . . . truly gentlemen now we are otherwise resolved for we will not suffer it noe longer for by your assistance, we are resolved to meet in Morefields betwixt eight and nine of the clocke in the afternoone on Mayday next therefore faile not for wee your brethren Apprentices and Journimen will not faille you for wee will not have them reigne in our Kingdom. Soe God save the King: and all the royall family procure what armes you can for wee are resolved to doe it.[37]

There is no record that an armed uprising of apprentices and journeymen did take place at Moorfields on May Day. But this pamphlet, full of brooding suspicion and violence towards 'forraigne' traders working within England, reveals something of the mood of London workmen with which the Huguenots had to contend when they settled in London in large numbers during the 1680s. And it gives a foretaste of conflicts still to come.

Precisely where these apprentices and journeymen lived in 1670s Spitalfields is not entirely clear. There were certainly meaner houses and courts in and around Petticoat Lane and Brick Lane, so presumably some of them dwelled here. Some may also have moved in to the newly built streets of relatively modest houses that are shown on Ogilby and Morgan's map of 1676 – for example 'Dean and Flower Street', later 'Flower and Dean Street', started in 1655 (intriguingly in the teeth of the then general presumption against building in or near London), and 'Dorset Street' from the early 1670s. Generally speaking their houses would have doubled as their places of work. It's a reminder both that not everyone in Stuart Spitalfields was prosperous and that even at this time it was becoming something of an industrial area.

This status is confirmed by the emergence and rapid growth of two significant businesses that had nothing to do with weaving: the wholesale fruit and vegetable market and Truman's Brewery.

In December 1672 Edward Nicholas and George Cooke leased the open 'Spittle Feild' – immediately to the north of 'Paternoster Row' – to John Balch and Henry Allen for eighty years. This was the field that they had previously claimed would be 'left unbuilt' when petitioning to build to its south, and so as a result the lease contained a restriction on building. The restraint, however, was lifted by Chancery decree in February 1683/4.[38] Balch was a silk thrower who had married one of the seven Wheler daughters (and so obtained control of one-seventh of the Wheler Estate, south of Lamb Street/'Browns Lane') and was also Edward Nicholas's cousin. On 20 July 1682, before the restriction on building was lifted (or indeed as part of the means by which the prohibition was lifted), he obtained a charter from the Crown stipulating that he could hold two markets per week – on Thursday and Saturday – on the 'Spittle Field' site.

Balch didn't live to enjoy the fruits of his proposed enterprise, dying in 1683/4. But Edward Metcalfe, to whom the land passed by the terms of Balch's will and who had been his partner in the silk thrower's business, wasted no time. Given Spitalfields' swelling population, a new market made complete sense. (In fact in 1682 the Crown, when selling the Old Artillery Ground, had initially hoped to include a market within the development but the proposal had faltered – either because Barbon did not want to pay the Crown for the Charter or lose house-building plots, or because the City objected, fearing a new market right on its edge might damage local businesses.)[39] Moreover, even though the area was becoming built-up, there were still plenty of open fields and market gardens that could supply large quantities of vegetables and flowers.[40] In 1684 and 1685, therefore, Metcalfe granted sixty-one-year building leases for the erection of shops and houses around a market house.

The layout he went for was both rational and symmetrical. As the *Survey of London* explains, there was:

> . . . a cruciform market-house, surrounded by stalls in the centre and four L-shaped blocks of buildings around it, each containing houses facing inwards on to the central market-place and other houses facing outwards on to the four streets surrounding the former Spital Field. The four blocks, each of which contained a courtyard with access to the market-place, occupied the corners of the 'square' and were separated by four streets, North, South, East and West Streets, which linked the central market-place to the surrounding streets.[41]

*A portion of Spitalfields Market in about 1840, showing structures and details dating
from the late seventeenth and eighteenth centuries.*

The central market house was later destroyed by fire, but because the market was proving so successful, its site was left open to ease congestion.[42] John Rocque's map of 1746 reveals that not only was the market house not rebuilt but that the four L-shaped blocks that framed it had also, by then, been removed to increase the area of the market square, which appears to have contained a number of free-standing stalls.

A few years before the market gained its charter in 1682 a brewery was established on Brick Lane that over the following years was to become not only the biggest single business in Spitalfields but also one of the largest industrial concerns in Britain. Its origins are, to a degree, lost in myth, but it seems most likely that the man who gave his name to it, Joseph Truman, started out by purchasing an already existing brewhouse on Brick Lane from a Thomas Bucknall in 1679.[43] The brewery seems to have achieved success almost immediately. A lease of 1694 granted to Truman refers to a 'messuage, brewhouse, granary, stable and two pieces of land in the occupation of John Hinkwell', which appear to have been served by passages leading between 'Pelham Street' (now Woodseer Street) and land on the east side of Brick Lane, by which it would seem Truman's brewing business was located on both sides of the lane.

To Truman's contemporaries beer was an essential everyday beverage, far safer than water, far cheaper than wine (which, of course, had to be imported), and until the nineteenth century at least, far more economical than tea or coffee. Moderate consumption was considered healthy and natural – as William Hogarth's wholesome and jolly 1751 engraving of 'Beer Street' suggests – certainly in contrast to gin. In rural areas many people still brewed their own beer. In urban ones over the course of the sixteenth and seventeenth centuries, townspeople were increasingly served by so-called 'Common Brewers'. By 1699, there were 194 of these Common Brewers in London, who between them produced most of the beer consumed in the capital.[44]

It's not difficult to understand, therefore, why Truman should have established a brewery in London, nor why it should have been successful. The question is why he chose Brick Lane. It would have been easy enough to bring in most of the raw materials by cart, but the one local resource beer requires is, of course, fresh water – of good quality and in enormous quantities – and that is not something one immediately associates with this part of East London. One can only assume that there must have been a series of wells or springs on or near the brewery and that by the late eighteenth century, when Truman's had become a vast enterprise, these were gushing water at an incredible rate. It may be that Truman's acquired the rights to the old monastic conduit – the 'Snekockeswelle'– that we know to have stood near Brick Lane (see page 20). Water divining on the Truman site and surrounding area in recent years has located a main spring on the south side of Cheshire Street ('Hare Street') and another within the brewery site itself, below the existing eighteenth-century Directors' House and immediately to its west.[45]

Under Truman's control the brewery flourished and, it seems, its profits allowed him to diversify his business interests. In about 1705, no doubt encouraged by the recent success of developments in west Spitalfields, he tried his hand as a speculative house builder, acquiring open land near his brewery (on the junction of 'Browns Lane' and Brick Lane) on which he swiftly built at least fifteen houses. These included a group on a court off Brick Lane that a few years later was extended west to become 'Princes Street' (now Princelet Street). Built on a large scale, and with a uniform design, they set a new standard for Spitalfields.[46]

Joseph Truman died in 1719 or 1720,[47] and the business was inherited by his eldest son, also named Joseph. Within a few years, though, for reasons that are now unclear, a younger son – Benjamin Truman – took control of the brewery, of which he had been made a partner in 1722. By 1724 he was living in a house in the newly laid out west end of 'Princes Street' (now numbered as 4 Princelet Street).[48] Meanwhile Joseph the Younger had retired to Trowbridge to live the life of a gentleman and when he died in 1733 was 'reputed' to be worth the considerable sum of £10,000.

Benjamin Truman was evidently a shrewd businessman and entrepreneur with an eye to the main chance, a sense of changing tastes in beer, and a recognition of the potential of rapidly evolving technology to enable the production of a quality product, quickly and in great quantities. In 1737 he supplied beer to the Prince of Wales and so started a connection with the Royal Family that culminated with Truman being knighted in 1761. He was also at the forefront of the development and promotion of porter, a pungent, strong, tasty and heavily hopped beer, made with dark brown malt, that captivated the palates of London's working men.

Truman's own house on the Brick Lane site no longer exists. But it probably stood near – or adjoined – what is known as the Directors' House, an architecturally impressive range of offices clad with giant brick-wrought Doric pilasters, ornamented with Venetian windows, and incorporating details made of fine, rubbed brick. Begun in the 1730s, it almost certainly combined commercial and domestic uses, its nine-bay pilastered elevation to Brick Lane proclaiming very publicly the ambitions of the Truman family.[49] By the mid eighteenth century when the first phases of the Directors' House had been completed (there would be additional embellishments in the 1770s), Truman's Black Eagle Brick Lane Brewery was the largest single business enterprise in Spitalfields.

Meanwhile, to complement Spitalfields' elegant new houses, and in marked contrast to its burgeoning commercial enterprises, a major new feature was evolving within the former northern precinct of the priory. On Ogilby and Morgan's 1681–2 map the oblong yard known then as 'Spittle Yard' occupied the ground that had once been the priory cemetery. But in about 1700 this was extended west, largely over the site of the nave/chancel of the priory church, to create what was soon known as Spital Square, or 'Spittle Square' as John Rocque terms it on his 1746 London map. This reconfiguring of Spital Yard into Spital Square created what was in effect a long and rather narrow court, with a sense of enclosure attempted by pinching in the connection to Bishopsgate at its west end. In the early 1730s the form of the 'square' became stranger still when a north–south arm was added to make it L-shaped. The extension work of c.1700 included levelling and to a degree raising the ground and replacing much of what remained of the Principal Tenement on the north side of the Yard with a terrace of six houses (eventually known as 4–9 Spital Square and demolished in the 1930s). These were of simple and regular design, three storeys high above basements and mostly three windows wide. The process of their construction is unknown but it was probably a speculation undertaken by the Bolingbroke family, the freeholders of the site.[50] A survey of the Spital Square area made in 1712/13 – when it was proposed to construct one of the Fifty New Churches on the corner of 'Bishopsgate Street' and 'White Lyon Street' – shows the new square in its early form. It is already called 'Spittle Square' not Yard – a reflection of the desire to upgrade its status and attract desirable residents – with the smart new terrace defining much but not all of its north side. Today, only 37 Spital Square, rebuilt in a handsome and substantial manner in about 1741, survives from this grand rebuilding.[51]

Above: *Spital Square in 1909, looking east. The terrace on the left dated from c.1700–4.*
The monumental house on the east side of the square was number 22 and dated from 1733.
Glimpsed in the distance is the pilaster-clad house of 1733 on Church/Nantes Passage.
Below: *Spital Square looking south, with number 22 at the far end.*

The remodelling of Spital Square stimulated the Bolingbroke family to rebuild its own home, Spital – or Spittle – House, in about 1700, retaining portions of the old structure but adding a new show façade, facing east over the garden, on foundations set nearly four metres west of the old frontage, presumably to reduce the bulk of the old house and enlarge the garden. This new house was U-shaped in plan, with a pair of wings stretching from its main body west towards Bishopsgate.[52] It was both ambitious and fashionable – and an attempt to match the aristocratic homes being constructed in London's West End at about the same time (for example, Clarendon House of 1665 on Piccadilly). Today its site is occupied by St Botolph's church hall, built in 1890, and by a modern block of flats with a ground-floor restaurant.

The newly remodelled house became the London home of the politician Paulet St John, 3rd (and last) Earl of Bolingbroke. His neighbours in the new square were mostly master weavers or merchants.[53] We know from documentary evidence, for example, that number 7 was occupied in 1727 and 1731 by James Dalbiac and number 8 by Simon Dalbiac, both members of a leading Huguenot dynasty of silk masters and merchants. Number 10 was home in 1727 and 1731 to John Lekeux, a 'gentleman', lawyer, and a member of a Huguenot family long established in England, which owned land on the edge of Lolesworth Field. The substantial houses built on the east side of the north arm of Spital Square from 1725 to 1733 (numbers 17 to 22, now all long demolished) counted among their early occupants James Dalbiac (who moved from number 7 to number 20 when it was completed in 1732), and Anthony Rocher, a weaver, who occupied number 21 in 1735, while number 24 was occupied in 1739 by Matthew Parroissien, a master weaver.[54]

The transformation of Spital Yard into Spital Square brought about a social as well as an architectural revolution in the priory's former northern precinct. Now the last, ad hoc remains of the precinct's monastic and early post-Reformation history – the Candle House and the Brick House – were swept away or buried. In their place was an elegant new square to house the most elegant of Spitalfields' new inhabitants.

SIX

'DISTRESSED STRANGERS'

The Arrival of the Huguenots

The spread of speculatively built houses in Spitalfields after the Great Fire was echoed in other parts of London as more people chose to relocate to the 'cheaper, cleaner and, often, safer suburbs'.[1] But in terms of scale and rapid progress the transformation of areas such as the Old Artillery Ground and swathes of the Wheler Estate was scarcely matched elsewhere, for their developers' ambitions very swiftly expanded to accommodate an ever-swelling body of able and ambitious immigrants: the Huguenots. Subsequent decades were to see an influx of Catholic Irish and Jews. It was the French Calvinist Huguenots, however, as they flooded in from France from the early 1680s onwards, who played the major role in accelerating the area's evolution from a semi-rural suburb to a densely built and richly occupied merchants' quarter.[2]

French Protestants had long been ill-treated in their homeland. The first wave of persecution had reached a bloody and shocking crisis in 1572, during the wedding in Paris of the Huguenot prince Henry of Navarre, when Catholics, perhaps with the support of King Charles IX, had launched what became known as the St Bartholomew's Day Massacre, slaughtering leading Protestants who had gathered for the wedding and then over the next weeks extending their murderous onslaught beyond Paris (as many as 30,000 Huguenots may have been killed). That period of persecution came to an end when Henry of Navarre, who had narrowly escaped assassination, and who inherited the throne in 1589 as Henry IV, approved the Edict of Nantes in 1598 which granted official toleration to the practice of the Protestant religion in France in an attempt to achieve civil unity (he himself, meanwhile, had converted to Roman Catholicism). But during the seventeenth century the levels of persecution Protestants experienced in France and its colonies gradually increased, coming to a head in 1681 when Louis XIV authorised the *Dragonnades*, the quartering of dragoons in Huguenot communities to suppress the Protestant faith through torment, terror and intimidation and to induce conversion to Catholicism. Initially, many French Protestants chose to remain in their homeland, hoping that the persecution would pass. When it became clear that it was only really possible to stay put if they renounced their faith, however, many chose to emigrate. It was an extremely risky path to take. To leave France without permission was illegal. If caught, Huguenots risked loss of property, imprisonment, enslavement in the king's galleys or even summary execution.

Huguenots fled in their tens of thousands to such Protestant nations as England, as well as to its colonies in America. A committee established in London in early 1687, charged with distributing charitable funds to distressed Huguenot refugees, estimated that by December 1687 13,050 French Calvinists had settled in the capital, mostly in Spitalfields.[3] Overall, between about 1670 – when the level of persecution started to rise significantly – and 1710 it has been estimated that around 50,000–80,000 Huguenots fled France, more than half of them coming to England, and, of those, more settling in London than in all other British locations combined. Of the capital's population of around 575,000 in 1700, Huguenots may well have formed 5 per cent.[4]

The attraction of Spitalfields to these new arrivals was due, in part, to its proximity to the long-established French Protestant church in Threadneedle Street in the City (other Huguenot refugees were drawn to the area near the French church in the Savoy, off the Strand, and so contributed to Soho's rapid and large-scale expansion and development in the 1680s and 90s[5]). And Spitalfields was, as we've seen, a focus for speculative builders and canny landowners from the mid seventeenth century onward so there were buildings there for the Huguenots to occupy and significant opportunities for expansion.

But Spitalfields also had something else to offer. The eastern parishes and Liberties of London had long been home to weavers, working with wool but also from the mid seventeenth century producing silk ribbon, too (see page 137).[6] In other words, there was already a significant native silk industry before the arrival of large numbers of Huguenots. Silk was hugely popular with the English (even if Daniel Defoe's claim, made in 1705 and 1722, that there were 50,000–100,000 silk-ribbon weavers in London is almost certainly an overestimate – 40,000 is possibly more likely).[7] At the time, though, no English-based industry was able to manufacture the more complex or wider fabrics required for much sought-after high-quality silk dresses, waistcoats and coats. The newly arrived refugees from France, many of whom possessed skills in the silk trade, therefore saw a business opportunity: they could create a new, high-quality, French-style silk industry in an area of London that was congenial to French Protestants, that possessed associations with the embryonic native silk-weaving industry and that presumably also contained the core of a workforce with some relevant skills.

Not all the Huguenots who came to England were silk weavers. Some worked with precious metals, producing exquisite objects in silver and gold. A significant number arrived with no practical trades, often being former landowners or gentlemen unused to industry. All, though, were driven by the determination to succeed in their new home. They knew the English had an insatiable appetite for high-quality and well-designed French-made silk as well as silver and gold artefacts. They also knew that while there was demand there was no ready supply that was not made prohibitively expensive through import taxes. The newly arrived Huguenots must have perceived with some excitement that they were ideally placed to give the English what they wanted at prices that undercut French competition and with delivery unaffected by the weather, civil unrest or military intervention. Those who did not have the necessary trading skills or time or ability to acquire them often possessed business acumen, or had good contacts, or had either escaped their homeland with capital or, through merchant connections or latterly banks, had access to it. How could the creation in London of French-style silk and silver industries fail?

It may perhaps seem a little paradoxical that such austere Calvinist believers – in many ways Puritanical in outlook (see page 173) – should have sought to devote their working lives to the production of visually seductive luxury goods and the amassing of personal wealth. The Huguenots, however, did not view their efforts in this light. They believed that wealth earned with a good heart and honest toil was godly, and that even the reasonable display of wealth earned through honest labour was 'not ostentation'.[8]

To understand the nature of the Huguenot community in London, and the speed with which it successfully established itself, it is necessary to remember that for decades these French Calvinists had been a hard-pressed, increasingly isolated and ultimately persecuted minority within their own homeland. This experience had established among them powerful traditions of self-reliance and mutual support. Family became all-important. Survival mechanisms became well honed. In London, therefore, they soon formed a tightly knit community – families and neighbours uniting in a common purpose, with marriages contracted almost invariably within the Huguenot community and the rearing of large numbers of children viewed as a duty and necessity (as exemplified by the Ogier dynasty in the early eighteenth century – see chapter 12).

One gets a clear sense of the tight-grained nature of the community from perusing the register of the Huguenot church of La Patente, founded in 1688, located in 'Paternoster Row'/Crispin Street by 1707, and from 1740 until 1786 in the still-surviving if much altered building in Hanbury Street (formerly 'Browns Lane') that had been built in about 1719. The register shows that many of the Huguenots who attended the church were already silk weavers or members of the silk trade when they arrived in London and a large number came from just two cities in France: Lyon and Tours. Many of them probably knew each other before they arrived in Spitalfields.[9]

From the point of view of the English monarchy, the arrival *en masse* of French people fleeing France during the early 1680s must have been something of an embarrassment. Charles II had been at odds with France in the early years of his reign (England and France indeed fought each other in 1666 during the Second Anglo-Dutch War). But by the time of the 'secret' Treaty of Dover of 1670, Charles was hoping for a rapprochement in order to secure financial aid from the French that would free him from financial dependence on Parliament. He had also fallen out with the Whig faction at Westminster (to whom, with their Protestant associations, the Huguenots were naturally sympathetic), and was reaching a personal reconciliation with Catholicism (as suggested by the Treaty of Dover). But although his relationship with France was ambiguous and his independence compromised he was a tolerant man who disliked the notion of brutish persecution for reasons of religion. Moreover as someone who had himself been an exile in earlier life, he clearly felt sympathy for the new refugees.

Consequently, although it could only hinder his maturing policies and private plans, he chose to offer the arriving Huguenots a warm and public welcome. Robin Gwynn – the acknowledged authority on the Huguenots in England – suggests that this indicates 'a genuine generosity of heart' on the king's part, and goes on to say: 'In 1666, even as he was declaring war on France, Charles chose to welcome French Protestants into his country. And when the *Dragonnades* began in 1681, he acted with speed and decisiveness in offering the Huguenots both a home and significant privileges, so that those who came to British shores were well treated for the four years before his death in 1685.'[10] The king also, perhaps, perceived that the arrival of the Huguenots offered economic benefits that outweighed possible political disadvantages and domestic difficulties.

The practical outcome of Charles' support was the issuing in 1681 of a *Brief*, designed to raise funds to relieve the more distressed of the newly arrived immigrants. In it the king talked of the religious persecution of the Huguenots, described how they were 'being forced to abandon their native abodes', and called them 'not only distressed strangers, but chiefly persecuted Protestants'.[11] This was emotive stuff. The poor and persecuted Huguenots were – by royal approval – evidently deemed worthy, indeed admirable, objects of charity and of national support. The *Brief* was read in churches around the land, and must have come as a great source of comfort, as well as practical help, to the newly arrived French Protestants.

Four years later, matters took an even worse turn for those Huguenots still living in France. On 22 October 1685 Louis XIV passed the Edict of Fontainebleau, revoking the Edict of Nantes that had granted French Protestants religious liberty. The *Dragonnades* had been bad enough. Now, at the stroke of a pen, Louis outlawed the Protestant faith in France altogether and initiated the closure and destruction of Protestant churches and the prosecution and punishment of all professing Protestants. The exodus from France intensified.

Not, however, to England in such numbers as previously, for in February 1685 Charles II had died and been succeeded by the pro-French and Catholic James II. A far less subtle and thoughtful individual than his brother, his determination to restore Roman Catholicism as England's official faith was to lead to his dramatic downfall in 1688. But in immediate terms his sympathies served to unnerve both the Huguenots already in England and those thinking of making their way there. Some certainly crossed the Channel and came to London. Others, though, took up the invitation issued by Frederick William, Elector of Brandenburg and Duke of Prussia. His extraordinarily enlightened and enterprising Edict of Potsdam – passed a week after and in response to the Edict of Fontainebleau – encouraged Huguenots to emigrate to Prussia by offering safe passage, freedom of worship and tax-free status for ten years. As a result Prussia – and Potsdam in particular – became a centre of Protestant European immigration, offering an attractive alternative to London for large numbers of Huguenots, as well as Dutch, Russian and Bohemian Protestants. Prussia was to benefit economically and culturally from the energy and commercial initiative of these migrant communities.

James II's attitude to the Huguenots was inconsistent and contradictory. He certainly saw them as a threat – not only to himself but to the very principle of monarchy since he was convinced that their Puritanical Christianity made them republicans at heart. But at the same time he did not like the way in which they were being persecuted. The lawyer and Whig politician Sir William Trumbull, when describing the king's disapproval of the *Dragonnades*, wrote that, 'though he did not like the Huguenots (for he thought they were of anti-monarchical principles) yet he thought the persecution of them was unchristian, and not to be equaled in any history . . . they might be no good men, yet might be used worse than they deserved, and it was a proceeding he could not approve of.'[12] James also knew that openly to ignore the Huguenots' plight would be to court trouble. Despite some initial alarm at their arrival in large numbers, the mass of English people generally recognised that the Huguenots were fellow Protestants who were being persecuted, and, what was more, were the victims of an autocratic Catholic monarchy that many in this country found particularly threatening, arrogant and repugnant.

So James II resolved to follow a two-faced approach. He contrived to appear to be continuing Charles II's sympathetic policies in order to appease the Protestant sensibilities of the majority of his subjects. But at the same time he wanted to satisfy his French masters by making life sufficiently difficult for Huguenots in England that some might leave and few would feel inclined to choose it as a place of refuge. Thus, for example, at the time of the Revocation of the Edict of Nantes, the king 'prohibited the captains and officers of English ships from taking French subjects on board unless they had passports – which they could not obtain – and punished at least one captain for disobeying this injunction.'[13] It's not surprising, therefore, that although, at his accession, he promised foreign churches in London the same protection and support they had enjoyed during the reign of Charles II, issued a *Brief* for a public collection on the Huguenots' behalf, as had been done in 1681, and continued to grant letters of denizenship (that is, the granting of certain rights to foreigners residing in Britain), the Huguenot community believed him to be 'shifty and untrustworthy, his actions but a front to placate English public opinion'.[14]

Some indication of James's Machiavellian propensities is given by his intervention during the drafting of a Parliamentary Bill in 1685 for the 'general naturalisation of French Protestants currently residing in England ... and such others as shall come over within a limited time'. The Court disliked the Bill. It therefore ensured that a clause was added that ordered all French churches and congregations to use only the Anglican liturgy translated into French. This was obviously unacceptable to Calvinist Huguenots – and was evidently intended to be so. They had given up all in their native land for the freedom to worship in their own manner and would scarcely agree to a course of action that compromised this freedom. Had the Bill become law unamended it would have destroyed all foreign nonconformist churches in England and – perhaps more to the point – would have put a total stop to the flow of persecuted French into the country. That it did not ultimately reach the statute book seems to have been largely a matter of chance. In June Charles II's illegitimate son the Duke of Monmouth, hoping to grab the throne, launched a Protestant rebellion against James II and in the aftermath of its defeat in early July the Bill lapsed and no more was heard of it. However, as Gwynn points out, this legalistic attempt on their religious freedom ensured that Huguenot 'elders were kept uneasy for the rest of [James II's] reign.'[15]

Something of the volatile atmosphere of the early years of the Huguenot settlement in London is captured in an extraordinary document compiled by Roger Morrice, a nonconformist vicar ejected from his living in 1660 for his Puritanical and Parliamentarian persuasions, who became a freelance political journalist. Morrice's *Entering Book* records the word on the street – both gossip and informed opinion – from coffee houses and taverns, for the edification of a small group of clients who evidently subscribed to the theory that knowledge is power.[16] Some entries are in code or shorthand, which may have been used for speed or secrecy. And one entry in particular, for Saturday 7 November 1685, serves as a reminder of just how much subterfuge James's policies at home and abroad involved.

So far as Morrice was concerned, the day was marked by a generous action on the part of the king. 'The last counsel day', he wrote, 'his Majestie was gratiously pleased to grant a Brief throughout the Kingdome, for the distressed Protestants fled out of France who conformes to the church of England.'[17] What Morrice could not have known, though, was that while the *Brief* was indeed ordered in Council on 6 November, it was not actually to be issued until 5 March and that even then its reading in London churches was to be delayed by several weeks. Morrice would have assumed that the *Brief* was all it appeared to be. In fact, it was evidently issued with an 'ill grace' and 'such procrastination troubled Englishmen as well as French'.[18] John Evelyn, the diarist and close observer of the political and social life of James's court, blamed the delay on 'the interest of the French ambassador and cruel papists'.[19] In addition, Gwynn records that 'Lady Russell, who had contacts in the refugee community, wrote that the Lord Chancellor, Judge Jeffreys, "bid [the *Brief*] be laid by, when it was offered him to seal."'[20] Jeffreys, it seems, informed his fellow Commissioners named in the *Brief* (who were those responsible for allocating the monies raised) that the king considered the refugees to be enemies of monarchy and episcopacy.[21] Evelyn was convinced that French agents were at work. And indeed Louis XIV had sent an agent to England – one Bonrepaus – who later told Louis that James was giving him all possible support.[22]

The delay in the public reading of the *Brief* was not the only evidence of royal meddling. Its wording was, too. Quite simply, it had been watered down from the *Brief* issued in 1681, which, as we've seen, made vivid reference to the Huguenots 'being forced to abandon their native abodes' and called them 'chiefly distressed strangers' and 'persecuted Protestants'.[23] The *Brief* of 1686 'said nothing about conditions in France, nor about persecutions, merely stating that the destitute French Protestants currently in England needed relief.'[24]

Worse still the *Brief,* and its promise of charitable disbursements, came with strings attached. It stated that the money raised through donations was to be used to 'benefit only those who lived in entire conformity and orderly submission to our government established both in church and state'.[25] No such phrase had been used in the 1681 *Brief.* The Huguenots wondered how this was to be interpreted. Did it mean that only those refugees who attended conformist French congregations or Anglican churches were to be offered relief? Would it be necessary for potential recipients of the bounty to produce a certificate to say they had received Communion according to the usage of the Church of England? Ultimately this ambiguous requirement did not prove a significant stumbling block for the Huguenots and was not comparable to the stipulation in the earlier and abandoned Parliamentary Bill that they must use Anglican liturgy. As Gwynn explains, 'since the continental Reformed churches accepted the Anglican Church as a true Protestant church, most refugees felt able to comply with this condition, but only after considerable heart-searching; they were, after all, refugees for the sake of religion, and had left their native land to be free to worship in their own way.'[26]

Despite its toned-down nature the 1686 *Brief* still provoked a most generous response from the public after being extended by an Order of Council in March 1687. Over £42,000 was raised. On 16 April a further Order of Council was made for a new general collection. This raised £200,000, forming a fund known as the Royal Bounty.[27] A lay French committee was entrusted with an annual distribution of £16,000 amongst poor refugees and their descendants, while a second ecclesiastical committee distributed £1,718 annually to 'distressed' pastors.

A note in Morrice's *Entering Book* for Saturday 21 November 1685 indicates why people should have been so generous:

> The persecutions and torments of the Protestants in France is still inexpressible, its writ over by an eye witnesse that Dragoons are sent even into all Countreys, and that in one part of a Province 18,000 Protestants, when the Dragoons came did generally run to the Churches for feare of the Gallies, Torments or Death, and there offered to renounce the Protestant Religion. The Papists would not take their renunciations till they had made the Protestants solemly to sweare that they did not make that renunciation for feare of torment or for any such selfish reason, but out of the sence of the great dishonour they had done God, and the scandall they had cast upon Holy Church by living in such damnable Heresies so long &c.[28]

Of the public's response to the *Brief*, Morrice recorded on Monday 3 May 1686: 'In many Parishes in London and in the Suburbs they have given liberally to the Collection for the French Protestants, but very many persons are confidently reported to have given five or ten times more than they have upon an exact enquiry.'[29] For James II, according to Gwynn, such generosity must have seemed 'little short of a slap in the royal face'.[30]

James's actions went beyond delaying and diluting the *Brief.* He also resorted to censorship. The official newspaper of the time, the *London Gazette*, maintained a silence about events in France in 1685 so deafening that it was hard for contemporaries not to assume some official cover-up. As Evelyn observed in his diary:

> One thing was much taken notice of, that the *Gazettes* which were still constantly printed twice a week, and informing us what was done all Europe over etc.: never all this time, spake one syllable of this wonderful proceeding in France, nor was any relation of it published by any, save what private letters etc. the persecuted fugitives brought: Whence this silence, I list not to conjecture, but it appeared very extraordinary in a Protestant country, that we should know nothing of what Protestants suffered.[31]

Thanks to the French agent Bonrepaus' reports to his superiors in France we know that James was fully complicit in this conspiracy of silence.[32] He even went so far as to order Jean Claude's *Account of the Persecutions and Oppressions of the Protestants in France* to be publicly burnt by the hangman at the London Exchange and its translator to be arrested. Ultimately, though, his heavy-handed approach backfired. As Gwynn observes: 'Public discontent was further intensified by the knowledge that James had been prompted by Barrillon [the French ambassador]. And concern was expressed that the French Ambassador should have, as Evelyn put it, "so mighty a power and ascendant here". Ultimately, James' actions merely increased public sympathy for the Huguenots.'[33]

In immediate practical terms, James's hostile approach did ensure that fewer Huguenots crossed the Channel in the early years of his reign than had done so in the years immediately after 1681. But even here he was ultimately to be hoist by his own petard. The Declaration of Indulgence that he issued on 4 April 1687 was designed to make it possible for Roman Catholics to worship openly and, by removing the obligation to swear allegiance to the Anglican Church before assuming positions in public office, allow them to start moving back into public life. But James's seemingly enlightened relaxation of theological controls had inadvertent side effects that were, from his point of view, most unfortunate. By suspending penal laws enforcing conformity to the Anglican Church, the king also made life easier for all other Christian denominations that did not conform to Anglican doctrine or liturgy – including the Calvinistic Huguenots. His actions were, understandably, opposed by the Anglican

Church and the Episcopalian Church in Scotland, who saw their dominant positions being undermined. At the same time this relaxation of
controls did not make the Huguenots any less distrustful of the king. The
following year they were to throw all their support behind his nemesis
William of Orange and were to remain opposed to the Catholic-tainted
Stuarts well into the eighteenth century and to the Jacobite uprisings of
1715 and 1745.

Nevertheless, the Declaration of Indulgence did open the way for a new
wave of Huguenot immigration. It had become law first in Scotland on 12
February 1687 and by early March – when it was known that it was soon to
become law in England – the Huguenots were already on the move, as if
a wave had suddenly burst the dam. On Saturday 5 March 1687 Morrice
noted: 'This last weeke it is very credibly reported there is full 2,000
French Protestants fled out of France into Plymouth, Falmouth, Sussex
and London whereof about 600 are Seamen.'[34] A couple of months later he
recorded gossip that he'd heard suggesting James was displaying – for
public consumption at any rate – yet more sympathy for the Huguenots.
On Saturday 14 May 1687 Morrice recorded in his *Entering Book*:

> It is said the King of England will Indenzion [that is grant denizenship,
> which conferred certain rights on foreigners residing in Britain] 200 French
> Protestants that lately made their escap thence hither, and ordered the ship
> that brought them to pay but half custome, that is according to the rate
> English subjects pay, when it was a French ship and otherwise must have
> paid double. How this will be resented by the French King we know not,
> but he will insist upon a privat Article with our King that he should deliver
> up all his subjects that were fled hither.[35]

Despite the official clampdown on coverage of news from France, some
details of the sufferings of the Huguenots in their homeland inevitably
slipped through. In an entry dated Saturday 14 May 1687 Morrice set down
what he understood to be going on:

> The torments [the King of France] puts them through are far worse than
> death it selfe, being more durable, and at last necessarily ending in death,
> as starving some, keeping others altogether without rest and sleep, Pier-
> cing others with sharp pointed iron instruments of cruelty, binding or in a
> sort roasting others at a distance from the fire till they dye &c . . . Some
> few Minsters they have burned of late by those slow fires . . . they generally

send the men to the Galleys, and the women to Nunneries or religious houses, where they are so tormented and disturbed by the Nunnes &c that many times it issues into death.[36]

So far as the English Huguenots were concerned, though, their uncertain position was resolved at a stroke in November 1688, with the ousting of James II and the accession of the Protestant William and Mary. Even if their sufferings in France were not ended, their long-term security and future in Britain was assured.

The generous responses to the royal *Briefs* reveal the extent to which the Protestant English middle class and aristocracy welcomed the arrival of their fellow Protestant and generally middle- or merchant-class French. This was predictable. These upper levels of society had nothing to lose and much to gain from the arrival of French craftsmen. Moreover there was political capital to be made from offering refuge (the word refugee was first coined at this time) to Protestant Frenchmen fleeing persecution in their own land, and simultaneously showing the autocratic monarchy of Catholic France in such a poor light.

But working people, notably journeymen weavers and smiths involved in the precious-metal trade, feared that they had much to lose. For them the Huguenots represented a potential or actual threat to their livelihoods. The historian Catherine Swindlehurst, who has made a close study of the reaction of journeymen weavers in the areas in which many of the French initially settled, particularly on the east side of London and in Norwich in Norfolk, notes that as early as 1681 one James Jeffries expressed fear of an uprising in Spitalfields against French refugees. Some Spitalfields residents, he observed, had amassed weapons, and '. . . those that have them say that those weapons are to defend themselves against the Papists and a Popish successor . . .'[37] The reference here to Papists may seem contradictory, but it should be remembered that for many uneducated English working people, being French was synonymous with being Catholic. They therefore tended to assume that the Huguenots – arriving in large and sudden numbers – were nothing less than an undercover French invasion force of Catholics and spies intent on causing mayhem in England.

At the same time there were those among the native labouring community who realised that there was an opportunity to be grasped here. They knew that, in comparison with France, England suffered from antiquated trade and manufacturing traditions and was unable to compete with the high-quality luxury artefacts being made on the other side of the Channel. Now they had in their midst skilled workers who could level the field for them. So, as Catherine Swindlehurst points out, 'France and the French silk industry were both the nemesis and the spur towards development of the English silk weaving trade in the late seventeenth century. For many London weavers, the French trade was something to be both revered and copied, as well as to be scorned and protected against.'[38] Despite the perceived cruelty and intolerance of its Catholic king, France was also, paradoxically, admired for its economic success and as a centre of taste and fashion. So the arrival of French tradesmen, enterprise and style in England promised the potential of successful competition with France in the production of luxury goods.

Despite the generally mixed response to the arrival of the Huguenots the long-established Weavers' Company seemed generally to take the view that the advent of the French represented – on balance – an opportunity for creative cooperation and self-improvement rather than a commercial threat. Its jurisdiction was limited in the early 1680s – it was not until its Royal Charter was granted in October 1685 that the company gained authority 'over all persons practising the art of weaving within the Cities of London and Westminster, the Borough of Southwark, and all other places within twenty miles distant'.[39] But even before that date, the company saw ways to reconcile Huguenot and English weavers, within Spitalfields and adjoining areas, to their mutual benefit. Thus, for instance, when John Larguier of Nîmes was granted the status of master by the Weavers' Company in 1684 it was not only because he had proved that he was 'fully inabled to weave and perfect lutestrings, alamodes and other fine silks as well as service and beauty in all respects as they are perfected in France', but because he had also agreed to the 'condition that he imply himself, and others of the English nation, in making the said alamode and lutestring silks for one year from this day'.[40] In other words, he had committed himself to share his skills, new technologies and trade 'secrets' and not, as many feared, keep them exclusively within his own community and employ only French apprentices and journeymen.

Many native weavers, though, remained suspicious. Their perception was that the Huguenots' skills, initiative, ambition and driving work ethic were threats to the practices of 'fair trade' – a notion that, among other

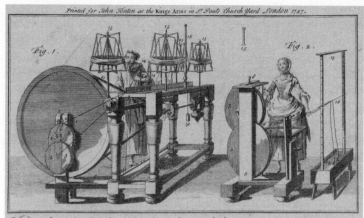

A Draught of the Silk-Windles or the method of Winding and Twisting of Silk for the Weavers

Above: *a print of 1747 showing silk being twisted into thread and wound onto bobbins or spindles for use by weavers. Below: the trade card of John Crozier, based in Widegate Street, 'Spittlefields'. Like Francis Rybot and Nicholas Jourdain, in nearby 'Raven Row', Crozier was a weaver and a mercer who made and sold 'all sorts of silks'.*

things, promoted and protected established practices of production and scales of wages. English workers in the silver and gold industry seem to have felt this equally if not more strongly, and made it clear that they viewed the arrival of a small number of Huguenots who were highly skilled smiths as a direct and immediate challenge. The fear that the French incomers would undercut their English rivals by accepting lower wages and charging less for their work was particularly marked, arising from a perception that earlier immigrant communities had done precisely this as they strove to establish themselves. As one pamphlet poem, published in 1681, observed: '... weavers all may curse their fates/Because the French work under rates ...'[41]

Tensions grew rapidly so that by early August 1683 riots in and around Spitalfields were feared. Among the State Papers various eyewitness reports survive, including one that states: 'the factious partt [of the weavers] thereabouts has been very bold and presumptuous this last week: and ... they do cabal together oftener than has been usual.' English weavers, it was observed, gathered in public houses 'in opposition to the French weavers in their neighbourhood', and it was feared that if the weavers 'can get a sufficient number together, they will rise and knock [the French] on the head.'[42] One informant told the authorities that he had '... found out the three houses of their meeting viz at the sign of the Poor Robin in Bishopsgate Street, at the sign of the Town of Hackney in the same street, and at the Cock in Whitegate Alley near the Fields' (what is now Widegate Street, according to Ogilby and Morgan's map of 1681–2). Some of the weavers attending these meetings were, warned the informant, 'not sober and rationull'.[43] Clearly, local taverns were a focal point for festering discontent.

The official response to such information was a controlled display of force. On 9 August 1683 Charles II ordered Horse Guards to be 'quartered about Islington, Hackney or Mile End to keep the weavers in order',[44] and the City's trained bands were kept in Devonshire Square, just off Bishopsgate (shown as 'Devonshire House Garden' on Ogilby and Morgan's map and located immediately to the south of Spitalfields). This tactic seems to have worked – certainly no assault on the Huguenots took place – but ill feeling simmered not far beneath the surface. On 25 August an informant reported that 'he was desiered by two journeymen weavers ... to meet in Swan Fields one Monday morning and he doth conclude is in order to some bad designe, it being the same method they took when they burned the ingin loombs.[45] The reference is to engine-loom riots in 1675 when Spitalfields silk-ribbon weavers rioted against the introduction of machinery that heralded automation and was therefore seen as a threat to the local workforce.

In London all proposed violent protest came to nothing, probably because the presence of armed troops was a sobering prospect and effective deterrent. There were, however, severe riots against the Huguenots in Norwich in August and September 1683. Francis Blomefield, writing some years later, described how:

> The Mob brake open one of their Houses. And misused a Woman so, that she died 2 or 3 Days after; the Pretence was, that these People would under-work them; however, the French that dwelt there were forced to quit the Street that Night . . . The Poor being still discontented at the French which were left in the City . . . and coming in a large Body into the Market Place, declared that the French came to under-work them, and accordingly going to Mr Barnham's in St Andrew's Parish, they pulled them and their Goods out of their Houses, abused their Persons etc.[46]

Soon after the August/September riots one Frenchman reported to a compatriot that the townspeople of Norwich believed the settlers to be 'only a troop of Papists masquerading as Protestants and would ruin their trade'.[47]

Antipathy to the Huguenots focused principally on the economic threat they were felt to pose. But there were also fears about the religion that they practised, about their desire to worship in their own churches in their own way, and about the impact this might have on Anglican observance. In his *Entering Book* for Thursday 29 March 1683 Roger Morrice noted that these fears had proved sufficient to provoke an official, defensive response. 'The last weeke', he wrote, 'the Bishop of London, and Mr Secretary Jenkins its said dined with Sir William Smith at his petty Sessions for the Hamletts of the Tower &c. and there they resolved to build 2 or 3 churches . . . about Spittle fields towards Stepney &c. that the Dissenters might not have such a faire colour to go to Conventicles &c. [unofficial religious meetings].[48]

In other words, the authorities were prepared to go to the expense of constructing new, and strategically placed, Anglican churches in newly created and administratively important parishes to protect areas such as Spitalfields from the dominance of Calvinism or other religious faiths outside the state control of the Church of England. In the event, because the necessary funds were in such short supply in the 1680s, the project failed to get off the ground. Revenue could have come from a national tax on coal that had been initiated in 1667 to help fund the reconstruction of the City after the Great Fire. The tax money was used especially for the reconstruction of parish churches and St Paul's Cathedral, and in the 1680s there simply was not a surplus to fund other building projects. But after 1710, when the reconstruction of the City was nearly complete, Coal Tax money became available for new churches and in 1711 the Act for Building Fifty New Anglican Parish Churches in London was passed. One of the targets of this Act was Spitalfields, where Christ Church was started in 1714 and a new parish created in 1729 when the church was finally completed.

When the construction of Christ Church began the Huguenots had been established in large numbers in Spitalfields for around thirty years, and by the time it was completed the Huguenots essentially *were* Spitalfields. Huguenot families were the ones that mattered, economically and culturally. They were the significant merchants and entrepreneurs; they occupied many of the area's largest and grandest houses; and they were a respected part of London society with many rising high in the professions and the Weavers' Company. They had command of Spitalfields' wealth and most of its wealth-generating industries and, although not members of the established Anglican Church, ran the area through the vestries and parish administration.

John Strype in his 1720 *Survey of London and Westminster* records the respect in which the Huguenots of Spitalfields were by now held and the reasons for this:

> The North west Parts of this Parish (Spittle Fields and Parts adjacent), of later Times became a great Harbour for Poor Protestant Strangers, Waloons and French; who as in former Days, so of late, have been forced to become Exiles from their own Country for their Religion, and for the avoiding cruel Persecution. Here they have found quiet and security, and settled themselves in their several Trades and Occupations; Weavers especially. Whereby God's Blessing surely is not only brought upon the Parish, by receiving poor Strangers (*Come ye Blessed of my Father, Etc, For I was a Stranger and ye took me in*) but also a great Advantage hath accrued to the whole Nation, by the rich Manufactures of weaving Silks and Stuffs and

Camlets: which Art they brought along with them. And this Benefit also to the Neighbourhood; that these Strangers may serve for Patterns of Thrift, Honesty, Industry, and Sobriety, as well.[49]

This was an extremely positive view of the benefits of the Huguenot arrival and settlement in Spitalfields. It was also, presumably, one commonly held in 1720. Certainly Daniel Defoe had expressed a comparable opinion in 1719 when, in a pamphlet supporting the native silk industry, he stressed the economic importance of the Huguenots' contribution to national well-being and emphasised the fact that the 'Silk Manufactures of this Kingdom' were, with the wool industry, 'the Staple of our Trade and the most considerable and essential part of our Wealth, the Fund of our Exportation, the Support of our Navigation, and the only Means we have for the Employing and Subsisting our Poor.'[50]

But even in the early eighteenth century, when Huguenot merchants, silk weavers and silversmiths were well established, seemingly accepted as part of London life with the bounty of their trades much valued, there remained characters who continued to view the settlers with deep suspicion. Perhaps the most curious of these was Jean-Baptiste Denis, a French immigrant himself and also a Calvinist. In fact he was more than that, which might explain his poisonous attitude to his fellow Frenchmen in early-eighteenth-century Spitalfields.

Denis had been born into a good family in Toul in about 1676 and was brought up a Roman Catholic. He took a law degree at the University of Pont-à-Mousson, was received into the Roman Catholic priesthood in Rome and became almoner and secretary to the Bishop of Meaux. But then he gave it all up. For reasons of conscience, it must be assumed, he found his comfortable life intolerable. He resigned his benefice at Toul in 1704, and then went to Berne where he abjured Catholicism and became a Calvinist. In about 1705 he moved to England and was soon preaching to the Calvinist community in Spitalfields. As a daring proselyte, who had given up all for his faith, Denis should have been a hero among the Huguenots. But he was not. There must have been something awkward, in a most deep-grained way, about his character. He had given up Catholicism and comfort in a Catholic country for a new faith. Now – as a refugee in Spitalfields – he turned against his new and adopted community, pouring out his spleen in a pamphlet, published in around 1722, with a long title that says it all: *A Plot Discovered: Carried on boldly, these many years by False Brethren Against the New Converts from Popery to the Protestant Religion . . . Wherein is set forth, the insolence and ingratitude, of the greatest part of the French Refugees, towards the English, their Benefactors.*

The feud between Denis and his fellow French Calvinists appears to have been sparked by a dispute over the location of his family's pew in l'Église de l'Hôpital, a Huguenot church or 'temple' in Black Eagle Street, Spitalfields. Even in the generally austere Huguenot faith, where you sat in church said much about your place in the hierarchy of the local community, and clearly Denis did not think the location of his pew bestowed upon him the status and esteem he believed he and his family were due. Since by 1717 he probably had around seven children, the size of the Denis family pew must have been of some consequence, too. However, the matter was not resolved to the mutual satisfaction of all – or at least not of Denis – and the vitriolic pamphlet seems to have been his extraordinary riposte to the slight he believed he had received.

But it went far beyond the matter of an inferior pew. The faults among his fellows that Denis perceived, and to which he chose to draw attention, included the 'general corruption that reigns among the refugees', their pride, ingratitude, injustice and ungenerosity towards proselytes. The Huguenot 'Master-Weavers in Spittle-Fields' were, he wrote, 'a people stiff-neck'd and uncircumcis'd of heart . . . Whose pride and ambition have tower'd to such a height, as to make their condition not only envy'd by the greatest merchants in the City, but have also made themselves formidable to the most antient and most powerful Companies of the nation.' In sardonic vein Denis observed what 'a glorious set of people indeed are these French master weavers . . . that ruin the body, of which they denominate themselves members, purely to enrich themselves by the ruin, the spoils of the unfortunate, not sparing their own countrymen . . . the greatest part of the refugees are a cast-out people, without honour or principle . . . a ridiculous concourse of vagabonds.'[51]

These are no doubt the exaggerated ravings of a disappointed and unbalanced personality. But, as with Strype's upbeat summary of the Huguenot character and achievement, Denis' perception could offer a clue to a wider undercurrent of opinion. If Strype reflects the commonly held positive attitude to the Huguenots, does Denis accurately capture the negative attitudes, prejudices and assumptions held by more xenophobic Londoners?

Denis' ultimate fate among his Spitalfields neighbours is not known, but it surely cannot have been happy. He abandoned his ambition to preach among them – which was probably just as well – and it seems he resolved to open a boarding school teaching Latin, French and Italian. He advertised the enterprise in his pamphlet and stated that the school was to be located in 'an airy house, with a garden', in 'Princess-street, Spittle-Fields'. Princelet Street – formerly 'Princes Street' – had not been completed at the time Denis' pamphlet was published. But the small group of buildings off Brick Lane and on what became the north-east corner of Princelet Street had been built by 1705–6 and by 1713 were known as 'Princesse Street',[52] and so it must have been in one of these new houses that Denis hoped to establish himself. It is now not known if his educational enterprise succeeded.

Even if Denis' views were shared by others in the early years of the eighteenth century they did not, ultimately, prevail. No doubt one of the main reasons for the eventual and fulsome acceptance of the Huguenots – even by journeymen weavers, who once felt themselves threatened – was the fact that the incomers had virtually invented a new and valuable industry in London. The high-quality silk they produced was unprecedented in Britain. Huguenot weavers and masters, and the trade they created, clearly had not directly supplanted a native workforce or local trade but – on the contrary – had created new markets, employment and skills, and generated wealth. The most dramatic evidence of the contribution the Huguenots made to the nascent London silk industry was the valuable trade secrets refugees brought with them. For example, an otherwise anonymous French weaver named Mongeorge brought the secret from Lyon of how to give lustre to silk taffeta. This allowed Spitalfields weavers to compete with new and desirable French-made products, even on occasion to surpass them in quality, as well as – for domestic sales – undercut them in price.

Huguenot sophistication and merchant skills enabled them to plead their cause effectively with legislators. For example in 1713 Huguenot weavers presented a petition to Parliament against a proposed commercial treaty with France, arguing that 'by the encouragement of the Crown and of divers Acts of Parliament' the silk manufacture of London had grown twentyfold since 1664, that '. . . good black and coloured silks, gold and silver stuffs and ribands, are now made here as in France', including black silk for hoods and scarfs 'that was not made here above twenty-five years ago [and] which before were imported from France'. The trade, the value of which 'amounted annually to above £300,000 for several years past', was clearly, pointed out the weavers, too successful to put at risk.[53] The weavers also succeeded, in 1721, in obtaining an Act of Parliament that encouraged the silk industry by offering a 'bounty' for successful trade. By exporting 'wrought silk', weavers received repayment of part of the duty they had paid on imported raw silk.[54]

All in all, by the 1720s the Huguenot-inspired and -driven Spitalfields silk industry was an economic and artistic triumph, moving towards the height of its first 'Golden Age'. But the system by which the industry flourished carried within it the seeds of its own eventual decline. As is so often the case, as the sun shone brightly distant storm clouds were gathering.

SEVEN

GOD'S CHOSEN PEOPLE

The Life of the Huguenot Community

The esteem with which the Huguenots were generally held by their new fellow countrymen, and in particular their reputation for honest hard toil, is hinted at in a series of twelve engravings by William Hogarth called *Industry and Idleness*. As the title suggests, the sequence offers a strong moral message about the rewards of the former virtue and the dire consequences of the latter vice, and it does so by following the very different paths taken by two 'Fellow 'Prentices', Tom Idle and Francis Goodchild.

Plate one of the series sets the tone. It shows the two apprentices in a weavers' garret evidently somewhere in Spitalfields (a large ale mug, from some local tavern and engraved 'Spittle Fields', balances on the loom of the idle apprentice). Tom is snoozing on his workbench while a cat molests his dangling shuttle and a discarded copy of the *Prentice's Guide* gathers dust at his feet. The admirable Francis Goodchild, by contrast, is toiling earnestly. Not surprisingly as the sequence of engravings progresses, Francis does, too. Pious, hardworking and trustworthy, he ends up marrying his master's daughter – Miss West – acquires wealth and finally becomes Lord Mayor of London. The lazy Tom Idle, by contrast, is dismissed by his master, takes to gambling, whoring and thieving, and ultimately is hanged at Tyburn. He represents the loucher side of Spitalfields life but also provides the shadow against which the virtuous Francis shines more brightly.

There was, as it happens, a Lord Mayor of London called Francis Child, who held office in 1731, and it is possible that Hogarth had been impressed by him and modelled the industrious apprentice on him. But since the engravings were published some years later, in 1747, it's also possible that Hogarth had in mind the man who held the office of Lord Mayor that particular year: Sir Robert Ladbroke. There is no evidence

Plate one of William Hogarth's 1747 series Industry and Idleness *shows the 'Fellow 'Prentices
at their Looms' in a Spitalfields weaving garret. The industrious Francis Goodchild
weaves while Tom Idle snoozes, his mug of beer and tobacco pipe on the loom in front
of him and, pinned above his head, a page from* Moll Flanders, *Defoe's novel
about a wayward adventuress.*

that Francis Child came from a Huguenot family but Sir Robert, who was a City merchant banker, and from 1754 a Member of Parliament, was a prominent member of Spitalfields' Huguenot community, married to the daughter and heiress of John Peck, a member of a dynasty of dyers who played a prominent role in the area's silk industry. Ladbroke's splendid monument, by John Flaxman and dated 1794, stands near the altar in Christ Church Spitalfields and shows him in his Lord Mayor's robes – an expression of great local pride and a very public celebration of the virtues and achievements of Spitalfields' Huguenot merchant community.[1]

It's tempting to think that in juxtaposing the vices of Tom Idle with the virtues of Francis Goodchild, Hogarth was criticising the laziness and profligacy of elements of the native workforce as well as paying tribute to the hardworking 'profitable strangers' who now occupied such a central position in London commerce. If so, then he must have believed, as did many others, that the Huguenots had useful lessons to teach their English neighbours. And if Francis Goodchild is indeed partly inspired by Sir Robert Ladbroke, Hogarth's engravings hint at another truth about the Huguenot community of his time: they may have been accepted by most Londoners, and the majority by the second quarter of the eighteenth century would have been English-born, but they were also identifiable as a discrete group that stood slightly apart from their non-Huguenot fellow Londoners.

This was a deliberate choice on the part of the Spitalfields Huguenots. They treasured their own cultural and religious heritage. They chose to preserve French customs and language. And they also continued to follow different Protestant rites in their own places of worship. By 1700 there were at least nine Huguenot churches or 'temples' within Spitalfields, including ones in Black Eagle Street and Spitalfields Market.[2] Further temples followed in the new century, including three that still survive today: the former L'Artillerie (now a synagogue) of 1766 in Sandys Row, La Patente in Hanbury Street, and L'Église Neuve, which stands on the corner of 'Church'/Fournier Street and Brick Lane. Of these L'Église Neuve is architecturally the most significant. It has a simple but elegant exterior, with elevations inspired by antique temples and crowned with large and noble pediments. The sundial within the Fournier Street pediment is dated 1743 and is inscribed with the motto '*Umbra Sumus*' – 'We are but shadow' – a reminder that all in the material world is transitory.[3] Inside, the church (which became a synagogue in the late nineteenth century and remained one for most of the twentieth) was, until its conversion to a mosque in the 1980s, furnished with high-quality joinery and with box pews and capacious galleries, as in contemporary Anglican churches (the appearance of this largely lost interior is preserved in *The Survey of London*).[4] It would have witnessed services largely free from the sort of ritual to be found in Church of England liturgy, though with ministers to officiate, prayers, scripture readings and even music. And it would have witnessed, too, an intensity and certainty of belief.

The Huguenots' Spitalfields churches were more than the setting for everyday services. They also staged baptisms and marriages, as the records of St Jean, which stood from 1687 to 1827 in St John's Street, confirm.[5] But – and this demonstrates just one of the ways in which the Huguenots were both separate from and part of the wider community – their baptisms and marriages tended to be registered in Anglican churches, too. These were the administrative centres of their parishes, not just their spiritual centres: in a sense, they were also town halls.

The vestrymen and the governing body of eligible and elected parishioners met in the church or vestry room to govern the parish: to raise local taxes to finance the lighting, cleansing and policing of the parish area, and to administer the Poor Law. So the church was very much an instrument of the state and the law. Since the sixteenth century parish churches had maintained – in a regular manner – registers of all baptised, married and buried in their areas, and these registers were the primary documents that gave the individual inhabitants of England a legal identity and civil rights. For example, to be a beneficiary of the Poor Law it was necessary to demonstrate the parish of birth. So the Huguenots, even if they did not worship in Anglican churches but in their own churches with their own ministers, were obliged to operate within the Anglican parish system to establish their identities and origins, just as they might serve as vestrymen at, say, Christ Church, even though they did not worship in the vast new church. Thus the *Actes* governing the Huguenot church of St Jean, St John Street, Spitalfields, for example, explain that certain baptisms were entered in the register of the parish church of St Dunstan's Stepney, at a charge of sixpence per entry, and that 'certain marriages were solemnised in the church "*selon le rite et formulaire de l'Église Anglicane.*"'[6]

What is not clear from this is why the records of only 'certain' and not all baptisms and marriages conducted in St Jean were registered with the Anglican parish church. It seems that the interrelation between Anglican

Above: *the sundial on L'Église Neuve on the corner of Fournier Street and Brick Lane. Built in 1743 as a Huguenot church it is now a mosque, having been a synagogue for most of the twentieth century. 'Umbra Sumus' – 'We are but shadow' – is a reminder of the transitory nature of the material world and that physical existence is but a shadow of the spiritual world. Below: tin-glazed tiles of c.1700 from a coffee house that probably stood in Brick Lane. By this date coffee houses had become the centres of business for eminent merchants of the sort that lived in Spitalfields.*

and French churches was somewhat inconsistent, which is strange given the requirement to make information about baptisms, marriages and deaths publicly available. As historian Eileen Barrett observes, on the organisation of charity and the operation of Poor Law and relief funds: 'There seems to have been little interaction between . . . the French Church of London and English parishes operating in the same area.'[7] Presumably it was assumed that the Anglican and French church records existed in parallel, with both available and open for inspection by those who were interested in establishing the baptism, marriage or death of an individual even if this did not always happen in practice.

Burials and interments were a rather different matter. Huguenot baptisms and marriages may usually have been conducted in their own churches, but the dead invariably found their final resting place in the crypts and graveyards of Anglican parish churches – as is revealed by the many Huguenot burials and interments in Christ Church including of various Ogiers, Louisa Perina Courtauld and James and Anne Ouvry. The reason for this was practical. Huguenot churches generally had limited space for interment, and while there were of course nonconformist burial grounds – such as Bunhill Fields just to the north-west of the Spitalfields boundary – these were few and far between. It therefore made sense, and was certainly more convenient, for Huguenots in Spitalfields to be buried in the vaults or graveyards of the Anglican parish churches of St Dunstan's Stepney, St Leonard's Shoreditch, St Mary's Whitechapel, St Botolph's Bishopsgate, St Botolph's Aldgate and, after 1729, in Christ Church Spitalfields.[8]

It was perfectly acceptable from a religious point of view, too: Huguenots accepted the Anglican faith, despite its ritual, as part of the true Protestant Church, and Anglicans accepted Huguenots as fellow Protestants. Besides, for most Calvinist Huguenots the final resting place of the mortal remains was of relatively little importance in comparison with the fate of the immortal soul. Interestingly, even Roman Catholics made use of Anglican churchyards, sometimes in specially demarcated areas, because there was often, for ordinary families in London, no alternative acceptable way of disposing of the body.

If this pragmatic and seemingly happy marriage of practical necessities suggests that ultimately there was not much difference in doctrinal terms between Huguenots and Anglicans other than their forms of worship, that is certainly not the case. Their beliefs, at a very fundamental level, were in striking contrast with one another. Conventional Anglicans believed in the divine gift of free will by which individuals can choose, strive for and attain salvation. They also believed in the concept that a person would reap what they sowed, and that divine punishment awaited those who made the wrong decisions or committed sinful actions on earth. The Huguenots, on the other hand, adhered to the doctrine of predestination. They held that God's control over the world is absolute and that the destiny of each person is ordained before birth. The founder of Calvinism, John Calvin, described the process as 'the eternal election, by which God has predestined some to salvation, and others to destruction'.[9]

It was a belief rooted in a very particular interpretation of biblical texts in which God nominates a 'chosen people' to 'consume' evil,[10] and, as their reward, to go on to enjoy salvation. In *Deuteronomy*, 7:6, for example, God tells His 'chosen' people that 'thou art an holy people unto the Lord thy God . . . chosen . . . to be a special people unto himself, above all people that are upon the face of the earth.' Believing they were the 'Elect' – the people 'chosen' by God, even before their birth, and privileged to recognise the one true faith and thus achieve salvation – Calvinists had merely to be true to their religion and the laws of the Bible to be saved. As with many radical faiths Huguenot Calvinism was exclusive: its adherents believed that they alone were right and that they alone would achieve salvation. As for what happened in life – whether good or bad – that was God's will.

To outsiders in late-seventeenth- and early-eighteenth-century England, Calvinism must often have seemed intolerant and unbending – even fanatical – not least because it embraced the Old Testament notion of a vengeful and jealous God who 'repayeth them that hate him to their face, to destroy them'.[11] Certainly, Huguenot Calvinists felt it was theologically and ethically acceptable to offer violence to what they perceived as the forces of evil – notably the forces of the 'anti-Christ', the Pope in Rome. But such attitudes went hand in hand with a stern sense of moral and ethical responsibility and a Puritanical regard for the strictures of the Ten Commandments (the more cynical might have assumed that since Calvinists believed they were assured of paradise, notwithstanding their conduct on earth, they were free to behave as they liked, but such was not their own view).[12] Thus, although they were successfully integrated into London's society, the Huguenots remained different.

They were different, too, from another highly significant Christian minority group in contemporary Spitalfields – the Quakers, who had emerged in the mid seventeenth century and who by the early nineteenth were to be among the area's leading tradesmen, especially in the brewing business. Superficially there were some similarities, and there must have been a degree of empathy between the two groups. Both were inspired by individual interpretations of very selective and specific biblical texts. Both believed they were people chosen by God (one of the key New Testament texts for early Quakers was 1 Peter 2:9–10, which talks of a 'chosen generation . . . an holy nation, a peculiar people', that together form a 'royal priesthood . . . the people of God'.) Both believed that hard work and honesty reflected an emotional purity inspired by Christ – with Quakers perhaps embracing more fully the Christian virtues of compassion and a philanthropy that recognised the responsibility man has to help all his fellow men – no matter their race or religion – when in want. And both saw no problems in pursuing trades that some might view as morally or ethically problematic – banking (the Bible tends to frown on usury), making and selling alcohol (albeit wholesome beer and ale rather than spirits), and manufacturing luxury goods such as silver and silk. Huguenots and Quakers alike would have argued that such enterprises were redeemed and purified by the honest intentions and actions of godly tradesmen.

But there were substantial differences, too. Quakers were pacifist by principle while Huguenots were not (indeed many Huguenots became successful soldiers). Quakers embraced a Puritanical simplicity of garb, demeanour and language that made them more obviously 'outsiders' in late-seventeenth-century London. They did not agree with the need for 'ordained clergy' to conduct effective worship nor with conventional religious ritual. They believed in the 'priest-hood of all believers', holding that all are capable of a direct and very personal relationship with Christ and of gaining spiritual power through ecstatic religious experience.

The Quakers' experience of wider society was different, too. By and large the Huguenots were accepted. The Quakers, by contrast, like other outspoken Dissenting sects, were proscribed. They suffered direct and sustained persecution, partly because their refusal to take oaths placed them outside the legal system, partly because their independence of mind and direct rejection of Anglican ritual made them appear more of a political challenge to the established social and political order and to the hierarchies of monarchy, state and church.

It was highly significant – and not a little radical in the 1660s, and much in the spirit of the Puritanical republican Levellers of the Civil War era – that Quakers practised a form of egalitarian democracy in their language as well as their behaviour, preferring to communicate in a Bible-inspired archaic language and to refer to all, be it king, bishop or fellow Quaker, as 'friend', and address all as 'thee' or 'thou' in what one of the Quaker founders, George Fox, termed egalitarian 'plain speaking'. They also rejected some notions of property ownership – most dramatically the institution of slavery, which they regarded as the simple evil of one man holding another in unnatural and unchristian bondage. Some Anglicans regarded them as heretics and their beliefs as no more than blasphemy. Attempts were made to suppress them through the so-called Act of Uniformity of 1662 that prescribed the form of public prayers to be used in places of worship, and the Conventicle Act of 1664 that aimed to prevent Dissenters from meeting by forbidding the gathering for unauthorised worship of more than five people not members of the same family. The Toleration Act in the late 1680s gave Dissenters some relief from persecution. Not the Quakers, though. The Act required oaths to be taken, and this was something the Quakers could not do.

So while the Quakers struggled for religious toleration, the Huguenots found that their system of belief did not embroil them in ethical and moral conundrums, and that their churches were accepted. They did not have to live on the edge of – or even outside – mainstream English society. The significant religious differences between the French incomers and the vast majority of their new fellow countrymen were compounded – at least initially – by their many other differences as French-speaking émigrés fighting to survive in a foreign culture. This sense of being distinct, but also of being the 'Elect' or 'chosen people', adrift among foreigners with far less certain spiritual futures, must have had a profound influence on their thinking and actions; and it is easy to imagine that through being one of the 'Elect' it would be tempting to believe oneself 'justified' in actions that others might perceive as sins. At any rate, it is essential to bear in mind the very particular mindset of the Huguenots when considering their attitudes to their fellows, to those outside the faith and the immediate family circle – and to those inside who transgressed.

The average Huguenot's approach to business transactions was no doubt tempered by a sense of Christian morality, but it was tough as well.

After all, the leading Huguenots were not only tradesmen and craftsmen but, in many cases, capitalist entrepreneurs and merchant adventurers, and the essence of capitalism is to utilise – even exploit within accepted boundaries – resources and people to maximise profit. The Huguenots drove hard bargains, and although their community was clearly God-fearing and protective towards its members, when it came to business Huguenot masters were happy to work their journeymen weavers very hard indeed. Some of these would have been fellow and less commercially fortunate co-religionists. Some would have been English weavers attracted to Spitalfields because of the wealth the industry there was now creating – the case of John Larguier mentioned earlier, and the obligation imposed upon him in 1684 by the Weavers' Company to employ English weavers, does tend to confirm that there must have been some friction between the two communities and that within years of the arrival of the Huguenots they had English weavers working for them.[13] By the 1730s considerable numbers of Irish weavers (see pages 260–3) were also working in the Spitalfields silk-weaving industry.

The Huguenot community was divided by success, wealth and power. But it was also a meritocracy. Journeymen – through industry, energy and art (and occasionally a good marriage) – were, at least in theory, able to rise through its ranks. And as with most close-knit communities, even those lowest in the pecking order were supported by a close and complex mesh of cultural, economic, ethical and religious as well as family bonds that kept the community together and safe in a foreign land. Membership, though, came with associated expectations and obligations. Those who abided by the community's strict rules could fare well. Those who transgressed could suffer a pretty dismal fate. The Huguenots' ethical code and religious doctrine was unforgiving of transgressors and, true to its Old Testament model, could be vengeful.

If the Huguenot community was critical to the welfare of the individual, it was also critical to the smooth running of business, for the silk industry in the late seventeenth and early eighteenth centuries was a highly complex, multi-tiered one, involving numerous individuals, tasks and levels of skill. Indeed the sheer number of stages involved in obtaining and transforming raw silk into beautiful dyed and figured garments was one of the main reasons why they were so expensive.

There were many tradesmen and craftsmen of various levels of skill – with wives and children often employed alongside them – involved in the production of silk fabric, its sale and its use. These included journeymen weavers, dyers, 'pattern drawers' or designers, mercers and retailers. And presiding over this industry were the entrepreneurs, the master weavers with the capital to risk and invest, who bought the silk, employed the workforce and oversaw – for the likelihood of a handsome profit – the creation of what was one of the finest fabrics the world has ever seen. And the glory of silk was not just that it could be intensely beautiful and the height of fashion; it was also a robust and, in many ways, very practical fabric.

The complex journey from raw material to finished artefact usually began with the silk importer or merchant buying and importing silk from China, India or Italy. Even at this initial stage, though, permutations were possible because imported silk might be raw or already reeled or coiled onto skeins, or already 'thrown' to produce silk yarn or thread.

Next in the process was the 'Silk Man', who bought the imported raw or thrown silk from the importer, and then sold it on. He might be considered no more than a warehouse-keeper but sometimes the same merchant undertook the importing and selling on of silk on his own account. From the silk merchant or 'Silk Man', the silk – if imported raw and not thrown – would go to the 'throwster' to undergo the first major operation in the silk-weaving process. The 'throwster' took the silk off the skeins, cleaned it and twisted it into a 'slight' yarn or thread known as 'singles', which were then combined to form 'organise' or 'tram'. An 'organise' consisted of yarns of silk tightly twisted and doubled while a 'tram' was usually two or three yarns lightly twisted together. The number of twists involved depended on whether the yarn was to be used as warp (threads running the length of the fabric on the loom) or as weft – the cross threads interlaced with the warp by means of a shuttle to form the woven fabric. 'Organise' was generally used for warp while 'trams' were generally used for weft. The twists of yarn were then sorted into different types or qualities and each wound onto bobbins, spools or spindles by 'winders' for use in the next stage of the process.

From 1722, when John Lombe introduced North Italian silk-throwing technology in his mill in Derby, this stage of the silk industry became an increasingly English-based activity, with Stockport, Macclesfield and Congleton becoming dominant centres by the mid century. Attempts to start up native silk production, however, were rather less successful. William III is often said to have played a key role here, but the fact is that silkworms did not particularly thrive on white mulberry trees in England and so in quality and quantity the home-grown product could not compete with imported silk. William's simultaneous encouragement of regular imports from Italy of raw and thrown silk was, on the other hand, rather more successful.

Where the government could prove most helpful to the native silk industry was in the legislation it passed to control foreign imports. For example in 1745/6 the excise on velvet and silk goods was increased, so discouraging the import of foreign-made silk fabric and artefacts and in consequence encouraging the import of raw or thrown silk for use by weavers in Britain. In 1750 the duty on raw China and India silk was reduced, and in July 1759 an Act for the 'encouragement of Silk Manufactures' stated that the higher duty paid upon 'raw short silk, or capitons and silk nubs or husks of silk' was to be made the same as the previously lower duty paid upon 'raw long silk'.[14] This legislation also lowered the duty payable on Italian silk to the level of duty paid on Chinese silk at a period when the majority of the silk used in Britain was imported from Italy.[15] Finally, in 1766, an Act was passed to prohibit the import of foreign woven silks.[16]

Once the bobbins had been prepared they were transported to weavers or, if the thread was to be coloured before weaving (as was usual), to dyers. Dyeing was among the most important and fascinating of all the many facets of the silk trade. Dyers were the trade's scientists, constantly striving to make dyes that produced strong and attractive colours that were as stable as possible. In the eighteenth century, though, they struggled to achieve total colour stability, with the result that people rarely risked washing woven figured silk fabric or garments made with different-coloured threads. Silk is washable but the chance that one of the dyes might run was simply too great a risk to take. Silk fabric, then, was rarely washed after being worn, and so consequently much use was made of washable linen undergarments.

At this stage, with silk made into yarn and dyed, the master weaver – if not already involved – took the lead role. He bought the prepared silk and organised its transformation into bolts of fabric. This involved commissioning designs from 'Pattern-drawers', such as Anna Maria Garthwaite who from 1728 lived in 'Princes' (now 2 Princelet) Street and is documented as working for several leading local master weavers, including her neighbour Peter Abraham Ogier (see chapter 12). The designs, prepared for weaving use, and the silk thread – readied for use – were then put out to journeymen weavers who wove the designs. These journeymen usually had limited capital and resources and often rented their looms from the masters for whom they worked. Traditionally, and certainly in the early days of the trade, the vast majority of journeymen worked from their own homes, although there are records of weaving factories being established in Spitalfields from the mid eighteenth century by enterprising, well-funded masters. For example John Sabatier had a 'warehouse' at the west end of 'Church'/Fournier Street that in 1750 contained fifty looms, later increased to a hundred.[17]

Clearly master weavers had great economic power – they purchased the prepared silk thread, they generally owned the looms on which the thread was woven and they put out the work to journeymen weavers. Daniel Defoe recognised that it was the master's role in this complex trade structure that was critical and on which the success of the other trades, and the prosperity of the industry's diverse operatives, depended. This was made crystal clear at times of stagnation: '. . . in Spittle-fields', he wrote, '. . . as soon as the Market stops [the Masters] stop; if they cannot sell their Work, they immediately knock off the Looms, and the Journey-men as immediately starve and want work.'[18]

As well as operating as businessmen and capitalists master weavers could also possess varying levels of trade skills, the most experienced being capable of producing highly complex figured fabric. As for the silk fabric itself, this came in an almost bewildering variety of types. A list of different silk fabric or artefacts produced in 1769 includes 'brocades, tissues, peruvians, damasks, satins, striped and corded tabbies, tobines, enamelled mantuas, armozians, ducapes and lusterings'.[19] Descriptions of a few of these types give a good idea of the sheer variety available: brocades are rich and heavy fabrics with raised floral or figured patterns, often emphasised by contrasting colours incorporating gold or silver threads; damasks are also heavy fabrics with contrasting pattern and backgrounds that originated in Damascus; a tabby is a type of watered silk with patterns created by calendering (pressing in rollers) or by weaving techniques that create varying tensions in the warp and the weft; ducapes are heavy corded, or ribbed, fabrics popular in dressmaking; while lustrings are fine, glossy fabrics favoured for use as linings.

Once woven, the bolt of fabric would be returned to the master weaver who would warehouse it, display it, perhaps in his house, and then either sell directly to the public (usually through a West End warehouse or shop, perhaps in his ownership), or, more commonly, sell the fabric wholesale to a mercer (it was usual to give a mercer twelve months' credit, allowing him to sell the fabric at a profit before he had actually to pay for it). For his part, the mercer then sold to a retailer, who in turn sold it to the public from his shop.

As if that chain wasn't complicated enough, it was also sometimes the case in the early eighteenth century for an individual known as a mackler to act as middleman between master weaver and mercer or to sell weavers' fabrics directly to shopkeepers. Macklers could also be weavers themselves, commission work from journeymen weavers directly or specialise in selling lengths of damaged silk – or any combination of these. There were also people known as 'piece-brokers', who bought remnants of silk from weavers, mercers or macklers. When it finally came to the buying public, what was on offer in the shops was, for the most part, not ready-made garments but fabric that they would then send on to tailors to fashion into garments to suit their size and taste.

On occasion mercers employed journeymen directly to make pieces to order from patterns supplied – usually cribbed from imported French silks. Even more occasionally mercers also operated as master weavers themselves. Francis Rybot and Nicholas Jourdain, for example, were both weavers who also retailed silk from the shops above which they lived at 3 and 4 'Raven Row' (now 56–8 Artillery Lane). Rybot's trade card describes him as a 'Weaver and Mercer who makes and sells all sorts of rich brocaded silks . . .'[20] The houses survive, one with a splendid mid-eighteenth-century shopfront.

Mercers were also responsible for commissioning patterns and designs from professional pattern-drawers, and these designers soon gave Spital-fields silk its distinctive appearance. A leading light here was Anna Maria Garthwaite. Born in Harston, Lincolnshire, she arrived in Spitalfields in 1728, with her widowed sister Mary, and set up home and workshop in a newly built house on the corner of 'Princes Street' and 'Wood Street' (now 2 Princelet Street). For over thirty years – until her death in 1763 – she produced patterns for many of Spitalfields' master weavers and during this period evolved a powerful personal style that combined naturalistic portrayals of plants with sinuous asymmetrical Rococo composition, incorporating C- and S-shaped forms inspired by nature, including the curved edges of shells. (The term Rococo itself is probably a combination of the French *rocaille* meaning 'stones' and *coquille* meaning 'shell').

From around 1742 Spitalfields designs started to diverge from the continental ones. In essence the motifs incorporated – almost invariably flowers, plants and fruit – became more realistic in appearance, whereas in France the motifs became more stylised and the colours less naturalistic. This Spitalfields tendency can be seen as a reflection of contemporary advances in England in botanical illustration. Or more directly, if prosaically, it can be seen as a consequence of the fact that Spitalfields silk designers shared the same streets as the area's long-established fruit, flower and vegetable markets. On a daily basis Anna Maria Garthwaite would have seen, virtually on her doorstep and when in season, inspiring displays of flowers such as carnations, geraniums and roses, exotic fruits such as pineapples and pomegranates, along with hops, wheat and barley. All of these make regular and repeated appearances in Spitalfields silk fabric, with the flowers being an inspiration for ornamental designs while the hops and cereal crops were perhaps incorporated in designs that were more symbolic, celebrating the wealth and prowess of Spitalfields' brewers, brewing industry and fertility in general.

Although, as mentioned before, there was some initial resistance to the Huguenot silk weavers, their skills and financial acumen soon won them a place in their new homeland. They were also swiftly accepted into the Weavers' Company where a number of them rose to positions of great prominence. The rather different experience of their fellows working in precious metals, however, shows how easily the Huguenots, as potential rivals and as a people apart from the mainstream, could meet opposition.

At first their craftsmen and merchants settled, logically enough, near Goldsmiths' Hall and Cheapside in the City of London, which were the capital's traditional centres for the silver and gold trade. Like their Spitalfields neighbours they had been attracted to the area by the established French Protestant church in Threadneedle Street. But whereas the English weaving establishment swiftly accepted its French counterparts, English silver- and goldsmiths were not so easily won over. Craftsmen proposing to work and deal in silver and gold needed to gain the Freedom of the City of London through a livery company in order to trade in the

City and in London generally, and the obvious livery company to join was the Goldsmiths'. The Goldsmiths', however, was controlled by London-born tradesmen, who were suspicious of the talented Huguenot arrivals. They were jealous of the newcomers' skills, daunted by their industrious nature and fearful that they would win many commissions. So they closed ranks and kept the Huguenots out.

The Huguenot precious-metal workers, though, were nothing if not canny and determined. From the late seventeenth century they started to build a community in south Soho around Gerrard Street, Great Windmill Street and the Newport Market area, and conveniently close to the French Protestant church off the Strand in the Savoy. In the process, they helped transform the area into a new merchants' quarter on the west edge of London. At the same time, faced with the intransigence of the Goldsmiths' Company, they decided to make jealousy their friend. Realising how much other livery companies disliked the arrogant Goldsmiths', the Huguenots played on traditional City rivalries and, by persuading companies that had nothing to do with their craft to allow them to join their guilds, managed to get themselves the necessary toehold. Peter Archambo, who in 1710 had become an apprentice to a fellow Huguenot silversmith named Jacob Margas with a workshop in St Martin's Lane (then the south-east boundary of Soho), in 1720 became free of the Butchers' Company. His contemporary Paul Crespin became free of the Longe Bowe Stringmakers. By doing so, both these leading members of the Soho trade gained the Freedom of the City.

One Huguenot craftsman who did manage to join the Goldsmiths' Company was Paul de Lamerie, one of the most able and successful Huguenot metalworkers and, according to the Victoria and Albert Museum, 'the greatest silversmith working in England in the eighteenth century'. But he was only able to do so after a number of run-ins. Born in April 1688 in 's-Hertogenbosch in the United Provinces (now the Netherlands), de Lamerie came to London with his immigrant family – of minor aristocratic ancestry – when he was just one year old. At the age of fourteen he was apprenticed to a Huguenot goldsmith named Pierre Platel and in 1712 opened his own workshop, probably in Great Windmill Street. The same year he was made free of the Goldsmiths' Company and registered his first mark (the symbol or emblem used to identify his work), choosing the first letters of his surname – LA – with a crown and small star above and a fleur-de-lis below.

Almost immediately, however, de Lamerie came into conflict with the Company, for just two years after he had set up shop, he was called before the Goldsmiths' Court for failing to have his work hallmarked. This was a serious offence. By the early eighteenth century silverware had by law to be stamped with various hallmarks to establish the date and location of its manufacture and the quality of the silver from which it was made. The latter mark – the most important – was only added to the piece after official scrutiny by the local assay office. In addition, but not mandatory, was the emblem to identify the manufacturer of the piece. Only makers who traded under their own names and whose association with a piece could enhance its value were in the habit of signing their work. By 1714 de Lamerie was such a smith, but since putting the necessary marks on one of his pieces would have led, almost inevitably, to an obligation to pay duty, he appears to have decided against doing so. For this offence he was fined a hefty £20.

De Lamerie's response seems to have been to seek further ways to challenge the Company's authority. In 1715 there was more trouble when they claimed that he 'covered Foreigners work and got the same toucht at ye hall'. It seems that de Lamerie was 'passing off as his own work pieces made by others, probably Huguenots, who were not free of the Company and did not have registered makers' marks, a service for which he would undoubtedly have charged.'[21] The following year he was up on the same charge again. In 1717 he was once more accused by the Company of making and selling large quantities of plate that he had not brought to 'be Mark't according to law'. He appears to have had an almost contemptuous attitude to authority.

The contest between de Lamerie and the Goldsmiths' Company was prolonged. But it does not seem to have damaged him professionally nor indeed to have irredeemably tainted his relationship with the Goldsmiths'. By 1716 he was appointed gold- and silversmith to George I and in the same year – presumably feeling his future was secure – de Lamerie married Louisa Juliott who was, as was usual within the French immigrant community, also a Huguenot. Eventually they had six children. Also in 1717, the year he was accused of making and selling unmarked plate, de Lamerie became a Liveryman – or full member – of the Goldsmiths' Company. It must be assumed this was mutually advantageous: de Lamerie gained acceptance; the Company hoped that by making him more fully a part of the precious-metal establishment, they would be better able to control him.[22] Their strategy appears to have worked. From around this time – 1719 or so – de Lamerie seems regularly to have marked his products.

By the 1730s he was dominant in his field, supplying the rich, powerful and titled in Britain and abroad with artefacts of consummate beauty – characteristically reflecting the favoured Rococo manner of the time – and of extraordinary expense. Part of his success was perhaps due to the fact that from the late 1720s and into the 1730s he employed William Hogarth to engrave some of his pieces, including the stunning silver salver of 1727/9, made for Sir Robert Walpole, that is now in the Victoria and Albert Museum.[23] If it is indeed an industrious Huguenot honoured in Hogarth's series of engravings *Industry and Idleness*, then de Lamerie is another potential inspiration for the successful apprentice Francis Goodchild.

It was during the time of his association with Hogarth that de Lamerie started his ascent within the hierarchy of the Goldsmiths' Company, being elected in 1731 to its Court of Assistants – effectively its governing body and therefore, of course, the body with which he had previously been at loggerheads. Poacher was turning gamekeeper. Another sign of de Lamerie's elevated establishment status was his move in 1738 to a new house (and probably workshop, too) at 40 Gerrard Street – then the best address in the heart of south Soho's silver and gold district. By the time he died in 1751 de Lamerie had become Second Warden in the Goldsmiths'. Only illness kept him from the top post. He was buried, like so many of his co-religionists, in an Anglican church: St Anne's Soho. Not that this choice of final resting place would have been of much importance to him. It was the fate of his immortal soul that mattered. And for him no doubt, as for his fellow Huguenots, the value of his soul was enhanced by the pursuit of a vigorous work ethic, characterised by hard toil and rewarded by the amassing of wealth and worldly goods.

That said, it would appear that de Lamerie was not entirely free from the less admirable qualities that so often accompany the desire for fame, glory and riches as one particular incident in his life demonstrates. In 1722 – when he was still consolidating his position as one of Britain's leading silver- and goldsmiths – his shop was visited by a chimney-sweep's boy named Armory, who had found a jewel and wanted to have it valued. De Lamerie's apprentice inspected the jewel and offered to pay only three-halfpence for its setting. When the boy asked for the return of the jewel along with the setting the apprentice refused, presumably on the grounds that the boy had found it rather than owned it.

Friends of the boy advised a court action and the verdict of the King's Bench set a legal benchmark. It ruled that although the boy did not have absolute title to the jewel, he had the right to keep it until its true owner was established. De Lamerie was therefore ordered to return the jewel or give the boy its value in money. To his credit de Lamerie did not pretend he had never received the jewel from the boy and even agreed to its being valued by others. They declared it to be of the highest quality and the boy was duly compensated. But the initial behaviour of de Lamerie and his apprentice – which was in effect an attempt at 'legal' robbery and exploitation of a humble youth – offers an insight, perhaps, into the ruthless practices sometimes employed by the Huguenot business community.

On the other hand, de Lamerie's actions did lead to a refinement of the law of personal property and so helped establish the custom of 'finders, keepers'.[24]

EIGHT

'BUILT NEW FROM THE GROUND'

The Creation of Georgian Spitalfields

The author of *Robinson Crusoe* knew Spitalfields well. As a child, Daniel Defoe attended a Presbyterian chapel in Little St Helen's on the edge of the suburb, run by the Puritan divine and former protégé of Oliver Cromwell and his son Richard, Samuel Annesley (see page 108). (Annesley, Defoe recalled in an elegy written after the Presbyterian Dissenter's death in 1696, 'charmed us with his Godliness, and while he spoke, we loved the doctrine for the speaker's sake.') Defoe also perhaps lived for a while in 'Hand Alley' off Bishopsgate, near what is now New Street; and the church in which he married in 1684 was St Botolph's Aldgate, on Spitalfields' south-east corner. He therefore had a local's memory of what the area had been like in the years before the coming of the Huguenots in large numbers.

He wrote in his *Tour Thro' the Whole Island of Great Britain*, published in 1724–6:

> The lanes were deep, dirty and unfrequented; that part now called Spitalfields-Market was a field of grass with cows feeding on it, since the year 1670. The Old Artillery Ground ... took up all those long streets, leading out of Artillery Lane to Spittle-yard-back-Gate and so on to the end of Wheeler-street.

So far as the northern and eastern reaches were concerned, he recalled how 'Brick-lane, which is now a long well pav'd street, was a deep dirty road, frequented by carts fetching bricks that way into White-Chapel from Brick kilns in those fields, and had its name on that account.'[1]

By the 1720s, however, the area looked very different:

> Within the memory of the writer hereof, all those numberless ranges of building, called Spittle Fields, reaching from Spittle-yard, at Northern Fallgate, and from Artillery Lane in Bishopsgate-street, with all the New

Streets, beginning at Hoxton and the back of Shoreditch Church, North, and reaching to Brick-lane, and to the end of Hare-street, on the way to Bethnal Green, East; then sloping away quite to White-Chapel Road, South East, containing, as some people say, who pretend to know, by good observation, above three hundred and twenty acres of ground, which are all now close built, and well inhabited with an infinite number of people, I say, all these have been built new from the ground, since the year 1666.

'In a word', Defoe concluded, 'it is computed that above two hundred thousand inhabitants dwell now in that part of London, where, within about fifty years past, there was not a house standing.' This was a vast overestimate given that the entire population of London at that time can only have numbered around 600,000 (a likelier number is 20,000 people housed in something over 3,000 dwellings). But Defoe's exaggerated number is a perhaps understandable reflection of the vast transformation he had seen wrought in his lifetime.

Two maps provide a vivid portrait of Spitalfields as it appeared shortly before and at the height of the expansion that so struck Defoe. Joel Gascoyne's map of the Parish of St Dunstan's Stepney, published in 1703, captures the area just as expansion was starting. Since the map shows only the part of Spitalfields within the parish of St Dunstan's, the Liberties of Norton Folgate, with its burgeoning Spital Square area (see page 143), and the Old Artillery Ground, with its houses and streets erected by that arch-speculator Nicholas Barbon (see page 129), are excluded. What is shown are many of the developments to which Defoe refers – notably 'Wheeler Street', and its southward extension Crispin Street, and the large number of new buildings – including the market area and on 'Red Lyon Street' – erected since 1666 between these two streets and Brick Lane to their east. Indeed this area was by 1703 almost entirely urban, as was much of the area east of Brick Lane towards the area known as 'The Hamlet of Mile End New Town'.

That said, significant areas had yet to be built upon, even west of the line of Brick Lane. The largest of these areas is named on the map as 'Slaughters Land', which straddled Brick Lane just south of 'Cock Lane' (as Redchurch Street and the western end of what is now Bethnal Green Road was then called), its portion to the west of Brick Lane being known as 'Swan Field' and its eastern portion 'Cross Field'. North of 'Cock Lane', 'Nicolls Street' (later Old Nichol Street) had been built by

1703 as the first element of what would become a dense development of two-storey terraces and courts of weavers' houses (and by the late nineteenth century a notorious slum). But beyond 'Nicolls Street' there were still large swathes of open ground, mostly in use as market gardens – notably 'Richardsons Garden' and 'Kemps Garden' – revealing that by the beginning of the eighteenth century the growing of flowers and vegetables was already a major Shoreditch industry. Gascoyne's map also shows that the heart of Spitalfields still contained significant areas of open ground – notably the 'Tenters' ground between 'Red Lyon Street' and Brick Lane and to its north, and separated from this by a row of irregular buildings (that mark the future site of Fournier Street) another field stretching north to 'Browns Lane'.

By the early 1720s – when Defoe was completing the text for his *Tour* – 'Swan Field' had been built upon, its main street – Sclater Street (named after the Sclater/Bacon family whose name was, seemingly, sometimes spelled as Slaughter) – having been started in 1718. Development of the 'Tenters' ground and adjoining land was also under way. Christ Church had been under construction since 1714, while 'Princes' (now Princelet) and 'Wood' (now Wilkes) Streets had recently been laid out and were being lined with houses.

And by time John Rocque's epic map of London was published in 1746 the development of Spitalfields was virtually complete. 'Prince' and 'Wood' Streets were completed as, by c.1730, was 'Church Street' (now Fournier Street) that replaced the row of irregular buildings shown on Gascoyne's map. And, of course, at the junction of the new 'Church Street' with 'Red Lyon Street' (later included in Commercial Road), the magnificent new parish church of Christ Church had been completed in 1729 to the design of Nicholas Hawksmoor. Also, by 1746 the development of 'Swan Field' was complete, buildings lined nearly three sides of the neighbouring 'Cross Field' and, immediately to the east, the new parish church of St Matthew's Bethnal Green had been completed, in the year the map was published, to the design of George Dance the Elder.

Rocque's map shows that the heart of the priory's former northern precinct – where until the 1730s a scattering of priory or late-sixteenth- and early-seventeenth-century buildings still existed – had been levelled and remodelled by its new owners, the Tillard family, into an elegant merchants' quarter. Key was the enlargement of Spital Yard into Spital Square, which by the late 1730s had become an enclave of ambitious merchant palaces.

In addition, a significant area of open ground in the Liberty of Norton Folgate, not shown on Gascoyne's map, had also been built upon by 1746. The ground was known as 'Porter's Close' and had once been the location of gardens and orchards belonging to St Mary's Priory (part of it, with rows of trees divided by a hedge, is shown on the 'Copperplate' map of c.1553). Shown clearly and named on Ogilby and Morgan's map of 1676, it had been developed by the Tillards from c.1722 to c.1730 with a grid of picturesquely named streets: Blossom Street, 'Flower De Lis' Street, Elder Street, 'Porter Street' and 'Porter's Field', names evoking the area's disappearing past and fading bucolic quality.[2] It was also during this period, of course, that Spital Square assumed its grandest form.

The houses built on and around Spital Yard to help form the new Spital Square, and on 'Porter's Close', had mostly been constructed on leases let to a collection of tradesmen and speculative house builders – notably William Goswell (a carpenter), Jonathan Beaumont (a mason), Thomas Bunce (a plasterer) and Thomas Brown (a pavior, or person who lays paving) – who appear to have worked almost exclusively on the Tillard Estate.[3] Tragically, most of Spital Square was demolished in the 1920s and 30s; one grand house, number 20, first inhabited by the leading Huguenot entrepreneur and master weaver James Dalbiac, survived until the early 1960s when it and adjoining early-eighteenth-century houses in the square and in Folgate Street were swept away.

Also significant in the 1720s upgrading of the old priory area was the widening of the east end of 'White Lyon Yard/Street' (now Folgate Street) and the construction in 1724 along its south side of a tall, uniform terrace, at least six houses long, that turned the corner into Spital Square. This handsome street became the main entrance from Bishopsgate into the Tillard's 'improved' Norton Folgate Estate because the entry into Spital Square itself remained narrow and restricted, to help protect the inhabitants from noise and nuisance.

The men responsible for this transformation were the owners of Spitalfields' various estates, both large and small. Some were personages of considerable consequence – noblemen and merchants, among them leading members of the Huguenot community. Others were less notable, but still well-to-do. What drove them all was the realisation that the burgeoning silk industry was attracting ever more people to the area, and that

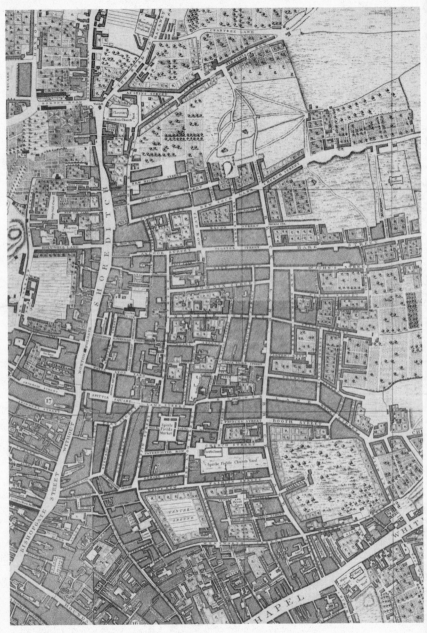

A detail from John Rocque's map of 1746, showing Bishopsgate running north. Spitalfields lies to the east Estate replace 'Joyce's Garden'; Elder Street and related developments

and its Georgian development is nearly complete. Christ Church and the surrounding Wood–Michell replace Porter's Close; and Spital Square has taken its final form.

the wealth it was generating was making it a newly desirable area in which to live.

It's hard to overestimate the value and national importance of the silk industry in the early eighteenth century, or at least overestimate the value it was perceived to possess. In 1719 Defoe had written that the wool and silk trades were the 'most considerable and essential part' of the nation's 'Wealth' (see page 163). In 1726 he refined and focused the thought: '. . . the manufactures of England, particularly those of wool . . . and of silk . . . amount to the greatest value of any single manufacture in Europe' and so not only 'employ more people, but those people gain the most money' and 'have the best wages for their work of any people in the world'.[4] Masters were clearly in funds but good wages meant working men and tradespeople could pay high rents and enjoy credit. So in the early eighteenth century Spitalfields must have had all the characteristics of a boom town – albeit a rather elegant one – with landowners being only too aware that the money available, combined with a demand for houses and workshops, meant there were potential fortunes to be made replacing – through the speculative building system – open ground or small ramshackle old buildings with larger and more stylish new developments, fit for the purposes of the affluent population of new Spitalfields.

Two particular events boosted the endeavours of these landowners: the 1713 Treaty of Utrecht, which put an end to the War of the Spanish Succession in a manner that was broadly favourable to British interests, and the accession in August 1714 of the first Hanoverian monarch, George I, to the throne. Together these events ushered in a period of peace, prosperity and political and financial stability that was only briefly troubled by such crises as the Jacobite rising of 1715. Stability was, of course, good for trade generally and, in particular, for speculative house builders, who could only thrive when money was on the move and investors' confidence was high. That this new confidence had a remarkably buoyant effect on the main landowners in Spitalfields is revealed by the development patterns of their estates there – large and small – which, after some initial growth soon after 1714, burst into building activity just before and just after 1720.

Among the leading local figures in this property boom was Isaac Tillard (from 1722 Sir Isaac), who in 1716 acquired the desirable Bolingbroke/St John Estate (see page 115) that covered much of the north precinct of the former priory and the Liberty of Norton Folgate.[5] His ancestors were Huguenots who had moved to England in the sixteenth century, settled in Totnes in Devon, prospered, and then moved to London. Sir Isaac himself became something of a pillar of the establishment. By the time of his death in May 1726 at his house on 'Spittle Square' – almost certainly the former Bolingbroke establishment – he had acquired a whole range of grand offices and titles: 'Colonel' of the 2nd Regiment in the Royal Hamlets; a Lieutenant for the City of London; Deputy Lieutenant for the County of Middlesex and the Tower Hamlets; a Justice of the Peace; a Commissioner for the Land Tax and for the Sewers; and a Governor of St Thomas's Hospital. His body was duly interred in the splendid Wren-designed church of St Stephen Walbrook with full City pomp and pageantry.[6] In his will, dated 1720, Sir Isaac 'of the Liberty of Norton ffolgate' left money to his mother and various relatives, property to Christ's Hospital, and £100 to the Governors of St Thomas's Hospital. He also left £100 to the 'Overseers' of the poor in the Liberty of Norton Folgate, to be used for the benefit of the Liberty with the provision that his wealthier tenants there – 'paying Twenty pounds per annum rent' – also made contributions.[7]

Upon Sir Isaac's death control of the estate passed to his brother William – whom he made his residuary legatee – with his youngest brother receiving £3,000. William, an officer of the East India Company, took up residence in Spital Square, where he remained until the late 1730s. It would seem that it was Sir Isaac's idea that the family should – in the optimistic spirit of the times – start to exploit their new estate, in particular 'Porter's Close', which had lain fallow during the decades of Bolingbroke ownership, because building leases for sites on Elder Street started to be granted in 1722. But the Close can have been little more than a collection of staked-out lots, at best largely a building site at the time of his death in 1726, with only a few completed houses mostly on its west side. Consequently it fell to William to steer the project to fruition.

Not all developments were as grand or as ambitious as those undertaken by the Tillards. When Robert Seymour updated John Stow's *Survey of London* in 1734/5, he commented that among the 'remarkable Places and Things' of the area were some distinctly unglamorous features: 'Spittle-fields-market' (where 'are sold Greens, Roots, etc . . .'), a workhouse in Bell Lane ('wherein the Poor are employed and maintained, who are in number about 120, and their chief work is winding of Silk for Throwsters'), and a hospital in 'Grey Eagle Street' ('in which the French maintain

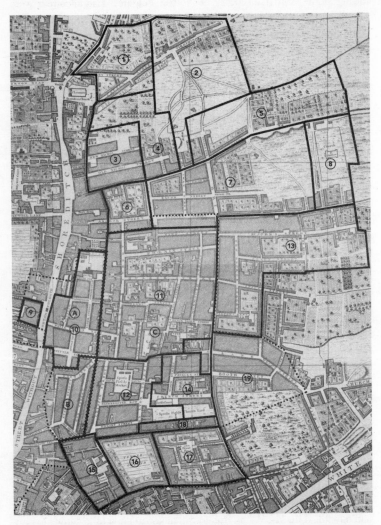

*A mosaic of the main Spitalfields estates developed during the seventeenth, eighteenth and early
nineteenth centuries. 1: Austen, 2: Fitch, 3: Nichol, 4: Snow, 5: Tyssen, 6: Byde, 7: Red Cow,
8: Wood Close, 9: Carpenters' Company, 10: St John/Tillard, 11: Wheler (north), 12: Wheler
(south), 13: Hare Marsh, 14: Wood–Michell, 15: Halifax, 16: 'Tenter' ground, 17: Fossan (Keate
and Tonge), 18: Captain Lekeux's Ground, 19: Halifax/Osborn. Also shown are A: Liberty of
Norton Folgate, B: Old Artillery Ground, C: Christ Church parish (to the right of which is a
piece of 'Joyce's Garden' on Brick Lane that Joseph Truman bought in 1705 for development).*

their own Poor').[8] And not all property speculators had the well-to-do exclusively in mind when they developed their estates.

The Tillards' fellow Huguenots, the Lekeux, for example, sought to cater for much-needed commercial and more modest domestic functions. Part of 'Captain Lecuse's Ground' – to the south of 'Joyce's Garden' – was thus developed to complement grander houses on nearby 'Church', 'Wood' and 'Princes' Streets and to continue the more humdrum surroundings of Brick Lane. According to the *Survey of London* the long narrow strip of 'Ground' – set between the south wall of the new churchyard adjoining Christ Church and the existing buildings on Fashion Street, and stretching east from 'Red Lyon Street' to Brick Lane – was owned by John Lekeux, described as 'of the Old Artillery Ground', who is recorded in 1727 and 1731 as living in 10 Spital Square and was probably a lawyer.[9] Lekeux leased the eastern portion of this ground in May 1711 to William Seager, a carpenter of Spitalfields, who built the Seven Stars public house (which survives in late-Victorian guise but, sadly, no longer functions as a pub) fronting onto Brick Lane. In December 1728 the remainder of the ground was leased to Simon Michell, who subsequently sublet it for the extension of the gardens behind the 'Church'/Fournier Street houses that he had developed and for the erection of 'stables, coachhouses and other buildings'.[10]

The Lekeux themselves, though, were clearly men of means, who lived in some style. The first eminent Spitalfields-based Lekeux seems to have been 'Colonel' Peter Lekeux, who was born in Canterbury in 1648, where he was apprenticed as a weaver, but had moved to London by 1675 when he was admitted to the Weavers' Company.[11] He became eminent in his trade and in the Company, and by the time of his death in 1723 had attained the same social eminence as his contemporary and neighbour Sir Isaac Tillard. His nephew and executor Peter Lekeux II, born in 1684 (and pre-sumably a cousin of the John Lekeux of Spital Square), also became a silk weaver and rose high in the Weavers' Company, being made an Upper Warden in 1728 and elected to its court of assistants – essentially the Com-pany's governing body – in 1734, and like his uncle was a captain in the London trained bands. On his death in 1743 he left money and his weaving business to his son, Peter Lekeux III, who carried on the family trade with notable success, concentrating on the most expensive silks for men, but did not go in for public service or office.[12] Peter III died in 1768 and left all his property to his wife Mary. There were, it seems, no children nor any partners to carry on the Lekeux family business.

Peter III's lasting legacy can be found on the north side of 'Church'/ Fournier Street at what are now numbered 1 and 3, built on family-owned land in 1755, and among the largest and most architecturally sophisticated houses to survive in Spitalfields (appearing, moreover, at a time when little else was being constructed locally after the boom years of the 1680s and 1720s). Peter himself chose to live in number 3 – an apposite symbol of his taste and wealth – where he remained until his death.[13]

The owners of other estates, too, opted to cater for humbler dwellings and workshops. One such was Thomas Bacon, who owned the Red Cow Estate – a holding that included 'Slaughters Land': largely open land at the beginning of the century, built up by Rocque's time. The 'Land' – and the estate – stretched south from Bethnal Green Road (called 'New Cock Lane' and Church Street) to the north side of 'Hare Street' (now Cheshire Street) and to the south side of Sclater Street; it stretched as far west as the east side of Club Row and as far east as the west side of Church Row, facing the church of St Matthew's Bethnal Green. Its spine was formed by the north portion of Brick Lane. The estate was named after a building – probably a farm – that once stood on the north-east corner of Brick Lane and 'Cock Lane' but had been demolished by 1703.

When Gascoyne published his map in 1703 there were just a few scattered buildings on the 'Land': at the north-west corner of Brick Lane and 'Cock Lane', along the east side of Brick Lane north of 'Hare Street', and along the north side of 'Hare Street' itself.[14] But from 1718, reflecting the optimistic and settled atmosphere after 1714, Bacon (formerly called Sclater; 'Slaughter' was presumably a corruption of the surname), leased out small portions of land on sixty-one-year building leases to London builders, mostly carpenters.

The development of the estate is related in detail by Peter Guillery in *The Small House in Eighteenth-Century London*.[15] As mentioned, its ambitions were modest. Evidently the landlord and his lessees did not seek to emulate the impressive scale of the developments getting under way in south Spitalfields – for example on the Tillard Estate – but preferred to construct smaller buildings that could serve as houses and workshops or even as buildings in multi-occupation.

Construction started on the portion of the estate called 'Swan Field' with Sclater Street being laid out in about 1718 to link with the east end of the mid-seventeenth-century 'Anchor Street'. Then building works started in Bacon Street in c.1720, and in 'Thomas Street' in 1723. Having commemorated himself and his family in the street names of the estate, Thomas Bacon seems to have slowed down works, with the north-east portion of the estate – the roughly rectangular 'Cross Field' – framed by buildings on only two and a half sides in 1746 and remaining largely undeveloped until the late 1760s. Only a handful now survive of the 300 or so houses that had been built on the estate by 1751.[16] This is partly because of the modest, economic and essentially flimsy nature of their construction, but also because the estate was overtaken by decay and neglect in the nineteenth century as it descended into poverty and very high-density occupation. Those few buildings that do survive confirm the generally utilitarian and mixed-use nature of the original development.

Until recent years a fairly large number of original houses still stood in Sclater Street. The most striking group, numbers 78–88, on the south side of the street, dated from c.1720. Constructed by various builders, they were similar in their plans and elevations, although not self-consciously uniform. Each was one-room deep and three storeys high above a basement, some with one- or two-storey rear extensions. Most had, at first-floor level, a single, wide window – set off-centre – and one very small window. The wide window was to light the weaver's living accommodation, although letting in enough light to permit this floor to be used as a workroom if required. The small window, characteristic of this type of building, lit a compact, winding and very utilitarian staircase that rose in one corner between the front and party wall – clearly the occupants of these buildings were not expected to be interested in making an ostentatious display with staircase halls and ornamental newels, balusters and tread ends. This staircase form also suggests the buildings were designed with multi-occupation in mind. Each tenant had merely to enter the front door and then turn immediately into the staircase compartment to ascend to the floor level desired. This arrangement appears, states Peter Guillery, 'to have been a long-standing vernacular practice associated with design for multiple occupation'.[17] The second floors of most of the buildings were lit with wide windows, stretching virtually from party wall to party wall. Generally these contained timber mullions framing fixed windows and casements. Originally these would have been formed with small panes of glass set in lead cames. These front windows – usually mirrored by similar windows in the rear elevation – served the weaving workshop. This Sclater Street group of houses was demolished in the early 1970s.

The way in which these houses were initially occupied is suggested by
the inventory attached to the will of Luke Miller, evidently a relatively
affluent member of the weaving industry, who died in 1735.[18] He occupied
an entire house located in Bethnal Green (its precise address is unknown),
which comprised five floors, described as one above the other. So the
house was one room deep, like the Sclater Street houses, but contained
one more floor. In Miller's house the basement was not used as a
kitchen – as was usual with larger Spitalfields houses – but as a coal cellar.
The ground floor – the 'lower' room – in fact served as the kitchen. The
first-floor room contained a bed, some silver, silk clothing and wigs. The
second-floor room had two beds and some books, and the garret –
presumably with wide windows and designed as a workshop – contained
'working tools' and two spice boxes. The 'tools' could have been related to
weaving but were almost certainly not looms, although the garret was
probably intended for them. Perhaps Miller was rich enough not to have
been obliged to have looms in his own house but could locate them elsewhere. Or perhaps he was a 'pattern' maker or designer and did not require
a loom to follow his trade within the weaving industry.

Today just a sprinkling of early buildings from the Red Cow Estate
survive, scattered here and there along Sclater Street, Brick Lane and
Bethnal Green Road. Some are in a very perilous state: 70–74 Sclater
Street, for example, which were built in about 1719 and re-fronted in the
late eighteenth and early nineteenth centuries, are now (as of autumn
2016) derelict, cocooned in scaffolding and mothballed for future repair
after being severely disfigured by floor-to-eaves graffiti. They are characteristically simple affairs: one room deep (some with ground-floor
rear-room extensions) and three storeys high above a cellar.[19] Numbers 125
and 127 Brick Lane on the north-west corner of Sclater Street are the best
preserved of the early buildings on the estate. Affixed to 125 is an ornate,
and somewhat Baroque name plaque inscribed 'This is Sclater Street'
along with a date, very weathered, that could be 1718 (in which case it has
come from another house and probably relates to the founding of the
street) but is usually interpreted as being 1778.[20] The house itself is a
remarkable survival, built as a mixed-use block, and no doubt for multi-
occupation. It's now three storeys high, but a watercolour of 1914 by E. A.
Phipson now in the London Metropolitan Archives shows that the building was originally four storeys high above ground. The upper-floor
windows are generally wide, while the now lost top floor was furnished

with a continuous row of weavers' windows looking onto Sclater Street and a wide window – comprising four sashes in a row – looking onto Brick Lane. The house was probably built for Daniel Delacourt, a distiller, in c.1778, replacing one built in c.1718, and its original mix of uses included a shop, weaving workshops and tenements that could be sublet.[21]

Since Brick Lane is now one of the best-known and most thronged streets in Spitalfields it is perhaps worth pointing out two other eighteenth-century Red Cow Estate survivals. The first, at 190, was built in 1778–9 by James Laverdure, a Spitalfields carpenter.[22] It was seemingly intended for residential use because its windows are of conventional width rather than wide weavers' windows, and clearly had pretensions because the first-floor room retains boldly detailed full-height panelling of some quality. The second is the now recently and tragically mutilated 194–8. This once splendid block was erected in 1763–5 by 'one of the area's landlord oligarchs, Peter Mansell [a tallow chandler] to provide what is best understood as a large mixed-use tenement block rather than as three separate houses.'[23] Externally only a small portion of the first-floor brick façade of 194 survives.

I managed to get inside the corner house, number 198, in the 1980s. It had no yard, was very plain internally and – being a corner building one room deep – had absolutely no windows on either of its inner walls, making it essentially a back-to-back building. It had very much the feel of a workshop or industrial building, giving a sense of how factory buildings might have evolved from domestic architecture. Wide windows – particularly on second and third floors – did much to compensate for the lack of any at the rear. On the ground floor were shops, no doubt an original arrangement, each with domestic space above at first-floor level – as revealed by the fact that the first floors of all the houses generally had standard domestic windows. The asymmetrical design of the elevations of these buildings was a direct diagram of their function and internal use.

Another important estate developed along relatively humble lines, again during the boom years of the early 1720s, was the Tyssen Estate, its focus now the stretch of Brick Lane north of Bethnal Green Road, then called 'Tyssen Street'. Development got under way when Samuel Tyssen – a member of a wealthy Hackney-based merchant family of Flemish origin – started to lease building plots, usually for terms of eighty years, from 1724. Leases were granted to bricklayers and carpenters, including William Farmer, and building started on 'Church Street' (as the eastern

194–8 Brick Lane was built in 1763–5 as a mixed-use tenement block, with shops on the ground floor, living space on the first floor and weaving workshops, with wide windows, on the upper storey. This semi-industrial group of buildings is in striking contrast to the more familiar elegant Georgian domestic architecture of Spitalfields. Shown here in the early 1970s these buildings have since been mutilated almost beyond recognition. Number 192 (far right), built in the late eighteenth century, has now been demolished.

portion of 'New Cock Lane' had become known) and in 'Tyssen Street', the southern end of which had been lined with buildings by 1728. By 1732 'Satchells Rents' (as named on Rocque's 1746 map and running north off Church Street) had been developed. Building proceeded along 'New Cock Lane' and 'Church Street', with plots at its west end leased in 1732 to William Farmer, in 1734 to Matthew Wright 'gentleman', and in 1735 to John Wolveridge, a plasterer. The Tyssen Estate continued to expand during the late eighteenth and early nineteenth centuries so that it contained 475 houses and workshops by 1836.[24]

Very little historic fabric now survives on the estate – with one notable exception. Numbers 113 and 115 Redchurch Street were almost certainly built in c.1735 by William Farmer, and are very rare and very important examples of the relatively humble buildings in which Spitalfields journeymen lived and worked.[25] Number 113 retains its original brick elevation (although now rendered), is four storeys high (including a garret) above a basement, and was at first only one room deep above the ground floor. The first floor has a pair of standard, segmental arched windows typical of the period, which no doubt lit the domestic accommodation in the house. At first-floor level, too, there is a narrow window lighting the cramped newel staircase that winds against the party wall and between the front façade and the side of the chimney stack. The front elevation at second-floor level has one wide, workshop window. The rear elevation has wide, shallow weavers' windows with lights separated by mullions. Internally elements of panelling survive at first-floor level, mostly on the fireplace wall, indicating how the staircase was screened from sight and entered from the upper rooms via doors. In the late nineteenth century the ground floor became a shop. Number 115 was similar but is more altered, with its front façade rebuilt in a crude manner. However it retains its wide weavers' window in the upper portion of its rear elevation. In autumn 2016 both these important houses stand derelict although 113 has, since 2009, been listed by the government as a building of architectural or historic interest.

It is fascinating to see how the era of political and financial stability after 1714 led to the transformation of even some of Spitalfields' oldest, smallest, and longest-developed estates. Back in 1630 the Carpenters' Company acquired a small estate on the north side of Norton Folgate for £660. They bought it as an investment, using rental income from properties already standing on the land 'for the relief of the Poor of the Company and for the aid and ease of [the Company's] taxes.'[26] But an estate survey of 1727 in the Company's archives shows that by that date the estate had been rebuilt, with seventeen major and separate structures being constructed on what was a relatively small piece of land. Judging from the plans of the buildings, most were likely to have been built in the early years of the reign of the new Hanoverian King George I. These buildings eventually gave way to the nineteenth-century commercial architecture that increasingly dominated Bishopsgate and, from the 1870s, to the railways.

Substantial improvements took place, after 1714, on other of Spitalfields' smaller, peripheral estates, but almost without exception these early-Georgian architectural ambitions gave way, barely more than a century later, not to the commercial expansion of the city but – by contrast – to decay and poverty that became a byword for urban squalor. For the most part these were estates to the north of 'Cock Lane'/'New Cock Lane'/'Church Street' (now Bethnal Green Road and Redchurch Street). To the west was the Nichol Estate, which comprised about five acres of land that had been bought by John Nichol – an entrepreneurial Gray's Inn lawyer with family connections to Bethnal Green – just before the Restoration. Presumably Nichol anticipated profits in house building after the demise of the Commonwealth (he was correct) and initially built a few houses himself on the land before leasing or mortgaging most of it for building to Jon Richardson, a London mason, for 180 years from 1680.[27] Slow and sustained development followed. Initially Richardson excavated brick earth, then he sublet building plots – typically relatively small in size (frontages were generally sixteen feet wide, with the largest only twenty feet wide) – so that the streets on the estate gradually became lined almost exclusively with two- and three-storey terraces containing weavers' homes and workshops. By the time of Gascoyne's map of 1703 only the terraces fronting south onto 'Cock Lane' and – parallel to the north – the pair of terraces forming 'Nicolls Street' were complete. But Rocque's map shows that most of two blocks to the north of 'Nicolls Street' (by then renamed Old Nichol Street) had been built, along with most of two blocks to the east, beyond the north–south aligned 'Nichol Street'. Much of this development was probably completed or initiated in the boom years after 1714.

To the east of the Nichol Estate was the Snow Estate, with a very narrow frontage on what is now Redchurch Street, which from the early eighteenth century was controlled by George Turville, a gentleman and landowner of Bethnal Green whose family had inherited the estate in the 1680s from Elizabeth Snow.[28] In keeping with the expansionist mood of the time from 1723, Turville granted building leases to various speculating builders for plots along the newly created 'Turville Street'.

To the east of the Snow Estate was the Fitch Estate, which also possessed a narrow frontage on 'New Cock Lane' (now the junction of Bethnal Green Road with Redchurch Street). The north boundary of the estate was formed by 'Crabtree Row/Lane' (essentially now Columbia Road), and the west boundary was defined at the point Castle Street became Virginia Row/Street. The Cock Lane and Virginia Row/Street frontages of the estate were developed from 1725 into the 1730s, but Rocque's map shows that, in 1746, the land between remained open. A portion of this was known as Friar's Mount – probably named after James Fryer who farmed the area in the 1720s – which was later commemorated by 'Mount Street', which, constructed between c.1799 and c.1819, ran south from the junction of Castle Street and Virginia Row.[29] By the 1890s, when Arthur Morrison came to write his semi-factual novel *A Child of the Jago* (see page 500), Friar's Mount was regarded as the epicentre of the destitute East End.

The nearby Byde Estate, south of 'Cock Lane'/Redchurch Street and centred on 'Anchor Street', with Club Row marking its eastern limit, represents one of the last of the boom-era developments. In 1736 Anthony Natt, a Spitalfields-born carpenter, acquired the estate at a time when the original leases were coming to an end. This offered a splendid opportunity for redevelopment, though it would appear that Natt opted to improve the quality of the buildings rather than pack more in because Rocque's map shows that extensive gardens – or at least tree-dotted open ground – survived behind the main street frontages. If this was Natt's approach, it would appear that it proved successful, for he rose in the hierarchy of the Carpenters' Company, and ended up as Warden in 1747. At about the same time he moved into one of a group of three large houses, each furnished in a genteel manner with a coach house, he had just built on Old Ford Road (these still survive and are now numbered 17–21).[30] For a Spitalfields-born carpenter and speculative builder to become Warden of a City Livery Company, live in semi-rural splendour and keep a coach was some achievement.[31]

Today, no very early fabric survives on the Byde Estate but there is, nevertheless, one very remarkable survival: a pair of houses, 3 and 5 Club Row, dating from 1764–5. They are three storeys high above a basement,

each presenting to the street one wide window per floor. Similar to the
Redchurch Street survivals, they are little-altered examples of the humble
houses in which Georgian journeymen silk weavers lived and worked.
Their internal layout is characteristic, the wide windows set off-centre to
allow for compact staircases, and, originally, staircase lobbies on each floor
so that the upper rooms could be reached without walking through the
lower – an essential requirement, of course, for multi- or mixed-use occupation.[32] Number 5 retains some original internal details, including
panelling at first-floor level on the fireplace wall.

The very few early buildings that survive on these small estates in north
Spitalfields – notably the pairs of houses in Club Row and in Redchurch
Street – are the fragmentary remains of a lost Georgian Spitalfields. Small
weavers' houses and workshops of the type represented by these buildings
once existed in their thousands throughout Spitalfields, Bethnal Green
and Shoreditch. Their architecture was humble and unglamorous – so in
consequence unappreciated, undervalued and unprotected. Yet they were
also fascinating social documents that did much to reveal how journeymen silk weavers and other tradesmen lived and worked. Now there are
barely two dozen such buildings left in Spitalfields.

- - -

Not every landowner took advantage of the property boom that changed
early-Georgian Spitalfields. For some the costs of development were
clearly deemed to outweigh the profits that might be gathered, and this
applied especially to the small estates on the south and west edges of Spitalfields that, adjoining the City of London, had generally been developed
during the second half of the seventeenth century. This certainly seems to
have been the case with the Halifax Estate, which occupied the south-
western portion of Spitalfields – with Artillery Passage and the Artillery
Ground development to the north, the ancient Petticoat Lane forming its
western boundary, and with the estate's main thoroughfare, Wentworth
Street, marking its southern edge. The estate passed through various
ownerships in the sixteenth and seventeenth centuries, notably in 1639
when it was sold by Thomas Wentworth, Earl of Cleveland and Lord of
the Manor of Stepney, to Henry Montague, Earl of Manchester. By the
early eighteenth century it had clearly declined from initial 'prosperous
domesticity' to become a place of small – low-value – tenements, workshops and industry.[33] Although the low value of the estate seems to have

discouraged investors in the boom years, the Earls of Halifax (members of the Montague family), who owned the estate by the second quarter of the century, did grant some leases for new buildings, including one in 1728 for the Spitalfield parish workhouse on Bell Lane.[34]

With the very small Fossan Estate (latterly embracing the Keate and Tonge Estates) to the east of the Halifax Estate, existing development seems to have served as a deterrent to new projects. Back in 1655, the Fossan brothers – who had acquired control of the estate in 1642/3 – granted ninety-nine-year building leases on two adjoining parcels of land to John Flower and Gowan Deane, bricklayers of Whitechapel. Within eight years this pair had completed 'Flower and Deane' (later Dean) Street, west of Brick Lane. The intensity of the development of this estate during the second half of the seventeenth century left, it seems, little reasonable opportunity for improvement in the early eighteenth. This was also the case with one of the more northerly estates, the Hare Marsh Estate, which extended east from Brick Lane into Mile End New Town, with its north boundary marked by the south side of 'Hare Street'. The estate had been acquired by the Carter family in 1653 and in 1669 John Carter leased building plots along the south side of 'Hare Street' to a carpenter named Josias Hill. He had built a number of houses by 1671, when he and Carter required the support of Sir Christopher Wren, Surveyor to the Crown, to enable them to complete their building project and to pave the road. Most of the streets on the estate had been laid out and built by 1682 or 1684. It must be assumed that the arrival of the Huguenot refugees from 1681 stimulated the final phase of the estate's development.[35] Given the relative newness of the fabric there clearly seemed little sense in tearing it down and starting again so soon.

I've tended to focus so far on the humbler parts of the Georgian new town, in part because they were – in terms of their extent and population – highly significant, partly because so little of their fabric survives. For those whose idea of the typical Georgian house is the grander, better-built and better-detailed sort that stood on the Tillard Estate, the very ordinary houses of north Spitalfields, often built of poor bricks, hastily assembled and with little evidence of craft-skill in their detailing and construction, can come as something of a shock. But to think of Georgian architecture only in terms of its better houses is to gain what Peter Guillery has called a 'skewed

representation of the house-building world of eighteenth-century London'.[36] These unremarkable houses were – in numerical terms, at least – far
more common. In the following century they were to be among the first
to degenerate into slums, and they were therefore among the first to be
swept away. What we're left with now therefore is, for the most part, the
more expensive type of house built for the more prosperous Londoner.

A very good example of such a house is the one now numbered 5 White's
Row that was built on the very small Tenter Ground Estate adjoining the
Halifax Estate. Some building here seems to have started in the mid seventeenth century but the estate was nevertheless largely undeveloped
when, by 1707, Nathaniel Shepherd, a gentleman of St Albans, had gained
an interest. But it was not until the period of the Spitalfields boom that
Shepherd, like so many of his fellow landlords and building speculators,
really got things moving. In November 1733 he granted a sixty-one-year
building lease to Henry Smith – a Whitechapel dyer – for a sixty-seven-
foot frontage on the south side of White's Row.[37] The surviving number 5
shows just how ambitious the scheme was.

It is five windows wide and five floors high with its ground floor raised
upon an elevated basement. Clearly the aim was to make the house as
monumental as possible – and this was achieved not just through scale but
also through detailing. The central door, reached by a flight of steps (sadly
recently rebuilt but originally rising parallel to the front elevation in a
most distinct and unusual manner), is an aspirational affair. Smith or
Shepherd, wanting the elevation of the house to be the height of fashion,
based the design of the timber door surround – including a keystone
sporting the visage of a river god – on one published in 1728 by James
Gibbs in his magisterial *Book of Architecture*. Gibbs, the designer nearly
a decade earlier of one of the most architecturally and socially important
churches in London, St Martin-in-the-Fields, was fashionable, successful
and influential, and the plates in his book inspired design not just in
Spitalfields, but in Britain generally and throughout the English-speaking
world, including New England in America and ultimately Calcutta and
Madras (where permutations of St Martin's were built). Smith and Shepherd's utilisation of one of his designs marks them out as pioneers, at the
cutting edge of what was then the fashion in building, and amongst the
first landlords and speculative builders to use Gibbs's book as a source for
the creation of aspirational modern homes.

But perhaps the best place to experience the upper end of the

early-eighteenth-century Spitalfields house-building market – for both
quality and quantity and because much has, by luck, been preserved – is
the former Wood–Michell Estate. The force behind the creation, after
1718, of the houses that survive on the streets north of Christ Church were
the canny and pushy Lincoln's Inn lawyers Charles Wood and Simon
Michell. Wood, who came from Luckham in Somerset, was admitted to
Lincoln's Inn on 25 June 1700[38] and in 1729 became one of the Commissioners of Sewers for the Tower Hamlets.[39] His partner Simon Michell
was also a Somerset man – from Brympton – and described as a 'gentleman' when admitted to the Middle Temple on 10 March 1704/5.[40] He was
admitted to Lincoln's Inn on 22 October 1714. He appears to have been
something of a serial speculator, responsible not just for developing land in
Spitalfields but for constructing 'Red Lion Street', Clerkenwell, in about
1719–21 (partly surviving as Britton Street) and rebuilding the Church of
the Priory of St John of Jerusalem (purchased 1721 and sold to the Fifty
New Churches Commissioners in 1723). He was also clearly disliked by
many in his local community in Clerkenwell. An account of the area published in 1828 recalls how: 'Notwithstanding that Mr Michell was a liberal
benefactor to St John's, the populace, by whom as a magistrate he had
been much disliked, were with much difficulty restrained on his interment here, from committing outrage on his remains.[41] The builders of
late-Stuart and Georgian London were rarely pleasant people.

The freehold interest that the two men acquired in the heart of Spitalfields had once been part of the ancient Lolesworth Field, subsequently
belonged to the Wheler Estate and, Gascoyne's map suggests, was largely
undeveloped when Wood and Michell took possession. Bounded by buildings on 'Browns Lane', 'Red Lyon Street', Fashion Street and by property
built by Joseph Truman on the west side of Brick Lane, the site was divided
into roughly equal north and south portions – 'Joyce's Garden' and the 'Tenters' respectively – by the irregular row of buildings, mentioned earlier, that
was to became 'Church Street', and later still Fournier Street. This north
portion, 'Joyce's Garden', was named after the London merchant Thomas
Joyce who in 1660/1 had acquired its lease, in an exceedingly complex and
contested manner, from a lessee of the Wheler Estate. Before Joyce's involvement in the land it had been conveyed in 1649 by William Wheler of Datchet
to Edward Nicholas and George Cooke in trust to raise portions (presumably dowries) for Wheler's seven daughters.[42]

The circumstances in which Wood and Michell acquired 'Joyce's

Garden' remain obscure. By the end of the seventeenth century ownership
of the land was shared among the six remaining Wheler daughters and
their heirs and, it seems, Wood and Michell obtained these shares gradually and by various means. By 1717 they were sufficiently confident about
the final acquisition of the entire estate to enlist the services of Samuel
Worrall as lead speculator and builder on the estate. Worrall was a carpenter by trade. Over time, though, he prospered and rose in social
position to become an overseer of the poor, a surveyor for the Land Tax
and a churchwarden. His professional success is indicated by the fact that
in 1745 he undertook to provide seven of his workmen in arms to resist the
'Young Pretender', something only the richer and more public-spirited of
Spitalfields' tradesmen were able and inclined to do.[43] His name first
appears in an agreement of 1717, and is referred to in a deed of September
1718, relating to building on all or part of 'Joyce's Garden'.[44] He witnessed
leases to other builders and was probably the chief contractor on the estate.
One of his earliest building projects on the estate was the construction of
his own house and building yard on a large plot near the centre of 'Joyce's
Garden', just to the north of the existing buildings that marked the site of
what would be the north side of Fournier Street. The house, freestanding,
two rooms wide and one room deep, is now the much-altered and renum-
bered 18 Princelet Street. It was probably started in late 1721 and occupied
by Worrall by April 1723. He occupied it until at least 1759.[45]

By 1718, when Wood and Michell felt able to grant building leases, a
simple grid of streets had been laid out, the irregular row of buildings in
the centre of the site had been removed and the ground had been levelled
and – judging by archaeological evidence – raised by a metre or so, presumably to match the ground level of Christ Church, under construction
since 1714. The grid was formed by a pair of streets running parallel to the
existing 'Browns Lane' and Fashion Street, linked by a cross street running parallel to 'Red Lyon Street' (now part of Commercial Street). The
more northern of the two new parallel streets was named 'Princes Street'
(now Princelet Street) and was an extension of a court built off Brick Lane
in c.1705–6 by the speculating local brewer Joseph Truman.

The parallel street to its south was named 'Church Street' (now Fournier
Street). It was so-called because in 1713/14 Wood and Michell had sold a
large parcel of the 'Joyce's Garden'/'Tenters' ground site, where it fronted
on to 'Red Lyon Street', to the Church Commissioners for the construction of Christ Church, one of the Fifty New Anglican Churches proposed

by an Act of Parliament of 1711. This was a sale of some complexity since it involved not just Wood and Michell as majority controllers of the site but various surviving relatives of the Wheler sisters. In fact, the sale required three Chancery decrees in July 1713.[46] Construction of the church started in 1714, to a design by Nicholas Hawksmoor, and its long and sublimely sculptural north elevation defined the frontage of the south side of the street. Running north–south, linking 'Church Street' to 'Browns Lane' (now Hanbury Street) and crossing the west end of 'Princes Street', was 'Wood Street' (now Wilkes Street), presumably named after Charles Wood.

Initially Wood and Michell granted building leases on gap sites in long-established 'Browns Lane', which was no doubt a sage move. This street had seen a recent flurry of new building. Joseph Truman's development of 1705–6 in future 'Princes Street' had continued north along Brick Lane to form the south-east corner of 'Browns Lane', and by 1710 an impressive block of houses, taller and more regular than was usual in Spitalfields, had been completed. In March 1712/13 Frances Paltock, one of the seven daughters of William Wheler, had conveyed to one Edward Peck six houses at the west end of 'Browns Lane'/Hanbury Street, a yard (that still survives between numbers 10 and 12 and is called Peck's Yard), and 'a small parcel of ground heretofore a Bowling Alley' that lay behind the houses, along with four more on adjoining 'Red Lyon Street'.[47]

This appears to have been a piece of last-minute property dealing undertaken before the surrender of control of the land, on terms that remain unclear, to Wood and Michell – and, of course, it's quite possible that the two lawyers might have resented this conveyance of property that they had perhaps hoped to acquire. If so they were far too shrewd to let on. Taking on the Wheler daughters would have been unwise. Taking on Edward Peck would have been positively foolish. Peck is described in the transaction as a dyer and so was a key player in the area's powerful weaving industry, almost certainly well connected, and with influential friends. His status is hinted at not only by the fact that he was able to invest in 'Red Lyon Street' – a good address – but also by his choice to take up residence in one of the houses he acquired, near the site of the existing Golden Heart public house, which probably also became his place of work (the adjoining Peck's Yard still retains a series of subterranean vats that no doubt were part of the dye works). Even more significantly, he was one of the Commissioners charged with overseeing the building of the Fifty

New Churches. Peck was therefore a man Wood and Michell needed to have on their side when negotiating the sale of the large site in 'Joyce's Garden'. Relations between them evidently flourished. Wood and Michell not only did their deal with the Commissioners but Peck laid the foundation stone of the new church and his splendid monument stands inside, in a place of honour near the altar.

The earliest leases that the two Lincoln's Inn lawyers granted on their newly acquired land, for the building of numbers 24 and 26 on the south side of 'Browns Lane'/Hanbury Street, were taken in 1717–18 by Joseph Saubere, a silk dresser. The houses may have incorporated some of the fabric of earlier structures on the site, but external and internal details, particularly the stout balusters of the staircases, look much like the standard components used by Worrall in his early buildings on the Wood–Michell Estate, so presumably these houses too were a Worrall project.

Further buildings on small plots on the south side of 'Browns Lane'/Hanbury Street followed, then the development of the north side of 'Princes'/Princelet Street (where work began in 1718), then the south side of 'Princes Street' and 'Wood'/Wilkes Street in the early to mid 1720s, and finally 'Church Street' from the mid to late 1720s. By 1728, or perhaps as late as 1730, the domestic development of the 'Joyce's Garden' Estate was complete. The best and largest of the houses were in 'Church Street', Christ Church itself being completed in 1729.

A number of speculative builders besides Worrall were involved in the development of the estate – notably William Tayler and Marmaduke Smith, both of whom in 1726 built large and architecturally ambitious homes for themselves, essentially 'show houses', on the superior south side of 'Church Street' (now number 4/6 Fournier Street for Smith and 14 Fournier Street for Tayler). But while these builders, and their teams of craftsmen, displayed their own individual tastes when it came to design details, the architectural vocabulary employed by all was fairly uniform – limited in range, but often sophisticated in conception and execution. Taken together the houses these men built offer a fascinating vignette of the architectural aesthetics of the time, and of the development of early-Georgian speculative housing at a critical moment in London's building history, at the height of the Baroque style and during a city-wide construction boom.

Regardless of individual taste, a driving concern among all speculators and their builders was economy of time and money, to keep construction

Above: *25 (left) to 39 Fournier Street – mostly constructed in 1725–6, with, on the corner with Brick Lane, the former Huguenot church of 1743. The timber-clad third-floor weaving garrets are almost certainly later additions.* Below: *the rear elevation of 25-37 Fournier Street. The upper (third) floors of most of the houses are provided with wide windows set within the original rear walls of the houses. This suggests the upper-rear rooms were, from the start, intended to serve as workshops.*

costs down. Details therefore tended to be limited and made the best use of cheaper materials (for example, pine rather than oak) and such techniques of mass production as were then available. At the same time, of course, the houses had to appear sound and reasonably fashionable – both inside and out – in order to attract the right sort of affluent occupier. Externally, therefore, the focus of design and workmanship was concentrated on brickwork – notably the form of window arches and the dressing to windows as well as the regularity and pointing of facing brickwork on street elevations, on the relative shape and proportion of window openings and on the timber doorcases that acted as temple-like portals to the homes they served. The speculative builders operating on the estate tended to take on pairs of buildings at a time, so as not to risk too much capital in one operation, an exception being 17–25 Wilkes Street, which is the surviving portion of a six-house terrace built in 1723–4 by Marmaduke Smith.

Most builders on the Tillard Estate (notably Thomas Bunce, Thomas Brown and Jonathan Beaumont), in a manner typical of early-Georgian London, tended to run up shells of houses, roofed and floored but with the interior left to the first occupier to fit out in a manner to suit his taste and pocket. William Goswell on the Tillard Estate tended to include interiors as well, and this was the more general practice followed by builders on the Wood–Michell Estate. Here, new houses (certainly those built by Worrall and Tayler) were usually fully panelled at ground and first floor, with varying details to reflect the status of the house and the house-style of the builder and his joiners, with a mix of full and half-panelling and plaster walls on the upper storeys. Water supply and sewage removal were limited.

As in Barbon's Artillery Ground development of nearly fifty years earlier, cesspits were located in rear yards but not connected to the sewer system, which was intended primarily to remove surface water and improve drainage (this was controlled by statute but, no doubt, liquid waste from cesspits was occasionally siphoned into the sewers). Fresh water was supplied by private water companies (from 1806 the East London Waterworks Company) via underground elm pipes, and later cast-iron pipes, that were charged with water at specified times during the week. Subscribers were connected to the pipes via lead 'quills' that allowed them to pump water into lead storage tanks within their houses, often set at basement level to serve the kitchen and washroom.

The earliest houses built on the Wood–Michell Estate – 24 and 26

Browns Lane, dating from 1717/18 – offer a clue to the planning aspirations behind the landlord's speculation. A memorial of the deed of conveyance of the land from Wood and Michell to Joseph Saubere suggests that any houses constructed there were to be designed to conform to a 'Modell or Plattforme'.[48] If this was the case then presumably the estate wanted to ensure uniformity and quality in its architecture and planned to get spec-ulators to build to agreed model elevations. This pair of three-window-wide houses have uniform elevations, recently much but accurately reconstructed. Their window arches are flat but with those to the first-floor centre of each house embellished with serpentine – Baroque – undersides, and the red dressings to the window jambs are linked vertically to form a continu-ous band rising through the height of the house. This was a popular detail in the architecture of late-seventeenth-century London. There are no string courses and a parapet replaces a timber eaves cornice as regulated in the 1707 Building Act. The ground floors of both houses have been recon-structed, so no evidence of early doorcases survives.

The next phase in the development of the Wood–Michell Estate was the extension of the court off Brick Lane, created in 1705/6 by Joseph Tru-man, to form 'Princes Street', and the construction of groups of houses along its north side from c.1718–20. The origin of the name 'Princes' is something of a mystery. It seems that as early as 1713 the court was known as 'Princesse Street', and, of course, it's quite feasible that this choice of name was a purely arbitrary one.[49] But there is another possibility. One of the surveyors active in early Georgian London was a man named John Prince. He had close connections with the 2nd Earl of Oxford, Edward Harley, and was involved with laying out the Harley Estate in Maryle-bone, as well as preparing an estimate for converting a barn adjoining Marylebone manor house into a 'French Chapell'.[50] It is possible that Wood and Michell, gentlemen and Lincoln's Inn lawyers, would have had connections with the Earl, and that if so they opted to make use of his surveyor John Prince and then acknowledged his involvement by naming the first new street on their estate in his honour. Wood and Michell's business partner Samuel Worrall might seem the more obvious candidate, but his glory days lay somewhat in the future (he was appointed main carpenter at Christ Church Spitalfields in 1723).

Prince's name doesn't appear in any contemporary documents related to 'Princes Street' (which suggests that, if he was indeed involved, it was on an informal basis), but his possible involvement in Spitalfields is suggested

by a stylistic link between the idiosyncratic use of giant Corinthian pilasters at Cound Hall in Shropshire (which Prince is thought to have designed
in around 1703 for Edward Cressett, a back-bench Tory MP and colleague
of Harley's) and the design of at least two Spitalfields houses. One of
these, Marmaduke Smith's home, now numbered 4/6 Fournier Street, has
a façade framed by a pair of giant pilasters – in this case Doric – rising
from ground to parapet, which are disproportionately spaced and purely
ornamental in the manner of Cound Hall's: they are not part of a system
of classical design and do not relate to other components in the façade.
The second example, which stood at the junction of Lamb Street and
'Church'/Nantes Passage and was built by Samuel Worrall in 1733, has
long been lost.

   Whatever the origin of these giant pilasters, they became something of
a theme in the architecture of Spitalfields and its environs, being employed
in the 1730s at the Directors' House, on the Truman Brewery Brick Lane
site, and in the early-eighteenth-century 190 Shoreditch High Street, built
on the Holywell Priory site, immediately to the north of Spitalfields.
These houses serve as a reminder that however much speculative building
of the period worked to certain prescribed forms, aiming at economy that
tended to lead increasingly to uniformity and minimal ornamentation,
there are frequent flashes of individuality, sometimes even ostentation. It
is these details, offering moments of unexpected variety, that give the surviving Georgian architecture of Spitalfields much of its appeal.

   Looking at the early buildings in these streets it is also fascinating to
see how the simpler standard designs evolved. Numbers 17 and 19 Princelet
Street, a pair built in 1718 by Samuel Worrall and a bricklayer called Samuel Phipps, have flat window lintels, but now embellished at first-floor
level with brick-wrought keystones, and each has continuous vertical
bands of red-brick dressings linking the window jambs.[51] Numbers 2 and
4 Princelet Street, built just a few years later, are different again. They
were built by Worrall under a ninety-nine-year lease from Wood and
Michell dated January 1723/4, but unlike houses built even just a year earlier they have window arches that, rather than being flat, form a curve
derived from a segment of a circle.[52] This particular feature appears to
have been of French Baroque origin and was introduced into England by
Sir Christopher Wren and other Francophile architects – it appears, for
example, if only fleetingly, in Wren's 1690s work at Hampton Court. From
1718 it started to appear in London's speculatively built streets, and by the

early 1720s was becoming standard in Spitalfields (5 and 7 Elder Street of 1725 by Thomas Bunce being rare exceptions). The previously popular flat arch did not start to return to fashion in London until the mid 1730s.

Another fashion of the 1720s was for doorcases with Doric pilasters and rusticated shafts (as, for example, at 17–25 Wilkes Street, 9/11 and 13 Elder Street, 10 Folgate Street and on the now lost 17, 18 and 19 Spital Square). These, with their mass-produced repeating details, rather than individual hand-wrought work, would have been economical to produce, but they also possess an artistic power that stems from the accuracy and erudition of their design. Again, though, these machine-made, mass-produced designs were far from universal in 1720s Spitalfields. Number 2 Wilkes Street, for example, built under a lease of March 1725 by William Tayler, referred to in various documents as a 'gentleman' or 'carpenter', had a doorcase (destroyed in the early 1970s) of the traditional handcrafted type, with serpentine brackets embellished with carved acanthus leaves and cherubs' heads. A similar approach was adopted at the contemporary Tayler houses, now numbered 17 and 19 Fournier Street. Their bracketed hood designs and cherub heads are reminiscent of Wren's late-seventeenth-century designs, and must have seemed rather old-fashioned when they were constructed. Both doorcases are now modern reproductions, but informed and very well executed.

Idiosyncrasies went beyond external details. William Tayler's houses, for example, are distinguished by simple internal detailing, and his staircases characterised by the use of alternating twisted and straight-shafted balusters – a simpler version of the design used in 1726 for the Christ Church Rectory at 2 Fournier Street, constructed under the direction of Nicholas Hawksmoor. The consistency of Tayler's structural and decorative approach is revealing for it suggests he used the same team of builders for his operations, and that he developed and applied a particular 'house-style'.

The first-floor windows on virtually all the surviving houses on the Wood–Michell Estate are the tallest ones, revealing that the builders wanted to evoke the fashionable Renaissance ideal of the *piano nobile*, in which important rooms are located on the first floor. (In Worrall's later houses, though, only just.) But as was common in London's early-Georgian architecture, the ground-floor rooms of some Spitalfields houses were superior to those on the first floor. This is particularly the case in Elder Street, where ground-floor windows and floor-to-ceiling heights can be a few inches taller than on the first floor (for example numbers 15 and 17), and where even the ground-floor window arches on some houses (particularly those by Goswell, such as 32–36 Elder Street) are slightly more ornate than those above first-floor windows.

But, of course, many of these Spitalfields houses fulfilled more than a purely domestic role: they were places of work as well as leisure. On the north side of Fournier Street (the last street to be built on the Wood–Michell Estate, from the mid 1720s), for example, the brick-built rear elevations of numbers 25–37 continue to the third floor while in the front elevation they stop at second-floor level with the top floor being a garret. And numbers 25, 29, 31 and 37 possess wide third-floor rear windows that were seemingly intended to light weaving garrets or workshops. In section these houses had, in their original form, five full-height rooms to the rear (including the basement) but only four full-height rooms to the front. To contemporary passers-by they would thus have presented stylish street façades while concealing the office and manufacturing space that existed at the rear of each building. They were, in other words, a fusion of elegant home and practical workshop. In the late eighteenth century, as Spitalfields declined in fashion and wealth, additional manufacturing space was added to many houses, to squeeze more activity into the building and so increase its value. In some cases, as with 31–37 Fournier Street, garrets were added to the front part of the house, to join the existing workshops at the rear of the third floor.

Even within a single street the relative status of individual houses could vary quite significantly. Thus in Fournier Street, the houses on the south side were clearly intended to be – and to look – superior to those on the north. Those on the south side have deeper gardens – some bordering the churchyard – and enjoy a sunny and open prospect from their rear rooms. Their basements are lit and ventilated by railed-off areas. The basements of those on the north side of the street, by contrast, have to make do with light wells and grilles. And there are more subtle expressions of superiority. Number 20, on the south side of the street, was built in 1726 by Edward Grange, a carpenter, and it has a fine doorcase of a type that Worrall appears to have introduced. It is a triumph of relative simplicity – being essentially an assembly of erudite classical joinery details – spiced up with a bold Baroque flourish. This is achieved by curving the architrave up through the frieze to the cornice, bringing to the streets of Calvinist Spitalfields a whiff of Counter-Reformation Rome. But being on the south

The diversity of Fournier Street doorcase designs shows a fusion of erudite, mass-produced joinery with idiosyncratic, hand-wrought details. Above: 14 Fournier Street, 1726; centre: 27 Fournier Street, 1725; below: 20 Fournier Street, 1726.

side of the street this Edward Grange design is a little more ornate than similar examples on the north side. It has the additional detail of dentils in its cornice, and this breaks forward over the pilasters that frame the composition. Similar doorcases on the north side have neither of these refinements.

In fact all doorcases on the houses on the south side of Fournier Street – no matter what their design – have something that none of the early doorcases on the other side possess. On the south side the doors within the doorcases are set within deep and generous panelled reveals. On the north side these panelled reveals are absent. It's a small thing perhaps, but one that reveals with great accuracy the houses' relative hierarchy. And the different houses also reveal something about the fleeting nature of taste: 8 and 10 Fournier Street, on the south side, although built by Samuel Worrall and furnished with his standard doorcase design (now embellished by dentils as on number 20), do not have the keystones sported by his houses on the north side of the street. Those on the north side were constructed by the end of 1725. The building lease for numbers 8 and 10 is dated 26 July 1726 by which time the houses were described as 'erected or now in building'.[53] Presumably during the six months or so since the north-side houses were completed, the fashion or demand for keystones had declined.

Fournier Street possesses five houses of unusually large size. Two of these are merely big, with their details being standard and their design and plans being vernacular in feel. These are both on the north side – 27 and 35 – although it must be said 27 possesses a richness of detail and generosity of space that makes it exceptional (see pages 343 and 397). The three big houses on the south side, on the other hand, are not only big but also architecturally ambitious. The Rectory of 1726–c.1730 was designed by Hawksmoor's office and executed by the building team working on the church. It is a fine and fascinating building, well constructed out of excellent materials and beautifully and carefully detailed. Immediately to its east stands 4/6 Fournier Street, the large and richly detailed house constructed in 1726 by Marmaduke Smith for his own use and which, with its early architectural use of mahogany on the staircase and its giant external pilasters, possesses something of an aristocratic and stately feel. It is no doubt significant that Smith probably had professional connections with architect Thomas Ripley, who in the early 1720s was working on the Admiralty, Whitehall and Houghton Hall, Norfolk – both with Prime

Minister Sir Robert Walpole, a great fan of mahogany, as client. (Interestingly in the Rectory and number 4/6 the ground- and first-floor windows are of virtually equal depth.)

To the east of number 4/6 is number 14 Fournier Street, also built in 1726 by William Tayler for himself. This in several ways is the most extraordinary house of the three, not because of its architectural sophistication but because of its sheer – almost barbaric – bravado. Inside, the panelling and staircase are of the highest quality, with much carving of telling details (Tayler was described as a carpenter and joiner), while the exterior is simply astonishing. Its front façade seems intended to be a display of the arts and crafts of the bricklayer, with beautifully rubbed and gauged segmental window arches – each complete with a triple keystone – and rubbed brick aprons below window sills. There are also profiled string courses between storeys, and perhaps originally a moulded brick cornice, although the existing one is modern and speculative in design. The doorcase is a unique concoction in which correct classical authority and pedigree are combined with bizarre invention. The lower portion of the design is conventional, with fluted Ionic engaged columns set on pedestals, placed against rustic blocks and framing a segmental door opening with an ornate keystone. All is correctly and quietly Baroque and designed and detailed as if made of stone.

Above the Ionic capitals is a doorcase design of very different conception. The lower portion of the design promises a conventional entablature and pediment. But instead the frieze above the capitals sprout – in surprising manner – small brackets that support a segmental hood that breaks forwards and, with its coffered underside, contrives to look like a portion of a dome. This flamboyant and inventive doorcase, which ultimately eschews the Palladian conventions and classical correctness of the period, combined with the richness of the brickwork – particularly the string courses – gives this elevation an old-fashioned if magnificent Baroque quality. It's as if Tayler, through the design of his house, wanted to grant himself the imprimatur of an ancient pedigree.

It seems appropriate that such a house should be erected so close to Christ Church – by far the most architecturally important structure to be erected in eighteenth-century Spitalfields, designed by the most important architect to work in the area: Nicholas Hawksmoor, protégé of Sir Christopher Wren and veteran of numerous significant building projects including St Paul's Cathedral, Greenwich Hospital (now the Old Royal Naval

Christ Church, from a print of c.1756 by Benjamin Cole. The church's spire was rebuilt in simplified form in the early nineteenth century. The rounded cobbles give an approximate idea of road treatment in early-eighteenth-century Spitalfields.

College) and various of Wren's City churches. Designed to impress with its 'solemn and awfull appearance', the church was to be 'a monument to posterity' and proclaim the power and the presence of the Anglican Church in an area occupied almost exclusively by nonconformists and Dissenters of one kind or another.[54] It was, in other words, very much state-sanctioned architecture, largely paid for by a national tax on coal and with its stones carrying a message from the government to the diverse inhabitants of Spitalfields. The location, great size and design of the church combined to make a single point.

Its noble Tuscan west portico (in fact a late addition to the design) and tall tower and spire occupied a visually dominant position in the heart of new Spitalfields, while the church's frontage looked across 'Red Lyon Street' and slightly askew down 'Paternoster Row' to Crispin Street – all important and long-established thoroughfares in 1720s Spitalfields. Inside the new church, above the altar, was a royal coat of arms, proclaiming the power and glory of the unified church and state. More particularly, when completed, a new parish was created for Spitalfields' splendid new Anglican figurehead, carved out of the ancient, huge and rambling parish of St Dunstan's Stepney. The new church might not have had a large and ready congregation – most inhabitants of Spitalfields in the 1720s went to their own Calvinist chapels or Dissenters' meeting houses – but it did, through its vestry, instantly become the centre of local government and administration and, for the wealthier Huguenots, the preferred place of interment or burial.

This great new church and the network of streets to its north containing large new houses became – along with Spital Square – the emblem of Spitalfields' enhanced status as a prosperous merchant quarter that, in its architectural ambition, possessed something of the character of contemporary and aristocratic West End developments. There were novel and pleasing prospects throughout the streets that elevated it from being an everyday tradesmen's suburb. There was the striking vista from Bishopsgate, east across Spital Square to 'Church Passage' and Lamb Street, that narrowed progressively to evoke the theatrical quality of a Baroque false perspective. And the new houses – large, regular in their design and relatively uniform – would have been in obvious contrast to the majority of the area's smaller late-seventeenth-century buildings. To appreciate the scale and drama of the transformation it is only necessary to compare the Spital Square area as shown on Rocque's map with the same area on Ogilby and

Morgan's map of 1676 – where the sixteenth-century Principal Tenement, Vaughan's Mansion, the early-seventeenth-century Brick House and the monastic Candle House can still be identified – and then with the almost bucolic rendering of the area to be seen on the mid-sixteenth-century 'Copperplate' map.

The high architectural quality of Christ Church and the fact that the project took fifteen years to complete (and cost vast sums, with the completion cost being just over four times Hawksmoor's April 1714 estimate of £9,129.16.0d) meant that it became something of a college of learning, yielding inspiration and a repertoire of useful details for Spitalfields craftsmen and builders – notably Samuel Worrall, who was carpenter to the church from 1723, and Thomas Lucas, who was one of the bricklayers and worked also on Hawksmoor's St George-in-the-East and St Anne's Limehouse, and during the first decade of the eighteenth century undertook the speculative development of the Baroque-detailed Albury Street, Deptford. In addition, Christ Church was, presumably, a building project on which many useful contacts were made.

But it also serves as a reminder of how quickly taste could change in the eighteenth century, for when Robert Seymour came to consider it in 1734/5 in his updated version of John Stow's *Survey of London*, just five or six years after the church's completion, he noted: 'The building here is very strong and substantial but greatly found Fault with by some Criticks in Architecture.'[55] The inventive, wilful and idiosyncratic Baroque classical architecture of Vanbrugh and Hawksmoor was in the process of being superseded by more orthodox Palladian design. A similar fate must have overtaken Spitalfields domestic architecture as taste moved away from the individualistic vernacular Baroque, characterised by variety and strong-coloured brickwork, towards more uniform, regular and simple street architecture. As James Ralph wrote in his *Critical Review of the Public Buildings . . . in and about London and Westminster* of 1734, 'Simplicity is generally understood to be the ground-work of beauty.'[56]

This new simplicity is expressed by the pair of houses opposite Christ Church. Numbers 1 and 3 Fournier Street were built in about 1755 for the prosperous and sophisticated silk master Peter Lekeux III (see page 195). They are tall, uniform, almost gaunt, wrought of cool yellow brick with a minimal Portland stone trim and with elevations distinguished by subtle first-floor *piano nobile* windows and topped (as was the vogue at that time) with square attic windows set above a shared cornice. Inside, the houses boast lofty internal volumes and generous staircases. They are in striking contrast with their neighbours, and reveal the then current urban ideal, which at that time was being expressed in such West End estates as that of Lord Berkeley in and around Berkeley Square. It is now curious to realise that the ambitious houses of Spitalfields' 1720s 'New Town', which when first built had put their late-seventeenth-century precursors in the shade, were by the 1750s already noticeably old-fashioned.

NINE

HOUSES AND PEOPLE

Elder Street's Early Years

E lder Street runs north–south across the former 'Porter's Close', once part of the orchard and garden belonging to the Prior of St Mary and, at the beginning of the eighteenth century, one of the last large open spaces in Spitalfields.[1] By the mid 1670s, a few buildings stood on what would become the south end of Elder Street, facing on to 'White Lion Yard' (now part of Folgate Street), but as late as 1711–13 when the survey for a proposed 'New Church' on the corner of 'White Lion Yard' and Norton Folgate was being drawn up, there were clearly no plans under way to develop a street here. But evidently intentions changed in 1716 when the Tillard family acquired ownership of 'Porter's Close' and adjoining land (see page 193).

Interestingly, though, it seems that, as elsewhere in Spitalfields (if not to the same extent), rubbish from the post-Fire City was dumped on 'Porter's Close' in the 1670s and 1680s. Fragments of an early-seventeenth-century Cologne-made earthenware Bellarmine or Bartmann jug have, in recent years, been discovered below 34 Elder Street, while excavations in the basement of number 15 – in which I've lived since 1977 – have revealed shattered slipware, spongeware and fragments of seventeenth-century Delft tiles. A small, domed, bone or ceramic medallion was also unearthed, bearing the lightly incised image of a T-shaped tau cross with a fox-faced serpent draped around its cross bar. This emblem – inspired by the biblical description of the brazen serpent wrought by Moses at God's instruction and set upon a pole to cure snakebite – had by the seventeenth century become a token to use against the spread of plague.[2] The condition of the ground surface of 'Porter's Close', whether strewn with refuse or perhaps poorly drained, might explain one of the oddities of the houses that were eventually built on it. In Elder Street, the principal and best-preserved of the streets built on the Close, ground floors are consistently raised significantly above ground level, and all front doors are reached by flights of three or four steps. This is in distinct contrast to most of the contemporary houses on the nearby Wood–Michell Estate.[3]

The first mention of a street 'intended to be called Elder Street' comes in May 1724, although initial building activity on its site had seemingly commenced a couple of years earlier.[4] In the early 1720s the rebuilding of 'White Lion Yard' or Street had begun, and by the mid 1720s the consolidation and extension of what was to become the architectural and social jewel of the Tillard Estate, Spital Square, was well under way. Elder Street was to form the main axis in a small new orthogonal grid of streets: the parallel but narrower Blossom Street to the west; Fleur de Lis Street, crossing Elder Street; and, at the northern end of Elder Street, 'Porter Street' (so named on Rocque's map of 1746 and later known as 'Blossom Terrace'), which in the late 1720s became the location for two almshouses, one for the Weavers' Company and another for 'decayed' residents of the Liberty of Norton Folgate. Both sets of alms-houses were demolished in the mid nineteenth century – along with the rest of 'Porter Street' and the north ends of Blossom Street and Elder Street – to make way for the construction of Commercial Street. Today the early buildings of Spital Square, bar one house, have all gone. No early houses survive in Fleur de Lis Street or in Blossom Street, and only a few scattered early-eighteenth-century houses survive at the west end of Folgate Street. But the south end of Elder Street – south of Fleur de Lis Street – remains largely intact.

The first houses completed in Elder Street were numbers 24 and 26, built as a pair under a building lease granted in July 1722 by the estate owner Sir Isaac Tillard to joiners Edward Osborne and John Burges. Number 26 is modest in size – only two windows wide – and while 24 is three windows wide, most of its ground floor is given over to a wide arch that served a walled yard created by Tillard. This suggests a utilitarian or even industrial purpose for the pair. Yet, if intended for the operation of the weaving industry, it is odd that wide weavers' windows are absent. Indeed the houses are generously proportioned, and do not have the feel of tenements or workshops, with ground floors being raised higher, and with ground-floor ceiling heights loftier, than in later adjoining houses. Also, externally, the pair are well detailed, with segmental arched windows formed with well-wrought rubbed bricks. No internal details survive and the plan form of the pair is altered. So far as 24 is concerned, we know that John Burges was not only its builder but also its first occupant.[5] He was, suitably enough, a man from the silk trade – a calender, that is a tradesman responsible for giving silk fabric a smooth and glossy appearance by rolling it between cylinders or using hot and cold presses to exaggerate the appearance of 'watered' silk. He was also clearly a man of at least local reputation because in 1744 he was a trustee of the Norton Folgate Court House.

It seems reasonable to speculate that since these were almost certainly the first houses in the street, they were completed to specifications laid down by the Tillard Estate and were thus intended to act as models for future developments. The Tillards had, of course, a long-term interest in Elder Street: under the prevailing system of estate development, while land owners received a low ground rent for the length of the first lease (in Elder Street, usually sixty-one years), the buildings became theirs when the lease terminated. It therefore benefited them if the houses, architecturally and structurally, were of good quality and likely to endure. As mentioned earlier, this desire could be – and often was – in direct conflict with the short-term interest of the speculative builders, who generally wanted to build as quickly and cheaply as possible, cut corners where practicable, reap what profits were forthcoming, and move on.

If 24 and 26 Elder Street were the approved model, then the estate must have been somewhat disappointed by what followed them. The pair now numbered 5 and 7 (previously 14 and 15) were built soon after, under a sixty-one-year lease granted in July 1725 to plasterer Thomas Bunce. These houses are smaller and archaic in design. On the other hand the pair now numbered 9/11 and 13 Elder Street – built soon after by Bunce, now working in conjunction with the pavior Thomas Brown – matched, and even exceeded, 24 and 26 in scale and detail. The speculative builder William Goswell also achieved a pleasing uniformity with 32, 34 and 36 Elder Street and three related houses in Folgate Street, on a building lease dated May 1725, as did Isaac Dupree with 28 and 30 Elder Street, which were completed by November 1724.[6] Dupree, interestingly, was a weaver as well as a speculative builder – which, perhaps strangely, was rare in early-eighteenth-century Spitalfields. But, although handsome, these houses are slightly smaller in scale than 24 and 26 Elder Street.

Interestingly the six-house project undertaken by Goswell on the corner of Elder and Folgate Streets incorporated an arch (through the five-bay 23 Folgate Street) serving a stable yard set behind the houses. Stables were uncommon in Spitalfields of that period. You can scrutinise Rocque's map

Above: the east side of Elder Street, built from 1725 to 1728. Numbers 5 and 7 are on the left. The white stucco-clad house in the distance is number 23. Below: a detail of the doorcase on 30 Elder Street. The house was built by 1724; the doorcase, of very correct Ionic classical design, must be a little later if based on designs published by Gibbs in 1728 or Batty Langley in his Builder's Jewel *pattern book of 1741.*

of 1746 and discover many yards and courts, some marked as 'Timber Yards' others as 'Brew House' (for example the large yard east of Elder Street), but none marked as stabling. Goswell's stable is not marked – but a stables it was because the building agreement of 1725 between Goswell and the Tillard Estate for 23–27 Folgate Street and 32–36 Elder Street states that behind the six houses were six stables containing twenty-eight stalls. The number of horses suggest this stables was not just for the occupiers of the six houses but that it was a livery stable. Two coach houses and stabling for six horses were also located next to the 'Brew House' east of Elder Street.[7] These stables and coach houses – and there must have been many more – were essential not only for the carriage and riding horses that the richer and more aspirational masters and weavers of Spitalfields must have owned or hired, but for the many working horses required to service and serve the area's population. The issue of stables has an architectural aspect because at the very time the grand new houses of Spitalfields were being constructed – in and around Spital Square and north of Christ Church – a very specific urban form, the 'block', incorporating houses, gardens/yards and stables facing on to a mews, was being developed on the main West End estates then under development. For example John Prince (see page 213) in his plan of 1719 for the aristocratic Harley Estate, north of Oxford Street, envisioned blocks of houses serviced by rear mews, and if you look at Rocque's map showing Grosvenor Square – developed from the early 1720s – you will be amazed by the degree to which, in striking contrast to contemporary developments in Spitalfields such as Elder Street, the estate was served by many and large 'mewse' set behind the principal terraces.[8] Of course, Spitalfields was a congested area and did not possess the open space necessary – and available on the green-field Grosvenor Estate – for generous service roads, courts, mews and stabling. Nor did it possess substantial numbers of residents with the wealth or desire for coaches and horses. But there is one surviving example of the West End fashion surviving in Spitalfields. The wealthy Peter Bourdon did indeed in 1725 arrange for what was almost certainly a coach house and stable to be constructed behind his Fournier Street house, although in the absence of a mews or service road this genteel appurtenance had to be reached by passing through the fabric of the house itself, by way of an arch and passage little more than six feet wide incorporated into it (see page 343).

The fact that there might have been some architectural master plan at work in the development of Elder Street during the 1720s is supported by the design of numbers 15 to 23. These houses suggest a subtle pattern. Constructed by three different teams of speculative builders – 15 and 17 by Bunce and Brown, 19 and 21 by Jonathan Beaumont, and 23 by William Goswell – they form a broadly harmonious group, notably with the sills of all first-floor windows aligned, seemingly to match those of the slightly earlier 28–36 Elder Street.[9]

But this seeming attempt at architectural harmony and concern for the public aspect of these houses must not prevent the appreciation of a brutal truth that characterises so much speculative building in London. The houses' 'private' or secret aspects – as represented by their generally concealed structure – are pretty shocking. Goswell's 32–36 Elder Street houses are a good example of this. The bricks forming their façades are of superb quality and very well laid, and details such as window arches are admirably crafted. But this beauty is painfully superficial. The façade is only half a brick (four inches) deep, with most of the apparent 'headers' in the handsome Flemish bond 'snapped' – and so, in fact, only half-bricks that do not tie in with the brick piers behind. This means that the bond between the skin of the façade and the structural piers is slight and very random. And since the structural piers and rear and party walls were designed to be concealed, the builders thought they could get away with using poor-quality brick for those.

The result is that half of the six houses in the group have had to be re-fronted, while number 36 Elder Street has such a large bulge – located at first-floor level and the result of the veneer of facing bricks buckling under an excessive load – that it's a miracle it has survived at all. The bulge has now been expertly secured by steel pins and has been preserved to astonish future generations. Tradesmen involved in the repair told me that the lack of bond between different brick-built elements seemed to be more than mere accident.[10] Some malevolent force appears to have been at work. Perhaps Goswell's ruthless behaviour as a speculator extended to the mistreatment of his workforce – and neglectful construction was their revenge. Whatever the truth, this small group of houses says much about building in Georgian London – skin-deep beauty hiding corruption, even deceit, like a mask of white lead face paint over a decaying visage.

In comparison with Spital Square, the houses in Elder Street are smaller and the inhabitants were generally less wealthy. In the 1740s and 1750s some were even brought before the manorial court for keeping pigs.[11] Nevertheless, most were sufficiently prosperous to be assessed for payment of the Land Tax, levied on the estimated wealth of an individual as represented by the rent on the property occupied and paid generally by the occupier of a building rather than its owner (it's worth bearing in mind that up to 30 per cent of the population of any given area would have been too poor to be assessed). A tax charge of £10 plus per annum in the mid eighteenth century qualified an occupier of the Liberty of Norton Folgate to serve as Headborough (equivalent to mayor) or in other of the Liberty's offices, such as Scavenger (see page 255). These were honourable offices but onerous and some residents paid a 'fine' to avoid serving when their turn came. Along Elder Street the going rate in the 1767 Land Tax assessments was twelve shillings on the valuation of the rent, dipping to nine shillings for those living in some of the humbler houses.[12] Larger, newer buildings in good repair would, of course, be rated for a higher tax than small, old or decrepit buildings.

The Land Tax assessments do more than simply give us a sense of the relative wealth of an area. They also let us know who lived where and when. They are, admittedly, not easy to use: street names are listed but not house numbers (indeed, houses tended not to be numbered until the late eighteenth century and the London numbering system was then changed significantly the following century). Houses on corner sites were allocated to the street on which they fronted, which can make identification difficult if those houses were subsequently demolished and their orientation therefore impossible to be sure of – though, at least, cross streets were noted where they occurred. And although the tax collectors, from one generation to the next, usually followed the same route through the area when noting information about individual houses, they didn't always start in the same place. The Elder Street assessors for the Land Tax assessments that survive from the eighteenth century – of which the earliest are 1743, 1759 and 1767 – seem to have walked west along 'White Lion Street', turned right (north) into Elder Street, and then walked north, listing first the houses on the east side. The house on the south-east corner of Elder Street was entered from 'White Lion Street' and so was presumably enumerated with it.[13]

The names recorded are suggestive of the mix of English and French

Huguenot-descended people who lived in the street in the decades after it was first constructed. On the one hand there are Tanners, Simpsons and Hunts, more likely than not English surnames; on the other, Hanchettes, Aubens and Martells, almost certainly Huguenots of French descent. Sometimes people make a fleeting appearance in one Land Tax assessment and have moved (or died) by the next: thus the house currently numbered 23 Elder Street was occupied in 1743 by Sar. Warry, who paid a rent of £1. But in 1759 the 'head tenant' was Richard Tonks and in 1767 it was Rich Hanchette, who was responsible for the payment of the twelve-shilling tax. Next door at number 21, John Fallowfield, resident in 1743, had given way to Jno. Tanner by 1759, who in turn was replaced by Lambert Dunnage in 1767. Sometimes, though, people stayed for rather longer. In 1743, 1759 and 1767 Benj. Hutchings was head tenant of number 19 (former 20) Elder Street, paying, in the latter year, the standard twelve-shilling tax.

Sadly, for the most part, the names listed in the Land Tax records remain just that: first names and surnames recorded on an official document, with a note of the level of tax the individual in question was subject too. But in a few cases, thanks to the existence of supplementary records, we get a fuller picture.

We know a fair amount, for example, about 'Fran. Bowlan', who in 1759 was listed as the head tenant of what was then the largest house on Elder Street and is now still numbered 9 and 11 (the house was divided into two separate dwellings in the early nineteenth century) despite being reunited as one house in the late 1970s. Five windows wide, and built in 1725/6 by Bunce and Brown, the house preserves a very finely detailed panelled interior and a superb marble fire surround in a ground-floor room. Francis Bowlan (or Boland) was a weaver – and a weaver of distinction. He wore linen shirts worth five shillings each – nearly the average weekly wage at the time for many journeymen weavers (see page 266) – hung a sword (the recognised emblem of a gentleman) on the wall in his parlour, and kept a footman. The reason we know all this is because in May 1765 a former footman, one Richard Riley, stole the shirts and the 'steel-mounted' sword, along with a 'silver boat' (presumably a sauce boat), valued at eight shillings, and two yards of velvet, valued at sixteen shillings, and ended up in court.[14] Francis Boland himself did not testify because he was 'in the country for his health', but his father, John Boland, who was also a weaver, was on hand to identify the items produced in evidence as his son's property: 'I can swear to the velvet and the boat . . . I have seen such a sword as this hanging in the parlour.'

Riley did not deny the charge of 'grand larceny' levelled against him. Apparently, when under arrest for the theft, he'd appealed to John Boland for help: 'he confessed to taking the things . . . he cried, and said he hoped I would forgive him. I said, I should be sorry to hang him . . .' And the confession was accompanied by the testimonies of pawnbrokers and old-clothes men who all confirmed that Riley had offered them the stolen items. Riley's defence, such as it was, was one of poverty: 'I was in distress, and took the things, but with intent to get them again as soon as I got money: It was through necessity; I did not sell any of them.' He was, pre-dictably, found guilty, but although the value of the stolen goods could have cost him his life, he was transported rather than hanged. Presumably his ready admission of guilt and his contrition saved his life.

Francis Boland (in this case spelt Bowland) makes an appearance in another legal document, this time dated 1760. At the Middlesex Sessions, Bowland, 'of Elder Street, Spitalfields, Esquire', and Thomas Cobb of Sadlers-Hall, London – an attorney-at-law – posted bail of £40 for a defendant, Mrs Frances Rooke, being prosecuted by the Crown.[15] There appears to be no record of the outcome of this case, heard at the Middlesex Sessions House, but the fact that Bowland was styled 'Esquire' confirms his relatively high social status. By the time the 1767 Land Tax was levied, however, Boland was no longer in residence in Elder Street – perhaps his sojourn in the country had failed to restore his health. Now Peter Abraham Auben was listed as head tenant of 9/11 Elder Street and was assessed to pay the higher tax of one pound.

Perhaps the most dramatic mention in contemporary records of some-one associated with Elder Street is that of Samuel Randall, a son – or perhaps just a relative – of Thomas Randall, who in the 1759 and 1767 Land Tax assessments was recorded as the head tenant of 24 Elder Street, and was listed as a 'Merchant . . . Thomas Randall and Son, Elder Street', in *A Complete Guide* of 1765. The late 1760s were difficult times in Spitalfields as journeymen weavers, worried about changes to the silk industry that, they thought, might threaten their security and livelihoods, organised them-selves into groups known as 'cutters' because their favoured action was to cut, and so destroy, the silk on the looms of those masters they believed hostile to their cause (see chapter 10).

In the early morning of 17 January 1771 when trials were still taking place in the wake of the journeymen's protests, and local tensions were running high, Samuel Randall was among a party of men and women walking along Shoreditch High Street when they collided with a group of drunken men. One of these, John Foy, it was later alleged, 'jostled' one of the women in Randall's group, and then got into a scuffle with her husband, Joseph West, which ended with Foy lying mortally injured. West and Stephen Paris, a midshipman on leave, were charged with his murder, and Samuel Randall, on the evidence of one Roger Fines, was charged with 'aiding, abetting, comforting, and maintaining [the accused] in committing the said murder'. Randall pleaded not guilty and his bail was set and paid by 'John Randall [or Randale] of Elder Street, Norton Folgate, "Tabby waterer" [tabby was a type of watered silk with a pattern created by calendering, suggesting Randall had taken over the business from John Burges], and John Fromont junr. of Wood Street, Spitalfields, Weaver.' A receipt for the bail still survives. 'Paid in £40. Paid out £20.'[16] Randall faced a potential death sentence.

The trial was held at the Old Bailey on 20 February 1771.[17] One of Foy's friends, a journeyman weaver and neighbour named Thomas Clark, who had been with Foy as he languished – conscious – for a day after the attack, described what Foy had told him in his final hours:

> I heard him say that the big man, West, knocked him down, and trampled upon his private parts; and the little man with the ribband in his hat [Paris] stamped upon his stomach. This was Wednesday morning, a little before he died.

This story was corroborated by another weaver – William Williams – who also visited Foy as he lay dying:

> . . . he was lying upon his back; his eyes were shut; sometimes he opened his mouth: I said, Jack, do you know me? He said, Yes, Will, very well: I said, I am sorry to see you so ill used: he said, Will, I am barbarously used; my heart is broke within me . . .

In his defence, West offered the following account:

> I, my wife, her mother, her sister, her two brothers, and her cousin, when near Holywell Lane . . . unfortunately met . . . these three men; they were all arm in arm, and running, and the deceased Foy run against my wife, and struck her on the breast. I then demanded the reason of it, a blow

immediately followed; one took my wife by the arm and snatched her off the pavement. I ran towards her, and two of them took me by the collar. I had a handkerchief tied round my neck, they got hold of it, and one on one hand, and the other on the other, squeezed my handkerchief round so that I could hardly speak, I could not utter any words. My wife screamed and cried out for the watch [i.e. watchmen], upon which some of my company that were behind came up to my assistance. I struck one of them, and then this Fynes blasted his eyes and swore the most bitter oaths, and then struck me. I was obliged to strike him, and do the best I could till the watch came up; then I gave charge of this Fynes, seeing him first: then they gave charge of me. The watchman took hold of me, and there was he with his fist over their shoulders and d - n - g and swearing at me, and wanted to get at me all the way to the watch-house, and abused us: he called my wife's mother old bawd, and said that my sister and all were a parcel of whores. The constable said, if he would not be easy he would put him in the cage . . . My wife had been ill almost five months. She was brought to bed about five months before this. The surgeon told her he did not know whether her arm would not be cut off. I had hold of her right arm, they came slap against us, and turned us out both against the houses.

Both parties, then, accused each other of being the instigators and escalators of the violence. But the circumstances of Foy's death clearly won the jury's sympathy, and West and Paris were found guilty and sentenced to death. Nothing was proved against Randall. Despite evidence that he had brandished a cudgel, he was acquitted and – no doubt feeling lucky to be alive – might well have enjoyed a night of celebration in 24 Elder Street. On the other hand he might have been in shock, trembling at the thought of his former drinking companions hanging on the gallows.

Clearly, Spitalfields in the second half of the eighteenth century could be a volatile place, but West's mention of the 'watch' shows that it was not wholly lawless. The quality of life in Elder Street at that time is suggested by the draft Act of Parliament of 1759 that aimed to raise local taxes to light, cleanse and 'watch' the streets of the Liberty of Norton Folgate (see page 235).[18] The local taxes were to pay for a beadle, six nightwatchmen, the daily collection of rubbish and a handsome array of globular street lamps, fixed to houses or standing on stanchions. In June 1759 the minute books record that twenty-eight residents (presumably trustees) were present at a meeting and 'resolved' to employ a beadle at £20 per annum. The beadle was to 'set the watch, attend at the watch house, attend collectors in collecting ye rates . . . keep the Liberty free of vagabonds and people making a shop to sell fruit etc. . . . keep the book which of the watchmen's turn it is to be on each stand [and] to be a constant resident of the Liberty.' It was also resolved that six watchmen (or charleys) were to be hired at £12 per annum each, and four stands erected. These watchmen were to 'Beat the round every half hour, watch from 9 o'clock in the evening to six in ye morning from Michaelmas to Ladyday, and from 10 in the evening to four in the morning from Ladyday to Michaelmas.' These watchmen were to be supervised by the Constable or his deputy (the beadle) or the Headborough.

A subsequent meeting of occupants of the Liberty determined how its paid workforce was to conduct itself. They were to 'apprehend and detain Malefactors, Rogues, Vagabonds, Disturbers of the Peace and all Persons whom they have just reason to suspect have any evil designs . . . deliver to the Constable or Headborough . . . or the Beadle' and then 'with all convenient speed . . . to . . . some justice or justices of the Peace to be examined and dealt with according to law'. The watchmen were especially instructed to 'apprehend any Person casting the night soil in the street and carry them to the watch house.'

Everyday life in Elder Street must, then, have been relatively orderly, the street well lit and clean, reasonably well policed and with all manner of 'Vagabonds' kept at bay. The only acceptable itinerant visitors were, presumably, street-traders who would regularly pass along selling their wares by means of distinctive song or chanted 'cries'.

That said, at times of unrest – and Spitalfields suffered several bouts of civic commotion during the eighteenth century – the local forces of law and order proved themselves unable to cope, and on occasion the area was wholly given over to the mob.

If contemporary documents reveal snippets about life in Elder Street, so, of course, does the physical evidence of its surviving Georgian houses. Many stand as reminders of their original dual function as both homes and businesses. Number 5 (formerly 14) is a case in point. Built in Elder Street's earliest days, in 1725, as a pair with number 7, which it mirrors, it

Above: *the door of 9/11 Elder Street, 1726, by Thomas Bunce and Thomas Brown. The Doric doorcase, framed by pilasters formed with rustic blocks, was a favoured Spitalfields design.* Below: *the marble fireplace in the ground floor north room of 9/11 Elder Street.*

is two windows wide, but with blocked windows shared between the houses that give a little extra frontage. The front door opens into a partly panelled entrance passage that leads directly to the rear door to the yard. Off this passage, roughly halfway down its length, is the staircase compartment that contains a somewhat cramped newel staircase leading to the upper floors and a winding flight down into the basement. It's an arrangement that has affinities with the lobby-entry plan form found in seventeenth-century vernacular architecture, and with a plan of a terrace house published in 1703 by Joseph Moxon in his *Mechanick Exercises*. The Moxon plan is intended to show a terrace house erected in accordance with the 1667 London Building Act. Number 5, then, is a little archaic for its time – as is confirmed by its use of flat rather than the more newly fashionable segmental window arches.

The basement, well lit, contains two rooms. The front room was without doubt the kitchen. The rear room, without a fireplace, would have been the 'wet' kitchen, where the water supply was organised and other household essentials stored. Until recently the floor was surfaced in utilitarian manner with brick paviours, was cambered to assist drainage and the rear window has steps to help with the manhandling of barrels.

The ground floor has two rooms. Both are fully pine-panelled with standard 'square' panelling, and both also have delicately profiled dado rails and handsome Doric box cornices. The rear room, with its chimney stack set in an angle against the spine and party walls, retains a simple early fire surround. The most striking original decorative detail is the curved-back china cupboard, with shaped shelves and glazed door, that survives in the front room. Another detail, minor but of interest, is an extra small moulding of semi-circular profile added to the corona of the 1725 box cornice. This feature – with evidence that it was once gilded – is a later enrichment that must reflect an occupier's desire to express their wealth, taste or sense of fashion. Certainly it is a sign of affluence.

The pair of first-floor rooms are treated differently. Only the front room is fully panelled, but lacks the extra details of the ground floor. It would seem that these rooms were of less importance than those on the ground floor. So, it must be assumed, the ground floor contained the parlours while the first floor contained the main bedroom and dressing room.

The character of the house changes dramatically above the first floor. The second and third floors have only one utilitarian, unpanelled room per level. In addition the rooms on both storeys are lit by long workshop windows set in the rear elevation, with the second-floor level also having a wide window onto Elder Street. In other words, it would seem clear that the lower three floors of the house were residential while the upper two were 'industrial' – presumably serving as locations for looms or work-shops for the generations of the silk-weaving family who lived and worked in this house. The Middlesex Land Registry document relating to the development of numbers 5 and 7 (formerly 14 and 15) Elder Street confirms that the Tillard building lease for the pair was granted to Thomas Bunce and that the mortgage was first assigned to a weaver, Francis Martell, for £250, with Martell providing a further £337.10.0. to complete the project.[19] Martell seems to have become involved very early on – a move that carried both risk and the potential for considerable profit – and perhaps retained Bunce as the builder.[20] It would also seem that Martell made number 5 his home and perhaps workplace.

The Martell name is attached to this Elder Street development in all three Land Assessments of 1743, 1759 and 1767. In the 1743 assessment a John Hunt is listed as head tenant of number 7 (formerly 15), but in 1759 Jas. Mar-tell is listed as being head tenant of two houses. Jas. Martell, presumably Francis's son, is listed in *A Complete Guide* of 1765 as 'James Martell and Son . . . Merchants' living in Elder Street. Five years later, in March 1770, James sat on a jury at the Middlesex Sessions with two Elder Street neigh-bours, Thomas Taylor and Miles Burkett or Burkitt, for the trial of Charles Hay, who had been accused of stealing a large and valuable parcel of clothes.[21] Another member of the dynasty, Isaac Martell, also lived at number 5 at one point – a silk design signed by him and dated 1757 is now in the collection of the Royal Society of Arts.[22] By 1805, according to the Land Tax of that year, the Martells had finally left 5 Elder Street, replaced as head tenants by either Susannah Moore or Widow Dubois.

My own house, number 15 (formerly 18), has a complex and puzzling building history and its early pattern of occupation is largely undocu-mented. We know that it was built as one of a pair with number 17 by Thomas Bunce in collaboration with Thomas Brown on a sixty-one-year building lease granted on the 28 June 1727 by William Tillard, then recently in charge of the estate's development. We don't know for sure, though, who it was built for. Nor is it entirely clear why the material used and manner of construction should be significantly inferior to the adjoining 9/11 and 13 Elder Street that Bunce and Brown had completed just a few months before. For example, the brick pier dividing number 15 from the adjacent number 13 is only a brick's width, suggesting that instead of building a proper party wall, the builders opted to fix the principal timber beam of number 15 directly on to the flank wall of the next-door house – a potentially very unsound bit of corner-cutting. Nor do we know why the facing bricks are slightly less fine than those of 13, nor why the window jambs are not dressed with red bricks, as was usual in the street. One has to assume that Bunce and Brown were in somewhat straitened circumstances when they started 15 and 17. Perhaps their next-door venture – spatially more ambitious, better detailed – had not delivered the rapid and profitable return on their investment that they had hoped for.

It's also not clear why Bunce and Brown should have chosen to build a pair of houses – both three windows wide – that do not (as is more usual and economical) mirror one another. Both have their front doors in the northern portion of their front elevations and both have their chimney stacks set within their south party walls. It would have been cheaper to construct a single, slightly larger, shared stack. Also puzzling (but admittedly not unprecedented in Spitalfields houses of the 1720s) is why the builders should have opted for a design in which the window heights on all floors (except basements) in both houses are virtually identical – although, as a subtle indication of hierarchy, the ground-floor windows are two bricks deeper than those above. But, combined with the fact that floor-to-ceiling heights in the house are unusually low, it must be assumed that the builders wanted to fit the maximum number of floors into the minimum house volume. It was all, it seems, a matter of money – getting the most for the least expenditure.

One very important clue to the early history of number 15 is provided by its finest external feature: its grand and glorious doorcase, which is quite different from the much more modest and much later door surround now on number 17 and was almost certainly not put there by Bunce and Brown. A few builders operating in Spitalfields – such as Marmaduke Smith and Samuel Worrall on the Wood–Michell Estate and William Goswell on the Tillard Estate – fully completed their speculations, including interiors and external details such as doorcases, and in the process used pioneering mass-production methods to save money and achieve a seemly visual uniformity. But Bunce and Brown appear to have pursued a varied strategy. On 5 and 7 and 9/11 and 13 Elder Street they seem to have finished the houses inside and out – certainly the panelling within each pair is roughly uniform and the doorcases on 9/11 and 13 are similar

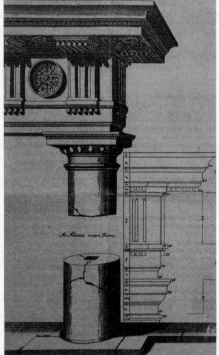

Above: *the doorcase of 15 Elder Street, built in 1727.* Below: *a plate from Evelyn's*
A parallel of the antient architecture with the modern . . . *of 1664 based on de*
Chambray's 1650 publication and seemingly the inspiration for the doorcase.

although not identical. They are of a favoured Spitalfields type – used by Smith, Jonathan Beaumont and others – with Doric pilasters with rusticated shafts framing the door opening and supporting a full Doric entablature, inspired perhaps by such East End and City constructions as Christopher Wren's Temple Bar, designed in 1669. When it came to 15 and 17 Elder Street, however, Bunce and Brown opted for that common early Georgian practice of reducing their capital costs and the financial risk of the speculation by completing the brick shell of the pair, plastering internal walls, installing the floor structure and roof, and then selling on the lease to the first occupier to complete. This explains the huge internal differences between 15 and 17 – and it also suggests very strongly that the responsibility for the doorcase on number 15 does not lie with them but with the house's first occupier.

The door surround – made of soft wood – is, like that on neighbouring 13 Elder Street, an essay in the Doric, but one fashioned with great erudition. Doric pilasters frame the door opening with the door itself set back in a panelled reveal, but here the pilasters are fluted, not rusticated, and the Doric entablature – that is, the ornamented horizontal lintel – they support is finely and delicately detailed. Notably the metope, or rosettes, on the Doric frieze within the entablature are formed by large, beautifully carved flowers; the projecting mutules or blocks on the underside of the cornice are formed with conic-shaped, peg-like drops or guttae; and between the mutules are smaller, delicately carved flowers. All, originally, would have been protected with paint, made with white lead, and almost certainly a pale stone in colour.

This incredible, classically correct and sophisticated design appears to be based on a very specific model. Architectural pattern books were not yet common in the 1720s among London builders – they would soon become so as printing developed and such books became cheaper and more available. But there were books, with inspirational plates, that could be referred to by the more learned. James Gibbs's immensely influential *Book of Architecture* of 1728 was one such (see page 206). Another – more rarefied – was Roland Fréart de Chambray's *Parallèle de l'architecture antique avec la moderne* published in France in 1650. Fréart de Chambray, who had spent some years in Rome and in 1641 published the first French translation of Andrea Palladio's seminal *I quattro libri* of 1570, collected an anthology – the *Parallèle* – of exemplary ancient and modern writers on the classical orders of architecture with the aim of improving 'modern' taste. The book contains a plate of an ideal Doric order – based on an ancient prototype at Albane near Rome – that clearly provides the model for the doorcase on 15 Elder Street. And Fréart de Chambray's book carries a particular message. He praises the Roman architect Vitruvius but criticises the orders the Romans evolved – the Tuscan and Composite – extolling instead the virtues of the three original 'Greek' orders, the Doric, the Ionic and the Corinthian, and claiming divine inspiration for classical architecture by arguing that the Corinthian order had been employed on Solomon's Temple in Jerusalem.

How would a humble Spitalfields joiner have known this book, or had access to it? Probably, of course, the reference was produced by the client – the first occupier or head tenant of 15 Elder Street – who must have been an educated and discriminating individual who desired his home to be adorned with an erudite example of French academic classicism. This comes as no surprise if he was, as in all likelihood, a Huguenot master weaver. But there was also a more local source. The English connoisseur John Evelyn, deeply impressed with Fréart de Chambray's book, translated it into English and published an edition in 1664 entitled *A parallel of the antient architecture with the modern* . . . And the creator of this Elder Street doorcase also must have had a copy of Palladio's *I quattro libri*, because the small carved flowers set below the capitals of its pilasters are derived from the Doric order as illustrated by Palladio.

What was this superb doorcase on 15 Elder Street intended to say? Obviously it expresses taste and cultural aspiration. It is a doorcase fit for a palace. Indeed it even refers to Solomon's Temple, which was then regarded as the greatest building ever made, designed by God Himself and the origin of beauty in architecture. The entrance portal to a man's home could hardly have better credentials.

So who was the first occupier of number 15 – the individual who commissioned the doorcase? We can't be sure. But it's possible that it may have been 'Jas. Payton', who was almost certainly in residence by 1741 and who is listed in the Land Tax records as being head tenant of '2 Houses' – seemingly 15 and 17 – in 1759 and (with his brother John Payton) 1767.[23] An indenture, or agreement – dated August 1741 – between 'Jonathan Troy of London and John Payton of the Liberty of Norton Folgate in the county of Middlesex, Weaver', which possibly relates to Troy becoming Payton's apprentice, also, intriguingly, seems to be related to the original 1727 lease of 15 Elder Street between Brown, Bunce and Tillard. If so, that takes

John Payton's involvement in the house back to the date of its initial construction.[24]

Payton was a man of some eminence. He was a 'shag weaver' (shag is a coarse, rough-woven silk, rather like plush but with a stiffer nap) and almost certainly a Huguenot. In addition he was a trustee for the Norton Folgate Court House (effectively, the town hall of the nine or so acres of the self-governing Liberty) in 1744,[25] and of sufficient wealth and standing to undertake to raise a body of forty-seven of his workmen – a considerable number – to resist the 'Young Pretender' in 1745 if the Jacobite army got as far south as London.[26] At some point between 1743 and 1745 it looks as though he moved next door, to number 17, leaving his brother James to occupy number 15.

The Paytons' involvement with Elder Street seems to have lasted until the 1770s (the will of Elizabeth Payton, widow, of the Liberty of Norton Folgate, was proved on 19 February 1770).[27] By 1777, though, their name is no longer listed as being in residence as merchants in the generally reliable *Kent's Directory*. The Land Tax assessments of 1785 show one Philip Gross in occupation of 15 Elder Street. We can never be absolutely sure what their early connection with the house was, but it does seem pretty certain that either John Payton, or possibly his brother James, commissioned the doorcase for number 15. And it is tempting to imagine – if the Peytons were indeed Huguenots – that Roland Fréart de Chambray's publication was a family heirloom, as well as a source of artistic inspiration, that had been carried to England when the family fled their native France.

It may seem strange that men of such apparent wealth and local prestige should have occupied two of the smaller houses in the south portion of Elder Street. Both numbers 15 and 17 were built just one room deep (until recent years 17 still possessed only one room per floor and has a very simple interior, with old-fashioned, vernacular panelling formed by tall panes set between flat posts or muntins).[28] But houses were expensive in early-eighteenth-century London and to possess even a modest but modern one was a notable sign of affluence. Moreover, number 15 was soon extended. In the front rooms of each floor beams visibly span between the party walls, and are set slightly off-centre towards the rear elevation. This offset was presumably to help define a volume for a newel staircase rising in a rear corner of the house, as conceived when it was to be only one room deep. Such a staircase survives in 17 Elder Street. But this beam must also have been intended to house a partition, if one was desired, to divide each upper-floor room to create a small front room and an even smaller rear room (such an arrangement exists at second-floor level within the one-room-deep 17 and 19 Elder Street).[29] The intention to place partitions to divide some of the upper-floor rooms is also suggested by the placing of the chimney breasts in 15 and 17 Elder Street. They are off-centre on the party walls, tending towards the front elevation, but would be central to a room defined by the front elevation and a partition set below the floor beam.

It is evident, however, that the first occupant of 15 thought the house as built far too modest for his ambitions and requirements and therefore had an additional rear room added at each floor level, to create a ten-room house. This was done in a structurally modest and most economical manner. The brick-built rear wall was left to act as a partition; window openings were extended down to floor level and made into doors; and the new rear portion of the house was constructed entirely of wood. A structural frame of pine posts and joists – prefabricated in traditional manner with joints marked for erection with Roman numerals – was clad externally with pine clapboard and internally with pine panelling at lower-floor levels and lath and plaster at upper levels. This extension contains the house's handsome staircase, which, like the panelling in the rear rooms, clearly dates from the late 1720s. At some point in the nineteenth century the clapboard on the extension's rear elevation was replaced with brick.

Further proof of the relative affluence of 15 Elder Street's first occupant is the level of rent he had to pay. It has been calculated that the cost of constructing the house was £180 but that its 'value', after its rear extension had been completed, was around £250, with an annual rentable value of around £18 (admittedly this construction cost was relatively little when compared with the £600–700 that Isaac Ware in his *Complete Body of Architecture* of 1756 claimed it cost to build the 'Common' London house).[30] Surviving eighteenth-century budgets suggest that, on average, about one-eighth of an annual income in London went on rent.[31] So the occupant of 15 Elder Street would have to have been worth (after taxes) about £145 per year. This was a lot of money when in the 1720s a journeyman building tradesman would have earned around £45 per year, a sum which the annual earnings of a highly skilled journeyman weaver might have matched in the boom years around 1760, though by the mid to late 1760s the average journeyman weaver earned only £15–26 a year.[32] So the house could only have been occupied by someone of the financial

The stair balustrade and newel, at ground-floor level, in 15 Elder Street, c.1727.

status of a highly skilled master weaver, who in the early eighteenth century earned enough to afford the rent and upkeep of the property.[33]

Internally the enlarged house was finished to a good standard. The
front basement room was the 'dry' kitchen, and was furnished with a
stone-flagged floor (fragments of which survive) and a splendid dresser,
with a top surface supported on diminutive Doric columns and sinuous
sideboards supporting shelves. This front basement room would originally
have housed a cooking range. The rear basement room has no fireplace
and must have been intended for storage. It was clearly a very utilitarian
room, used originally for water storage, for washing plates, cooking uten-
sils and clothes. It was the 'wet' kitchen.

The most elegant part of the house is the ground floor. Its entrance passage is fully panelled, with flat panelling set in frames formed by rails, stiles
and muntins, all embellished with ovolo, or quadrant-moulded edges, and
joined with pegs. A Doric box cornice tops the panelling and a pair of plain
pilasters – with rudimentary Doric capitals – mark the junction of the
entrance passage with the staircase compartment. The ground-floor front
room has panelling of similar design, as does the adjoining rear room. Both
are furnished with Doric cornices, but in the front room these have an additional dentil course, marking this room as the best in the house, a status
confirmed by the fact that its floor-to-ceiling height is slightly more generous than that of the floors above. It probably contained the best parlour – made
into a dining room by simply opening a gate-leg dining table. The first-floor
room above could have been another parlour or reception room but was
probably the best bedroom with a dressing room to the rear.

As a key feature of the house that all visitors would have seen, the portion of the staircase that reaches from the ground floor to the first half
landing is, appropriately, the most ornate. It is organised as a straight
flight with the balusters – formed with twisted columns set on tablets and
gadrooned urns – arranged as a fashionable open-string construction.
Once beyond the view of the visitor, however, the staircase starts losing its
grandeur. The columns on the stretch from the half landing to the first
floor are no longer twisted, and thereafter as the staircase ascends the
house further, serving rooms for family or servants alone, it gets yet more
basic and more old-fashioned.

The wall panelling of the higher floors not only reveals their humbler
original functions but also shows that, as a rule, front rooms were more
important than rear rooms. Thus, for example, the front room on the first

floor, like the staircase compartment on the landing, is lined with ovolo-moulded panelling, and has a full box cornice; but the rear room, while it, too, has a box cornice, is lined with flat panelling with no ovolo. On the second floor the front room has flat panelling with no ovolo and no full box cornice while the rear room has only half-panelling. And the third-floor rooms possess no panelling at all, except for the partition between rear room and staircase, which has plank and muntin panelling of vernacular, seventeenth-century type.

This top floor was probably intended as a workshop, its large windows letting in plenty of light for those weaving or otherwise toiling there. A wide opening originally linked the first and front rooms, which suggests that they were used as one. The floor level of the rear room is slightly lower than that of the front and the fact that this should be the case says much about the very economical way in which the rear extension was built. A proper roof truss on the rear extension would have been more expensive than the option the builders actually went for: a shallow mono-pitch that is a continuation of the rear slope of the roof over the main house. This sloping mono-pitch roof – known colloquially and for obvious reasons as a 'cat-slide roof' – gives the rear room a sloping ceiling and reduces ceiling height. So to gain a little extra headroom the floor level of the room has been lowered. The top rear room has a fairly large and wide casement window, again suggesting workroom use. Indeed the very roof form appears to proclaim light industrial use for cat-slide roofs are (or were) a common feature of the rear portions of houses built partly for weaving use, for example 5 and 7 Elder Street and 3 and 5 Club Row of 1764–5. Within a nineteenth-century fixed cupboard in the third-floor front room is a blocked door leading into 17 Elder Street – evidence of the shared occupation of 15 and 17 Elder Street in the mid eighteenth century by the Payton family.

The plot of 15 Elder Street measures around seventeen feet by forty, with the house itself now being just under thirty feet deep. As originally conceived it would have occupied almost half the plot, with the yard occupying the remainder. The yard would no doubt have been paved and largely utilitarian, although Horwood's map of 1799–1819 suggests a garden. What is certain is that the yard contained a latrine in the form of an outhouse placed over a cesspit. There may indeed have been two, one in each corner. One survives in the south-east corner of the yard. There would also, no doubt, have been fuel-storage bins (the houses in Elder Street do not possess coal vaults) and butts for storing rainwater. The house could have been connected to a commercial water-supply company for a certain number of hours each week.

Throughout the house there are reminders of the way in which it evolved over the years, as each new generation adapted it to their particular needs. The most immediately visible are the two blocked windows, at first- and second-floor levels. Sometimes windows were blocked from the start and were there simply to give the building a pleasing rhythm. The blocked window at first-floor level between 5 and 7 Elder Street, for example, could never have been open because it straddles the party wall. But this is not the case with 15: the fact that both these windows were once fully functioning is confirmed by the vertical straight joints in the panelling behind. They must therefore have been blocked to avoid the payment of Window Tax.

This was a property tax, dating from 1696 and based on the simple notion that the richer you were the bigger your house must be, and the bigger the house the more windows it must have. It was an almost brutally simple tax in conception. In application, though, it was fairly complex and fluid. Houses were charged a flat rate of two shillings tax per window and an additional sum based on the number of windows. Houses with ten to twenty windows had to pay an additional four shillings and houses with over twenty windows an additional eight. Naturally the number of houses with ten or twenty windows decreased rapidly because to fall below the tax threshold it was only necessary to block one window. Perhaps significantly 15 Elder Street seems to have had nineteen windows when built. In response to the blocking of windows and to retain tax revenue, the threshold for additional tax payments was lowered in 1766 to include houses with seven windows or more. After 1778 the tax became linked to the value of the house rather than its size, and so was often calculated in relation to Land Tax; and in 1825 the threshold for the additional level of taxation was raised to houses of eight windows or more. It is reasonable to assume that windows in 15 Elder Street were blocked subsequent to its completion in an attempt to avoid tax.

Inside, brass mounts and levers at first- and second-floor levels show that at some point in the very late eighteenth or early nineteenth century a wire-operated system of bells was added. Clearly, at this time, the house contained a family or families with servants. Other internal evidence, however, reveals that these days of elegance were relatively short-lived. The first-floor rear room contained within its fireplace a mid- to late-nineteenth-century cast-iron cooking range, with oven and hot

An early-nineteenth-century fire surround and cast-iron grate in the third-floor front room of 15 Elder Street. The top bars on the grate hinge to make a cooking surface.

plates (a similar range survives in the ground-floor room of 19 Elder Street). An early-nineteenth-century cast-iron hob grate set within a simple fire surround can be found in the front room of the top floor. The grate has a grille that hinges flat to create a cooking surface. Presumably this had become a bed/sitting room, with cooking potential, in a multi-occupied house. And, as the years of multi-occupation continued, the throngs of people pounding up and down the staircase – some in working men's hobnailed boots – gradually tore away at its treads. In time, those on the flight of steps up to second-floor level wore out completely and were crudely replaced with planks.

Who some of these later tenants were is indicated by the pinholes, set at a diagonal, that can still be seen on the reveal of the front door, and on door architraves on the ground and first floors, which mark where mezuzahs were once fixed. Mezuzahs are hollow cylinders containing prayer scrolls that fulfil the biblical command that the faithful fix the Shema – a passage from the Torah – on the door 'posts' of their houses. The texts written on the scrolls are taken from Deuteronomy, 6:4–9, and 11:13–21: 'Hear, O Israel, the Lord our God is one Lord. And thou shalt love the Lord thy God with all thine heart, and with all thy soul, and with all thy might. And these words . . . shall be in thine heart . . . And thou shalt write them upon the posts of thy house, and on thy gates . . .' In Jewish households it is customary to fix a mezuzah next to a house's main doors (sometimes just the front door) where it can be touched upon entry in similitude of prayer. These mezuzahs, as census records reveal (see appendix), must have been fixed in the house some time after 1880.

And then, in the second-floor front room, is something altogether more enigmatic. Here, roughly square notches have at some point been cut on the outer edge of the inner leaves of the window shutters. When the shutters are closed the notches form informal peepholes, allowing the occupant of the room to watch – unseen – the windows of the house opposite, or to scrutinise, without attracting attention, a portion of the pavement. I suppose they can be seen as part of the security of the house – permitting limited observation of the immediate area without revealing the spy and provoking retaliation.

But there could be more to it than that. This second-floor room has long served as my bedroom, and one morning when I first opened my eyes I saw an image on the panelled wall opposite the windows. At first there appeared nothing out of the ordinary about it, but then I realised that it was a

perfect, sharply focused – but inverted – image of a second-floor window of
the house opposite. Whether by accident or intention the notches cut in the
shutter leaves formed a perfect *camera obscura*, projecting a powerful image
when the shutters were closed and the room darkened. Since the front-
room windows of 15 Elder Street face west, the light cast by the rising sun
has to bounce off the glass of the windows opposite, which would have
required a degree of ingenuity on the part of any would-be creator of a
camera obscura here. Such ingenuity, however, would not have been beyond
a member of the Spitalfields Mathematical Society – or another of the area's
learned societies – who might once have occupied this room.

Using buildings – their form, mass or materials of construction – as
pieces of large-scale scientific apparatus to conduct experiments was
familiar practice in the seventeenth and early eighteenth centuries. Sir
Christopher Wren and Robert Hooke, in their design of the Monument
in the City, managed to contrive an open-well staircase that could house
a zenith telescope and be used for gravity and pendulum experiments, while
the evenly spaced steps – each six inches high – could be used for barometric
pressure studies. Wren probably also had some scientific ideas in mind
when he created the 'whispering gallery' within the drum supporting the
dome of St Paul's Cathedral. It's tempting to think that, in its more modest way, the second-floor front room of 15 Elder Street played a part in the
intellectual life of Georgian London.

As the nineteenth century approached several generations had come and
gone since Elder Street was first conceived. Most of the surnames recorded
in the 1794 Land Tax assessment (which survives only in part for Elder
Street) are unfamiliar from earlier records: Sam Murdock, Rob Bottle,
Sam Frith, Richard Jones, Thomas Cockshead, Richard Spindellow, Ed.
Smith, J. Jessie, J. Barker, Peter Dubois. The street, though, was still prosperous. Analysis of the Land Tax assessment for 1805 suggests that 19
Elder Street, to take one example, was home to Samuel Prosser 'Gent'[34] –
possibly the same man as the Samuel Prosser who, according to the Old
Bailey proceedings of a trial on 12 April 1809, owned a shop in Bedford-
bury (Covent Garden) from which Catherine Hagan, aged thirty-two,
stole seven yards of kerseymere cloth, valued at £4. The prisoner offered
no evidence in her defence, nor did she call character witnesses. Consequently she was found guilty, confined to fourteen days in Newgate and

fined one shilling. And Prosser – 'woollen draper and man's mercer' – recovered his valuable kerseymere (fine woollen cloth with fancy
twill weave).[35] Samuel Prosser also emerges as a member of a jury at a
coroner's inquest on 23 October 1799 considering a suspicious death near
Leicester Fields.[36] If the two men are indeed one and the same as the connection between Spitalfields and cloth retailing would seem to suggest,
then Prosser was clearly a man of some substance: for an individual to be
eligible for jury service he needed a certain respectability and reliability.

An insurance policy for 19 Elder Street from the Sun Insurance Company dated 16 April 1808, and covering the period to Lady Day 1809, would
seem to confirm Samuel Prosser's standing in the community.[37] Its valuation of the house and contents runs as follows:

Samuel Prosser, at no 20 [i.e. now 19] Elder Street Spitalfields – Gent.
On his household goods in his now dwelling house only situated as aforesaid
Brick, not exceeding One Hundred Pounds:
Printed Books therein only not exceeding Thirty Pounds
Wearing Apparel therein only not exceeding Thirty Pounds
Plate therein only not exceeding Twenty Pounds
China and Glass therein only not exceeding Twenty Pounds.
Total value. Two hundred pounds.
W. C. Shawe F. Ladbroke C. G. Thornton [assessors].

The value of the contents, equal to the value of the house, seems high, suggesting that Prosser lived in some style. As for the house itself, valued at
£100, it was probably in 1809 worth little more than 50 per cent of its original construction cost. Still standing today, it's a fine five-storey and
five-room brick house built as one of a pair with 21, on a sixty-one-year
lease dated 28 June 1727 from William Tillard to Jonathan Beaumont, citizen and mason. Externally, it possesses some of the details favoured by the
English Baroque: the façade is framed by pilaster strips, and the windows
have fluted keystones and stone sills supported by ornamental stone brackets. Inside, it is finished in handsome style, with a high-quality raised and
fielded overmantel to the fireplace of its first-floor room and fine sculptural
stone fire surround, suggesting that this, rather than the ground-floor
room, was originally intended to be the grandest in the house. It's tempting
to think that the craftsman who created such an outstanding fire surround
was influenced by Hawksmoor's work at Christ Church. Whatever the
case, eighty years later, the house retained its appeal for the well-to-do.

By the time of the 1831 Land Tax assessment number 19 was occupied by John Troake, whose name still survives, in signwriter's hand, next to the house's front door, along with the old house number – 20 – and his trade: 'Straw Chip & Leghorn Presser' (these are types of straw used for hats and bonnets, Leghorn – from Livorno, Italy – being a high-quality fine smooth straw popular in the Regency for ladies' bonnets). Presumably Troake not only lived in the house but also traded from it – either selling ready-made bonnets or more likely wholesaling straw into the hat trade or even making bonnets on the premises. This occupation was not unusual for early-nineteenth-century Spitalfields where milliners were relatively common. Judging from contemporary commercial directories, John Troake had been in business for some time before the 1831 Land Tax assessment. For example he is listed as of 20 Elder Street in *Pigot and Co's London and Provincial New Commercial Directory for 1828–9* under 'Straw, Leghorn, etc, Hat Bleachers and Pressers'. Troake is not listed in *Johnstone's London Commercial Guide* of August 1817, suggesting he arrived after this date. But it can't have been long after because the style in which the trade sign is written is suggestive. The middle 's' in 'Presser' is written as an 'f' – implying a Regency, i.e. pre-1820 date. The fact that the sign has been renewed suggests that Troake traded from this house for some time.

Silk weavers still lived in Elder Street during the era in which Troake took up residence. And they were still reasonably well-to-do. A Sun Insurance policy and valuation, dated 27 July 1815, for number 6 (now 26) is indicative of the kind of wealth they could build up. Listing the possessions of Francis Hewitt the valuation states:

> On his household goods, wearing apparel, printed books and Plate in his now dwelling house only situate aforesaid. Brick, one hundred and eighty pounds. £180.
>
> China and glass therein only twenty pounds. £20.
>
> Stock utensils and goods in trust therein only seven hundred pounds £700.
>
> Total value: £900.[38]

Francis Hewitt's occupation is confirmed by *The Post Office Annual Directory* of 1815, which lists him as a 'Silk-weaver' of '6 Elder-street, Norton-falgate'.

The 1805 Land Tax assessment records that Joseph Neale was head tenant of 18 Elder Street (now 15), who in *Kent's Directory* of 1800 is listed as a

'Weaver' of 28 Spital Square, while the 1812 Land Tax assessment records that 14 Elder Street (now number 5), once the home of the Martell silk-weaving family, was occupied by William Symonds or Symons, also part of a silk-weaving family. Nearly thirty years later the family were still there, the 1841 census recording that the 'head' of the family in 14 Elder Street was Mary Symons, then aged fifty-five, who is described as a 'Silk Weaver' (given her age then, she might well have been in residence in 1812, too). Also present was William Symons, aged twenty-five, probably Mary's son, and like her a 'Silk Weaver'. So it seems that this house, pur-pose-designed in 1725 for weaving with its two upper floors organised as well-lit workshops, remained a silk weaver's residence as long as the trade lasted in Spitalfields.

It's a similar picture with 1 (now 36) Elder Street. 'Jno. Gammon' lived there at the time of the 1828 Land Tax assessment, and he was still there when the 1841 census-taker visited and recorded him as a silk weaver. The house retains a weaving garret, which was presumably used by Gammon as his place of work. Other silk weavers living and working in Elder Street recorded in *Johnstone's London Commercial Guide*, 'corrected' or updated to 1 May 1818, were: Richard Horsley, silk-trimming manufacturer at number 8 (the now-demolished 22); Tharp & Bradley, silk weavers at number 9 (the demolished 20); and Nicolas Racine, silk manufacturer, at number 21 (still numbered 21).

People with occupations allied to the weaving trade also lived in the street. A policy and valuation with the Sun Insurance, dated to Christmas 1803 and relating to a building later destroyed to make way for Commer-cial Street, reveals that it was taken out by one 'Joshua Hopkins in Elder Street Spitalfields, Dyer'.[39] The valuation reads: 'On his Millwork, stock, Liquor Back and Pump in his open shed, timber, and open Yard adjoining in Quaker Street Spitalfields not exceeding four hundred pounds – £400.' Hopkins also had possession of, and insured, 'Two Houses and Offices adjoining in Fleur de Lis Court near Wheeler [sic] Street in the tenure of no hazardous Trades. Brick not exceeding one Hundred Pounds on each – £200.' The £600 valuation was signed by C. Berrick, W. Hamilton and J. Chake. The premium Hopkins had to pay on this is not mentioned.

But what early-nineteenth-century records further show is that by now a wide range of people from other professions or skilled trades were also living in Elder Street. The 1812 Land Tax assessment shows that number

13 (formerly 17) was occupied by Jno. Wallen, a surveyor and architect also based at 4 Spital Square in partnership with George Ferry.[40] Wallen was a pupil of D. A. Alexander, the civil engineer, architect and designer of the London Dock from 1796 to 1820 and Dartmoor gaol in 1806–9 for French prisoners-of-war; one of Wallen's many pupils was Horace Jones, who was to become City architect and designer of Tower Bridge and Smithfield Market.[41] In 1813 Wallen and his partner Ferry worked on repairs to the Norton Folgate workhouse.[42] According to *Johnstone's London Commercial Guide*, 'corrected' to 1 May 1818, a solicitor named Stephen Auber lived in number 2 (now 34); Elaine Valentine & Co., Dry Salter was at number 7 (now 24, with a yard behind reached by the large arch); William Hind fancy-trimmings manufacturers were in number 13 (the demolished 3); Joseph Bouen, chair manufacturer, was living in number 15 (now 7), and Joseph Steel, painter and glazier, was based in number 18 (now 15).[43]

A similar picture emerges from the 1841 census. But by this time something else was happening, too: the houses were starting to become more densely occupied. Thus, for example, 15 Elder Street (formerly 18) is listed as containing twelve people on the day of the census, probably organised in two separate households. One of these families was headed by Ebenezer Swain, a fifty-year-old painter. His twenty-year-old son Joseph was an engraver, who pioneered the precise reproduction of artists' work and set up business in the house. In 1842 he was made manager of the engraving department at *Punch* magazine.

There must still have been a sense of community in Elder Street at this time, for some people stayed for quite a long time and so presumably got to know each other well. The 'Straw Chip & Leghorn Presser' John Troake is one example; the painter and glazier Joseph Steel another.[44] But Elder Street's growing population and the humbler trades pursued by some of its newer incumbents were indications of things to come. In the 1820s, though, its fall from grace was still some years away.

TEN

SPITALFIELDS' DARK UNDERBELLY

Crime and Riot in the Eighteenth Century

Disputes between masters, business entrepreneurs and the workforce of journeymen weavers characterised life in Spitalfields from the very earliest days of the industry. As Lindsey German and John Rees point out, 'The silk weavers were among the most pugnacious sections of London society, strongly organised to protect their trade and repeatedly forced to defend themselves'.[1] In August 1675 – even before Huguenots had arrived in significant numbers – London silk weavers rioted against the introduction of new machines and production techniques and against 'strangers', who it was feared were working for lower wages than generally agreed and had not completed proper apprenticeships: the Venetian ambassador reported a rumour that 'they were going to massacre all the French'.[2] The riot lasted three days, during which mobs of weavers roamed the City and Spitalfields smashing machine looms and occasionally abusing and assaulting – but not fatally – their perceived French rivals. Some were said to have worn green aprons or carried sea-green banners – a colour with radical political connotations since it had been the emblem of the republican Levellers, who had been active during and immediately after the Civil War. The authorities were, not surprisingly, deeply worried. But, as it turned out, whatever revolutionary aspect the riots might have possessed, nothing significant materialised.[3]

Just over two decades later, in 1697, riots broke out again, this time aimed against the import of foreign silks. Weavers lobbied Parliament, laid siege to the Leadenhall Street headquarters of the East India Company, a major importer of woven silk and cotton from India (which represented clear competition for London-woven silk), and threatened to destroy the home of Sir Josiah Child, the fabulously wealthy and ambitious Governor of the Company.

The spirit of ruthless exploitation on the part of masters and capitalist entrepreneurs at the top end of the industry and their relentless quest for profits help explain one the paradoxes of life in eighteenth-century Spitalfields. Even during the 'Golden Ages' of silk weaving, roughly the seventy years after 1690 and the two decades after 1800, there was not only great wealth evident in the area but also, lurking in the shadows, the spectres of poverty, distress and dissent that in a moment could be expressed in sudden and tumultuous upheaval.[4] There was also the brooding indignation of workers against unscrupulous masters and the forces of authority that supported them. As in the 1670s and 1690s this indignation could, and occasionally did, flare into riot and serious violence. The immediate spark might often be a fear of unemployment, but the burning and no doubt justified sense of oppression and inequality was constant.

Fear of unemployment could be ignited by one of two factors. It might be spurred by the introduction by masters of new labour-saving technology that would result in fewer journeymen being employed. Or, even more futile than this Luddite protest in the face of inevitable change, it could be set off by a public change of taste or by its desire for cheaper fabrics. Thus, for example, in 1719 the Spitalfields weavers, worried by a slump in their trade, rioted against the dramatically increasing popularity of cheaper and washable Indian-made cotton fabric (called calico because by tradition it was woven in Calicut, south-west India). Essentially they wanted the import of foreign-made fabrics controlled and were willing to intimidate consumers and Parliament to achieve this goal.

The 1719 riots also show how easily and speedily protests could get out of hand in a city that had virtually no police force beyond parish constables, nightwatchmen and beadles, and where, if things escalated, the only option for the authorities was to call in the military. On 13 June around 4,000 weavers paraded through the streets of Spitalfields and the City, protesting against the import of cheap cotton. Soon, however, the protest turned nasty, as demonstrators started to unleash their fear and fury on innocent bystanders. Before long all women encountered wearing calico or muslin dresses, or even linen – indeed anything other than silk – were subject to attack, generally by having their dresses torn off or doused in ink or in corrosive *aqua fortis*, a liquid used in alchemical experiments that contained nitric acid. The Lord Mayor therefore had to call out the City's trained bands and the Horse Grenadiers to suppress the weavers, and the Riot Act, recently passed in 1714 in response to a series of major civil disturbances, was read in an attempt to disperse seemingly threatening crowds.[5] Large numbers of disgruntled weavers also gathered in Old Palace Yard, Westminster, hoping to put pressure on Parliament to support the silk industry by passing protectionist legislation that would reduce the quantity of calico imported. Here they accosted peers as they passed into the House of Lords and begged them 'to commiserate the poor weavers'. Parliament, however, responded much as the City had done and called for military protection. When the Horse Guards arrived the weavers dispersed, but not before they had 'unrigg'd a few Callico Ladies'.[6]

During these widespread disturbances numbers of rioters were arrested and taken to the Marshalsea prison. Soon an excited mob had gathered outside and proceeded to attack the prison, seeking to free the demonstrators held there. More troops were called from Whitehall. They fired blank cartridges to no significant effect. Then a soldier – perhaps fearful for his safety – fired a ball and three rioters were wounded. The protests subsided. Over the next few days the authorities attempted to make arrests, but conclusive evidence against specific individuals was seemingly hard to obtain, and eventually just four members of the mob were arrested. They were committed to Newgate for riot, with two of their number additionally charged with felony for tearing the gown off one Mrs Beckett.[7]

The spur for the riots was the growing ubiquity of cheap calico. But the demonstrators had other concerns too. Women were not only spending their money on cheaper material, but, along with their children, were also increasingly competing with men for jobs in the weaving industry. Moreover, London's silk weavers faced competition – as they had in the sixteenth and seventeenth centuries – from country weavers moving to the capital in hope of higher pay. As one agitating pamphleteer asked provocatively in 1719: 'How many country weavers come daily to town, and turn their hands to different kinds of work than that they were brought up to?'[8]

In the years after the riots, continued but lower-level agitation was accompanied by more considered lobbying, such as the publication in 1721 of a broadsheet entitled *The Spittle-Fields ballad: or, the weavers' complaint against the calico madams*.[9] The result was a modicum of success: in the same year as *The Spittle-Fields ballad* was published the Calico Acts – in existence since 1690 to control the import of cotton fabric – were reinforced by an Act[10] that, to protect the native weaving industry, prohibited the sale of most cottons, with the exception of thread and raw cotton, and effectively banned the wearing of this fabric.[11] Where violent and lawless riot had failed, satire and the pen had succeeded.

Daniel Defoe, writing immediately after the riots, offered some observations on the whole affair. In a pamphlet published in 1719 he broadly supported the aims of the weavers but deplored their methods. As he put it, 'had the poor Weavers . . . brought their Complaints against the exorbitant Wearing of Calicoes in regular and justifiable manner [they] would, perhaps, have met with more Friends.' But, Defoe explained in their defence, 'the Weavers suffer under the general Calamity of Trade [and] they, and even the whole Manufacturing part of the Nation, are oppres'd by the exorbitant growth of clandestine Trade, and the unreasonable pouring in of East-India Wrought Goods upon us.' Defoe, in part, blamed the all-consuming power of whimsical fashion, which – he argued – resulted in a people acting against their own long-term interest. It's an interesting observation that echoes through the ages. Defoe told his readers that:

> . . . the Humour of the People, *as too often is the Fate of Nations*, seem'd, at that time, possess'd against their interest, and being hurry'd down the Stream of their Fancy, they ran headlong into the greatest Neglect and Contempt of the Growth and Manufactures of their own Country and People, and embrac'd, with a Violence in their Temper, not to be resisted, the Silks and Callicoes of India, in a manner even ridiculous to themselves, as well as fatal to their Interest . . . Ladies converted their Carpets and Quilts into Gowns and Petticoats . . . and dress'd more like the Merry-Andrews [clowns] of Bartholomew-Fair, than the Ladies and the Wives of a Trading People.

The consequence was 'the Ruin of our Manufactures . . . the stagnation of our Trade, the stop of Employment, and the starving of our Poor.' The outcry was 'universal' and justified and Defoe pointed out that 'not the Spittle-fields Weavers only, felt it; the Calamity was general . . .' His view was that the government could and should intervene to protect the trade, pointing out that in the past 'no sooner was the Flux of foreign Manufactures stopp'd, and the East-India Goods prohibited, but the trade reviv'd.' His wish was granted for, as we have seen, the Calico Acts were indeed strengthened in 1721 to reduce the import of woven cotton.[12]

But the tranquillity that this protectionist legislation ushered in did not last for long. Attempts by the masters to maintain low wages in a commercial enterprise where profits had become uncertain persisted. And then a new cause of conflict started to make itself felt. Irish immigrants had been coming to London since the early seventeenth century. In the early 1730s, their numbers sharply increased.[13]

Ireland, like England, had gained from the exodus of Huguenots from France in the late seventeenth century, but in Ireland's case it was not a silk industry that was enriched and extended but a long-standing linen industry that was given new life. A key figure here was Louis Crommelin from Armancourt in Picardy. After the Revocation of the Edict of Nantes in 1685 he took refuge in the Netherlands where his personality, skills and practical business acumen so impressed the Prince of Orange that, when he came to the throne of Britain as William III, he persuaded Crommelin to move to Ireland to improve its linen industry. Crommelin arrived in Lisburn in 1698 as 'Director of the Royal Manufactories of Irish Textiles', set about his task with energy and in 1711 helped establish the Board of Trustees of the Linen Manufactures of Ireland, with statutory power to nurture and control the industry.

But whereas the efforts of Crommelin's fellow Huguenots in England generally benefited the wider community, in Ireland linen-weaving was very much a Protestant-owned and -managed concern and those who gained tended, by and large, to be members of the Protestant community. It was, of course, no mere chance that Crommelin chose to settle just a few miles outside Belfast, in the secure and Protestant-friendly Lisburn in the heart of Protestant Ulster.

The country's native Roman Catholics, by contrast, found themselves an increasingly disadvantaged majority. Persecuted since the sixteenth century, their sufferings increased dramatically after the Protestant William III's victories over the Catholic James II at the Battle of the Boyne in 1690 and the Battle of Aughrim in 1691. The unequal nature of the 'Settlement' that followed is made crystal clear by a few statistics. In 1688 – at the time of James II's flight from his throne – Catholics retained 22 per cent of the land in Ireland. Confiscations following the Protestant triumph of the 1690s reduced the proportion to 14 per cent. By 1776 Arthur Young, the agricultural improver and avid collector of social statistics, estimated that Catholics possessed only 5 per cent of the land despite representing 75 per cent of the population.[14]

Matters for the native population were made even worse by the operation of anti-Catholic legislation that sought to subjugate them totally – to rob them of power, dignity and civil rights and to make them, in every sense, second-class citizens in their own land. For contemporary Protestants, this represented an elemental battle to the death between not only two religions, but between two different peoples and cultures – as the Protestant Bishop of Derry wrote, 'either they or we must be ruined'.[15] In 1695 the Irish Parliament initiated a Penal 'Code' aimed at preventing the 'Further Growth of Popery' that prohibited Catholics from 'bearing arms, educating their children and owning any horse above £5 in value'.[16] In 1704 it went a step further, voting to banish monks and friars from the land, and allowing Catholic priests to remain only if they were 'registered' with the Protestant authorities. Since being registered usually meant the priests were obliged to take an oath – imposed in 1710 – to abjure the authority of the Pope, they were effectively left with the choice of staying and being spiritually impotent or leaving the country and so abandoning their flocks. The majority chose to stay but not to register, and so they became illegal. The punishment proposed for them was extraordinary. In 1719 the Irish Privy Council explained: 'The Commons [of the Irish Parliament] proposed the marking of every priest who shall be convicted of being an unregistered priest . . . remaining in this Kingdom after 1st May 1720 with a large "P" to be made with a red hot iron on the cheek. The council generally disliked that punishment, and have altered it into that of castration which they are persuaded will be the more effectual remedy.'[17] Fortunately this absurdly barbarous proposal did not become law.

The final Penal Law, passed in 1728, deprived Catholics of the vote. It was the terminal blow to their ambitions. They were left with few chances for wealth, social eminence, higher education and political power in their native land. They could not buy land, could not hold leases running more than thirty-one years, and, if they did own an estate, on their death had to divide it equally amongst their sons. They could not join the legal profession or achieve high rank in the army. All public offices were closed to them. They were, effectively, left to remain in ignorant subjugation so as to provide servants and labourers for the Protestant elite. The only opportunity left open for the most enterprising Catholics with capital or access to funds (and there were very few of them) was to invest in commercial ventures.[18] Edmund Burke – born in Dublin in 1729 and brought up a Protestant, though with a mother who was a Catholic – described the Penal Code as an elaborate mechanism 'as well fitted for the oppression, impoverishment, and degradation of a people, and the debasement in them of human nature itself, as ever proceeded from the perverted ingenuity of Man.'[19] Even Samuel Johnson, an English Tory, Anglican High Churchman and xenophobe, observed after a visit to Ulster: 'The Irish are in a most unnatural state, for we see there the minority prevailing over the majority. There is no instance . . . of such severity as that which the Protestants of Ireland have exercised against the Catholics.'[20]

The Penal Laws did not lead as one might imagine to the mass conversion to Protestantism by pragmatic Catholics. Only 5,500 Catholics officially converted between 1703 and 1789.[21] Instead, it led to the paradoxical situation whereby Irish Catholics came to the conclusion that they would have more of a future in an England filled with potentially hostile Protestants than if they remained in a country largely populated by their co-religionists. Increasingly, therefore, after 1728 they decided to try their luck in London, many settling in the rookeries of St Giles Holborn and near St George-in–the-East, just east of the Tower where by 1746 – according to Rocque's map – the east end of Cable Street had become known as 'Knock Furgus'. In the process, these new arrivals greatly added to the capital's existing Irish population. In the early 1780s a Dr Bland, having analysed records relating to the City of Westminster, concluded that one-fourth of the population was born in London while one in eleven had been born in Ireland. No doubt a similar investigation of St Giles or Whitechapel would have revealed a higher proportion of Irish inhabitants.[22]

Of course, many impoverished Irish migrants settled in Bethnal Green and Shoreditch, on the outer edges of London's Spitalfields weaving quarter. And for good reason. As M. Dorothy George observes in *London Life in the Eighteenth Century*, 'the Irish in London were for the most part unskilled labourers [but] there were also Irish weavers' and, as she also notes, 'there was a close connection between the silk trades in London and Dublin, and linen weavers came over from Ireland and took to silk weaving.'

One has to assume that these Irish migrants retained their Catholic faith. After all, faced with a choice between flight or conversion to a faith that would have made their earthly life more convenient, they – like the Huguenots before them when facing a similar choice – had chosen flight.

But precisely where these settlers worshipped is not clear. The building of Catholic places of public worship was illegal in Britain for much of the eighteenth century. It was not until the Papists Act of 1778, which started the process of emancipation, and Acts of Parliament in 1782 and 1791, that church building became possible for Catholics; and the magisterial and authoritative *Survey of London* volume on Spitalfields makes no mention of a purpose-built Catholic church until the construction of St Anne's in the 1850s.[23] It has to be assumed, therefore, that Catholic communal worship in early-eighteenth-century Spitalfields was an 'underground' affair, albeit one that, according to the practices of the religion, would have required the presence of an ordained priest, particularly during the celebration of the Mass. Discreet Catholic churches certainly do seem to have existed near early-eighteenth-century Spitalfields: there was, for example, a chapel in Ropemakers Alley, off Moorfields and only a few minutes' walk west from Spitalfields, though it was virtually destroyed during the anti-Catholic Gordon Riots of 1780. Access to such semi-clandestine chapels was carefully controlled: as a rule, people had to pay a penny to a man behind a grille before they were allowed in – a charge that presumably gave such establishments the private status enjoyed by embassy and country-house chapels and the security that went with privacy.

A penny, however, was a not insignificant sum: in the early eighteenth century it could buy a decent meal.[24] So whether or not clandestine chapels would have been visited by the poorest of the new Irish settlers is a moot point. Perhaps as in late-seventeenth- and early-eighteenth-century Ireland, the poorer Catholics in Spitalfields and Shoreditch set up 'Mass Stones' – that is stones, possibly from a ruined medieval and once Catholic church, placed on a site deemed to be sacred and used as a focus for informal open-air worship. Spitalfields and its surrounding area must have been full of monastic stones and was certainly rich in former monastic sites – once consecrated to Catholic worship – that could have been viewed as sacred. Some of these sites, like that of St Mary's Priory, were too public and too developed, but the more remote churchyard of St Leonard's Shoreditch, around which an Irish community gathered, had been consecrated ground since at least the mid twelfth century. Can a 'Mass Stone' once have stood here? Would the Protestant incumbent of the church, and his congregation, have permitted informal Catholic worship in their churchyard? It seems unlikely, but possible.

Often underpaid, unemployed, embittered, persecuted and embattled, Irish migrants became a new fixture of life in Spitalfields and Shoreditch.

But simultaneously they became a new focus for resentment from the already beleaguered native weavers. In the past, masters had been pitched against their journeymen. Now an additional set of battle-lines were established: between Catholic Irish and Protestant English and French. Many Spitalfields weavers feared – as London tradesmen generally had when the Huguenots started to arrive in large numbers in the 1680s – that these Irish newcomers would undercut them by working for lower wages.[25]

A sense of the tensions that quickly sprang up is revealed in most dramatic manner in a 1736 pamphlet entitled *Spittlefields and Shoreditch in an uproar, or, the devil to pay with the English and Irish*. Purporting to be a 'full account of the . . . bloody battles . . . fought between the English and Irish in Spittlefields, and Shoreditch, on Monday and Tuesday nights last etc.' it includes 'an exact List of the Names of the persons kill'd and wounded on both sides'.[26] But in fact it is essentially a xenophobic tirade against the newcomers:

> It is shocking to behold the Cruelty or Impudence of some People, who, even in a strange Country, by the Natives thereof they get their Living; yet these ungrateful wretches are ever belching out their most dreadful oaths, Curses and Imprecations against those very People by whom they have Subsistence. The Truth of what is said here will evidently and plainly appear, by a genuine Relation of the fights which have happened between the English and the Irish in Shoreditch and Spittlefields, which will set forth in true light the Insolence of the Irish, who were Aggressors in this hitherto unheard of Action. It is hoped that proper Means will be taken by the Majestrites to quel those audacious Rioters, and to put a Stop to their wicked, cruel, and inhuman Purposes.

The apparent cause of the 'battle' was the demolition of the medieval Shoreditch church and its replacement by a new building designed by George Dance the Elder. Labourers were needed by the bricklayers to clear away rubble and, according to the pamphleteers, the response of the Irish workmen on hand revealed their dastardly tendency to undercut the English. As the pamphlet puts it: 'some Irish weavers . . . offered to work at half the price of the English', who were angered and voiced 'Disgust'. Insults must have been given and received, and indignation roused on both sides. The Irish then went to lunch at 'one Goulding's, an Irish Cook's in Shoreditch, where they told their story, at which the Woman of the House wrapt out a great Oath, and said, That she should mind it no more to cut up an English Man's Heart, than to cut up the Buttock of Beef that was before her. She likewise encouraged them to proceed in the Quarrel, and her husband told them, he would give them ten Guineas for a Pint of an English Man's Blood.'

The result was 'a sharp and bloody battle' on the night of Monday 26 July 'in which several were most cruelly wounded on both sides, but none were quite killed this Time.'[27] The next day 'one Francis Martin, going through Shoreditch, was met by 8 or 10 Irishmen, who asked him what Countryman he was, he said an Englishman; upon which they drew out Knives, and stab'd him dangerously in three Places' and the following day 'another Battle was fought, far more sharp and dreadful than the other, both Parties being enraged to the highest Degree.' This 'bloody Engagement', presumably taking place in the fields and burial ground around Shoreditch church – a particularly precious site for the Irish if it did indeed contain a 'Mass Stone' – was finally quelled by 'the Train'd Bands of the Tower Hamlets, Constables, Watch Etc.' During the fighting 'numbers' were wounded and one English boy – Thomas Larkin – 'was shot dead on the Spot'. In response the English tore 'Goulding's House almost to Pieces, and he is gone away, as they likewise to the Houses of several others.' The casualties, according to the pamphlet, were seven English 'dangerously wounded' and ten Irish.

No French names are mentioned in the pamphlet. Indeed this appears to have been a purely English and Irish affair, an affray amongst a certain type of bellicose journeyman weaver – ready to take offence – who at earlier times had rioted against new technology or imported fabrics. So serious was this sustained and bloody running battle that it even came to the attention of the Prime Minister Sir Robert Walpole. In a letter to his son Horace he described how 'this complaint against the Irish . . . is founded upon greater numbers than ordinary [of them] being here . . . letting themselves out to all sorts of ordinary labour considerably cheaper than the English labourers have, and numbers of them being employed by the weavers upon like terms . . . They are building a new church . . . where, I am told, the master workman discharged at once a great number of all sorts of labourers and took in . . . Irishmen who served for above one-third less per day.'[28]

No specifically religious dimension is mentioned in the pamphlet or by Walpole, but it's hard to believe that there wasn't one.[29] Certainly, in future years, the mix of Calvinist Huguenots, Irish Catholics and English Protestants was to prove a far from happy one.

The next explosion of violence came only three years later. This time it was not between Englishmen and Irishmen but, in more traditional manner, between seemingly exploited journeymen and a profiteering master. According to a press report of 6 November 1739, 'A great Number of Journeyman Weavers assembled in Spital Square before the House of an eminent Master Weaver, and endeavour'd to destroy the same.' This outburst was 'occasion'd by a Report of his being concern'd in a Combination to oblige the Journeymen to wind in their Silk gratis with their Work [i.e. to carry out more work for the same pay]'. A body of Guards was summoned from the Tower and the Riot Act read. But the journeymen 'not dispersing within the limited Time ten of them were taken and committed to Newgate to be prosecuted on the Riot-Act.'[30]

The disputes between master weavers and their journeymen, exacerbated by Anglo-Irish tensions, rumbled on, reaching crisis point in the early 1760s. With hindsight it's possible to see that the industry's ailments – which sparked the violent outbursts – were terminal and beyond the control of journeymen, masters or even government. Spitalfields silk was, largely due to the complex process of its manufacture and through duties imposed upon the import of raw silk, expensive, while its physical nature imposed problems and limitations: it was inherently complex to manufacture, almost impossible to wash without its dyes running, and unsuitable for certain garments – such as the light and practical dresses that increasingly became the vogue. It was gradually being driven from the market, not only by Indian calico and muslin, but by silk from China and by linen. After the end of the Seven Years War in 1763 it also faced direct competition from French silk. And the overmanning of the industry and the intense competition for work were driving wages down.

By 1761, according to the *Parents Directory* of that year, 'the best hands among the journeymen [were] seldom able to get above 15s. a week', and even highly skilled brocade weavers could not expect to earn above twenty shillings a week. And this was 'a time of great prosperity' in the trade. These levels are partly confirmed by the *Gazetteer and Daily Advertiser* for 14 March 1765, which states that average wages in Spitalfields for child workers were then two shillings to six shillings per week; 'Others 6 shillings to ten shillings per week', with 'much the greater part' not exceeding ten shillings to sixteen shillings per week. 'Very few' earned twenty shillings to thirty shillings per week.[31] By comparison journeymen of middling skills in the building trades – such as joiners, bricklayers and carpenters – were earning on average eighteen shillings to £1 per week.[32] So even before the silk industry entered its final long years of decline its wages were relatively low, and their steep and rapid fall between around 1761 and 1765 – from as much as £50 per annum for a skilled weaver to as little as £15.10s for an ordinary weaver – helps explain the riots that occurred from the mid 1760s.

Continuing technological advances made a bad employment situation worse. John Kay's 'Flying Shuttle', patented in 1733, enabled a single weaver to make much wider fabrics than before, and when mechanised – as became increasingly the case – led to 'engine-looms' that were even more productive and less labour-intensive. The culmination of engine-loom technology and automation was the Jacquard mechanical loom developed in France by Joseph Marie Jacquard, first demonstrated in 1801, which entered the British weaving industry during the second decade of the nineteenth century. Utilising a continuous chain of punched cards, the loom could, at speed and with a single operator, produce complex patterned fabrics such as brocades and damasks.

These innovations meant that not only was there now conflict between masters and journeymen, but tensions between opposing groups of journeymen – those who were 'single-hand' or 'narrow' weavers and those who utilised various forms of engine-loom. For example, in 1768 single-hand and engine-loom weavers attacked each other, admittedly not primarily because of the use of labour-saving technology but because one group accused the other of 'working at an under rate'.[33] Many traditional weavers had to give up their own looms, which they had previously operated at home as 'outside' weavers with the freedom and sense of pride such independent industry encouraged, and work instead as 'inside' weavers, toiling under the supervision and regulation of masters. Even those hand-loom weavers willing and able to acquire their own modern looms had a problem because mechanisms such as the Jacquard loom were too large and heavy to fit within a traditional weaving garret or workshop. The move towards 'inside' weaving and new and large technology made factory production inevitable.

In the 1760s the wholesale mechanisation of Spitalfields silk weaving lay in the future. But the industry's increasing problems and the wage cuts these led to were bringing journeymen to the point of starvation.[34]

Resentment increased. In a desperate attempt to improve their situation, journeymen weavers organised themselves into 'combinations' – trade associations organised for mutual benefit and a prototype for the trade unions that were to spring up in the following century. These were funded by levies – collected by force if necessary – to maintain themselves and to fund protests against the capitalists and masters. And they could be both deeply intimidating and very violent. In October 1763 several thousand journeymen weavers assembled in Spitalfields, broke into the house of a master, destroyed his looms, paraded his effigy around and then hung it in chains on a gibbet and burnt it.[35] In early May 1765, when the king attended Parliament to give assent to the Regency Bill, the weavers formed a procession from Spitalfields to Westminster, carrying red and black flags and banners to protest against the importation of French silks. Many prowled the streets around Parliament, intimidating the House of Lords into adjourning its business, and they also jostled the Duke of Bedford's coach. The mob was initially dispersed by cavalry that had been stationed in New Palace Yard, but then made its way, with evil intent, to Bedford House, on the north side of Bloomsbury Square. There it attacked the Duke's house and grappled with its guards. Its selection of the Duke of Bedford as a target was not coincidental. He had played a central role in agreeing the unpopular Treaty of Paris of 1763, which ended the Seven Years War on terms that could have been more favourable for Britain, and as Lord President of the Council had opposed a bill that aimed to place a high import tax on Italian silk-made fabrics. He was therefore, not surprisingly, an unpopular figure in the Spitalfields weaving community.

Rioting by the weavers continued, on and off, for a month. Alarmed West Londoners and City dwellers enrolled in militias as a means of protecting their property, streets and neighbourhoods from the threat posed by militant weavers from the eastern environs of the city. Troops from the Horse Guards were stationed in Bloomsbury Square and Albemarle's Dragoons set up a road-block in Tottenham Court Road and mounted patrols in Islington and Marylebone. This military action was organised by Welbore Ellis, the Secretary at War and a somewhat lacklustre political creature whom Horace Walpole dismissed as an 'incorrigible placeman'. In July Ellis lost his job, suggesting that the use of military force on London's streets to suppress protesting tradesmen was, in the government's view, an ill-judged action that could do more harm than good.[36]

The events of May 1765 inspired a satirical and sardonic pamphlet entitled *A Letter from A Spitalfields Weaver, to a Noble Duke.*[37] The duke referred to was, naturally, the Duke of Bedford:

> ... may it please your Grace, in the name of the whole body of Spitalfields Weavers, to beg that you will be pleased to accept their sincere thanks for all the services you have done them in. First, forming a resolution never to wear any thing manufactured in France. Secondly, for discouraging the same in your own family, and in those noble families who have the honour of your Grace's acquaintance ... It has been said your Grace has asserted, 'That was you a Spitalfields Weaver, you could live upon Ten-pence a day' ... Ten-pence a day! Ten-pence a day ... is a princely allowance. Oh that I had Ten-pence a day for life, and I would not envy your Grace ...

Having explained, in a lavishly sarcastic manner, how ten pence a day might keep a man fed and clothed – '... Breakfast 2d., Dinner 4d., Supper, after a hard day's work, 2d. ...' – the pamphleteer goes on to point out that the daily sum makes no provision 'for those imprudent wretches who have been indiscreet enough to get themselves married, and in consequence, some of them have six or seven children.'[38] But it proposes a solution to this problem. Seemingly inspired by Jonathan Swift's satirical pamphlet of 1729 entitled *A Modest Proposal for preventing the Children of the poor people in Ireland becoming a burden to their parents or country*, the anonymous 'Spitalfields Weaver' suggests that a market should be opened at the Royal Exchange 'for the sale of all such children who have parents that are unable to provide for them'. There, it proposes, 'people of fashion and fortune may go and provide themselves with as many infants as they think proper, just in the same manner as they would bargain for a quarter of lamb.'[39] One advantage of this scheme is that 'it would encrease the care and tenderness of mothers towards their children, when they were sure of a certain sum of money for them, when they arrived at one year old: and I make no doubt but we should soon see an honest emulation among women, which of them could bring the fattest and finest child to the market.' The *Letter* is dated 18 May 1765, about a week after the attack upon the Duke's house. (The passing of the Act of 1766 that banned the import of foreign woven silk shows that the authorities were not entirely deaf to such protestations.)

The journeymen weavers' more usual form of protest was not open riot but sabotage that involved attacking the looms of masters or destroying or cutting the silk on the looms. It was potentially a very dangerous tactic. Following lobbying by master weavers, an Act was passed in 1765 that made it a felony punishable by death to break into any house, or shop, with the intent to maliciously destroy, or damage, any silk in the process of manufacture. (The law also stated that, to preserve the staple of the silk manufacture, 'each piece of silk should be stamped at each end with the maker's name, the number of yards in each piece, and the breadth thereof in inches and half inch, and this regulation to be enforced by proper penalties.'[40]) But the new deterrent did not prove effective against the 'cutters' – as the protesting weavers were termed – and in 1768 simmering anger erupted in a series of terrifying riots and moments of mob-rule that – for a time – made Spitalfields one of the most dangerous places in Britain.

'Combinations' of dissatisfied journeymen weavers stalked the streets heavily armed. They pressurised their fellow journeymen to support the protest, and 'cut' the silk in the looms of those weavers who it was perceived had 'broken the book' of fixed prices and worked at lower rates to undercut their fellows. Master weavers were attacked, and in some cases their houses ransacked and their looms destroyed, if they refused to make a contribution to the funds being collected to support protesting journeymen.[41] One group of journeymen – calling themselves the 'Bold Defiance' – demanded money from masters in a most intimidating manner. One master who refused to pay received a threatening letter: 'Mr Obey, we give you an Egg Shell of Honey, but if you refuse to comply with the demands of yesterday, we'll give you a Gallon of Thorns to your final Life's End.[42] The 'cutters' committees were well organised: funds were raised at local taverns as well as through intimidation. And committees even on occasion managed to obtain advantageous prices in the London food markets.[43]

All this took place in a city that was already on edge. In the early spring of 1768 jubilant London crowds – including Spitalfields weavers – marched through the City to celebrate John Wilkes's return to Parliament. Wilkes, an exile and outlaw since February 1764 following his trial and conviction for libel against the Crown, was popularly perceived as a radical challenge to the dictatorial rule of the established authorities and as a spokesman for the rights and liberties of working men and women. The government cowered as the people took to the City streets, shouting 'Wilkes and Liberty' while smashing windows in the Lord Mayor's Mansion House and forcing merchants to light candles in their windows in token of 'celebration'. The excited crowds – the 'mob' to those who felt threatened by the exercise of popular power – controlled the City for two days before things quietened down.[44] Then things flared up again on 10 May when crowds gathering in St George's Fields in support of Wilkes were fired upon by troops. Seven people were killed and fifteen injured.

The significant role played in all this by Spitalfields journeymen weavers, with their reputation for militant protest, is suggested by a slightly panicky Memorandum sent by a member of the government to Lord Shelburne – a leading Whig politician and at the time Southern Secretary in the government of William Pitt. In it he noted that the weavers had 'united into Combinations of a very dangerous and alarming Nature . . . they amount to several thousands and are reduc'd to the most exact Discipline under their Leaders, they plant Centinels in all ye Neighbourhood of Spital Fields and are ready to collect themselves upon any Alarm. They disguise themselves with Capes and are arm'd with Cutlasses and other Weapons. They write threatening Letters in the form of humble Petitions to the Master Manufacturers and they deter by Threats those labourers from working at an under Price who would be otherwise glad to be employed.' Having then described their sabotaging tactics, the author of the Memorandum suggested that 'they are learning the discipline of regular Troops . . . they have their Watch Words and a cant Language understood only by themselves.'[45] These journeymen weavers were clearly well organised, and as Peter Linebaugh has observed, 'were a formidable force that . . . played a major part in the political and social upheavals of the time.'[46]

But in the end the often justified protests of the journeymen did not result in significant political reform, nor did they of course end in revolution of the sort that liberated American colonists during the 1770s and early 1780s and transformed France in 1789. Their dispute with authority remained focused on trade regulations, wages and job security. Just possibly – had the protests been more effectively targeted and embraced principles that attracted wider support and solidarity from the city's trade community – the uprisings among Spitalfields journeymen weavers in the 1760s could have led to a defining moment in the history of Britain. Instead the movement was stalled and suppressed, with leading members of the combinations and committees tracked down and prosecuted – some betrayed by colleagues, some the victims of informers. In the process it is likely that many innocent people suffered, their lives destroyed by *agents provocateurs* or people prepared to perjure themselves to remove competition, settle scores or gain reward money. Hangings took place – often in the teeth of wild public protest – and after the hangings the mob returned to exact vengeance on those it held responsible for the execution of innocent – or at least honourable – working men.

This last phase of the Spitalfields uprising was in many ways the most disturbing because it ended in the spring of 1771 with a man being hunted through the streets, gardens and wasteland of Shoreditch and Spitalfields, beaten without mercy by a baying mob, and – naked, bloody, bound and abused – casually killed in full public gaze. It was a moment of appalling cruelty that reveals to the full the forces of anger and deep resentment that existed within the Spitalfields silk industry.

The first steps on the path that led to this tragedy were taken many months earlier. On 7 August 1769, it was later alleged, the silk on the looms of a weaver named Thomas Poor was cut by a group that was led, so it was claimed, by weavers named John Doyle (or D'Oyle) and John Valline, both reputed to be leaders of the 'Bold Defiance'. Valline was also said to have headed a mob of 1,500 who attacked seventy-six looms belonging to an affluent Huguenot master weaver named Lewis (or Louis) Chauvet, who lived in 40 Crispin Street, because he would not make contributions to the committee's funds. The authorities, prompted in part by Chauvet's connections, felt compelled to take action. Consequently, when they got a tip-off in September that silk weavers would be gathering at the Dolphin Inn on Bishopsgate to collect contributions, they sent troops to break up the meeting. The soldiers duly attempted to do so, but the weavers fought back and shots were fired. When the tumult subsided two weavers lay dead, and while most of the others managed to flee, four were taken prisoner. Spitalfields now fell under the grip of the military. Chauvet and other affluent master weavers paid for soldiers to be billeted in the area, and revenge on the troublesome journeymen was plotted. Evidence was collected and, as later events suggest, a crude conspiracy was put in motion to ensure that the journeymen's 'ringleaders' were punished in exemplary fashion. The initial move was the arrest of Doyle and Valline who on 18 October 1769 were put on trial for their lives at the Old Bailey, charged with 'Theft and Housebreaking'.

The south wall of the charnel house of 1320. The ribs were originally part of a stone vault supporting the chapel above.

Excavation photograph of the Brick House of c.1600, once the home of Doña Luisa de Carvajal y Mendoza. Folgate Street is in the background.

Seventeenth-century objects found on and around the site of the northern precinct of St Mary's Priory. Top: a horncore, used as a cheap building material; centre top: slipware jar, flanked by bowls used for the preparation of medicine; centre below: a clay wig curler, flanked by fragments of earthenware tin-glazed plates and bowls; bottom: a range of clay pipes from c.1660 (left) to soon after 1700.

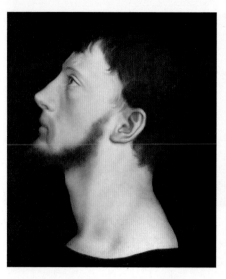

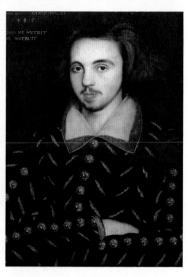

People of Spitalfields. Sir Thomas Wyatt the Younger. He lived within the former St Mary's Priory buildings and was executed as a rebel in 1554.

Christopher Marlowe, who lived in Hog Lane, in the Liberty of Norton Folgate, and was killed in 1593.

Doña Luisa de Carvajal y Mendoza. She lived in the Brick House, Spital Yard, and died a martyr in 1613.

Sir Benjamin Truman, painted in 1770–4 by Thomas Gainsborough. He lived near his Brick Lane brewery and died in 1780, aged 80, having retired to Hertfordshire.

Peter Ogier III, a silk merchant and entrepreneur who lived in Spital Square and died in 1775.

Louisa Perina Courtauld, the daughter of Peter Ogier II and sister of Peter III. Brought up in Spitalfields, she flourished as an independent gold- and silversmith and businesswoman and died in 1807, aged about 77.

A robe of brocaded satin in coloured silk, with sprays of rosebuds, morning glory and auricula; woven in 1744; the robe updated in c.1780. The pattern was designed by Anna Maria Garthwaite who lived and worked in Princelet Street from 1728 until 1763.

The junction of Steward Street (coming in from the left) and Fort Street, on the Old Artillery Ground, in 1914 (by E. A. Phipson). Most of the houses shown are typical of those built here in the early 1680s.

Edward Peck, the eminent dyer of Red Lyon Street, Spitalfields, as portrayed on his Baroque memorial of 1737 in Christ Church.

Eighteenth- and early-nineteenth-century objects found in the Elder Street area. Top: tiles, probably from Delft in the Netherlands and made in c.1725, found in debris in and near 15 Elder Street; centre: fragments of eighteenth-century tiles, those on the left probably English, those on the right probably Dutch, with Chinese import 'blue and white' porcelain bowls in the middle; below: clay pipes from c.1700 to 1840.

Left: a broken fragment of the Chinese-made porcelain 'wedding service' that was found among debris of c.1820 in the cesspit belonging to 24 Fort Street. *Right:* a late-seventeenth-century Chinese porcelain ornament showing a copulating couple under observation by a third party. This was apparently disposed of in the privy serving 21 Duke Street.

Silver cup presented in 1823 by a group of 'operative silk-weavers' of Bethnal Green to their solicitor Robert Brutton for his 'indefatigable labour' in defending the Spitalfields Acts. The Spitalfields silk against which the cup is set dates from c.1755 and shows ears of wheat.

People of Spitalfields. The philanthropist Annie MacPherson who in 1868 opened the 'Home of Industry' on Commercial Street.

The clergyman Canon Samuel Barnett and his wife Henrietta, who were instrumental in the foundation of Toynbee Hall in 1884 and the Whitechapel Art Gallery in 1901.

The outsider, American author Jack London, whose impassioned yet erratic *The People of the Abyss*, published in 1903, remains a defining text about East End slum life in the late Victorian age.

The social researcher and reformer Charles Booth, who in 1889 published the first volume of his detailed enquiry into poverty.

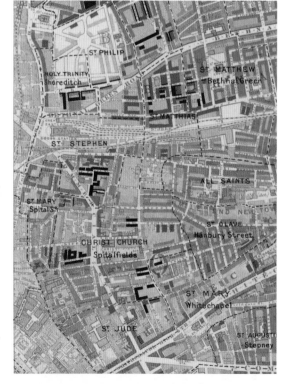

A detail of Booth's revised map of 1898/9 showing Spitalfields and Shoreditch. The income and poverty of the residents of London's streets were coded by the use of seven colours. The poorest houses and streets were shown black: 'Lowest class. Vicious, semi-criminal'; then dark blue, light blue, purple, pink, red, and finally gold for 'Upper-Middle and Upper-Class. Wealthy'. This area of Spitalfields has many black and dark blue streets.

Tenants of the Rothschild Buildings, in the very early 1970s, chatting in an entrance off Flower and Dean Street.

The author in conversation with Sandra Esqulant, of the Golden Heart, in the saloon bar of her Commercial Street public house.

The key prosecution witnesses at the trial were the Poor family.[47] According to their testimony fear, intimidation and blackmail had become a way of life in 1760s Spitalfields. Thomas Poor asserted that he was 'obliged to pay six-pence a week to these people the cutters for each loom, that is, three shillings and six-pence a week . . . by which means I thought myself safe.' But he was, it seems, disappointed in that belief. In early August, he claimed, a body of men arrived at 11.30 at night at the house he occupied with his wife Mary and son William (who at the time was sleeping 'in the shop'), threatened violence, and then destroyed silk (owned by one Thomas Horton) and weaving equipment (owned by Poor).

Mary Poor, for her part, was very specific in her accusations: 'I remember the night very well . . . we were between sleeping and waking, and my husband said, Here are the cutters . . . They came to the door and cut at it with their swords . . . I got up, and said, Gentlemen, don't cut the door; I'll let you in . . . The first man that entered my door was John D'Oyle, with a pistol in one hand, and a sword in the other. There were seven of them came in. I pushed the sword from my stomach, that D'Oyle held. The other went up to the room. They said, Get out, you old w – e [whore] get out of the shop. I said, You know I know you all very well, I will not go out. I was in my shift all the time. Valline cut the work, the property of Mr Horton; and D'Oyle had a pistol standing along side me at the time. D'Oyle was a neighbour of mine; he lived within three doors of me. I said to Valline, You are known in this alley, why do you come here?'

William Poor corroborated much of his mother's evidence and, in addition, described the arrest of Valline: 'I and some constables went and took Valline at Highgate; (he is a militia man), he had soldiers clothes on. I knew him then, though in a different dress, and told the constables that he was the man.'

Doyle's defence was that Mary Poor – 'that wicked woman' – held a grudge against him. After a difference of opinion between Doyle, a friend and Poor, 'she began to call us a parcel of thieves, robbers, and cutters. I took a warrant for her, and had her before the justice. She wanted a warrant against me, but the justice would not grant one.' For the record Doyle stated that, 'I never was in her house before I was taken up, neither was I there with [Valline] that night.' The connection between the men was that Valline was Doyle's tenant.

Valline's defence was simply that the Poors were lying and – specifically – that he had not collected protection money for the cutters

The penultimate plate of William Hogarth's Industry and Idleness *set of prints of 1747 shows the 'Idle 'Prentice' on his way to execution at Tyburn. Like the Spitalfields 'cutters' who were executed in 1769, this fictional apprentice was trained as a weaver in Spitalfields. He is being escorted to his execution, among a tumultuous crowd, by a body of armed soldiers.*

from them as accused. Certainly Valline's decision to join the militia – which he stated he 'entered' on 14 April – would surely have been an odd move (or a cunning ploy?) if he was a cutter since the militia had been assembled to suppress them.

Witnesses were called who gave evidence that contradicted the Poors' accounts and who stated that Doyle and Valline were both of good character. The prosecution also produced witnesses to give negative character references. Most of these witnesses had, seemingly, nothing to do with the case but all were evidently master weavers of Huguenot origin. Peter Traquan, a neighbour of Chauvet's in Crispin Street, stated that 'D'Oyle was one of the cutters [not] a working, industrious man', while Valline, was 'certainly riotous'. A Mr Dumoissur stated that Valline's character was that of a rioter and finally a John Chauvet (presumably Lewis Chauvet whose looms had been destroyed earlier or a relative) took the stand to tell the court that he knew Valline, and that he was 'of a riotous disposition'. Doyle and Valline were found guilty and sentenced to be hanged.

At related trials on 18 October 1769 James Fessey – an 'engine-loom' weaver – was found guilty and sentenced to death for 'feloniously, and with force, breaking and entering the dwelling house of John Dupree . . . in St John Street, Bethnal Green . . . with intent to cut and destroy a certain silk manufactory on a certain loom' on 22 September.[48] Peter Perrin, on similar charges, was condemned to death for destroying 'four certain instruments called looms' on 4 January 1768 owned by 'fancy-weaver' John Clare.[49] Both of these men's sentences were 'respited' and both were transported for fourteen years.[50]

On 13 November 1769 Doyle and Valline were hanged, not at Tyburn as was usual, but near the scene of their 'crime'. This was intended to act as a stark warning to the militant weavers of Spitalfields, Shoreditch and Bethnal Green.[51] Clearly the authorities and master weavers such as Chauvet believed that such a visible exercise of retribution would help break the spirits of the more recalcitrant journeymen weavers. But it was also a risky step to take – one that could lead to more riot and large-scale civic unrest.

The place of execution chosen was the heart of the area where, in the 1760s, journeymen weavers lived and worked, the gallows being erected at the junction of Bethnal Green Road and 'Dog Row', Bethnal Green (now Cambridge Heath Road), outside a tavern – which survives in rebuilt form – called the Salmon and Ball. A huge crowd gathered, seething with fury and on the verge of violence. Stones and insults were thrown at the soldiers guarding the condemned men. For a moment it even seemed as if they might be rescued. Amidst uproar and great groans from the crowd, though, the executions went ahead.

Before he died, according to a subsequent newspaper report, Doyle had declared:

> I John Doyle do hereby declare, as my last dying words in the presence of my Almighty God, that I am as innocent of the fact I am now to die for as the child unborn. Let my blood lie to that wicked man who has purchased it with gold, and them notorious wretches who swore it falsely away.

These words, if they were heard by the crowd, can hardly have calmed it. In its fury and frustration, it tore down the scaffold when the hangings were over and carried it to Spitalfields where it was re-erected in front of Chauvet's house in Crispin Street. Chauvet either escaped or had wisely gone into hiding, but his house was stoned, windows smashed and furniture grabbed and burnt.[52]

The decision to execute Doyle and Valline in Bethnal Green provoked something of a legal crisis. It had been made by James Eyre, Recorder of the City of London and one of the judges on the bench during the trial. Eyre had made his reputation in 1763 defending the radical politician John Wilkes when he spoke powerfully and effectively against the evils of General Warrants – documents that gave the authorities the power to search places or seize people or property without drawing up specific charges. But after this bravura libertarian performance – which ensured that General Warrants were never again used to arrest people – Eyre slipped into the role of conservative-minded hanging judge.[53] City Sheriffs claimed that Eyre's decision to choose an irregular and intimidating place of execution was an 'unconstitutional innovation' that set an alarming precedent. If sites of execution could be chosen at will then not only were exemplary executions possible but also – more sinisterly – 'secret' ones. The Sheriffs also condemned the use of troops in Spitalfields and Bethnal Green to ensure that the executions were carried out. They were, presumably, echoing the discomfort felt in 1765 at Welbore Ellis's use of the military in a civil matter. Eyre's actions were ultimately sustained but his long-standing and profitable relationship with the City Corporation – he had been one of its legal counsels since 1755 – was over.[54]

Violations of legal procedure in the trial and the irregularities in Eyre's conduct and his sentencing were also asserted by John Horne Tooke in a pamphlet entitled *Copies of All the Letters . . . Relative to the Execution of Doyle and Valine* (sic). Tooke, a veteran radical parliamentary reformer and a former supporter of John Wilkes, had been gaoled for one year in 1777 for libel following the publication of an appeal for funds to aid the families of American colonists killed in the early stages of the Revolution. These men, wrote Tooke, 'preferring death to slavery', had 'been inhumanely murdered by the King's troops'. Despite this somewhat lurid past Tooke, who as well as being a lifelong radical was also a clergyman and a lawyer, was respected by many and the points made in his pamphlet were well reasoned.[55]

Tooke's pamphlet helped, no doubt, to keep the mood in Spitalfields dark and dangerous for some time to come. Journeymen believed themselves betrayed – both by some of their masters and by some fellow journeymen. Two men had died, in the most harrowing circumstances, and the working community of the area was unforgiving. There was almost certainly a racial and class aspect to the disturbances, too. Most of those accused were Irish and impecunious, while, of course, the influential master weavers – like Chauvet and Thomas Horton, who owned the silk being woven by the Poors – were Huguenot or English. But the Irish community itself was divided, with the beleaguered journeymen on one side fighting to protect their livelihoods, and on the other the richer Irish, like the Poors, who owned looms and were tempted to side with the Huguenots and English.

Meanwhile the authorities inexorably pursued others accused of involvement in the disturbances. On 6 December 1769 William Horsford, an Irish weaver, was tried and sentenced to death for his role in the attack on the Poors' workshop. Again the conviction was largely based on evidence from Thomas and Mary Poor. Whether or not their testimony – predictably almost word-for-word the evidence given at the trial of Doyle and Valline – should once again have been taken at face value is open to question, particularly given some of the new details they let slip. It emerged, for example, that Chauvet had offered rewards to those who could identify and help convict 'cutters' and that he had paid the Poors to give evidence at both trials. Indeed Mary Poor admitted, under cross-examination, 'that she heard there was 500 l. advertised for a discovery about cutting Mr. Chauvet's work; and that she applyed to Mr. Chauvet, having heard he was a sufferer'. It was even alleged that she had tried to extort money from people by threatening to accuse them of being 'cutters' and offering to swear false evidence for a price. She denied this, though she did reveal that she had tried to obtain 'fifty-three shillings' from a Mr Horton (in this trial named as Joseph not Thomas Horton) in an attempt to make him take responsibility for the damage done to the looms.[56]

Her husband similarly revealed that he had 'heard of a reward two years ago for apprehending the cutters'. He further admitted that he 'made a discovery [accusation]' because he was driven to poverty 'by those people the committee men' – by which he meant the committee running the combinations of cutters. Personal animosity between the Poors and some of the accused also seems to have been a factor. Certainly allegations and counter-allegations flowed pretty freely as the Poors and their opponents tried to use the law to settle grudges and collect reward money. The warrant that Doyle had obtained against Mary Poor – which resulted in her being sent to the Bridewell – must have been an added cause for vengeance, as was the fact – according to Poor – that 'Valloine' had also taken out a warrant against his wife because she had 'abused him'. So, seemingly in retaliation, Thomas Poor had made his 'discovery' to Sir John Fielding, the famed Covent Garden magistrate who ran the detective force of constables known as the Bow Street Runners, naming the men he held responsible for attacking his house and workshop.

Given all this, neither Thomas Poor's nor his wife's evidence could exactly be said to be objective or beyond question. Nevertheless, the description of the night of the attack that Poor offered at Horsford's trial does give us a particularly powerful sense of the tensions at large in Spitalfields and Shoreditch at this time. In an incidental way, it also provides a fascinating insight into the appearance and arrangement of a Georgian weaver's house and workshop. During his testimony Poor explained that:

> I kept seven looms there at that time in my house [in Stocking-frame Alley in Shoreditch] . . . On the beginning of August I went to bed about ten o'clock . . . My wife and I had been about an hour and an half in bed [then] heard a great noise of people coming up stairs; they came thundering and rapping at the outward door of the house. At the passage coming in, they cried out, Mary Poor, you old whore, open the door! . . . Then she came out and opened the door. We lay up one-pair-of stairs. She did not go down stairs after we came out of our chamber. Our street door is on our right

hand, within about two feet of the chamber door. We heard them come up stairs; there is no outward door; they kept thundering at my room door. There is no fastening but only my room door. You come up one-pair-of stairs, the door is right before you. When the door is open, there is a little passage on the right hand to go into the shop by my room.

Clearly, Thomas Poor's house doubled as his workshop. It appears that there was no front door, or at least the 'outward' door was not locked, and that the house was in shared occupation (Poor revealed, under cross-examination, that he paid £8 a year rent to a Mr Dean, who had a wool 'warehouse' on the ground floor and let the upper floor to wool 'combers', who reached their rooms via a different staircase). The 'chamber' in which the Poors slept was at first-floor level. It was 'very small, only for a bed, a chest of drawers, and a chair' and was accessed via a narrow, winder staircase leading to the Poors' door and an internal lobby with a passage that led to the workshop at the back. It would also seem that the street door entered into a lobby that was communal – serving tenants on the ground floor as well – or that was viewed almost as public and virtually as part of the street, a tradition continued in nineteenth-century blocks of industrial dwellings where entrance halls, staircases and galleries had open access from the street. This description, with a utilitarian staircase set immediately beside the street door and intended to serve a house designed for multiple occupation and mixed use, is broadly supported by the physical evidence offered by the few surviving eighteenth-century buildings in Spitalfields and Shoreditch that originally housed weavers' families and workshops, for example 3 and 5 Club Row of c.1764.

Poor's description of the actual wrecking that then took place gives some idea of the set-up of a weaver's workshop. Lit by a large window 'with three or four square panes in a row' that reached 'all along' one side (and so providing enough light for him to be able to identify all the saboteurs), it was thirty-six feet long and contained seven looms. 'I did not go up till I heard the weight stones fall,' he recalled. 'My wife was then in the shop with them. I believe the stones fell in about two minutes after they were there.' Poor explained that the weight stones 'keep the work stiff to work. The weight is hung to the cane roll. I believe there may be about three quarters of a hundred weight, or near a hundred weight upon the roll.' He calculated that the 'cutters' were in his workshop for 'about eight or ten minutes', then 'past near me when they came out. I saw seven come out in the whole. The prisoner was one of them; he, and two more of them, came in about two steps into my chamber, and shook hands with my wife, and said, Good night, mother Poor . . . After they were gone, I struck a light, and went into the workshop. There were some pieces all lying about . . . I found the work cut, hanging, some by one cord, and some by another. It was cut cross. It was bombazeen [twill fabric woven from silk and worsted]. The cane was all silk . . . It is shot down with worsted . . . about a yard distance from that that was cut [was another] of all silk; that that was made and rolled on the roll, was then not worth a pin to make any use of it. It was not worth a penny to anyone . . .' Poor then explained the damage to the 'tackle' or 'harness' that 'we tread . . . up and down with our feet . . . that . . . makes the work', and to the reed that 'we strike . . . in at every shoot.' The tackle belonged to Mr Horton, as did the silk, and 'the reed is not worth a pin now. They gave it a cut with a hanger.'

Poor went on to describe his next and very poignant meeting with the accused:

> I saw the prisoner after he was taken before Sir John Fielding, which was, I believe, the last day of the last sessions . . . They told me he was there in the name of Stroud. He was sitting there, he reached out his hand, and shook hands with me. I said, Will Horsford, how are you? He shook his head at me, and spoke in Irish for me to have compassion on him . . . I repeated in English, Will, you had no compassion on me when you destroyed me, and when you was of the Defiance sloop [asked to explain this term, Poor said it was the name 'they gave themselves . . . these men the cutters']. [Horsford] told me I was doing this [giving evidence] for the sake of money. Sir John opened the door, and asked if Poor was come. The man said I was. Sir John asked me if I knew the prisoner Stroud. I said, I did not know Stroud, but I knew the prisoner William Horsford. Sir John asked him then how he came to change his name? He came up to the bar and said: It is true, William Horsford is my name.

Poor was emphatic in his identification of the seven 'cutters' who had entered his workshop: 'John Doyle, Bill Duff, Joe Colman [who commonly went by the name of Jolly Dog], Andrew Mahoney, Thomas Pickles, William Horsford, the prisoner, and John Valloine [sic], all weavers.' But it was apparent that Poor paid a price for the accusations he had levelled against them. Since his wife had been released from the

Bridewell, he told the court, he had not 'followed his business' but had been 'supported by the goodness of every gentleman that would give him something'. He hoped, though, to be 'rewarded' when the Old Bailey session was over 'with what the government would allow him' that 'he should be put in a way of business' and that 'promises [had been] made him by gentlemen'. He claimed, however, not to know who these gentlemen were.

On the same day at the Old Bailey – 6 December 1769 – William Eastman was tried for entering the house of a weaver named Daniel Clarke, who lived in 11 Artillery Lane, there attacking his looms and the silk on them, which was owned by Thomas Cook.[57] Eastman vigorously denied the accusation, claiming hardly to know Clarke. Clarke's evidence, however, was pretty unequivocal. He described how on Monday 11 September, between one and two in the morning, he was awoken by a voice calling 'Where does Clark the pattern drawer live?' Going to the window, he asked, 'Gentlemen, what do you want?' The people in the street below told him to open the front door, but Clarke, dressed only in a shirt and night-cap, decided to wait downstairs in the yard until he could be sure that they were determined to come in.

Soon he could hear them hacking away at the door, and so fearing that 'the lives of my family would be in great danger', he agreed to draw the spring-lock back and let them enter. Five of the intruders went upstairs, the sixth stayed to argue with Clarke, who recalled: 'I fell to telling him I had a good right to have looms worked, and they had no right to cut mine, for I was willing to pay . . . They demanded two shillings a loom, which we were obliged to pay, or have the goods destroyed, and the master's work also.' Clarke agreed to these terms, and so the sixth man, Mr Gusset, called the others down and they left. Very quickly, though, they seem to have changed their minds, for they re-entered the house (the lock had been so damaged that Clarke had been unable to fasten the door) and, as he stood outside in the yard, attacked his looms and materials. Clarke could, so he claimed, hear Eastman saying 'Here it goes', and identified him as a man he had known for four or five years: 'I . . . have often discoursed with him about weaving; he was no particular acquaintance of mine, far from it; though he never affronted me in his life before.' Finally, as the clock struck two, the men left, and when Clarke got up a few hours later he went to inspect the damage:

I found the mountear cut all to-pieces . . . that is a tackle that causes the flowers to be made in the work; it is used in making flowered silk; it will make all manner of flowers (*produced in broken pieces*) and (*two pieces of sattin produced*) this is the work. It is called the Leopard spot. (*The lingoes produced.*) . . . They are about the bigness of the tube of a tobacco pipe, about six or eight inches long, fastened to a small cord or thread, at one end. (*A piece of a shuttle, and the reed broke in three pieces produced.*) There were two shuttles, they broke one in two pieces, and damaged the other; the reed is entirely spoiled. The quill-wheel is a large thing; I have not brought that, they broke that; the use of that is to wind quills on pipes, which pipes or quills are put into the shuttle; that is a particular tool used in weaving all broad silk; the shuttle and quill-wheel were my property. (*A brass point to a scabbard of a hanger or cutlass produced.*) This I found in the room the next day.

The accused man, Eastman, seems to have been well liked in Spitalfields and three character witnesses spoke up for him. James l'Homme, who was a 'foreman' and lived in Wilkes Street (a northern continuation of modern Wilkes Street, now part of the Truman brewery site), said Eastman was 'a very hard working man, very honest, and very civil. He has earned upwards of 50 l. a year, one year with another'. Daniel James, 'a silver buckle maker; living in the Kingsland Road', told the court that the prisoner 'is reckoned in the neighbourhood to be a very honest quiet man. I live but four doors from him', while John Nash stated that Eastman 'is a peaceable quiet neighbour . . . I have known him between one and two years.' Even a friend of Clarke's – James Williams – spoke up for Eastman. Williams told the Court that he had supper with Clarke soon after the attack, during which Clarke had stated that, 'he knew never a man of [the attackers], so as to swear to them, he wish'd he could'.[58] But this evidence did no good. Eastman was convicted, largely on Clarke's evidence, and condemned to death.

By Christmas 1769 four weavers had been hanged – Doyle, Valline, Horsford and Eastman – and two – Fessey and Perrin – had each been transported for fourteen years, as terminal a punishment as execution for those the exiles left behind. For his part, Clarke was the object of considerable bitterness in Spitalfields. It was generally believed that he had abused the law, that he was in the pay of that *éminence grise* Chauvet and that he had perjured himself for money or to gratify some obscure but deadly grudge against Eastman. Moreover he was almost certainly an Englishman and, if so, was an Englishman who had given evidence against Irishmen on trial for their lives. His own life after the trials and the hangings cannot have been easy and it is scarcely surprising that the local Justices of the Peace should have advised him to carry pistols in his pockets 'for fear of being attacked'.[59] To no avail. Eighteen months later, on 16 April 1771, fate caught up with Daniel Clarke.[60] Barely three months later, on 3 July 1771, three people were brought to trial for 'feloniously and wilfully, and of their malice aforethought, being present, aiding, abetting, assisting, comforting, and maintaining, certain persons unknown' to murder him.[61] Their names were Henry Stroud, Robert Campbell (also spelled Cambell) and Anstis Horsford – the widow of William Horsford, who had been hanged in 1769.

According to the trial records Clarke's final, terrible ordeal started just after noon as he walked along 'Half Nichols Street', 'Spital-Fields', with Benjamin West, a weaver of 'Fleet Street', which lay just to the east of Brick Lane. West explained that Clarke 'used to draw patterns for me' – that is, make designs for silk – and that on that morning the two men had met at Clarke's house before setting out 'to look at some work'. Once they got to 'Half Nichols Street', however, Clarke was recognised and 'attacked by two men', after which 'people increased very fast'. The mob – the instrument of popular retribution – was coalescing. The cry went up: 'There goes Clarke, that blood-selling rascal.' This attracted yet more people. Clarke's reaction was to 'turn round to speak to them', to attempt to reason with the swelling mob and calm it down. It was a misjudgement. 'They threw stones at him . . . we ran . . . I did not look behind me till I saw him upon the ground . . . I saw two men knocking him down . . . after I came into Cock-lane' – now Bethnal Green Road or Redchurch Street.

The court was anxious to establish the identity of the assailants and so West was closely questioned. He described how: 'I saw him down, with his hat and wig off' and that 'I saw two or three men' with him, 'one man kicking him: I cannot tell what kind of a man he was; I saw Clarke get up, and he ran into Mrs Snee's house: that is all I saw of him; then I came away.' West decided it was best to go to Clarke's house to summon assistance. The walk from 'Cock-lane'/Redchurch Street to Artillery Lane would have taken about eight minutes. When West arrived he 'told the person [Clarke] lived with, which I understand now is not his wife; that he was at Mrs Snee's, that he had been attacked and lost his wig: I desired her to take him a wig.' This recommendation suggests that West did not fully appreciate the extreme danger Clarke was in. He seems to have thought the prime concern was the preservation of Clarke's dignity and appearance, though he did tell the woman at Clarke's house, 'I thought it would be necessary to take his pistols, for fear he should be attacked again.' He did not explain – nor was he asked – why he did not seek a Justice of the Peace or local constables for assistance. No doubt the latter would have been hard to find, and those in the Liberty of the Old Artillery Ground – where Clarke lived – would probably have been unwilling in any case to take on a potentially very dangerous mob gathered in the parishes of St Leonard's Shoreditch or St Matthews, Bethnal Green – areas that were beyond their jurisdiction. (The only police force in London that regularly operated city-wide without regard to parish boundaries was magistrate Sir John Fielding's highly trained and efficient Bow Street Runners.) What West was unable or unwilling to do was to identify any of the people involved in the running attack – which he said lasted 'not above half an hour' before Clarke gained refuge in Mrs Snee's house. Given what he saw happen to Clarke – a man accused of being an informer – West's reticence at turning informer himself is hardly surprising.

Mary Snee was next called, and the evidence she gave was exceedingly dramatic. She confirmed that she lived in 'Cock-lane' and that she had seen Clarke 'five times before' he 'opened my latch and ran in . . . bloody: he was cut over his eyes, and had no wig on; I said, Lord have mercy upon me what is the matter Mr Clarke: he said, I'm beset; I said "who has beset you?"' The record of the evidence at this crucial point is imperfect but it seems that Clarke said that he didn't know. He then said, '"Lock the door, for God's sake, lock the door." I did, and shut the inside shutters of my windows.' Then 'he walked about the house, we gave him water and washed him . . . he was very disconsolate . . . he said, "this is the finishing stroke; this crowns the work": He desired me to send for his wife [as evidently he called the woman he lived with] for he had no wig, he asked me to let my daughter bring his pistols: my daughter went and met Mrs Clarke coming in Shoreditch with his pistols; she brought them, he desired her to go back and fetch him a wig, and bring his powder box with his gun powder, which she did.' Clarke's 'wife' did not return for half an hour, and while she was away Mrs Snee could hear the mob outside her door, 'now and then; but they turned down the corner of the street', yet 'several times' people 'peeped thro' the window and said, "D—n him, there he is: turn him out, let us hang him, or burn him, or any thing, let us do something with him."'

By the time Clarke's 'wife' returned, however, the street was pretty quiet. So, after taking refuge for an hour, Clarke, his 'wife' and a little boy – presumably their child – left the house, 'with his hands one in one pocket and the other in the other, upon his pistols'. They proceeded, according to Mrs Snee, 'not half a stone's throw, and when the mob saw the corners of the streets beset they came running round him; I was at my own door, I saw a great mob, then he run back again.' Clarke was alone – the woman and the boy had made their escape. 'He stood at my door, he took his pistols out; a fellow coming up to him, he said, "I will shoot you," the fellow took his stick and held it up to his face, and said, "D— you do." Mr Clarke could not let the pistol's off, so he pushed into the house, and I shut the door and locked it.'

The mob had grown in number and in fury. It wanted its prey. 'There were I believe, a hundred,' estimated Mrs Snee. 'I said, for God's sake what must I do; the outside shutters were not shut at all; they throwed a great brickbat at the door, and when they had done that, they throwed another and broke four panes of glass and the frame, and all of the windows. They said, "D—n him, turn him out, and they would hang him, or burn him, or drown him, or do something or other to him; d—n him turn him out."' Again Mrs Snee asked Clarke whether he knew these people that 'beset' him. He replied that he didn't, 'but I know them that does'.

The mob kept beating the door and window. Clarke beseeched Mrs Snee, 'For God's sake do not open the door.' He then asked her if she had a cellar. She did, so Clarke 'went down into the wash house, and then down into the cellar.' When he was in the cellar, and hiding, Mrs Snee opened her front door to – as she explained – 'let in a friend'. But as she did, she told the court, one of the fellows came in . . . pushed into the kitchen to me, and said, "D—n you, where is he." I said he is not here.' The court then directed Mrs Snee to 'look at the prisoners and recollect if you saw either of them there?' Mrs Snee replied, 'no, I was in a great fright'. Like West, she was unable or unwilling to identify any individuals in the mob or to accuse the people on trial. Mrs Snee described how the man, who had pushed his way in, 'ran up stairs and met my daughter and said, "D—n my blood, if I don't kill all in the house if they don't find him.' The daughter, seemingly with great calmness and presence of mind, replied, 'As I hope to be saved, he is not up stairs.' Which of course was true.

At this point Clarke made an attempt to escape. He left the cellar, via the kitchen, and jumped over the garden wall. But he was spotted. 'There he goes, there he runs,' bayed the mob in the street, and ran into the garden. This, explained Mrs Snee, was not her garden, but 'a great garden, belonging to a gardener' (John Rocque's map of 1746 shows a large garden, with walks and trees, behind the houses on the south side of 'Cock Lane').

The story was now taken up by John Marsh, a shopkeeper who lived in Norton Folgate. It seems that from 'Cock Lane' Clarke fled south, presumably along Shoreditch High Street and Norton Folgate, towards his home in Artillery Lane. But, just a couple of minutes from his front door, he was once more 'beset'. As Marsh explained, 'I had just dined and heard an extraordinary noise, which occasioned me to look out of my window; there I saw a man, which they tell me, was Clarke . . . at the corner of White Lyon street [now Folgate Street], at Mr Woodrow's corner, surrounded by a number of people.' Marsh made a point of stating that 'I saw nobody strike him then' – like the other witnesses he must have wanted to make it clear that he was not going to risk identifying any of the accused as being among Clarke's assailants – but he did say that he saw an unidentified man, who seems to have been just a passer-by, lash out with a whip, possibly at Clarke. 'I saw no more,' John Marsh concluded. 'I know nothing of the prisoners; I did not go out of my shop.' It would seem that Marsh was a reluctant witness. Certainly it seems improbable that a shopkeeper on one of the area's busiest streets could not identify anyone in a local mob. And John Marsh was not the only unwilling eyewitness. The Mr Woodrow he referred to in his testimony – another Norton Folgate shopkeeper – failed to appear in court at all.

One witness of the action in and around Norton Folgate and of subsequent events who did turn up in court was Thomas Gibson. A 'silk dresser' living in Norton Folgate, Gibson first saw Clarke 'in Norton Falgate' soon after two o'clock, surrounded by about a hundred people, and he witnessed him being savagely whipped for 'perhaps a minute'. This savage treatment seems to have moved no one to pity, or at least prompted no one to intercede on Clarke's behalf. No doubt, with the mob in such a bloody and vengeful temper, it would have been extremely dangerous to attempt to save him. In any case, Gibson made no effort to intervene: 'I went away to my shop; I work in Blossom-street [off 'White Lyon Street' (Folgate

Street)] [and] I lost sight of him [but] got sight of him again in about four or five minutes, in Wheeler-street, the next street to White Lyon-street.' It seems that Gibson joined the mob, no doubt as a discreet observer, gripped by horror and curiosity.

'The people were pursuing him; they had got him up in a corner and were throwing dirt at him, and striking him.' Now the melee, with Clarke at its centre, turned east along Quaker Street and away from Clarke's home. 'He never seemed to try to get away,' said Gibson, 'but seemed to go with them; he was in the middle of a great number of people.' Clearly Clarke was stunned and confused, as well as being frightened and in pain. 'About the middle of Quaker's-street somebody came and gave him a blow, and said, D—n your blood: and Clarke fell down.' But once again he rose and Gibson said that he followed Clarke to 'the Broad way' (presumably Brick Lane) and then into 'Hare Street' (now Cheshire Street) where against a brewhouse, in about the middle of the street, he was stopped and stripped. 'I cannot say how much they stripped him, he had his breeches and stockings.'

Finally, the mob dragged Clarke into a field at the north-eastern end of 'Hare Street', on to a 'Brick-field, where there is a pond, occasioned by digging out the bricks', threw him into the icy cold water and then proceeded to pelt him with 'earth and brick-bats, and any thing they met with'. Rocque's map of 1746 shows a number of ponds in a field to the north-east of 'Hare Street', around a courtyard building named Coate's Farm. It was perhaps around one of these ponds – or one further to the south, created since 1746 – that Clarke suffered. By the time the mob, with Clarke in its midst, had reached the pond Gibson estimated that it had swelled to include as many as two or three thousand people. And the weather, Gibson remembered, was cold: 'It snowed at times as fast as I ever saw it in my life.'

At last, the horror and savagery of the almost ritualistic stoning to death proved too much for some of the onlookers – including, it seems, Gibson: 'There was a parcel of boys and girls about him; I went, and said, You little brats you will kill this man, and some of you will get hanged for it. A man came up and assisted me . . . we pulled him out [and] dragged him four or five yards from the place.' To show compassion at this moment was brave – and very dangerous. Gibson told the court that some of the mob accused him of being one of Clarke's 'confederates' and threatened to push him into the pond. 'I slipped away at a distance from the mob,' said

Now standing approximately on the site of the ponds that are shown to the north-east of Hare Street on Rocque's 1746 map, this circle of trees frames a shallow mound surmounted by a pile of boulders arranged like a primitive altar. This curious, elemental composition inadvertently commemorates the possible site – the 'pond occasioned by digging out of bricks' – where Daniel Clarke was brutally and publicly murdered by a blood-thirsty mob in 1771.

Gibson, 'some advised me to go home, and said I should get myself ill used.' But he decided to risk staying – until the bitter end. He saw Clarke, now lying 'about nine or ten yards from the water . . . down upon the sand-heap' with people 'throwing sand on the top of him'. This lasted 'about a quarter of an hour, or twenty minutes . . . and then they came and throwed him into the water again . . . he was crawling like upon his hands and knees, at times, striving to keep himself from drowning; they kept throwing brick-bats and stones at him . . . I saw half a brick, as it appeared to me, come and strike him on the left side of his temple, and the blood poured out as fast as if he had been pricked with a lancet, and the water was discoloured with the blood.'

The court enquired if Clarke did or said anything during this terrible ordeal. Gibson answered, 'He put his hand upon his head, and wiped the blood off and said, "Oh, gentlemen, you use me cruelly."' Another witness, Robert Baldwin, added a further emotive dimension to this tale when he told the court, 'I saw Mr Gibson help him over; I said, that man was doing good for evil; for he had told me the deceased had wronged him out of about two pound.' Or perhaps, more prosaically, Gibson wanted Clarke alive so that he could get his money back.

Only now did the forces of authority make an appearance – in the person of the 'keeper of Whitechapel prison . . . [or] a turnkey or something belonging to the prison'. This was enough to cow the mob. The violence stopped. It was, however, too late for Clarke. Gibson got him out of the water for a second time, but as he went to summon help to get him to an infirmary 'somebody came up again, and said, he is dead . . . I went to look again,' Gibson said. 'I saw he was dead; we drawed him away from there to the sand house.'

Telling details about Daniel Clarke's last moments were offered by the man who helped Gibson drag the dying man's body from the pond, a 'fruiterer' called Francis Clarke, who lived in 'Grey Eagle Street'. Even during his torment 'the people talked to [Daniel Clarke] about hanging the cutters,' recalled Francis Clarke, '. . . and about Chevat [sic] [and] he made answer and said, Chevat is worse than me.' According to his name-sake, Clarke then pleaded, 'Let me go home, for God's sake; I will freely forgive you.' But he was clearly not believed. 'One man said, "D—n you, you said you would swear against twenty" . . . some of them d—d and cursed him . . . all the mob were against him . . . I heard very few people that were pitying of him,' the witness added; 'they said, "He was a very

bad man, and would swear peoples lives away."' Francis Clarke claimed
that when the victim had been pulled from the pond the first time, people
put a cord over his head and dragged him along – something that Gibson
had apparently not observed. He also testified that a man 'in a shirt' had
tried to push Daniel Clarke's head under the water.

People joined the mob for different reasons. Some, as Francis Clarke's
testimony suggests, were clearly out for revenge. William Atkins, a gardener who gave a character reference for one of the accused, Henry Stroud,
described how when he asked his maid what was going on, she explained
that they were 'ducking . . . Clarke that hung the cutters'. Clearly, that was
how he was viewed locally – as the man whose conduct had condemned
innocent people to death. Some of Clarke's tormentors, like the man who
possibly hit out at him with a whip, were casual onlookers caught up in the
fury of the moment. And some were merely curious bystanders. John
Winterson, another gardener who offered a character reference for Stroud,
watched as events unfolded but did absolutely nothing either to help or
hinder, being, as said, more worried about the snow and the state of his
master's cucumbers ('So the cucumbers were the reason of your not protecting this man's life?' the Council for the Crown caustically suggested).
Winterson did, however, intimate why so many of the crowd should have
been passive onlookers when, so far as the court was concerned, to do
nothing was little short of being an accomplice. 'They were afraid to
meddle or make,' he said; 'a man would not venture himself among
the mob.'

The key issue for the court, of course, was whether any of the witnesses
could – or would – identify those responsible for the murderous attack on
Clarke. Gibson said he recognised the prisoners at the bar, but although
he specifically picked out Campbell as having been near the pond during
Clarke's last moments alive, he did not suggest that he had actually taken
part in the fatal assault. Indeed, since he wavered in his view of what
Campbell had been wearing that day, it wasn't even clear that it was
Campbell he'd seen. (Was he in a coat, as Gibson claimed at one point, or
in a shirt similar to the one worn by the man seen pushing Clarke's head
under the water – or, as later testimony seemed to suggest, did Campbell
take off his coat just before entering the water to press Clarke's head
down?) One small detail Gibson mentioned, though, was significant. He
thought 'Campbell' had been holding 'a bit of a hoop stick, or some such
thing'. Were Campbell to be positively identified as one of the assailants,

the suggestion that he had been holding some kind of weapon could be enough to hang him.

As for Francis Clarke, he didn't recall having seen Campbell before – but he did recognise the other two defendants: the woman Anstis Horsford and Henry Stroud. He had seen Anstis Horsford, he said, standing by the pond, wringing her hands. A woman near her had asked her, 'What do you cry for, you see satisfaction.' Horsford had responded, 'What is that for the loss of my husband and for my fatherless children?'

So Francis Clarke, like Thomas Gibson, did not directly incriminate anyone. But, as the trial proceeded, it became increasingly apparent that he was a far from trustworthy witness. When, for example, he told how he had tried to get Daniel Clarke out of the water, he mentioned that 'somebody came behind me and put their knees under my backside and said throw him in for his namesake.' That one little detail shows that Francis Clarke was well known locally – hardly surprising given that Spitalfields was a relatively small community. Yet he for his part seemed wholly unable to identify anyone unequivocally. Like other witnesses, he must have believed that giving evidence that might help to hang a 'cutter' was just too dangerous an undertaking.

But there was more. In the general absence of a professional and independent body of criminal investigators and detectives in the eighteenth-century legal system, very little objectively gathered or forensic evidence was offered in English courts. Instead, by tradition, great reliance was based on sworn evidence, not least because the serious sentences imposed for perjury were seen as adequate deterrents to prevent those tempted, for whatever reason, to lie in court while under oath. And since the person who swore first was more likely to be believed, the accuser had an inherent advantage over the accused. The evidence of a man like Francis Clarke therefore carried disproportionate weight. If he chose to offer evidence against Campbell that Campbell disputed and that could not be corroborated by another witness it would, of course, be just one man's word against another. But in this circumstance, by the legal conventions of the time, the court would tend to favour and give more weight to Francis Clarke. This gave Clarke potential power and laid him open to bribery or to the corrupting temptation of rewards that were routinely offered for successful convictions, and as subsequent evidence and cross-examination revealed, an attempt was almost certainly made to bribe Francis Clarke.

The first hint of this came in answer to a question put to him by Robert Campbell. 'Where was you a drinking upon the 17th of the same month?'(the day after the killing of Daniel Clarke). Clarke said that he had been with a Mr West (whether this was the same West as Clarke's companion on the day of his murder is not known). Campbell asked Clarke what they spoke about and Clarke admitted that West 'asked me if I would be made a man of; he said, I need not carry fish [presumably he meant fruit] any more; I might be made a man of for ever.' Had West offered him money, then? No, but he had been approached by an officer of the law – a constable based in Whitechapel – who had said that he would be given 'fourscore pounds' by a lawyer's clerk if he went to Sir John Fielding in Lincoln's Inn Fields and formally identified Campbell as one of the assailants. Clarke claimed that he was 'frightened' by this proposal and that he said, 'God forbid I should go to swear against a person I do not know.' The law officer for his part, when cross-examined, denied that he offered a reward and said simply, 'I was sent by the Bench to serve the summons on this man and another.' It is now impossible – as with so many details of this bewildering case – to know exactly what was going on here and who was perjuring themselves under oath and who was not. However it is possible that Campbell, fearing Clarke's potentially damning evidence, simply wanted to undermine his credibility as a witness.

So, assuming that Clarke was broadly telling the truth, for whom was the lawyer's clerk who offered the £80 acting? Given the circumstantial evidence and hearsay surrounding this strange tale it is reasonable to assume that it was Lewis Chauvet. Daniel Clarke had perhaps been his creature (certainly going by what was said during the attack it seems this was assumed to have been the case by members of the mob and explains why he was attacked so mercilessly) and Chauvet wanted to make sure that at least one of Clarke's alleged killers was convicted – no matter how that conviction was obtained. If this was the case, was Fielding in on the conspiracy and was the lawyer's clerk operating with his knowledge? Can it be that Fielding had been convinced of Campbell's guilt by a party unnamed and was prepared to see a man die, although accused on dubious evidence and therefore convicted in a legally unsafe manner, to create a fearful example to help quell the dangerous civil unrest sparked by the actions of the Spitalfields weavers?

It seems scarcely credible, but Campbell certainly could have been the target of a possible legal conspiracy. Under cross-examination by counsel, presumably acting for Henry Stroud, Clarke confirmed that the constable had made it clear that it was 'Bob Campbell' he was supposed to identify. When it came to Stroud, however, Clarke, far from picking him out as an assailant, claimed that in Daniel Clarke's final moments Stroud had 'offered to carry the deceased to the Infirmary upon a brick barrow'. According to Clarke, Stroud 'appeared in as much anxiety as I was'. He was, so Francis Clarke thought, solicitous for Daniel Clarke's safety and Francis did not see him throw anything at him.

Clarke's testimony, however, was not sufficient to clear Stroud, for now one Joseph Chambers, who worked at a brick kiln, was called to give evidence, and positively identified Stroud as one of the people who had thrown bricks at Clarke. Given that Stroud was clearly physically very distinctive – tall and with a squint – this eyewitness account must have seemed conclusive. But even here there were wheels within wheels. Chambers, it soon emerged, was married to a professional informer and was himself clearly in it for the money. The local Bethnal Green justice, Mr Wilmot, had put up a ten-guinea reward for the apprehension of those responsible for Clarke's death, and had stated that an additional £40 reward was on offer (though he did not say from whom). Chambers had therefore decided, it would seem, to go into league with two distinctly unsavoury characters to secure it.

One, James Knight, a gardener who worked in Vauxhall, had, it was alleged at the trial, already resorted to attempted extortion: on encountering Stroud in the Axe public house one day shortly after the murder, Knight had told him to give him a pot of beer or he would 'swear it against him, and take him up [have him arrested]'. The other was one David Higgins, an acquaintance of Knight's. At the trial, however, each man hopelessly contradicted his acquaintances, leaving us to suspect that each now saw the others not as fellow conspirators but as rivals for the reward money. The most plausible account came from Higgins: Chambers, he said, had been offered a reward to find someone involved in the killing of Clarke, had latched upon Stroud as a likely victim and source of reward money, had realised that to achieve his goal he would have to swear he had seen Stroud in the act of attacking Clarke (which he clearly had not), and that – while happy to perjure himself – he had wanted to get Knight and Higgins to agree that Stroud was a likely contender. According to Higgins:

When I went to [Chambers'] house, he was talking about Knight . . . He said, Where is he, for he wanted him on particular business. I said, does he owe you any thing? He said, No, he did not want him upon that account. One thing brought up another. I mentioned the words [Knight] said about Stroud at the Axe. Chambers said, did you know Stroud? I said, I did know him. [Chambers] said, he saw a man throw very much at the pond, in a frock, a very little man. Chambers said, he thought it was Stroud. I told him it was not him, for Stroud was a great man, and cross-eyed. He asked me if I knew him; I said, Yes. He said, would I tell him where he was; I told him where he was, and then he said Mr Wilmot had bound him in a forty pound bond to find somebody that had been concerned in the murder, and he must take up somebody, and he would be obliged to me to tell him. I told him I saw nothing of the affair, and could say nothing at all about it.

Higgins' own role in all this, though, was clearly less than admirable – as his astonishingly confused, hedging responses to subsequent questions revealed.

The question is why should Stroud, out of all the people at the pond that day, have been picked out as one of the primary instigators of violence? It's perhaps understandable why Robert Campbell should have been put in the frame for Clarke's murder: he was, after all, a fellow weaver and consequently a possible 'cutter'. Stroud, however, was, like Knight, a gardener. But, it emerged, he was connected with the weaving fraternity, because he was the brother-in-law of William Eastman, one of the weavers who had been hanged back in 1769. This connection offers a possible explanation as to why William Horsford – tried and condemned for his role in the attack on Daniel Clarke's workshop on the same day as Eastman was condemned for his role in the attack on the Poors' workshop – chose to use the alias Stroud when brought before Sir John Fielding. Horsford was evidently trying to shift possible blame away from himself onto Eastman's brother-in-law. Precisely why we will never know.

There are therefore various reasons why Stroud ended up in the dock. He was connected through family to the hanged Eastman and this alone might have been sufficient reason to ensure his selection as a victim of exemplary punishment. He might have been the victim of a vendetta between the Horsford and the Stroud/Eastman families. Or, of course, he actually was one of the people who attacked Clarke and therefore was guilty as charged.

There's another possibility, too. In December 1750 Stroud had been tried for the murder of one Richard Chamberlain. During the trial it was revealed, and evidently believed by the jury, that Chamberlain was a drunken oaf and bully who habitually beat his wife and his daughter. On one occasion Stroud 'endeavoured to prevent the deceased beating his wife' upon which Chamberlain struck Stroud 'several blows with his fist, and tore his coat'. The wife's brother then entered the room and 'struck the deceased upon the eye' upon which Chamberlain 'stripped' and prepared to attack his brother-in-law. Stroud intervened, saying, 'Dick, you have hit me several blows, now I have a great mind to hit you one . . . then struck the deceased upon the breast two or three times, with his fist; upon which the deceased fell, and never spoke more.' This account of events was supported by several witnesses, including Chamberlain's wife, who said 'she believed there was no malice between them, or any design for mischief'.[62] Other witnesses gave it as their opinions that Stroud interposed 'in order to make peace'. Consequently Stroud was cleared of murder but the jury found him guilty of manslaughter and he was punished by being branded upon the hand. It is possible that this brand upon his hand, and his reputation as a man-killer, made Stroud the natural target for reward-hungry and unscrupulous scoundrels like Chambers and Knight looking for a plausible victim to falsely 'swear' away for profit.

The fact is that it's impossible to be certain of anything in this astonishingly convoluted case. Some witnesses were clearly too scared about possible repercussions to offer truthful testimony. The trial records note, for example, that one Elizabeth Breech 'trembled, and seemed much frightened' and despite reassurances ('Don't be afraid, there can no harm happen to you for any thing you are to do here') said she was wholly unable to identify any individual present at Daniel Clarke's murder. Other witnesses seem to have been pursuing their own private agendas or were in it for the reward money. Consequently, when it comes to those crucial moments on the afternoon of 16 April when Clarke was subjected to his final torments, it's possible to chart fairly accurately what happened, but not who was responsible.

Stroud and Campbell were defended by some; accused by others. Gibson said Campbell had done nothing. Robert Baldwin, by contrast, while generally reluctant to give evidence against the prisoners, said that he had seen Campbell go up to Clarke and ask him 'whether he had known the executed man William Eastman', and that when Clarke had been thrown back into the pond 'Campbell came stript in his shirt' and 'came and seized him on the top of his head, and plunged his head under water several times.' Knight in his testimony claimed he had seen Stroud throwing bricks. A gardener named Bath said that he had not seen Stroud throw anything at all and that since he was with Knight at the time, Knight could not have witnessed Stroud throwing bricks either. Francis Clarke said that Horsford's widow Anstis did nothing to harm the wretched weaver: 'she did not do any thing, to my knowledge'. Another witness, Ann Jackson, on the other hand, said that she saw Mrs Horsford throw a brickbat at Clarke: 'she said this was the man that was the occasion of her husband's death; she said her poor husband lost his life by this man in the pond; she was crying shockingly'. Judith Morris, for her part, denied that Mrs Horsford had had anything at all in her hand, painting instead a portrait of a woman almost prostrate with grief:

> ... I put my hand under her arm, and said, Mrs Horsford, come home, for you are a woman, that will be remarked here; I beg you will go home with me: she said she would go and look at him; I turned back, and followed her; I kept as close to her as ever I could ... I don't think she was out of my sight during the time ... I saw her go to the pond, and speak to him; she said, Clarke, Clarke, I am left a widow; my child is fatherless on account of you, and more of your companions ... I believe she said, Do you remember poor William Eastman? Clarke was naked in the pond, begging for mercy, and praying to God.

Henry Stroud was invited to offer a 'Defence'. He was brief and to the point:

> I am as innocent of the affair as ever was a child in the world. I neither handled brick, stone, tile, nor anything, so help me God.

Robert Campbell's defence, by contrast, was long, confused, confusing and far from the point. He claimed he had spent the day looking for work ('I am a weaver, and sometimes a seaman'), drinking with friends, looking again for work, wondering whether he 'could do better at sea than as at present', and only then, hearing that Clarke had been attacked, going 'to the edge of the ground, and no farther'. Finally, he said, he went home to his wife. It was an unconvincing performance.

Both men produced character witnesses. Dawson, who kept the Angel Inn in the City Road and for whom Stroud had worked, stated that his 'general character is very good; he is as humane a man as any I know in the world'; William Townsend, of 'Little Pater-noster row, Spitalfields', who had known Stroud 'eight or ten years . . . and his mother before him', said 'he was always a hard working, honest man'; John Wolridge, the owner of the market garden where Stroud had worked for three years, had never seen 'any impeachment of his humanity, or saw him quarrel, or given to quarrel, in my life'. Campbell's character witnesses included Joseph Driver, who had known him for eight years, and had 'never heard any thing amiss of him' and believed 'he kept his family well'; William Westman, a journeyman weaver, who had known Campbell three or four years and had 'never heard but that he was a very quiet, peaceable man . . . of good character'; and William Hilbery, another journeyman weaver, who had 'never heard any thing but that he was an honest man . . . a very peaceable man'.[63]

We don't know how the judge summed up for the jury, but we do know that despite the unsatisfactory and contradictory nature of the prosecution evidence, and the implications of bribery, Stroud and Campbell were found guilty and sentenced to be hanged in 'Hare Street' – 'the very heart of the residence of the perpetrators' – rather than at Tyburn.[64] This was intended, of course – as in the case of John Doyle and John Valline – to set a salutary example for the local weaving community and to terrorise would-be 'cutters'. Evidently the criticisms of James Eyre's conduct of the executions of Doyle and Valline had not been heeded by the authorities. The fate of Anstis Horsford is unclear. She is not listed at the end of the trial proceedings as having been found guilty or not guilty and is subsequently lost to history. Perhaps she was released during the course of the trial.

The Ordinary of Newgate's Account states that Stroud and Campbell were executed on 7 July 1771 (presumably a misprint for 17 July, since the trial lasted eight days). The Ordinary's account also notes that Stroud and Campbell suffered the additional punishment of having 'their bodies delivered to Surgeon's hall to be dissected and anatomised'.[65] This was a refinement of the sentence of capital punishment reserved for murders deemed to have been extraordinarily wicked. Since Christian beliefs in the eighteenth century held that the soul could only undergo resurrection at the End of Days if the body was preserved largely intact in consecrated ground, a sentence of hanging combined with dissection and dispersion of the corpse was not just a physical death sentence but a spiritual one, too. The authorities clearly intended Stroud's and Campbell's deaths to be as frightening as possible.

Stroud maintained his innocence to the moment of execution. *The Proceedings of the Old Bailey* describe this as a 'remarkable circumstance' because in the absence of a post-trial confession the innocence of the condemned remained a possibility and could – in such fraught cases – inflame popular opinion and lead to riot and protest. However there was in the 1770s a practical reason not to plead guilty or admit guilt after conviction. Prisoners who admitted being guilty of murder forfeited their property to the Crown. The heirs of those who maintained their innocence to the bitter end retained, in principle, their right to inherit. It was therefore in the interests of the authorities to get prisoners to confess, and they might well put them under considerable pressure to do so. In the case of Stroud, the authorities were so angered that a decision was made to publish information about the earlier trial in which Stroud had been involved, which, it was hoped, would suggest he was given to violent outbursts and, by implication, confirm his guilt in the Clarke killing.

Despite the shambolic nature of the trial, the possible injustice of the verdict, and the spectacle of Stroud and Campbell's public execution in Bethnal Green, violence did not flare again in Spitalfields. The cycle of killing stopped. There was no public hunt for the men who helped to hang the pair. There is no record of Chambers or Knight being assaulted. As garden labourers rather than weavers they had little or no trade connections with Spitalfields and so could easily – and no doubt did – move out of the area never to return. Also the lengthy and rambling trial was – if far from a model of legal procedure – perhaps something of a cathartic exercise for Spitalfields. No matter what one's personal beliefs, the public and brutal killing of Clarke was clearly a shameful affair. Perhaps the lengthy trial, where so much opinion was expressed by so many, was something of a relief and helped the people of the area, collectively, to move forward.

And a few years after the killings of Doyle, Valline, Horsford, Eastman, Clarke, Stroud and Campbell, the conditions that helped to provoke their deaths and cause the troubles in Spitalfields changed. In response to the turbulence and violence that characterised London's silk industry during the 1760s, and in an attempt to bring peace and tranquillity to the weaving districts of London and more financial security and stability to the lives of journeymen weavers, the government in 1773 passed the Spitalfields Act. This Act, such as it was, represented the fruit of years of agitation and anxiety on the part of journeymen and master weavers. Essentially, it aimed to regulate wages and working conditions, and to protect the domestic market from overseas competition by controlling the import of foreign-woven silk.[66] More specifically the Act of 1773, and a supplementary Act of 1793, ruled that the wages of journeymen silk weavers within the legally recognised boundary of Spitalfields should be fixed by magistrates at quarter sessions, with penalties inflicted on masters or journeymen who paid or demanded above or below the agreed rate. Moreover, competition within the trade was reduced by limiting to two the number of apprentices a silk weaver could have at any one time. To satisfy masters, 'combinations' – perceived by authority as one of the main causes, rather than the consequences of, the troubled times – were outlawed. An additional Act of 1811 extended the provisions of the earlier Acts to female weavers.

The Acts were, for the increasingly troubled Spitalfields silk industry, a temporary stay of execution.

ELEVEN

RADICALS AND ENTHUSIASTS
Spitalfields' Intellectual and Cultural Life

By the 1770s a new radicalism had found its way into English intellectual life. The Unitarian preacher and scientist Joseph Priestley, for example, who in 1774 had been the first to identify oxygen, wrote a pamphlet in the same year entitled *Address to Protestant Dissenters of all Denominations, on the approaching Election of Members of Parliament, with Respect to the State of Public Liberty in General and of American Affairs in Particular*, which attacked the British government for depriving the American colonists of their natural rights and liberties. A few years later, in 1782 and 1786, he wrote pamphlets on Christianity that were so scathing about received views of theology (Unitarians denied the Holy Trinity and argued that Christ was not part divine in his nature but entirely human) that one of them, *A History of the Corruptions of Christianity*, was publicly burnt. Other radicals took similarly sceptical views on important matters of eighteenth-century church and state.

But it was the outbreak of the French Revolution in 1789 that really galvanised radical sentiment. Priestley, by now living in Birmingham, argued that events in France would increase the 'goodwill among all nations' for they marked the triumph of 'the Liberal, the Rational and the Virtuous' and heralded an 'empire of reason that will ever be the reign of peace.'[1] He also held that it was time to change the system of monarchy in Britain, to make the sovereign the 'first servant' of the people and 'accountable to them', a view so incendiary that a mob – probably put together and led by government agents and reactionary figures in Birmingham Corporation – sacked Priestley's house, destroying not only most of his papers but also his laboratory. (A shattered man, Priestley fled to London and thence, in 1794, to America, where he died in 1804.)

Many radicals argued that for far too long power and wealth had largely resided in the hands of a relatively small aristocracy whose behaviour had proved overbearing, arbitrary and – ultimately – unproductive. They found the new spirit of revolution intoxicating. On 4 November 1789 the moral philosopher, nonconformist preacher, political pamphleteer and radical republican Richard Price, who had given vocal and consistent support to the American colonists during their successful revolution, delivered a memorable sermon entitled 'A Discourse on the Love of our Country' – at a meeting house in Old Jewry, just a quarter of an hour's walk from Spitalfields – to the Society for Commemorating the Revolution in Great Britain (known informally as the Revolution Society), which concluded with the stirring words:

> Be encouraged, all ye friends of freedom and writers in its defence! The times are auspicious. Your labours have not been in vain. Behold kingdoms, admonished by you, starting from sleep, breaking their fetters, and claiming justice from their oppressors! Behold, the light you have struck out, after setting America free, reflected to France and there kindled into a blaze that lays despotism in ashes and warms and illuminates Europe! Tremble all ye oppressors of the world! Take warning all ye supporters of slavish governments and slavish hierarchies . . . You cannot now hold the world in darkness. Struggle no longer against increasing light and liberality. Restore to mankind their rights and consent to the correction of abuses, before they and you are destroyed together.

The Revolution Society had been established ostensibly to commemorate the 'Glorious Revolution' of 1688 that brought William and Mary to the throne of Great Britain, but the society's members were soon arguing that the French Revolution – with its watchwords of '*Liberté, Égalité, Fraternité*' – was no more than the natural extension of Britain's earlier upheaval.

In a similar vein, Wordsworth, who in 1791 had been inflamed and inspired by the experience of walking through a recently emancipated France still flushed with the first thrill of its own self-liberation (and whose own emotions were also no doubt stirred by falling in love with a Frenchwoman – Annette Vallon – who was to bear their child), later recalled that early enthusiasm in his autobiographical work *The Prelude*:

> . . . A glorious time,
> A happy time that was; triumphant looks
> Were then the common language of all eyes:
> As if awaked from sleep, the Nations hailed
> Their great expectancy.[2]

Various books in defence of the French Revolution were issued between 1789 and 1791 by the London publisher Joseph Johnson, employer and publisher of William Blake. Johnson also, for a decade from 1788, put out a journal, the *Analytical Review*, that became a forum for radical political and religious debate and pressed the case for political reform. (Johnson even planned, in January 1791, to publish Tom Paine's dangerously radical *The Rights of Man*, but got cold feet over the almost inevitable legal consequences, leaving the way open for J. S. Jordan to publish the first part of the epoch-making work some weeks later in March.)

One of Johnson's authors was the Spitalfields-born Mary Wollstonecraft, whose grandfather was an affluent weaver living in 'Primrose Street'. Her 1792 work *A Vindication of the Rights of Woman* was followed two years later by *An Historical and Moral View of the Origin and Progress of the French Revolution*, a text that supported the basic revolutionary principles even as it criticised the mounting levels of violence. Blake himself wrote a verse narrative in 1791 entitled 'The French Revolution' that, in the fragment that survives, supports the uprising and, among other things, features a debate between king and nobles modelled upon the assembly of Satan and his legions in Milton's *Paradise Lost*. He must have realised the poem could be interpreted as seditious and it was never published.

London in the spring of 1792 was gripped by revolutionary fervour. Supporters of the new regime in France wore their hair short and unpowdered and dressed in simple clothes to mark the spirit of the new egalitarian age of liberty. Blake wandered the streets sporting the Phrygian cap or *bonnet rouge* of liberty. Radical organisations sprang up including the Society of the Friends of People for Parliamentary Reform and the London Corresponding Society, the latter working closely with the revived Society for Constitutional Information, whose membership included many artists and craftsmen. The general aim of such groups was to secure basic rights for all working men – the vote, liberty and fair wages – but the means of securing these were usually predicated on reform rather than revolution. Support of Revolutionary France, however, could take more extreme forms. At a dinner of the Revolution Society in November 1792 the Marseillaise was sung, and the words 'Liberty' and 'Equality' started to appear chalked on walls around London.

British society became deeply divided in its opinions of the situation in France and about what the nation's response should be. While some citizens of London gladly learnt the Marseillaise others of their countrymen trembled. One of Britain's future war heroes, Horatio Nelson – in 1792 an unemployed naval officer languishing on half-pay in his native Norfolk – listened with alarm to farm labourers talking on his father's land at Burnham Thorpe and in the village pub, the Plough, and on 3 November and 10 December 1792 wrote letters about his concerns, and his proposed solution to the problem, to the Duke of Clarence – an old naval friend and the future King William IV:

> . . . if I may judge from this county, where Societies are formed, and forming, on principles certainly inimical to our present constitution, both in Church and State, of which our Dissenters are the head . . . near Norwich . . . the Clubs are supported by Members of the Corporation; and they avow that till some of the Nobles and others in Parliament are served as they were in France, they will not be able to get their rights.

Nelson warned the Duke about the outspoken preacher Joseph Priestley, and the use of village inns for radical meetings. He wondered why the magistrates did not annul the licences of 'those public houses who allow of improper Societies meeting in them, and take up these incendiaries who go from ale-house to ale-house advising the poor people to pay no taxes etc.' Nelson asked the local Justice of the Peace why Priestley was not arrested. His answer was that: 'No justice would render himself unpopular at this time . . . for that his life and property were gone if the mob arose.'[3] In January 1793, as the crisis between Revolutionary France and Great Britain came to a head, Nelson was recalled by the Admiralty and put in command of the 64-gun HMS *Agamemnon*. As a man of action this appointment must greatly have eased his mind.

The government became increasingly concerned by the tenor of public opinion, and as 1792 progressed an air of menace settled over the capital as the authorities pondered legislation to suppress revolutionary thoughts and actions. In May 1792 a Royal Proclamation was issued against 'divers wicked and seditious writings and publications', prompted by the appearance the previous February of the second part of Tom Paine's *The Rights of Man*. Arrests on charges of sedition and causing public unrest began to be made, with a warrant for Paine's arrest issued on 21 May. English and German troops were barracked around the capital. In December 1792 Paine – who in *The Rights of Man* had declared that every man had the natural right to freedom of thought and action – was tried for seditious libel in absentia (having fled to France just before the warrant for his arrest was served). He was found guilty, which ensured to the government's satisfaction that one troubling radical at least was kept out of Britain. The guilty verdict also encouraged the government to believe that further successful prosecutions should be possible as part of its campaign to suppress radical thinking and control the population.

This was also the year, however, when opinion in Britain – and presumably in Spitalfields – began to shift away from sympathy for the French Revolution. Many individuals, particularly Dissenters, were concerned by the escalation of violence in the late summer of 1792 and, especially, by the 'insurrection' of 10 August that brought about the downfall of the monarchy. By the autumn of 1792 Blake had discarded his red bonnet. Soon a cooling of enthusiasm was replaced by outright Francophobia. People were horrified by the execution of Louis XVI in late January 1793; and they were appalled by the Terror that seized France in early September 1793 (by July 1794 16,600 people had been guillotined, 2,600 of them in Paris, and there had been perhaps another 25,000 summary executions). Most fell in with Prime Minister William Pitt the Younger's decision to confront the new revolutionary government and join an anti-French coalition. In response, France declared war on Britain and the Dutch United Provinces on 1 February 1793.

A report in *The Times* of Monday 10 September 1792 gives a good sense of the repugnance for revolution that was by now starting to overtake English thinking:

> ... we have no precedent of such wanton and disgraceful excesses ... Many of the facts have been related to us by a gentleman who was an eyewitness to them, and ... the facts stand not in need of exaggeration. It is impossible to add to a cup of iniquity already filled to the brim ... on Wednesday, the MASSACRE continued without abatement. The city had been a scene of bloodshed and violence without intermission since Sunday noon, and although it is difficult and indeed impossible to ascertain with any precision the number that had fallen victims to the fury of the mob during these three days, we believe the account will not be exaggerated when we state it at TWELVE THOUSAND PERSONS—(We state it as a fact, which we derive from the best information, that during the Massacre on the 2d instant from SIX to EIGHT THOUSAND Persons perished) ... the unhappy victims were butchered like sheep at a slaughter house ... When the mob went to the prison de la Force, where the Royal

attendants were chiefly confined, the Princess DE LAMBALLE went down on her knees to implore a suspension of her fate for 24 hours. This was at first granted, until a second mob more ferocious than the first, forced her apartments, and decapitated her.

The circumstances which attended her death were such as makes humanity shudder, and which decency forbids us to repeat . . . and for two days her mangled body was dragged through the streets . . . The heads and bodies of the Princess and other Ladies—those of the principal Clergy and Gentlemen . . . have been since particularly marked as trophies of victory and justice!!! . . . Are these 'the Rights of Man'? Is this the LIBERTY of Human Nature? . . . Read this ye ENGLISHMEN, with attention, and ardently pray that your happy Constitution may never be outraged by the despotic tyranny of Equalisation.

But although the public as a whole was turning against revolutionary sentiment, the government remained nervous, taking ever more draconian steps to suppress and punish those factions of British society that were deemed to support political upheaval. The Act of Habeas Corpus was suspended in the spring of 1794 – which meant that the government now had the power to arrest and detain without trial – and in 1795 two Acts were passed against 'Treasonable and Seditious Practices' and 'Seditious Meetings and Assemblies'. These in turn were reinforced by the Unlawful Societies Act of 1799 (laws which effectively marked the end of open and organised radicalism in London). The war with France added a further dimension to official fears: revolutionary sympathisers were now, more than ever, perceived to be a potential fifth column.

In London many of Blake's friends – including Thomas Holcroft (also a friend of Tom Paine) and William Sharp – were arrested or questioned, and in 1799 Joseph Johnson was imprisoned for seditious libel for selling a pamphlet written by Gilbert Wakefield that, in general, attacked the privileged position of the wealthy and, in particular, targeted an anti-radical tract by the Bishop of Llandaff. Sedition trials became commonplace, creating an atmosphere of suspicion, intrigue and fear, made worse by the hearsay, vindictive denunciation and secret reports by eavesdropping government agents that informed the prosecutions. In 1803, when Blake was charged with high treason for uttering seditious words against the king, it was on the vengeful evidence of a poorly behaved, probably drunk and apparently trespassing private soldier whom he had ejected from his garden.

Punishments for treason and sedition were potentially ferocious. In practice, though, they were generally confined to short periods of imprisonment and fines: juries were very reluctant to condemn people to death or transportation for years simply for voicing their opinions. Johnson, for instance, was sentenced to six months' imprisonment. Blake, who had been accused by the soldier of damning the king, all his subjects and all his soldiers, and stating that if Bonaparte should invade 'I will help him' and he would be 'master of Europe in an hour's time', was quickly acquitted in January 1804 by a sympathetic jury – a verdict greeted by applause in the crowded court.

The government's sustained efforts to control popular opinion in Britain, far from calming the situation, served only to worsen the divisions in society that the legislation was intended to remove. When the king opened Parliament in October 1795 his coach was actually barracked by the mob. Francis Place – a self-educated London tailor with a taste for radical politics – was in St James's Park and outside the Houses of Parliament during the opening and records that many in the crowd hissed the king, calling out: 'No Pitt, No war, Peace, Peace, Bread, Bread.'[14] Others claimed that there then followed an 'attack' on the king's coach. Place's rather less sensational account, however, seems more convincing. While it was passing through a narrow street near St Margaret's Church, he records in his autobiography, a pane of glass in the royal coach window broke – either by chance or by being hit by a stone (but certainly not by a pistol ball as the authorities suggested at the time) – after which John Ridley, a bootmaker of Covent Garden, 'stepped from the footpath into the road way the better to ascertain the cause of the noise . . . his foot slipped, he was thrown towards the carriage . . . and to save himself he thrust his hand against the coach door to push himself back so as to escape the wheel.' This 'attack' was used by the government as a justification for the harsh actions that had already been taken against those suspected of harbouring sympathy for French Revolutionary principles and paved the way for the repressive sedition acts of 1795. As Place observed, 'had Ridley been apprehended he would probably have been hanged for attempting the King's life and, as he was a delegate from one of the Divisions of the London Corresponding Society it [would have been seen by the government as] a plot got up by the leaders of the Society.'

A far more severe test of government authority was to come in April and May 1797 when elements of the Royal Navy mutinied. Those at

Spithead, Portsmouth, principally sought an improvement in their living conditions and a pay rise. But those who followed suit at the Nore demanded not only better service conditions but radical political changes as well, including an end to the war with France. The Spithead mutineers were treated leniently by the Admiralty and pardoned, but the Nore mutineers were not, with thirty sailors who had been identified as ringleaders executed and many others flogged, jailed or transported.[5] Government suppression at its most severe was demonstrated the following summer in Ireland in the wake of an uprising led by the middle-class and Protestant-dominated United Irishmen. Supported somewhat belatedly with French aid, the rebels sought liberty from England and the creation of an independent republican government, based on religious tolerance and fraternity. The uprising started in late May 1798 but by mid July all was over bar the suffering and the ruthless and vengeful suppression that saw many United Irishmen and Irish patriots executed, often in dreadful circumstances.

Given the authorities' terror of sedition and revolution it is hardly surprising that they should have been constantly concerned about the mood in Spitalfields, with its recent history of riot and insurrection. Their assumption seems to have been that the majority of the local working population would be in sympathy with the republican, egalitarian, anti-monarchist principles of the French Revolution. Superficially, the histories of the people making up a large proportion of the population of Spitalfields suggested this would be the case. The area's large population of non-Anglicans – including those of Huguenot descent – were essentially the 'Dissenters' that Nelson feared because, he assumed, they were republican in their outlook. The increasingly paranoid authorities must have been particularly worried by the Huguenots because their ancestors had been the victims of an arbitrary and ruthless wielding of royal power, while Spitalfields' Irish population, particularly if Catholic, had little reason to revere the British monarchy. Consequently when in February 1793 Britain found itself at war with Republican France, Spitalfields was kept under close scrutiny as a likely breeding ground for sedition and treason.

Particular attention was paid to the activities of the London Corresponding Society (LCS), an organisation with strong links to the area. The LCS had been established in January 1792 by Thomas Hardy, a

Scottish-born shoemaker, for the promotion of the reform of Parliament. Its aims were relatively modest: universal suffrage, annual Parliaments, wages for MPs to allow them to operate independently of patronage or private means, and the freedom to form popular associations. Membership of the LCS was drawn mainly from the ranks of artisans and tradesmen such as Francis Place, who in the early 1790s became a member of its Executive Committee. Its methods were decidedly non-violent. It wanted to debate, to lobby, to correspond with like-minded organisations and achieve change through reform not through bloody revolution. But, even if itself an advocate of non-violence and reform, the LCS could be provocative. The toasts proposed in its committee room on 23 January 1794 were 'To the Rights of Man – and may Britons never want spirit to assert them', 'Success to the arms of Freedom against whomsoever directed, and confusion to despots with whomsoever allied', to 'Citizen Thomas Paine – may his virtue rise superior to calumny and suspicion, and his name still be dear to Britons', and 'A speedy and honourable peace with the brave Republic of France'.[6]

Hardy was arrested in 1794 and put on trial for high treason.[7] But he was fortunate. Many trials after 1794 were to be conducted without a jury, but Hardy's case was heard before his fellow citizens and they found him not guilty. This, at the time, was a notable victory for common sense, marking a popular reaction against the government's increasingly repressive penal policies. As John Ashley, Secretary of the LCS, wrote in a pamphlet in December 1795: 'Let us remember, that we are not YET deprived of trial by Jury:- The English Juries have long been celebrated for their Opposition to cruel laws.'[8]

Official files now lodged in the National Archives reveal the lengths to which the government went to find out about the LCS and its membership.[9] The documents that tumble out of the dusty folders still make chilling reading. A letter of 12 January 1796 from James Powell to Richard Ford is a case in point. On one level it seems harmless enough: the letter is little more than a note apologising for a failure to keep in touch due to illness. But one phrase is very revealing: 'I would have sent [the letter] to you before but this is the first day I have been able to go out and had nobody I could trust to put it into the post on account of the direction.' Powell, it transpires, was a government informant within the LCS and Ford an under-secretary within the office of the Secretary of State for Home Affairs based in Whitehall. Powell, in other words, was part of a

Above: *Gillray's print of April 1798 depicts members of the London Corresponding Society skulking in a cellar, reading of 'State Arrests'. The name at the top of the list is, predictably, Irish – 'O'Conner'. The portraits on the wall are of 'Horne Took' and 'Tom Payne'. Although Gillray regularly caricatured the king he was a conservative and promoted the government's line by constantly attacking radicals.* Below: *the obverse of the 1795 London Corresponding Society medallion. It shows the Roman fasces – a bundle of twigs bound together – representing the belief that by 'corresponding' together parliamentary reformers would gain strength through unity.*

government fifth column within what they perceived to be a fifth column. Francis Place was later to describe Powell as 'an easy, silly fellow . . . but honest . . . whose relations were gentlefolk, well informed respectable people'. Given what Powell was up to, this doesn't seem a particularly penetrating character study.

In a letter to Ford of 11 June 1796 Powell describes a meeting of LCS members; 'Most violent among them was Harpin, an Irishman, by trade a shoemaker, by Religion a Roman Catholic. He knew the Catholics of Ireland to be staunch friends of Liberty and Equality and enemies to Tyranny and Oppression. They were blood to the backbone and would jump mast-high if they had an opportunity of fighting for Liberty.' This Irish patriot cursed 'what was called the Glorious Revolution of 1688 when a bloody foreigner was brought over here to be a tyrant over this country and Ireland', damned the 'thieves and murderers who had succeeded him' and declared he was 'willing to lose the last drop of his blood in fighting the bloody Pope [meaning, presumably, the prime minister or king] of this country.' Powell offered a mild excuse for Harpin by declaring that he 'appeared to be a little heated with liquor' but this statement provided enough evidence to jail the man – or even to hang him.

By October 1796 Powell was in financial trouble and seems, through ill health, to have failed to attend LCS meetings. He thus had little to report to his masters, and was clearly worried that in losing his importance to them he might also forfeit his government 'allowance'. A letter dated 28 October, addressed from 3 Ossulston Street, Somers Town – then an artisan area of North London – is both a plea for understanding and an admission that he had been betraying his friends and the LCS on a regular basis, for money. 'Since my first being employed by you, Sir,' he writes, 'I am certain I have done everything in my power to fulfil my duties of that employment. During the whole of the last year, the greatest part of which time I was in office in the Society, I am sure, Sir, I was always regular in my reports to you & anxious to do everything in my power for the service of government.' Powell points out that, 'at the time of the great general meetings you always found me ready to do everything you wished, and that during the passage of the Treason & Sedition Bills when the Committees met three or four times in a week . . . you yourself believed Sir had I been discovered it would have been attended with much personal danger.'

He pleads:

> [A]ll I wish, Sir, is that I may still be continued in my employment [and]
> still have my £10 per month. You will find Sir I am able to be of greater
> service from my absence as it must do away every lurking suspicion against
> me (& there were certainly some) ... I am actually without any money
> whatever [but] am certain Sir you will find nobody so ready or willing, &
> from situation, I may say abilities, has it so much in his power to serve gov-
> ernment as myself.

Powell's begging letter worked. He retained his status as government spy
and also managed to rise within the ranks of the LCS. In a letter to Ford
of 10 December 1796 he boasts of 'having been elected to the Executive
Committee ... I last night took my seat [and] was elected reporter, the
principle officer in the society, except the Secretary as all the correspondence and all the business of the Society must go through my hands.'

The Privy Council records include names, addresses and occupations of
LCS members that must have been compiled by Powell and other informers. They also include minutes – actual or copies – of the meetings of the
Executive and General Committees and of 'Division' meetings. One of
these minutes, which records the Executive Committee meeting of 9
December 1796 (the one at which Powell was elected 'reporter'), also
reveals the way in which a powerfully placed *agent provocateur* could get
the society to incriminate itself. Powell, who 'presided' over the meeting
that night, proposed that 'the names of the members of the committee
appointed to write or to answer letters or to do any other business for the
Society be reported to the General Committee.' One of the members present – John Bone – opposed the proposal because 'in the case of any
prosecution [of the LCS] it would be a clue to the Attorney General to
get evidence.' Bone was right of course, but his opposition was rejected
and Powell's proposal carried.

Place tells an extraordinary tale about a meeting that took place in
London in January 1798 that reveals the lengths government *agents provocateurs* were prepared to go to in order to entrap members of the LCS.
Apparently, a man named 'O Quigley' had come over from Ireland to
advise on the setting up of an active cell of the LCS based on the model
of the Society of United Irishmen that was soon to embark on its bloody
and ultimately fruitless rising against English rule. To be associated with
an organisation committed to armed resistance was to court disaster, as
Powell was no doubt well aware. He therefore managed to get himself

made 'coadjutor' of the fledgling Society of United Englishmen and, at this initial exploratory meeting, as Place discovered to his horror, the organisation committed itself to armed resistance, its 'object' being 'to produce a revolution'. In Place's view 'a more absurd and ridiculous project never entered the heads of men out of Bedlam' and he quickly realised that the organisers of the meeting had been 'prompted by emissaries of government who were well informed of all their proceedings'.

Virtually all those present were seized. Powell, however, managed to 'escape'. Curiously this did not alert Place to his coadjutor's treachery. He was of the view that Powell was 'the most dangerous man among them' but only because he was so gullible and immature: 'There was no absurdity ... that Powell did not eagerly go into, nothing which any villainous spy could suggest that he would not adopt.' Had Powell been taken and questioned, concluded Place, 'he would have told all he knew, and altho' he knew no more than any spy ... it would have been from the mouth of one of [the society].' Powell's cover was clearly superb: Place had no idea that the 'emissary' of government who orchestrated the fatal meeting was Powell himself. In fact, Place hid Powell and then helped him to 'escape' to Hamburg. O Quigley – or properly the Reverend James O'Coigly – was not so lucky. While attempting to escape to France in February 1798 he was captured at Margate, with a store of gold and an incriminating letter headed 'The Secret Committee of England to the Executive Directory of France'.[10] He was tried for treason, found guilty and executed on 7 June. Philip Anthony Brown, in *The French Revolution in English History*, published in 1918, called O'Coigly an 'undoubted revolutionary', but also an 'heroic figure'. His arrest was perhaps the work of Powell. The brutal sentence was, no doubt, partly the consequence of the violent actions of the United Irishmen just then being quelled in Ireland.[11]

Powell's genteel background made him an unusual figure in the LCS. Most members were far more humble. A breakdown of the trades of the membership of one of the Westminster 'Divisions' in 1794/6 shows that of the twenty-three members, five were smiths, four were shoemakers and two were bricklayers. Numerous LCS members came from Spitalfields. At an Executive Committee meeting attended by Powell on 10 July 1794, mention is made of Charles Pretty of 68 Shoreditch, and Jno. Thompson of 56 Norton Folgate. In the Home Office files kept in the National Archives is a 'True List of the names of the members of the 25th Division as taken from the Book of the Division', dated 20 February 1794 and signed

'George Beire, Delegate', that includes among its eighty-three names and addresses many who lived in such streets as Brick Lane, 'Great Pearl Street', Wheeler (sic) Street, and Norton Folgate, Elder Street ('Tho. Sanders' at number 14) and 'Fleur de Lis Court' (Jos. Butler at number 6).[12]

The membership of the division seems to have been fluid, local weavers joining and leaving its ranks on a regular basis. Certainly quite a few names mentioned at a meeting held on 9 December 1796 had not featured on the 20 February 1794 list. By now membership of such a society was far more dangerous than it had been two and a half years earlier so the men mentioned in December 1796 must have been amongst the LCS hard core in Spitalfields: 'David Jones, 36 Bishopsgate-within, Taylor; George Prichard, 12 Flower de Lisle Street, Norton Falgate, weaver; Alexander Prichard, 12 Flower de Lisle Street, Norton Falgate, weaver; James Lesbourgeon, 2 Artillery Street; William Page, Steward Street, Bishopsgate; Jo. Lambourne, 29 Rose Street, Spitalfields, Robt. Berry, West Street, Spitalfields Market, weaver.'

These lists offer a fascinating geography of political radicalism in Spitalfields in the volatile mid 1790s and hint at a profile of the area. Most of the members lived in the smaller, older and more humble streets, courts and alleys of Spitalfields – such as Wheeler (sic) Street, 'Great Pearl Street', 'Phoenix Street', 'Smock Alley' (now Artillery Passage) and Brick Lane – with none based in what were the still-grand streets inhabited by master weavers and merchants such as Spital Square, 'Church' (now Fournier) Street and 'Wood' (now Wilkes) Street, and very few in the main streets of the Old Artillery Ground such as Steward, Gun, Duke or Fort Streets or adjoining Crispin Street. Although the houses in these Artillery Ground streets were relatively small and old, in the 1790s they were generally still prosperous and the homes, warehouses, shops and workshops of master weavers and merchants.

The names on the list were evidently journeymen not masters, people who had suffered decades of poverty and uncertainty toiling on the periphery of the weaving industry. They had perhaps been 'cutters' and potential anti-authority rioters in the 1760s – men who believed that the application of the principles of the LCS would greatly improve their own lives and, perhaps idealistically, the lives of all working people. There are few French names on the various lists, mostly no doubt because the weaving community had been greatly expanded by the large numbers of English and Irish workers entering its lower echelons during the eighteenth century. Only one eminent Huguenot name is included: Jn. Jervis, living in

'Great Pearl Street' and mentioned in the February 1794 list. The Jervises had been a distinguished family of master weavers in early-eighteenth-century Spitalfields, based in White's Row.[13]

Of all the houses mentioned in the LCS records only one, it seems, still survives: the home of Thomas Sanders at 14 Elder Street (now number 5 Elder Street), included in the February 1794 list. Built in 1725 the house has a handsome and regular elevation, is four storeys high above a basement and would have contained about eight rooms, those on the lower two floors being well panelled (see pages 235–8). For Sanders to have occupied the entire house in 1794 would have required considerable personal wealth. Land Tax assessments of Elder Street in the late eighteenth and early nineteenth centuries, however, do not mention him among the 'head tenants' of the house. Presumably, then, he was a subtenant or a humble live-in employee of the head tenant.

Another Elder Street connection with the LCS still survives. In the 1990s the historian Raphael Samuel, who lived at 19 Elder Street – a house built in 1727 and formerly numbered as 20 – lifted a floorboard and found a large bronze medallion emblazoned with the name of the London Corresponding Society, dated 1795 and bearing the image of a dove of peace and the legend 'United for a Reform of Parliament'. Presumably it had been loyally retained and hidden – rather than cast away – when the LCS was declared illegal and to be associated with it was to court danger. The medallion remains in the possession of Samuel's widow.

Reports of the chillingly named 'Committee of Secrecy' of the House of Commons, which gathered information on allegedly subversive political societies such as the LCS, appeared in 1794 and 1799. They included reprints of LCS pamphlets as well as minutes and letters acquired by spies such as Powell. A quotation from a pamphlet by Hardy was included in which he raised the question: 'Will you wait till Barracks are erected in every village, and till subsidised Hessians and Hanoverians are upon us?' For the authorities this was a clear echo of the revolutionary struggle of the American patriots twenty years earlier. It is not surprising, therefore, that the 1794 report should have concluded, after considering the 'evidence' gathered, that the proceedings of the LCS 'become everyday more and more likely to affect the internal peace and security of these kingdoms and to require, in the most urgent manner, the immediate and vigilant attention of Parliament.'

Despite government harassment, persecution and anti-French propaganda, however, the LCS continued to enjoy support from large numbers of working men throughout the mid 1790s. In November 1795 an estimated 300,000 supporters were said to have attended a meeting called by the society. In this context one can only wonder with what bitter contempt ordinary Londoners would have viewed such sensationalist cartoons as James Gillray's 'Promis'd Horrors of the French INVASION' of 1796 in which leering French troops are seen goose-stepping, flogging and butchering their way along St James's Street. Another crude Gillray cartoon of 1798, showing a brutish band of LCS members gathered in a cellar and each stricken with 'alarm' due to a 'guilty conscious', seems to be further evidence of the now commonly held view that he was a government man and presumably a committed and well-paid propagandist.

Finally, in 1799, the government dropped its mask of pained tolerance. With the Unlawful Societies Act, given royal assent in July, the LCS was finally outlawed and its leaders dispersed. Hardy had already retired from active campaigning; Place had left the society some years before. Now the remaining activists were forced to abandon the public expression of their convictions. As historian E. P. Thompson explains in his seminal 1963 study *The Making of the English Working Class*, after 1799 ordinary working men were seemingly left with no means of demanding a reform of Parliament. For would-be radicals the position was made worse by a swelling wave of patriotism. The threat of a French conquest of Britain rather than its fraternal liberation – which became a real possibility after 1797, when the newly powerful General Napoleon Bonaparte made the political and military subjugation of Britain a prime aim in the French plan for world domination – reunited British society and marginalised radicals. In the mounting ferment arguments for parliamentary and social reform were sidelined while Britain fought a battle for survival. Napoleon's declaration 'let us . . . annihilate England [so that] Europe is at our feet' possibly saved Britain from another revolution.

Some sense of the paranoia of the time, and of the likely mood in Spitalfields, is given by an account of the trial by jury of one Thomas Breillat in the Middlesex Sessions House on Clerkenwell Green on 6 December 1793, charged with uttering seditious words. Breillat lived in the parish of St Leonard's Shoreditch in the county of Middlesex and was a pump-maker. Pumps were elegant court or dancing shoes for women and men. Men's pumps usually had uppers made of patent leather or a dark material such

Gillray's vision of October 1796 of the 'Promis'd Horrors of the French INVASION', showing French troops goose-stepping along St James's Street as Tories are tossed off the balcony of White's Club and St James's Palace burns. In the foreground the Whig Charles James Whig Fox thrashes the Prime Minister William Pitt, while Thomas Erskine (in legal wig and gown), who represented Tom Paine when tried for seditious libel in December 1792, stands in front of a guillotine mounted on the balcony of the Whig 'Brookes's' club, holding a burning copy of the Magna Carta while also brandishing a 'New Code of Laws'.

as black velvet. Women's, on the other hand, could have ornamental uppers of silk and so Breillat could therefore be considered a member, or at least an adjunct, of the Spitalfields silk industry. It is also possible, but not provable, that Thomas Breillat was related to the 'Sam. Breilet' of '2 Maidenhead Ct., Spittlefields' mentioned in the February 1794 list of members of the 25th Division of the London Corresponding Society. Maidenhead Court, now entirely obliterated, was immediately north of Fleur de Lis Street.

Men such as Breillat – independent-minded and educated tradesmen – were among the more enthusiastic supporters of the French Revolution in its early days. And with Breillat this support may have had an additional dimension. His surname suggests that his ancestors were among the Huguenots who fled to London in the late seventeenth and early eighteenth centuries and, if so, he is unlikely to have felt any sympathy for the ousted royal regime in France, would most probably have welcomed the Republic and favoured a more wide-reaching democracy in Britain. Breillat, who later events connect with the London Corresponding Society, no doubt believed he was doing no more than exercising his right to speak his mind in a free country when he supported the arguments for parliamentary reform. But if this was the case, then in late 1793 he found himself confronted by a paranoid government, inflamed and perhaps misled by informers, which regarded free speech of a certain kind as a criminal act worthy of merciless punishment. The ruthless suppression directed against Breillat in 1793 could only have confirmed him in the opinion he no doubt held that there was something rotten in the state. After the trial he had the short-hand transcript published, presumably to reveal to the wider world the injustice he felt to be lurking beneath the formal veneer of the law.[14]

The indictment of Breillat, which took the form of eleven similar and interrelated counts, was that he was 'a malicious, seditious, and ill disposed person . . . wickedly and seditiously devising and intending to move and incite the liege subjects of our said lord the King to hatred and dislike of the Constitution of the Government of this Realm, and to cause the said subjects to wish for, and to endeavour to procure a subversion of the said Constitution.' The evidence for this charge came from a 'certain conversation' between Breillat and others which took place in St Leonard's parish and which was overheard – and duly reported – by 'divers liege subjects of our . . . lord the king'. The 'malicious, seditious and inflammatory words' that Breillat was alleged to have said 'with a loud voice' were that

'Reformation cannot be effected without a Revolution' – a 'subversion', the prosecution claimed, 'of the Constitution of the Realm in contempt of our said lord the King and his laws, to the evil and pernicious example of all others.' The reference to Breillat using a 'loud' voice is significant. There is all the difference, legally, between a private, quiet and intimate conversation between friends and a public harangue. What is permissible when said conversationally can become an offence when voiced publicly.

Breillat is then alleged to have made numerous other statements – overheard and reported by 'liege subjects' – which, in the eyes of the law, were at least equally seditious. These included: 'We have no occasion for kings', 'There never will be any peace or good times until all kings are abolished from the face of the earth', and 'It is my wish that there were no kings at all'. More sensational was his alleged declaration that: 'I wish the French would land one hundred thousand men in England to fight against the Government Party.' Britain was, of course, at war with France when the statement was alleged to have been made.

Breillat pleaded not guilty.

The counsel prosecuting for the Crown – a Mr Silvester – told the jury that a 'more inflammatory set of words could not be got together by the wickedest subject of the kingdom'. The wish for a liberating French army to invade was particularly criminal: 'gentlemen . . . can there be a worse subject existing than the man who could harbour these ideas in his breast for a single moment? Would not Government, or those persons employed under the Government to protect our lives and liberties, have neglected their duty if they had not brought such a man forwards . . .?' The only question the jury had to decide, said Silvester, was whether Breillat spoke any of the words alleged in the indictment. If so then he must be found guilty. But Silvester was not content just to offer the jury this simple piece of advice. He continued his speech by making a further attack, calculated to make Breillat appear almost perverse in his wickedness.

> What will you say Gentlemen, when I tell you that that man is a man of property, is a man in a situation of life to have influence in his neighbourhood . . . possessed of land and houses . . . he is a man of fortune [and] has had the honour to sit in that box that shall screen him today . . . Here you have not a low man, it is acknowledged that he is a man of property, that he is in a good situation in life, that he is your equal, and therefore becomes the more an object of danger.

As the prosecution case unfolded, more facts – and alleged facts – came to light. Breillat's home, it emerged, was in Holywell Lane (although called Street in the report), a street running west off Shoreditch High Street, just on the boundary between Shoreditch and Spitalfields. He also had another house on the nearby Hackney Road. His offence, the prosecution claimed, had been committed 'at the house of a Mr Goodman, publican'. Goodman stated in his evidence that he did not immediately raise the alarm but waited until he heard reports in Spitalfields – 'where there are thousands of inhabitants, who are of the lower class and of the poorer sort of people' – of a meeting to be held on Breillat's property, which evidently incorporated a field, on the Hackney Road. Here, stated Goodman, 'they boasted that they would have thousands of persons to come, whose sense they were to take upon the propriety of a reform.' When magistrates and constables entered the premises on 24 October they found 'a thousand people, pretty nearly, assembled in Breillat's field, with himself there; and by their exertions, they dispersed the meeting and no harm was done.'

Cross-examination conducted by Mr Vaughan, counsel for the defence, established that Goodman was not only a publican and victualler, but a police officer. Mr Vaughan accused Goodman of withholding information, questioned his sobriety and his memory of the incident, his ability to hear the conversation and his reasons for believing that Breillat intended 'to work on the minds of the people through the proposed meeting in Hackney'. It emerged that Goodman never learnt the true nature of the meeting. 'Don't you know', asked Vaughan, 'the purpose of the meeting was to petition for a reform in Parliament, or take some measure for that purpose?' 'No,' replied Goodman. The defence counsel also pointed out that 'notice was given to such magistrates and that their attendance was particularly desired by the people who ordered the meeting [in Hackney]'.

Vaughan took the prosecution's ignorance of the actual circumstances and intentions of the meeting as the basis of Breillat's defence. He argued that Breillat's statement that 'there would not be good times till all Kings were abolished from the face of the earth' could not be taken as evidence of sedition on the part of the defendant as it had been read from a book, and therefore could not be charged as anything other than a libel. Indeed a defence witness was to testify the book Breillat read from was actually the Bible, the thoughts expressed being inspired by Chapter 11 of the apocalyptic Book of Revelation of St John the Divine, which states that in the visionary 'new heaven' and 'new earth' – the 'New Jerusalem' – 'the

kingdoms of this world are become *the kingdoms* of our Lord, and of his
Christ, and he shall reign for ever and ever' (11:15). Breillat, explained
Vaughan, interpreted this text as a prophecy relating to current affairs in
France. There was no conversation, said Vaughan, about the abolition of
kings from the face of the earth.

As for the prosecution's assertion that the Hackney meeting resembled
the Protestant Gordon Riots of 1780, Vaughan argued that 'so far was this
meeting at Hackney from bearing any such character, that it was constructed upon a different model, and I will tell you what model, not of
tyranny – not of fanaticism – not of fire and sword', but, as he explained,
modelled on, and aimed to uphold, the principles of freedom enshrined in
the 'Glorious Revolution' of 1688. This was a good point well made because
it allowed Vaughan, inspired by the arguments of the Revolution Society,
to remind the court that the notion of revolution could, in certain circumstances, be regarded as beneficial.

It was true, admitted Vaughan, that Breillat had said that 'a reformation
cannot be effected without a revolution', but 'revolution', argued Vaughan,
does not mean 'a subversion of the government . . . Gentlemen . . . it means
the revolving of things and returning to the point from which they first set
out.' Referring back to the Glorious Revolution, that removed the Catholic
and increasingly autocratic James II, Vaughan suggested to the court that
a return to first and better principles 'was done at the revolution. James
wanted to ruin the constitution; when James abdicated the throne and
William had delivered this country from slavery, then took place the revolution; then was the glorious revolving of things; then it returned to its
original state, and then it was that our benefits were complete.'

Vaughan was scathing about the contemporary culture of denunciation:

> . . . we live in times which are somewhat strange. We live in times when
> word-catching and libel-catching seem to be the fashion of the day; when
> men seem to think they recommend themselves and to suppose it the gen-
> teelest thing in life to call down others for their unguarded expressions,
> and to dignify the character of an Englishman with that of a spy and an
> informer . . . Gentlemen, there are, as we all know, a monstrous number of
> committees of those bodies who call themselves associations against repub-
> licans and levellers, but they would give themselves a far better name by
> calling themselves associations for receiving information – anonymous let-
> ters and carrying on prosecutions. These gentlemen have 150 committees in

different parts of the capital . . . there is not a word spoken by any of you in a butcher's shop, or any other, but it may be carried to the office of these gentlemen, exactly as at Venice, where you may throw a piece of paper into the mouth of a lion.

Breillat's counsel continued by defending the right of free speech: 'God forbid that I should think likewise that reform cannot be effected without revolution, but . . . I have a right to say so.' And the fact that this right was being eroded, he stressed, 'is what I am assured of from every observation which I have been able to make; from conversations, and particularly the conversations of those who are the most active in opposing this reform, and in bringing forward this disgrace to our country, this gang of spies and informers, and to place their fellow-citizens in imprisonment and ruin them by fines.'

In conclusion, Vaughan argued that the case against Breillat had not been proved.

The judge, though, was clearly not convinced. In his summing-up Mr Justice Mainwaring addressed the jury thus:

> Certainly we cannot but admit that no man is punishable for the discontent and dissatisfaction of his own mind; men have a right to their own opinions . . . but no man in a discontented state of mind is to infuse that discontent into the minds of others, by which he disturbs the public tranquillity . . . I would have you . . . take into consideration, not merely whether he said the words, but the intent with which he uttered them . . . it has been said by the learned counsel of the defendant that a reform is necessary, and that he thinks so; he has a right so to think; but the question is, what method is to be taken to obtain it: a man wishing to bring about a reform has no right to enforce it by violence, by force of arms, that is no less an offence than high treason . . . it is asked, what is a revolution? A revolution does not mean a subversion of government, it means a revolving of things. It may have that meaning in some cases; but you must take the subject matter; if it is applied to the government of this country, it is a subversion, a total change in the government of the country, there cannot be two opinions about it.

This was the nub of the case. To lobby for change, for a 'revolution' of affairs, might be acceptable. But, so far as the authorities were concerned, to advocate and attempt to orchestrate a violent revolution of government was sedition.

The jury retired to deliberate for about three hours. Their verdict was that the defendant was guilty of all except the last two counts in the indictment, though they recommended leniency. Had Breillat been found guilty of high treason, he could theoretically have been subjected to the barbarous ritual of being hanged, drawn and quartered. Even conviction on a lesser charge could have resulted in a long term of imprisonment or even transportation. As it was the court sentenced him to twelve months' imprisonment, a £100 fine, and required security for his good behaviour for three years, with Breillat himself paying a £500 surety and two others standing sureties of £250 each. Speaking one's mind in the mid 1790s could be an expensive business. But at least the good sense of the people of Britain – even when under pressure from the government, with its repressive emergency laws and informers – ensured that it was rarely a truly ruinous or lethal activity.

While Breillat was probably still in gaol the rather more high-profile government-sponsored trial of Thomas Hardy took place. In November 1794 the LCS founder and secretary was charged with high treason, along with his associates the radical John Horne Tooke (see page 277) and the rabble-rousing revolutionary John Thelwall. Breillat's defence lawyer Mr Vaughan appears to have been present during at least part of the trial because, following a complaint by a prosecuting counsel, he was questioned by the court about his actions as adviser to the defence team during the cross-questioning of witnesses. And Breillat, too, received a mention: an item offered as evidence by the prosecution stated that: 'At a General Meeting of the London Corresponding Society held at Citizen Breillat's Hackney-road, 23th October 1793' two 'Correspondents' – LCS founding member Maurice 'Margaret' (in fact Margarot) and Joseph Gerrald – were elected as 'delegates' to represent the LCS 'at an ensuing Convention to be held at Edinburgh for the purpose of obtaining a thorough reform in the Parliament, and equal representation of Great Britain.'[15]

Hardy, Tooke and Thelwall were all acquitted by the three separate juries charged to hear evidence. A curious aspect of the case is that James Eyre – who had in 1769 orchestrated the public hangings of Doyle and Valline in Bethnal Green and had been criticised by Tooke for his action – was one of the judges at the trial of Tooke, Hardy and Thelwall. When he addressed the Grand Jury before the trial Eyre argued there was a case to answer because the accused were, in his view, open to the charge of being part of 'a traitorous and detestable conspiracy . . . formed for subverting the existing laws and constitution, and for producing the system of anarchy and confusion which have so fatally prevailed in France'. Eyre reiterated some of his assertions after the trial when summing up the case against Thomas Hardy, although – seemingly not a man to bear a grudge – in Tooke's case he summed up for an acquittal. The jury evidently took Eyre's advice in the case of Tooke and ignored him when it came to Hardy.[16]

Given the fate that had befallen Breillat such a result was unexpected and highly significant, suggesting a popular repudiation this time round of the government's repressive policies. The trial proceedings also reveal a little more about the purpose of the meeting held at Breillat's Hackney Road property – referred to during the trial as 'Breillat's Yard' – and would seem to confirm his important role in the LCS. As subsequent events proved, Breillat actually got off quite lightly. At their trials in January and March 1794 Maurice Margarot and Joseph Gerrald – the men elected in 'Breillat's Yard' – were found guilty of sedition and each transported to Australia for fourteen years. And in 1803 Colonel Edward Despard – an LCS member of Irish Huguenot descent and former British military hero of the American War of Independence – was actually sentenced to be hanged, drawn and quartered after being found guilty of plotting to assassinate George III. For fear of exciting public outrage the sentence was commuted to mere hanging and beheading. Horatio Nelson, an old fighting companion of Despard's, gave evidence at the trial as a character witness. These were 'somewhat strange' times indeed.

The radicalism of many in the Spitalfields community helped to mark them apart from the majority of their fellow Londoners during the last tumultuous decades of the eighteenth century. The same is true of their cultural and intellectual interests. One of the defining features of Spitalfields life through the centuries is the extent to which it has constantly embodied paradox: great wealth alongside appalling poverty, beauty juxtaposed with squalor. And in Georgian Spitalfields, intimidation, violence and cruelty existed alongside an appreciation of nature and of learning. Indeed throughout the later eighteenth century and well into the nineteenth, the area was home to various learned societies – the fruits of its earlier decades of wealth when weavers had time and money to indulge their curiosity. Moreover, among many weavers, or at least among those with enquiring minds who were committed to self-improvement, there was a love not just of subjects such as mathematics but of natural beauty, natural history and, more specifically, flowers and birds. Often, political radicalism, intellectual curiosity and a love of nature went hand in hand.

Of the twin passions for flowers and birds it was probably flowers that were most important to the mental well-being of Spitalfields' weavers. Indeed by the 1790s some observers saw the weavers' passion for flowers as emblematic of their community and their pattern of work. It was a cultivated interest that distinguished them as skilled and prosperous artisans who enjoyed moments of well-deserved leisure and which raised them above the ranks of mere labourers, condemned to a remorseless and brutalising hand-to-mouth existence. Robin Veder has suggested in an illuminating essay that perhaps 'artisans grew flowers' and 'labourers did not' because labourers 'lacked the moral fibre to resist the time-consuming vices of gambling, drink, and thievery'.[17] Be that as it may, the skilled and painstaking pastime of rearing flowers could be seen as a critical activity. If a weaver could raise flowers successfully he was not only distinguishing himself from a common labourer but also utilising and displaying those talents that made him a skilled and useful artisan – manual dexterity, the power of concentration, self-discipline and aesthetic taste. All of this suggested that weavers, as a community, were intellectually sophisticated. Mixed in with their dreams of liberty and equality was a love of aesthetic pursuits.

As early as 1795 one local man at least regretted that such people, their interests and their way of life, were under threat. John Thelwall who, with Thomas Hardy and John Horne Tooke, had enjoyed a near-miraculous escape in November 1794 when tried for high treason, was the radical son of a Spitalfields silk mercer. He was, as well as a London Corresponding Society and Jacobin activist, an inflammatory public orator on all matters revolutionary. In addition – as if to demonstrate the interface between politics and art – Thelwall was something of a pastoral poet.

In his 'On the Causes of the Late Disturbances', Thelwall wrote in September 1795 of a world where 'local leisure pursuits and places' such as flower gardens were being lost. He recalled a time in Spitalfields 'when a man who was a tolerable workman in the fields, had generally, beside the apartment in which he carried on his vocation, a small summer-house and a narrow slip of a garden, at the outskirts of the town, where he spent his Monday, either in flying his pidgeons, or raising his tulips.' All this, however, was changing: 'those gardens are now fallen into decay. The little summer-house and the Monday's recreation are no more; and you will find the poor weavers and their families crowded together in vile, filthy and unwholesome chambers, destitute of the most common comforts, and even of the common necessaries of life.'[18]

Thelwall was, to a significant degree, echoing the sentiments of Oliver Goldsmith – a poet he greatly admired. In 'The Deserted Village' of 1770, Goldsmith extols the virtues of innocent bucolic existence, celebrates the invigorating character of the countryside 'where health and plenty cheered the labouring swain', reveals a deep suspicion of the city – a place of temptation, poverty and oppression for the dispossessed villager – and bewails the 'desolation' that overtakes his idyllic village. The dark agents of change and the destroyer of innocence in his Eden are the modern worlds of trade and industry and the selfish, greedy and exploitative pursuit of excessive wealth and personal pleasure at the expense of common people. In the abandoned glades and village 'the tyrant's hand is seen' as 'one only master grasps the whole domain'. Goldsmith warns that while princes and lords may come and go, 'a bold peasantry, their country's pride, when once destroyed can never be supplied' and that while 'trade's proud empire hastes to swift decay' a 'self-dependent power can time defy, as rocks resist the billows and the sky.'

Thelwall's perception is inevitably a more urban one, but he clearly saw in the decline in floristry among Spitalfields weavers and their loss of gardens and countryside living examples of the grim prophecy enshrined in 'The Deserted Village'. The once 'self-dependent power' of the weaving community was being eroded, the pride, skill and independence of journeymen weavers was being diluted, and in the process they were gradually slipping into the degraded position of exploited and oppressed labourers. Nearly thirty years later, John Claudius Loudon – the botanist, garden designer and author – made much the same point. To him the potted flowers he noted in weavers' windows represented the last expression of their independence: a 'symbol' of 'territorial appropriation and enjoyment' and of what Veder terms 'the inherent pride and pleasure derived from the happy rural life of working the "soil"'.[19] Thelwall saw in this decline a clarion call for action. According to Veder, he wanted weavers, deprived of their flowers and gardens, to transform themselves 'into Jacobin rebels' prepared to 'fight for artisanal independence and proportionate distribution of wealth.'[20]

It was a somewhat idealistic aim. But it was also based on a misreading of the situation, for Thelwall's elegy was premature. Forty-five years later Edward Church, a solicitor and resident of Spital Square, dated the demise of flowers and gardens in Spitalfields, not to the 1790s but to the period between 1810 and 1840 when the area's decline into squalor was fully under way.[21] Robin Veder confirms the continuation of Spitalfields' floricultural traditions long after the 1790s. She cites William Tallack's observation in 1865 that in about 1815 many weavers still had allotment gardens and window boxes full of flowers,[22] and an article published in 1863 in the *Illustrated London News* that confirmed floristry thrived in Spitalfields in the late 1830s and that all who visited the area then would be sure to remember the 'prize tulips and dahlias'.[23] Indeed in June 1838 when James Mitchell was compiling his report 'The East of England' for the Parliamentary Commission on Hand-loom Weavers he stated that he had been able to tour the market gardens on the north edge of Spitalfields and see for himself the floristry that still thrived. The gardens he toured included the six-acre Saunderson's Allotment Garden, one of the many large plots of 'Gardens' and 'Garden Grounds' shown immediately to the north and east of Spitalfields on Horwood's map of 1799–1819. Saunderson's Garden was divided into 170 plots, on which weavers grew – mostly – flowers and some vegetables.[24] Mitchell's account of Saunderson's Garden makes it clear that, even in a time of general poverty, weavers preferred to use their plots to grow flowers rather than food:

> Some of the gardens had cabbages, lettuces, and peas, but most of the cultivators had a far loftier ambition. Many had tulip-beds, in which the proprietors not a little gloried, and over which they had screens which protected from the sun and from the storm. There had been a contest for a silver medal amongst the tulip proprietors. There were many other flowers of a high order; and it was expected that in due time the show of dahlias for that season would not fail to bring glory to Spitalfields.[25]

At this period the East London Amateur Florists' Society and the East London Horticultural Society met at the Salmon and Ball tavern, at the east end of Bethnal Green Road. It seems that, by the 1830s, some weavers were starting to diversify their business activities and make appreciable profits from dealing in their prize flowers. They could sell them at Spitalfields Market – which had long dealt in flowers because 'the weavers have always had a turn for window-gardening'.[26] There was also a flower market in 'Hares Lane', running north from Bethnal Green Road. This appears to been subsumed by the massive Columbia Market that opened in 1869 and is now continued by the Sunday-morning flower market in Columbia Road, which adjoins 'Hares Lane', now named Barnet Grove. The value of the weavers' trade in flowers is suggested by William Bresson, a Spitalfields velvet-weaver and 'loom-broker' of Huguenot descent, who in July 1838 told the House of Commons Parliamentary Commission on Hand-loom Weavers that: 'A tradesman, named Bartlet, a butcher, had a bed of tulips valued at 2,000 pounds; and not long since I knew an operative weaver who was able by the proceeds of his tulip-bed to set up a beer shop, which could not have cost him less than 40 pounds.'[27]

Henry Mayhew, the campaigning journalist and social observer, when writing about Spitalfields in the late 1840s, similarly remembered the weavers' 'former' reputation as avid gardeners but also observed that 'their love of flowers to this day is a strongly marked characteristic of the class'. He described workshops with spinning wheels and three looms in operation and flowers growing inside and out. 'Along the windows, on each side', observed Mayhew, 'were ranged small pots of fuchsias, with their long scarlet drops swinging gently backwards and forwards, as the room shook with the clatter of the looms.' The adjoining gardens, he recorded, were 'filled with many-coloured dahlias'.[28]

At roughly the same time Dr Hector Gavin, the tireless sanitary reformer (see page 382), visited gardens on or near the site of Saunderson's Garden – including the 'extensive' Whisker's Gardens, just north of Bethnal Green Road – and noted that:

> The choicest flowers are frequently raised here, and great taste, and considerable refinement, are evidently possessed by those who cultivate them. Now, among the cultivators are the poor – even the very poor – of Bethnal Green, for the few gentlemen who likewise have their gardens here are inconsiderable in number . . . The weary artisan and the toil-worn weaver here dedicate their spare hours, in the proper seasons, to what has always been considered a refined, as well as an innocent recreation, the cultivation of beautiful flowers.

Gavin was puzzled by the dramatic contrast between the poor weaver's beautiful and ordered garden and his often squalid and chaotic street, home and workshop:

The love of the beautiful, and the sense of order which are readily accorded to the artisan, or weaver, in his neat garden, surrounded by the choicest dahlias or tulips carefully cultivated, are denied to him when visited in his filthy, dirty street. When seen in his damp and dirty home, he is generally accused of personal uncleanliness . . . yet in his garden, he displays evidences of a refined taste and a natural love of beauty and order.

Gavin concluded that since the love of beauty and order 'is natural and spontaneous, we are irresistibly led to regard the personal uncleanliness of the poor, and the impurities which surround their houses, as the result of agencies foreign to the individual.' This contrast between urban squalor and almost sylvan beauty was for Gavin particularly striking because adjoining Whisker's Garden was Pleasant-place, which he described as the 'ne plus ultra of street abomination . . . utterly filthy . . . the street . . . a black, slimy, muddy compost of clay and putrescent animal and vegetable remains.' (Soon this garden would be transformed into ad hoc slum dwellings, later criss-crossed by a grid of mean streets.) Gavin observed that many weavers had erected 'wooden sheds, cabins or huts' on their garden plots to serve as 'summer-houses' and noted that 'it is very greatly to be regretted that the proprietors of these gardens should permit the slight and fragile sheds in them to be converted into abodes for human beings.'[29] Twenty years after Mayhew and Gavin's accounts of weavers' homes and workshops, Isaac Taylor remembered – in 1869 – that 'in a single room I have seen as many as twenty or thirty plants, carefully trained with sticks or trellis-work.'[30]

Weavers often opted to grow flowers that were demanding. The auricula was a particular favourite. As Veder explains, 'These plants are "miffy" (florists' slang for "easily mismanaged"), requiring strongly fertilised soil, controlled moisture, good drainage, frequent ventilation, and mild sun exposure [and] during the blooming period . . . had to be turned, shaded, pinched back, and trained on wire supports, requiring attention at least once a day.'[31] In other words the weavers liked plants that required skill and time. But while the industry was in its prime they had both. Senior and superior weavers – masters or well-established journeymen – could set their own hours. They were still essentially part of a cottage industry, not yet part of a ruthless and unforgiving factory system. So, paid for work measured by the 'piece' and not by the hour or week, they were at liberty – if work was regular and money reliable – to allocate time during the working day to their flowers and to arrange their working week to accommodate their wider interests. They could take Sundays off and – as was a custom in the eighteenth century among skilled workmen in secure employment – also observe 'St Monday' as a full or part holiday, usually to compensate for the use of Saturday as a working day.

As Commissioner Hickson pointed out in 1840 in one of the reports produced for the Parliamentary Commission on Hand-loom Weavers, 'At any moment the domestic weaver can throw down his shuttle and convert the rest of the day into a holiday, or busy himself with some more profitable task'.[32] It must also be remembered that silk weavers' working conditions suited plant growing. It was usual to work with the windows of the weaving garret closed to trap internal moisture so that silk would not dry out and become brittle or lose the sense of 'weight' which added to the fabric's value. This naturally could create a hot-house atmosphere similar to florists' bell jars and cold frames. In addition, panes of glass in the wide windows that were sometimes papered over to protect coloured silks from fading were ideal for protecting petals from direct sunlight.[33]

Contemporary views about why the Spitalfields weavers should have been so devoted to their flowers differed. Gavin suggested that their love of floral beauty revealed their innate character. Mayhew, when compiling the volumes of *London Labour and the London Poor* during the late 1840s and 1850s, came to the conclusion that 'the presence or absence of flowers' in the homes or workplaces of artisans simply 'marked the difference between the well-paid and the ill-paid workman'. For Mayhew, flowers were not so much a badge of taste and the cultural emblem of a skilled artisan as a token of affluence and the possession of a disposable income.[34] Later writers took different stances, too. As Robin Veder points out, for some social historians such as M. Dorothy George whose pioneering *London Life in the Eighteenth Century* was first published in 1925, weavers' floristry was the luxury of the 'labour aristocracy; and evidence that industrialisation was slow and did not significantly affect or reduce the quality of life of most working people in Georgian Britain.' But for others, such as E. P. Thompson in his *Making of the English Working Class* of 1963, the weavers' love of flowers and the countryside were emblematic of an independence that was eventually destroyed by industrial capitalism and Free Trade legislation.[35]

Whatever it was that drew weavers to their flowers, it also seems to have attracted them to bird-keeping. Thelwall talks of pigeon fanciers, but caged birds seem to have been more popular and were often kept in weavers' garrets in the eighteenth and early nineteenth centuries, as this description in the Victoria County History volume on Middlesex reveals:

> The houses occupied by the weavers are constructed for the special convenience of their trade, having in the upper stories wide, lattice-like windows which run across almost the whole frontage of the house. These 'lights' are absolutely necessary in order to throw a strong light on every part of the looms, which are usually placed directly under them. Many of the roofs present a strange appearance, having ingenious bird-traps of various kinds and large bird cages, the weavers having long been famed for their skill in snaring song-birds. They used largely to supply the home market with linnets, goldfinches, chaffinches, greenfinches, and other song-birds which they caught by trained 'call-birds' and other devices in the fields of north and east London.[36]

The goldfinch mule became particularly popular with weavers, replacing the canary as the most melodious songbird of choice. It is hard now to say precisely what the most successful mules actually were because – as the name implies – they were hybrids, specially and selectively bred for their look and their song. It is probable that the most popular cross was between goldfinches and canaries but generations of careful selective breeding must have produced birds that were of unique quality. As with the rearing of flowers, the rearing of birds appealed to something deep within the weavers' psyche: it required skill, knowledge, patience and an aesthetic appreciation of the beauty and wonder of nature. It also engendered a relationship with, or memory of, the countryside that was, in popular memory, the repository of human dignity.

Songbirds became an integral part of East End life. Augustus Hare observed in the late 1870s that 'in a walk through Spitalfields no one will fail to be struck with the number of singing-birds kept in the houses . . . often [in] a large cage near the roof'.[37] And the pastime of collecting, selling and displaying birds outlived the demise of the silk industry. Indeed it survived, albeit in a greatly reduced way, until the late 1970s. The focus of trade and display became Club Row market, at the western end of Bethnal Green Road at the junction with Sclater Street, where, every Sunday morning, the Knave of Clubs public house would be full of caged

The north side of Sclater Street in around 1900. To the west is Bethnal Green Road and Club Row. This Sunday market specialised in the sale of animals and – in particular – birds. The early-eighteenth-century houses, with their wide weaving windows and small windows lighting utilitarian newel staircases, were demolished many years ago.

birds for sale or just for display. Predictably the pub acquired the informal name of 'the Bird Cage'. The building – a fine late-Victorian building – survives. It is now an expensive restaurant.

If birds and flowers were hobbies, albeit hobbies that represented the weavers' pride in their status as skilled and independent artisans, their deep-rooted love of flowers also fed directly back into their trade. As mentioned in Chapter 7, by the early 1740s the London Huguenots were not only matching French silk in quality but starting to develop their own distinct style. In broad terms Spitalfields became famed for its 'figured' (floral-patterned) silk, featuring clusters of flowers and various plants depicted in a manner that was startlingly naturalistic in comparison with contemporary French designs that often included flowers but depicted them in a far more stylised manner.

Because Spitalfields designs were more truthful to nature the attributes of individual plants came into play. For example, wheat was evidently symbolic of fertility, plenty and the classical goddess Flora, while other plants such as hops might celebrate the local brewing industry. The fact that the plant imagery in Spitalfields silk of the mid eighteenth century was often rendered with botanical accuracy raises intriguing possibilities. Could the naturalistic Spitalfields style have been inspired by the ready supply of specimens of flowers, fruits and vegetables available in the markets that opened in the heart of Spitalfields just as the Huguenots started to arrive in large numbers in the mid 1680s? Or – far more likely – was the naturalism of the Spitalfields silk designs yet one more expression of the weavers' love of floristry? It seems self-evident that the flowers the weavers grew and displayed in their lofts and gardens as part of their world of recreation would also provide artistic inspiration for their world of work. According to Deborah Kraak, by the mid eighteenth century naturalistically rendered florists' flowers – the tulip, rose, iris, auricula, carnation, pink, polyanthus, hyacinth and anemone – 'became the core of a tasteful vocabulary of motifs used in disproportionate numbers on English textiles and embroideries'.[38]

This connection between natural history and Spitalfields silk designs is illustrated by the works of two of the area's leading pattern-makers – Joseph Dandridge and Anna Maria Garthwaite (see page 180). Dandridge was born in 1665, lived in Moorfields and was a leading pattern-

maker or silk designer, working for such leading Spitalfields masters as
James Leman, who was of Huguenot descent and whose family had moved
to Spitalfields from Canterbury. In 1702 James Leman was apprenticed
to his father Peter and lived and worked in Steward Street (sometimes
referred to as Stewart Street) in one of the houses recently constructed by
Nicholas Barbon on the site of the Old Artillery Ground. Leman was
himself a pattern-maker as well as a weaver, an unusual combination in
Spitalfields. The fact that he employed Dandridge suggests that he appre-
ciated the designer's special ability, which gave added value to the Leman
output, an ability almost certainly connected both to Dandridge's knowledge of natural history (he was a skilled illustrator, specialising in drawing
plants and insects) and to his talent for using this knowledge to produce
silk designs that were both decorative and popular. He was probably one
of the founders of the Society of Aurelians, a rather grand name for students and collectors of butterflies. A volume of Dandridge's drawings of
c.1700–10 of arachnids (a class of insects that includes spiders, mites, ticks
and insects with silk or poison glands) survives in the Sloane Collection in
the British Museum and shows how skilful, meticulous and informed he
was as a natural historian.[39]

Dandridge's near contemporary Anna Maria Garthwaite was also a
botanical illustrator, but she was the more striking designer, her composi-
tions often possessing notable visual punch and making use of the points
rentrés weaving techniques pioneered by the Lyon master Jean Revel in
1730, whereby colours merge and dovetail in tone to create astonishing
three-dimensional effects. Garthwaite's office ledgers survive – now
lodged in the Victoria and Albert Museum – and offer fascinating insights
into her working methods. The ledgers include design sketches, samples
of silk woven to her designs and the names of the master weavers with
whom she worked. These include Peter Abraham Ogier who lived near
her, in what is now 19 Princelet Street (see Chapter 12).

The popularity of 'figured' silk started to decline from around 1775 but
it continued to be made in Spitalfields, in significant quantities, well into
the nineteenth century. (According to the House of Commons Commission on Hand-loom Weavers of 1840 there were 500 workshops in Spitalfields
employing figured-silk weavers in 1838.) Some might argue that this simply
shows that Spitalfields weavers lost touch with prevailing fashions as their
trade declined and that they continued to rely on hand-production because
weaving silk of this kind was highly skilled and difficult to mechanise.

But the survival of figured silk can also can be seen as a demonstration of their continuing love affair with their flowers, which remained a joy and an inspiration for as long as the trade existed.

This enduring love of flowers and of gardens developed – as James Mitchell and Edward Church observed in the late 1830s – within the context of a wide range of learned societies.[40] Even as the economic status of Spitalfields slowly declined its learned societies – fruits of its earlier decades of wealth when weavers had time and money to indulge their curiosities – continued.

Many of the weavers, journeymen as well as middling masters, were wedded to the notion of self-improvement through education. Spitalfields' weaving community was complex, divided by rank, money, religion and ethnic origin. There were masters, middling weavers who owned their own looms, journeymen who did not, and then the less or unskilled members of the industry who were little more than labourers. It's tempting to assume that it was the more prosperous weavers, the ones who, as Natalie Rothstein has observed, owned their own looms, were 'intelligent, skilled and enlightened within limits' and who were 'generally anxious to be accepted as "gentlemen"', who would largely have made up the membership of Spitalfields' learned societies.[41] Quite where this leaves the journeymen who rioted, were 'cutters' and who intimidated other weavers through the threat of physical violence, is unclear. It is of course possible that such men, fighting ruthlessly for the way of life they knew – indeed for survival – could still, during moments of calm within the storm, have pursued the leisure interests traditional to their trade.

After flowers and birds mathematics seems to have been of most universal interest within the Spitalfields weaving community, perhaps because numbers and calculation were integral to the weaving of fine figured silk. Indeed Thomas Simpson (1710–61), the son of a weaver, and a self-taught mathematician and astronomer, not only went on to become a Fellow of the Royal Society but evolved a mathematical formula called Simpson's Rule. His Spitalfields contemporaries may not have reached quite such heights, but a number, including Simpson himself, were active in such local groups as the Mathematical Society – a select group of enthusiasts who by 1784 were holding their gatherings 'at the sign of the Black Swan in Brown's-Lane, Spitalfields'. A small pamphlet published that year contains a list of the 'Articles' governing the organisation and gives a very good sense of how it operated:

> I. The number of members . . . shall not exceed the square of eight. II. This Society shall meet every Saturday, between the hours of seven and ten; when each member present shall pay fourpence. III. Between the hours of eight and nine, silence shall be kept in the room, and every member present shall employ himself in some Mathematical exercise, or, after admonition from a Steward, shall forfeit twopence for neglect. And if any member be asked a question in the Mathematics by another, he shall instruct him in the plainest and easiest method he can, or forfeit one shilling . . . XV. Every member shall pay sixpence per quarter, towards defraying the expences of the Society . . . and every absent member (except sick and disabled . . .) shall forfeit one penny for each night he is absent . . . XVIII. Visitors permitted, if agreed by Stewards and upon paying six pence . . . XXVI. This Society shall not be removed above half a mile from Spitalfields Church.[42]

The Articles are followed by a 'Catalogue of the Books, Pamphlets, Droughts, Maps and Instruments belonging to the aforesaid Mathematical Society' that runs to over sixty pages. There is also a short history of the society itself, 'which originally consisted of sixty-four members' and which 'was first established at the Monmouth's Head in Monmouth Street, Spitalfields, in the year 1717, by the diligent and successful endeavours of Mr Joseph Middleton, who was a generous encourager of Mathematical Learning.' Monmouth Street, which ran parallel to and west of Brick Lane, was destroyed for the expansion of Truman's Brewery and the railway.

John Timbs in his *History of Clubs and Club Life* of 1872 states that the society was largely made up of 'tradesmen and artisans'. Thomas Simpson was not its only success story. Another member, John Dollond (1706–61), the son of a local Huguenot silk weaver who in his youth worked as a weaver himself, went on to devise improvements to the refracting telescope and to become a pioneering optician. His sons followed in his footsteps, building a company that would, after various changes of ownership, ultimately become Dollond & Aitchison. According to Timbs, alongside its library of over 3,000 volumes, the Mathematical Society possessed air pumps, telescopes, microscopes and electrical machines, and 'long cherished a state for exact science among the residents in the neighbourhood of Spitalfields'. By the late eighteenth century the society was also offering a wide range of public lectures. Its Notebook for 1804 records that 'in the year 1798 a few respectable members of the Society generously stepped forward and gave the public at large an opportunity of increasing their knowledge, on terms so easy, as to be within the reach of every individual, who has a taste to cultivate, or curiosity to gratify.'[43]

This was a difficult year for the society. The silk industry was in a very depressed condition, and suspicion of sedition among the Spitalfields workforce had made the government extremely jittery about all types of societies, not just the political ones. Inevitably, a 'gang of informers' duly infiltrated the Mathematical Society to report on its activities to the authorities. Nothing untoward appears to have been discovered, but the forces of law and order nevertheless seem to have been determined to close the Mathematical Society down just in case, which the 1795 sedition acts potentially gave them the power to do. They therefore accused it, in its promotion of public lectures, of taking money for 'unlicensed entertainment'. The society fought back, there was a court case and it won – although the legal process proved a heavy drain on its resources. But by 1804 it had recovered to the extent that it even broke one of its own 'Articles' by increasing its membership number to the 'square of nine'. In 1821 it fielded five different lecturers to give twenty-two lectures on an impressively wide range of topics: mechanics, hydrostatics, pneumatics, optics, astronomy, chemistry, magnetism, electricity and galvanism. A ticket for each lecture cost one shilling – a not insignificant price.[44]

It's possible to see in the Mathematical Society the roots of an impulse that in the nineteenth century was to lead to a flourishing network of Mechanics' Institutes. This particular movement had its origins in Glasgow in the 1790s when Professor John Anderson left a sum of money to start a second university in the city, to promote 'useful learning' and teach 'practical subjects' for the 'good of mankind' (this became the Andersonian Institute in 1796 and is now the University of Strathclyde). In 1800 George Birkbeck started to lecture at the institute. He was a Quaker, had trained at Edinburgh University as a doctor of medicine, and was the institute's Professor of Natural Philosophy. After his lectures he was often asked – by working men or 'mechanicals' – about the apparatus he used. Thus he perceived that there was a hunger for knowledge among ambitious, intelligent and curious but poorly educated adults. So Birkbeck started to hold free public lectures on Saturday evenings on the 'mechanical arts' – mostly science and technical subjects. These proved very popular and Mechanics' Institutes were duly opened in Edinburgh in 1821 and in Liverpool in 1823. In November 1823, Birkbeck, who by now had moved to London, opened the capital's first Mechanics' Institute and became its president. This London Institute revolutionised access to education in science and technology for ordinary people (it is now part of the University of London), although its charge of one shilling per lecture must, as with the Mathematical Society lectures, have put it beyond the reach of the poorest and neediest of weavers.

But even before founding London's first Mechanics' Institute, Birkbeck had been active in Spitalfields. He and fellow Quaker philanthropists – including Peter Bedford, the brewer Thomas Fowell Buxton, and Joseph and William Allen (see page 389) – were alarmed by the widespread illiteracy amongst the poor children of the area. Their enlightened response – typical of Quakers at that time (see page 393) – was to assume responsibility for remedying this, raise funds and organise a school for 1,000 boys and 500 girls which duly opened in 1812 in 'Spicer Street' (now part of Buxton Street), running east off Brick Lane. The school was open to all children – no matter their race or religion – aged between six and fourteen, on payment of one penny a week or by nomination by a subscriber. Practical and basic education was the aim, pure and simple. The harshness of the times is demonstrated by the fact that it soon proved impossible for many local families to pay even the penny fee and the school struggled until its closure in the late 1830s.[45] Nevertheless, despite its difficulties, this was a noble and pioneering enterprise that, together with the Spitalfields learned societies, distinguished by their long-established principles of self-improvement, provided inspiration and the model for the Mechanics' Institute movement.

Most tellingly, Spitalfields itself did not acquire a Mechanics' Institute. While institutes were being constructed during the 1830s in cotton-rich cities like Manchester and Liverpool, Spitalfields' silk industry – post the repeal of the protectionist Spitalfields Acts (see pages 363–7) – was in final and terminal decline. Not only did Spitalfields not acquire new institutes of learning, during the 1830s its own and venerable Mathematical Society was faltering. As the area's wealth vanished so did its once elite, skilled, proud and educated workforce. By 1845 the society had only nineteen members. Accepting that its dissolution was inevitable, but wanting to keep its library intact, the society offered it to the Royal Astronomical

Society, which was 'grateful' for 'this act of judicious benevolence', regretted that the 'ancient' Mathematical Society was on 'the eve of dissolution
and decline' and instantly elected its nineteen surviving members as members for life of the Royal Astronomical Society.[46]

In 1838 James Mitchell observed that the weavers who from 1773 to 1824
had worked under the protection of the Spitalfields Acts had been – in the
rosy glow of memory at least – something of an aristocracy of labour. 'The
weavers of that day', he suggested, 'were a different class of men, both
intellectually and physically, from the weavers of the present day.' And as
a 'decided proof' of this he cited 'the societies for amusement and instruction which flourished among them.'[47] Edward Church, quoted in Mitchell's
report, described the range of societies that had once been in existence:
not just the Mathematical Society, the Floricultural Society and the
one dedicated to fancy bird breeding, but also societies for history, ento-
mology, music and poetry. The demise of these societies, and the end of
often vociferous – sometimes riotous – trade activism and political radicalism, signified the final disappearance of a whole and very distinctive way
of life within Spitalfields.

TWELVE

PEOPLE OF SPITALFIELDS

The Ogiers and Their World

Peter Abraham Ogier was born Pierre Abraham in 1690 at Chassais-l'Église near Sigournais in Bas-Poitou. He was one of fourteen children, of whom at least ten lived beyond babyhood. His parents, Pierre and Jeanne Ogier, had chosen to remain in France after the Edict of Nantes was repealed in 1685, but in around 1697, in trouble for attending Protestant *assemblées* and with her husband recently dead, a heavily pregnant Jeanne decided to flee to England. She brought with her perhaps eight of her children, leaving two sons behind in France. One, Daniel (born 1683), remained as a Catholic while the other, Pierre (born 1680), struggled as a merchant at Moncoutant until 1730, when he left for England. (Peter was a popular name in the extended Ogier family in London and so Pierre is now generally known as Peter II.) Whether or not Jeanne immediately took up residence in Spitalfields is not known, but given how swiftly the area was being developed at that time, it is perfectly possible.[1]

She evidently recognised that the silk industry offered the prospect of wealth and security for her family (the Ogiers had not been notable silk weavers or merchants in France) and used some of her money to apprentice Peter Abraham to Samuel Brule, a foreign master. In time, Peter Abraham himself became a successful master weaver, a freeman of the Weavers' Company in 1716, and a liveryman in 1741. He also became an elder of La Patente, the French church located first in 'Paternoster Row', within the fruit and vegetable market, and then in 'Browns Lane', now Hanbury Street.[2] His success as a weaver is reflected in the fact that in 1745 he was able to offer twenty-eight men to serve the Crown in the face of Bonnie Prince Charlie's advance into England. Overall, the Ogier dynasty and their six companies were able to volunteer a force of 164 workmen.[3]

In 1712 Peter Abraham married a Frenchwoman – Esther Dubois

(Duboc) – from Normandy at St Dunstan's Stepney (the parish church that served much of central and east Spitalfields until the creation in 1729 of the parish of Christ Church) and the couple went on to have twelve children (seven of whom died young). By the 1740s, if not earlier, he and his family were living at 19 Princelet Street (originally 18 'Princes Street'). The house had actually been built some years before, in 1718/19, and is fairly typical of the period: one room wide, two rooms deep and three storeys high, plus a basement kitchen, pantry and scullery. There would also have been an attic, though probably smaller than the one that can be seen today, which is almost certainly, at least in part, a later-eighteenth-century addition. The internal details of the house are standard products of the workshop of its builder, Samuel Worrall, in his initial Spitalfields houses.

On its lower floors it once contained full-height panelling that was generally without moulded enrichments but was topped by box cornices of Doric profile. The staircase is furnished with full-bellied and sensuously profiled column balusters and square-topped newel posts in the form of a bulbous column set upon an urn. These details are unusual and particular to early Worrall houses but, in the standard manner for medium-sized early-eighteenth-century Spitalfields houses of the better sort, the staircase is set in a rear corner and is of dog-leg form – a space-saving solution in which alternate flights return on each other and are connected by landings or winders. Although a standard product of Worrall's early building practice, number 19 is unusual because, for reasons unknown, the Wood–Michell Estate, on which the house is built, conveyed it freehold – not leasehold – to Worrall. To raise money he conveyed the house in 1721/2 to a consortium comprising a 'drugster, a draper and a glover', who with Worrall made a further conveyance in 1722 to a 'needleworker'. By 1743 the house was confirmed to be in Ogier's occupation.[4] So the fabric of the house predates his influence – but with one remarkable exception. In the first-floor front room there formerly stood a fine timber-made French-style Rococo fire surround of c.1745–50, which Ogier must have added in the last years of his life. It shows that his taste in architectural details was, like his taste in silk designs, refined and inspired by French models. The fire surround was stolen in the early 1980s but was later recovered and is now in storage awaiting repair and reinstatement.

The house has, for Spitalfields, an unusually large rear garden (it's one of the distinctive features of the houses on the north side of Princelet

Number 19 Princelet Street, built in 1718/19 by the speculating builder Samuel Worrall and by 1743 occupied by Peter Abraham Ogier – an eminent master weaver – and his family. In the early 1860s the house was adapted to house a synagogue, at which time the ground floor elevation was remodelled. On the right is part of 21, which dates from 1705/6.

Street and the houses on Fournier Street). This would no doubt have contained a 'house of office' set over a cesspit and have served other practical purposes such as a location for fuel and water storage. But it was large enough to have been ornamental as well and, since Huguenots included gardening amongst their many cultural interests, would probably have been laid out to flowerbeds with plants in tubs set between gravel paths. The plants – including varieties of roses and jasmine – would probably have come from the Shoreditch and Hoxton market gardens of such flowermen and nurserymen as Thomas Fairchild, author in 1722 of *The City Gardener*. As for the lavatory, this might well have been disguised as a plant-veiled pavilion, with roses, perhaps, twined around or in front of it. This was not unusual in the eighteenth century, hence the euphemism for going to the lavatory – to 'go pluck a rose' – as explained in verse by Jonathan Swift:

> The bashful Maid, to hide her Blush;
> Shall creep no more behind a Bush;
> Here unobserv'd, she boldly goes,
> As who should say, to Pluck a Rose.[5]

When completed in the mid 1720s, Princelet Street with its tall houses of regular design and relatively large rear gardens was one of the best streets in Spitalfields. For a successful master weaver and silk merchant such as Peter Abraham Ogier it was therefore a suitably prestigious address.

The Land Tax returns of 1743 for Christ Church Middlesex[6] give a very good sense of the community in which Peter Abraham Ogier lived. The assessors – of whom one was Samuel Worrall, who himself lived in a house in the large yard between Fournier Street (formerly 'Church Street') and Princelet Street ('Princes Street') – noted eleven neighbours for Peter Abraham on the north side of Princelet Street. They were clearly well-to-do: valuations of tax on their houses range from £9 to £14, with one as high as £20, suggesting that in some cases named occupants might well have been in possession of two houses. Ogier himself was assessed to be liable for the average tax paid of £14. (The returns also make it clear that he was, in addition, the occupant of a house in Hanbury Street, probably the one backing onto his Princelet Street house.[7]) Most of the names listed in the returns are French, as one might expect given the period and the location. So, for example, what is now number 1 Princelet Street – on the corner with Wilkes Street – was occupied by Jno. 'Bellynew'. Other residents included Sam. Delors, John Baptiste Bowe, Daniel Pilon, and Rene Turguan.

Thanks to his will, made on 29 October 1761, we know quite a lot about Daniel Pilon, one of Peter Abraham's near neighbours who lived in what is now 15 Princelet Street (formerly 20 'Princes Street').[8] Like Ogier, he was a member of an extensive and successful Huguenot dynasty and may have been given the house as a marriage gift in the 1720s when he married the daughter of the successful master weaver Peter Bourdon, whose own large house survives today, now numbered 27 Fournier Street.[9] Pilon was clearly very well connected. Listed among the trustees of his will, for example, is John Sabatier, who lived virtually opposite Pilon in Princelet Street and who is known to have owned one hundred looms (journeymen weavers who either worked in his warehouse using his looms or worked in their homes using looms owned by Sabatier or hired from him).[10]

Daniel Pilon's daughter Jane was married to Obadiah Agace – a member of another leading Spitalfields weaving family, specialising in fabric formed of silk mixed with worsted. They had three sons, all with splendid Old Testament names: Obadiah, Zachariah and Daniel, and through a network of sisters and numerous cousins and nieces Pilon was also related to many other successful influential people in the area. Pilon was, in short, a rich and successful man who, profitably enmeshed in the upper tier of Spitalfields Huguenot society, prospered in the silk industry to the extent that, in 1745, he was able to muster as many as forty-nine of his workmen. At the time of his death in 1762 Pilon left stocks and shares in the East India Company and the South Sea Company; property in London and Barking; and looms, cloth, frames and his 'wearing goods' to his son, Nicholas Peter. He left his house to his widow – complete with furniture, 'brewing vessels', and 'coppers' for washing clothes – but also granted Nicholas Peter the right to 'enjoy' the house 'for the term of his natural life'. A year later the 1763 edition of *The Complete Compting-House Companion or, Young Merchants and Tradesman's Sure Guide* lists 'Nicholas-Peter Pilon' as being based in 'Prince's Street, Spitalfields', which makes one wonder whether the son actually ousted his mother. According to the records of the Huguenot Society, he died in 1788, apparently leaving no will or documents of administration.

As the Land Tax returns show, Peter Abraham was part of a similar closely entwined network of family and business associates. David Godin, a partner in the silk-weaving firm of Godin and Ogier, by 1759 lived at nearby 24 Hanbury Street (which still survives, although much altered internally).[11] This firm was large enough to muster sixty of its workmen in 1745.[12] In 'Red Lyon Street', widened and slightly realigned in the mid nineteenth century when it became part of Commercial Street, lived John Ogier, probably Peter Abraham Ogier's younger brother, who married Louise Françoise Maillard in 1719 and died in 1777.[13] In 'Church Street' (Fournier Street), probably in the now lost 24 or 26 at the south-east end, there lived 'Thomas Tryquett', who was in all likelihood involved in the silk-manufacturing firm of Ogier, Vansommer and Triquet based in Spital Square.[14] And, crucially for Peter Abraham, in Wilkes Street, on the south-east corner where the road joined Princelet Street (and now numbered 2 Princelet Street) resided Anna Maria Garthwaite (see pages 180–1), the acclaimed pattern-maker or silk designer employed by many of the leading masters of Spitalfields – including Peter Abraham Ogier. The building was Garthwaite's home and workplace from 1728, when she moved in, until her death in 1763.

Peter Abraham's activities as a master weaver were complex and his roles varied. But one thing he would almost certainly not have done, when in his prime as a master, was actually weave. He was no doubt a skilled weaver and had worked as one in his youth, but as a master he would have been more of an entrepreneurial businessman. He would have acquired raw materials, organised their complex processing, commissioned fabric designs and employed journeymen weavers to make the silk before he oversaw its wholesaling to mercers.

Peter Abraham's business activities must have had a direct influence upon the way he and his family occupied 19 Princelet Street and on the arrangement and appearance of its interior. But weaving almost certainly did not take place there during his occupancy. In the first half of the century the Ogiers would have lived in the house in some style and with a number of servants. Business activities would have been limited to meetings with suppliers, designers, weavers and mercers, presumably in one of the ground-floor rooms (now lost) that would have served also as a dining parlour – and perhaps for the occasional display of the latest products. The small attic room, probably at the rear, that existed before its replacement by the existing well-lit weaving garret, would presumably have been used for some practical purpose, perhaps as a counting room.

Sadly there are no records of life in 19 Princelet Street during Peter Abraham's occupation, or indeed detailed records of the daily and domestic lives of any Spitalfields Huguenot families at the time. To attempt a portrait we have to assemble and ponder what physical or documentary evidence survives, and speculate. We know the Huguenots made and admired fine silver ornaments, clocks and furniture, and these – combined with their beautiful silks – must have made the interiors of the principal Huguenot family houses impressive. Furniture is a feature of Daniel Pilon's will, for example, while the 1732 will of the master weaver Peter Bourdon of 27 Fournier Street mentions 'household goods [and] all my plate', which he left to his 'beloved wife Margaret', along with his 'linen, rings and jewels' and, most tellingly, £3,500 in 'lawful money' – a very significant sum at the time.[15] The more affluent of these Spitalfields master weavers were rich indeed.

Archaeological investigation of 19 Princelet Street, and of comparable and contemporary houses in Spitalfields, suggests that their panelled interiors were painted in soft and simple stone colours – either light ochres, pale blue/green greys or 'drab', all realised through the mixing of earth pigments such as 'Oxford Ochre' and umber, organic indigo dye, soot (called 'lamp black') or copper carbonates with white lead ground in linseed oil. Strong, dark colours could be also achieved with these pigments ('lead' colour, for example, olive green, 'wainscot colour' or blue or green verditer) but these seem to have been reserved for very occasional use only, on doors, on skirting or in kitchens or workshops (on plaster as well as timber) from the 1720s to the 1740s.[16] Such a pale, uniform and simple scheme – and most certainly mouldings or panels were not picked out in different colours – would have acted as a splendid foil for rich walnut (and latterly mahogany) furniture, with strongly coloured silk or needlework upholstery, sparkling silver and burnished brass, and prints or family portraits. The high style of the (originally pale-coloured) Rococo fire surround in the first-floor front room of 19 Princelet Street marks this as the main reception room and also confirms Peter Abraham's enduring taste for refined and exquisite French design.[17]

The prosperous Ogiers would, of course, have eaten well, too. And, judging from a late eighteenth-century recipe book that once belonged to

Mrs Merceron, a member of a Huguenot family from Spitalfields or
Bethnal Green (see page 369), they would have enjoyed culinary treats
as well. Her collection largely features speciality dishes, such as 'Port
wine jelly' for the infirm, but it also includes a great many cake recipes –
'common cakes', 'excellent cakes' – suggesting that Huguenots had rather
a sweet tooth. Some idea of the diet of a well-to-do member of the community a couple of generations or so later is contained in the diary of
William Tayler, a footman who worked for Mrs Princeps, née Auriel, the
widow of a City alderman. Breakfast at the Princeps home in the West
End was, he recorded, a fairly simple affair, consisting of rolls, toast and
'fancy' bread, served with tea and chocolate. For lunch there would be cold
meat and vegetables. A normal supper would involve fish, mutton, chicken,
vegetables and rice. But when guests came to dinner, they were entertained
on quite a lavish scale – a reflection, no doubt, of long-standing Huguenot
traditions of hospitality. In May 1837, for example, Mrs Princeps gave a
dinner for two gentlemen that involved 'fish, soop, saddle of mutton, piece
of veal stewed, spinach, two sorts of potatoes and a bowl of salad. For
second course, a roast duck, stewed coliflour, gooseberry tart, orang jelly,
custard pudding, two dishes of oranges, one of apples, one of sponge
cakes, one of cracknels, one of pruins, one of raisons and almonds, wine
&c, &c.'[18] The soup Tayler mentions could have been oxtail, held by tradition to have been invented in Spitalfields in the late seventeenth century
by frugal Huguenots whose culinary skills were such that they were able
to put cheap offcuts to delicious good use. It was perhaps the oxtail soup
served at the Maison de Charité de Spittlefields, founded in the winter of
1689/90, that gave the establishment its popular name, La Soupe.

Peter Abraham died in 1757, and it is not currently known where he and his
wife Esther are buried. Some members of the family were certainly interred
in the public vault located in Christ Church, others more probably in its
churchyard – including their daughter Mary (1734–8) and another daughter,
Esther (1723–1803), who specifically asked in her will to be buried at Christ
Church 'in the best ground'. But when the vaults were emptied in 1984–6 no
trace of Peter Abraham or Esther could be found. It seems most likely that
they found their final resting place somewhere in the churchyard.

Peter Abraham's eldest son – also called Peter (now distinguished as
Peter IV) – was also a weaver. He was born in 1716 and died in 1754. He

married Elizabeth Cadet and they had five children but all died young. Peter Abraham's second son, Abraham (1717–84), a 'notary', lived over his business premises in Pope's Head Alley, in the City opposite the Royal Exchange. He had eight children with his first wife Martha Tarquand, five of whom died young. Their son Joshua (1761–1825) was also a notary and one of the last male Ogiers descended directly from Jeanne Bernardin.

One way and another, the Ogier family became extraordinarily rich and powerful members of the French merchant community in eighteenth-century London. It was, as already suggested, a tightly knit society that retained its coherence because virtually all marriages and most significant business partnerships were kept within the Huguenot community. Indeed most business partnerships were between men (and occasionally women) related by blood or through marriage. And the Ogiers were an extensive family: just three members – Peter II, Peter Abraham and Peter III – had twenty-nine children between them, most of whom lived to adulthood, many occupying houses in virtually adjoining streets. They also made some strong and long-lasting alliances.

Louisa Perina, for example, who was the daughter of Peter Abraham's brother Peter II (born in 1680) and Catherine Rabaud, married Samuel Courtauld, a Huguenot goldsmith, in 1749.[19] She was a remarkable character. Smuggled out of France in 1730 at the age of one in a sack of potatoes when her father eventually decided to flee to England (an illegal action that could have ended in confiscation of property, gaol, even execution), Louisa prospered – no doubt partly because in 1740 her wealthy father left her £2,560 in his will. When Samuel Courtauld died in 1765, Louisa – by then the mother of eight children – oversaw the growth of the Courtauld precious-metals business from a goldsmith's shop in Cornhill and laid the foundations for a commercial empire that soon expanded to include silk. Louisa had a home in Essex, where she lived the life of a country gentlewoman, and latterly in Clapton, where her will was addressed and dated. For her burial, though, she wanted to return to what had been the Ogier family's London power base. In 1807 therefore Louisa Perina's earthly remains were returned to Spitalfields to be interred in the vault beneath Christ Church. Here she rested until the mid 1980s when her skeleton – and around 2,000 others interred between 1729 and 1851 – was removed and archaeologically investigated. Her bones resided for some time in the Natural History Museum, under the catalogue number 2309.

Louisa Perina was obviously a most able woman who forged a successful life for herself in her adopted country. But this, of course, was not
exceptional. Her brother Thomas Abraham (Abraham was another very
popular Ogier name) was, in his own way, just as successful. He was born
in France in 1716, but with his family fled to England in 1730 where he
became a master weaver. Married in 1740 to Magdelaine Barnard at Christ
Church, they went on to have seven children (four of whom died young),
with Thomas Abraham becoming a stalwart of the Spitalfields Huguenot
community, helping to take responsibility for the maintenance, security
and quality of life of the area. He, along with Zachariah Agace (a grandson
of Daniel Pilon and manufacturer of black silks and gauze), gave evidence
in 1759 to a Parliamentary Select Committee over paving in Norton Folgate,[20] and he was a trustee under the Norton Folgate Local Act of 1759,
which organised the 'government' (watching, cleansing and lighting) of
the Liberty in which he, and numerous other Ogiers, lived and worked.[21]
He also actively supported – and defended – the interests of the weaving
community. He held high office in the Weavers' Company and was instrumental in securing a total prohibition on the import of French silk that
lasted until 1826, when the legislation following the 1824 repeal of the Spitalfields Acts took effect. Along with Lewis and Peter Ogier III, Thomas
Abraham Ogier was one of the Spitalfields master weavers who gave evidence to the Parliamentary Committee at the end of Seven Years War.[22]
He must have lived in considerable style at 24 Spital Square, erected in 1733
and one of the largest and most modern and fashionable houses in Spitalfields. Certainly, the story that he is supposed to have lost £10,000 as a
result of the 1755 Lisbon earthquake but was not ruined by the disaster
seems to point to very considerable wealth. He died in 1770.

The intermarriages between the Ogiers and other Huguenot families
and the resulting close and complex family and business alliances were
clearly a source of great social and financial support. But this close-knit
society, defined by religious beliefs and shared ethics, could, as suggested
in Chapter 6, also be inhibiting and was certainly judgemental. Huguenots reconciled their Calvinistic brand of Puritan belief with the material
world – they worked hard to make money and they produced silk of ostentatious, almost sensual, visual and tactile beauty: this was deemed
acceptable if the toil that produced it was honest and in the interest of the

family. They also drove their workforce hard, hence, in part, the industrial unrest that led to violence throughout much of the eighteenth century.

Master and journeymen Huguenot weavers worshipped at the same churches – equal before God, but not, it would seem, when it came to business. It would therefore be scarcely surprising if those at the bottom of the heap sometimes behaved in a manner somewhat different from their sober, thrifty and hard-working superiors. Certainly weavers had, by the early eighteenth century, acquired a reputation for being riotous, rumbustious, and drunken, and presumably this included French journeymen as well as the English and Irish. The Anglo-Dutch political economist Bernard de Mandeville observed in 1714 that 'Every Body knows that there is a vast number of Journey-Men Weavers, Tailors, Clothworkers . . . who if by four days labour in a Week they can maintain themselves, will hardly be persuaded to work the fifth [and] who will . . . disoblige their masters, pinch their bellies and run into debt, to make holidays'. Mandeville asked, as perhaps exasperated master weavers in Spitalfields also did, 'when Men show such an extraordinary proclivity to Idleness and Pleasure, what reason have we to think that they would ever work, unless they were oblig'd to it by immediate necessity',[23] and of course by the severity of master towards employee.

And if people such as the Ogiers were tough with their workers, they were also tough with any members of their own family who broke their strict code of conduct. One such transgressor was Andrew or André Ogier, one of Peter Abraham's thirteen siblings. Andrew, who was born in 1695, seems to have been a very different character from his elder brother. In 1736 he married a Huguenot woman – Marianne Hanrot – who was then aged about thirty-eight, a rather mature bride for the time (though, of course, she may have been a widow); and after their marriage they lived in 'Wood Street' (now Wilkes Street), a fine new street and a good address. Andrew, however, was clearly not very successful in the world of weaving for by 1738 the couple had moved to an older, and perhaps humbler, house in Wheler Street. Here Marianne died in 1738/9; and less than a month later Andrew married an Englishwoman – a spinster of thirty-seven – called Susan Craven.

For reasons that remain obscure, the Ogier family disapproved of the new match. It could be that they felt Andrew had remarried too swiftly or that Susan was an unsuitable wife (the speed at which he married her suggests Susan might formerly have been his mistress). It could simply be that they disliked the fact that she was English and therefore presumably an Anglican rather than a Calvinist. At any rate, Andrew's actions led to his rejection both by his family and by the community. Generally speaking, Huguenot families and the community as a whole could be expected to rally to their own if they got into trouble. But this was not so in Andrew's case. Although his financial position was evidently desperate, his family did not bail him out or use its influence with his main creditors, some of whom are likely to have been friends, clients or relations of the Ogier dynasty. They let him fall, and within a month of his remarriage Andrew was declared bankrupt. He lived on for many years, the black sheep and failure of the family, and was finally admitted insane in 1771 to the French Hospital, La Providence, near Old Street. He died in the same year.[24]

It would appear, then, that the Ogier dynasty – like the wider Huguenot community – offered great support to those who respected and followed its ethical codes and religious doctrine. But it was unforgiving – even vengeful – to those who did not. And while offering charity to the deserving, it also followed – in its business activities – hard-nosed and even ruthless practices. The story of Andrew Ogier reveals just how hard life could be for a member of the community who ignored its conventions or failed to live up to its particular set of standards.

Hanging in La Providence – the institution in which Andrew died (now located in Rochester, Kent, and still offering care to those of Huguenot descent)[25] – is a portrait of another Ogier family member whose life took a very different turn and whose career shows what could, with talent and judgement, be achieved by working creatively within the nurturing constraints of the Huguenot society. The portrait is of Peter Ogier III, the son of Peter Abraham's elder brother, Peter II, and his wife Catherine Rabaud, and so a nephew of the ill-fated Andrew.

Peter Ogier III is a fine example of a successful Huguenot merchant. He was born in France in 1711 and in 1730 came to England with his father, mother, brothers and sisters – including Louisa Perina. Peter III married a Huguenot girl – Elizabeth Gatineau (they had eight children) – was naturalised in 1749, elected to the Court of Assistants of the Weavers' Company in 1756, became Renter Bailiff in 1758, and in 1760 achieved the highest office of Upper Bailiff.

Peter Ogier III was in the top tier of the Huguenot silk trade not because he was himself a highly skilled practitioner but because – as was usual – he was a pre-eminently successful silk master. He was an entrepreneur who played the laws of supply and demand with brilliance. He orchestrated the supply of raw material, its processing, and the production and eventual sale of the shimmering silk product. He made and realised fashions and helped create the marketplace that allowed silk to be made and sold for a handsome profit. His success in the industry is shown by the fact that in 1765 he insured stock worth £3,000 and had premises in Pall Mall, St James's and in Bath.[26] Peter III was the 'grandest of the Ogiers in the mid eighteenth century'[27] and was the chief partner in the firm Ogier, Vansommer and Triquet, 'flowered silk weavers'.

Like many successful Huguenot merchants, he also felt a sense of responsibility for the welfare of his community, especially for its members who, while loyal to its creed, were less able or successful. This is revealed most obviously by the fact that in 1761 he became one of the Directors of the French Hospital of La Providence, but it's also suggested by the brave and resigned way in which he faced the illness and slow, painful decline that culminated in his death in 1775 when he was sixty-three. Many years later, in 1817, his nephew George Courtauld recalled his extraordinary fortitude. 'My Uncle Peter Ogier', he wrote, 'was a pattern of patient suffering for some years before his death. After lying on his couch in agony for quarter of an hour at a time the drops of sweat running down his face from extreme pain – a few minutes relief would induce expressions of pious gratitude for the ease he experienced, and he would speak with his wife and family about their several concerns: then when another paroxysm was approaching he would resignedly lie himself down and mildly say God's will be done.' And so did a brave Huguenot die in the eighteenth century.

It is thought that Peter III lived and died at 37 Spital Square,[28] which adjoins the Old Artillery Ground, and today is the square's only surviving Georgian house. If so, then the well-ordered and handsome panelled rooms in which he suffered and died, with a stoicism and sense of divine omnipotence that was perhaps typical of the Huguenot community, can still be seen.[29] He had bought a country estate in Lewisham, but was, like his three sisters, interred in the vault below Christ Church. Today his skeleton resides in the Natural History Museum.

In 1767, some years before his death, Peter III was party to an agreement to establish a trading house in Canada – then newly acquired from the French (by the Treaty or Peace of Paris of 1763) and a new market full of export opportunities since English goods, notably silk, were now welcome. Other members of the consortium were – typically – all cousins. These included the failed Andrew's son Abraham (born 1728). It would appear that in the Huguenot community the sins of the father were not visited upon the son – but Abraham was nearly forty and this was his first big business break. Presumably he had been hampered but not fatally compromised by his father's unfortunate business and marital history. Another of the partners was also called Abraham Ogier, son of the Abraham Ogier who was Peter Abraham's son and the notary living and working in Pope's Head Alley in the City.

One of the cousins in the consortium was called John Renaud, so the agreement set up for five years to run the consortium as a partnership ordained that the new enterprise be called Ogier, Renaud and Company. John Renaud and Abraham Ogier (the son of Andrew, not of the notary) were to go to Quebec to set up a 'house of trade' with £10,000 capital provided by Peter Ogier III and such sums as the others could raise. Peter III was to be in charge in London, shipping out the goods to Canada, and if all went well Peter III's son – called Peter Abraham (born 1742) – was to be taken into partnership. Profits were to be divided in the ratio of two-fifths to Peter III, two-fifths to John Renaud and one-fifth to Abraham – confirming his relatively junior role. However, the partnership was dissolved after only six years in 1773 so was presumably not a great success.

Abraham, the son of the failed Andrew, was evidently accepted by the Ogier clan and the Huguenot community. But he seems to have lived somewhat on the edge, perhaps because, like his father, he married an English girl. She was named Mary Cooper, fifteen years old at the time of marriage and probably the daughter of Abraham's landlady. Their first child, Louise, was born in 1755. Despite the fact that Abraham's first big family-based business had folded, he decided to stay in the New World, moving from Quebec to Camden, Knox County, Maine – this was something of a pioneering decision since the town was then just being settled in a daunting wilderness – and finally to Boston where he died in 1798. Abraham's son Lewis (1760–1849) is said to have fought in the American War of Independence as a patriot, serving with the Scots-born Colonel John Allan and the Massachusetts Militia. If true this perhaps reflects his father's independent disposition. What is more certain is that Lewis had twelve children and started a wool mill in Camden, Maine.

The Ogier family's North American connections are significant because it was not only Abraham and his son Lewis who settled there. Louis Ogier (1719 or 1726–80), a brother of Peter III, was a master weaver of flowered silk who according to the Rate Books of 1758 and 1763 lived in 2 Spital Square and had a son called Thomas (1755–1833), who in time moved to Carolina to live and work. His memorial survives in the First (Scots) Presbyterian Church in Charleston, its inscription proclaiming how Thomas, in his 'life and manners afforded a practical illustration of the Christian Faith and Charity' and in his death 'evinced THE HOPE THAT MAKETH NOT ASHAMED. Revere his memory – Imitate his Virtues.' Thomas has direct descendants still living in Charleston, but not with the surname Ogier.

Through the late eighteenth century and into the nineteenth the Ogiers continued to diversify their business interests and expanded their activities far beyond Spitalfields. Into Canada and the North American colonies, of course, but also – somewhat less exotically – into far-flung Clapton, Hackney and the upwardly mobile Huguenot happy hunting grounds of west Essex. In 1766, for example, Abraham Ogier (1716–84) – the son of Peter Abraham and Esther Ogier – took on the lease of the Hackney Corn Mills and Water Works on the River Lea.

During this period of family success, however, one more black sheep did rear its head. On 26 April 1786 one Peter Ogier – presumably a nephew of Peter III – stood in the dock at the Old Bailey on a charge of 'grand larceny'.[30] He had, so it was alleged, stolen furnishings and contents from a set of chambers – including carpets, books, a bowl, 'five pair of silk stockings', a tray, and a china tureen and dish with a total value of £6. It was a serious accusation. If found guilty of a theft on that scale, Peter Ogier faced a potential death sentence.

The Ogier family name clearly rang bells with the court, for when Peter came to offer a defence he was asked, 'What part of the world did you come from?' Peter answered, 'Originally from Spital-fields,' and the judge, Sir James Eyre, observed that he knew 'there was a very respectable man of that name' living there. Ogier replied, 'It was my father.'

The circumstances of the case were straightforward. The Rev. William Jackson, who had chambers at Lyon's Inn, had employed Ogier as an 'amanuensis, to transcribe various things that I used to send to the press.' Lyon's Inn was an Inn of Chancery, attached to the Inner Temple and

located in Wych Street. By the late eighteenth century it had a poor reputation and was generally used by disreputable or disgraced lawyers. Jackson
explained that Ogier was 'recommended to me as a person in great distress, but who belonged to a very respectable family, and whose misfortunes
he had not contributed to by any bad action'.

The case against Ogier was presented by the newly qualified William
Garrow, soon to make his name, ironically, as a very robust defence counsel before reverting to the role of prosecutor (often for the government in
cases of treason) and, ultimately, becoming Attorney General in 1813. Garrow called various pawnbrokers to give evidence that Ogier had offered
the stolen items to them for cash. Ogier, for his part, never denied that he
had taken the fittings and furnishings from Jackson's chambers, but
pleaded mitigating circumstances. He 'did not mean to steal the things',
he told the court. He 'only took them for a temporary relief; I was in hopes
by applying to my friends to have got sufficient money to replace them all.'
The reason for his rash action was that he had been driven 'to the very
greatest distress, I had not a shirt to put on my back.' A character witness
stated that Ogier 'had been a broker, and he has been a clerk with me
and . . . was very honest.'

Ogier's remorse and the character witness's testimony did him no good.
He was found guilty. Presumably because he had admitted the theft,
though, he was spared execution and instead was transported for seven
years. Nothing more is known of him. How he had fallen into such financial distress, and why his family did not assist him, remains a mystery.
Presumably, like Andrew Ogier before him, he had in some manner
broken the Ogiers' code of conduct. If so, the price he paid was bitter
indeed.

By the early decades of the nineteenth century the Ogier name seems to
have disappeared from Spitalfields – certainly it does not appear in the
significant annals of the area – and the former Ogier homes were no longer
the grand affairs they had once been. In 1851, according to the census of
that year,[31] 19 Princelet Street (then 18 'Princes Street') was occupied by
two households. One was headed by John Broadbridge, a thirty-year-old
'Surveyor' who lived with his wife Sarah, twenty-nine, born in 'America'.
The second household comprised, on the day of the census at least, Elizabeth Carter, aged seventy, the 'House Proprietor', born in East Elm,

Essex. The Ogiers appear entirely absent – although the 'American' origin of Sarah Broadbridge, and Elizabeth Carter's birth in Essex, where Louisa Perina had once resided, suggests the remote possibility of Ogier connections.

The low density of the occupation of 19 Princelet Street – three people in a house with about ten rooms – was most unusual in mid-nineteenth-century Spitalfields and implies that the house remained in some form of genteel occupation. More typical was the life being led within nearby 23 Princelet Street (16 'Princes Street'). In stark contrast this house, built in about 1705 and roughly the same size as 19, was occupied by five households and contained eighteen people on the day of the census: Edward Hall, a thirty-year-old 'Vullum binder' and his thirty-seven-year-old wife; William Frost, a 'Foreman salesman', his wife, two children and mother; Sarah Anne Spraggs, a forty-two-year-old widow and 'silk winder', and her 'errand boy' son; Francis Lewis, a fifty-seven-year-old turner, his wife, two children and two apprentices; and Tho. Meller, a twenty-four-year-old butcher, his wife and a fifteen-year-old female servant. And the neighbouring property – 17 Princelet Street (former 19 'Princes Street') – was occupied by thirteen people in three households, including the ninety-six-year-old former parish beadle Thomas Hart.

But all was soon to change for 19 Princelet Street, too. In 1862, or thereabouts, a synagogue, relocated from Fashion Street, was created within the house for Russian and Polish Jews.[32] Given that Eastern European migrant Jews did not start to appear in large numbers in East London until after a wave of Tsarist pogroms got under way in 1881, it's a surprisingly early date for such a place of worship. The house was transformed. The main congregational room of the synagogue (called the United Friends Synagogue in the 1871 *Post Office Directory*) was built upon the garden, taking the form of a double-height hall top-lit by roof lanterns and containing galleries supported by cast-iron columns. Below the hall, and dug out of the garden, was a large meeting room used primarily by the Loyal United Friends Friendly Society created in September 1870 in association with the synagogue and intended to support needy members of the congregation. The works also involved the complete remodelling of the ground floor of the 1718/19 house to create a 'Saturday' school in the front room, with the rear room added to the volume of the synagogue's hall. Externally the house was given something of the appearance of an institutional building by covering the ground-floor elevation with stucco and

A photograph of the synagogue at 19 Princelet Street taken before it fell into disuse.

by replacing the two ground-floor windows with a single, large, semi-circular arched window adjoining a wide, arched door. In 1893 it became the 'Princes Street' Synagogue. According to the 1891 census 19 Princelet Street, in common with much of the street, was more densely occupied than earlier, containing thirteen people in three family groups (see page 536).

The history of 19 Princelet Street in the second half of the twentieth century was mostly one of neglect. For nearly forty years, until 1969, the garret floor was home to the reclusive and enigmatic Jewish scholar David Rodinsky, who disappeared one day almost without trace, leaving his home an undisturbed chaos of newspapers and learned volumes on languages and the Cabbala.[33] As for the synagogue, this ceased to function by the late 1960s. It then suffered decades of abandonment and dereliction until acquired in the early 1980s as a tottering but deeply moving and atmospheric semi-ruin by the Spitalfields Historic Buildings Trust. Today the building is secure, and although its long-term future use as a museum of 'Immigration and Diversity' is still evolving and repairs are ongoing, the former home of Peter Abraham and Esther Ogier stands as a monument to the aspirations and achievements of generations of people – mostly migrants escaping persecution in their homelands – who have lived and ultimately thrived in Spitalfields.

PART THREE

A PLACE OF POVERTY

From the Regency Era to the First World War

THIRTEEN

SPITALFIELDS IN PERIL
The Battle for the Silk Industry

The last decade of the eighteenth century saw the working conditions of journeymen weavers become increasingly harsh, with long periods of unemployment, extreme insecurity and terrible poverty. In 1793 nearly 4,000 looms in Spitalfields were calculated to be standing idle, and desperate journeymen were having to beg the area's master weavers for work in an ever-declining trade. Some masters responded by exploiting an already grim situation, renting looms to journeymen at premium rates and then driving them hard.[1] The position of journeymen weavers was further weakened in 1799 by the passing of the Combination Act, which, although not specifically aimed at silk weavers, effectively outlawed any attempts on their part to organise and banned collective bargaining. Clearly, the Spitalfields Acts, passed from 1773 (see pages 298–9), were failing to protect the trade from the desperate circumstances that now beset it. As William Hawes, a dispensary doctor, recalled in 1802, when describing his work amongst poor weavers in Spitalfields in the early 1790s: 'It is not in the power of language to describe their long and continued miseries, miseries not brought on by idleness, intemperances or a dissolute course of life, but human wretchedness, absolutely produced by want of employment . . . whole families without fire, without raiment, without food . . .'[2]

And then there was a respite. The long war with Napoleonic France created a temporary boom as continental competition was effectively removed from British shores for two decades. It was a boom that even weathered Napoleon's Milan Decree of 1807 by which France, as part of its system of economic warfare, sought to ban all European or 'Continental' trade with Britain including, of course, the export of Italian raw silk.[3] As the historian M. Dorothy George observed, the years from 1800 to 1826 'were referred to as the "Golden Age" of the trade'.[4] It must have appeared to contemporaries as a new dawn. Tragically, it turned out to be a false one.

One surviving house seems to capture this brief moment of hope, and also reveal the complex nature of Spitalfields society and the silk industry in the early years of the nineteenth century. Number 15 Princelet Street (formerly 20 Princes Street) was constructed in 1718/19. Until the 1760s it was occupied, or leased out, by members of the Pilon dynasty of Huguenot silk weavers (see page 343). And then in the early decades of the nineteenth century, during Spitalfields' second 'Golden Age', it was rebuilt in grand and fashionable manner.

Such a dramatic development – perhaps surprising given the generally uncertain nature of the silk industry over the previous years – has two possible explanations. It can be seen as clear physical evidence of early-nineteenth-century optimism, as some masters came to the conclusion that the good times had returned to stay. Or it can be interpreted as a show of continuing commitment to the area by one of its more affluent silk-weaving families. For many their Spitalfields houses were essentially ancestral homes, occupied by the same family for generations. The area still exerted a strong emotional pull – which is why, presumably, Louisa Perina Courtauld left instructions in her will that she be interred in Christ Church Spitalfields, even though by the time of her death in 1807 she was living in rural Hackney (see page 347). Of course the two explanations are not mutually exclusive – far from it.

Whatever the precise reason for the transformation, at some point between 1800 and 1820, 15 Princelet Street was substantially refashioned. Its front elevation was rebuilt in a most up-to-date style, using cool yellow bricks. Its three-windows-wide elevation was replaced by a two-window-wide elevation with then-popular wide brick piers to give the house a more authentic Italian Renaissance, rather than vernacular Dutch, feel. And inside, the ground-floor front room acquired an elegant scheme of delicate and high-quality frescoed decoration of a modish Regency type rarely found elsewhere today in Spitalfields (although something comparable does survive in the first-floor front room of 15 Wilkes Street).

Land Tax returns reveal that the head tenants/occupants of the house during the period when reconstruction took place were Robert Mason from 1793 to 1806; a Mr Edges in 1807; James Dupree from 1808 to 1811 (listed in trade directories with the house being given as his residence rather than place of work); John Edger from 1812 to 1821 (also listed in trade directories); and John Gregory, 1822–5.[5] The question is: which of these was responsible for the rebuilding work?

In fact there are two likely contenders. The first is James Dupree, whose family seemingly had a long-established relationship with Princelet Street, stretching back at least to the first half of the eighteenth century. He himself was evidently a property-owning gentleman, living in Spitalfields off inherited money and investments rather than working there.[6] Certainly, therefore, he had the money to upgrade the house, and his ancestral links to the area would doubtless have exerted a sufficient pull to make him wish not only to live in the area but to make his chosen house as elegant as possible, despite the increased poverty and overcrowding that had started to become a feature of life in Spitalfields (see chapter 15). If this is the case then Dupree's works are clear evidence that old Huguenot families liked to go on living in their ancestral territory.

The other possible candidate is Dupree's successor in the house, John Edger, described as a 'silk manufacturer' in *Robson's* directory of 1820, who was in occupation by 1812 (according to Land Tax returns) although not listed in trade directories until 1816 (which could be interpreted to mean that he was having the house reconstructed during those four years).[7] The length and timing of Edger's stay fit well with the practicalities and the style of the reconstruction. On the other hand, Dupree's relatively high social status for early-nineteenth-century Spitalfields makes him in some ways the more likely candidate for the remodelling of 15 Princelet Street, although, of course, he was only there for three years. Either way, 15 Princelet Street was, between 1808 and 1821, still in the hands of someone connected with the silk trade – directly in Edger's case, indirectly in Dupree's – who had an eye for fashion and money to splash around.

But if the house's rise in the world was swift, its decline was equally rapid, for the head tenant after Edger's departure was a far humbler man, and moreover one with no connection whatsoever to the silk trade. John Gregory, contemporary trade directories make clear, was a potato salesman, with premises in 1835 at 40 Crispin Street, Spitalfields. Potatoes are not the stuff of fashion nor, surely, would their sale provide the stimulus for the transformation wrought in 15 Princelet Street. Gregory was presumably the beneficiary of all the recent hard work. His presence, though, is an intimation of the transitory nature of Spitalfields' Regency boom. A house that for over a hundred years had been associated with the upper echelons of the silk trade suddenly became the home of a potato salesman.

Even by the early 1820s things were changing. And as they did so, a fiercely fought debate arose over the best way to see the silk trade through what was clearly going to be a difficult future. Some argued for the status quo, advancing the view that the Spitalfields Acts offered a much-needed degree of protection to the area's now beleaguered workforce, ensuring that foreign competition did not become overwhelming, that wages of journeymen weavers were regulated so that they could not work for, or be paid, under the agreed rate, and that not too many apprentices entered the trade. Others, though, saw things very differently. The competition the trade sought to avoid, they argued, should actually be embraced. It would remove unnecessary shackles, allow the strong to flourish, and ensure greater profits. Trade was, after all, a remorseless fight for survival and supremacy. It resembled Tennyson's 'Nature, red in tooth and claw', as contemplated by the poet in the 1830s, in which new science-based evidence revealed a natural world operating apparently without moral or divine intervention.[8]

The rights and wrongs of the two opposing schools of thought are now difficult to untangle. The Spitalfields Acts sustained the traditional idea that, through government regulation and taxation, a trade could be protected from relentless market forces and so helped to flourish. Things may not have turned out that way, but, given what did ultimately happen, it's possible to argue that the Acts delayed, even if they did not halt, the demise of the Spitalfields silk trade. On the other hand, it seems clear that even while the Acts were in operation, journeymen weavers found themselves in an increasingly difficult situation. Since legislation prohibited them from working at reduced rates, when downturns did occur journeymen weavers were simply thrown out of work by masters who could see no profit in operating in such a constrained environment.

Resistance to the call for the Spitalfields Acts to be repealed came from master weavers who felt not just that they themselves would suffer if unregulated free trade were to be introduced, but that journeymen weavers would, too. One such master weaver was William Hale, who in 1822 published *An Appeal to the Public in Defence of the Spitalfields Act: with*

Remarks on the causes which have led to the Miseries and Moral Deterioration of the Poor.[9] He was 'in a considerable way of business', employing from 300–400 looms.[10] It seems very likely that he lived at 4 'Wood Street' because the address appears on a letter dated 22 November 1806 that he wrote to the famed police magistrate and social reformer Patrick Colquhoun, enclosing a copy of his open letter to Samuel Whitbread MP on the subject of the poor of Spitalfields in which he expresses 'a deep concern of the infinite obligation this parish is under to you.'[11] Today 4 'Wood Street' survives as 6 Wilkes Street, a large, five-window-wide house, partly two rooms deep, which was built in 1723/4 by Samuel Worrall. The ground floor appears to have been altered in about 1790, with an elegant cornice set above windows and door, to serve as a showroom or office – presumably for Hale.

His *Appeal* stresses 'the essential community of interest between employers and employed and the relative industrial peace which had prevailed in the past when prices and wages had been regulated.'[12] He certainly wasn't an anti-capitalist, but he was very critical of the abrogation of responsibilities that he felt had resulted from untrammelled competition and the ruthless quest for profit. In short, he was, arguably, a capitalist and merchant entrepreneur with a social conscience. In his review of the history of the Spitalfields silk industry Hale concluded that many of its ailments were the result of 'masters tied together by sordid ties of common interest'.[13] Cooperation was what was required, within the workings of existing protective legislation.

Hale sought to 'prove' in his *Appeal* that the Spitalfields Act of 1773 had 'conferred some of the greatest blessings and benefits, both upon the numerous and industrious poor of Spitalfields [and] upon their employers'.[14] Reflecting on the murderous riots of the 1760s and early 1770s he argued that 'the passing of the Spitalfields Act, at the request of all the manufacturers RESTORED ORDER. The poor were employed, and were paid according to a fair rate of wages; – and, as the natural consequence peace and happiness reigned throughout the whole of this populous district.'[15] He emphasised his point by claiming that 'there is no district in the empire where so many thousands of the lower classes are congregated in so small a space; and yet there is no district more peaceable'.[16] Even from 1792 to the spring of 1793, which Hale identified as a 'time of universal depression in the silk trade', the 'Spitalfields Acts, preserved the poor weavers from utter ruin ... and its advantages proved to be far beyond all calculation.'[17] Somewhat bafflingly, he calculated that in 1808 three-quarters of Spitalfields weavers were unemployed – a strange argument to make in defence of the status quo, particularly given that 1808 falls near the mid-point of the industry's Regency 'Golden Age', but clearly he felt that on balance the Spitalfields Acts were a force for good.

He concluded his case by referring to a request put to him by a Select Committee of the House of Commons that was attempting 'to ascertain the general opinion of the manufacturers of Spitalfields with regard to the Acts which regulate the trade'.[18] This he had done, he said, and the 'unqualified opinion of a great majority of the silk manufacturers, and those of the first respectability . . . practical weavers' was that the Spitalfields Acts were beneficial and that 'an extension of the silk Acts to the country at large, would be attended with the same advantages as we have'.[19] Hale listed eighty-eight weavers or companies in support of the Acts, including himself of course. In 1822, the year the pamphlet appeared, he had been in the trade thirty-four years. John Edger, his near neighbour at 15 Princelet Street who is named as a supporter of the Acts, is described as having been in the trade twenty years.

Evidently Hale was in very good company in his campaign to save the Spitalfields Acts. This is confirmed by a large and beautiful urn-like silver cup of splendid neo-classical design made by Thomas Bateman that the Spitalfields Historic Buildings Trust currently has in its ownership. The cup was commissioned by a group of 'Operative Silk Weavers of Globe Fields, Bethnal Green and its Vicinity' that was opposed to the repeal of the Act, and commemorates the moment – in 1823 – it believed it had won. The cup was presented by the group to its solicitor, Robert Brutton, for his 'Indefatigable Exertions . . . at both Houses of Parliament . . . whereby the Spitalfields Acts were Supported and the Price of their Labour secured to them.' Named on the base are the weavers who made the gift of the cup, and opposed the repeal of the Acts. They include eminent masters and members of some of the leading and ancient Huguenot weaving families of Spitalfields, such as James Ouvry.

The case against the existing Acts was loosely based on the new economic theories formalised by Adam Smith in his *Inquiry into the Nature and Causes of the Wealth of Nations*, first published in 1776. Smith's work contrasts controlled markets – of the sort created by the Spitalfields Acts – with free markets driven by the exigencies of supply and demand and unhindered by protectionist Acts of Parliament or manipulation of trade through customs duties and taxation. The free trade outlined by Smith was, argued his supporters in Spitalfields, ultimately best for both masters and journeymen because the Acts, unintentionally but as a result of the nature of competitive trade, priced Spitalfields silk out of the market and so undermined the job security of journeymen. They therefore created the very conditions they were designed to prevent: ruthless competition, unemployment and poverty. If wages were set by the market-place, on the other hand, they would certainly fluctuate but at least journeymen would stay in work, even if their incomes decreased. Hale was not convinced. When pondering Smith's writings, he asked, more in sorrow than in anger, 'what would this great man have thought' if he had realised the consequences of the 'cruel' economic system his theories promoted?[20]

The views of the advocates of free trade are well expressed in a pamphlet of 1822 entitled *Observations on the Ruinous tendency of the Spitalfields Act to the silk manufacture of London*. Editions of this document include 'a reply to Mr Hale's Appeal to the public in defence of the act'[21] and Hale's own *Appeal* also contains a response to the *Observations*, whose anonymous author, he observes, had put forward a 'popular' argument with 'considerable talent'. So the debate was evidently circular, with arguments from both sides well circulated before publication in final form in pamphlets.

The *Observations* stressed the urgency and extreme nature of the problems that were perceived to face the Spitalfields silk industry: 'The present state of the London Silk Manufacture is such as to call for the serious consideration of all who are interested in its welfare. The duty of the raw material being great, the wages of labour high, and the pressure of taxation heavy, the manufactured commodity is necessarily very much enhanced in price.' There then followed an analysis of one of the key causes of the problem: 'the vigilant competition of foreigners who, in consequence of labour being cheap, and taxes few in their respective countries, are able to produce an article at a much lower rate than ourselves [making] all competition, under present circumstances, totally impossible.' Foreign competition, the author of the pamphlet argued, has 'to the great regret of every well-wisher to the prosperity of this country – swept away almost the whole of our Foreign Trade in Silks; and by means of smuggling, which it is found impossible totally to prevent, they are enabled to interfere to a very considerable extent with the home market.'[22]

However – in the view of this supporter of Adam Smith, at least – the problem was made worse by existing legislation: 'The silk manufacture in

A PLACE OF POVERTY

London and Middlesex is regulated by the Act 13 Geo. III. c. 68, under which the Lord Mayor, magistrates &c. have a power of settling and regulating the wages to be paid to journeymen weavers by persons residing within limits therein prescribed, and by which heavy penalties are imposed upon persons so residing and employing, for the purpose of evading the Act, weavers who live beyond those prescribed limits.'[23] One consequence of this, the argument ran, was that because wages in London were 'very much above that of the country', country manufacturers were able to undercut their rivals in the capital: 'recently the country silk trade has so far increased as to make its competition dangerous, and it is the Spitalfields Act which arms that competition with all its powers of mischief to the London manufacturer.'[24] Macclesfield, Manchester and Reading were listed as rival silk manufacturing centres.

The answer, according to the *Observations*, was to repeal the legislation that safeguarded journeymen's wages at a level that free-traders saw as prohibitive, and to remove the taxes that made raw material so expensive. If this could be achieved, then alongside 'a more extensive use of machinery' London silk weavers 'would immediately be placed on a level with those of the country, and an important point gained towards the ultimate design of competing with the foreign manufacturer.'[25] And the *Observations* offered additional grounds for optimism about the industry if the protectionist Acts were repealed: 'As we have now free access to the raw material through our Eastern colonies – an almost unlimited command over capital and machinery – and artisans whose industry and skill cannot be surpassed – it is conceived we have it in our power ultimately to triumph over foreign competition.'[26]

Such arguments prevailed and in 1824, the year after the optimistic weavers had presented their cup to their solicitor Robert Brutton, the Spitalfields Acts were repealed.

With hindsight it can now be seen with burning clarity that working and living conditions after the repeal rapidly worsened for Spitalfields journeymen weavers rather than improved. Their 'labour was devalued . . . and the related legislation to allow foreign imports into the domestic market in 1826' – the year the repeal became effective – 'greatly undermined the trade', according to one account.[27] As the historian Marc Steinberg explains, after 1824 the Spitalfields trade suffered 'progressively worsening cycles of depression' with 'brief plateaus of respite' until it 'succumbed to those successive blows, throwing thousands of weavers into destitution and reducing the once honourable trade to sweated outwork.'[28] The capital-rich masters were able to diversify into other trades or markets, as the leading Huguenot families had done from the mid eighteenth century or earlier.[29] The impoverished journeymen had no such option.

They also seem to have been crushed into silence. Most of the talking about the Spitalfields Acts, on both sides, was done by the masters. Journeymen protests and action – of the sort familiar in 1719, 1765 and 1768 over calico imports, engine-looms and wages – were either absent or subdued, going little beyond lobbying Parliament. It seems that years of poverty after 1770, culminating in the dreadful conditions of the 1790s, had broken the spirits of the journeymen, while the Combination Act of 1799 made organised direct action difficult if not impossible. Their learned societies lingered through the 1820s, as did flower and bird fancying (see chapter 11), but generally, by the early nineteenth century, weavers' behaviour seems to have been characterised by the extremes of boisterous escapism or lethargy rather than by self-improvement or trade activism.

Some of this lack of purpose and focus might, perhaps, reflect the rural origin – and increasing lack of education – of many of the weavers by now living in Spitalfields, their condition exacerbated no doubt by poverty and harsh working conditions. The Rector of St Matthew's Bethnal Green, located just north of 'Hare Street' (Cheshire Street), took a fairly dim view of them when describing a typical Sunday there in 1816. The parish consisted, he wrote, 'of a population of about 40,000, generally the lowest description of people, the overflowing population of Spitalfields', and 'every Sunday morning, during the time of Divine Service, several hundred persons assemble in a field adjoining the church-yard, where they fight dogs, hunt ducks, gamble, enter into subscriptions to fee drovers for a bullock . . .' It seems that the Rector's weaver parishioners preferred to spend their leisure time on a Sunday not in prayer but indulging in blood sports, bull-baiting and gambling. This was largely due to Joseph Merceron, a Brick Lane-based pawnbroker of Huguenot descent who, in the early nineteenth century, became the focus of organised crime in Spitalfields. It seems he arranged – for a hefty profit – the bull-running and dog fights. Spitalfields – along with the majority of its inhabitants – was changing for the worse.[30]

The radical tailor Francis Place (see page 306), contemplating the many

A detail of Richard Horwood's London map, published and revised between 1799 and 1819. ...of 'Fleet Street', east of Brick Lane – has not yet been laid out; and in the Nichol

The 'Tenter' ground south of White's Row has yet to be developed; Pedley Street – a continuation
area, to the north, most of the north side of 'Half Nicols Street' is still an empty site.

weavers assembled in Palace Yard, Westminster after the repeal of the
Acts in 1826, made a telling observation. They were, he wrote, when 'compared with other trades, a physically degraded people [and] their manners
are coarser than that of any other tradesmen'.[31] In 1838 a leading Spitalfields weaver told a parliamentary inquiry, when describing his fellow
weavers, that 'perhaps the majority are not able to read or write'.[32]

The 1840 House of Commons Commission on the working conditions
of hand-loom weavers reported that by the late 1830s, although unemployment in the Spitalfields silk industry was very high, there were still around
17,000 looms in operation, with the vast majority of the area's operative
weavers working at home, and with 20 per cent of Spitalfields' population
employed in family-run hand-loom workshops containing two looms.[33]
Only 3 per cent of the workshops contained more than five looms. As
Robin Veder points out, it must be concluded that most weavers – despite
the ever more desperate conditions – 'resisted the transition to the factory,
preferring to remain in the same environment, determine their own hours,
and keep their traditional habits as long as possible.'[34]

And things grew worse for them. Writing just a quarter of a century
later, in the mid-1860s, Thomas Archer explained that: 'Unfortunately the
cheapness of the French and German silk and velvet which is now exported
free of duty, and the operation of the country factories as well as those of
the large towns, have combined to reduce the London weavers to a very
deplorable condition.'[35] A later historian, A. K. Sabin, argued that '. . . when
the Commercial Treaty was made with France in 1860, thousands of [work-
ing weavers in Spitalfields] were told that from the day the Treaty was
confirmed no further work would be given out, since foreign silks could be
purchased at a cheaper rate than they could be made in England . . . and
that part of the struggling Spitalfields industry which produced the lighter
cheaper sorts of silks webs received its death blow.' He continued:

> A few large firms which had adopted the factory system, and a small num-
> ber of master weavers who produced work of a high order and kept on their
> books a number of families of first-hand operatives, were less affected by
> the Treaty and continued to work, but the industry generally, which had
> given employment in a more or less remunerative way to hundreds of thou-
> sands of silk weavers during nearly two centuries, was practically brought
> to an end, and impoverished weavers were plunged into the direst distress.
> The Spitalfields weavers never recovered from the blow.[36]

The man who helped negotiate the 1860 treaty with France, Richard Cobden, was also the man who had done so much to champion free trade.

It's conceivable that the champions of unregulated free trade did not fully understand the implications of the repeal of the Acts. More disturbingly, it's possible that they did, but were not concerned. If journeymen weavers were to be driven to the wall, free-traders might have thought, this was no more than the application of that ruthless natural law that had so disturbed Tennyson. It was exploit or be exploited. The suffering of weavers was perhaps seen as a short-term evil leading to long-term benefits. So their situation, long precarious because of the cheaper and more practical alternatives to silk, such as calico and muslin, now became virtually untenable.

Some superior weavers did manage to ride the storm. William Bresson, for example, interviewed by one of the parliamentary commissioners looking at the state of hand-loom weavers in the late 1830s, seems to have been reasonably well-to-do. He lived in 'Daniel Street', off Orange Street, located in a now long-lost network of weavers' streets north of Bethnal Green and immediately east of the Nichol;[37] he was a skilled velvet weaver, the great-grandson, he claimed, of Raymond Bresson, a Huguenot who had taken refuge in England after 1685. Bresson was a successful capitalist, who had managed to acquire about 200 looms from which he made a sizeable income by hiring them out at between threepence and fourpence a week.

When he spoke to Commissioner W. E. Hickson in July 1838 he confirmed that 'few weavers' then earned more than fifteen shillings a week and that in 1823 – in the 'Good Times' before the repeal of the Acts – many had earned as much as twenty shillings per week. Bresson's estimate of a weaver's weekly earnings in 1838 seems to have been somewhat optimistic, however. He says 'few' achieved that sum whereas Mayhew, writing in 1849, states that the average wage in 1839 'would have been . . . about 7s. a week per hand', while what he calls 'plain weavers' earned eight shillings and sixpence per week. Presumably the difference between the totals is that the lower average wage includes all operatives in the silk trade, including the less-skilled non-weavers.[38] But Bresson's house, though cramped and lacking basic amenities (it had no cesspit or sewer), did have a flower garden in front measuring ninety feet by twenty, and inside three small living rooms shared with his wife and son. A fourth room contained six looms. He paid £16 a year rent for the house and £2.5.0 for the flower garden.[39]

Other streets and houses in the area, however, stood in very stark contrast to this. A particularly bleak example was Pedley Street, just east of Brick Lane and in the early nineteenth century a relatively recent development. Rocque's map of 1746 shows a 'Fleet Street' off Brick Lane. By the time of Richard Horwood's map of 1799–1819, some of the market gardens around 'Fleet Street' had been built upon but the street itself had not been pushed further east. During the next ten years or so, the market gardens disappeared under bricks and mortar and, from its east end, 'Fleet Street' was extended by the newly laid out Pedley Street. This development was, presumably, the somewhat belated fruit of the optimism that had characterised the silk industry in the first decades of the nineteenth century until the repeal of the Acts.

One of the weavers living here had also given evidence to the Parliamentary Commission, and it was to his testimony that the journalist Henry Mayhew turned in the late 1840s when he was gathering information about the Spitalfields weaving community for a series of extraordinary and revelatory articles for the *Morning Chronicle* that in 1851 were included in the three volumes of his *London Labour and the London Poor* (see pages 424–5). The weaver's name was Thomas Heath and he lived at number 8 Pedley Street. The report that Mayhew quoted explained that Heath had been 'represented by many persons as one of the most skilful workmen in Spitalfields' and submitted a 'detailed account' of his earnings during the last eight years. This averaged out at a gross income of about fifteen shillings a week. The master weaver William Hale, in his *Appeal* of 1822, had stated that 'the average price which I pay for labour to all the men I employ, does not exceed seventeen shillings per week.'[40] After the payment of rent, the wages to a boy to wind quills and the purchase of candles, Hale's calculation was that the average Spitalfields weaver in 1822 had about fifteen shillings per week clear. In 1839 Heath – a superior weaver – had, after expenses 'for quill-winding, picking, etc.' – a net income of, on average, a mere eleven shillings and sixpence a week. Heath's wife's earnings were three shillings a week. The superiority of Heath's trade status is confirmed by Mayhew's estimate that – as we have seen – the average weekly wage for a weaver in 1839 was seven shillings to eight shillings and sixpence.

Above: *a weaver's house in Spitalfields in the mid nineteenth century. Note the entry to the weaving workshop via a trapdoor, the long, leaded 'light', the profusion of plants and, of course, the dominance of the loom, with its complex mechanism.* Below: *a late-nineteenth-century photograph of the houses of Florida Street, just north of Pedley Street, which were probably built in the 1820s and which were typical of the buildings of the now long-lost weaving district of Bethnal Green.*

Mayhew published his account of Heath's deteriorating financial position ten years after the skilled journeyman had revealed it in his evidence and asked his readers to consider how much worse things had become in the interim: 'what must be the condition and feeling of the weaver now that wages have fallen from 15 to 20 per cent since that period!' By Mayhew's calculation the average weaver's wage in 1849 was five shillings and sixpence.[41]

Mayhew was particularly struck, when reading Heath's evidence, by his bitter and forlorn answer when asked if he had any children: 'No; I had two, but they are both dead, thanks to God.' When asked why he was pleased his children were dead, Heath replied that by their deaths he was 'relieved from the burden of maintaining them, and they, poor dear creatures, are relieved from the troubles of this mortal life.' Such was the dreadful situation of a skilful weaver in 1839.[42]

Heath's house has long since been destroyed and much of the site of Pedley Street itself has been recently obliterated by the construction of the new overground railway route that now cuts through the former junction between 'Fleet Street' and Pedley Street. However, Heath, his family and his house – as well as his neighbours – hover like spectres in the 1841 census for St Matthew Bethnal Green.[43] Here he is described as a weaver, aged forty-five, born in Middlesex, living with his wife Ann, aged thirty. They have no children listed. In the same house, which must have been small – probably no more than two or three storeys high – there appear to have been three other families and eleven people in occupation on the day of the census. There was Robert Connell, thirty, a weaver; Richard Willett, thirty-five, also a weaver, his wife Maria, aged thirty-five, who was a 'Silk Warper' and their four children; Sarah Poole, aged sixty, and John Poole, twenty-five, presumably her son, who mended shoes for a living.

The six houses adjoining number 8 offer a composite portrait of mid-nineteenth-century Pedley Street. There were forty-nine people living in them on the day of the census. Add to this the number in Heath's house and there were sixty inhabitants in a row of seven small, adjoining houses, so on average between eight and nine people per house. Of these sixty people, twenty-seven were involved in the silk-weaving or fabric industry. One house, three doors distant from number 8, was populated by a single family – nine in number – of 'Fringe makers'. The eldest was the father, James Haine, aged fifty, and the youngest his daughter Ann, aged nine. The house adjoining was occupied by a family of silk weavers six strong, headed by George Potts, aged forty, accompanied by his wife and two elder sons. Presumably their looms were kept on the upper floor and garret of the house while the family lived on the lower floors. Another house, with fourteen residents seemingly organised in six family groups, included a husband and wife team of 'Engine weavers' – Edward Farrington, aged thirty-five, and his wife Mary, of the same age. Amongst the residents of these houses there was a straw-bonnet-maker, Sarah Seddons, aged twenty-two, and a shoemaker, Robert Parkin, aged fifty. Both of these were common Spitalfields trades at the time.

In his exploration of the Spitalfields weaving quarter in 1849 Mayhew chose a house at random (he does not say in which street), knocked on the door and was 'ushered up a steep staircase, and through a trap in the floor into the "shop".' This proved to be 'a long narrow apartment, with a window back and front, extending the entire length of the house.' Here Mayhew found a velvet weaver, making drab velvet for coat collars. He pulled up a chair so they could talk as the weaver worked. The weaver said he had a family of six; that he could get three shillings and sixpence a yard for the work he was engaged on but could weave only half a yard a day. If all his three looms were working and all his family employed he could earn twenty to twenty-five shillings per week, 'but one loom is generally out of work.' The weaver told Mayhew that 'up to 1824, the price for the same work as he is now doing was 6s. The reduction, he was convinced, arose from the competition in the trade, and one master cutting under the other.' He continued, 'the workmen are obliged to take the low prices, because they have not the means to hold out, and they know that if they don't take the work others will . . . people are [now] compelled to do double the quantity of work they used to do, in order to live.' As for the masters that employed him, the weaver told Mayhew, 'they will never advance wages . . . it's been a continuation of reduction for the last six-and-twenty years, and a continuation of suffering for just as long . . . Manufacturers may be divided into two classes – those who care for their men's comforts and welfare, and those who care for none but themselves.'[44]

After visiting several other journeymen in their homes, Mayhew went to a tavern where 'weavers who advocate the principles of the People's Charter [the Chartists, who advocated wide-scale political reform] were in the habit of assembling.' These weaver Chartists told him that the 'primary cause of the depression of the prices . . . was the want of suffrage' and because 'labour is unrepresented in the House of Commons . . . the capitalist and the landlord have it all their own way.'[45]

After this discussion, and because it was 'now getting late', Mayhew 'was anxious to see some case of destitution in the trade, which might be taken as a fair average of the state of the second- or third-rate workman.' The weavers he had met so far were, despite their troubles, relatively superior artisans. Mayhew's guide therefore took him to a three-storey house in a 'narrow back street' near Shoreditch church. It was getting dark when they arrived. They saw 'a light shining through the long window in the attic', knocked and were eventually admitted. After groping their way upstairs – keeping away from the banisters because they were 'rotten and might give way' – they arrived at the top floor and entered the garret. The weaver greeted them 'from between the curtains of a turn-up bedstead' – presumably a bed that could be folded or disguised as a cupboard or other piece of furniture during the day – while a girl lit another lamp. 'Never', admitted Mayhew, had he 'beheld so strange a scene. In the room were three large looms', and a clothes line – stretching from the bed to one loom – from which 'hung a few ragged shirts and petticoats'. Another clothes line, with linen drying on it, was stretched below one of the looms, and on the floor was 'spread a bed, on which lay four . . . boys, two with their heads in one direction and two in the other . . . covered . . . with old sacks and coats. Beside the bed of the old man was a mattress on the ground without any covering, and the tick positively chocolate-coloured with dirt.'

The old weaver revealed he had been ill with cholera: 'I couldn't work! Oh, no! It took all the use of my strength from me.' He told Mayhew: 'I hadn't got any money to buy anything. Why, there's seven of us here . . . all dependent on the weaving here, nothing else. What was four shillings a yard is paid one and nine now, so I leaves you to judge, sir . . . My work stopped for seven days . . . and we had nothing to live on. God knows how we lived. I pawned my things – and shall never get 'em again – to buy some bread, tea, and sugar, for my young ones . . .' He then described the family's living conditions: 'there's four on us here in this bed. One head to foot – one at our back along the bolster; and me and my wife side by side. And there's four on 'em over there. My brother Tom makes up the other one.'

As well as suffering the toll of illness, overcrowding and poverty, the weaver was also exhausted by the ruthless competition imposed by the unregulated market. 'The prices of weaving is so low, that we're ashamed to say what it is, because it's the means of pulling down other poor men's wages and other trades . . . Some of the masters is so cruel, that they gives no more than 1s. and 3d. [a yard] – that's it. But it's the competitive system; that's what the Government ought to put a stop to.' The weaver gave it as his opinion that the weavers of Spitalfields were being 'brought to that state of destitution, that many say it's a blessing from the almighty that takes 'em from the world . . . And this is to have cheap silks . . . Everybody is becoming brutal – unnatural.' The old weaver then cast his mind back to the condition of trade before the repeal of the Spitalfields Acts: 'Yes, I was comfortable in '24. I kept a good little house . . . I could live by my labour then, but now, why it's wretched in the extreme. Then I'd a nice little garden and some nice tulips for my hobby, when my work was done.'[46] Mayhew's research revealed that in 1838 there had been 9,302 looms at work in the area with 894 unemployed.[47] He reckoned that every two looms employed would occupy five hands 'so that the total number of hands engaged in the silk manufacture in Spitalfields, in 1838, must have been more than double that number – say 20,000.' But the 'depreciation in the value of their labour' during the decade after 1839 meant only suffering for this large, underemployed workforce.[48]

That there were still weavers scratching a living in Spitalfields well into the second half of the nineteenth century is clear from the 1851 census returns. A sample of just nine houses[49] in 'Hare Street' (now Cheshire Street), for example, shows no fewer than twenty-seven weavers, 'handloom weavers' and 'silk-winders' in residence, along with single members of a large variety of other trades and occupations including ginger-beer-maker, joiner, bricklayer, dyer, dressmaker, fishmonger, linen draper, confectioner, toymaker, butcher, shoe-binder, milliner, and even a surgeon – a John Lea Beddingfield.[50] There were also two cabinet-makers and two shoemakers. Today, Cheshire Street, which lies off Brick Lane and is immediately to the north of Pedley Street, contains one early house, number 46, which was built in the 1670s and re-fronted and altered in the early nineteenth century.[51]

It can be very difficult to match up old and new addresses but, with the use of Richard Horwood's map of 1799–1819, it would seem that at the time of the 1851 census this was 92 'Hare Street'. If so, it was a house that in 1851 still maintained a link with Spitalfields' weaving past, for a 'silk weaveress', forty-eight-year-old spinster Phoebe Jollick, was living there, no doubt using one of the house's weaving floor's wide windows as was originally intended. The other occupants of this particular house, though, had nothing to do with the weaving trade: they were a 'victualler' named Robert Kele, aged forty, his wife Ruth, aged forty-four, a son and a daughter, and a twenty-two-year-old servant named Jane Norton.

The fact that Kele was a 'victualler' suggests that perhaps this census return relates to the neighbouring building to the west of 92. This had been the White Horse pub and, although no longer licensed premises, the building still exists. We know that the White Horse tavern was in operation before the existing building was constructed in the 1860s because it is mentioned in May 1836, during John Sheering's trial for perjury, when the 'beadle of Bethnal-green' told the jury that since it was his 'business to see in what state the public-house are kept during Divine service . . . I went to the White Horse, in Hare-street, at a quarter before twelve [and found] the house was quiet and orderly, not a soul there . . .'[52] If 92 'Hare Street' was indeed the White Horse then we should look at the census returns for 91, which possibly relate to the existing 46 Cheshire Street – the altered 1670s weaver's house. On the day of the census number 91 contained seven families and an astonishing forty-three people, eleven of whom – six women and five men – were in the silk industry. There were two 'silk winders', one 'weaveress', and eight 'hand-loom weavers in silk'. The people crowded into this house must have been living in desperate circumstances.

But the street was, apparently, a place of stark contrasts in 1851 and not all in the silk industry living there were impoverished. For example, number 94 was occupied by William J. Paxman, a 'silk dyer and master' who employed six boys and thirty men – a considerable enterprise for the period. Aged thirty-one, he lived there with his wife Eliza, thirty-two, two sons, and a twenty-eight-year-old servant named Susannah Cook. His father, also named William, who appears to have built up the business, had recently died (his will, dated 12 November 1850, is preserved in The National Archives),[53] and Paxman Junior had clearly come into a substantial inheritance.

One gets a sense of what Paxman Senior was like from evidence he gave at a trial held at the Old Bailey on 14 February 1816. In the dock stood a prisoner, accused of stealing £450 worth of silk from a dyer called Thomas Meadows, who had premises in 'Princes Street', now Princelet Street[54] (the

On the right is 74 (formerly 79) Hare Street (now Cheshire Street). Built in the late seventeenth century as a weaver's workshop and home, perhaps with a shop on the ground floor, it was described in the mid nineteenth century as 'abominably dirty and foul'. The photograph was taken in the mid 1920s just before the building was demolished.

house has since been rebuilt and is now numbered 26 Princelet Street) and to whom William Paxman was apprenticed. 'I live in [Mr. Meadows'] house,' Paxman explained; '. . . after I put the dog in the dye-house, I went to bed. I got up at about twenty minutes before seven on Sunday morning; the dye-house was all safe then: I locked it [and] then went down to the Plough, at Mile-end [where] I met my brother (and later left him) at the corner of Old Montague-street, he saying . . . he was going into Whitechapel . . . and I went to breakfast at my master's [and] found the gate of the yard open . . . the dye-house open . . . I looked into two drawers, but they were empty . . . ' When cross-examined Paxman admitted that 'the prisoner is my brother.' Thanks in large part to Paxman's testimony his brother John was found guilty and sentenced to be transported for seven years. Ruthless honesty and loyalty to trade and master, beyond loyalty to a family member who erred, were presumably attributes that were both respected and necessary for success in the hard-bitten business community of Spitalfields.[55]

Despite the presence of the Paxmans, however, it's clear that by the time of the 1851 census 'Hare Street' was on its way down in the world. Indeed when the sanitary reformer Dr Hector Gavin came to look at it in the late 1840s, he found to one side of the Spitalfields workhouse (located at the east end of the street) 'a night-man's yard' containing 'a heap of dung and refuse, about the size of a pretty large house' – hardly what one would expect to find in a well-to-do street. But then night-men's yards were becoming a common sight in the East End. The men who ran them had the unpleasant job of emptying cesspits, carrying their ordure away (a task usually performed under the merciful veil of night, hence the name), and selling it on to farmers as fertiliser. For this they were well rewarded (Noddy Boffin – the 'Golden Dustman' in Charles Dickens's *Our Mutual Friend* of 1864–5 – actually makes his fortune from waste). For their neighbours, on the other hand, this source of cash was a scene of squalor and potential danger to health.

Next to the heap Gavin noticed 'an artificial pond, into which the contents of cesspools are thrown. The contents', he noted grimly, 'are allowed to desiccate in the open air; and they are frequently stirred up for that purpose.'[56] This was perhaps the pool in which, nearly eighty years earlier, Daniel Clarke had met his death (see page 287).

Of 'Hare Street' itself, Gavin recorded that it was 'abominably dirty and foul', with 'the back yards of the houses . . . in a most scandalous state'. He was particularly drawn to 'the backyard of number 79' which was 'in a perfectly beastly state of filth; the privy is full and smells most offensively. There is a large cess-pool in it, one part of which is only partially covered with boarding; the night-soil was lately removed from it, but the stench arising from it is still very great.' He noted that in this particularly foul and desperate habitation 'a pig-stye has lately been removed . . . the wife of the present owner lately died of fever' and 'none of the inhabitants are well', with 'three cases of fever and one death . . . clearly traceable to the abominable filthiness of this place.'[57]

One cannot but wonder what on earth the long-demolished hell-hole at number 79 was like, and who could have lived there. According to Horwood's map the house was on the south side of the street, on Hare Marsh Estate land, on the corner with '3 Cow Court', which ran south to St John Street. The court or alley still exists but on the corner site once occupied by 79 there now stands a modern and utterly characterless residential building. The passage, as it happens, is far from characterless. In fact, it's one of the best things of its kind in the area. It leads to a ruthlessly utilitarian pedestrian bridge of some age that crosses the main railway line, and in the process offers a stunning view of the towers of the City, before descending, via a cranked staircase, to a cobbled street. This is the stunted remains of Fleet Street Hill, which runs south towards Pedley Street through a large and echoing arched opening in a now redundant and oddly truncated railway viaduct.

The 1851 census, compiled about three years after Gavin's observations, offers a profile of the community then living in number 79. There were nine people in occupation at the time the census was conducted. John Brown is listed as the 'Head' of the household. He was a thirty-six-year-old bootmaker born in Bethnal Green. Living with him was his thirty-seven-year-old wife Lydia, also born in Bethnal Green, their three sons, their daughter and three apprentice bootmakers: John Welsh aged nineteen, William Collins aged seventeen, and James Wilson aged sixteen. All the children and apprentices had been born in Bethnal Green.[58] It would appear that this was not the family that had occupied the house when Gavin made his visit, when the wife of the 'present owner' had recently died. That stricken family had presumably moved on and the Browns had installed themselves.

As well as getting a glimpse of the people who lived in the house in the mid nineteenth century it is also possible to see what the building itself looked like, thanks to a splendid photograph preserved in the collection of the London Metropolitan Archives of number 74 (as 79 had now become) and number 76.[59] The photograph was taken in about 1925 just before the buildings were demolished and shows a pair of three-storey buildings, with mirrored plan, standing on a corner site. Each house has a wide weavers' window at second-floor level, and at first-floor level a single conventional window lighting the living quarters flanked by a small one lighting the cramped newel staircase constructed against the front façade. This pair of buildings were probably built in the late seventeenth century and, despite being slightly extended and altered in the late eighteenth century, were typical of the street's original structures.

Given the depressed nature of these streets east of Brick Lane, where poverty stalked and competition for limited resources was extreme, it comes as no surprise to learn that tension sometimes spilt over into violence. In late October 1850, for example, in an argument over money, two beerhouse-keepers, with premises on opposite corners of Fleet Street Hill and Pedley Street, had a confrontation, in the course of which James Cousins butted George Smith so violently in the body that Smith sickened, took to his bed and died a month later. The fight was a very public affair and at the subsequent trial many people gave evidence. Cousins was found guilty, not of murder but of 'felonious killing', or manslaughter, and was sentenced to only three months' gaol, largely because the prosecutor himself recommended mercy and because in court Cousins had 'received a good character'. It all reads like something from the Wild West. The men had had an argument about 'lead', then a slang word for money, due to publicans, with Smith demanding a share and publicly insulting Cousins. The law of the street resolved the dispute in an open and deadly fight and the law of the land turned virtually a blind eye.[60]

When Charles Booth, the social reformer, walked down Hare Street with his policeman guide and escort Sergeant French nearly fifty years later, on 22 March 1898, things had, if anything, got worse. The area was more crowded, old buildings more ruinous, and virtually all craft trades such as weaving had been replaced by more mundane – sometimes desperate – modes of life. In his notebook Booth confirmed that the street should remain shaded dark blue (the second from worst of the seven colour-coded categories by which he classified the conditions of the occupants of London's streets – see pages 519 and 522) as designated on his map of ten years previously. He observed 'some Jews, shops underneath, the rest rough, thieves.' The pair then went 'south down 3 Colt Corner, black in map [the worst category] now dark blue on west side only . . . to a bridge across the Great Eastern Railway train lines'.[61]

***

The death throes of Bethnal Green's ancient but hard-pressed weaving community are captured in the *Illustrated London News* of 24 October 1863,[62] which paints a poignant picture of skilled workers trying desperately to retain their traditional and admirable standards of craftsmanship and respectability, even when faced with destitution: '. . . wherever the weaver is found his personal cleanliness and the tidiness of his poor room offer a striking contrast to those of many of his neighbours,' it noted. This view echoed the opinion of the journalist George Dodd, expressed twenty years earlier, that the impoverished silk weavers of Spitalfields and Bethnal Green were 'intelligent and communicative' and still 'retained some humanity' in contrast to 'the less honourable persons attracted to the area by public bounty'.[63]

As the *Illustrated London News* observed, the average weaver still occupied very much the same sort of premises that his predecessors would have done a century and more earlier: '[His] work requires a "long light" or leaden casement, so that he most frequently occupies garrets originally designed for his trade.' But living conditions had changed wholly for the worse: 'Poor, suffering, nearly starved, and living in a house which shares with the rest the evils of bad or no drainage and insufficient water supply, his business requires at least some amount of personal cleanliness, or the delicate fabrics on which he is employed could never come out unsullied from the touch of coarser hands.'

A couple of years later, Thomas Archer repeated this view word for word in his book *The Pauper, the Thief and the Convict* (suggesting either that he was a shameless plagiarist or that he was the author of the *Illustrated London News* article). But he also added some telling additional details. Although usually clean and tidy, observed Archer, a weaver's rooms were often 'pervaded by a strong ammoniacal smell from the animals which most of them keep, whether they be pigeons, white mice, cats, rabbits, fancy dogs, or singing birds. Of these pigeons and singing birds are the most common, the former being kept in the lofts, and flying from dormers on the tiles, where their masters spend a great part of their spare time, and notably their Sunday mornings.'[64] Archer also noted the defining sound of a weaver's house – 'the click of the shuttle' that could be 'heard all day long while the weaver has work to do'. By the 1860s, though, that shuttle was all too often silent. 'When [the weaver] is "at play" (the term used to express the period while he is waiting for a fresh "piece" or "cane", as the web of silk is technically called),' Archer observed, 'his time is spent in waiting his turn at the warehouse of his employer till he obtains work again. [This] "play time" which formerly denoted a time of relaxation . . . now signifies a fireless hearth and hungry children . . .'[65]

But Archer also discerned a sense of family pride and the distant memory of more prosperous times: 'In one of these long "shops" [where] a whole family and all their live stock will sometimes live . . . amidst the turned up stump bedsteads or the roll of blankets on the floor'. Among 'the few pieces of broken crockery, and the rickety furniture, some of which is generations old,' he writes:

> there is often seen some sort of order and decency which is worthy of a better fortune . . . a cracked china cup, an ivory carving, a silver-keyed flute, a flawed and riveted punch-bowl . . . a scrap or two of old point lace – such things have I seen here and there . . .Two years ago I used to notice a board outside a window near Club Row, amidst the pigeon shops, which intimated that there was, somewhere close by, 'A Day school both in French and English,' but I miss it to-day, and the last remnant of the old weaver colony seems to have floated away with it . . . into the great sea of oblivion.[66]

It is, of course, curious to contrast these views – no doubt romantic and sentimental – with the more brutal portraits of the decaying Spitalfields weaving community offered in the early nineteenth century by such as Francis Place. And it is predictable that over a decade before Archer published his account Charles Dickens, a man more than a little prone to the sentimental, had also spotted and been moved by similar reminders of better days in the weavers' houses he visited (possibly in or near Pedley Street), in which silk looms so dominated the interiors that 'the children sleep at night between the legs of the monsters.' The weavers also, observed Dickens, kept pigeons and grew green runner beans. But, he ruminated, 'while birds could fly and escape, their owners could not. The bean stalk allowed Jack to escape in the fairy tale but the "Jacks" of Spitalfields will never, never, climb to where the giant keeps his money.'[67]

FOURTEEN

SOUP KITCHENS AND BODY-SNATCHERS

Spitalfields in the Late Regency Period

The increase of poverty in Spitalfields throughout the 1830s was linked not only to the repeal of the Spitalfields Acts in 1824, which served to reduce wages and increase unemployment, but also to a sharp rise in its population figures. Until the first meticulous census was conducted in 1841, it's difficult to be sure of exact numbers, but it seems likely that the population of Spitalfields (along with the Liberties and those parts of surrounding parishes that had become part of the area generally regarded as Spitalfields) more or less doubled in the period 1801–31 to between 65,000 and 80,000.[1] This was a pattern reproduced nationally. In the same period, as the first phase of the Industrial Revolution took hold, the population of England and Wales grew from 9 million to nearly 14 million. And just as Spitalfields buckled under the strain of a larger but more impoverished population, so areas of extreme deprivation spread across the country as a whole.

The response of government was to attempt to create a more efficient mechanism for dealing with the poor (a process that was to continue throughout the nineteenth century). And efficiency equated with toughness. Under the terms of the Poor Law Amendment Act of 1834, and subsequent and related legislation, the system of poor relief was tightened to ensure a more cost-effective use of resources. Poor people who sought help could no longer live at home and receive funds, as they once had. Instead, they had to resort to workhouses whose regimes were specifically designed to deter malingerers and offer assistance only to the truly destitute. These institutions, in other words, were intended to be so unpleasant that only the desperate would want to take refuge there. It was a form of state punishment of the poor underscored by an assumption that their poverty was not only their own fault but, in a sense, a crime against society – an unhappy state of affairs that greatly antagonised such liberal-minded people as Charles Dickens. Several of his novels, from *Oliver Twist* (serialised 1837–9) onwards, were to highlight the evils of the workhouse system.

A key expression of this streamlining of poor relief was the uniting of different parishes into Unions and, simultaneously, the replacement of scattered, smaller parish workhouses by fewer, larger Union institutions. In Spitalfields and Whitechapel, a new Union workhouse was built in 1842 in Vallance Road to replace the old parish workhouses serving Spitalfields that had stood in Bell Lane from the late 1720s (see page 193) and in 'Charles Street' (as Vallance Road was originally named) in Mile End New Town. The new Whitechapel and Spitalfields Workhouse served nine parishes and Liberties, including – together with Christ Church Spitalfields and St Mary's Whitechapel – the Liberties of Norton Folgate and the Old Artillery Ground as well as the parish of St Botolph's Aldgate. The workhouse was enlarged in 1859 in gaunt and forbidding manner to comprise three large wards, with males and females segregated to ensure, among other things, that families were broken up and effectively made miserable. There were also a kitchen, offices, laundry, infirmary – including a ward for 'imbeciles' – and a 'casual' ward where vagrants would be given food and accommodation for the night providing they did a fixed amount of work for the Union. With the passing in 1867 of the Metropolitan Poor Act that, among other things, required workhouse infirmaries to be housed on separate sites from the workhouse itself, the Whitechapel and Spitalfields Union was relocated to South Grove, off the Mile End Road, and the Charles Street building became the workhouse infirmary and then St Peter's Hospital until it was demolished in the 1960s.[2]

The workhouse system was brutal; it was calculated to be so, and its harsh policies ensured that it failed to help many of the nation's poor. Instead it humiliated its inmates, broke up families, and persuaded many desperate people to take their chances and fend for themselves as best they could. This, of course, led in turn to vagrancy, begging and destitution of the sort that Henry Mayhew noted in *London Labour and the London Poor*, published in 1851, when describing the lives of London's 'street-folk' (see pages 424–5), and which Dickens's Ebenezer Scrooge so strongly condemned in *A Christmas Carol* of 1843. Scrooge's view – and it was presumably one commonly shared – was that institutions that taxpayers already funded should deal with the poor: 'Are there no prisons?' he asks. 'And the Union

The Spitalfields and Whitechapel Union workhouse, as photographed by Jack London in 1902 and reproduced the following year in his The People of the Abyss. *Here men are waiting for admittance to the 'casual' ward of the 'Spike', hoping for a night's lodging in return for labour.*

workhouses? . . . Are they still in operation?' He did not think that individual acts of philanthropy were required: 'I help to support the establishments I have mentioned –' he maintains '– they cost enough; and those who are badly off must go there.'

Fortunately, not everyone felt this way, and in the course of the nineteenth century – both in contrast to the blunt operation of the Poor Laws and paradoxically in response to them – there was a marked increase in individual philanthropic initiatives in the fight against poverty. Inspired for the most part by Christian beliefs, these took the form of well-meaning 'missionary' crusades and the establishment of charitable educational and medical institutions in poor areas. Spitalfields, with its swelling ranks of the poor, not surprisingly proved to be fertile ground for these philanthropists.

One of the earliest of the large-scale local charitable enterprises emerged from within the area's own weaving community. This was a soup kitchen founded by William Allen, a Quaker and the son of a silk merchant, whose life is described in a curious book of 1884 entitled *The Spitalfields Genius: The Story of William Allen*,[3] written by one J. Fayle. He clearly had no love of Spitalfields: he describes it as 'as one of the unsavoury districts of London', a haunt 'of costermongers, cadgers, and thieves . . . home of disease, begotten by Dissipation and Dirt! [where] the children of the poor are still dragged up in poverty, hunger, and dirt; in fact, a place of little credit to London'.[4] He did, however, clearly admire William Allen and *The Spitalfields Genius* is a faithful account of what he achieved.

According to Fayle, Allen was born in 1770 in Plough Court, off Lombard Street, in the City.[5] He used his inherited wealth to study chemistry and to create a highly successful pharmaceutical company that allowed him in 1841 to found and become first President of the Royal Pharmaceutical Society. But he was also clearly a man with a strong moral conscience, the product of an age in which brutal working conditions and poverty not only stimulated great benevolence amongst Evangelical Christians and Dissenters but also among rational men of science – like Allen and Joseph Priestley – who evidently viewed inaction in the face of human suffering as unnatural and unjust as well as ungodly.

'In the year 1797', Fayle explains, 'the attention of [William Allen] was particularly directed to the best means of affording relief to some

thousands of industrious poor families in Spitalfields in great misery and
destitution, from the stagnation of trade and the high price of provisions'.
Twenty people 'met at the house of a Friend' (meaning a Quaker and presumably the Allen house, almost certainly in Steward Street) and 'a
working Society was formed, a "Ladling Society" we might call it, for
every member of the committee had to take his turn on duty, and actually
help to ladle out the soup at this new centre of active benevolence, [in]
Brick Lane, Spitalfields'.[6] This 'little band' was able to 'serve out daily over
3,000 quarts of excellent soup, money taken, tickets marked, and all in the
short space of two hours and a quarter'.[7] It was not the only philanthropic
enterprise that Allen undertook. In 1805 he became a committee member
of the Society for the Abolition of Slavery; in 1812 he was involved in the
opening of the Spicer Street school in Spitalfields (see page 337); and in
1824 he founded the Newington Academy for Girls.

The soup kitchen's activities fluctuated according to the condition of
the poor in Spitalfields at any given time: 1812 was a particularly bad year.
Six thousand people therefore needed to be fed daily, and the quantity of
soup sold monthly averaged 80,000 quarts.[8] In the same year Allen
founded the Spitalfields Association for the Relief of the Industrious Poor,
which established a shop in Spitalfields Market selling salt fish and pork
at almost cost price.[9] He was joined in this enterprise by William Hale,
the local master weaver who in 1822 was to argue powerfully but ultimately
unsuccessfully against the repeal of the Spitalfields Acts (see pages 364–7).
Another supporter was Samuel Hoare, a rich Quaker merchant and
banker, who lived in nearby Old Broad Street in the City, was one of the
founding members of the Society for the Abolition of the Slave Trade,
and – upon Allen's third marriage in 1827 – became his brother-in-law. It
would seem that the defence of journeymen weavers from the ruthless
forces of unregulated capitalism were – to enlightened Quaker philanthropists at least – acts of conscience synonymous with helping the
destitute and campaigning against slavery.

The premises on Brick Lane used by the admirable 'Ladling Society'
survive – now generally unrecognised and uncelebrated. Numbers 106 to
122 are a block of houses and shops dating in part from the late eighteenth
century. Between 114 and 116 is a door, formerly numbered 53 Brick Lane,
that evidently leads to a corridor or alley,[10] and above it is a large but mutilated cartouche that bears the date – in slab-like sans-serif numerals – 1797.
This was the entrance to the 'Spitalfields Soup Society' (as the 'Ladling

Above: *soup being prepared and served in the Brick Lane soup kitchen, as depicted in the* Illustrated London News *in March 1867.* Below: *the volume of the building survives behind the late-eighteenth-century 114–16 Brick Lane. The date over the central door, 1797, is the year the soup kitchen was opened on the site.*

Society' became known), which survived until 1883, when the running of the soup kitchen was taken over by the parish.

An illustration of it in operation was published in the *Illustrated London News* for 9 March 1867.[11] It shows a large, single-storey, barn-like structure, with a steeply pitched roof over an open space. A row of huge steaming vats of soup stand to one side and a teeming but orderly crowd to the other. They are being served by women at tables in the centre of the room, ladling out soup from large urns. Also in the middle of the room is a stocky and rather mysterious vertical structure – presumably part of a chimney related to the large range on which the soup is being heated. The illustration is captioned: 'Distress in the East of London: The Spitalfields Soup Kitchen'.

Today, the door to the former soup kitchen leads to upper-floor flats. The kitchen itself, however, can still be reached via number 112. It's now a large room that houses Taj Stores, the major Bangladeshi supermarket in Brick Lane. No traces of the soup kitchen are visible except perhaps for some of the external wall to the east. But the space, now seemingly characterless, is immensely evocative. Wandering along the aisles stacked with spices, packets of food, the frozen carcasses of huge fish from the Bay of Bengal and exotic kitchen implements, it is impossible not to feel the presence – even if very faint – of outcast Spitalfields, the shades of the desperate people who gathered in this space for nearly one hundred years.[12]

A lengthy description of the soup kitchen and its mode of operation was published in an 1812 issue of a periodical that Allen had launched the previous year, entitled *The Philanthropist, or Repository for Hints and Suggestions calculated to Promote the Comfort and Happiness of Man*.[13] 'In Spitalfields and its neighbourhood, many hundreds of families of industrious poor are not able to procure as much bread as is necessary to satisfy the cravings of hunger. They only who visit these districts, and go from house to house, can have any adequate idea of the misery that prevails during a scarcity of corn, or a stagnation of trade.' It goes on to explain how William Allen, inspired by the operations of Count Rumford in Munich, decided to set up the soup kitchen; how successful it was from the start ('the applicants paid the penny per quart with cheerfulness, and carried home a supply of food which they could not have prepared of equal quality themselves, for four or five times the sum'); and how costs were kept down by buying at wholesale prices: 'every thing is done . . . from the purest and most disinterested motives, there are no salaries for clerks, no commission to agents: the only expense beyond that of the ingredients of the soup is the rent of the premises, the hire of the servants to prepare the soup . . . and a moderate allowance to the superintendent'. The institution's committee embraced different religious denominations – 'here Dissenters and Churchmen forgetting their little differences of opinion on other respects, unite cordially together in the work of Christian benevolence' – and met once a fortnight at the 'Soup House' to manage affairs. It was, proclaimed *The Philanthropist*, 'one of the triumphs of philanthropy'.

Committee members were obliged to take turns attending the daily making and distribution of the soup, which, given the number of members, was not too onerous – in 1812 only once every three weeks. A list of the committee members' supervisory duties for 'the present season, 1811–1812' reveals that soup was issued six days a week (not on Sundays) with the cycle starting on a Monday with William Allen and his son-in-law Cornelius Hanbury (both of whom are listed as of Plough Court, Lombard Street), and with volunteers who represented a virtual roll call of the good and the great of contemporary Spitalfields. They included the eminent Quaker philanthropists Peter Bedford (of 32 Steward Street); William Hale (of 'Wood Street' (Wilkes Street)); John Fry of Whitechapel; and William and Joseph Fry of St Mildred Court in the City. The Frys were, of course, members of the eminent Quaker dynasty that included Elizabeth Fry, née Gurney, the prison reformer. William Allen's son-in-law Cornelius Hanbury, too, came from a dynamic and successful Quaker family. The Hanburys were closely involved with Truman's Brick Lane Brewery, managed for nearly fifty years by Sampson Hanbury, who introduced steam power there in 1805 and who brought his brother Osgood and his nephew Thomas Fowell Buxton into the business. Buxton was also a Quaker, political activist, reformer, Member of Parliament from 1818 and the brother-in-law of Elizabeth Fry. Elizabeth's mother was a member of the Barclay banking family. So this group of Spitalfields 'soup ladlers' had connections among the most powerful and influential in the land. Scarcely surprising then that their efforts should have been supported by perhaps the most famous of all English philanthropists: William Wilberforce.[14]

The Philanthropist calculated that in 1812 the soup kitchen furnished a nourishing meal to 7,000 persons every day from supplies that included 856 pounds of beef; 426 pounds of barley; 317 pounds of split peas; 40 pounds of onions; 3 pounds 14 ounces of pepper and 62 pounds of salt. It also noted that 'the difference between the cost of the soup and the money paid by the poor occasions a loss to the Institution of more than 15ol. per week', and noted that this is 'supported by subscriptions from various benevolent individuals, by liberal contributions from the bankers, fire-officers, merchants and principal tradesmen, aided by donations from the City of London and the Bank; a committee at Lloyd's coffee-house for the relief of the Industrious Poor, the East India Company, the West India Dock and Mercers' Companies, the Royal Exchange Assurance, and other corporate bodies.'

The heroic activities of the Soup Society and the huge demand for the food it offered reveal very clearly the limitations of the Poor Laws. But perhaps more sobering is the fact that the organisation was intended to offer relief only to those labelled, with a whiff of condescension, the 'industrious poor' or, as they would be known slightly later in the century, the 'deserving poor' (see page 441). These were people judged to be in need through no fault of their own, who laboured hard in badly paid jobs or who were clearly physically incapable of work. The method by which such individuals could be identified and separated from their less deserving brethren taxed the ingenuity of many a nineteenth-century social reformer and philanthropist. It certainly concerned the committee of the Spitalfields Soup Society. They therefore decided to 'obtain more exact information of the particular circumstances of every poor family to which the soup was distributed'. In this way, presumably, they hoped to be able to take a view about the nature and cause of individual cases of poverty and perhaps, if satisfied that a particular person or family was 'deserving', offer more regular and wide-ranging help. One industrious member of the society's committee consequently amassed the addresses of and basic facts about all families buying tickets for soup and compiled a 'book', in which 'particulars of 1,504 cases were entered'. This, records *The Philanthropist*, 'furnished a valuable body of evidence, as to the state of a considerable part of Spitalfields and the neighbouring parishes.'

Early in 1812 a subcommittee resolved to make a 'visitation' of the area, using the information assembled in its book. It discovered that 'imperfect' or false directions meant that many families could not be found, while others were 'removed' and a 'considerable number gone into different workhouses'. But a fascinating social profile of poverty was nevertheless put together through what was, in effect, a small and informal census, and in the process those streets and parts of Spitalfields in the most desperate straits were identified. It is perhaps worth remembering that although this was the time of silk industry's second 'Golden Age' (see page 361), 1812 itself was a bad year: Napoleon's earlier Berlin and Milan Decrees had closed the Continent to British trade, making the acquisition of Italian raw silk very difficult.[15] When supplies dried up, masters simply stopped the looms and laid off the workforce. Destitution was rife.

The largest area of poverty uncovered by the 'visitation' was in the north and north-east portion of Spitalfields, around Wheler, Quaker, Pearl, Phoenix, Bacon and Sclater Streets. But poor streets, and enclaves of the poor, could also be found in the more affluent parts of the area, for example in 'Fleur de Lis Court' near Elder Street, in 'Brown's Lane' (Hanbury Street) and in 'Dorset Street' near the market. There was also a poverty-stricken quarter in the south-east part of Spitalfields, centred on Fashion Street and 'Flower and Dean Street'. As might be expected, the grander streets in Spitalfields such as Spital Square, 'Church Street' (now Fournier Street), 'Wood Street' (now Wilkes Street) and Elder Street do not feature in the list.

The overall survey of 1,504 families revealed that just under half of them (725) were involved in the silk trade. As for religious affiliation, nearly half (725) were Anglicans, 492 were Dissenters, and 276 families had 'no religious Profession'. Seven hundred and two families had no Bibles. Only thirty-four families were Catholics – a puzzlingly low number given the long period of Irish immigration into Spitalfields, Shoreditch and Bethnal Green, suggesting that Catholics did not tend to use the soup kitchen either because they were discouraged or because they could not afford to do so. In terms of levels of poverty, 352 families were 'much distressed for work', 649 were in 'distress', 216 were in 'greater distress' and thirty-one needed immediate 'relief'. A 'fearful amount of ignorance' was uncovered, too, as perhaps the lack of Bibles suggests: well over a third of the adults surveyed could not read.[16] This realisation seems to have galvanised an initiative launched the previous year by the Quaker Peter Bedford (also an active member of the Soup Society) to establish, with Allen's help, the school in 'Spicer Street', for it opened the same year as the 'visitation'.

The Soup Society was particularly interested in the plight of the Spitalfields weaving community, noting that 'at the present time a large proportion of them are out of work, in great part, if not wholly arising from the difficulty of procuring a certain description of silk from Italy.' It calculated that there were 'above 10,000 looms in Spitalfields and its neighbourhood' but reckoned that 2,852 of them were unemployed, 'and that the persons in families depending upon those unemployed looms amounts to 9,700.' 'If, to this, looms not half employed were added,' *The Philanthropist* later reported, 'the number would be at least doubled; and if we further add the dependents on weavers, as winders, dyers, warpers, quillers etc., we may have some faint idea of the distress that now prevails.' The society's visitation subcommittee evidently made observations about the homes it saw, and passed these to *The Philanthropist*: 'Upon the weavers and their dependents the pressure is particularly great ... they have been ... obliged to pledge, sell, and make away with the little property acquired by industry and care in better times; some of them are reduced nearly to nakedness, and deprived of every domestic convenience, while grief and dejection in unequivocal characters are stamped on their countenances; some, in their struggle to hold out as long as possible have sold their looms, beds, bedsteads, stoves, and other articles ... The whole proves, that from whatever cause it may have arisen, the present are indeed calamitous times.'[17]

It might indeed have been an exceptionally bad year, but the fact that such high and dreadful levels of poverty and unemployment existed over a decade before the repeal of the Spitalfields Acts demonstrates that, overall, the legislation was not very effective. This of course contradicts the evidence put forward by supporters of the Acts such as William Hale. Since he was himself involved in Allen's 'Ladling Society' and must have been aware of the facts gathered in 1812, one has to ask whether he simply chose to ignore them when writing his upbeat 1822 review of the silk industry under the protection of the Acts, or whether he disputed the facts that the Society had gathered and publicised.

The continuing plight of Spitalfields weavers into the mid nineteenth century – and well after the protectionist Acts were repealed – is confirmed by the activities of another devotee of the charitable soup kitchen. Alexis Benoît Soyer was born near Paris in 1810, became a chef at Versailles in 1821 and in 1831 moved to London where he cooked for various members of the British aristocracy. In 1837 he became chef of the newly created Reform Club in St James's where he pioneered the use of gas for cooking, and made his name in June 1838 when he cooked breakfast for 2,000 guests at Queen Victoria's Coronation. In 1847, at the government's invitation, he opened and operated a soup kitchen in Dublin during the Great Famine, mass-producing cheap but nourishing food. This gave him a taste for such enterprises and after writing a fund-raiser book, *Soyer's Charitable Cookery or, The Poor Man's Regenerator*, published in 1848 and sold for sixpence a copy (one penny of which was donated directly to poor relief), he opened a soup kitchen in Spitalfields.[18] Soyer went on to cook for visitors to the 1851 Great Exhibition, travelled to the Crimea in 1855 to help reorganise catering in hospitals in Scutari and Balaklava and died in London in 1858 – probably from a fever caught while in the Crimea. Where his Spitalfields soup kitchen was located from the late 1840s currently remains a mystery.

If the Soup Society served the local community's stomachs, then the London Dispensary – which worked along similar philanthropic principles – sought to minister to its health. Its base was what is now 27 Fournier Street, a fine house of 1725 built for, and first occupied by, Peter Bourdon, a successful weaver who in 1712 had been elected 'headborough' of the hamlet of Spitalfields. It was, and is, a grand house, five windows wide and once with a building (now demolished) in its large rear yard or garden that may have served as Bourdon's coach house and stable.[19] Peter Bourdon himself died in 1732, a wealthy man – so wealthy, indeed, that he was clearly concerned his widow might attract fortune-hunters, and consequently stipulated in his will that 'in case my wife happen to marry again . . . before such marriage she shall be obliged to place in the name of my executors [in] some public funds or other security the sum of £1,000 sterling, the interest whereof shall be paid to her during her natural life and after her decease the said capital shall go to my children or their descendants by equal portions.'[20] After his death the house passed through the hands of various other successful Spitalfields families, including Obadiah Agace, son-in-law of Peter Abraham Ogier's neighbour Daniel Pilon (see page 343). But by the 1820s this former merchants' palace was coming down in the world. In 1829, its days of glory behind it, it became home to the London Dispensary.

The Dispensary had been founded in 1777 in Primrose Street, just west of Bishopsgate and opposite Spital Square, before moving in 1809 to what is now 41 Artillery Lane and from there to Fournier Street.[21] Like the Soup Society it offered help that was subsidised but not free, issuing medicines and medical advice at minimal charge to the area's poor and needy.

Minutes of meetings of the committee regulating the Dispensary, which are kept in the London Metropolitan Archives, reveal the scope and scale of its activities.[22] By 5 January 1827 (the date of the first surviving minutes) the Dispensary had 'admitted' 145,304 people. Of these 137,494 had been 'cured/relieved'; 2,076 had died; 5,198 had been 'discharged'; and 538 patients were still 'under cure' when the minutes were compiled. So it was handling on average nearly 2,800 patients a year. By 7 December 1831 it had 'Admitted' 157,665 patients.

The use of the word 'admitted' is potentially deceptive. The Dispensary did not have wards and in-patients but merely medical stores and preparation areas, dispensing rooms and – perhaps – consultation and treatment rooms. The internal alterations at 27 Fournier Street (since removed) suggest the way in which the ground floor was organised to create public areas within which patients could gather and medicine be dispensed while segregated from more secure areas where staff could work. For example the original entrance hall and ground-floor front parlour were united to form a large waiting room separated by a wall from the staircase leading to staff accommodation.[23]

In 1839 the physician and future public-health reformer Charles James Berridge Aldis became involved with the Dispensary, perhaps as its surgeon (he was then only thirty-one). He wrote about his experiences in 1835 in *An Introduction to Hospital Practice* that led the *Medical Times and Gazette* to observe that there was nothing so 'noisome, monotonous, thankless, useless and hopeless as that of attending the dregs of the pauperised classes in Spitalfields . . .'[24] By 1841, according to that year's census, the house (then numbered as 21 'Church Street') was occupied by forty-year-old William Gayton – who was by then the 'Surgeon' – his wife and four children and two female servants aged seventeen and nineteen. Interestingly, no in-patients or medical staff are listed.[25] Thereafter Gayton became something of a fixture, still in place as late as 1871 when he was living in the house with his wife and two married daughters, along with one 'domestic servant'.[26] The London Dispensary continued its work in Spitalfields until 1946 when the National Health Act and the creation of the National Health Service made it redundant.

As I've already said, the period 1800–23 is sometimes referred to as Spitalfields' second golden age. But the very fact that a need was felt for enterprises such as the Soup Society and the London Dispensary shows that, if a few prospered in these final glory days of the silk industry, ever more were suffering. And these, of course, included many beyond the reach of either organisation. After all, the Soup Society and the London Dispensary existed to help the 'industrious poor': people who, for the most part, were in work, or at least trying to work, and who could be regarded as respectable. Such philanthropic enterprises were not there to help Spitalfields' growing underclass of the desperately poor – people who lived in slum areas such as the Nichol in Shoreditch (see pages 428–31) and the area immediately to its north, on the outer edge of London, where places such as Crabtree Row and 'Nova Scotia Gardens' became notorious as the desolate domain of the destitute and the criminalised. The poorest of Spitalfields' poor lived in shanty-dwellings and huts marooned in wastelands that had once been market or flower gardens (see page 188), within a diabolical landscape dotted with mountains of stinking offal, smoking brick-kilns and dark and slimy pools of ordure.

The circumstances that brought one particular local man – John Bishop – to achieve a degree of fame in the 1830s say much about the degraded way of life of the underclass. They also shed light on one particular trade practised by some of the less deserving poor. During the eighteenth century there was a burgeoning demand for human cadavers. These were required primarily by doctors seeking, through dissection, to increase their knowledge of the working of the human body and so enhance their ability to cure ailments and disease. Cadavers were also, to a lesser degree, sought after by artists wishing to improve their understanding of human anatomy. But bodies were in very limited supply, largely because Christian doctrine insisted that only if they were kept intact after death, and stored safely in consecrated ground, could resurrection take place at the Last Judgement and the soul have a chance of eternal life. So to steal, dismantle, disperse or discard parts of a human body was, by Christian perceptions at the time, an unconscionable act. Indeed it was tantamount to inflicting a second and terrible death – the murder of the eternal soul. This helps to explain why in the eighteenth and early nineteenth centuries it was primarily the bodies of executed murderers that were legally available for dissection: such an ultimate fate for the condemned felon was both a terrible punishment and a fearful deterrent.

Such problems with supply meant that human bodies became rare, desirable and highly expensive merchandise. For the desperate and non-squeamish they therefore offered a potentially very lucrative trade, particularly since the law relating to the removal and ownership of dead bodies was very imprecise. Essentially, since a body was the creation of God, it could not – after death – legally belong to any person. Taking a corpse from a grave was not technically a theft because, being no one's property, it could not be defined as a stolen item. This did not mean that body-snatching was without any hazards. The obvious one was the risk of encountering an outraged mob or relatives of the dead. To fall into their hands would be to endanger the body-snatcher's own life. And then there were the legal niceties. A dead body might be no one's property, but 'interfering' with a grave was a 'misdemeanour' that could be punished by a fine or imprisonment, and stealing the coffin, grave goods or shroud was a 'felony' that could be punished with transportation or death. So bodysnatchers – or 'resurrection men' – had to be very careful about any items they carried away with them. To be safe, it was best just to make away with the naked corpse in a sack and leave anything else behind.

By the late eighteenth century body-snatching had increased to epidemic proportions in Britain and was a national scandal. One reason for this increase was – somewhat paradoxically – that the mellowing judicial temper of the times meant fewer people were being executed and so fewer bodies were being made legally available for dissection. Individual parishes were therefore forced to take action, lighting and patrolling their graveyards and erecting watch houses on their perimeter walls. Fragments of a watch house survive at St Leonard's Shoreditch and a handsome and intact example of 1826 at St Matthew's Bethnal Green. This church also retains the rattle and blunderbuss that were issued to its watchman. He was paid ten shillings and sixpence a week, was given an additional reward for apprehending any resurrection man, and granted permission to fire at suspicious characters in the churchyard, providing he sounded his rattle first.

Some resurrection men – intoxicated by the money to be made selling fresh flesh to the medical profession – went beyond grave robbing. Since it was difficult and dangerous to acquire recently buried bodies from graveyards, it was tempting to turn predator among the living and to seek out suitable and vulnerable healthy specimens to be turned into dead meat. This was what Irish immigrants William Burke and William Hare had done in Edinburgh in 1828, when they murdered sixteen people and sold their bodies to the incurious anatomist Dr Robert Knox, and it was what Thomas Williams and John Bishop did in Shoreditch and Spitalfields in

1831. The area, with its crowded and expanding slums, seemed to be awash with anonymous and defenceless potential victims few would miss or mourn if they quietly disappeared. A good fresh body could fetch between eight and twenty guineas at a time when a silk weaver might earn as little as 5/- for a six-day week. The temptations were therefore huge. And Wiliams and Bishop were poor.

London resurrectionists worked in gangs, but how many of these there were and how many members each gang contained remains unclear. The historian Sarah Wise observes, in her definitive book on Bethnal Green body-snatchers, that in the early 1830s 'there may have been as many as seven London gangs, but with infighting a common feature of resurrection life, the gangs were likely to have been constantly breaking up, re-forming and disintegrating again'. A 'gang', she concludes, 'could have comprised as few as two men or as many as fifteen',[27] with the vast majority of members being only part-time or amateur body-snatchers. But what is certain is that there was a Spitalfields gang. It was 'notorious' and is mentioned in contemporary accounts and reports.[28] For example the *Morning Advertiser* of 16 October 1827 mentions that a William Davis was a member of the Spitalfields gang, and had been offered as much as twenty guineas by surgeons for the body of a young female who had died in an insane asylum. Davis was arrested by parish watchmen while digging up the young woman's body at Wigginton's private burial ground in Golden Lane, and thus his activities found their way into the press.[29] The Spitalfields gang was also mentioned to the 1828 Parliamentary Select Committee on Anatomy during evidence being given by a 'professional' resurrectionist identified merely as AB. This man, who said he knew the Spitalfields gang, had once been shot at by a graveyard guard, had served six months in gaol and claimed to have snatched a hundred corpses in a good year. AB could conceivably have been John Bishop, who also served a six-month sentence, but this is now impossible to prove.[30]

Bishop's partner in crime Thomas Williams lived, as did Bishop, at 3 Nova Scotia Gardens, part of a remote cluster of cottages just north of 'Crabtree Row' (now Columbia Road), south of Hackney Road and a few minutes' walk from St Leonard's Shoreditch. The cottages appear to have been little more than sheds standing among rank gardens pitted with ancient excavations from which brick earth had been long ago extracted. In the 1830s these excavations were known euphemistically as 'laystall', but were in fact repositories of filth and sewage from local cesspits dumped by night-soil men. This excrement might, in moderation, have been good for the market gardens of Shoreditch but here it simply accumulated, coagulating, filling the excavations and gradually collecting, flowing together and growing into a mighty mound of putrescence.

The remote nature of their base, the offensive surroundings that must have kept casual visitors at bay and the proximity to the mean streets of Shoreditch and north Spitalfields teeming with vagabonds provided Bishop and Williams with the tempting prospect of acquiring valuable bodies without the risk or trouble of digging them up. But their arrant stupidity, their avarice, and the drunken indiscretions of an accomplice named James May, by trade – appropriately enough – a butcher, proved to be a fatal combination, and on 1 December 1831 Williams, Bishop and May found themselves standing trial at the Old Bailey.[31] They were charged with the 'wilful murder' of two people. One was, according to the indictment, the 'Italian Boy' – a street performer of about fourteen named Carlo Ferrari, aka Charles Ferrier. The other victim was described as a 'certain male person, whose name is unknown'.

The first witness called by the prosecution revealed how the arrest was made. His name was William Hill and he was a porter at 'the dissecting-room at King's-college, Somerset House'. As Hill told the court:

> On Saturday, the 5th of November, about a quarter to twelve o'clock, the bell of the dissecting-room rang; I answered it, and found Bishop and May at the door – I knew them before: May asked if I wanted any thing – I said not particularly, and asked what he had got; he said a male subject: I asked him what size – he said it was a boy about fourteen years of age; I asked the price: he said twelve guineas – I said I could not think of giving that price for it; we did not care much about it, for we did not particularly want it, but if he would wait I would see Mr Partridge, who is the demonstrator of anatomy ... [Partridge then appeared and haggled over the price.] May said he should have it for ten guineas ... Mr Partridge ... told them he offered nine guineas; May said he would be d—d if it should come in for less than ten guineas: he was tipsy at the time – May stood outside the door, for a necessary purpose [i.e. urinating], Bishop called me aside, and said, 'He is drunk, it shall come in for nine guineas within half an hour'.

May and Bishop then left, but:

> returned the same afternoon, about a quarter-past two o'clock, in company with Williams and a person named Shields; they had a hamper – they came to the room appropriated for them; I was called – I went to the door,

unlocked it, and to the best of my recollection the hamper was off the head of Shields, the porter; (I knew him as such) – all four persons stood round the hamper: it was on the ground; they all four came in . . . May and Bishop carried the hamper through into the other room, they opened it . . . and in it was a sack, containing the body in question; May turned it out of the sack very carelessly, as he was tipsy; I looked at it, and both May and Bishop observed that we could not have a fresher, or that it was a very good, one – I said Yes, it was certainly fresh; I observed that it was particularly fresh, and . . . I asked the prisoners what the body had died with: they said they did not know, it was no business of mine or theirs – I cannot say which said so; it was said in the hearing of both.

The court then asked Hill if the body, when produced, 'was . . . in such a form as it would be if it came from a coffin?' 'No,' answered Hill, 'the left arm was turned up stiff, and the fingers clinched – I went to Mr Partridge, and detailed to him what I had seen, and what I thought; he returned with me to the room where the body was, [then] Mr Partridge . . . went to the secretary . . . some of the students saw the body, and their suspicions were created.' Meanwhile the three purveyors of the body of the boy were warming themselves by a fire in the adjoining room.

By now the game was up. The only question was how to detain them until help arrived. Partridge had a ploy. He returned to the prisoners, 'showed them a 50l. note, and said he must get that changed and he would pay them . . . Bishop said, "Give us what money you have got, and I will call on Monday for the remainder." May said if the note was given to him he would get it changed.' But Partridge 'smiled and said, "Oh no!" and left them without giving them any money – they remained there.' 'Partridge', Hall went on, 'returned in a quarter of an hour or twenty minutes . . . with the Police, and they were all taken into custody.' Hall told the court that while they waited for Partridge's return, 'Bishop said that when I paid them I was to give him only eight guineas, in the presence of Williams, and to give him the other guinea, and he would give me half a crown.' Such was the abject criminality of resurrection men. But then, if a man was prepared to murder a fourteen-year-old boy for money, should he be expected to behave honourably towards his partners in crime? Hall also observed that when he 'delivered the same body, hamper, and sack to Mr Thomas, the superintendent; I know the body had not been laid out in a coffin, for there was no saw-dust about the head.'

Richard Partridge gave evidence to confirm Hill's account and explained that when he looked at the body 'the external appearances were suspicious, which induced me to go to the Police – I observed the swollen state of the face, the blood-shot eyes, the freshness of the body, the rigidity of the limbs, and a cut over the left temple; the lips were swollen'. Partridge explained that he examined the body more closely the next day, at the police station in Covent Garden, and during dissection of 'the spinal part of the back of the neck ... found ... internal marks of violence ... sufficient to produce death – I believe violence had been exerted to have the effect on the spinal cord ... I think a blow from a stick on the back of the neck would have caused those appearances, and think it would produce a rapid death, but perhaps not an instantaneous one'. Numerous medical men were called to support Partridge's interpretation and confirm that the body delivered in a sack or hamper had indeed died a recent, sudden and violent death.

The obvious question that one would ask now was not, it seems, deemed worth putting in 1831. Why were Partridge and the hospital receiving and paying for dead bodies on a regular basis from such men as Williams, Bishop and May? Why did they not – until this occasion – question thoroughly the sources of these bodies and their causes of death? The answer, accepted at the time, was that the hospital had no legal requirement to do so and – incredible as it now seems – these medical men generally felt no ethical obligation to pry too deeply. As far as they were concerned, all the purveyors of corpses had to do was to state – but not prove – that the 'subject' for sale had died of natural causes. We may well think it extraordinary that leading surgeons would knowingly deal with human vultures. Yet they were clearly happy to do so, and would no doubt have argued that they had no choice if the cause of science were to be advanced. Sir Astley Paston Cooper, the distinguished surgeon and anatomist of Guy's Hospital, who knew the Quaker philanthropist William Allen and had been a member of his enlightened scientific debating club called the Askesian Society that until 1807 had met in Plough Court, was not only a voracious acquirer of dead bodies but even seems to have directly employed a gang of body-snatchers in Great Yarmouth, Norfolk. The most casual of surgeons, though, would have baulked at murder. If foul play was strongly suggested by the condition of the corpse then it had to be reported, because to turn a blind eye to a suspicious death could incur the charge of being an accessory to it. And in London in the 1830s such a report must be made to the recently formed Metropolitan Police.

Above: *the handsome watch house, dated 1826, on the south-west corner of the churchyard of St Matthew's Bethnal Green. The watchman, who occupied the house, was armed by the parish with a rattle and blunderbuss to deter body-snatchers.* Below: *3 Nova Scotia Gardens, leased by body-snatcher and murderer John Bishop in July 1830 and where he and John Williams lived, along with their respective families. This view of the cottage – and of the well in which the men's victims were suspended – was made soon after the pair had been convicted of murder in 1831.*

Joseph Sadler Thomas, superintendent of the division based in Covent Garden, gave a lengthy explanation of the circumstances of the arrest:

> ... I told May he was charged on suspicion of having improper possession of a subject – he said, in the presence of the others, that he had nothing at all to do with it, that the subject was that gentleman's property, pointing to Bishop, and that he had merely accompanied him to get the money; I asked Bishop how he got the body – he said he was merely removing it from Guy's-hospital to King's-college; I asked whose it was – he said it was his own; I then asked Williams what he had to say – he said, 'I know nothing at all about it; I merely went to King's-college, out of curiosity, to see the building': I asked Bishop, when he said the body was his own, what he was – he said he was a bl—y body-snatcher; I should observe, that the prisoners were under the effects of liquor in my judgement – I ordered the body to be taken out of the hamper, which was done in my presence, and laid on a table; it struck me it was the body of a person who had recently died, as there was blood trickling from the mouth; the front teeth were all out – in consequence of further information I went to the house of Mr Mills, Newington-causeway, on the Tuesday following, and received from him twelve teeth, which I now produce.

Healthy young teeth were a valuable commodity in their own right, much sought after by dentists making expensive dentures for wealthy but tooth-less clients.

Aware that he was now investigating a murder, Thomas went to Bishop and Williams's home at 3 Nova Scotia Gardens on two occasions in search of evidence. He found a trunk 'and in the front parlour ... a hairy cap, covered with dirty linen.' At the trial it was felt necessary to have a full understanding of the arrangement of house, outbuildings and gardens in order to assess whether other people living there were, or were not, aware of what was going on (since the location and circumstances of the murder were not yet known it was generally assumed that Williams's and Bishop's wives were accessories). One of architect Sir John Soane's assistants was therefore commissioned by the prosecution to make a model for use during the trial. It showed a set-up typical of many of the humbler cottages in the area. In his evidence Bishop described it as consisting of 'three rooms and a wash-house, a garden, about twenty yards long, by about eight yards broad, three gardens adjoin, and are separated by a dwarf railing'. An outhouse containing a lavatory was set, in most unceremonious manner, against the house's front elevation.

The evidence of a twelve-year-old boy named George Gissing, whose father kept the nearby Bird Cage tavern in 'Crabtree-row' (Columbia Road), suggested strongly that Williams's house was indeed a key setting for his crimes. Gissing described how:

> ... on Friday evening, the 4th of November, about half-past six o'clock, I saw a yellow-bodied hackney chariot draw up opposite my father's house. Bishop's cottage, No. 3, Nova Scotia-gardens, is a short distance from my father's house; I did not see who got out of the chariot [but] saw Williams standing on the fore-wheel, talking with the coachman ... then I saw a man, whom I did not know, carrying a sack in his arms; Bishop had hold of one end of it, coming on abreast ... they put the sack into the chariot – it appeared to have something heavy in it ... Williams helped them ... Bishop and the other man then got into the chariot; Williams remained there – it drove up Crab tree-row ... towards Shoreditch church and Bishopsgate.

Gissing had, it appears, witnessed the removal of the body from the site of the murder. He also added an interesting detail: 'I believe Bishop is Williams' father-in-law; I recollect one Monday, when it was said he had married Bishop's daughter, they came to our house for beer.' The Bird Cage, incidentally, still survives in Columbia Road. It's a fine early-nineteenth-century building that may well have been frequented by Williams.

Staff from Guy's Hospital and Grainger's anatomical theatre, Webb Street, Southwark, revealed to the court that the accused men had tried to peddle their body-in-a-sack to them before ending up at King's College. Thomas Davis, a porter at Guy's, saw Bishop and May – 'I knew them both before' – and declined the 'subject' but agreed to store it overnight, during which time he saw 'a foot, or a portion of a foot, obtrude from' the sack, and judged it to be 'the foot of a youth or a female, it was not large enough for a man'. James Appleton, the 'procurator' at Grainger's, stated that he knew 'all the prisoners', that they turned up at the theatre 'and told me they had a subject for sale; I asked what it was – they said a very fresh subject, a boy about fourteen years of age; I declined to purchase.'

Was this because it appeared to be a suspicious death? If so, Appleton evidently did not alert the authorities, suggesting that not everyone felt a compunction to report bodies that turned up in dubious circumstances.

Thomas Mills gave evidence to clear up the mystery of the loose teeth:

On the 5th of November May called and offered me a set of twelve human teeth – there were six of each jaw . . . he asked me a guinea for the set; I said one of the front teeth was chipped, which lessened the value, and I would give him 12s.; I said . . . I did not believe they belonged to one set . . . he declared, upon his soul, to God, they all belonged to one head, and not long since, and that the body had never been buried – he at last agreed to take 12s., which I gave him, and he left; I examined them particularly afterwards, and found a portion of the gum, and some part of the socket attached to them – I cleaned it off: from that circumstance it appeared to me that the teeth had certainly been wrenched from the jaw by violence – they were so firmly attached I had great difficulty in separating them; I remarked to May that they had certainly belonged to a young subject, or a female – he said, 'The fact is, they belong to a boy between fourteen and fifteen years old'.

The court now sought to establish the identity of the alleged murder victim and ascertain where, when and how he went missing. Witnesses were therefore called to confirm whether, he was, as was generally suspected, the Italian teenager called Carlo Ferrari, commonly known in the area as Charles Ferrier. The evidence of Augustine Broom, the man who had actually brought Ferrari/Ferrier over from Italy a couple of years earlier, was inconclusive. Speaking through an interpreter, he explained that the boy had lived with him for about six weeks, but that he could not be sure of the identity of the body shown to him at the burial ground near Covent Garden on 19 November: 'I can only say that I suppose it to be the boy of whom I have spoken, by his size and hair, but the face I cannot give an opinion upon, from the state it was in, and the teeth were taken out.'

The evidence of Joseph Paragell, who 'played an organ and pandean pipes about the streets with my wife and three children', was, however, more conclusive. He was confident that the body he had viewed at the 'station-house' was that of Ferrier whom he had last seen alive four weeks before in the Quadrant, Regent Street. Paragell also revealed a little about the dead boy's occupation. Like Paragell himself, the boy was a member of the fraternity of Italian street performers that were, in the early nineteenth century, a common sight on London's streets. The Quadrant was a fashionable, if somewhat louche, shopping location, popular with shoppers and promenaders as well as with superior street prostitutes, their swaggering bullies and the flashier, low-grade bucks and dandies. It must have been an excellent location for beggars or street performers like Ferrier who, when last seen by Paragell, 'had a little cage round his neck, and two white mice in it.'

Paragell's wife – Mary Paragelli (sic) – confirmed the sighting and the identification. She also offered a little more information about Ferrier's mode of entertaining passers-by: 'he had a little cage, like a squirrel's cage, which turns round, with two little white mice in it.' Evidently Ferrier presented brief shows with his mice, persuading them to do tricks. Andrew Coller – a birdcage-maker – also confirmed the identity of the body in Covent Garden police station, and added to the pathetic image of Ferrier's 'profession'. As well as a cage with white mice in it, he also had a tortoise that he must in some way have included in his act. Ferrier was one of the type of 'street-folk' that Mayhew was to interview and include later in his *London Labour and the London Poor*. Ferrier would also have made an unexceptional companion for the exotic band of beggars and street performers that J. T. Smith described and illustrated in his picturesque volume *Vagabondia or, anecdotes of Mendicant Wanderers through the streets of London*, published in 1817. Andrew Coller identified the cap and trousers found in 3 Nova Scotia Gardens as belonging to Ferrier.

A series of witnesses were called who placed the boy outside 3 Nova Scotia Gardens a few days before Guy Fawkes Day. One, eleven-year-old Martha King who lived in 'Crabtree-row', remembered seeing 'an Italian boy near the Bird Cage public-house . . . on the Wednesday or Thursday before Guy Fawkes' day, and about twelve o'clock . . . he was standing still opposite the Bird Cage, with his box slung round his neck, and a cap on his head; the cap was just like this: Bishop's house is about a minute's walk from our house – I have never seen the boy since.'

Rebecca Baylis, who lived opposite the Bird Cage, stated that, on 3 November, she:

> . . . saw an Italian boy . . . he was very near my own window, standing side-ways; I could see the side of his face and one end of the box, which he had in front of him: I think it was slung round his neck he had a brown fur or seal skin cap on, a small one rather shabby; I could see the peak was lined with green, and cut off very sharp [looking at the cap], it was this colour . . . a cap much like this; I cannot swear whether this is it: he had on a dark blue or a dirty green jacket, and grey trousers . . . very shabby . . . these have the appearance of the trousers he had on. About a quarter of an hour after . . .

I went a little way down Nova Scotia-gardens to look for my little boy; I saw the Italian boy standing within two doors of No. 3.

William Woodcock, Williams's neighbour in 'Nova Scotia Gardens', recalled that:

... on the Thursday, before the 5th of November, I went to bed about half-past nine o'clock ... and suppose I had been asleep four hours, or four hours and a half; when I was awoke, (I was half asleep) – I sleep in the front parlour; I heard footsteps, and thought it was somebody at the back of my premises [but] I found it was not in my house, but in the adjoining parlour, No. 3 – I distinctly heard three men's footsteps; I remained laying in bed ... I heard a scuffle, which might last about a minute or two at the furthest, and then all was silent – the scuffling was in the same room as I heard the foo'steps – before I entirely went to sleep again I heard the side gate open ... I am positive I heard the footsteps of two leave the house, and I heard them run back again – before they returned I heard the foot-steps of one person within the house; the two returned in about a minute, and then I distinctly heard the voices of three persons – I knew the voice of one to be Williams; after that all became silent, and I went to sleep.

Joseph Higgins, a policeman, told the court that on

... the 9th of November I went to No. 3, Nova Scotia-gardens, about five o'clock in the evening, I searched the house, and found two crooked chis-els, a brad-awl, and a file – there was some blood all over the brad-awl, which looked fresh ... on the 19th I went again to Bishop's house ... searched the garden, behind the house ... and found something rather soft, [dug] and the first thing that came up was a jacket and trousers, and a small size shirt [then] dug in another part of the garden, and found a blue coat, a pair of trousers, with braces attached to them, a striped waistcoat, which appeared to have been a man's, but was taken in at the back, as if to fit a boy – it had marks of blood on the collar and shoulder; also a shirt, which was torn right up the front.

Edward Ward, a six-year old boy living in 'Nova Scotia Gardens', told the court that on Guy Fawkes Day he went to Bishop's house and saw his children playing with 'two white mice – one little one and one big one ... in a cage, which moved round and round.'

Statements that the accused had made under caution during the coroner's inquest on 8 and 10 November on the body in the sack were read out in court. In his statement thirty-three-year-old Bishop claimed that he could not:

> . . . account for the death of the deceased; I got the body out of a grave: the reason why I do not like to say the grave I took it out of is, there are two watchmen in the ground – they entrusted me; they are both men of family, and I do not wish to deceive them; I took it for sale to Guy's-hospital, and as they did not want it I left it there all night and part of the next day, and then I removed it to the King's-college. That is all I can say about it.

His written defence, which was read out to the court, contained an admission that he had been procuring bodies for twelve years, but also a protestation that all had died a natural death. He claimed to 'know nothing at all about the various articles of wearing-apparel that have been found in the garden', and while he acknowledged the existence of the cap, he stated that it was not Ferrier's at all, but 'was bought by my wife of a Mrs Dodswell, of Hoxton Old-town, clothes-dealer, for my own son, Frederick' (Mrs Dodswell corroborated this in court). He further claimed that: 'May and Williams know nothing as to how I became possessed of the body.'

For his part, May admitted to selling bodies, and admitted to working with Williams and Bishop, but denied having had anything whatsoever to do with the death of Ferrier. On the Thursday night that the teenager had been killed, he said, he had been with one Rosina Carpenter in Golden Lane – an alibi Carpenter herself corroborated. The following day, he had met Williams and Bishop at the Fortune of War tavern in Smithfield (in his written defence he described it as 'a house that persons of our calling generally frequent'), had given them advice on how to get the best price for the body they said they had obtained, and then helped them sell it. His written defence stated that he was 'thirty years of age . . . married, with one child . . . and received a moderate education; I was not apprenticed, but followed the calling of a butcher in the earlier part of my life . . . I first became engaged in the traffic of anatomical subjects six years since, and from that period, up to the time of my apprehension, have continued so, with occasionally looking after horses.' But he also claimed that 'during all the years that I have been in this business, I never came into possession of a living person, nor used any means for converting them into subjects for the purposes of dissection; I admit that I have traded largely in dead bodies, but I solemnly declare that I never took undue advantage of any person alive, whether man, woman, or child, however poor or unprotected.'

Williams's statement was brief. He confirmed that he lived at 3 Nova Scotia Gardens, was a glass-blower by trade, and that he met 'Bishop last Saturday evening, in Long-lane, Smithfield . . . we then went to the Fortune of War public-house [then] we went to Guy's-hospital [and] . . . to the King's-college; then May and the porter met [Bishop] against the gate, then Bishop went in, and I asked him to let me go in with him – a porter took a basket from the Fortune of War to Guy's-hospital, and I helped him part of the way with it. That is all I have got to say.' His written defence gave a few further details. He, was, apparently, 'twenty-six years of age . . . a bricklayer by trade, and latterly worked at the glass-blowing business, as a fireman.' He swore that he had never procured dead bodies before until 'the present melancholy business' when he had been 'invited' by Bishop. And he also swore that: 'I am entirely innocent of any offence against the laws of my country.'

A magistrates' clerk at Bow Street and a Covent Garden policeman added gruesome details that they had observed during the initial examination of the prisoners and during the inquest. The clerk said that in the examination, when May was shown the brad-awl, he admitted that it was 'the instrument which I punched the teeth out with'. The policeman told the court that:

> . . . at the time the Inquest was held on the body of the lad; I saw all the three prisoners in the front room – there was a printed bill stuck up there, referring to this supposed murder . . . Bishop leaned his head over Williams to speak to May, and observed, in a low tone of voice, 'It was the blood that sold us' . . . he then got up, looked at the bill, read it over a second time, and sat down with a sort of forced laugh, and said, 'This states marks of violence, the marks of violence were only breakings out on the skin.'

All three were found guilty by the jury and all were sentenced to death by the judge.

But that was not the end of the story.

On Sunday 4 December, the day before their execution, Bishop and Williams went to the prison chapel and afterwards, while both in the same cell, they confessed to their crimes. Their statements were recorded by the prison Ordinary or chaplain and by the under-sheriffs of London.[32]

Bishop admitted stealing and selling up to a thousand bodies in twelve years, confessed to murder and revealed the modus operandi pursued at 'Nova Scotia Gardens'. With Williams, he said, he picked up vagabonds and children, took or enticed them to 'Nova Scotia Gardens' on the promise of work, food, drink and shelter. The victims were rendered unconscious with a hefty dose of rum and laudanum and then, in dead of night when family and neighbours were asleep, a rope was tied around the victim's ankles and they were lowered down a nearby well where they were left for some time to drown or suffocate. This operation not only killed the victims with minimal noise or struggle but, said Bishop, allowed the rum and laudanum to trickle out of the bodies. It was a logical, if grue-some, tactic. If a corpse stank of rum, or rum and laudanum were found in its stomach, dissectionists might fear the worst and sound the alarm rather than risk the prospect of being accused of being accomplices to murder.

As well as the murder of a boy on 3 November 1831 Bishop admitted the murder on or about 9 October of one Fanny Pigburn whom they found sleeping rough in Shoreditch. Evidence subsequently collected suggested that Pigburn was last seen leaving the house of 'Mr Campion in Church Street, Bethnal Green, at half-past nine o'clock on the night of Saturday 8th October . . .'[33] While Fanny hung dying in the well Bishop and Wil-liams went for a drink in the London Apprentice (the pub survives, rebuilt, on Old Street, a few hundred yards west of Shoreditch church). On 12 October, the pair confessed, they also murdered a boy called Cunning-ham. He was about ten or eleven and had run away from home a year earlier. His body was sold for eight guineas. The bodies of these two vic-tims were sold to Grainger's and to St Bartholomew's Hospital.

Some confusion remained about the murder victim of 3 November. Bishop insisted his victim was not the 'Italian boy' but a boy from Lin-colnshire whom he had picked up in the Bell, Smithfield, tempted to 'Nova Scotia Gardens' with the promise of lodgings and when there drugged in the usual way with laudanum and rum. While the boy was slipping into unconsciousness, Bishop said, he and Williams had gone for a fortifying drink in the Feathers, near Shoreditch church, then returned to 'Nova Scotia Gardens' and pitched him into the well with the rope around his ankles. He struggled briefly, they let him hang for a bit then hauled him up, stripped him and put the body in a sack.

Bishop's and Williams's confessions cleared May of murder, so he escaped the hangman's noose and was instead detained at His Majesty's pleasure. Bishop and Williams, however, were hanged at Newgate. Their execution proved an immensely popular affair: resurrection men were greatly loathed and feared and so around 30,000 people attended the spectacle. With grim and intended irony Bishop's body was then sent to King's College for dissection and Williams's to Dr William Hunter's anatomy theatre in Great Windmill Street, Soho. In response to popular demand, the Metropolitan Police opened Williams's house in 'Nova Scotia Gardens' to people willing to pay for admittance. Souvenir hunters then virtually stripped it bare.

As it happened the trial and execution of Bishop and Williams virtually marked the end of body-snatching in Britain. In the following year – 1832 – the Anatomy Act was passed, which by making many more bodies legally available for dissection destroyed their financial value and so removed the temptation to trade illicitly in them. From now on, not only were the bodies of executed murderers handed over to medical institutions, but so were those who died – without funds and whose bodies were unclaimed for burial – while residing in parish institutions such as workhouses, infirmaries or in various asylums or prisons. Now it was the abandoned and the poor, those without the means to pay for their own funerals, who were to forego the chance of resurrection and paradise.

In 1848 the social and sanitary reformer Dr Hector Gavin explored the region of 'Nova Scotia Gardens' and confirmed that not much had changed in its infernal landscape since Bishop and Williams's time. Most notably there was still 'a table mountain of manure' towering over a 'lake of liquid dung'.[34] In 1859 George Godwin visited, illustrated and described 'Nova Scotia Gardens' and its nearby mountain of garbage. He wrote:

> an artistic traveller, looking at this huge mountain of refuse which had been collected, might have fancied that Arthur's Seat in Edinburgh . . . had suddenly come into our view . . . and the dense smell which hung over the 'gardens' would have aided in bringing 'auld reekie' strongly to the memory. At the time of our visit, the summit of the mount was thronged with various figures, which were seen in strong relief against the sky: and boys and girls were amusing themselves by running down and toiling up the least precipitous side of it. Near the base, a number of women were

arranged in a row, sifting and sorting the various materials placed before them. The tenements were is a miserable condition. Typhus fever, we learnt from a medical officer, was a frequent visitor all around the spot.[35]

In the 1860s the rich philanthropist and social reformer Angela Burdett-Coutts took an interest in this dreadful region. She had acquired a familiarity with such urban horrors – and a determination to bring about change – while taking night walks through London slums in the 1840s and 50s with her friend Charles Dickens.[36] The scene that confronted Burdett-Coutts was described by Princess Mary Adelaide, Duchess of Teck: 'There was a large piece of waste ground covered in places with foul, slimy-looking pools, amid which crowds of half-naked, barefooted, ragged children chased one another. From the centre arose a great black mound . . . the stench continually issuing from the enormous mass of decaying matter was unendurable.'[37]

Very bravely the Baroness purchased the site of 'Nova Scotia Gardens', cleaned up the area and in 1869 built the monumental if gloomy Columbia Market, intended to encourage honest trade, thrift and industry among the working people of the area.

FIFTEEN

'A DISMAL SQUALID DISTRICT'
Victorian Views of Spitalfields

F ew parts of London can have been as closely scrutinised in the nineteenth century as Spitalfields, Bethnal Green and Shoreditch. For journalists, the area offered a rich source of sensational stories. For novelists such as Charles Dickens it provided information about outcast life and – more importantly – inspiration. It was an object of study for social reformers and philanthropists. For political writers and theorists it represented a reproach to society as a whole. All saw the East End as a place apart. It appeared wild and alien, unchristian and frightening – an unknown country even.

'[A]s there is a darkest Africa is there not also a darkest England?' the founder of the Salvation Army, William Booth, asked in his book *Darkest England and the Way Out* (1890). His question and the comparison he made were, at least in part, inspired by the enormously popular *In Darkest Africa*, published earlier that year by the journalist and explorer H. M. Stanley, in which, in the course of documenting the sensational Emin Pasha Relief Expedition (which Stanley led), he sought to evoke the solemn, awful and unsettling atmosphere of the interior of the 'dark continent'. Booth's thinking was also inspired by the 74th Psalm: 'Forget not the congregation of thy poor . . . Have respect unto the covenant: for the dark places of the earth are full of the habitations of cruelty.'[1] At the end of the decade the narrator in Joseph Conrad's *Heart of Darkness* (1899), when contemplating London from the Thames estuary, observes, '. . . this also . . . has been one of the dark places of the earth'. The reader might suppose the narrator is referring to Roman times but Conrad's implication is that darkness is timeless and enduring. For him the supposed darkness of London in the past was made tangible by the popularly proclaimed darkness of London in the 1890s.

Poverty was scarcely unique to the East End of London in Victorian times. Plenty of industrial towns had their own slums, and deprivation was not unknown in the countryside either. But few areas of England could exhibit within the matter of a mile or two – from the City and the 'Heart of Empire' to the dungheaps and hovels of Shoreditch – such an extreme contrast between affluence and want, and it was this contrast that threw the sufferings of the East End into particularly stark relief and made it an area of fascination to observers, social and political reformers, and sturdy and curious urban explorers. David Bartlett, an American who visited London at the time of the Great Exhibition, wrote of the 'great gulf' that yawned 'almost like that between heaven and hell' between the rich and poor of London.[2]

In his *The Condition of the Working Class in England*, published first in Germany in 1845, Friedrich Engels, the German-born political theorist and friend and collaborator of Karl Marx, quoted an article from *The Times* of 12 October 1843 that well illustrates why the East End should have become the object of such appalled fascination:

> . . . let all men remember this – that within the most courtly precincts of the richest city of God's earth, there may be found, night after night, winter after winter, women – young in years – old in sin and suffering – outcasts from society – ROTTING FROM FAMINE, FILTH, AND DISEASE. Let them remember this, and learn not to theorise but to act. God knows, there is much room for action nowadays.[3]

Engels' own view of the area was unremittingly bleak: '. . . in this overcrowding,' he wrote, 'it is nothing unusual to find a man, his wife, four or five children, and, sometimes, both grandparents, all in one single room of ten to twelve feet square, where they eat, sleep, and work . . .' One particular location – Quaker Court, Spitalfields – drew his attention:

> On Monday, 15th January 1844 two boys were brought before the police magistrate because, being in a starving condition, they had stolen and immediately devoured a half-cooked calf's foot from a shop. The magistrate felt called upon to investigate the case further, and received the following details from the policeman: The mother of the two boys was the widow of an ex-soldier, afterwards a policeman, and had had a very hard time since the death of her husband, to provide for her nine children. She lived at No. 2 Pool's Place, Quaker Court, Spitalfields, in the utmost

poverty. When the policeman came to her, he found her with six of her children literally huddled together in a little back room, with no furniture but two old rush-bottomed chairs with the seats gone, a small table with two legs broken, a broken cup, and a small dish. On the hearth was scarcely a spark of fire, and in one corner lay as many old rags as would fill a woman's apron, which served the whole family as a bed. For bed clothing they had only their scanty day clothing. The poor woman told him she had been forced to sell her bedstead the year before to buy food. Her bedding she had pawned with the victualler for food. In short, everything had gone for food. The magistrate ordered the woman a considerable provision from the poor-box . . .[4]

Such then, according to Engels, was the life lived in the 1840s in these once handsome and productive late-seventeenth- and early-eighteenth-century streets and courts around Quaker Street. In the 1660s and 1670s Wheler Street had been the most architecturally important – and most affluent – new thoroughfare in Spitalfields, which, with the houses in neighbouring streets, had formed something of a self-contained and harmonious new town. Now, in common with much of Spitalfields, the density of occupation in this area had started to increase dramatically as rows of cramped, ill-lit, ill-ventilated and generally ill-built cottages of small scale were constructed in what had been open courts, yards and even gardens. The result was an urban labyrinth, with secreted courts of cottages threaded around large and ancient houses that were usually multi-occupied, in mixed use and neglected. For Engels this proved a larger point about contemporary Britain: that it had, more than ever before, become a profit-driven land where entrepreneurs and industrialists had forged a selfish, materialist and heartless society in which the poor – if deemed unproductive – were suffered to starve, even within the heart of one of the richest cities in the world.

Today virtually all the alleys and courts of small cottages have been cleared away, so no sense of this dark, dank, urban maze survives in Spitalfields; nor does any of the earlier, more salubrious late-seventeeth-century fabric in the Quaker Street area. The major reasons for their loss relate to the growth of industry in the area and from the 1830s the construction of roads and railways in north Spitalfields. Truman's Brewery on Brick Lane expanded to the west, and from 1839 railway construction, initially for the Eastern Counties Railway (ECR), then the Great Eastern Railway (GER), led to the creation of viaducts and cuttings to the north of Quaker Street. What does still survive, at the north end of Wheler Street, is a short section of one of the viaducts. Dating from 1838–40, and designed by railway pioneer John Braithwaite, it is one of the earliest things of its kind to be built in London.

Interestingly, such viaducts as Braithwaite's came to play a role in the way in which Spitalfields was perceived. They provided travellers with elevated vantage points from which they could take a broad view of the area and experience its character from the safety of their railway carriages. George Dodd, a jobbing journalist and contributor to Charles Knight's verbose multi-volume series *London*, published from 1840 to 1844, was one of the first to do so. He recorded his impression of a train journey into the ECR terminus at the junction of Norton Folgate and Shoreditch High Street, which opened in 1840, describing how the railway traveller approaching from the east could see rooftops and garret windows and bird-cages giving way to 'dismal streets in which no traveller dared to tread.'[5] Later in the century the artist Gustave Doré and author Blanchard Jerrold took a similar journey, noting in 1872 that any visitor travelling by rail 'east from the City' could look out over the 'dirty, poverty-laden streets' of an ancient neighbourhood that 'remains an exotic one'. They observed that: 'The German, the Jew, the Frenchman, the Lascar, the swarthy native of Spitalfields, the leering thin-handed thief, the bully of his court, the silly-billy [a clown-like street entertainer] of the neighbour-hood ... with endless swarms of ragged children, fill the roads and pavement. The Jewish butchers lounge – fat and content, in their door-ways; the costermongers drive their barrows slowly by, filling the air with their hoarse voices.'[6]

From his elevated railway carriage, George Gissing gained an even bleaker view of the East End in 1889 for his novel *The Nether World*, a pes-simistic account of poor families trapped in slum conditions: 'over the pest-stricken regions of East London,' he wrote, 'across miles of the city of the damned ... above streets swarming with a nameless population crue-lly exposed by the light of heaven; stopping at stations which it crushes the heart to think should be the destination of any mortal, the train made its way beyond the utmost limits of dread.' The sights Gissing evokes on the streets of this 'city of the damned' are lurid in the extreme and

Gustave Doré noted in 1872 in London: A Pilgrimage *that any visitor travelling 'east from the City' by train on an elevated viaduct could look out over the 'dirty, poverty-laden streets' and observe 'the German, the Jew, the Frenchman, the Lascar, the swarthy native of Spitalfields'. These, according to the journalist George Dodd a few years earlier, were 'dismal streets in which no traveller dared to tread.'*

mercilessly unforgiving. If the object was to shock his readers with bleak descriptions of hopeless East End poverty then Gissing surely succeeds.

Charles Dickens, a London obsessive and an uncontrollable and at times melodramatic romantic, had, it seems, got to know – and pluck inspiration from – the murky world of Spitalfields as early as the mid 1830s when writing *Oliver Twist*. His central villain Fagin, the Jewish fence and 'kids-man' (a man who lured children into crime and trained them), was probably based on Isaac Solomon, who was born in Houndsditch and by 1810 had a shop in Bell Lane, Spitalfields, which he used as a front for trading in stolen property. During the next two decades Solomon became notorious for his crimes, arrests, trials and bold escapes – most notably in Petticoat Lane in 1827 from a hackney carriage that was taking him to Newgate prison. After a trial in 1830 – much like Fagin's fictional trial – Solomon was transported to Van Diemen's Land, where he remained until his death in 1850. In Dickens's novel, published in instalments from 1837, Fagin's brutal partner in crime, Bill Sikes, lives in Bethnal Green, and Dickens powerfully describes Oliver's first visit 'through many winding and narrow ways' to Sikes's house, hidden 'in a maze of the mean and dirty streets which abound in that close and densely-populated quarter'.[7]

Dickens returned to Spitalfields during 'The Great Exhibition of the Works of Industry of all Nations', which opened in Hyde Park on 1 May 1851. Among other things, the Exhibition was intended to proclaim the industrial might of progressive British society, and Dickens – ever topical – no doubt saw an opportunity to place the Exhibition's ambitious claims in realistic and gruesome context: the new juxtaposed against the old, unreconstructed and often impoverished world of British labour. He publicised what he had seen in the weekly journal *Household Words*, which he part-owned and edited and which espoused the cause of the poor and of working people but was, predictably enough, calculated to be read by, and pluck the heartstrings of, the middle classes.

In edition number 54, published on 5 April 1851, Dickens asked his 'dear readers' if they had 'any distinct idea of Spitalfields . . .?' He answered his own question: 'A general one, no doubt . . . an impression that there are certain squalid streets, lying like narrow black trenches, far below the steeples, somewhere about London – towards the East End perhaps – where sallow, unshorn weavers who have nothing to do, prowl languidly about, or lean against posts, or sit brooding on doorsteps . . .' So the picture Dickens painted of Spitalfields was sinister, perhaps dangerous, a place where unemployed tradesmen were wont to 'prowl' and where life – in the long term – was hopeless, and poverty and uncertainty unremitting. He noted that the weavers occasionally 'assemble together in a crowd to petition Parliament or the Queen; after which there is a Drawing-Room, or a Court Ball, where all the great ladies wear dresses of Spitalfields manufacture.' Then, as he put it, 'the weavers dine for a day or two', but soon 'relapse into prowling about the streets, leaning against posts, and brooding on doorsteps.' Spitalfields was, in Dickens's forlorn assessment, 'the grave of modern manufacturing London'.[8] His bleak view of the area was supported by *Tallis's Illustrated London in Commemoration of the Great Exhibition of 1851*,[9] which simply dismissed Spitalfields as 'a dismal squalid district'.

A couple of months later, in the 14 June 1851 edition of *Household Words*, Dickens followed up his grim description of the East End with an account of his latest intrepid expedition into hostile and foreign territory, this time led by the 'imperturbable' Inspector Field of the Metropolitan Police's detective force and a number of seasoned sergeants and constables. The party made a night-time foray into London's underworld, going to places such as St Giles, the Mint, Borough and, in the early hours of the morning, finally arriving in Whitechapel 'to unveil the mysteries of Wentworth Street'. There they met a couple of locally based constables who led them by the 'flaming eye' of bull's-eye torches to the lodging house they were seeking. This was 'hidden in a maze of streets and courts', almost certainly in or near Spitalfields' infamous Thrawl Street and 'Flower and Dean Street' 'Rookery' – the general term used at the time to describe overcrowded and decayed slum areas tainted by a reputation for endemic and often dangerous crime.

They found the establishment 'fast shut', so they knocked at the door and 'tapped at a window' until the 'landlord' of the lodging house sent a 'Deputy' to let the party in: 'Deputy is heard to stumble out of bed. Deputy lights a candle, draws back a bolt or two, and appears at the door. Deputy in a shivering shirt and trousers by no means clean, a yawning face, a shock head much confused externally and internally.' The police told him they had come to look for someone. The 'Deputy' replied that they could 'take 'em all'. The police searched among the sleepers in the 'labyrinth of airless rooms' with 'each man responding like a wild beast, to the keeper who has trained him, and who goes into his cage.' The police search party returned empty-handed to the entrance where a woman 'mysteriously sitting up all night in the dark by the smouldering ashes of the kitchen fire' told them: 'it's only tramps and cadgers [shop lifters-cum-beggars] here: it's gonophs [Yiddish for "thieves"] over the way.' The truth of this advice seemed to be confirmed by a man who, 'walking about the kitchen all night in the dark' told her to 'hold her tongue'.

The hunt was on again. Field took the woman's words as a hint that they should try a nearby establishment run by 'Bark, lodging-house keeper and receiver of stolen goods', and so to Bark's the party went. This second expedition turned out to be a much tougher proposition. Bark was asleep 'in an inner wooden hutch, near his street-door' but as the police entered the house he flew out of bed, 'a red villain and a wrathful, with a sanguine throat that looks very much as if it were expressly made for hanging'. He tried to resist the police's attempt to search the inner parts of his lodging house, but they carried the day, descending into his 'low kitchen . . . crammed full of thieves, holding a *conversazione* there by lamp-light.' It was, Dickens thought, 'by far the most dangerous assembly' his party had yet seen. They re-ascended and told Bark that they intended to go upstairs. He once again resisted; they pushed on; Bark cried that if the 'coves [men] in the kitchen was men they'd come up now, and do for you!' Suddenly a door closed and the party found itself 'shut up, half-a-dozen of us . . . in the innermost recesses of the worst part of London, in the dead of night.' But despite the house being 'crammed with notorious robbers and ruffians', not a man stirred. For Dickens this suggested that those down below knew 'the weight of the law . . . and Inspector Field and Co, too well.'

And so Dickens lived to tell this tale of derring-do and the triumph of law and order to his avid weekly readers.[10] He seems to have been so impressed by Inspector Field that he almost instantly reinvented him as a fictional character – the indefatigable Inspector Bucket – for his next published work, *Bleak House*, which appeared from 1852. It serves as a reminder that Dickens's fiction and journalism were not necessarily worlds apart.

Without doubt the greatest work on London to appear in the year of the Great Exhibition was Henry Mayhew's *London Labour and the London Poor*. During the 1840s Mayhew had published a series of investigative and campaigning articles in the *Morning Chronicle* that explored and revealed the lives of the generally neglected outsiders and outcasts of London life: the poor, the street-traders and practitioners of mean and humble livelihoods such as 'pure' or dog-excrement gatherers, sewer-scavengers and mudlarks. These articles were then collected and enlarged upon in the three-volume set published in 1851.

Mayhew's publications were an immediate and great success. He did no less than turn the world upside down and present a new portrait of London as a city with a vast underworld and pauper population in the last extremes of poverty and despair. As he explained in the introduction to volume three, in which he recapitulated the main conclusions of the previous volumes, the 1841 census suggested there were little over 2,000 'street-folk' in London – that is, people making a living by or in the streets. But Mayhew revealed that, according to his pioneering investigations, there were actually no fewer than 40,000 such people and that the annual turnover of their activities was £2.5 million, and thus of considerable economic significance for the city.[11] At the same time, in his exploration in 1849 of Spitalfields' weaving quarter – notably the area west of Brick Lane and south of Shoreditch church – he shone a light on the desperate struggle for survival of the area's once proud weaving community (see pages 374–9).[12]

London Labour and the London Poor was a breathtaking and radical undertaking, rich in authentic observation, investigation and apparently verbatim interviews with 'street-folk'. But it is important to remember that Mayhew was not trained as a social reformer, and was not a philanthropist, historian or academic. He was, like Dickens, a journalist and a storyteller, with an eye for the novel and the sensational. According to his own testimony, his books were 'the first attempt to publish the history of a people, from the lips of the people themselves – giving a literal description of their labour, their earnings, their trials, and their sufferings, in their own "unvarnished" language; and to portray the condition of their homes and their families by personal observation of the places and direct communion with the individuals.'[13] But the authenticity of Mayhew's interviews was never fully established and his sources remained mostly – perhaps significantly – anonymous. How much is objective observation and how much journalistic embellishment is therefore impossible to establish.

A seemingly more measured description of the area was given by the sanitary reformer Dr Hector Gavin (see pages 382–3). He had Mayhew's eye for the telling detail and was – like Dickens – a man with a humanitarian mission, but unlike his peers he had a more practical goal. Mayhew was an observer, not a reformer. Dickens wanted, through his fiction and journalism, to expose the brutal reality of the lives of many Londoners so as to bring about change, but he did not seek to explain how that change might be achieved. Gavin, by contrast, wanted to collect evidence – street by street – to prove to the legislators at Whitehall the need to do something about one particular aspect of the lives of many Londoners: the filthy and insanitary conditions that they had to endure. He also wanted to make a larger point. It was, he argued, poverty that begets evil, and not evil or slothful dispositions that lead people to lives of poverty. For Gavin the poor of the East End were not depraved. They were basically 'good' people oppressed by poverty. And, as he argued in *Sanitary Ramblings, Being Sketches and Illustrations of Bethnal Green*, published in 1848, he believed that if the authorities were to 'cleanse ... streets, remove the dust and garbage-heaps from the houses and dwellings of the poor, and cleanse ... the filthy cesspools and privies which everywhere pollute the surface of the dirty parish' they would 'effect an amount of good of which they have no conception' and receive 'the blessings of thousands of the neglected and suffering, yet patient poor.'

Typical of his approach to his task is his description of the houses that stood in Pedley Street just east of Brick Lane (see page 374) and adjoining thoroughfares:

KNIGHTLY COURT ... in a very dilapidated state. In it there are two privies in a beastly state, full, and the contents flowing into the court. There is one dust reservoir [ash from coal fires, among other refuse, was collected by 'dustmen']. One stand-tap supplies the seven houses. The court at the further end of this court is quite unpaved, and in a nasty filthy state; two cases of severe typhus lately occurred here, one died. These wretched houses are let at 3s. 6d. per week. PETLEY-ST [Pedley Street] The roadway is broken up and full of holes, and more resembles the remains of an ancient Roman road, than a modern roadway. FLEET-ST ... most abominably filthy, the gutters are full and partly cover the street with foetid, black, slimy mud; garbage is frequently thrown over its surface; the houses are elevated, consisting of several flats, with different families in each; the ventilation of the rooms is most imperfect, and the smell from them most disagreeable. It will be observed that fever and the other

THE DWELLINGS OF THE POOR IN BETHNAL-GREEN.—THE STATE OF THE WATER SUPPLY.

Above: *women and children waiting to gather drops of precious water, as depicted in 1863 by the* Illustrated London News *in an article on 'The Dwellings of the Poor in Bethnal Green'.* Below: *women sifting through rubbish and ashes at one of the vast mounds of garbage that in the mid nineteenth century disfigured the landscape of the north-east fringes of London.*

epidemics are rife in this dirty place. Horse-ride in Fleet-street, is very filthy. FLEET-ST. HILL . . . a great part of this place is most abominably filthy.

Just how rundown this area was by Gavin's time is indicated by an incident that took place in Fleet Street Hill and its environs a few years before. In September 1826, at about half-past seven in the evening, a surgeon named Henry Fuller was walking along Fleet Street Hill when he was attacked by a gang of about twenty men. According to Fuller, when giving evidence in court six weeks later, two of the men pinioned his arms while another fastened them to his body by a rope. Fuller claimed that many brandished sticks to terrorise him and one shouted 'if the b—r speaks, knock his b—y brains out.' Fuller's pockets were rifled, his surgical instruments grabbed, and then he was released and the gang ran off. But it's what happened next that is particularly telling.

As Fuller explained in court, after being untied and while the gang made off, 'I raised a cry of Stop thief!' Nobody in the street, however, responded or picked up the cry. Fuller chased the thieves for about ten yards, calling 'Stop thief!' when 'some persons came up and begged me to hold my tongue, saying the gang was so desperate, they would murder me if I did not.' These streets appear to have been lawless places after dusk, stalked by street gangs that were, no doubt, bred out of the poverty and unemployment of the collapsing silk industry. Eventually four men were charged with the violent 'highway robbery' of Henry Fuller and tried at the Old Bailey. Three were acquitted for lack of evidence against them but one – James Bishop – was found guilty and was hanged. He was eighteen years old.[14]

Gavin was notably forthcoming about one particular area of Spitalfields – the Nichol Estate – an area that, with its terraces of weavers' cottages, was by the end of the nineteenth century to become one of the most desperately decayed, dangerous, impoverished and overcrowded areas in London.[15] Established in the late seventeenth century (see pages 187–8), it was based on an orthogonal grid that, by the time of Rocque's map of 1746, comprised the east–west streets of Old Nichol Street, New Nichol Street and the south side of 'Half Nichol Street'.[16] These three streets were bounded on their west ends by the north–south-running arm of 'Cock Lane' (later called Boundary Street) and on their west ends by 'Nichol Street', which later became 'Nichols Row', then 'Nichol's Row' by the time of the 1872/3 Ordnance Survey map and connects with Club Row.[17] At the time of Richard Horwood's map of 1799, only the south side of 'Half Nichol' (or 'Nicols' as it was then called) Street had been lined with buildings,[18] but by the time of the 1872/3 Ordnance Survey map the built-up area of the Nichol had been extended to the north by a grid of streets built on the Snow Estate (see page 203). This development included the north side of 'Half Nichol's Street' (by this date an apostrophe had been added to all the Nichol street names) and a set of parallel streets named after the naval heroes and engagements of the Napoleonic Wars: the eastward extension of 'Half Nichol Street' was called 'Trafalgar Street', and then there were 'Vincent', 'Nelson' and 'Collingwood Streets'. The streets and building-plot widths were similar to those of the Nichol Estate with the exception of Vincent Street, where plots were even narrower. Overall, in fact, it's clear that by the 1870s development on the Nichol had become generally denser, with courts and cottages created on land behind street frontages. A new, very narrow north–south street – called 'Cross Street' – had been cut through the centre of the area. Its main purpose appears to have been to create yet more street frontages and building plots, and to open up backland for development. The area was also festooned with numerous small courts, meandering alleys or cul-de-sacs reached through narrow arches in street frontages.

What nineteenth-century maps of the Nichol only hint at, of course, is the density of the population, the terrible physical condition of the streets, courts and houses, the paucity of the area's services and the turmoil, cacophony, stench and meanness of its fetid daily life. But Gavin's account does, and it also reveals for the first time the condition of some of the many small courts, squares and alleys created behind the main street frontages.

Club Row – the original Club Row including the lost portion south of Bethnal Green Road and one of the best streets in the Nichol area – he called 'perfectly beastly' with its street surface like that 'of a pig-stye [with] scattered heaps of garbage and collections of mud.' Swan Court, immediately east of Club Row, was 'abominably filthy' with 'three open privies belonging to it . . . full and most disgusting . . . dust heaps, ordure, and garbage are scattered about, as are also shallow pools of liquid foetid filth.' 'The houses convey the impression of desolation,' Gavin wrote, shocked by the sense of 'great moral debasement and degradation among the occupants'. He went on: 'The medical officer at one time attended here six cases of fever, being all the occupants of one room; they all lay in one bed . . . All this disease was mainly attributable to the impure atmosphere.'

In 'Half Nichol's Street' he found the surface of the street 'bountifully strewn [with] all kinds of dust, dirt, refuse, and garbage', because the inhabitants, 'in order to get rid of all their refuse, solid as well as fluid, are compelled to throw it on the streets, there to putrefy and be mixed up with the mud.' 'In consequence of the free exposure of the animal and vegetable remains in a pasty state to the sun,' he went on to record, 'the muddy compost becomes most offensive to the smell, and a constant cause of disease and death to the inhabitants. Invariably, wherever such filthy streets are found, so likewise are fever and the other zymotic diseases.' The filth was the consequence of a vicious circle. The inhabitants had nowhere to dispose of their rubbish but the street itself; the rubbish collectors refused to remove it unless paid, but the inhabitants would or could not pay; and so filth increased as – presumably – did the price of the labour for removing it. 'The inhabitants of this street', stated Gavin, 'complained bitterly that "the people in it never died a natural death, but were murdered by the fever"'.

A particularly alarming state of affairs prevailed in Shacklewell Street where some houses were located 'within a few feet south of Gibraltar Chapel grave-yard'. On entering one Gavin found 'the smell was most offensive, and was compared to that from a close-confined vault in which the dead had long been retained.' These evils – water polluted by filth from privies and by decomposing cadavers – were soon to be identified as among the main causes of London's cholera epidemics. Evidently the Nichol in the 1840s was a prime breeding ground for the disease. Gavin noted that '3s. 6d. and 4s. a week are paid for these two-roomed houses.' And that '12s. appears to be the extreme of the weekly earnings of the inhabitants; it was stated that not one earned 14s. a week.' He also noted dryly that 'Sir James Tyrrell is the ground landlord of this street. Since the property has come into his possession no remedies have been applied to the discreditable condition of things which exists here.'

Gavin perhaps meant Tyssen not Tyrrell since Shacklewell Street was on the Tyssen Estate, but this does not matter because he was touching on a general point that was applicable to much of the slum of Friars Mount (the general name given to the area of which the Nichol formed the major portion). As with so many of the East End's worst slums the ultimate landlord – the person who benefited from the rents paid by these wretched tenants – was invariably wealthy enough to have been able to improve conditions had he or she so chosen. In the case of much of the Nichol, the responsible party was the family of the Duke of Chandos, who owned the five-acre estate at the heart of the area from 1753 and still retained a sizeable interest after selling a large portion in 1827. When the whole area was purchased by the London County Council in the late 1890s for demolition and replacement by the Boundary Estate, one of its principal landowners was Mary, Baroness Kinloss, the daughter of the last Duke of Buckingham and Chandos, sometime owner of the vast Stowe House in Buckinghamshire and a dedicated churchwarden.[19]

Fifteen years after Gavin's exploration of the streets and houses of the Nichol, the area was under scrutiny again, this time by journalists and building and medical experts as well as sanitary authorities. In 1863 the *Illustrated London News* recorded a shocking event that had recently occurred in the bucolically named but very far from country-like Hollybush Place, off Bethnal Green Road. Here an impoverished shoemaker, living in a garret with his family, had lost two children. They had died, in the terminology of the time, from a 'putrid fever' and 'blood poisoning' caused, at least in part it was assumed, from 'the impure state of the dwellings' and their 'extreme filth and squalor'. In simple terms the children had died as a result of the deep, ingrained and fatally polluted filth of their homes, their street and their way of daily life – from the water they were obliged to drink, from the air they were compelled to breathe, and from the cows and pigs – with their 'filthy exhalations . . . their special diseases [and] general abominations' – that were their close neighbours.[20]

More, and specific, details about 'Holybush Place' appeared in the *Medical Times and Gazette* of 22 September 1866. Evidently by this time – a few years after the death of the children – Hollybush Place had become something of a *cause célèbre*. The article explained that the place contained fourteen houses, each of which typically contained 'two small rooms, one above the other, with a staircase in the corner [and] no passage or backdoor', with the bedroom low and ventilation very limited. The house's 'closet accommodation' was communal, with all houses sharing 'two small garden privies . . . without any water supply or means of flushing [that] empty into a cess-pit under the entrance.' The *Gazette* also reported a coroner's inquiry into the recent death of an inhabitant of 'Holybush

ROOM OCCUPIED BY A MILITARY TAILOR AND HIS FAMILY, AT NO. 10, HOLLYBUSH-PLACE.

A 'military tailor' and his family at work in the room they occupy in a cottage in Hollybush Place, Bethnal Green. From the Illustrated London News, *1863.*

Place' – James Hubbard, forty-one, a labourer. The report stated that 'he used to sleep in a miserable room on the ground floor, close to the closet from which foul emanations were perpetually exhaling, and in the yard close by was the only receptacle for water – the half of a butter-firkin – which did duty as a water-butt and from which the deceased drank immediately before his rapidly fatal attack.' The cause of death was cholera.[21]

The *Illustrated London News*'s damning account of Hollybush Place in its 24 October 1863 issue was contained within a broader article entitled 'Dwellings of the Poor in Bethnal Green'. 'The disgusting details which have lately been revealed to that portion of the public who have only heard of Bethnal-green as a low neighbourhood where the weavers live, some-where in the far east of London, have been the steady growth of years,' the paper baldly stated. It noted that the population of the district 'has for years been subject to all the foulest influences which accompany a state of extreme filth and squalor'. It also claimed that 'those whose duty it has been to point out their inevitable consequences have treated them with indifference . . . and even now the owners of the putrid sties in the purlieus of Friars-mount and other centres of pestilence may well believe that neither board, nor commission, nor sanitary officer will trouble them if they can only let inquiry itself die.' The article was, accordingly, a call to arms. The *Illustrated London News* was determined to do its best to ensure that the public did not forget the horror of the Nichol and neigh-bouring slum areas and to compel the authorities to enforce change and improvements.

The newspaper's own inquiry and report – seemingly based on a first-hand and detailed investigation of the area – was harrowing and sensational. It reminded its readers that only twenty-five years before the area's now 'ruinous tenements reeking with abominations' were 'outlying, decent cottages, standing on or near plots of garden ground, where the inmates reared prize tulips and rare dahlias in their scanty leisure, and where some of the last of the old French refugees dozed away the evenings of their lives in pretty summer-houses, amidst flower-beds gay with Vir-ginia stocks and creeping plants.' Now, however, Spitalfields' 'worst features have been exceeded by the wretched maze of streets and alleys' immediately to its north.

The newspaper then took its readers on an exploration of the dark, alien and dangerous area of Friars Mount. Its fearless and intrepid reporter started at Bishopsgate Station, the terminus of the Great Eastern Railway on Shoreditch High Street – easily reached and bustling with city life. From here, observed the reporter, the 'earnest visitor' had only to traverse 'Club-row – the Sunday morning resort of pigeon and bird fanciers ... cross the road and turn up Nichols-row to find himself in as foul a neighbourhood as can be discovered in the civilised world (savage life has nothing to compare to it), and amongst a population depressed almost to the last stage of human endurance.'

These bird fanciers, incidentally, were not necessarily as innocent as they sound. Thomas Archer, who was exploring the area at much the same time – and may indeed have been the *Illustrated London News*'s reporter (see page 385) – noted 'bird, dog, and pigeon-fanciers' in Sclater Street (which by now had train tracks and viaducts leading into Bishopsgate Station immediately to its south) and Club Row but thought there was something threatening about them. He described how they would 'lounge, exchange or sell birds and pigeons, criticise dogs, [or] make appointments for a singing match between rival birds at the "Queen of Spades" in Hare Street.'[22] But it was also his view that: 'Many of these, if not thieves, are at the same time amongst the dangerous class which is found occupying a position between the pauper and the convict ... shambling, tight trousered, sleek haired, artful.'[23] They were perhaps members of the 'swell mob' or pickpockets active in the East End of Victorian London. Archer also noted the more 'regular thieves' who were attracted to Club Row on market day: '. . .I have counted eleven as I stand here by the corner, and I know that I am the cause of their uneasy shifting hither and thither, and that they are watching me as closely as I am looking at them. Theirs is a poor trade. Its poverty is manifest by their threadbare or coarse and mended clothes, the superficial cleanliness of their appearance not withstanding.'[24] Loitering for prey on a busy street, they could, of course, take refuge in a moment in the lawless and labyrinthine courts and alleys of the nearby Nichol.

The stark contrast between the bright and busy thoroughfares of Bethnal Green Road and Shoreditch High Street and the dark quarter that lurked beyond was touched on in the *Illustrated London News* report. Before describing 'the dens' of Friars Mount, the journalist noted one of the reasons why its horrors were not better known to other Londoners was that the appearance of the main streets, and the shopkeepers on them, could be deceptive: 'It is true that several of the main thoroughfares, though dirty and ruinous enough, do not indicate externally the teeming and filthy rooms [that lie behind]. There are still the remains of poor respectability in some places; and ragged, dirty children, and gaunt women, from whose faces almost all traces of womanliness have faded, alternate with the clean-looking and even well-dressed families of some of the shopkeepers.' However: 'let the traveller penetrate further, and he will enter upon a maze of streets each of which is a social crime, and each of which contains tributary hovels many degrees worse than itself. They are not always easy to find, since, if they have ever had any names, the names have been obliterated except from the memory of the police and the City missionary, the doctor or the landlord; and the entrance to most of them is by a covered alley not wider than an ordinary doorway.'

The journalist then took his reader into a typical 'blind court' to see 'a number of black and crumbling hovels forming three sides of a miserable little square, like a fetid tank with a bottom of mud and slime; or an irregular row of similar tenements, mostly of four small rooms, fronted by rotten wooden palings.' There were, observed the journalist, 'three peculiarities which are common to the great part of the whole neighbourhood. The miserable rooms are underlet [sublet] and teeming with inhabitants to an almost inconceivable extent. The water for some fourteen or fifteen houses is frequently supplied from one tap in a dirty corner, where it runs for only a short time every day; and the places are mostly undrained.' The unsavory atmosphere was made worse by the stench of decaying vegetable matter, of pigs and 'that sickly odour which belongs always to human beings living in such a state.'

The food for sale in the area also caught the journalist's attention, as if it were that of a distant land, or of an alien population that, through years of poverty, had developed strange – perhaps unhealthy – appetites: 'All through this teeming neighbourhood of Bethnal-green the visitor will have noticed a surprising number of shops where the coarsest parts of meat seem to share the space with what butchers call offal. Cow-heels, bullocks'-hearts, kidneys, and livers, thin and poor-looking tripe, and sheep's-heads are amongst the uncooked portion of the stock; while the cooked viands are often represented by piles and chains of bruised, and often damaged-looking, saveloys, black-puddings, and a sort of greasy cake of baked sausage-meat, known as "faggots", sold for a penny or three farthings, and made of the harslet and other internal portions of the pig.'

The epicentre of the area's physical decay and seemingly alien life – the spot which contained 'the greater part of the vice and debauchery of the district' – was 'Friars-mount . . . represented by Nichols-street, Old Nichols-street, and Half Nichols-street'. But it was not wholly unique. In a 'score of places', noted the journalist, 'extending over Bethnal-green parish for more than a mile in length and half a mile in breadth', similar scenes of degradation could be found. In such areas:

> from garret to cellar whole families occupy single rooms, or, if they can find a corner of available space, take a lodger or two. In some wretched cul de sac, partly inhabited by costers, the fetid yards are devoted to the donkeys, while fish are cured and dried in places which cannot be mentioned without loathing. Bandbox and lucifer-box [matchbox] makers, cane workers, clothespeg makers, shoemakers, and tailors, mostly earning only just enough to keep them from absolute starvation, swarm from roof to basement; and, as the owners of such houses have frequently bought the leases cheaply and spend nothing for repairs, the profits to the landlords are greater in proportion than those on a middle-class dwelling.

There was, concluded the journalist, 'nothing picturesque in such misery; it is but one painful and monotonous round of vice, filth, and poverty.'

A week after the *Illustrated London News* published its article, *The Builder* – the eminent organ of the construction industry – felt obliged to conduct its own investigation of the Nichol and parts of Spitalfields. Evidently the Nichol slum had become the hot topic of the moment and journalists were suddenly vying with each other to condemn an area that had been festering – largely ignored – for decades: 'Notwithstanding all that has been said on the subject elsewhere,' *The Builder* announced, '. . . the horrible condition in which a vast population are living is not yet understood and realised by the public.' So it set itself the task of publicising the ghastly horrors of the area and its environs as a first step towards change: 'Nothing short of a personal examination, indeed, under proper guidance, can convey a complete idea of it. We must endeavour . . . to urge on the authorities the absolute necessity for immediate steps with a view to bringing about a better state of things.'

The familiar litany of horrors followed: overcrowded and filthy houses, people forced to live in basements at two shillings weekly rent, water taps that had to serve two houses but that might only work for ten or so minutes a day.

One house – '59 Nichol Street' – came in for particular attention. 'The plaster has fallen from the walls and the ceilings, the narrow staircase is rotten and shaky, the general colour is of a dingy smoky black, with peeps of indifferent brickwork and broken laths. At the back there is a large open space, in a most filthy condition; damp refuse of all kinds is piled up against the wall; there is no supply of water; the people have "to hunt for it"; nor is there any distinct closet accommodation for this home.' And in the dark basement, lit by a small window overlooking a rubbish-filled area and with a ceiling height of less than six feet, 'two figures' were discovered, 'on a broken truckle, seemingly naked, with the exception of some black rags which passed across the middle of their bodies'. They were asked who and what they were. A small female voice replied: '. . . here are two of us. Mother is out.' But there was more. 'Gradually, as the eye became accustomed to the gloom two other figures were to be seen lying in a corner upon rags.' The reporter established that the room's 'inmates . . . were a widow and her four children: one a girl twenty years of age, another girl eighteen, a boy of fourteen, and a boy of twelve.' 'We returned from the inspection saddened and ill,' the article concludes. 'We have written of it coolly, but it was a sight to move indignation.'[25]

It's a heartbreaking account. It's also quite a difficult one to authenticate. Only twelve houses in Nichol Street (actually called 'Nichol's Row' by this time, when for no obvious reason Nichol had become Nichols or Nichol's on many maps) are listed in the 1861 census, so it would appear that the journalist recorded the address incorrectly. But even assuming that he actually meant Old Nichol's Street – the one 'Nichol'-related street to contain a number 59 – it's hard to square what he found with what appears in the census return. This shows that 59 Old Nichol's Street – probably dating from the late seventeenth century like most houses in the street – was occupied by four families, with ten people being present on the day of the census. There was Peter Shaw, a thirty-three-year-old 'sealmaker', his thirty-two-year-old wife Mary and their thirteen-year-old son; Henry Brown, a forty-four-year-old 'Carman' and his wife Elizabeth, a needlewoman; William Robinson, a thirty-year-old woodcutter and his twenty-eight-year-old wife Frances, a tailoress, and two-year-old daughter Elizabeth; and thirty-six-year-old Henry Hobbs, a 'deal' porter, and his wife Ann, a laundress of the same age. It was certainly a full household – it's even possible that it had to accommodate one family per room. But even so this does not seem as desperate as the picture painted by *The Builder*, nor are any widow and her four children mentioned. Was the paper describing a different house? Was its report an exaggeration?

It has to be said that, overall, the 1861 census returns for the Nichol slum do not present as black a picture as the accounts given in the *Illustrated London News* and *The Builder*. Take, for example, 'Half Nichol's Street'. It lay at the heart of the Friars Mount slum and was, seemingly, typical of the area, with houses (judging from the 1872/3 Ordnance Survey) that were generally less than sixteen feet wide and perhaps two rooms deep. Those on the south side dated from the early eighteenth century and generally seem to have been larger than the houses on the north side, most of which were probably built during the first half of the nineteenth century. All were generally two storeys high above ground, with basements. Some perhaps had small garrets. Those constructed for journeymen weavers, would, of course, have had wide first-floor windows to light the looms.

According to the 1861 census number 1 Half Nichol's Street was occupied by just one family: James Border, a baker, aged thirty-six; his wife Ann, aged thirty-nine; his widowed sister Ann Edward, aged thirty-seven, and her son James, aged seven and listed as a 'scholar'; and an unmarried servant, George Darrit, who was also a baker.[26] So this house, perhaps containing as many as eight or nine small rooms, was seemingly occupied by only five people. Number 2 Half Nichol's Street tells a similar story. Number 4, by contrast, contained thirteen people organised as four separate households. There were William Must, aged thirty, a 'glass bead maker', his twenty-nine-year-old wife Mary and their three children aged one to nine. There was a married couple, twenty-eight-year-old George Brown and his thirty-one-year-old wife, both of whom pursued occupations typical of London's poorer-paid population: George was a labourer, while Charlotte was a 'hawker', who sold goods in the streets, 'crying' her wares. Then there was a household headed by thirty-one-year-old George Lancaster, also a 'hawker', who lived with his twenty-eight-year-old wife Ann, their six-year-old-daughter and Ann's twenty-one-year-old brother Richard Wickers, another 'hawker'. Finally there was Robert Oxford, a thirty-four-year-old 'toymaker', and his forty-year-old wife Jane. All were clearly forced to live somewhat cheek by jowl, although it's also possible that number 4 was rather larger than its neigbours. Number 21 Half Nichol's Street was also crowded in 1861, with twenty people organised in three households, thirteen of whom were aged sixteen years or younger. Interestingly, the 'Heads' of all three households, along with two of their wives, one of their children and one of their lodgers, were 'silk weavers': even now, the trade on which Spitalfields had built its fortune retained a toehold in the Nichol. Arguably, the density of population of number 21 most closely approximates what journalists seem to have regarded as standard for the area.

New Nichol's Street – mostly dating from the expansion of the estate in the early eighteenth and the mid nineteenth century, seemingly a notch down the social scale from 'Half Nichol's Street' – also contained some houses that appear to have been seriously overcrowded. Number 1, for example, contained nineteen people organised as eight households on the day of the 1861 census. These included Thomas Bramley, a twenty-year-old 'Lighting man' (or could the census read 'Fighting man'?), living with his nineteen-year-old wife Susan, whose occupation was given as 'silk weaver', and their two-month-old son; Thomas Williams, a fifty-year-old 'hawker'; Elizabeth Priddy, a fifty-seven-year-old unmarried mother and 'needle woman'; Mathew Tot, a thirty-eight-year-old 'Tinman' and his forty-year-old wife Mary who was a laundress; and John Benfield, a thirty-four-year-old 'Hawker' and his thirty-year-old wife Jane, who was a 'Fancy box maker'. Judging from the 1872/3 Ordnance Survey the land behind the houses on both sides of the street was occupied by courts, alleys or buildings, while the north-west corner of the street was formed by a cluster of small cottages. These were set back-to-back and so apparently without rear windows and were entered from New Nichol's Street, Boundary Street or from very narrow rear alleys. They were among the worst of the worst.

And yet when a rough calculation of the population density of New Nichol's Street is made on the basis of the census (and taking into account empty houses and buildings – such as a 'cabinet factory' – that were in industrial use) it doesn't match the bleak assessment made by the reporters of the *Illustrated London News* and *The Builder*. The journalists seemed to imply a standard pattern of one family per room – so perhaps twenty people in a single house. The true number, though, seems to have been closer to ten to eleven people per house. That's not to say that there were no houses in the Nichol packed in the way that the journalists described – number 21 Half Nichol's Street is a case in point. Nor should it be suggested that people were living in anything other than cramped and often very squalid conditions. But the reality does not appear quite to match the blackness of contemporary accounts.

Whether *The Builder*'s grim description of '59 Nichol Street' is accurate is therefore very much open to question. On the one hand, it's not borne out by sober contemporary statistics. On the other, it is certainly consistent with other accounts of the time, and they surely can't all have been untrue: that would imply a conspiracy to present London's slums in an even worse light than the bleak reality.

But, then, perhaps that was what was indeed going on. Descriptions of desolation, of utter degradation, of dungeons with naked girls entombed in darkness, sold newspapers, and the prurient reading public revelled in them. There can be no doubt how deep and terrible the poverty of Victorian Spitalfields and Shoreditch was, but to get people to read about this required something more. Slums had to be made the horror movie of the age. Their inhabitants had to become creatures that could be contemplated, and shivered over, from the safety and comfort of middle-class homes.

SIXTEEN

DOING THE LORD'S WORK
Victorian Philanthropy

Some reports of the squalor of Victorian Spitalfields, along with neighbouring parts of Shoreditch, Bethnal Green and Whitechapel, may have been exaggerated, but they nevertheless touched on a fundamental truth: this part of London was becoming more overcrowded and run-down, sanitation was appalling and living standards low. Attitudes varied towards those forced to endure these terrible conditions. Some observers, like Dr Hector Gavin, argued that the poor were the victims, not the cause, of their distressing circumstances, and that the crime rife in the East End arose from desperation (see page 426). Henry Mayhew, by contrast, summed up with simplistic clarity the more commonly held mid-century view when he made a distinction in *London Labour and the London Poor* between 'those that *will* work, those that *cannot* work, and those that *will not* work'. It was a notion that embodied a very black-and-white view of society: on the one hand, there were the industrious and 'deserving poor', who worked, kept a decent home, went to church, lived a regular family life and stayed sober; on the other, there were the 'undeserving' poor, who did none of these things and who, it was assumed, preferred to beg and sponge rather than attempt any form of toil. The circumstances of the 'deserving poor' were not their fault. The circumstances of the 'undeserving poor' were entirely their own doing.

From here it was only a small step (which many took) to arguing that poverty was almost a form of genetic laziness, and that if crime and immorality flourished among the poor it was because many of them were not only 'undeserving' but also degenerate. This was a clear case of muddling cause and effect. Those who disparaged the 'undeserving' poor refused to acknowledge that poverty and its far-reaching consequences were generally the result of a set of unremitting difficulties that reduced most sufferers to a state of demoralised despair. They assumed instead that the 'undeserving' brought their problems on themselves.

The ranks of the unsympathetic included – perhaps unsurprisingly – those who had themselves formerly experienced privation, such as the California-born writer Jack London, who veered between Socialistic sympathy and ferocious contempt in his attitude towards London's underclass (see chapter 20). More curious still was the case of novelist George Gissing, whose apparent lack of sympathy for the poor seems especially startling given his own early circumstances. He had endured social ostracism and first-hand experience of low life when he had been imprisoned in 1876 for stealing money to give to a woman who was almost certainly a prostitute. He had then married her, and she fairly promptly left him. Yet his own suffering seems to have made him impatient with that of others. He was, of course, a novelist who wrote for dramatic and poetic effect, to make a point and tell a story, and it would be absurd to automatically assume that the views expressed by his characters were his own. Nevertheless it is surprising that in novels such as *The Nether World*, published in 1889, he should choose to be so pitiless in his portrayal of the East End – the 'city of the damned' – and display so little sympathy for the outcasts of society. Perhaps his own familiarity with want and despair had made him unsentimental. Be that as it may, his descriptions of deprivation still retain the power to shock. Take, for example, one particularly brutal passage in *The Nether World*: 'On the doorsteps sat little girls, themselves only just out of infancy, nursing or neglecting red-eyed doughy-limbed abortions in every state of babyhood, helpless spawn of diseased humanity, born to embitter and brutalise yet further the lot of those that gave them life.' There's no trace of compassion here.

The assumption that the indigent were often the architects of their own downfall underlaid the provisions of the Poor Laws (see pages 387–8). It underpinned much of Victorian philanthropy, too. In essence there was a widely held conviction that indiscriminate giving could cause more harm than good – reinforcing malingerers in their shiftless ways and robbing the more industrious-minded of the incentive to work. As J. R. Green, one-time vicar of Stepney, argued: 'It is not so much poverty that is increasing . . . as pauperism, the want [i.e. lack] of industry, of thrift or self-reliance', qualities which 'melt and vanish . . . before the certainty of money from the West . . . Some half a million people in the East End of London have been flung into the crucible of public benevolence and have

come out of it simple paupers.'[1] Charitable urges were therefore tinged by
a desire to separate worthwhile sheep from those perceived as incorrigible
goats.

As the century progressed, and the area's woes continued, attempts were
nevertheless made – often uncertainly and inconsistently – to ameliorate the
worst of the suffering and poverty in Spitalfields. In a few instances, official bodies were involved. More often, however, the initiative was seized
by philanthropic individuals and privately run charitable organisations.
Some like the late-eighteenth-century Soup Society subsidised nutrition
for the poor. Other bodies provided refuge, homes, training and education –
even intellectual and artistic inspiration – while a very few offered the
prospect of liberation from the area's mean and oppressive streets. Most of
the philanthropic institutions and organisations were religious enterprises,
like William Booth's Salvation Army, founded in 1865 as 'The Christian
Mission', seeking in one way or another either to save souls through missionary activity or to provide decent lives for their co-religionists.

The one major public work of social improvement undertaken in the
mid century was the construction of the wide and sinuous Commercial
Street that cut roughly north–south through the area, dividing Spitalfields
approximately in half and ultimately linking Old Street in the north with
Aldgate in the south. Conceived by the Commissioners of Her Majesty's
Woods, Forests and Land Revenues to a master plan by James Pennetho-
rne, construction began in 1843, the portion south from Christ Church
being completed in 1845[2] and the stretch north from Christ Church to
Shoreditch High Street being undertaken between 1849 and 1857,[3] initially
by the Commissioners of Woods and after 1851 under the auspices of the
newly founded Metropolitan Board of Works.[4] The intention was to
improve communication between Spitalfields Market and the established
thoroughfares of Whitechapel High Street and Road, and between North
London and the docks. But, as is clear from the evidence offered to the
relevant Parliamentary Select Committee and in the reports of the commissioners, the new road was also envisaged from the start as a mechanism
for slum clearance, its route – as far as was practicable – being deliberately
directed through the area's worst streets and enclaves.

In 1836 a Mr W. Cotton suggested to the Select Committee that a new
road slicing through the heart of Spitalfields would give the authorities

*Commercial Street, in front of Christ Church in 1907, looking north when the
Spitalfields fruit and vegetable market – its 1880s gabled buildings are on the left – was in
operation. Left foreground is the Britannia beerhouse, on the corner with Dorset Street.
Right is the Ten Bells public house, on the corner with Fournier Street, where in 1888 Annie
Chapman was last seen before her murder in Hanbury Street.*

the opportunity to keep under surveillance a 'low population' that was 'without any respectable persons to keep them at all in check'. In similar fashion, Reverend William Stone, Rector of Christ Church, told the committee in 1838 that a new road was desirable because it would enable 'public observation' of the 'exceedingly immoral population' of the area. Such views evidently had a profound influence on the Commissioners, who in their Fourth Report of 1845 argued as part of the rationale for the proposed road that it would result in 'the destruction of a neighbourhood inhabited by persons addicted to vices and immorality of the worst description'.[5]

Slum clearance by road construction, though, didn't address root causes or offer solutions to the essential problems of slum housing. To make matters worse, no reasonable efforts were made initially to ensure the welfare of displaced slum dwellers. Charles Dickens complained in *Household Words* in 1851 of 'our . . . new streets, never heeding, never asking, where the wretches whom we clear out, crowd.'[6] The policy of targeting slum streets and buildings also meant that the new road purposely ploughed through blocks of buildings and widened existing streets, so that old terraces would be tumbled away and light and air let in. In the process, ancient thoroughfares were truncated or eradicated and well-established routes destroyed. The southern portion of Wheler Street, for example, disappeared and part of its course was widened and incorporated into the new road, while the western part of Quaker Street was obliterated and its connection with Fleur de Lis Street severed. Needless to say the time-honoured urban geography of much of Spitalfields was transformed and disoriented, especially in the north where the new road cut diagonally through the existing right-angled grid of streets.

There was, however, one almost tangential benefit that resulted from the cutting through of Commercial Street: the construction works created large adjacent sites that the commissioners could then dispose of for various profitable uses calculated to improve the economy and social tone of the area. Capacious workshops now sprang up, along with warehouses, shops with flats above, public houses, a music hall (the Royal Cambridge, open from 1869), a large police station (see page 488), a couple of churches and even a multi-storey stable called Stapleton's – complete with tiers of loose boxes and a ramp-like equine staircase – that, according to an ornate 'Jacobethan'-style terracotta panel that still graces the building, was 'established' in 1842. Other sites the commissioners leased or sold went, perhaps at a discount, to worthy bodies for the building of new charitable or philanthropic buildings. George Peabody (see pages 464–5) – who dedicated much of his fortune to the construction of 'improved dwellings for the poor' – was one of those who took advantage of some of the land now freed up.

Another venture to benefit from the Commercial Street project was the Jews' Infant School, founded in 1841, and from 1858 based near the junction of the new street and Wentworth Street, in a handsome building (numbered 43) that comprised a centre block embellished with tall windows set within a two-storey classical arcade, framed by a pair of wings, slightly set back.[7] By 1861 it was providing education for 560 pupils drawn from the local community (though not from among the poorest families, since a small charge was made for each child). Among its later alumni was the playwright Arnold Wesker (1932–2016), one of whose memories of the place was 'looking up the skirt of one teacher' (he was, he said, 'sexually precocious').[8] The school closed in 1939, but the building survives substantially intact though now in commercial use.[9]

Grand construction projects apart, when it came to providing direct and practical help for slum dwellers, official bodies generally had little to offer beyond the often heavy hand of the Poor Laws or the grim prospect of the workhouse. It was therefore mostly voluntary charitable bodies that took the strain. This was a slightly mixed blessing. In London during most of the nineteenth century the spheres of private charity and philanthropy were inspired or administered by a wonderful if often strange (and generally ambitious, sometimes almost fanatical) galaxy of characters. But while their work, particularly the raising of donations, might be godly it was also, in its own way, very worldly. Charity was big business. It offered careers for the ambitious. It could help to make reputations, forge useful connections and garner honours. It was also fiercely competitive, with rival philanthropic bodies competing often ruthlessly for funds in a distinctly ungodly manner. Parish and public authorities with responsibility for the poor, who customarily depended to a degree on individual donations, were from time to time alarmed by the proliferation of private charities. They worried at their lack of accountability and at the way in which charismatic or high-profile characters could attract funds that, in different circumstances, might have been expected to find their way into the public purse.

The activities of some charities were made even more questionable by their relentless quest for publicity. All charities, of course, had to make a noise. They needed to highlight social evils in order to attract funds, and provide evidence of success in tackling those evils in order to ensure continuing support. But an overly insistent desire for constant public attention could attract the wrong sort of notice. Some philanthropists seem to have classed promoting a cause and promoting themselves as almost inseparable activities. Moreover, in order to attract attention – even for the best of reasons – some had a tendency to exaggerate, or distort, both the ills that they encountered and the cures they claimed to effect. And nowhere was this more apparent in Victorian Spitalfields than in the use some made of that technological wonder of the age – the photograph.

The vogue for photographs of child poverty in Spitalfields and the East End appears to have been initiated in the mid 1860s by Annie MacPherson (or McPherson as her name is sometimes spelt), the daughter of a Scottish Quaker teacher. She moved to London in 1865 and almost at once became 'appalled by the conditions in which children were forced to work, and shocked in particular by the plight of those who laboured for intolerably long hours gluing and sticking matchboxes.'[10] She channelled her outrage in a most practical manner, and in 1868, with the help of George Holland, launched her own enterprise to help poor children: the 'Home of Industry' in Spitalfields.[11] In her new role she became closely involved with the East End evangelical movement, but clearly kept her Quaker connections too, for a few of the photographs she commissioned of poor children in Spitalfields are now in in the archives of Hoxton Hall, a former music hall acquired by the Quaker Bedford Institute in 1893 (see pages 458–9) as a base from which to work within the impoverished community around Hoxton Street.

MacPherson's pioneering *City Arabs in the Wild and Brought Home*, which she issued from her 'Home of Industry, Spitalfields', consists of a series of images of street children, which take the form of 'before' and 'after' photographs. Hand-written inscriptions on their backs identify the individuals and the transformation wrought. There is, for example, a photograph of one Billie Griffin, 'a genuine London Arab' – which was the term used at the time for a begging, roaming, ragged street urchin – and another of him, looking well groomed, 'after a few months in the house'. It was a very immediate and effective form of propaganda.

Through her work Annie MacPherson came to know William Booth, the Methodist preacher and founder with his wife Catherine of the Salvation Army, and Thomas Barnardo, who was to become one of the most celebrated Victorian philanthropists. Indeed, as Gillian Wagner explains in her perceptive biography of him, before Barnardo was fully occupied with his own charity work and homes for street children he helped 'Annie McPherson at her Home of Industry, and there are references to him drilling her boys. Monthly prayer meetings took place at the home and Barnardo would have come into contact with many others engaged in mission work on these occasions.'[12] Within a few years of her arrival in East London, then, Annie MacPherson was – very clearly – a leading light in the missionary work of the area. An article celebrating the power of prayer to change life in the East End that appeared in *The Revival* – the organ of the evangelical movement – in its edition of 29 October 1868, gave her a place of honour in its litany of local philanthropic champions and ventures, alongside W. J. Lewis's evangelising Gospel Hall, Barnardo, and 'above all' William Booth's East London Christian Mission.[13]

For his part, although Barnardo started out helping Annie MacPherson, he was soon, as *The Revival* article makes clear, undertaking charitable work on his own account. And as he did so, he took the use of 'before' and 'after' photographs of street children several stages further. Annie MacPherson must presumably have been an influence. But, according to Gillian Wagner, Barnardo was also clearly inspired by the activities of the US evangelist Dwight Moody. As she points out: 'Two photographs exist showing Moody with his Sunday School, both taken in 1862. The first shows him with a group of ragged children . . . the second . . . shows the same children, neat and tidy.' She goes on to explain that Barnardo met Moody, and that soon afterwards he 'started to issue his own famous series of "before" and "after" photographs' and these 'were stylistically so similar to those taken by Moody that it is difficult to avoid the conclusion that Moody had brought his photographs to London with him and that Barnardo had seen them.' 'Recognising their powerful appeal in terms of publicity,' Gillian Wagner concludes, 'Barnardo adapted the idea to suit his own needs. Advertisements announcing the sale of the photographs in aid of the East End Juvenile Mission first appeared in *The Revival* in 1869. The earliest known surviving photograph is that of a boy crouching in rags on a doorway.'[14] For sheer scale of ambition, Barnardo's deployment of photographs of street children soon surpassed anything that Annie MacPherson had sought to achieve.

No. 5.—"I've got no work to do."
(Same lad as in No. 6.)

No. 6.—"I'm in work now, you know!"
(Same lad as in No. 5.)

A pair of Barnardos 'before' and 'after' photographs promoting, and fund-raising for, his 'Home for Working Lads'. The 'before' photograph is entitled 'I've got no work to do', while the 'after' (with the boy in a sailor's uniform) is labelled 'I'm in work now, you know!' The caption states that both are images of the 'same lad' – which is no doubt the case – but in 1877 it emerged that many of these 'before' and 'after' shots were staged, with the transformation being achieved merely by a bowl of water and a change of clothes.

In our age of heightened sensitivity about the sale of photographs of children, especially those in ragged or scanty attire, Barnardo's policy seems dubious. Certainly the process of making photographs of child poverty commercially attractive must be classed as one of the more reckless actions of arguably high-minded but money-oriented Victorian philanthropists. The temptation to manipulate truth for monetary ends – in essence to produce fake 'before' and 'after' photographs to encourage donations – was evidently hard to resist. A noble end might be viewed as 'justifying' ignoble means, but the whole enterprise was clearly teetering on the edge of an abyss of amorality. Setting aside the issue of paedophilia, even an innocent purchaser of the photographs was more likely to buy images of attractive rather than of dirty or diseased children, and of street children who had been miraculously saved and transformed rather than those still in need. Certainly, the temptation to provide the money-giving market with the images it wanted was to get Barnardo into serious trouble.

He was a great self-publicist who documented his whole life – his actions, beliefs and campaigns – in the columns of the popular press and soon also the pages of his own publications. He had a facility with words – a 'flair for publicising his work'[15] – and was willing and able to write about his actions and attitudes in a compelling and readable manner. He had a habit of retelling stories about himself and his achievements in a selective manner, and was certainly not averse to self-promotion – he was indeed an early master of 'spin'. It paid off.

The press in the 1860s and 70s was not as it is now. Papers and periodicals were a major means of popular entertainment and had little competition. There were therefore numerous local publications, national daily newspapers and papers and journals serving specialist-interest groups. These all appealed to the relatively large proportion of the population prepared to read lengthy articles on a wide variety of subjects. Letters, announcements and notices were devoured, too, and since these were placed by individuals it was pretty easy for men like Barnardo – engaged in interesting enterprises – to make their views and actions known to the public on a regular basis through the press. This was particularly easy if the contributor had a pre-existing relationship with the paper or its editor, or if – as in Barnardo's case – his activities related to the interests of the paper's specialised readership. Since the evangelical movement was large and nationwide it had several publications dedicated to its activities and so

Barnardo – a notable evangelical engaged in pioneering charity work –
had no difficulty getting his name into print. He could easily appeal for
funds to house, feed and educate destitute children, tapping into a deep-
rooted zeal among many to do what little they could to help social problems
that could not be tackled by the Poor Laws or the workhouse.

From the beginning Barnardo displayed a showman's sensationalist
approach to photography, using it primarily not to record objective truth
but to create emotive and calculated recreations of 'truth'. His earliest
photograph, he later admitted, was a staged recreation. He claimed that
he had stumbled over the boy huddled in that position in the street and
then 'made him take up the pose again to be photographed.'[16] A slippery
slope indeed.

Barnardo's showmanship and self-promotion angered many and in 1877
he became embroiled in a bitter row with his critics that led to an 'Arbitration', a formal process similar to a trial and conducted under oath. Since
he had raised much public money over the years for his charitable activities, it was felt necessary to discover how it had been used and if any of it
had been misused. The child photographs, of course, begged the question
of how he had raised the money in the first place. If, as those critical of
him claimed, he had made use of 'photographs representing children in a
state of fictitious destitution before admission to the homes to attract support', this was fakery with the intention of securing financial gain:
operating under false pretences at best, fraud at worst.[17]

Barnardo offered three lines of defence for his acquisition of these
images of children. The first was that he wanted 'to obtain and retain an
exact likeness, which being attached to a faithful record in our History
Book of each individual case, shall enable us in future to trace every child's
career, and to bring to remembrance minute circumstances which, without a photograph, would be impossible.' The second was that he needed to
make it easy to recognise boys or girls who 'committed criminal acts or
absconded from the homes'. It was, of course, his third reason – 'to aid us
in advocating the claims of our Institution, now containing nearly 500
children, with the Christian public' and, in his words, 'to sell all such
photographs for the benefit of the Institutions' – that caused the arbitrators to examine minutely the circumstances in which children had been
photographed.[18] And they soon discovered anomalies. One image, for
example, entitled 'The Raw Material', showed a group of ragged boys
being overseen by a lamp-toting beadle, who appeared to have just come

across them. In reality, the boys had not been found together but had been assembled for the photograph. This slight manipulation of the truth was revealed by the beadle himself, one Edward Fitzgerald, who had been sacked by Barnardo in October 1876 for drunkenness and immorality.[19]

Barnardo was never accused of selling sexually explicit or provocative pictures of children. Ultimately, though, the Arbitration did rule that they were 'deceptive', and that the famed 'before' and 'after' images had, in actual fact, often been taken on the same day, with just a wash and change of clothes to effect the transformation. There was also unhappiness with his refusal to answer a number of key questions under cross-examination. Given the legal status of the Arbitration, his recalcitrance was technically an offence.

The Arbitration's overall verdict was somewhat ambiguous. It did not find against Barnardo, but nor did it specifically clear him of all the charges brought against him.[20] In essence the Arbitrators decided that the best all-round policy was to offer broad, if cautious, approval: 'We are of the opinion,' they concluded, 'that these Homes for destitute boys and girls, called Barnardo Institutions, are real and valuable charities, and worthy of public confidence and support.'[21] The mood of the moment was captured well by Lord Shaftesbury, the leading light of the evangelical Christian charitable movement. Shaftesbury, who had long been courted by Barnardo and had previously shown some interest in his work, recorded his doubts in his diary: 'Dr Barnardo is acquitted after a fashion by the Arbitrators. Is it a just acquittal? If so I rejoice. The pressure on funds is frightful. If he was guilty I lament that iniquity has triumphed. The language of the Report, and especially of the conclusion, is like an effort of men who dare not call him innocent, and yet are zealous not to call him guilty. What will be the public response? Will he regain lost confidence? Will money flow in? Will the reaction make him greater or less great?'[22]

Within a few years of the humiliation of the Arbitration the ebullient Barnardo seems to have bounced back. But the cloud under which he had struggled for much of the 1870s was not fully dispelled and it seems to have become standard practice, within the world of London philanthropy, to assume the same stance as Shaftesbury and view Barnardo with caution and some concern. In the 1892 edition of his *Life and Labour of the People in London*, Charles Booth voiced these generally held mixed feelings: 'The work of Dr Barnardo is most remarkable,' he wrote. 'There is, I believe, nothing in the world like it. But, with such dimensions [as the] work has assumed ... special dangers show themselves. His interventions may begin to be counted on, and if so, it may tend to increase the troubles it sets out to cure.'[23]

The American novelist Jack London, on the other hand, was rather more easily impressed. His sensational *The People of the Abyss* (1903), written in only seven weeks and based on a mixture of first-hand observation and hurried research (see chapter 20), perceived Barnardo as a great hero. He was, London argued, the 'noble exception' to the otherwise futile efforts of charitable people 'who try to help'. London was impressed by the 'facts' – given to him presumably by the Barnardo office – that 'every twenty-four hours in the year Dr Barnardo snatches nine waifs from the streets.' As if copying uncritically from a Barnardo press release, London gushed, '[T]he people who try to help have something to learn from him. He does not play with palliatives. He traces social viciousness and misery to their sources. He removes the progeny of the gutter-folk from their pestilential environment, and gives them a healthy, wholesome environment in which to be pressed and prodded and moulded into men.'[24]

Barnardo had, however, learnt one lesson. After 1877, as Gillian Wagner records, he 'never sold photographs of the children for the benefit of the institutions, and the famous series of "before and after" photographs came to an end. Thenceforward children were simply photographed for identity purposes, although their photographs frequently appeared in Barnardo's publication *Night and Day*.' She also points out that 'after 1885 the Barnardo photographer took to writing the names of the children and the dates when photographed on the face of the photograph itself, thus formalising them still further.'[25]

A generation later, the series of photographs of impoverished Spitalfields children taken by Horace Warner in the early 1900s continued something of the theme of the Annie MacPherson and early Barnardo photographs, but without the crude artifice or direct pecuniary intentions. Warner was a Quaker and it would seem reasonable to assume that he photographed the children living around the Bedford Institute, on the corner of Wheler and Quaker Streets, of which he was a trustee.[26] But although this was one of the most deprived areas of the East End, the children Warner depicts, while generally ragged, also appear to be reasonably healthy. Obviously posed, they were presumably meant to document child poverty, and so to aid philanthropic work, but it would also appear that they were intended not so much to shock as to demonstrate the triumph of resilience over desperate circumstances. The children he depicted generally possess dignity and a zest for life rather than appearing as haunted spectres of poverty, disease and degeneration. They give rise to optimism rather than despair. Some hold pets, others are doing charmingly adult things like washing windows, chopping wood or looking at paintings, while others still are playing or looking impish. Occasionally the same children appear in different locations, and in one case a young urchin with a cheeky smile wears the photograph's generously brimmed and artistic-looking hat. Tantalisingly, the majority of locations in which the children were photographed are not clear. Most appear to be posed in paved courts, lined with cottages, often with large sash windows and sills very near ground level, suggesting the cottages were small and the courts narrow – indeed much like those south of Quaker Street, within a few minutes' walk of the Bedford Institute. Some of the houses look to be late seventeenth century and are furnished with wide weavers' windows. Many are ruinous. And, most fascinatingly, the humble lives and occupations of the inhabitants of these courts and streets are suggested by the paraphernalia of daily life, such as costers' carts and lines of washing draped between buildings.[27]

Annie MacPherson's philanthropic career is not as famous nor as sensational as that of Barnardo. But she was a pioneer in her field, in her way equally controversial, and had far more direct involvement with the destitute children of Spitalfields than Barnardo did. The 'Home of Industry' which she opened in 1868 – some two years before Barnardo's first home for boys – offered refuge, work, education, and practical 'industrial' training (rather as Barnardo's boys' home in Stepney Causeway offered training in carpentry, metalwork and shoemaking), as well as providing food to poor and orphaned children. It occupied a large warehouse (and former cholera hospital), organised around an inner court, off Commercial Street. Clara M. S. Lowe, MacPherson's biographer writing in 1882, described its acquisition in tones of near-religious ecstasy:

> The needed building was provided in a way that could have been little
> conjectured, but the Lord had gone on before. Along the great thorough-
> fare leading from the Docks to the Great Eastern Railway, lofty warehouses
> had taken the place of many unclean, tottering dwellings formerly seen

there. During the fearful visitation of cholera in 1866 one of these had been secured as a hospital by Miss Sellon's Sisters of Mercy, and the water and gas had been laid on every floor, and every arrangement made for convenience and cleanliness . . . in the following year Mr Holland saw how well it would be to secure it for a Refuge. The doors had been closed twelve month when Mr and Mrs Merry and three other friends entered the long-deserted dwelling, and joined in prayer that where death had been seen in all its terrors, there souls might be born to God.[28]

Lowe, like many nineteenth-century evangelists – including 'General' William Booth with his 'Salvation Army' – saw the struggle against Satan in military terms of battles and forays. To her the refuge was 'a post far advanced into the enemy's territory, for the adjoining streets are known as the "Thieves Quarter." Three thousand, it is supposed, have their headquarters here. In the square mile in the midst of which the refuge (now called "Home of Industry"), is situated 120,000 of our poorest population are to be found . . .' She recalled the enthusiastic efforts to make the Home of Industry a reality: 'Every hour of the day, and even far into the night, the voice of praise and prayer has been heard in some part of the building. Even in the vaults beneath the pavement was a little sanctuary made . . . In February 1869, the Lord granted us the desire of our hearts, and the Home of Industry was opened with praise and prayer.'[29] Holland had been too busy to take on the task of repairing and adapting the building, so Annie MacPherson, who had recently been to New York and seen how women worked there to relieve distress, decided to do the work herself.

She herself described the Home of Industry and its opening in *The Christian*, 22 February 1869, and in so doing revealed the familiar middle-class and West End fear of the alien East.

Last night I felt it right to sleep at the Refuge for once, so as to be able to enter into all its needs. No words can describe the sounds in the streets surrounding it throughout the night; – yells of women, cries of 'Murder' then of 'Police' – with the rushing to and fro of wild, drunken men and women into the street adjoining the building, whence more criminals come than from any other street in London. At three o'clock the heavy rumble of market wagons commenced, and then the rush of the fire-brigade . . . On the other side of the building is an empty space, known as 'Rag Fair', filled in the morning with a horde of the poorest women selling the veriest old rubbish.[30]

Annie MacPherson's Home of Industry was only part of her charitable endeavours. From the start, under the influence of Maria Rye, a social reformer and supporter of women's rights, she also pursued a policy, later known as the 'Home Children policy', of sending destitute East End children – ultimately some 14,000 of them – from the Home to live and work in Canada, Australia, New Zealand and South Africa.

The fairest thing that can be said of MacPherson's involvement with this policy is that she was naïve: she was convinced that in plucking children from the slums she was sending them to big bright lands to embark upon rosy futures. She does not seem to have calculated that on arrival the children were no doubt frequently disorientated, homesick, frightened and confused; that since the policy was not initially well monitored, they had no protectors and were at the mercy of the people with whom they were placed; and that, tragically, the world being what it is and was, abuse could and did take place.

Maria Rye's initial operation, which had started in 1867, had involved organising the emigration of poor women to Canada. Then it had moved on to children. Rye's early efforts – or at least intentions – were approved by the Archbishop of Canterbury. But there were sceptics even then. When rumours reached England of the ill-treatment of children and even of profiteering by the overseas organisers of the schemes, the London Board of Governors of the Poor Laws – who had nominal jurisdiction over many of the younger London children sent abroad – resolved to investigate. In 1874 the Governors sent a representative – Andrew Doyle – to Canada, where by that time MacPherson had also established three 'distribution centres' for her arriving children. Doyle visited the centres, spoke to some of the children and wrote a report that praised the organisers – particularly MacPherson – and their staff, recognising they were inspired by the highest motives, but condemned virtually all the practical aspects of the enterprise. Doyle criticised the way workhouse children, generally of good character, were grouped with street children, who were generally thieves. This policy, he recorded, led to nothing but trouble. He also pointed out that the checks made on children after they had been placed with employers – mostly farmers who could be inclined to view the poor children contemptuously and as little more than cheap labour – were practically non-existent. His conclusion was that, 'because of Miss Rye's carelessness and Miss MacPherson's limited resources, thousands of British children, already in painful circumstances, were cast adrift to be overworked or mistreated by the settlers of early Canada who were generally honest but often hard taskmasters.'[31]

Doyle's report, issued in 1875, caused much controversy in Britain and Canada. A Select Committee was set up by the House of Commons to examine the schemes. Its findings were inconclusive. Consequently, while some changes were made, the schemes were allowed to carry on – not just Rye's and MacPherson's but also those initiated by other institutions, including Barnardo's homes. The naïve and the romantic praised the enterprise. As late as 1903 the woefully unperceptive Jack London, in his hastily produced *The People of the Abyss*, was extolling the apparent virtues of dispatching East End waifs to the prairies of North America and – displaying little or no understanding of the possible consequences of these actions – commending Barnardo in particular:

> Dr Barnardo is a child-catcher. First, he catches them when they are young, before they are set, hardened, in the vicious social mould; and then he sends them away to grow up and be formed in another and better social mould. Up to date he has sent out of the country 13,340 boys, most of them to Canada, and not one in fifty has failed. A splendid record, when it is considered that these lads are waifs and strays, homeless and parentless, jerked out from the very bottom of the Abyss, and forty-nine out of fifty of them made into men.

The final and official acknowledgment that these schemes probably did far more harm than good came on 23 February 2010 when the then British Prime Minister Gordon Brown issued an official apology for the 'shameful' and 'misguided' child resettlement programme. This formal apology was in part prompted by research carried out by Margaret Humphreys, who estimated that around 150,000 children had been 'resettled' by the various 'Home Children' schemes, often being sent abroad without their parents' knowledge or after being told – falsely – that their parents were dead. Humphreys also suggests that one of the prime motives for the schemes was not charitable but financial: it was, quite simply, far cheaper to maintain a child in the colonies than in Britain.[32]

By the early 1880s the adventure of the 'Home of Industry' on Commercial Street was over, and in 1884 its buildings were replaced by Toynbee Hall. Founded by Canon Samuel Barnett and his wife Henrietta and named after their friend, the Oxford University-based economic historian Arnold Toynbee, who had died in 1883, this was a philanthropic exercise of a very different stamp. The Barnetts and Toynbee were social reformers with a shared vision of bringing rich and poor together within a harmonious, interdependent community. Their idea was that those with education and culture could help those who had neither but who would – the reformers believed – greatly benefit from both. As Charles Booth explained in 1892, Toynbee Hall aimed to 'bring University culture into direct contact with the poorest of people.'[33]

Poverty was not, in the view of these visionaries, just an oppression of the body but also of the mind. The body required nourishment in order to survive. The mind – the soul – needed culture, beauty, education and inspiration. The Elementary Education Act of 1870 had led to the creation of the London School Board and the construction of hundreds of light, lofty and handsome new schools, usually designed in the then fashionable Queen Anne style by the board's brilliant architect E. R. Robson. These schools were intended not only to offer enlightening education but to beautify the streets in which they stood and be inspiring and uplifting to all who saw them. Generally they succeeded, and prompted Arthur Conan Doyle to proclaim them – through his character Sherlock Holmes – 'beacons of learning' within the drab urban landscape.[34] The Education Act and the Board Schools it created did bring about significant improvements in the number of children educated and in the quality of their education. But in the opinion of many reformers, such as the Barnetts, much still needed to be done, particularly among the large numbers of the truly abject poor who were beyond the reach of legislation such as the Education Act.

Something of a precursor to this was the Bedford Institute, established by the Quakers on land acquired in 1867 from the Commissioners of Works who had recently constructed Commercial Street. (There is a tradition that there was a Quaker meeting house located near the site from the late seventeenth century; a Quaker Street appeared in Gascoyne's survey of Stepney in 1703 and its location conforms to part of the larger eighteenth-century street.) Named after Peter Bedford, a Quaker philanthropist and silk weaver who lived in Steward Street and started the Society for Lessening the Cause of Juvenile Delinquency,[35] the Bedford Institute sought to promote education, religious guidance and moral training, and to offer relief to the infirm and destitute. It seems to have flourished, for in 1894 the Quakers constructed a new and handsome building on the site from which to continue their work on a larger scale. This was a bold move for the Quaker Street area was then one of the most desperate slums in London, and the institute was intended not just to help its impoverished neighbours in a practical way but also – through its joyous Flemish-style Renaissance architecture – to offer artistic and spiritual inspiration. The Quakers continued to occupy the building until 1947. It still survives but is currently empty and decaying.

A more immediate spur for the foundation of Toynbee Hall may well have been a pamphlet written in 1883 by Andrew Mearns, a Congregationalist clergyman, that focused on the 'abject' poor of the city. Published in the pages of the influential *Pall Mall Gazette*, Mearns's emotive text galvanised – and shocked – public opinion. Entitled *The Bitter Cry of Outcast London: An Inquiry into the Condition of the Abject Poor*, the pamphlet explored the East End and described not just the physical horrors of poverty and slum life but also the moral decay that can accompany overcrowding – sensationally suggesting incest was a significant consequence of slum life. For Mearns poverty, and its resultant evil, was a cancer in the heart of society and, by implication, represented a fatal threat to all: '. . . seething in the very centre of our great cities, concealed by the thinnest crust of civilisation and decency, is a vast mass of moral corruption, of heart-breaking misery and absolute godlessness, and . . . scarcely anything has been done to take into this awful slough the only influences that purify or remove it.' Mearns's emphasis on the need to deal with the spiritual and moral evils of poverty and slum living must have been a prime influence on the Barnetts, as it was on others establishing city missions with the aim of spreading light and education amongst the poor. Mearns's writing was also a significant influence on the establishment in 1884 of the Royal Commission on the Housing of the Working Classes and subsequently on the Housing of the Working Classes Act of 1885.

Within this context Toynbee Hall was pioneering. It was the first of many such 'University Settlements' where volunteer middle-class 'settlement workers', including privileged students from Oxford and Cambridge Universities, made a social contribution by spending some time working among the East End's poor. Barnett was the Hall's first Warden, and the building, designed by Elijah Hoole to replace MacPherson's bleak warehouse conversion, speaks volumes. It was conceived as a university college-type building, informal, gabled, in vaguely early-seventeenth-century 'Vicarage-Gothic' style, with the hint of a great dining hall, and it looked onto a little garden quadrangle that was approached – college-style – from a gatehouse on Commercial Street.

Toynbee Hall and the 'University Settlement' movement was described in 1902 in somewhat light-hearted manner by Howard Angus Kennedy: 'The wise men came from the East; and now, thank heaven! a few of them are going back there – back to the . . . East-End of London. In that densely-peopled wilderness they are settling, in little colonies, to live helpful and simple lives among the poor, not as missionaries or as "superior persons" but as neighbours, brothers, and fellow-citizens.' Kennedy invited his readers to visit Whitechapel and suggested that when . . .

> . . . you have passed through the arched entry of Toynbee Hall you might imagine yourself in the 'quad' of some old college at Oxford or Cambridge. There is a feeling of refinement and distinction in the very air. In front, an ivy-clad porch; on one hand, a turreted library rising from its cloistered foundation; on the other, a dove-cote and a clock-tower. The illusion is deepened when you enter the spacious dining hall and hear the unmistakable 'Varsity accent of the diners; but . . . these Oxonians and Cantabs have become naturalised and enthusiastic Londoners – for London's sake.

Kennedy then described the varied after-dinner missions of the diners:

> . . . three or four have gone off to manage clubs for working-men or for the 'old boys' of some neighbouring Board school; one is going round arranging for parental payments to the Children's Country Holiday Fund, and another is presiding over a conference on old age pensions, or the water supply . . . while a couple of others have volunteered to patrol the streets – narrow and gloomy like mountain gorges, bounded on either hand by the forbidding fronts of common lodging-houses – to investigate a complaint that the street lighting is not equal to the needs of such a doubtful locality. Festoons of fairy lamps begin to twinkle and glow among the creepers that beautify the 'quad'; and presently the people of the neighbourhood will flock in to enjoy an open-air concert.[36]

Much of Toynbee Hall survives today and it continues its work, although now modified in response to the changing times. But sadly the gatehouse and the building on Commercial Street behind which the Hall had sheltered – and which must have done much to create the cloistered and collegiate atmosphere – were destroyed by bombing in the Second World War.

Toynbee Hall was not the only example of what Charles Booth was to describe as 'University Culture'. For in 1892, Barnett, in collaboration with a rich and enlightened benefactor named Passmore Edwards, opened a handsome public library on Whitechapel High Street, just to the south of Toynbee Hall. And less than a decade after that, in 1901, Barnett opened a public art gallery next to the library.

The roots of this enterprise lay in the mid 1880s when Barnett and his wife Henrietta took to holding exhibitions of paintings each Easter in St Jude's Church, next to Toynbee Hall on Commercial Street. Barnett firmly believed that artistic beauty had to be brought to the East End, to counter the 'paralysing and degrading sights of our streets' and, as he put it, to cater to the 'souls' needs' of his humble 'neighbours' in Spitalfields and Whitechapel.[37] While the exhibitions were on, Barnett would explain the works on show to anyone who would listen. But he clearly felt these occasional exhibitions were not enough, and the creation of a permanent gallery became his great – and crowning – project. He was determined to demonstrate that 'East Enders were just as capable of appreciating good pictures as West Enders', indeed were perhaps more receptive to them because, as he argued, 'Drab streets, dark rooms and the litter of a crowded life' had made people less, not more, colour blind.[38] He managed to raise the £6,000 needed to buy the site in just a fortnight in 1897.

The new Whitechapel Art Gallery not only contained art but, as designed in inventive Art Nouveau manner by Charles Harrison Townsend, was a work of art itself. Much like Robson's earlier Board Schools – and in the manner promoted in the 1880s by the novelist Walter Besant with his fictional East London 'Palace of Delight' – the art gallery embodied the notion that the introduction of architectural beauty of the highest possible order within the dismal East End streets was a key means of elevating East End society. And it was popular. In 1901 Horace Warner took photographs in the gallery of local children contemplating morally improving and escapist work by Sir Edward Burne-Jones. Presumably it was Warner who had taken the children there, but if so he was only doing what the gallery's founders had intended.[39]

Barnett was not the only enlightened churchman in the area who wanted to make manifest the truth of the biblical aphorism that 'Man shall not live by bread alone' (Matthew 4:4). Reverend William Rogers of St Botolph's Bishopsgate, whose City parish extended north-east into Spitalfields, also believed that his religious duties involved education and social work. In the early 1890s he drew together funds and various of the parish's charitable endowments to pay for the construction, on the City edge of Spitalfields, of what became known as the Bishopsgate Institute. The building – offering information and inspiration – aimed to cater for City workers and the poor of a particularly impoverished part of Spital-fields, including the adjoining slum quarters of Frying Pan Alley, Petticoat Lane and 'Dorset Street' (see page 529). There was a main door on Bishopsgate for the respectable and aspiring City clerks and a rear door on 'Duke Street' (now Fort Street) for the costermongers and market workers intent on self-improvement. Inside were a hall for lectures, concerts and public meetings, a reading room where journals could be perused and a library for more serious study. Completed in 1895, the institute anticipated the Whitechapel Art Gallery by being a building that not only had a noble cause but also a noble appearance, intended to beautify the city. Again the architect was Charles Harrison Townsend working in a wonderful, individual, ornamental and free-form historicist style. The Whitechapel Gallery and the Bishopsgate Institute continue to play vital roles in the artistic and intellectual life of Spitalfields and the East End, indeed in the life of London – as originally intended – which is a powerful testament to the wisdom and sound thinking of their founders.

However praiseworthy some of these philanthropic enterprises may have been, they did not, of course, really address the physical problems of the East End with its run-down streets, slum dwellings housing a teeming population, and wholly inadequate sanitation. But during the second half of the nineteenth century, some attempts were made to improve the built environment and to create decent homes for Spitalfields' working people, or at least for the portion of the area's poor that was perceived, by their philanthropic betters, to be industrious and 'deserving'.

One of the many thousands of items on display at the Great Exhibition of 1851 was an experimental 'Model Dwelling' for the urban working class. Supported by Prince Albert himself in his capacity as President of the 'Society for Improving the Condition of the Labouring Classes' and designed by the society's 'honorary architect' Henry Roberts, it was pre-served when the Exhibition closed and was re-erected on Kennington Common, where it can still be seen. It's a modest two-storey dwelling – essentially a modular design capable of extension horizontally or vertically

The Bishopsgate Institute, on the corner of Bishopsgate and Brushfield Street, soon after it opened in 1895. With its library, reading room and lecture hall it was intended to bring intellectual and spiritual light into the dark and dismal slums and commercial enclaves of Bishopsgate and Spitalfields. Designed by Charles Harrison Townsend for the Reverend William Rogers, the enlightened Rector of St Botolph's Bishopsgate, it continues to make a significant contribution to life in the City and the East End.

to create terraces or tall tenement blocks – and was clearly intended to be economical and utilitarian. Even so, the prototype dwelling still boasts functionally unnecessary ornament – diluted Elizabethan in manner – to give it a cultural pedigree and so, by the conventions of the time, to elevate the construction from mere building to architecture. This, presumably, reflects the Prince's influence and taste. But far more important than its decorative flourishes is the staircase serving the first-floor flats, which is exposed and open to the elements. The idea behind it was to render the staircase secure by making it visible, so that police could see if vagrants were squatting there, and to make it more hygienic by allowing it to be well ventilated and washed by the rain. And it was this open staircase, functioning much like a vertical street, sometimes combined with open-access galleries rather than internal corridors, that became one of the key strategies in the design of later-nineteenth-century working-class dwellings.

Not that it was a wholly novel idea at the time of the Great Exhibition. Since the mid 1830s Roberts had been involved in the design of experimental housing blocks, mostly for the 'labouring class', and in 1849 had given his ideas mature expression with a scheme for the Society in Streatham Street, Bloomsbury. Three blocks were set around a courtyard, with each incorporating cast-iron-fronted access staircases and open stairs of masonry, which in addition to being secure and hygienic were supposed – in theory at least – to be fire-resistant. In addition each of the forty-eight family apartments had its own water closet – an unheard-of amenity at the time for such humble homes – with some shared amenities, such as coal storage. The open-staircase design became a key feature of several Spital-fields philanthropic housing schemes – notably, as we shall see, in the Rothschild Buildings, completed in 1887 in the heart of the 'Flower and Dean Street' slum.

Tenements designed by philanthropic bodies for the labouring classes and the 'deserving' poor made an early appearance in Spitalfields. One of the first was the gaunt five-storey Albert Family Dwellings erected in Deal Street in 1848. More impressive and important was the large block constructed in 1863 on the corner of the newly extended Commercial Street and 'White Lion Street' (now Folgate Street). This was the initiative of the American banker, merchant and philanthropist George Peabody and was the first of his many London tenement dwellings 'to ameliorate the condition of the poor and needy' of London, 'and to promote their comfort and happiness.[40] Designed by Henry A. Darbishire, the block did not incorporate the novelties of open staircases and access galleries – instead access was internal in traditional manner – but it was solid and handsome. Formed of two ranges meeting at a curved corner on the junction of 'White Lion Street' and Commercial Street, the scheme was given a significant, if economic, urban presence. The simple flats were 'subsidised' by the creation of shops along Commercial Street. In somewhat Renaissance manner there is a mezzanine storey above the shops, which is topped by minimal cornicing and set in a rusticated wall so that the Commercial Street frontage looks – strange as it may seem – rather like a rudimentary palazzo. Also there's a spattering of robust, brick-built classical detail around the curved corner, and a number of Baroque gables. Inside there were water closets on landings, one per pair of flats; and the top storey, with its ranges of closely spaced windows, contained communal laundries, drying rooms and bathrooms.

The block when complete must have appeared a paradise on earth to those still crowded into the slums surviving nearby to the east of Commercial Street, notably around 'Great Pearl Street' and 'Flower and Dean Street'. True, there was some contemporary adverse criticism of the accommodation: *The Builder* complained that the flats had no entrance lobbies and that only living rooms had fireplaces. The *Survey of London*, on the other hand, concludes that these flats, in the forefront of London's tenement building programme, were 'an important step towards the proper housing of the poor of East London.'[41]

The word 'poor', however, requires some qualification here. Those housed in this block were the upper echelons of the industrious 'deserving poor' of Spitalfields. They were not its most desperate inhabitants (though perhaps it was hoped that the flats' attractions would spur on the poorest to aspire to them). The rents per week in the block ranged from two shillings and sixpence for a single room to five shillings for a three-roomed flat. Most of the flats contained two rooms and cost three and sixpence or four shillings per week. To afford such accommodation the family breadwinner had to be in reasonable and regular employment and, of course, lead a respectable life in order to pass the vetting process overseen by Peabody's trustees. The financial, and perhaps the social, requirements ensured that the flats were beyond the grasp of the most humble artisans, even if in regular employment, at a time when a labourer earned about £1 a week – or perhaps twenty-five shillings if he possessed a few basic skills.

The Peabody Buildings, on the corner of White Lion Street/Folgate Street and Commercial Street, soon after their completion in 1863. This was the first of George Peabody's philanthropic housing projects in London and provided flats, of various sizes, for the Spitalfields 'industrious' and respectable poor. On the ground floor, on Commercial Street, were shops. Communal facilities – such as laundries and drying-rooms – were provided.

And those few journeymen silk weavers still active in Spitalfields, who had earned on average as little as five and sixpence per week in 1849 (see page 376), would have received little more in the mid 1860s, particularly given that their trade had been further undermined by the abolition in 1860 of duties on imported silk, notably from France.[42] For such people, living in a flat in the Peabody Buildings must have remained a pipe dream.

If enterprises such as the Peabody Buildings – serving the 'aristocracy' of the Spitalfields poor – could do little to help the poorest inhabitants of Commercial Street, then what was to be done about those who lived in the Nichol slum in Shoreditch, or in the festering 'Flower and Dean Street' Rookery near Toynbee Hall, or in the road running at right angles to Commercial Street that in 1901 was to be described as 'the worst street in London', 'Dorset Street' (see pages 543–9)? This was a question that pre-occupied many Londoners in the 1880s.

'Flower and Dean Street', along with neighbouring Thrawl and Went-worth Streets, had originally been laid out and constructed in the late seventeenth century, and by the early 1880s all of them had long-established and wretched reputations as places of physical decay, danger, squalor and vice. The construction of the southern portion of Commercial Street spelt the end for some bad streets, courts and houses, but it seems likely that their populations simply migrated to what was left of 'Flower and Dean' and Thrawl Streets, which – in consequence – became worse. In 1883 the journalist and social observer James Greenwood, writing of 'Flower and Dean Street', noted that it had been a slum street for fifty years and that, despite its location 'within a short distance . . . of the heart of the centre of the City of London' and despite recent improvements to the area, it was 'perhaps the foulest and most dangerous street in the whole metropolis . . . as appalling a stronghold of ruffianism and vice as ever disgraced civilisation.' Greenwood described the physical extent and bound-aries of the rookery: ' . . . from Commercial Street . . . to Brick Lane . . . a square quarter of a mile' comprising 'Thrawl Street and Great and Little Keat Street . . . all knitted together in a tangle of alleys and courts of the worst kind', with the 'ugliest . . . of all' being 'Flower and Dean Street'.[43]

Jerry White, who has written the definitive history of the 'Flower and Dean Street' Rookery, explains that the essential problem besetting the twenty-seven courts, streets and alleys packed into the square quarter-mile of the neighbourhood 'revolved around casual or seasonal employment, starvation wages, a heartless system of poor relief and brutalising living conditions.' The prevailing contemporary view of the rookery was expressed by the *Tower Hamlets Independent* on 19 November 1881 when it proclaimed: 'Flower and Dean Street, Spitalfields, is associated in most people's minds with vice, immorality and crime in their most hideous shapes, and rightly so, for ... there is no street in any part of the Metropolis that has for its inhabitants a like number of the dangerous class.' The street was packed with common lodging houses of the lowest sort, where a place in a communal bed could be purchased for a few pence a night and where prostitutes could with ease entertain their clients. Using census returns White has calculated that the thirty-one common lodging houses in 'Flower and Dean Street' in 1871 contained 902 people, with the total population of the street on the day of the census being 1,078.[44] About ten years earlier, probably in 1860, John Binny – Henry Mayhew's collaborator on volume four of *London Labour and the London Poor*, published in 1861 – toured the 'Flower and Dean Street' area while compiling his text about London's 'street-walkers'. Protected by police officers he entered a house in 'George Street' (later Lolesworth Street, running south off 'Flower and Dean Street') to discover it 'principally occupied by females from 18 to 30 years of age, all prostitutes', and in Wentworth Street went into a brothel 'kept by a woman, a notorious character ... repeatedly in custody for robbing drunken men ...'[45]

In 1883, in *The Bitter Cry of Outcast London*, Andrew Mearns evoked the horrors of slum living without referring to specific examples, but it seems highly likely that the descriptions he used to startle and activate his God-fearing middle-class readers were inspired by descents into the 'Flower and Dean Street' Rookery and the Nichol:

> Few who will read these pages have any conception of what these pestilential human rookeries are, where ... amidst horrors ... tens of thousands are crowded together ... To get into them you have to penetrate courts reeking with poisonous and malodorous gases arising from accumulations of sewage and refuse scattered in all directions and often flowing beneath your feet; courts, many of them which the sun never penetrates, which are never visited by a breath of fresh air, and which rarely know the virtues of a drop of cleansing water. You have to ascend rotten staircases, which threaten to give way beneath every step ... You have to grope your way along dark and filthy passages swarming with vermin. Then, if you are not

driven back by the intolerable stench, you may gain admittance to the dens in which these thousands of beings . . . herd together.

The average size of many of the rooms in these rookery houses was, suggested Mearns, 'eight feet square', with walls and ceilings . . .

> . . . black with the accretions of filth which have gathered upon them through long years of neglect . . . it is running down the walls; it is everywhere . . . should you have ascended to the attic, where at least some approach to fresh air might be expected to enter from open or broken window, you look out upon the roofs and ledges of lower tenements, and discover that the sickly air which finds its way into the room has to pass over the putrefying carcases of dead cats or birds, or viler abominations still . . . as to furniture – you may perchance discover a broken chair, the tottering relics of an old bedstead, or the mere fragment of a table; but more commonly you will find rude substitutes for these things in the shape of rough boards resting upon bricks, an old hamper or box turned upside down, or more frequently still, nothing but rubbish and rags.

Mearns then turned to the inhabitants of these dreadful places. His observations are emotive and calculated for effect but now seem odd in their generality and the absence of any reference to place, date or specific source:

> Every room in these rotten and reeking tenements houses a family, often two. In one cellar a sanitary inspector reports finding a father, mother, three children, and four pigs! In another room a missionary found a man ill with small-pox, his wife just recovering from her eighth confinement, and the children running about half naked and covered with dirt. Here are seven people living in one underground kitchen, and a little dead child lying in the same room. Elsewhere is a poor widow, her three children, and a child who had been dead thirteen days. Her husband, who was a cabman, had shortly before committed suicide . . . Here you are choked as you enter by the air laden with particles of the superfluous fur pulled from the skins of rabbits, rats, dogs and other animals in their preparation for the furrier. Here the smell of paste and of drying match-boxes, mingling with other sickly odours, overpowers you; or it may be the fragrance of stale fish or vegetables, not sold on the previous day, and kept in the room overnight.

But Mearns had worse to offer in his dramatic – perhaps melodramatic – rendition of the lives of London's 'abject poor'. 'Wretched as these rooms are they are beyond the means of many', who:

. . . take refuge at night in one of the common lodging houses that abound. These are often the resorts of thieves and vagabonds of the lowest type, and some are kept by receivers of stolen goods. In the kitchen men and women may be seen cooking their food, washing their clothes, or lolling about smoking and gambling. In the sleeping room are long rows of beds on each side, sometimes 60 or 80 in one room. In many cases both sexes are allowed to herd together without any attempt to preserve the commonest decency. But there is a lower depth still. Hundreds cannot even scrape together the two pence required to secure them the privilege of resting in those sweltering common sleeping rooms, and so they huddle together upon the stairs and landings, where it is no uncommon thing to find six or eight in the early morning.[46]

Poverty could have appalling consequences, and Mearns was only one of many in the 1880s who felt obliged to draw them to the public's notice. In 1889 the playwright and journalist George R. Sims, in *How the Poor Live*, also revealed in unsettling manner how they died. He reported the findings of a sanitary inspector named Mr Wrack who seems to have been forever stumbling upon decaying cadavers in Spitalfields houses, their families too poor to afford a burial. At 24 'Princes Street', Spitalfields (now 5 Princelet Street and only a few blocks north of 'Flower and Dean Street'), for example, Wrack 'found in the second floor front room the dead body of an aged woman, who died on Christmas Day.' She had been dead ten days but the room continued to be occupied 'by the daughter of the deceased . . . who lived and slept in the same room.'[47]

Such heart-rending suffering should, surely, have been sufficient in itself to persuade people of the need for action. But what ultimately prompted the Victorian professional classes, legislators and philanthropists to do something was not so much pity as embarrassment and fear, or, as Jerry White puts it, 'street crime, prostitution, the threat of revolt, expensive pauperism, infectious disease spreading to London – the whole panoply of shame of this "boldest blotch on the face" of the capital of the civilised world.'[48] The destruction of the 'Flower and Dean Street' Rookery had long been contemplated. Small inroads had been made in the late 1830s and the construction of Commercial Street, lined with large modern warehouses, factories and commercial premises, had nibbled off the western edge of the rookery. But more drastic action was required. In June 1875, therefore, the Cross Act, named after Richard Cross, the

Conservative Home Secretary, was passed to increase the state's power of compulsory purchase and thereby to help eradicate London's most criminalised, overcrowded, squalid and structurally decaying slum areas.

As Jerry White notes, the passage of the Bill through Parliament had been 'watched with keen interest by members of the Whitechapel Board of Guardians, already notorious among the East End casual poor for their ruthless operation of the Poor Laws.'[49] The Guardians included among their members Canon Barnett, the future co-founder of Toynbee Hall and Rector of St Jude's, whose parish included part of the 'Flower and Dean Street' Rookery. Under the new Act, twelve ratepayers could demand an area be destroyed if they could prove it was 'unhealthy'. Barnett took the lead and on 25 January 1876 the Whitechapel Board of Guardians represented the whole of the area from Fashion Street (immediately north of 'Flower and Dean Street') south to Whitechapel High Street as an 'unhealthy area'. It included the site of the future Toynbee Hall. Barnett and sixteen other Guardians signed the representation, emphasising that 'the said Area is fruitful of sickness, misery, pauperism and crime within the Whitechapel Union.'[50]

As Jerry White observes, the Guardians' recommendation meant the 'destruction of an area at that time home to an estimated 4,354 people . . . all of whom would be made homeless if the Guardians' plea were accepted.'[51] But the new legislation had a flaw – at least as far as the moral crusaders were concerned. Buildings could not be demolished if they were merely in immoral or unsavoury areas – they had also to be shown to be unfit for human habitation. The Whitechapel Medical Health Officer therefore became involved, and by the time the Guardians' representation for demolition was forwarded to the Metropolitan Board of Works (MBW), the body responsible for demolition, two-thirds of the 'Flower and Dean Street' Rookery had been removed from the clearance scheme.[52] The order for the Improvement Scheme was finally signed by Richard Cross on 14 May 1877, but delays in carrying out evictions, and fears about the consequences of making at a stroke over 1,800 people homeless, meant that demolition did not actually take place until the autumn of 1883. Even then only a quarter of 'Flower and Dean Street' was destroyed and 'much of the worst [of the area] still remained – including the majority of the common lodging houses'.[53] Ironically, although these lodging houses were the buildings put to the most immoral use in the area (most were, at least in part, low brothels), they were also generally the soundest: their profitability meant that their owners were generally inclined to maintain them, and they had, in any case, been made subject to police supervision since the early 1850s.

In a further twist of fate, within only a few decades the huge and gaunt tenement blocks built on the site of the 'Flower and Dean Street' Rookery, mostly to house Jewish families flooding into East London to escape persecution in Tsarist Russia and Poland, had themselves become slums (see page 617). Rebuilding and rehousing, it was to become apparent, did not in themselves root out poverty.

THE CHILDREN OF THE GHETTO
The Jewish East End

The fate that finally befell the remains of the 'Flower and Dean Street' Rookery is one of the strangest stories of Spitalfields and relates not just to the new mechanism of funding and constructing philanthropic housing, but also – and more dramatically – to events that had their starting point many hundreds of miles away. Just as a wave of religious persecution in France brought the Huguenots to Spitalfields in the late seventeenth century, so in the nineteenth the brutal pogroms in Eastern Europe resulted in tens of thousands of Jews moving into the area. In the process, the East End was once again transformed and remade.

A Jewish community had, in fact, been well established in the East End long before the late nineteenth century. Its founding father, Antonio Fernandes Carvajal, who was Portuguese by origin, though long based in the Spanish Canary Islands, settled in London as early as 1635. He was a wine importer, and also appears to have been a Marrano – that is, a Jew who had been obliged to convert to Christianity. His adoption of Catholicism and, in the process, a non-Jewish name, possibly suggests a connection with his namesake, the Spanish missionary Doña Luisa Carvajal (see chapter 4), although no clear links have ever been established.[1]

This was not the safest of times for someone from such a background. The Jews had been expelled from England in 1290, and under the terms of the 1401 Act Concerning the Burning of Heretics (*De Heretico Comburendo*), to be a religious Jew was an offence potentially punishable by burning at the stake. Carvajal therefore regularly attended Mass at the embassy chapel. It was a move that freed him from any obligation to attend Anglican services, and, of course, made it absolutely clear to the authorities that he was not a practising Jew.

Times, though, were changing. In 1641 the Long Parliament repealed the 1401 Act. Then, in 1654, the Republican Commonwealth under Oliver

Cromwell held a conference at Whitehall Palace to discuss the possible readmission of Jews to England. This was a commendable act of religious toleration. It was, however, not an entirely altruistic one. That year bitter commercial and trade rivalry between England and Spain spilt over into war, which led to an unlikely alliance between Cromwell's Protestant Republic and the Catholic French monarchy. The Commonwealth government, noting the valuable trade with Spain and its South American colonies established by Portuguese and Spanish Jews in Amsterdam, clearly saw a commercial opportunity for a competing mercantile endeavour if Jews from the Low Countries could be encouraged to move to England. No doubt acting under Carvajal's advice, Cromwell invited Rabbi Menasseh ben Israel from Amsterdam's Portuguese synagogue to London, to explore in detail the possibility of a Jewish community being established in the city. The Whitehall Palace conference confirmed that there was no law against Jews living in England. This in turn opened the way to resettlement. Carvajal now felt sufficiently at home to take English citizenship and, as the ban on Jewish worship in his new country was lifted, he also seized the opportunity to convert to Judaism. He seems to have had a close relationship with the Lord Protector and his regime, and probably acted as an informer on Royalist activity in the Low Countries.

With Cromwell's blessing and protection, a small group of Portuguese and Spanish Jews, mostly from Amsterdam, started to move to the capital, and under Carvajal's leadership, established themselves in and around Duke's Place, Aldgate, a strategically significant location on the edge of the City. They were allowed to meet privately for prayer here and to lease land for a cemetery. They were also given permission to settle in English colonies. Immigration was nevertheless carefully controlled. Only 'recommended individuals' were allowed to settle in this new homeland.[2]

The close association between the new Jewish community and the Commonwealth regime could have spelt trouble for the settlers when the monarchy was restored in 1660, particularly as in that same year the City of London petitioned for the expulsion of the newcomers on the grounds that, by the simple expedient of selling cloth more cheaply, they were managing to export more of it than their English merchant rivals. Sensibly, however, the new Royalist government chose to ignore the City and to admire instead the Jews' business acumen in achieving better profits from bulk sales at low rates than from meagre sales at high rates. For their part, the Jewish community, realising that the City as an institution had to be mollified, started a tradition of annually presenting a gift of plate to the Lord Mayor. In 1664 Jewish merchants were confirmed in their right of habitation provided they conducted themselves 'quietly and peaceably with due obedience to His Majesty's laws and without scandal to his Government.'[3]

A quarter of a century later, in 1689, a successful petition against the levying of high taxes from the Jews revealed that by now the community consisted of sixty to eighty families, most of the merchants among them being endenizened, or 'naturalised', with the privileges and civil rights of Englishmen. It was at about this time that the Great Synagogue was built by Ashkenazi Jews in Duke's Place, Aldgate (Ashkenazi being the medieval Hebrew word for German). It was a public declaration of the status of the community, the legitimacy of its religious practices and of its intention to stay. (The Great Synagogue was later rebuilt in grand neo-classical style in 1788 to the designs of James Spiller but was destroyed by bombing in 1941.) Another synagogue, Bevis Marks, built by Sephardi Jews, followed in 1701 (Sephardi being the medieval Hebrew word for Spanish). Bevis Marks still survives as one of the most intact and beautiful of London's earlier sacred buildings.

But if the community was now firmly established it nevertheless continued to be a very small one. In London in 1695 there were a mere 560 Portuguese or Spanish Sephardi Jews and 200 German Ashkenazi.[4] Compared with the 20,000 or so Huguenots settled in nearby Spitalfields by 1710 their numbers seem almost insignificant. This new Jewish population nevertheless had certain features in common with its French predecessors. Like the Huguenots, the Jews were generally viewed by Londoners as a respectable merchant community. Like the Huguenots, their religious practices were accepted whereas Dissenters – such as Quakers – were penalised. Perhaps not surprisingly there seems to have been a certain empathy and mutual respect between the two immigrant populations, based in part on a shared belief in the virtues of honest trade and in Old Testament teaching, and inspired by a history of shared suffering at the hands of Roman Catholic authorities. This empathy must have resulted in significant mercantile collaborations that are, sadly, seemingly undocumented.

For the next half-century or so, the number of Jews in London continued to rise slowly. By 1753, it has been calculated that there were perhaps 2,000 Sephardi Jews and 4,000 Ashkenazi in the capital, mostly still living in the largely Portuguese-speaking 'village' of Duke's Place.[5] At this point in the community's history they enjoyed 'far more social accept-ance in Britain than in most European countries',[6] those who were not merchants worked in the few professions open to them, most notably as doctors or notaries. Thereafter, thanks to the stability and prosperity of this community, its numbers started to rise exponentially, and as they did so, and as the notion of entry for 'recommended individuals' only had col-lapsed with the demise of the Commonwealth, more and more migrants were attracted. The community inevitably became more diverse. Once, it had consisted of only the successful and prosperous. Now, while a signifi-cant rich and powerful stratum continued to flourish at the top, it was increasingly mirrored by a lower stratum of marginal and criminalised Jews who found themselves living among, and competing with, the poor-est elements of the English and Irish communities in London.

The more questionable element of this lower echelon is well represented by Isaac Solomon – the Spitalfields-based fence and renowned escapee from justice who almost certainly provided Charles Dickens with the model for Fagin in *Oliver Twist*. Rather more admirable, though still from the humbler end of the social spectrum, was the pugilist Daniel Mendoza. Of Portuguese Jewish origin, he was born and lived in Bethnal Green (a blue plaque marks his former home in Paradise Row, off Bethnal Green Road), worked in Aldgate for a tea dealer and then achieved heroic status as a prize-fighter. He achieved twenty-seven knock-out victories in a row and in 1792 was declared the boxing champion of England. In the process he not only revolutionised boxing technique by introducing nim-bleness and fighting tactics, or 'scientific style', into a sport that had been basically little more than a slogging contest previously, but also – as a brave, intelligent and skilled fighting man – did much to win Jewish peo-ple popular respect.

Even though he retired in the 1820s his reputation survived, and surely influenced the very positive appreciation of East London's Jewish com-munity that appeared in 1840 in the Parliamentary report into the working conditions of 'Hand-Loom Weavers'. James Mitchell, who compiled the section on the 'East of England', noted that 'physically the Jews are very strong', attributing this to the fact that 'they love good eating' while being 'very moderate as to drink'. Mitchell also observed that 'every information respecting the institutions amongst the descendents [sic] of the signally distinguished ancient nation of Israel, cannot fail to be interesting . . . to

Above: *an illustration of a 'Jew Old-clothes Man' that appeared in Henry Mayhew's* London Labour and the London Poor *in 1851. Below: Fagin and Bill Sikes get their first view of Oliver Twist, inside a well-secured room in a London rookery. Fagin was modelled on the Spitalfields-based fence Isaac Solomon.*

those ... looking forward to what may be the future destiny of that people', and was particularly impressed by 'the greatest efforts ... made by the more opulent to afford to their poorer brethren the means of education, both civil and religious, and also the means ... taken to teach the boys industrious trades by which they ... may become more useful members of society.'[7]

In the late 1840s the poorer sector of London's Jewish population naturally drew the attention of Henry Mayhew when he was compiling the research that he would use in *London Labour and the London Poor*, published in 1851. He noted that 'the number of Jews now in England is computed as 35,000' of whom 'more than one half, or about 18,000, reside in London.'[8] He also observed that 'foreign Jews' – meaning itinerant Jews originating from such places as Smyrna – were 'always numerous in London', with two-thirds residing 'in the city, or the streets adjacent to the eastern boundaries of the city.'[9] His view was that Jews 'prefer to trade in such commodity as is not subjected to a fixed price, so that there may be abundant scope for speculation, and something like a gambler's chance for profit or loss', and recorded that 'wholesale trades in foreign commodities ... now principally or solely in the hands of the Jews, often as importers and exporters, included watches and jewels, sponges – fruits ... such as oranges, lemons ... shells, tortoises, parrots and foreign birds ... snuffs, cigars and pipes.'[10] Among the 'street-Jews' he listed dealers in old clothes (for example, in Petticoat Lane) and 'street Jew-girls' (some of them stallholders) who, he observed, were 'often pert and ignorant [but] not unchaste.'[11] When he explored Petticoat Lane he found, in addition to the old-clothes trade, a thriving business in 'Jewish sweet-meats' and 'highly-glazed cakes and pastry', which were much prized by gentile children.

Another of Mayhew's culinary observations may well be linked with the early days of what is now regarded as a quintessentially British dish: fish and chips. While walking in the vicinity of The Lane, Mayhew wrote, he heard the cry of: 'Fish, fried fish! Ha'penny; fish, fried fish!' – clearly a sufficiently exotic cry for him to feel it worth recording.[12] Now, fish fried in 'the Jewish fashion' – in other words, battered – is a Spanish/Portuguese Jewish culinary tradition that was probably introduced into London during the second half of the seventeenth century. A hundred years later Thomas Jefferson mentioned eating it during his visit to London in 1786, and in the late 1830s Dickens describes Fagin as living near a 'fried fish warehouse'. At what point battered fish started to be served with baked potatoes or fried chips is not clear, and where it was first served is much disputed: both Lancashire and East London have claimed the honour. Some argue that the first shop to sell fried fish and potatoes was opened in Cleveland Street, East London in the early 1860s by a Jewish immigrant named Joseph Malin. Others have challenged every element of this and put forward a competing claim for Oldham. Be that as it may, if chips were being sold in the early 1860s then these would have been known as potatoes prepared by 'the French method'. And if the fish was battered in the Jewish manner, an intriguing proposition emerges for the origin of the great British meal of fish and chips. Arguably it's a marriage of battered and fried fish 'in the Jewish fashion', brought to London in the late seventeenth century by Portuguese Jews, and of potatoes prepared by 'the French method' and perhaps introduced in London at the same time by Huguenots – with both elements arguably brought together by an immigrant Jew in East London in the mid nineteenth century.

The arrival of fish and chips virtually coincided with the period when the composition of London's Jewish community began to change dramatically, as more Jews started to arrive from Russia and Tsarist-controlled Poland to escape increasingly harsh discrimination there. In contrast with London's established Jewish community these new arrivals tended to be of rural origin rather than urban, to be peasants rather than merchants, to possess few industrial skills, and although possessing rich cultural traditions, to lack more than elementary education. Needless to say, they were invariably miserably poor.

After 1881 their numbers greatly increased. In March of that year Tsar Alexander II was assassinated in St Petersburg by young revolutionaries. There was an immediate and vengeful reaction on the part of the authorities. And as police searched for culprits, civil liberties and personal freedom were suppressed, protesters of all kinds were arrested and the traditional victim – the Jew – blamed and crushed by officially orchestrated pogroms and anti-Semitic legislation. The initial flurry of spontaneous persecution was formalised by the May Laws – or 'Regulations concerning the Jews' – of 1882. These 'Laws' decreed that Jews were forbidden to settle anew outside towns or boroughs but must remain only in existing Jewish agricultural colonies; they could not obtain mortgages or deeds or leases on property, nor were they allowed to obtain powers of attorney to manage or dispose of their property; and they were forbidden to transact business on Sundays or on principal Christian holidays. Life was to be made difficult, if not impossible, for Jews within the Russian empire's 'Pale of Jewish Settlement', where these 'temporary' laws – as they were called – held force and where the majority of Jews lived. The natural reaction of Russian Jews was to flee, and by the summer of 1882 emigration from the 'Pale of Settlement' had reached immense proportions. Further pogroms followed, notably in 1903–6. It is now estimated that around 2 million Jews fled Russia and its empire between 1880 and 1914.

Of these desperate refugees several thousand arrived on the eastern edge of the City of London – in Whitechapel, Spitalfields and Aldgate – to join or to be near the East End's existing Jewish community. It must be said that they were not always welcome. A significant number of Jews who had been long established in London were less than delighted by the sudden influx of poor Russian and Polish peasants. They feared that the horde of newcomers could inspire a wave of English anti-Semitism and undo much that had been achieved during the previous two centuries or so to integrate the Jewish community into wider London society and win praise and respect. As the *Jewish Chronicle* argued on 12 August 1881, when discussing the arrival of the Eastern European Jews:

> Our fair fame is bound up with theirs; the outside world is not capable of making minute discrimination between Jew and Jew, and forms its opinions of Jews in general as much, *if not more*, from them than from the Anglicised portion of the Community. They retain all the habits of their former home and display no desire to assimilate . . . they appear altogether to forget that in accepting the hospitality of England, they owe a reciprocal duty of becoming Englishmen.[13]

The powerful, anglicised Jewish community had several options to prevent the anti-Semitic backlash it dreaded. It could dissuade Eastern European Jews from coming in the first place. It could encourage families that had arrived to return. It could persuade families to move on to the United States or the British colonies. Or it could deploy some of its resources to house as many Jewish families in London as it could, in reasonable accommodation and in a manner that would not provoke native Londoners.

Brushfield Street, although created only in the 1780s, marks the historic heart of Spitalfields. It runs from Roman-era Ermine Street (now Bishopsgate) across the edge of the Roman great north cemetery that later became the southern precinct of the twelfth-century Priory of St Mary and later still the Old Artillery Ground, which was built upon in the early 1680s to become Spitalfields' first large and coherent urban development. This view east along Brushfield Street shows the 1680s Gun Street on the right, 1920s and 1880s market buildings on the left and, in the distance, Nicholas Hawksmoor's Christ Church.

The north end of Brick Lane, at the corner of Sclater Street, with its traditional Sunday morning market still in operation. The corner building – number 125 Brick Lane – with its wide weavers' window at second-floor level, was built in 1778.

The south side of Fournier Street, built mostly from 1726 to 1730, with Christ Church at the west end. Number 20 is at the left.

23 Wilkes Street was built in 1723 by the speculating builder Marmaduke Smith. The design of the doorcase, with rusticated Doric pilasters, was popular in 1720s Spitalfields.

A very narrow court, running south of Fleur de Lis Street, photographed in the early 1970s and soon after demolished, with all trace of it obliterated. This was the last example in Spitalfields of once common late-eighteenth- or early-nineteenth-century cramped (in some cases, back-to-back) courtyard housing.

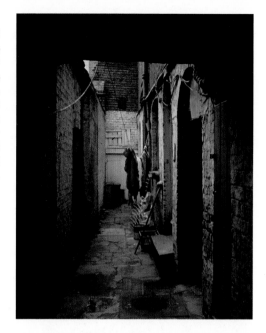

The trade sign of John Troake, a 'Strawchip & Leghorn Presser' (a supplier or maker of straw bonnets), who started business in 19 Elder Street some time soon after 1817. The house was then numbered 20, as can be seen. In the background is 36 Elder Street.

The staircase, from ground to first floor, of 27 Fournier Street, dated 1725. The house was built for the affluent master weaver Peter Bourdon, probably by William Tayler and Samuel Worrall. The details – twisted balusters, ramped handrails and carved tread ends – are very fine.

The basement kitchen of 36 Elder Street, built in 1725 by William Goswell. The room has partly been reconstructed in authentic manner; elements of the dresser are original.

The enfilade, at first-floor level, in 36 Elder Street (1725). The house is six windows wide at this floor level and the photograph is taken from a closet, looking across a parlour and stair landing, to a room on the corner with Folgate Street.

The first-floor front room of 15 Elder Street, built in 1727 by Thomas Bunce and Thomas Brown, and perhaps first occupied by the Payton silk-weaving family.

The splendid first-floor vaulted corridor created in the 1770s within the earlier Truman Brewery Directors' House on Brick Lane. This corridor was part of a sophisticated architectural route through the building that terminated at the first-floor boardroom, furnished with a fine mid-eighteenth-century Rococo ceiling, in which hung Gainsborough's portrait of Sir Benjamin Truman.

The galleried, top-lit synagogue – created in about 1862 – in the garden of the early-eighteenth-century 19 Princelet Street. The interior, notably the cast-iron stanchions supporting the gallery, appears to have been created using mass-produced, off-the-peg components.

Handsome tenement blocks forming Arnold's Circus at the heart of the former London County Council Boundary Estate. This pioneering example of public housing in London was opened by the Prince of Wales in 1900.

The Whitechapel Art Gallery, championed by Canon Barnett and intended to cater to the 'souls' needs' of his humble 'neighbours' in Spitalfields and Whitechapel. It was opened in 1901.

View looking west along Folgate Street, with Spital Square to the left and Elder Street to the right, showing the commercial towers spreading from the City of London and encroaching upon the historic core of Spitalfields.

Those who embraced the latter option felt a strong sense of urgency. They were worried that if the problem of mass immigration was not tackled swiftly there would be social unrest. In 1884, therefore, the Board of Guardians for the Relief of the Jewish Poor – founded in 1859 – set up a Sanitary Committee, to tackle the increasing problem of Jewish poverty in East London. This committee was soon joined by Baron Nathan Mayer Rothschild, later created 1st Lord Rothschild of Tring, the leading member of the most elevated circle of the Anglo-Jewish community. It was largely thanks to his involvement that the housing issue started to be tackled. In 1885 Rothschild became chairman of the East End Enquiry Commission, set up by the Council of the United Synagogue, and in this capacity oversaw the production of a report that concluded, much as the *Jewish Chronicle* had suggested, that the foreign 'poorer classes of the community' must 'upon arrival . . . imbibe notions proper to civilised life in this country' and that 'the physical conditions of the poor and their surroundings must be improved.'[14]

On 9 March 1885, six days after the report had been presented to the United Synagogue, Rothschild chaired a meeting at his banking house in the City that brought together 'the aristocracy of Anglo-Jewry: Lionel Cohen (president of the Jewish Board of Guardians), F. D. Mocatta (the philanthropic bullion broker), Claude Montefiore (the wealthy Biblical scholar and philanthropist), and Samuel Montagu (later Lord Swaythling, MP for Whitechapel).'[15] The meeting resolved to realise the recommendations of the report by forming a building company to be called 'The Four Per Cent Industrial Dwellings Company'. Its capital was to be £40,000, with 1,600 share issues of £25 each producing an average dividend of 4 per cent. This was a by now standard way to finance the construction of philanthropic working-class housing projects, and its ingenuity lay in its mix of altruism and capitalism. Those putting money into such a project were certainly not giving it away. On the other hand, to further a good cause, they were showing a willingness to accept possibly a lower return for their investment than they could achieve elsewhere.[16] It was an approach to building solid, economically constructed and hygienic, if generally not beautiful, subsidised housing. This would in due course be taken over in London in the 1890s by the newly formed London County Council and lead to one of its first great public-housing enterprises: the replacement of the seething and decaying Nichol with the splendid Boundary Estate (see pages 515–18).

Even so it was to be over a year before all the shares were sold and further money raised to allow building projects to start. By this time the site for the company's first project had been chosen – the cleared portion of the 'Flower and Dean Street' Rookery in what had become 'the heart of the Jewish quarter'.[17] Rothschild had purchased the site personally from the Metropolitan Board of Works in May 1885 and by October the plans of N. S. Joseph (who had been present at the meeting in Rothschild's bank and who became the Dwellings Company's architect) were accepted. Work finally began in mid 1886. The first of the 'model' buildings to be constructed was named Charlotte de Rothschild Dwellings, in memory of the mother of Nathan Rothschild, who since June 1885 had been Lord Rothschild, the first professing Jew to be a peer of the realm.

Soon known to their tenants simply as Rothschild Buildings, the scheme consisted of two parallel blocks of flats linked by a cross-wing, each six storeys high, above tall basements. The blocks were extremely sturdily built, with fire-proof concrete floors supported on iron joists, and with open entrance galleries containing staircases. Economy was the governing factor in their construction, with the result that the blocks were gaunt, with minimal ornamentation, and by their nature unlovely and unlovable. Ultimately these economic constraints led to maintenance problems. Rothschild Buildings were typical of much utilitarian working-class housing constructed in late-nineteenth-century London, which, as George Haw had observed, was 'more like warehouses than homes.'[18]

By the beginning of April 1887 the blocks, containing 198 flats, were complete and most had been let, at average rents of about five shillings per week, which was higher than anticipated but necessary to give the company's shareholders their 4 per cent return. The first tenants were largely Jewish immigrants, but there were also five policemen and a clergyman.[19] This community, within its tall blocks of flats, was initially marooned in a sea of decay and wasteland, with 'Flower and Dean Street's' surviving tottering buildings and common lodging houses still occupied by the remnants of the rookery's desperate slum dwellers.

The year after its completion Rothschild Buildings became part of the backdrop to events that were shaped by the old rookery buildings still surviving in portions of 'Flower and Dean Street' and its environs – and by their desperate occupants.

*The first blocks of the Rothschild Buildings – gaunt and forbidding if immensely
sturdy – were completed in the spring of 1887. This photograph, taken in 1902 from the
Commercial Street end of Thrawl Street, appeared in Jack London's* The People of the
Abyss, *published in 1903, where it is titled 'Working men's homes near Middlesex Street'.*

On the night of 31 August 1888 Mary Ann 'Polly' Nichols was found murdered in 'Buck's Row' (now Durward Street), Whitechapel, on the threshold of a gated stable yard, next to a handsome new London Board School. She had been grievously mutilated around the abdomen after being killed by a slashing cut to the throat. There was much blood on the scene, confirming that she had been attacked where the body was found. Shortly before her death Nichols was reported to have been 'living in Flowery Dean Street'[20] but on the night of her murder had been refused entry to the common lodging house she used at 18 Thrawl Street because she lacked the necessary fourpence for a bed.

Early in the morning of 8 September Annie Chapman found herself without enough money to pay for her night's lodging in 'Dorset Street' and so went out on the streets to earn a few pennies. Earlier she had probably been drinking in the Ten Bells public house on Commercial Street. At around six o'clock her body was found in the rear yard of 29 Hanbury Street, just beyond the threshold of the house's back door leading to the yard. Chapman had been killed and mutilated in a similar manner to Nichols, but had also had her uterus removed. Blood at the scene suggested she had been killed in the yard, but the sixteen people resident in the house at the time of the murder later told police they had heard nothing. Chapman was living at the time of her murder at 35 Dorset Street – a lodging house known as Crossingham's – but was also well known in many of the common lodging houses of the area.

On 30 September Elizabeth Stride was murdered at 'Dutfield's Yard', 'Berners Street' (now known as Henriques Street) off Commercial Road, and Catherine Eddowes was murdered in Mitre Square, Aldgate, near the Great Synagogue in Duke's Place. Both these women lived in 'Flower and Dean Street' – Stride at number 32, a common lodging house surviving opposite Rothschild Buildings, and Eddowes at number 55, a lodging house known as Cooney's. She had lived in the street with her common-law husband for seven years.

Stride's body was near the threshold to the yard and blood was still flowing from her neck when she was discovered. This – and the absence of any mutilation to the abdomen – suggested that the murderer might have fled before he could complete his grisly work. It was not absolutely clear if Stride had been killed where the body was found or if – for some reason – it had been deposited on that particular site after death. Eddowes, seemingly killed about an hour after Stride, was terribly mutilated – her

Number 29 Hanbury Street (the third house from the right) became infamous in September 1888 when Annie Chapman, the second of Jack the Ripper's 'canonical' victims, was found dead and mutilated in its back yard. This photograph was taken just before these houses were demolished in 1970.

face disfigured, ear cut, throat cut, disembowelled and a kidney removed and taken. The circumstances of this killing are the most intriguing of them all. Because police regularly patrolled the square, and thanks to the evidence of several passers-by and an alert ex-policeman watchman working near the crime scene, it was clear that the mutilated body was not in the square at 1.35 a.m. (when a woman answering Eddowes' description was apparently seen talking to a man there) but was at 1.45. Yet the injuries were such that they could scarcely have been inflicted in ten minutes. Moreover the notes of Police Surgeon Frederick George Brown who arrived at 2 a.m. suggest a suspicious absence of blood at the scene: he recorded that there was no evidence of 'spurting blood on the bricks or pavement around. No marks of blood below the middle of the body . . . there was no blood on the front of the clothes' although some 'clotted blood' was found 'after the body was removed'.[21] It therefore seems most likely that Eddowes was murdered elsewhere and that her body was dumped on the Mitre Square site, presumably from a carriage or cart.

The dual murders of Elizabeth Stride and Catherine Eddowes brought the East End to the point of hysteria. They also made the apprehension of the murderer a national political priority. A contributing factor here was the concern that mounting public fear was stoking and unleashing anti-Semitic frenzy. This had started to surface after the second murder – that of Annie Chapman. Eastern European Jews were relatively new in the East End, certainly in such large numbers, and the grisly and seemingly unprecedented nature of the murders made them appear – to many Londoners – to be the work of strangers. As the *Daily News* observed on 11 September 1888, the murders were 'foreign to the English style in crime'. It was in response to this growing wave of anti-Semitic feeling in the East End that Samuel Montagu – the Whitechapel MP and colleague of Lord Rothschild – offered a £100 reward for the discovery and conviction of the murderer.

Racial and religious tension was increased by the third and fourth murders. The body of Elizabeth Stride was found in a predominantly Jewish area of Whitechapel, and a Jewish connection to the death was implied by a witness (himself Jewish and named Israel Schwartz) who claimed to have seen a woman answering Stride's description being roughly handled by a pair of men, one of whom was apparently called 'Lipski'. Eddowes' body was found near a synagogue, not something that excited much immediate comment in itself, but an hour or so after her murder, at roughly

2.55 in the morning, a police constable found a dirty, blood-speckled rag (later confirmed as coming from the apron Eddowes was wearing at the time of her death) in the entrance to a tenement dwelling in Goulston Street, in the intensely Jewish area around Wentworth Street and Petticoat Lane. In the entrance there was also a chalk-written message stating: 'The Juwes are the men who will not be blamed for nothing.'

There was no evidence to connect this message with the murderer, and it's far from clear why the constable should have thought that a dirty rag discarded in the entrance to a tenement and an illiterate scrawled message were related to the Stride or Eddowes murders. Nor has it ever been explained why the police should have believed this obscure message to be so inflammatory that they immediately erased it, even before it was photographically recorded or authoritatively transcribed (several versions of the enigmatic wording exist). The assumption often made is that the message was obliterated because it was deemed to suggest that the murderer was Jewish and therefore might have inflamed local gentile opinion. But, if anything, the message seems to imply that the person who wrote it was anti-Semitic and therefore that Jack the Ripper (if he was its author) was not himself a Jew (assuming that the curious word 'Juwes' is indeed a misspelling of Jews). The whole episode – like so many other aspects of the Ripper murders – remains shrouded in mystery.

Curiously Thomas Barnardo, as he himself admitted, visited 32 Flower and Dean Street four days before the murder of Elizabeth Stride. He claimed to be there to gather information preparatory to establishing a scheme to save children from the 'contamination' of such low lodging houses. After Stride's murder Barnardo went to view her corpse, to confirm she was one of the women present during his visit. The police noted his presence in 'Flower and Dean Street' and in Whitechapel in general, along with his age and the medical training he had received that could have given him the ability to slice bodies with reasonable precision. Perhaps not altogether surprisingly, he was, for a while, regarded by the police as a person 'of interest' in their inquiries.[22]

The last of the five 'canonical' murders allegedly committed by Jack the Ripper took place on 9 November. The victim was Mary Jane Kelly and the location was her own lodging, in Miller's Court, off 'Dorset Street', just a few minutes' walk from 'Flower and Dean Street'. For some years Kelly had lived in Lolesworth Street (formerly 'George Street') running off 'Flower and Dean Street'.[23]

The Jack the Ripper murders reveal the darkest shades of late-nineteenth-century Spitalfields. All the victims were poor, vulnerable, and worked occasionally or regularly as prostitutes. Owing to the area's poverty and density of habitation, and to the predominantly itinerant and outcast proportion of its population, it was possible for a serial murderer to lurk there and strike unnoticed. The presence of a large police station (dating from the 1870s) on the corner of Commercial Street and Fleur de Lis Street, which would serve as the local headquarters for the hunt for the murderer (or murderers), proved no deterrent to the Ripper. Indeed the sites where Chapman's and Kelly's bodies were found were both less than four minutes' walk from it. And even though 'Flower and Dean Street' had been subject to recent improvements, it remained one of the most desperate locations in Spitalfields, its surviving collection of lodging houses the natural resort of the poor, dissolute and defenceless women who were the murderer's chosen victims.

One other thing is suggested by the geography of the murders. Elementary observation reveals that when their locations are marked on a map the first four 'canonical' murder sites generate a distinct geometrical form usually associated with the design of sacred buildings: if connected they form an almost regular lozenge or rhombus because, seemingly significantly, the murders took place – or bodies were placed – at roughly equal distances apart. The sites can also be connected to form a cross, with its two long arms and its two short arms being of equal lengths each side of its crossing point. This geometry could, of course, be accidental but it is more likely that it was carefully calculated because within the north–south axis of the rhombus a pair of overlapping circles can be described, which define a vesica piscis – one of the prime geometric forms of sacred geometry – while a larger vesica piscis, touching the murder sites, can be drawn to embrace the entire rhombus. The curious thing about this large, outer vesica piscis is that it cuts through Miller's Court, 'Dorset Street' – the site of the fifth and final 'canonical' murder.

The fact that the sites where the bodies were found can be linked to define a geometrically regular and significant form, and that this geometric form itself can be used to pinpoint the final murder site, suggests that the murders were ritualistic and, for whatever reason, blood sacrifices. There is also the sexual aspect to them. All the victims were involved in the sex industry and some of the mutilations can be seen as sexually motivated. It is perhaps significant that, in traditional Christian sacred geometry, the vesica piscis was sometimes used as the symbol of the vulva, the passage through which the Virgin gave birth to mankind's Saviour. It is possible that, in the tradition of black magic where benign or sacred symbols are reversed into the malign or sinister, the murderer could have desired to describe a vesica piscis, with its points marked in the blood of 'desecrated' as opposed to virginal females, as part of a satanic ritual.

The satanic intent behind these serial killings is suggested, in very direct manner, by one of the letters related to them. Most of the contemporary letters associated with the Jack the Ripper case were not, and still are not, regarded as having been written by the murderer. But one, postmarked 15 October and sent to George Lusk, the head of the Whitechapel Vigilance Committee, is both more convincing and more chilling. It is crude and simple and, if authentic, its only purpose seems to have been to goad the authorities. The misspellings it contains are such as to suggest that the murderer was ill-educated, possibly Irish (the seemingly phonetic spelling of 'Sor', for example, seems to indicate this) – though this may have been a calculated ploy to deceive. Addressed 'From hell' to 'Mr Lusk' it reads:

> Sor I send you half the Kidne I took from one women preserved it for you tother pirce I fried and ate it was very nise I may send you the bloody knif that took it out if you only wate a whil longer. Signed Catch me when you Can Mishter Lusk

The letter came with a small box containing a piece of kidney that was evidently human. A kidney had indeed been removed from Eddowes. Whether they were one and the same was impossible to verify medically in 1888, and since by the time the letter was posted the circumstances of the murder were well known it is always possible that it was the work of a trickster. But if the letter is genuine, it does suggest very strongly that the killer was indeed operating within the framework of a hellish ritual. The suggestion has moreover been made that the murders tended to be associated with thresholds – even the body in Mitre Square, it could be argued, was deposited on a threshold between the City and the East End, and Kelly's house was at the threshold of 'Dorset Street' and Miller's Court. Thresholds occupy a powerful place in popular folklore, being regarded as symbolic representations of the passage from one world to another. The ritualistic nature of the murders comes as no surprise, and is certainly not a new idea.[24] But if this surmise is correct, what precisely the ritual was, who devised and executed it, and why, remain a mystery.

The Jack the Ripper murders spelt the end of what survived of the 'Flower and Dean Street' Rookery. The fact that all the victims were associated with the street or the rookery did not escape the public's notice and intense pressure was brought to bear on the owners of the surviving buildings to improve them or clear them. 'My hope', Canon Barnett was quoted in the *Daily Telegraph* on 16 November 1888 as saying, 'is that, as they realise that the rents are the profits of vice, they will either themselves take direct action to improve this disgraceful condition of things, or sell their property to those who will undertake the responsibility.' Much of the freehold land in the 'Flower and Dean Street' area had been in the hands of the Henderson family for generations, and those Hendersons around at the time of the murders were the 'epitome of respectability': as Jerry White points out, in 1888 Kenneth Henderson was 'an army officer', Henry was 'an active member of the Conservative Club, St. James's St', and other family members were 'in the church'.[25] The family had kept a low profile for years but now, under the spotlight of the Ripper murders, offered parts of its estate for sale.

The Four Per Cent Industrial Dwellings Company continued its activities in 'Flower and Dean Street', building Nathaniel Dwellings, which were completed in 1892 to Joseph's designs. What had been one of the most dangerous and desolate areas of Spitalfields thus expanded the heartland of the area's new Jewish community, housed in 'model' manner. In addition other philanthropic companies built on cleared sites in adjoining streets. The East End Dwellings Company, for example – of which Canon Barnett was a founder member – built on Wentworth Street. By the close of 1894 nearly all of 'Flower and Dean Street' had been rebuilt, as had Lolesworth Street and Wentworth Street. As Jerry White observes, within six years, 'Jack the Ripper had done more to destroy the Flower and Dean Street Rookery than fifty years of road building, slum clearance and unabated pressure from Police, Poor Law Guardians, vestries and sanitary officers.'[26]

The writer Israel Zangwill offered a poetic perspective on the wider Jewish community in Spitalfields as it struggled to establish itself in the later nineteenth century and deal with endemic poverty and a sense of alienation within London. Born in London in 1864, Zangwill was educated in the Jews' Free School next to Frying Pan Alley, near the Old Artillery

Ground, and in 1892 published a novel, *Children of the Ghetto: A Study of a Peculiar People*, that was evidently semi-autobiographical and instantly captured the imagination of readers in Britain and the United States. At a stroke he became the philosophic chronicler of the plight that had befallen Eastern European Jews as they escaped persecution in their homeland only to fall into poverty and isolation in the world's new ghettos. His book offers an insider's view of the Jewish East End, and seeks to give its people a voice.

The 'Proem' to Zangwill's novel sets the hopes and aspirations of the East End's Jewish population in historical context. He starts by observing that the new ghetto of London's East End is unlike a traditional ghetto. It is without gates, and 'its narrow streets have no specialty of architecture; its dirt is not picturesque. It is no longer the stage for the high-buskined tragedy of massacre and martyrdom'. It is, however, a place 'for the obscurer, deeper tragedy that evolves from the . . . long-drawn-out tragi-comedy of sordid shifty poverty'. It is also 'a world which hides beneath its stony and unlovely surface an inner world of dreams, fantastic and poetic as the mirage of the Orient where they were woven, of superstitions grotesque as the cathedral gargoyles of the Dark Ages in which they had birth.'[27]

As for the 'folk' – the 'children of the Ghetto' – they are the product of the 'hovering miasma of persecution', and of 'that long cruel night in Jewry which coincides with the Christian Era . . . Into the heart of East London there poured from Russia, from Poland, from Germany, from Holland, streams of Jewish exiles, refugees, settlers . . . all rich in their cheerfulness, their industry, and their cleverness . . . rich in all the virtues, devout yet tolerant, and strong in their reliance on Faith, Hope, and more especially Charity.'[28] Zangwill reveals the heart of gold within even the darkest and most deprived ghetto slum, an attribute that generally eluded the observation of even the most sympathetic gentile observers. They were so overwhelmed by the dismal trappings of the outer life of the ghetto that they missed its inner vitality. To Zangwill, the Jewish immigrants – poor and abandoned as they were – had something precious in their cultural continuity and religious belief, a sense of self-worth and identity that enabled them to endure the privations and indignities of ghetto life.

Children of the Ghetto also offers an insider's perspective on life within the ghetto bounds. At its heart were Petticoat Lane and Wentworth Street. Zangwill writes that:

The Lane was always the great market-place, and every insalubrious street and alley abutting on it was covered with the overflowings of its commerce and its mud. Wentworth Street and Goulston Street were the chief branches, and in festival times the latter was a pandemonium of caged poultry, clucking and quacking and cackling and screaming. Fowls and geese and ducks were bought alive, and taken to have their throats cut for a fee by the official slaughterer.[29]

During Purim, a Jewish holiday commemorating escape from an ancient massacre and celebrated by exchanges of gifts, donations to charity, feasting, drinking, masquerades and fancy-dress parties, 'a gaiety, as of the Roman carnival, enlivened the swampy Wentworth Street' where 'confectioners' shops . . . were besieged by hilarious crowds of handsome girls and their young men, fat women and their children, all washing down the luscious spicy compounds with cups of chocolate.'[30] Of other streets, Zangwill notes, 'a dead and gone wag called the street "Fashion Street", and most of the people who live in it do not even see the joke . . . it is a dull, squalid thoroughfare . . . connecting Spitalfields with Whitechapel, and branching off in blind alleys,' with 'its extremities . . . within earshot of the blasphemies from some of the vilest quarters and filthiest rookeries in the capital of the civilised world.' Like Dickens before him Zangwill understood that demolition was a simplistic approach to the problem and did little to cure the cause of the slum. He notes that 'some of these clotted spiders'-webs have . . . been swept away by the . . . social reformer [but] the spiders have scurried off into darker crannies.'[31]

He also describes the trades and aspirations of the people of the ghetto, and in the process reveals a society far richer and more complex than that suggested by the somewhat patronising and two-dimensional portrait offered by Mayhew nearly fifty years earlier when he explored the same streets. Zangwill notes that there were 'Hawkers and peddlers, tailors and cigar-makers, cobblers and furriers, glaziers and cap-makers,'[32] confirming that most of the trades followed within the ghetto were only marginally skilled and that many depended on mental rather than physical dexterity, and on the well-honed business instincts of the merchant and market trader. Some of the key mercantile characters that Mayhew had noted were 'the Jew Old-Clothes Men' who traversed 'every street, square and road, with the monotonous cry, sometimes like a bleat, of "Clo! Clo!"'[33] By the late nineteenth century this occupation had grown in scale so that '"old clo" men plied their trade in ambitious content'[34] throughout the streets of London and were among the dominant tradesmen in many East London street markets. In Petticoat Lane and its environs this was, as it happens, a calling with an ancient pedigree because as early as 1598 a character in Ben Jonson's *Every Man in His Humour* castigates the old-clothes dealers from Houndsditch.

As for the aspirations and character of the Jewish tradesmen, Zangwill observed, in high poetic manner, that they carried 'with them . . . the odour of the Continental Ghetto' and bore 'in their eyes, through all the shrewdness of their glances, the eternal mysticism of the Orient, where God was born.' He noted that 'in sum their life [was] to pray much and to work long; to beg a little and to cheat a little; to eat not over-much and to "drink" scarce at all; to beget annual children by chaste wives (disallowed them half the year), and to rear them not over-well; to study the Law and the Prophets . . . to know no work on Sabbath and no rest on weekday'.[35]

The gentiles' inability fully to understand ghetto life is made clear in a book that was, in a sense, a homage to *Children of the Ghetto*. The author was Robert Blatchford, a man of humble birth, whose learning was a product of earnest self-education and who was himself no stranger to the privations and uncertainties of poverty. By 1899 Blatchford was an author and journalist with socialist allegiances – after spending some years in the regular army – and in that year published *Dismal England*. This is a highly personal, emotional and sympathetic first-person account of the poverty gripping the working people of England, a muted cry of rage and despair. The first chapter, surely in direct reference to Zangwill, is entitled 'The Children of the Ghetto', and takes the form of an exploration of the Jewish East End. But Blatchford – sympathetic observer though he is – sees little beyond the outward trappings of poverty:

> We entered the Ghetto. The children swarmed about us. They were swarthy, yet had on their faces the unwholesome pallor peculiar to London. They talked with volubility and eagerness . . . Jewish they all were, but of different nationalities, the prevailing language . . . was Yiddish. It was a strange experience: within half an hour's walk of the City boundaries we were in a foreign country.

This reference to the distance travelled suggests that Blatchford's exploration took him into the Jewish area between Whitechapel Road and

Commercial Road – no doubt having passed through Spitalfields along
Wentworth Street and Old Montague Street – rather than just being
focused on the Jewish alleys and courts around Artillery Lane and Petticoat Lane, which were on the City's border.

The perceived plight of the children, understandably, obsessed
Blatchford:

> Poor little people, how they swarm! There are crowds of them in the nar-
> row streets . . . I see the women here at the bars drinking with the men, and
> the little ones playing hide-and-seek in and out of the doors of the hateful
> dens. What can one do for the babies? Do you love children? Have you
> children of your own? . . . But I saw more children than even Christ could
> comfort, and many more women whom only Christ could bless . . . I came
> away perplexed and sad: I came away feeling many years older . . .

He was not alone in his incomprehension. When Henry Walker, author of
an 1896 evangelical tract on the East End, visited the 'Spitalfields Ghetto'
at the suggestion of Mr Scott, rector of Christ Church Spitalfields, he
was astonished by what he saw. In less than two minutes' walk from the
church:

> [An] almost impossible scene is before us. We seem to be in a world of dis-
> solving views. We suddenly find ourselves in a foreign land. The streets we
> enter might be streets in Warsaw or Cracow. We have taken leave of every-
> thing English, and entered an alien world. Wentworth Street . . . is the
> market of the thickly-herded, poorer immigrant Jews – Ashkenazi Jews
> from Poland, Russia, Germany and Holland. It is the East London coun-
> terpart of the poorest and meanest of the Continental Ghettos . . . In the
> heart of London, it is yet like a foreign town, with its own liberties of trade,
> own segregated peoples, religions, customs and industries.

Walker, like so many other outsiders, could not see beyond the crowding
and superficial veneer of material poverty, and found the controlled
behaviour of the Jewish poor almost uncanny. 'Strange as it may seem',
he observed when describing the Wentworth Street Sunday market, 'there
are no scenes of disorder, and nothing approaching to ruffianism. The
people are peaceable and law-abiding.'[36] This solemn air of dignity within
poverty plainly puzzled and confused him because it was in such stark
contrast to the strident, uncouth and largely lawless English and Irish
street markets and slums of the late-nineteenth-century East End – the

Nichol of course being the pre-eminent example. The calm, assured dignity and industry of the Jews perhaps also puzzled Walker because it threw doubt on the then conventional assumptions about the innate superiority of the 'Anglo-Saxon race' and Christian religion.

As for Mr Scott, he was faced with poor English Protestants who, by and large, didn't want to go to church; Anglo-Irish locals, many of whom must have been Roman Catholic but with whom, at least, he seems to have been popular; and Jewish people who had no interest in him or his church whatsoever. And the general peacefulness of the Jewish community must have seemed in strange contrast to the aggression he encountered elsewhere. Scott suggested that 'the late Mr Montague Williams' – magistrate and QC – had been quite correct when he had characterised Brick Lane as 'a land of beer and blood'. He himself lived in the Rectory in 'Church' (now Fournier) Street and 'sometimes', the seemingly disillusioned cleric told Walker, 'I have to stop free fights under my own window'.

Significant physical remains of this ghetto are now very few. There is the handsomely detailed 'Soup Kitchen for the Jewish Poor' in Brune Street, immediately south of White's Row, dated 5662/1902 (Hebrew and Gregorian calendars respectively), but closed for business since 1992, and there is the evocative and utterly haunting presence of two synagogues – the last of many that once dotted the area. One located in 19 Princelet Street – already described (see pages 355–7) – dates from the late 1860s and has long been closed. Fading inscriptions on its interior gallery testify to the fact that 'N. M. Rothschild & Co.' donated £50 at some point in the 1880s, while Samuel Montagu MP gave £31. 10. 6d. The last dated donation is from a Mrs R. Cohen on 2 September 1956. The second synagogue – still functioning – is almost a history in microcosm of eighteenth- and nineteenth-century Spitalfields. It stands in the narrow Sandys Row, which was once the north end of Petticoat Lane, and it was originally built in about 1766 as a Huguenot church. Because it stands near the Old Artillery Ground it was called L'Église de l'Artillerie (see page 169). Later it became a Baptist church and then in 1867 was bought by a Jewish society named *Hevrat Menahem Avalim Hesed v'Emeth* (The Comforters of Mourners Kindness and Truth Society) that had been founded by Ashkenazi immigrants – mostly Dutch – in 1853 as a mutual aid and burial insurance society that evolved into a synagogue. The original rear elevation, which forms virtually one side of Parliament Court, still survives, as do many eighteenth-century internal details including fine galleries

Above: *the St Petersburg kosher restaurant and its proprietor, Boris Schneer. The restaurant was located at 31 Hare Street, now Cheshire Street, which was – when this photograph was taken in the early twentieth century – a convivial market street and a focal point for Spitalfields' Jewish community. Just visible behind Schneer is a poster advertising a performance at the Yiddish Pavilion Theatre in Whitechapel. Below: the 'Soup Kitchen for the Jewish Poor', dated 1902, in Brune Street, which runs south of White's Row.*

supported on Doric columns. The somewhat utilitarian front to Sandys Row was built in the mid nineteenth century, but as a whole the building remains well worth seeing.

The various, often conflicting, communities in the East End constituted a potent mix. By 1901 London contained around 135,000 residents who were foreign by birth – about 3 per cent of the population – as opposed to 13,000 or 1 per cent of the population in 1841.[37] As the historian Jerry White observes, by 1901 London was 'the main Old World beneficiary of people displaced by a turbulent century'.[38] And this increased 'foreign' population – and especially the increased Jewish population that was made particularly distinct by its religious and cultural practices – helped fuel the fear that Jews were taking local jobs by accepting low wages and pushing up rents by creating an unquenchable demand for accommodation. One manifestation of this xenophobia was the formation in 1902 of the anti-immigration and paramilitary British Brothers League in East London. Its slogan – 'England for the English' – reveals the League's broad-brush approach. It does not appear to have been specifically anti-Semitic, certainly not initially; rather it was against the admittance of all poor foreigners to Britain, no matter what their race or religion. By 1914 the League had become a conduit for mounting anti-German feelings. It even received a donation from Sir Arthur Conan Doyle.

Worries about large-scale immigration and fear of the civil unrest to which it might lead provoked discriminatory legislation. In 1905 the Aliens Act was passed. Ostensibly it was intended to prevent criminals and paupers entering the country, but it was no secret at the time that its intention was also to control Jewish immigration from Central and Eastern Europe. Later strengthened by the Aliens Restriction Act of 1914, it introduced controls, and systems of registration and deportation. It also put the Home Secretary firmly in charge of what was to remain a key political issue throughout the century and into the next.

EIGHTEEN

DEMOLISHING THE 'FEVER DENS'
Victorian Slum Clearance

Although the demolition of slums and their replacement with 'improved' or 'model' dwellings was under way in Spitalfields by the 1860s, progress was slow and intermittent, and in the short term, at least, things seem to have got worse before they got better. A chapter entitled 'Curiosities of "Alley" Life' in James Greenwood's *Low-Life Deeps* (1881), for example, presents a picture of the Nichol so bleak as to suggest that it was, if possible, even more run-down and overcrowded than it had been just a couple of decades earlier. Greenwood, a tireless chronicler of London poverty, was struck not just by the squalor of the area, but by the number of people in each house, and the high rent paid for each room. 'Shepherd's-court', an alley off Old Nichol's Street (the apostrophe in the Nichol Street names appeared in the late nineteenth century), was fairly typical in this regard. It consisted of an 'irregular cluster of human habitations, the sight and smell of which are enough on an August afternoon to make one gasp for breath.' Greenwood ventured upstairs in one of these houses and found:

> but one bedstead in the room – a mite of a place . . . and yet it was made to accommodate mother, father, and eight children; some of course would have to lie on the bare boards, the bedstead, which was barely of the ordinary size, could not have contained them all. The room was in a shocking condition, with holes in the rotten floor and damp patches on the walls and ceiling. For this the weekly rent was two-and-ninepence.

Earlier accounts of overcrowding may sometimes have been exaggerated (see Chapter 15). But the density of occupation suggested by Greenwood does not appear to have been an overestimate when compared with late-nineteenth-century census returns. For example, the 1891 census for 40 Half Nichol's Street shows that it was inhabited by forty-four people organised in ten family units.[1] Twenty of the occupants were aged twelve or under, with only four aged sixty or over. Just six of the residents were born other than in Bethnal Green, Spitalfields, Whitechapel or Shoreditch (as elsewhere in the Nichol, none appear to have been Jewish; the 1899 map of Jewish East London, compiled after the Nichol had been largely demolished, shows most of the surrounding streets to the north and east as less than 5 per cent Jewish). Since the size of the house can no longer be determined, it is impossible to know precisely how densely packed 40 Half Nichol's Street was, but if the plots shown on the 1872/3 Ordnance Survey map are anything to go, it looks as though it might have been an eight-roomed house accommodating two families of seven in two rooms, and an average of five people in each of the other rooms.[2]

By the time the census was compiled moves were under way that were to lead to the levelling of the Nichol. In 1887 government inspectors confirmed that there were almost 6,000 people crammed into around thirty streets and courts of small, old and decaying buildings where the mortality rate was nearly twice that of the rest of Bethnal Green. The inspectors also confirmed Greenwood's claim that the rents were high, making these unlikely streets some of the most lucrative real estate in London. Sarah Wise, in her magisterial analysis of the Nichol, has done much research into the area's rents which, in turn, reveals much about the economy and morality of late-Victorian London: 'Per cubic foot', she suggests, 'the rents of the Nichol were between four and ten times higher than those of the finest streets and squares of the West End, averaging between 2s 3d to 3s for a single room and around 7s 6d for a three-room lodging'. As Wise points out, this startling fact meant that 'some 85 per cent of the working-class households in London spent one-fifth or more of their income on rent' while 'half of them paid between a quarter and half of their income to their landlords.'[3] This increasing intensity of occupation was in large part an unintended consequence of haphazard slum-clearance projects. As both Dickens and Zangwill had earlier observed (see pages 445 and 492), when bad streets and houses were cleared the displaced merely packed themselves into the nearest surviving slum houses, the rents of which became ever more expensive.

This shockingly opportunistic exploitation of the capital's shortage of housing for the poor meant being a slum landlord was potentially very good business indeed. Such speculators were generally loathed. Henry Lazarus, in his 1892 book *Landlordism*, called them 'the vampyres of the poor',[4] while the *Pall Mall Gazette* registered shock and dismay that 'these fever dens are said to be the best paying property in London, and owners . . . are drawing from 50 to 60 per cent on investments in tenement property in the slums.'[5] But, Wise points out, 'the *Gazette* had underestimated the money that could be made, and profits as large as 150 per cent per annum were not uncommon.'[6] This astonishing level of profit was confirmed by evidence given to the Royal Commission on the Housing of the Working Classes 1884–5. So too was the high proportion of their income paid as rent by the poor.[7]

The occupations of the residents of 40 Half Nichol's Street were predictably varied and humble: there was one bootmaker; two needleworkers; one 'general dealer'; one 'Japaner' (a type of varnisher in the furniture trade); one carman; one printer; two 'Fancy Boxmakers'; two errand boys; one French-polisher; one firewood cutter; one toymaker; one shoe-binder; two hawkers; and one matchbox-maker. Greenwood noted that matchbox-making was a common activity in the area, with 'every member of the family, down to the little child four or five years old, lending a hand as they squat in a ring on the filthy, uncarpeted floor.' For this industry, he wrote, 'they receive twopence halfpenny for making twelve dozen boxes, and out of this have to provide paste. By working very hard and without reference to the clock, a woman and three or four children so employed may earn fifteenpence a day'. The small rooms of the area's houses not only provided 'a refuge for a family', but also a workplace for 'at least three-fourths of the wretched tenants earn their bread at home.' Greenwood also pointed out that crime played an important role in the local economy. 'Old Nichol-street is not a particularly honest neighbourhood,' he wrote. 'There may probably be found within its limits a greater number of thieves – petty and other – than a square mile of any other parish could produce.'

Crime – violent crime, in particular – is what dominates one of the oddest, and now best-known, books about late-nineteenth-century London slum life: Arthur Morrison's *A Child of the Jago*. It was published in November 1896 and can be seen either as factual observation masquerading as a novel or as a novel masquerading as fact – or just as a piece of sensationalist, topical fiction, inspired by fact, that draws on some of the conventions of the historical novel. P. J. Keating, an authority on

Victorian 'working-class' fiction, had a high regard for Morrison, whose work, he claimed, was 'an amalgam of [Walter] Besant, who supplies a new image of the East End; Charles Booth, who clarifies the class structure of that image; and Kipling, from whom Morrison derives his objective, amoral, literary method. To these diverse influences he brings considerable personal experience of working-class life, carefully acquired skill as a reporter, and a simple but vivid prose style.'[8]

The novel tells the story of Dicky Perrott (a surname with strong Huguenot overtones) in three acts, each separated by a period of four years. In the first act Dicky is aged eight or nine. His father is a thief – perhaps a violent robber – and a prize-fighter; his mother undertakes sweated labour at home – stitching sacks or assembling matchboxes. Dicky is soon a hardened pickpocket and street thief, never has enough to eat, and becomes progressively more closely involved in and corrupted by the area's clan warfare – conducted with ghastly brutality – endemic criminality imposed by privation, and culture of deception, betrayal and revenge. Morrison does not concoct a happy ending. The moral is that despite the best intentions – and Dicky does attempt to escape the dreadful cycle of criminality leading to want leading to yet more thieving – all endeavour will be left unrewarded and any hope of redemption ultimately destroyed by remorseless poverty and by the heavy price exacted by living within a criminal and unjust society. Much as Hector Gavin had argued fifty years earlier (see page 426), Morrison's point is that the poor ought to be pitied not pilloried because, in their wicked or wretched ways, they are the victims of brutal circumstances and not the begetters of their dire circumstances.

To tell his tale Morrison created a fictional world that was an obvious echo of the real one. The 'Jago' of his invention was the Nichol, a fact that is made abundantly and immediately obvious because the book includes a street plan of the Jago, which is simply a street plan of the Nichol area but with street names slightly changed, usually by substituting Jago for Nichol – hence Old Jago Street, New Jago Street and Half Jago Street. 'Nichol's Row' becomes Jago Row, Boundary Street becomes Edge Row, 'Cross Street' becomes Luck Row, Church Street becomes Meakin Street and 'Orange Court' becomes Jago Court. Bethnal Green Road and 'The Posties' – the passage leading into the Nichol from Shoreditch High Street – retain their true identities.

These name changes, since they were not intended to conceal true locations, can be seen as a literary mechanism. They would appear to be telling the reader that the story told is symbolic rather than actual, and that while it is inspired by the real world, the book is not a literal account but an artistic creation that illuminates reality through the skilful evocation of a shadow world. The extremes of brutality the book portrays – the street violence, clannish drunken brawling, neglected children, sickness, poverty and horrid death – seem emblematic, with many of its more lurid descriptions merely exercises in poetic licence.

Morrison, though, did not concede this. He argued from the start that the book, although couched as a novel with fictional characters and narrative, was intended as an accurate reflection of reality, that it was an essentially truthful portrait of the suffering of the very poor and a plea, on their behalf, for understanding and help. The reading public seems generally to have accepted the book at this level – at least initially – and the work received immediate and general praise, both for its dramatic power, its 'reality', and for its philanthropic intent. Robert Blatchford praised both the book and Morrison in a 1900 article entitled 'On Realism' in *My Favourite Books*.[9] H. G. Wells, too, expressed admiration and was provoked to ponder the origin of the social evils the book chronicled. Were they the consequence of nature or of nurture? For Wells they were the result of environment, 'neither ignorance, wrong moral suggestions, nor parasites are inherited . . . the Jago is not a "black inheritance", it is a black contagion,' he wrote.[10]

Given that Morrison evidently wanted his book to carry an urgent and topical social message one might wonder why he did not simply write a documentary narrative about the Nichol. The most likely reason is that, as a typical product of the literary conventions of the time, he favoured the presentation of historical fact as almost historical fiction, not least because such an approach enabled him to indulge the maudlin and sentimental tastes of the reading – and book-buying – public. Dickens, of course, was a master of the genre, but he was certainly not the only well-known exponent. From the mid to late nineteenth century William Harrison Ainsworth churned out a succession of hybrid works on such subjects as Old St Paul's Cathedral, the Tower of London and Windsor Castle – all a blend of historical novel and fact-based research. Morrison himself had attempted a mix of fact and fiction before *A Child of the Jago* with *Tales of Mean Streets*, published in 1894, a collection of short stories that sought to evoke something authentic about the tough, uncertain and brutal nature

Above: *a street in the Nichol – probably Boundary Street. The small, early-nineteenth-century terrace houses, shown here as they were in the 1890s, were evidently built for the silk industry. They possessed, in their remorseless and sustained repetition, a spare utilitarian and almost sublime beauty.* Below: *Boundary Street today. Despite the former nineteenth-century pub in the left foreground and parts of the LCC Boundary Estate on the right, Boundary Street is now sadly characterless.*

of working-class East London life. The result is not a work of great or lasting literary merit, but it did at the time prove a publishing success.

The uncertainty of the boundary between fiction and journalistic observation makes *A Child of the Jago* a problematic read from a historical point of view. Morrison's own character is a further complication. He was born in 1863 in Poplar and raised in a series of East London 'mean streets', with a father in uncertain employment who died when Morrison was eight.[11] The family then became itinerant for a while, possibly while still living in the rougher parts of the East End. In his early twenties Morrison secured himself a position as a clerk in the People's Palace on the Mile End Road – an extraordinary enterprise, opened in 1887, that aimed to inspire, educate and entertain the more curious-minded among East London's working people and that was itself inspired, at least in part, by Walter Besant's *All Sorts and Conditions of Men: An Impossible Story* (1882). Besant's novel told the fairy tale of a rich and very bright couple from Mayfair who moved to East London to build a 'Palace of Delight' for the local people, with concert halls, reading rooms, picture galleries and art and design schools. The young Morrison must have been inspired by the idea that the power of the imagination could achieve wonders. By the late 1890s, however, he seems to have regarded the People's Palace as an expression of the patronising values of self-important philanthropists for he appears to parody it in *A Child of the Jago* as the 'East End Elevation Mission and Pansophical Institute'.

By 1889 Morrison had become a journalist and in 1891 a published author. He moved to West London, then to rural Chingford and Loughton, became a collector of, and authority on, Japanese art – then highly fashionable – and gradually drew a veil over his impoverished East End past. For example, the 1904 edition of the *Dictionary of English Authors* describes Morrison as having been born in Kent and educated at private schools and his father is elevated from engine-fitter to 'engineer'. Presumably this information came from Morrison himself who, on the census returns for 1891 and 1901, first claimed he was born in Sheerness, Kent, and then in Blackheath.[12] As Vincent Brome observed, it's 'almost as if the man who so vividly evokes the horror, the poverty, the seaminess of late nineteenth-century London, wanted to forget or run away from his own roots.'[13]

This move to disguise his origin in East London poverty is understandable given the social values and snobbery of the time. But Morrison's somewhat cringing response to contemporary notions about class and respectability, and the determination to forge himself more genteel origins in Kent, surely rob him of a certain degree of authority as a chronicler of East End slum life. Morrison himself was to argue that he knew the East End well, had even lived there (though in unspecified circumstances), and that the facts and opinions expressed in *A Child of the Jago* were the result of recent and intensive objective research. But it's hard to judge how objective he was really being. And since he clearly had personal and painful memories of growing up in East London poverty – or at least in impoverished areas – it's difficult to know to what extent *A Child of the Jago* relates to the true condition of the Nichol at the time, and to what extent it is autobiographical or perhaps inspired by events that took place elsewhere.

These ambiguities are embodied in the novel's main protagonist Dicky Perrott, a potentially decent human being ultimately destroyed by poverty and injustice. To what extent is Perrott based on the young Morrison? It is possible that through Perrott's story Morrison is expressing the fears that dogged his own early life. As P. J. Keating has suggested, Morrison's loathing of the Jago, and the prose this loathing inspires, must be due to 'some personal source'.[14] At the same time, Perrott seems, in part at least, to have been inspired by the story of Charles Clayton, who was stabbed in July 1892 in a street fight in the Nichol and died of peritonitis a few days later. He would appear, then, to be an amalgam created from personal recollection, direct observation and the novelist's imagination.

Another odd thing about *A Child of the Jago* is its timing. It is now generally accepted that Morrison spent most of 1895 and part of 1896 researching and observing the Nichol before sitting down to write his book.[15] This is what Morrison himself suggested after publication. But by early 1895 much of the Nichol area had already been demolished – clearance had begun in 1893 and the population had started to be evicted a year or so earlier, with perhaps one-fifth gone by the end of 1895. So Morrison was writing about a place that was ceasing to exist and one must wonder exactly what he did see – or could see – from 1895 and into 1896: presumably a vast demolition and construction site. Perhaps he witnessed the majority of the displaced Nichol population squeezing itself into surviving and surrounding slum streets, like Pedley Street, Weaver Street and Sclater Street. Perhaps he visited the area a couple or so years earlier.

Answers to some of these questions were offered by Morrison himself in the wake of the excitement following the publication of the book. Not all reviews had been uncritical. Henry Duff Traill, in the *Fortnightly Review* for January 1897, had claimed that Morrison's portrait of the Nichol – as personified by the Jago – was unrealistic and exaggerated.[16] Traill observed, with studied sarcasm, that 'the original of the Jago has, it is admitted, ceased to exist. But I will make bold to say that as described by Mr Morrison, it never did exist.' For Traill, 'the total effect of the story is unreal and phantasmagoric' with Morrison creating a 'fairyland of horror'.

Traill's criticism provoked Morrison to write a defence that appeared as a preface, dated February 1897, to the third edition of *A Child of the Jago*. In this preface Morrison claimed that he was 'a simple writer of tales, who takes whatever means lie to his hands to present life as he sees it', but made a point of defending the essential 'realism' and facts enshrined in his novel: 'the plan and intention of my story,' he wrote, 'made it requisite that, in telling it, I should largely adhere to fact, and I did so.'[17] In support of his claims to veracity he pointed out that 'for certain years I have lived in the East End of London, and have been, not an occasional visitor, but a familiar and equal friend in the house of the East-Ender in all his degree'. He also referred to those who had 'vindicated' the accuracy of his story – 'in particular, the devoted vicar of the parish which I have called the Jago', who had 'testified quite unreservedly to the truth of my presentation.' And he stated again what motivated him to write: 'It was my fate to encounter a place in Shoreditch, where children were born and reared in circumstances which gave them no reasonable chance of loving decent lives: where they were born fore-damned to a criminal or semi-criminal career. It was my experience to learn the ways of this place, to know its inhabitants, to talk with them, eat, drink, and work with them.'

'For the existence of this place, and for the evils it engendered,' he argued, 'the community was, and is, responsible; so that every member of the community was, and is, responsible in his degree'. Since he himself had neither the wealth nor political power to help, his contribution was to write 'a tale wherein I hoped to bring the conditions of this place within the apprehension of others.' As he said: 'observation is my trade.'

The 'devoted vicar' whom Morrison thanked was Arthur Osborne Jay, the vicar of Holy Trinity Church, which had been built in Old Nichol's Street in the 1880s (and which was destroyed by bombing in May 1941). The vicar's support is perhaps not surprising since it was Jay who, after reading *Tales of Mean Streets*, had invited Morrison to write about the people and poverty of the Nichol and it was to him that Morrison dedicated *A Child of the Jago*. In addition Jay appears within the book as Father Sturt, its most (indeed only) heroic, energetic and admirable character.

Jay had made something of a name for himself as an active battler against the physical and spiritual evils of poverty and in 1891 published a pamphlet – in response to one published by William Booth (see page 417) – entitled *Life in Darkest London: A Hint to General Booth*. In this publication Jay offered a manifesto for rigorous parochial relief work and a critique of Booth's fund-raising methods that moved resources away from the Church of England's poverty-relief programmes.

P. J. Keating outlines the working method that Morrison evolved after his meeting with Jay: 'For a period of eighteen months he made frequent trips to Shoreditch where, under Jay's guidance, he met all of the characters later to appear in his book, talking with them . . . drinking with them in local pubs, visiting their homes and even learning how to make matchboxes.'[18] Given the ambiguity that surrounds much of the creation and intention of *A Child of the Jago* it is important to note that this description of Morrison's relationship with Jay and his method of gathering material was given by Morrison himself in an interview for the *Daily News*.[19]

The mutual regard between Morrison and Jay is perhaps reflected by Morrison's rebranding of the Nichol as the Jago, which, of course, is a phonetic rendering of Jay-go, presumably meaning the place where 'Jay goes'. Indeed Morrison's relationship with Jay probably holds the answers to many of the puzzles of the book. Quite simply, he must have been the source for a considerable number of the tales told by Morrison in his book. It was a connection noted at the time. The anonymous review in the *St James's Gazette* of 2 December 1896 described *A Child of the Jago* as 'an illuminated version' of Jay's *Life in Darkest London*.[20] The view of Nichol historian Sarah Wise is that: 'Morrison's had not been an eyewitness account but a faithful regurgitation of tales told to him by Father Jay, some of which, what's more, had come to Jay at second hand. "Typical facts were all I wanted," Morrison had protested to his critics. Instead, he had retold atypical, and legendary, Nichol events, from which he constructed his fairyland of horror.'[21]

Morrison's defensive preface was not the last of his war of words with Traill. In March 1897 he published an essay in the *New Review* entitled 'What is a Realist?' in which he challenged Traill to 'trot out his experts'[22] if he wanted to prove *A Child of the Jago* a fantastic exaggeration and compilation of urban horror stories. Traill took up the challenge. In *The New Fiction and other Essays on Literary Subjects* (1897) he published the opinions of 'experts' ready to refute Morrison. As Sarah Wise explains:

> Woodland Erleback [one of Traill's 'experts'] had been a manager at the Nichol Street Board School for thirty years and stated that 'the district, though bad enough, was not even thirty years ago so hopelessly bad and vile as the book paints it. The characters portrayed may have had their originals but they were the exception and not the rule.' J. F. Barnard . . . told Traill that he had carried cash to and from the Nichol Street Penny Bank since 1874 and had never once been robbed. The textiles firm of Vavasseur, Coleman and Carter, whose warehouse in New Nichol Street stored bolts of valuable silk, had never had a break-in. Two more Board School managers; a pastor at the non-denominational London City Mission; a Poor Law guardian who had been resident in the Nichol for several years, and two women who ran local Mothers' Meetings came forward to Traill to defend the people of the Nichol.[23]

In her own review of police reports of crime in the Nichol in the 1890s, Sarah Wise made a discovery that is perhaps surprising if the portrait of the Nichol presented by Morrison is taken seriously. Although it is possible that many crimes were never actually reported, Wise found that the vast majority of offences in the Nichol that were officially recorded were mundane rather than murderous: 'The truth of the matter', she writes, 'is that drunk-and-disorderlies, fights between man and wife, missing dogs, the ill-treatment of birds for sale in Club Row, parental failure to comply with compulsory child vaccination and school attendance orders, and pub licensing contraventions, form the dreary bulk of police and magistrates' records of criminal activity in the Nichol in the 1870s, 1880s and early 1890s.'[24]

A Child of the Jago, then, must be treated with great caution as a source of authentic information about life in the Nichol. Much in it seems to belong to the world of Victorian melodrama and to be a product of Morrison's desire to produce a tale that would grip the imagination of the public and spread the word about the evils of poverty to the widest possible audience. Nevertheless, passages can be found that possess the ring of truth and offer an insight into the life – and death – of the Nichol. One such is the community's fearful response to the demolition of the area, not least because demolition and eviction must have been one of the main topics of conversation when Morrison was exploring the area. When

Father Sturt announces that Jago Court is to be demolished to make way for a new church, for example, the description of the locals' reaction is entirely convincing:

> Many held it a shame that so much money, destined for the benefit of the Jago, should be spent in bricks and mortar, instead of being distributed among themselves. They fell to calculating the price of land and houses . . . it was felt to be a grave social danger that Jago Court should be extinguished . . . but mainly they feared the police. Jago Court was an unfailing sanctuary, a city of refuge ever ready, ever secure. There were times when two or three of the police, hot in in the chase, would burst into the Jago at the heels of a flying marauder. Then the runaway would make straight for the archway, and, once he was in Jago Court, danger was over. For he had only to run into one of the ever-open doors . . . and out into the back yards and other houses, or, better, to scramble over the low fence opposite, through the back door before him, and so into New Jago Street.[25]

This passage conveys a sense of the true labyrinthine geography of 'Orange Court', which can be related to the outlines on contemporary Ordnance Survey maps. Morrison probably did not know 'Orange Court' himself – it had been demolished before 1895 – but he seems to have gleaned this authentic-sounding description from someone who did.

Another passage about the demolition of the Jago represents a scene and circumstances that Morrison could well have witnessed and recalls sentiments he could well have felt:

> And the wreckers tore down the foul old houses, laying bare the secret dens of a century of infamy; lifting out the wide sashes of the old 'weavers' windows' – the one good feature in the structures; letting light and air at last into the subterraneous basements where men and women had swarmed, and bred, and died, like wolves in their lairs . . . But there were rooms which the wreckers . . . flatly refused to enter; and nothing would make them but much coaxing, the promise of extra pay, and the certainty of much immediate beer.[26]

One particular street described by Morrison – 'Meakin Street' (Redchurch Street, formerly 'Church Street') – survived the demolition of the Nichol. To Morrison, it was a place of 'chandlers' shops with sugar in their windows, and cook shops with puddings.'[27] It was also a place where the shopkeepers 'knew their neighbours too well to leave articles unguarded'.[28] Because of that it was not a place of easy pickings for the Nichol children, but it did contain Fagin-like fences – receivers of stolen property – one of whom was to be the cause of Dicky Perrott's downfall.

Curiously enough another, and strikingly similar, image of 'Meakin'/ Redchurch Street is offered by a man who, born in 1885, would have been about the same age as the fictional Dicky Perrott in 1896. Arthur Harding was born in Boundary Street and grew up in the Nichol, and in the late 1970s told his life story to Spitalfields-based social historian Raphael Samuel. Harding's memoirs were eventually published in 1981 and the voluminous notes and taped interviews Samuel conducted are now lodged in the archives of the Bishopsgate Institute.

Harding's tales of life in Spitalfields and Shoreditch in the years just before, and the decades just after, 1900 are wonderful. They are also a challenging array of that mix of verifiable fact and seeming fantasy that perplexes many when contemplating *A Child of the Jago*. Years ago, after first reading Harding's memoirs, I asked Samuel if he believed them. It was a naïve question to which Samuel replied that his job was to record memoirs, not to judge their truthfulness. But it's fascinating to see the extent to which Harding's description of Redchurch Street chimes with Morrison's 'Meakin Street'. As Harding describes it:

> the high heaven of everything in the Nichol was Church Street . . . now called Redchurch Street . . . where all the shops were. The whole place was crooked, even those who kept shops . . . The White Horse pub stands on one corner, and on the other corner was a big men's and boys' tailor shop, known as Lynn's . . . On each side of Church Street there were food shops, used mostly by the people of the Nichol. The first was a fish and chip shop right opposite Boundary Street; the people could send the children for 'a penny bit and haporth' – one penny bit of fish and a halfpenny worth of chips or fried potatoes. This was the usual dinner and supper meal.

Samuel notes that 'the directories list James Julier as fried fish shop at no. 19 from 1890 to 1896'. Harding continues, 'next to the fish shop was a small timber yard . . . on the corner of Ebor Street . . . was [another] pub outside of which stood a street bookmaker waiting for punters to bet their fancy on horses . . .'[29] This pub, called 'The Jack Simmons . . . at the corner of Church street and Ebor street', was, recalled Harding, 'the most famous pub in the East End of a Sunday morning' and the favoured resort of the 'swell mob' and the 'sporting' fraternity. 'All the top Johnnies were in there, the prize fighters, and some of the music hall artists. It had a great big bar at the front, with a little private bar round at the side. Of a Sunday morning they used to do a rare old trade. The boxers and the prize fighters and the racing people used to go in there. All the rogues and the villains – the three-card mob and all that lark.' Later, Harding remembered, this East End gin palace 'was turned into a Jewish Synagogue'.[30]

Harding's Church/Redchurch Street, then, like Morrison's 'Meakin Street', had its criminal element. Charles Booth also testified to this in his 1898 account, where he described a pub on a corner site near Redchurch Street, called 'The Blue Anchor', as being 'the most noted thieves' resort in London', which 'every Sunday' was their gathering place 'from all parts of London' (see page 54).

But at the same time it's apparent that Redchurch Street was also a vibrant and bustling place, full of shops, pubs and eateries, generally affluent and, superficially at least, respectable. Certainly that's the picture that also emerges from the census returns of the period. Take, for example, the block of ten buildings – none later than c.1890, several much older – that still survives on the north side of the east end of Redchurch Street, at its junction with Bethnal Green Road. In 1881, six out of ten of these buildings were occupied by respectable shopkeepers, one was a manufactory, one solely a family home, and two were home to publicans, their families and staff (there was a pub at each end of the row).[31] The census returns also suggest that the density of occupation was not particularly high – only one building was occupied by two families as opposed to a single one – and of the eleven families living in the houses, no fewer than seven had at least one domestic servant. Trades represented included tobacconist (at number 105), pork butcher (107) and a chemist at the large mid-nineteenth-century 109 and 111, in the person of Alexander Dorrington Hicks, who lived there with his wife and two young children, his sixty-nine-year-old aunt, his forty-six-year-old sister, who was 'seeking [a] housekeeper's situation', his twenty-four-year-old cousin who was a 'Journeyman silk weaver', and nineteen-year-old lodger who was a 'journeyman Druggist' and who presumably worked for Hicks (in the 1861 census the premises were inhabited by a 'Pharmaceutical chemist' named William Fox, so perhaps Hicks purchased the business as a going concern). Number 113 – a house of c.1735

The east end of Redchurch Street – former Church Street – at its junction with Bethnal Green Road, in the mid 1970s. On the left is number 111; centre – with wide weavers' window – is number 113, built in about 1735 and in the late nineteenth century occupied by a family of twine manufacturers. In the distance is the former Van Tromp public house.

with wide weavers' windows on the upper floor – was occupied by Elizabeth Sturman, a fifty-eight-year-old widow and 'twine manufacturer', and
four family members (Elizabeth must have lived there for at least thirty
years, since her name first appears in the 1851 census[32]). Number 115 was
occupied by George Pottier, a wood dealer (resident in the house since at
least 1861), with four family members and a seventeen-year-old female
servant. At 117 there lived George Hanrick, a hairdresser, his wife Leah
(both were from Poland and the only foreign-born residents in the block),
their six children, two male 'assistant hairdressers' and a thirty-year-old
female domestic servant. At 119 there was a labourer, George Bonning,
along with five family members, and a seventeen-year-old male servant.
Number 121 was 'The Van Tromp' public house, occupied by F. E. Davey,
'Licensed victualler', his family of seven, a sixty-five-year-old nurse, a
sixteen-year-old domestic servant, two live-in barmen, a billiard marker
and a potman. All eminently respectable people.

Redchurch Street may not have been typical of many of the streets
within the purlieus of the Nichol. And, no doubt, the street possessed a
diverse range of households along its length, with its east end being, perhaps, the best section. But it is interesting that, even in the early 1880s,
when the Nichol's fortunes were at their bleakest, the census reveals that
this particular stretch was neither densely occupied nor in decay but flourishing and productive – and that some at least of its inhabitants were
happy to live there for many years as their names appear in earlier records.

A map of 1892, produced by Charles Booth and included in his *Life and
Labour of the People in London*, adds a touch more detail to what life in and
around Redchurch Street must have been like towards the end of the Vic-
torian era. The intention of the map was to pinpoint the institutions that
Booth believed defined urban living, ranging from places of worship to
five types of public house, and Redchurch Street and its immediate vicinity seem to have been able to offer examples of just about every type.
There was a Board School adjoining a site that would soon become Arnold
Circus at the heart of the Boundary Estate. There was also a Church of
England church and two nonconformist missions. The nearest synagogue
was to the south on Quaker Street and the nearest Roman Catholic church
still further to the south, St Anne's on Underwood Road. And then in or
very near Redchurch Street there were ten fully licensed pubs and
one 'beerhouse' with 'on' and 'off' licences (where beer could be drunk on
the premises or bought and taken away). So while churches of all faiths

were few and distant, virtually every small block in Redchurch Street contained one or two pubs. When Charles Booth returned for a further exploration in 1898 he was unimpressed, noting 'thieves' and 'prostitutes', and shops on both sides that were known to be 'receivers' of stolen property. He gave it his worst possible grade – 'Lowest class. Vicious, semi-criminal'.

So Redchurch Street was a street of contrasts, where petty criminals congregated but where respectable businesses and people co-existed with them. We have to imagine a street packed with life and with shops, some honest, many 'crooked'; all by the 1890s, like the pubs and gin palaces dotted around them, sparkling with light from dusk until late at night. Add to this illumination the flickering and undulating light from the gas lamps, the moist horse dung and general ordure on the glistening cobblestones, the street music and the street cries, and you have a fair approximation of the almost theatrical setting for late-Victorian life in the environs of the Nichol. And, despite the poverty, decay and general filth, this was evidently a place of some magic and romance.[33] Redchurch Street connected at its west end with Shoreditch High Street, the main shopping promenade of the area with a lively street market and a place of display and parade – which Arthur Harding remembered as 'our Champs Élysées'.[34]

During the second half of the 1890s, most of the Nichol slum was obliterated and then replaced by a new development that was, in its way, revolutionary.[35] Completed in 1900, the group of buildings known collectively as the Boundary Estate marked a profound change in the manner in which subsidised homes were in future to be provided for London's working populations. Previously the main initiatives had been undertaken by dwellings companies, which were partly philanthropic exercises but which also undertook to pay investors dividends, and which – like the Four Per Cent Industrial Dwellings Company – often catered for special-interest groups. But in 1889 the London County Council (LCC) was formed, and the political terrain of the capital changed forever.

The LCC was a city-wide, publicly elected and accountable local authority that shouldered most of the tasks previously fulfilled by parish vestries, the Liberties and the Metropolitan Board of Works. It took over responsibility for planning, the provision of 'council' housing for the working class, public transport and essential services such as the fire brigade, adding education to its remit in 1903 (and so replacing the London School Board). By assuming responsibility for public housing the LCC made new initiatives on the part of the dwellings companies increasingly unnecessary. But quite how the new authority would realise its housing responsibility was initially unclear. Would it simply build the type of utilitarian blocks run up by most dwellings companies, or would the LCC attempt something more architecturally and socially ambitious, more inspiring and comprehensive in its aims?

The LCC's first two schemes showed that it planned to think big, and that it was visionary in its aspirations for improving London and the lives of at least the more industrious portion of the capital's working people. Its first slum clearance and housing task embraced the replacement of the Nichol terraces with an entirely new urban quarter. This was soon followed by a similarly ambitious new housing project on Millbank, Westminster. Both schemes were large in scale and combined a determination to provide hygienic new homes with a desire to do so in a manner that was architecturally noteworthy and that conferred at least a degree of dignity upon the occupants. In this sense the new housing schemes continued the architectural principles established from the early 1870s with the design and construction of London's Board Schools: they were to be functional and handsome.

In 1893 the LCC's new architecture department established a small team to design its working-class housing projects. The architects were young, idealistic and inspired by the Arts and Crafts principles of Philip Webb, Norman Shaw, and W. R. Lethaby. They believed in the use of tried and tested traditional materials that were tough and low-maintenance, but were ready to combine them with modern building technology – concrete and iron – when it was practical to do. They also embraced the use of ornament and traditional forms, to confer upon their designs the dignity and pedigree of history. And they showed a willingness to learn the lessons gained from the previous fifty years of philanthropic housing initiatives. Some of the earlier projects offered useful models but most, in their soulless, bleak and barracks-like utility, were object lessons in what to avoid.

The redevelopment of most of the Nichol was decided upon in 1891 but demolition did not start until 1893. Construction then got under way in 1895. The plan of the Boundary Estate was, for its location, utterly extraordinary. In place of the grid of narrow streets, courts and alleys framed largely by two-storey houses, a Parisian Beaux Arts quarter sprang up with, at its heart, a large circus from which radiated broad, tree-lined avenues. Around the circus and along the avenues were placed tall, free-standing blocks of tenements. These rose directly from the line of the pavements, clearly defining the new streets and giving a distinct and powerful urban quality. Between the blocks were generous courts or gardens, ensuring a sense of space and light and allowing the free circulation of air. The communal doors to each housing block were generally placed off one of these courts or gardens, ensuring, among other things, that children could be more easily supervised and could not dash out into the streets. In a similarly practical way, the ground-floor elevations facing the circus were clad with glazed bricks so they could be easily cleaned of the horse dung that would inevitably spray up from the streets.

The blocks were of varied design, each largely tailored to its specific site, to avoid a sense of repetition. Most were given internal communal staircases and access corridors, but in a few – notably Henley House and Walton House – the bottom flight of the communal staircases burst into the outside court through open arches. There seems to have been a sense of experimentation in the design of the Boundary Estate blocks – no doubt part of a quest to find ideal forms for future schemes. What the buildings have in common is that they are faced with load-bearing brickwork, are more or less ornamented, and adopt an early-seventeenth-century Flemish gabled style (a permutation of the then fashionable 'Queen Anne' style, thought particularly appropriate for practical or residential buildings) that marries classical detail with Gothic freedom of composition. The architect in charge was Owen Fleming.

The estate was almost exclusively residential. There were two Board Schools, constructed just before the development of the area and integrated into the design of the circus. The front of one, the Rochelle Street School, now bears the date 1899, which suggests it was adapted or extended during the construction of the estate. There were also rows of workshops, a very handsome communal laundry block and a row of shops along one avenue. No public houses or off-licences were permitted.

Residents started to move in during the course of 1897. But they were not the people who had been displaced by the demolitions. This scheme was for the 'deserving' and 'industrious' poor, and for what are now termed 'key workers' – police, teachers and nurses. Of the 5,100 people eventually housed on the Boundary Estate when completed in 1900, only eleven had been among the 5,710 residents of the Nichol made homeless when the slum was swept away in readiness for its utopian replacement.

As early as 1900 George Haw concluded that the new LCC was, as a house provider for London's poor, much like the earlier artisan dwellings companies. 'Block buildings', as he termed tenements, 'never entirely re-house the people displaced from cleared sites. These people overcrowd into the already overcrowded smaller properties that lie around.' As far as Haw could see, 'chief among the offenders is the London County Coun-cil, as its high rents hold the poorer classes at bay.' Haw had discovered, from the Chief Sanitary Inspector of Bethnal Green, that 'the Boundary Street scheme turned over 3,000 people into the other overcrowded quarters of his district, very few of whom returned to the new block dwellings.'[36]

Jack London formed a very similar impression of the new estate in late 1902. In *The People of the Abyss* he mentions that he 'visited the municipal dwellings erected by the London County Council on the site of the slums where lived Arthur Morrison's "Child of the Jago",' and observes that 'while the buildings housed more people than before' and were 'much healthier', this was because they were 'inhabited by the better-class work-men and artisans'. As London put it, echoing Morrison and Booth, 'the slum people had simply drifted on to crowd other slums or to form new slums.'[37]

With the troublesome poor excluded and with a teetotal regime in place, the LCC revealed a grim determination not to let its exemplary estate descend into anything resembling social chaos. The importance of the estate as a model, and the interest shown in it when completed, is revealed by the sentiments expressed by the Prince of Wales when he inaugurated the housing in March 1900: 'Everyone', said the Prince, 'who takes any interest in the improvement of homes for the working classes has heard of [this] scheme undertaken by the London County Council.'

To proclaim the new respectability of the Nichol area and its conver-sion to conventional middle-class aspirations, a bandstand was erected on a mound in the middle of the circus. This was intended for polite Sunday entertainments and to encourage the residents of the estate to emulate their social superiors and promenade in sedate manner along the paths around the mound and in the surrounding streets. The social engineering was well meant but naïve. It was also brutal. Those who had once lived in the Nichol but who were too poor to pay the rents of these pleasant new homes, or were deemed 'vicious' or undeserving, were simply exiled from this new paradise. It is easy to understand the anger and alienation these exiles must have felt. Booth, the veteran campaigner for the welfare of the London poor, who had visited the area in spring 1896 while the resettlement was taking place, merely observed that 'the Boundary area is better because the old class has left and a new and more respectable one has come in.' He knew that the 'old class' had gone to swell the desperate populations in the slum streets that still survived on the periphery of the Boundary Estate. But evidently he – like many of his fellow middle-class philanthropists – did not perceive a simple truth. Slum clearance and rebuilding projects that did not involve the rehousing of the slum dwellers meant that the core problem of urban poverty and deprivation had not been solved. The problem had not gone away, it had simply been moved on.

This, of course, was precisely the point made by Arthur Morrison in 1897 when writing the somewhat defensive preface to the third edition of *A Child of the Jago*. He was aware that it might appear odd that his book was campaigning against the evils of the Nichol after the decision had been taken, and action was well under way, to remove that particular trouble spot. His explanation in the preface both explains his intentions and highlights the fundamental problem with a policy that envisages the provision of architecturally handsome but expensive – and ultimately exclusive – working-class housing. For Morrison the specific evil of the Nichol might soon be gone but the essential evil remained and so the battle was not yet over. 'The Jago, as mere bricks and mortar, is gone,' he wrote. 'But the Jago in flesh and blood still lives, and is crowding into neighbourhoods already densely over-populated,' which meant, for Morrison, the 'Jago difficulty' had still not been solved.[38]

NINETEEN

UNDER THE MICROSCOPE

The Streets of Victorian Spitalfields

While the rebuilding of the 'Flower and Dean Street' Rookery was under way, Spitalfields – along with the rest of central London – was the subject of a very detailed and revealing social survey. Charles Booth was a philanthropist and social reformer determined to help alleviate the plight of the poor in London. And to do this, he believed, he needed data that would assess grades of poverty and identify where the poor lived, in what numbers and in what condition. So he set himself the task of documenting the capital's working-class life as a means of producing objective facts and information to support arguments for reform. His survey, when focusing on the streets of Spitalfields and Whitechapel occupied by the Jewish community, offers not just a fascinating snapshot of the area in the mid 1890s but also a revealing companion piece to Israel Zangwill's emotive description of the same area. Zangwill gives an insider's view, suggesting the unseen world beneath the vivid and very visible images of the ghetto. Booth offers an outsider's view. He primarily notes the external appearances – the physical condition of the area and the state of its inhabitants – and does not venture far towards interpretation or explanation. These two accounts combined give us a remarkable insight into the metaphorical body and soul of Spitalfields' Jewish ghetto in the last decade of the nineteenth century.[1]

Central to the gathering of information was the collation of maps – the so-called 'Poverty Maps' – and these have proved of great and lasting worth for the vignette they present of the relative wealth of the inhabitants of London's streets, and some idea of the physical condition of these streets, at a critical moment in the history of the capital. The residential buildings shown lining the streets were coded with one of seven colours to record their social status – the 'general condition of the inhabitants' – and hint at their state of repair. Buildings coloured gold were 'Upper-Middle and Upper-Class. Wealthy'; red were 'Middle-Class. Well-to-do'; pink

Parts of the Ordnance Survey maps of Spitalfields (1873) and Shoreditch (1872). The west end of Bethnal era, in particular the cramped courts and alleys of small cottages created in the late eighteenth

Green Road is now Redchurch Street. The maps show the building density of the area in the late Victorian and early nineteenth centuries within spaces left open in the initial development of the area.

were 'Fairly comfortable. Good ordinary earnings'; purple denoted 'Mixed. Some comfortable, others poor'; light blue meant 'Poor. 18 shillings to 21 shillings a week for a moderate family'; dark blue were 'Very poor, casual. Chronic want'; while black meant streets or buildings were of the 'Lowest class. Vicious, semi-criminal'.

This final categorisation is disconcerting. It implies that, for all his reforming instincts, Booth was locked into the late-Victorian pseudo-science of eugenics, viewing the dire poverty of outcast Londoners as being in some way synonymous with being 'semi-criminal'. Entirely non-residential buildings – such as warehouses, manufactories, markets and public buildings – were not colour-coded. (The first map covering East London was published in his first volume of 1889, *Life and Labour of the People* and entitled the 'Descriptive Map of East End Poverty'. In 1891 the map was expanded to four sheets to cover most of central London, and in the late 1890s Booth published a revised edition of the 1889 map.)

One obvious problem with Booth's system is that it is fairly crude – gradations of wealth within a street, or within an individual building in a street, were difficult to record and show (although occasionally attempted by using one colour for a block and outlining it in another). But despite being somewhat broad-brush the map produced by Booth's system of categorisation nevertheless presented a startling physical representation of the location of the rich, the poor and the middling classes in late-nineteenth-century London.

Looking at the 1889 colour-coded map of Spitalfields two things are instantly – and predictably – apparent. Better classes of dwellings line new or major thoroughfares; poorer houses cluster in back streets, courts or alleys that often contain older buildings; and the juxtaposition of rich and poor households can be dramatic and extreme. For example, all the buildings that are colour-coded along Commercial Street are red or pink. There is just one exception, a block of buildings on the corner with 'Little Pearl Street'. These are coloured black. Most black-coded buildings in the area cluster around the courts and alleys south of Quaker Street (itself mostly purple) and 'Dorset Street'. The then still surviving buildings in the 'Flower and Dean Street' area are shown in black, while blocks of the new Rothschild Buildings are all coded as purple. The streets of the Nichol are generally black or dark blue, with Old Nichol's Street being worse than New Nichol's or 'Half Nichol's Street', and with 'Nelson Street' – coded light blue – being, apparently, a notch up.

In 1898 Booth took a detailed tour around Spitalfields so that he could check or revise the colour coding on his earlier maps, perhaps compiled as much as ten years earlier. He noted his observations, and the document (still owned by the Booth family and currently lodged in the London School of Economics) is a vital and compelling testament to the street life of Spitalfields, south Shoreditch and Whitechapel in the spring of 1898. The exploration was conducted in phases and the fifty-eight-year-old Booth was always escorted by a local police officer familiar with the ways of the inhabitants and local street life. He was clearly there both to guide and protect, but Booth also used his escort to gain, whenever possible, detailed information about the streets they walked through, the buildings they saw and the people they met.

The first Spitalfields walk started on Thursday 17 March from the Commercial Street police station that had, ten years earlier, been the local headquarters in the ultimately unsuccessful hunt for Jack the Ripper. Booth was accompanied by Sergeant French who had 'been 13 years in the Whitechapel service', had 'started in this division as a constable' but had been back only five years as a sergeant, 'coming here from Westminster'. Booth described French as 'middle height, sturdy, moustache, rather heavy face, very willing'.

From the police station the pair turned west down Fleur de Lis Street. Booth noted that 'it had been red on map; but was now not so good'. He sketched a bit of the street's history. It had, he wrote, been 'formerly inhabited by weavers, Houses 3 and 2 stories. 3 families in each. Jews beginning to come in, respectable market porters & labourers, get drunk on Saturdays'.[2] Booth concluded, presumably acting on French's advice, that the street in 1898 was 'not better than purple'.

Then south down Blossom Street, the west side of which had been largely rebuilt as workshops and warehouses by 1898. Booth noted 'pink on map, wash houses on west side. 3 storied tenements & houses on east side. Rough, cockney Irish.' Like Fleur de Lis Street, Blossom Street had gone down in the world – 'now dark blue'. On the west side was a small, cul-de-sac court called 'Blossom Place'. Booth recorded that the court contained '11 houses, 2 & 3 storied, & boot makers, quiet', and that it was pink on the map but should be downgraded to purple. The court survives, as indeed do the wash houses – although derelict in the autumn of 2016 and threatened with demolition (see page 633) – but all the cottages have long gone. The court is now part of a public house.

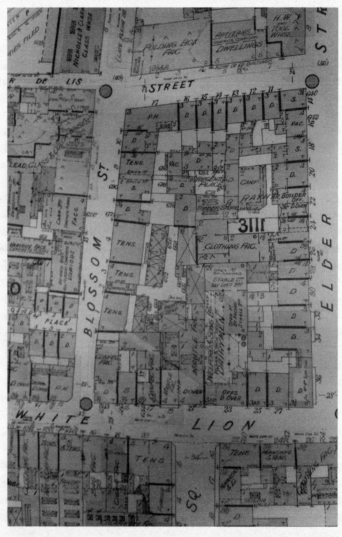

A detail of the fire insurance plan produced from 1886 by Chas. E. Goad Ltd. showing the west side of Elder Street and part of Norton Folgate. These maps primarily record structure and uses, and were constantly updated. This version dates from the 1890s. It shows the courts and alleys created around c.1800 between Elder Street and Blossom Street (D means a building in domestic use) and also west of Blossom Street. Also striking is the mix of uses, including a 'Cigar Factory', a 'Mantle Factory' and a 'Dairymen' on White Lion Street, a 'Furriers' on Spital Square, and a 'Folding Box Factory' on Fleur de Lis Street.

East of Blossom Street ran the long-lost 'Blossom Passage', also in 1898 lined with small and humble cottages. Booth noted four houses here, '2 & 3 storied', inhabited 'by Irish, rough' – a surviving enclave of the old Irish community in backstreets that were gradually seeing an increase in Jewish settlement. It is worth noting, though, that this portion of Spitalfields never fully became part of the Jewish quarter that flourished to the south around Wentworth Street and in Whitechapel. The 1899 map of 'Jewish East London' showed Jewish habitation in these north Spitalfields back-streets as 25 to 49 per cent, but contemporary census returns suggest the percentage was, in fact, 25 per cent or less. Once again Booth downgraded a category from pink to dark blue.

Such alleys and courts formed by terraces of small cottages were once common in Spitalfields, as scrutiny of the 1872/3 Ordnance Survey map makes clear. They had been created on former open courts and yards, even gardens, as the social and economic status of the area declined in the late eighteenth century and its population of poor people expanded, or even during the brief boom in the silk industry between 1800 and 1820. All the cramped and humble cottages they once contained have now gone. I remember the last small group, reached through a narrow arch off Fleur de Lis Street and located, back-to-back fashion, with a structure adjoining the yards of 5–7 Elder Street. The cottages, probably dating from around 1800, were two storeys high and looked across an alley barely more than a metre wide at a blank brick wall. Today the last flavour of this lost Spital-fields life is hinted at by a group of early-eighteenth-century, relatively large cottages in Puma Court, off Wilkes Street.

Booth and French then walked east along 'White Lion Street' (now Folgate Street) towards Commercial Street. Booth noted 'respectable tradesmen, Jews principally, respectable 2 & 3 storied houses.' There was no need to change the red category already shown on the map. Then he passed the turning into Elder Street: '3 ½ to 4 storied, Old Queen Anne houses with ornamental porches, workshops, furriers, Jews, red [as] on map.' Booth observed that on 'the corner of White Lion street (north side) & Commercial street, is a block of Peabody dwellings.' Interestingly he demoted these from red, as on the 1889 map, to purple.

The two men then turned down into a portion of Spitalfields that was decayed in 1898 and had now been completely transformed, with streets and courts lost and buildings swept away. First they entered the southern portion of Wheler Street – which had been Spitalfields' premier street when laid out around the time of the Great Fire (see pages 114–15) and which was subsequently truncated by the mid-nineteenth-century construction of Commercial Street. In 1898 Booth noted the street was 'rough', with 'several ticket-of-leave men living here' (that is, paroled convicts, licensed to live and work outside jail as on probation). There was 'mess on street, bread, old boots, paper, windows dirty & broken. Irish thieves.' Booth downgraded it from purple to dark blue. He then described the long-gone 'Chapel [Place] on the west side, near the alley now named Nantes Passage.' There he noted, 'houses 4 storied with long weavers' . . . windows at the top' standing in small courts and alleys and integrated intimately with the larger silk merchants' houses that once stood on 'White Lion Street' and nearby Spital Square. By 1898 these former weavers' cottages were slum dwellings, and Booth confirmed that they should be coded 'dark blue as map'.

He and French returned to 'White Lion Street', via Church Passage and Chapel Place,[3] which he thought 'clean' but deserved to be coded purple. They walked west to Spital Square, which still contained the largest and grandest collection of early-Georgian houses in Spitalfields. Booth observed, '4 storied, all Jews, red rather than pink on maps. Cigarette factory, well-to-do, better than White Lion Street, German synagogue on east side & the Central Foundation School on the south side.' He upgraded this location – largely commercial rather than residential – from pink to red. The pair proceeded east along Lamb Street to Spitalfields Market – then bounded by Lamb Street, Commercial Street, Brushfield Street and Crispin Street: 'flowers, fruit & vegetables. Lamb Street . . . small shops, owners living above, also market salesmen.' He downgraded Lamb Street from red to pink. On the north side of the street the pair explored 'a rough court, called Lamb Court', and here Booth noted, 'Irish, one barefoot boy, bullies or ponces.' This court he downgraded from purple to dark blue. In Crispin Street he simply noted 'market shops' and upgraded it from purple to pink. Brushfield Street he left 'pink as maps'.[4]

Booth and French now penetrated into the narrow streets of modest houses constructed in the early 1680s, under the control of the speculative builder Nicholas Barbon, on the Old Artillery Ground (see page 129). First they walked north up Gun Street, which Booth found 'very rough', with a 'mixture of dwelling houses & factories. 3 storied & attic houses.' At the north-west end of Gun Street he observed 'a Jewish common lodging house . . . where the Jew thieves congregate . . . called "The poor Jews home" on the board outside.' The south end of Gun Street – which is the surviving portion south of Brushfield Street – Booth thought 'rougher than the north end'. The street was 'narrow, 18ft across from wall to wall' with 'old boots & mess in it', the habitation comprised '4 ½ storied houses & a lodging house at the S.E. end.' The denizens of the street, Booth recorded, were 'dilapidated looking, ticket-of-leave men', but he conceded that the place was not 'particularly noted' for prostitution. Nevertheless, he downgraded it from purple to dark blue.

One local child Booth might have seen playing or loitering there during his visit was the future painter Mark Gertler, who had been born in a house in Gun Street in 1891 to Louis Gertler, a Polish Jewish master furrier. The father had then taken his family to Poland in 1892, but when his business endeavours failed, all returned to London in 1896. In later years, after a flirtation with the Bloomsbury and Camden Town groups of artists, intellectuals and patrons, Mark Gertler – troubled, ill and depressed – gravitated back to Spitalfields and lived in 32 Elder Street before committing suicide in a Hampstead studio in 1939.

Now Booth crossed from the north end of Gun Street into Fort Street, which he regarded as 'fairly well-to-do' with a 'few middlemen' residing in it. Steward Street, parallel to Gun Street, was similar. He upgraded both to pink from purple. Duke Street, also parallel to Gun Street, was a different story. Booth recorded that the street 'has houses on east side, the west side is all factories & warehouses', and that 'Costers, flower & fruit sellers in Liverpool Street come from here! Inhabitants a mixture of Jews & Irish.' He downgraded its 'character' from purple to 'dark blue to light blue'.

The two observers proceeded south into Artillery Lane, where Booth noted a synagogue on the west side,[5] and 'dwelling houses on east side, purple to pink'. This synagogue had just opened when Booth passed by, within a mid-eighteenth-century former Baptist chapel. It remained in use until 1948 when the building – crudely re-fronted – became a warehouse. It survives in office use, its front recreated in eighteenth-century style, its splendid ceiling incorporating plaster-clad dome still intact. They proceeded 'west along Artillery Passage', which Booth described as 'all Jews, rather narrow . . . with shops on either side, pink as map.' In 'Artillery Court' (now Parliament Court) off the north side of the passage, Booth noticed 'ragged children, fish curers, rough', and coded it dark blue. Then 'east along Artillery Lane' (in fact Artillery Street or still 'Raven Row' according to the 1894 Ordnance Survey map) to 'the Roman

Catholic dormitory at the corner of Bell Lane.' This was a night refuge, run by nuns, in a large and gaunt building, facing the west end of 'Dorset Street', which in the mid 1890s was one of the worst streets in Spitalfields. When Booth passed by 'the hour was only one PM' but, to his surprise, 'there was already a crowd of 30 men & 2 women waiting to be taken in, though the doors do not open till 4. French said they were a set of scoundrels, but they did not look as if they belong to the worst class, all fairly clothed, one or two old cripples.'

'Dorset Street' received a damning judgement: 'Black in map, still black. The worst street I have seen so far, thieves, prostitutes, bullies, all common lodging houses. Some called "Doubles", with double beds for married couples, but merely another name for brothels. Women draggled, torn skirts, dirty, unkempt, square jaws [presumably meaning defiant, aggressive, unrepentant, even drunk], standing about in street or on doorsteps.' Booth knew that 'the majority of the houses' were owned by one of the major characters of late-nineteenth-century 'low-life' Spitalfields, 'Jack McCarthy,[6] keeper of the General shop on the north side of the street'. McCarthy seems to have had a finger in many pies, all of them unsavoury, and to have been something of a 'Godfather' in the fraternity of late- Victorian Spitalfields gangs. As far as was known, he lived off immoral earnings – either as a pimp or through renting out houses to serve as brothels – was a slum landlord, and with his extended family and associates ran public houses and other places of entertainment.

Booth and French also explored the narrow courts and alleys reached from the north side of 'Dorset Street', some connecting with Brushfield Street. These, including Miller's Court where the Ripper victim Mary Jane Kelly had rented a room from McCarthy, were the worst parts of the 'Dorset Street' area. Booth mentioned 'New Court, 3 storied houses . . . black', and in 'Dorset Court' observed that the 'back rooms of a common lodging house for men & women come through into the court from the front of the street' with 'open basins & taps on the west side of the court for washing purposes.' In 'Old Dorset Court', 'now . . . done up', Booth noticed 'Irish & negress at a wash tub, windows dirty & broken, narrow 2 storied houses, also black.' In 'Little Paternoster Row' he saw a '2 & 3 storied common lodging house, ragged women & children [with] holey toeless boots, windows dirty, patched with brown paper & broken. Prostitutes, thieves & ponces – Black on both sides.' These buildings, recorded Booth, were also 'owned by the notorious Jack McCarthy of Dorset street.'

Booth and French next explored White's Row, parallel to 'Dorset Street'. He declared it mostly black 'by reason of . . . thieves & bullies'.[7] They then passed south under the early-nineteenth-century 'Shepherd's Place Arch', at the west end of White's Row into the Tenter Ground district, which Booth thought 'very rough' with its population 'all Jews, poor, fairly quiet though rowdy for Jews.' He downgraded it from pink to purple.[8]

In Wentworth Street, 'thronged every day by stalls', Booth noted that 'both buyers and sellers nearly, but not altogether, Jews. Women bare headed, bewigged [this presumably refers to the *sheitel*, which is a wig or half-wig worn by some orthodox Jewish married women], coarse woollen shawls over shoulders, more like a foreign market scene than anything English'. But, Booth observed, 'no poor here, except in the courts.'[9] He and French then went north-west and inspected Frying Pan Alley, with the Jews' Free School behind its south side. The alley was 'narrow' and 'poor', and coded light blue, like nearby Sandys Row.[10]

On Friday, 18 March 1898 Booth and French started from the Commercial Street police station on their second Spitalfields walk. This time they headed east along Quaker Street – along with 'Dorset Street' one of the worst locations in Spitalfields. Booth observed 'along Quaker street' three-storied houses inhabited by 'rough, Irish' with 'brothels on both sides.'[11] The pair then turned into the network of alleys and courts that survived to the south of Quaker Street (those to the north had been destroyed in the 1830s for the building of the railway). They went first into 'Pope's Head Court', south-west of Quaker Street. This narrow court is marked on Richard Horwood's map of 1799 when it contained ten or twelve houses (Booth talks of '1 or 2 storied old houses still remaining with long weavers' windows in the higher stories') and in more detail on the 1872/3 Ordnance Survey map. Entered through a narrow arched opening off Quaker Street, the court was just a few feet wide and lined with about fourteen small cottages. This court in turn was linked, via another arched opening, to an equally narrow but shorter court called 'Union Place' that led, via a further arched opening, into Wheler Street.

To the east of 'Pope's Head Court' – connected by a passage – was another court, shown on the Ordnance Survey map to contain a 'pump' that was no doubt the only source of water for these court-dwellers. Lavatories were probably located in the tiny rear yards that some of the cottages appeared to possess. And to the east of the court with the pump was 'New Square', where Booth noted two-storey houses and one single-storey

*A group of children photographed by Horace Warner in c.1902 in 'Crown Court',
which was one of the more secluded courts in the labyrinth of spaces off
Quaker Street and 'Great' and 'Little Pearl' Streets.*

house, 'dogs chained to each garden' and 'thieves'. Back in 1805 1 'New Square' (or 'New Court' as it was then known) had been home to the parents of a fourteen-year-old pickpocket named Elizabeth Taylor, arrested in Shoreditch High Street while lifting a pocketbook, convicted at the Old Bailey and transported for seven years. So impoverished were her parents that they had previously placed her in the workhouse.[12] Evidently, the square's deprivation was of long standing.

In 'Pool's Square' – which must formerly have been 'Pool's Place' and the location of the house of abject poverty that in 1844 so shocked Friedrich Engels (see pages 418–19) – were '3 storied houses', 'one house with wooden top storey, windows broken', and 'rough women about, Irish'. All was coded dark blue. 'This', observed Booth, 'is the last of an Irish colony, the Jews begin to predominate.'

The 1891 census puts flesh on Booth's thumbnail sketch of deprivation in 'Pool's Square', listing the names of individuals and families crammed, often several together, into the small houses. Among them are a scattering of people from Ireland, including at number 2 Patrick Carroll, aged forty-five, a 'working builder' who had been born in Cork; at number 4 John Crawley, a costermonger aged sixty, also born in Cork and now living on his own; and at number 6 Daniel Callaghan, a 'general labourer' aged sixty-two, with his family of four. And one of Horace Warner's photographs of c.1902 seems to show some of the children who lived in 'Pool's Square'. A long row of them sit on a wall with behind them the rear elevation of an early-eighteenth-century weavers' house, its rear rooms covered with a typical mono-pitch cat-slide roof. In front, standing on the cobbles, is another row of children. All are young, none probably more than thirteen or fourteen. They are captioned, by Warner, the 'open air concert group'.[13]

Booth and French also explored the area south of Quaker Street and around Christ Church Spitalfields. They went to 'Corbet's Court', just north of the church, where Booth noted '2 storied . . . Irish brothels on either side of north end . . . by no manner of means respectable . . . now dark blue to black.' In neighbouring 'Great Pearl Street' were 'common lodging houses with double beds, thieves, bullies, prostitutes like Dorset Street . . . black on map.'[14] In 'Little Pearl Street' were 'old houses with long, small paned weavers' windows to top stories. Some boarded up.' In houses in the middle of the street lived 'a few Jews'.

As the census returns and Booth's survey strongly suggest, the inhabitants of these poorer portions of Spitalfields were – in the late nineteenth

Horace Warner's photograph of c.1902 showing a group of children and captioned an 'open air concert group in Poole's sq. Quaker st.'.

century – very territorial. There were streets, courts and small areas inhabited almost entirely by poor Jewish families, mostly towards Whitechapel Road, and others by poor Irish or English families. These latter two groups tended to mix while the Jews almost always remained separate, part of the informal and wall-less ghetto described by Israel Zangwill (see pages 490–3). The people of these small courts off Quaker Street, such as 'Crown Court', are a case in point. The census shows a mix of Irish and English poor, with the English forming the majority (so not an 'Irish colony' as Booth seems to have thought), and in 'Pool's Square' only one surname – Shearman – that could conceivably be Jewish (this seems unlikely, though, since an isolated Jewish family here would have felt itself very exposed). Also seemingly absent is the Huguenot legacy. Only a few of the surnames sound French, such as the Lebeau family at number 8, seemingly confirming that by the end of the nineteenth century the area's once dominant French community was but a distant memory, its members having been assimilated or obliged to leave Spitalfields when its decline became general.

Also a distant memory in the 1890s – certainly in its poorest enclaves – was the once ubiquitous silk industry. Of all the people living in 'Pool's Square', with their diverse trades and occupations, only one – thirty-nine-year-old Mary Ann Maynards, who lived at number 1 – worked with silk. But the presence of a Sarah Adelaide Stillwell, a sixty-year-old charwoman, also at number 8 and who appears to have lived alone, poses some haunting possibilities. In the 1830s a James Stillwell lived in what is now 16 Folgate Street – a fine house of 1724 – and is said to have woven the cloth-of-gold for Queen Victoria's Coronation robes. He was regarded as the last of Spitalfields' 'old-time prosperous master silk weavers . . . on whose death in the early sixties his class became extinct.'[15] Can Sarah Adelaide Stillwell have been descended from a branch of this once illustrious Spitalfields family, her humble occupation echoing the decline of the area's once valuable silk industry and of its great merchant dynasties?

During their Friday walk Booth and French came face-to-face once more with Spitalfields gang life. In 'Dorset Street' they had encountered Jack McCarthy, who headed an Irish Catholic and English gang. Here, 'on the west side of Little Pearl Street', Booth writes, 'lives F. Gehringer. "Barrows to let" – the owner of all the houses' in a district that 'remains as

black as it was ten years ago. As the Dorset Street district belongs to a
dweller in it, MacCarthy [sic], so this bit belongs to "Geringer" [in fact
Frederick Gehringer] an inhabitant of Little Pearl Street.' The majority of
the properties in both these streets were common lodging houses for men
and women, containing 'doubles' – or double beds – that to observers like
Booth made them little better than brothels, so it is scarcely surprising
that he should have listed the inhabitants of the street as 'Thieves, bullies
and prostitutes'. According to historian Fiona Rule, Gehringer was of
German stock and controlled the area bordered by Quaker Street, Commercial Street and Grey Eagle Street – what Booth termed 'the Little
Pearl Street district'. His gang was, presumably, German/Jewish. As well
as running common lodging houses and brothels, he had a legitimate front
operating a haulage company and hiring out market carts or barrows, ran
the City of Norwich pub in Wentworth Street, and 'no doubt had business
connections at nearby Spitalfields Market'.[16] Booth dismissed the 'Little
Pearl Street district' as 'a thoroughly vicious quarter', partly because 'the
presence of the Cambridge Music Hall on Commercial Street makes it a
focusing point for prostitutes.'

From here Booth and his companion walked south down Commercial
Street, where Booth looked into Puma Court, a paved court (with alms-
houses on its north side) leading to Wilkes Street, which he coded as
purple and pink. They then explored 'Fournier Street – late Church Street',[17]
which with Spital Square contained the best large early-Georgian houses
to survive in Spitalfields. Booth noted the houses were the homes of
'well-to-do Jews' who 'keep servants', and that 'the large Wesleyan chapel
at the end of [the] street is now being converted into a synagogue.' (The
1899 map of 'Jewish East London' confirms that the houses on both sides
of Fournier Street were in '95% to 100% Jewish occupation'.) Sergeant
French told Booth that – most unusually for the area – there was 'one
family to each house'. Booth upgraded the street to 'red rather than pink
on map.'

Booth and French then walked north along 'Wilkes Street, late Wood
Street' – also of course lined on both sides with early-Georgian houses
(see page 210), though none as large as the best houses in Fournier Street.
The character of this street was a notch or two down from that of Fournier
Street, and the 1899 map suggests that the proportion of its residents was
between 75 and 95 per cent Jewish. Booth noticed on the street's east side
'a lodging house, frequented by ex-convicts'. French explained that the

house had 'six or seven rooms, old lags living there now'. There was, Booth reflected, 'no shame about having been in prison here.'

They then turned east along 'Princelet Street, late Princes St', where Booth noted 'Jews'. The 1899 map shows the same proportion of Jewish occupancy as Wilkes Street. At the east end of the street, on the corner of Brick Lane, Booth observed 'two common lodging houses (4d a night, 2/- a week)' used by 'thieves, prostitutes, bullies'. 'One of Cooney's houses,' his companion informed him.[18] Booth had evidently heard of John Cooney, perhaps because his name had been linked ten years earlier with one of Jack the Ripper's victims, Catherine Eddowes, who had lodged at a Cooney-run establishment at 55 Flower and Dean Street (he noted that Cooney 'has many common lodging houses of doubtful reputation in the neighbourhood'). French told him that 'Marie Lloyd the singer is a relation' of Cooney's and that she 'often comes down visiting here in a smart brougham.' The music-hall star, it seems, liked to visit her cousin at either of the pubs he owned in Hanbury Street – the Sugar Loaf at number 187 or the Weaver's Arms at number 17 – after performing at the nearby Royal Cambridge Music Hall. No doubt on such occasions she also ran across other members of Spitalfields' 'swell mob', including the notorious Jack McCarthy.[19] Cooney, incidentally, makes an appearance in the 1891 census,[20] where the then thirty-five-year-old is noted as living at 54 Flower and Dean Street, described as 'Part Private House and Part lodging house'.

In his 1898/9 re-survey Booth's map downgraded the houses on both sides of the east end of Princelet Street to black. The surviving houses on the north side, which might have included Cooney's lodging house, are among the very few structures once coded black by Booth still to be standing. A look at the 1891 census suggests why he took this action. Number 17 'Prince Street' (now 21 Princelet Street) was built as a five-storey ten- or eleven-room house between 1705 and 1706 and on the day of the census contained an astonishing forty-eight people, organised as eight family groups. The 1872/3 Ordnance Survey map shows a large structure in the house's generous rear yard. This could have been in residential use in 1891, but was more likely a workshop or in light industrial use.

Booth describes the occupants of the houses he colour-coded black as the 'Lowest Class. Vicious, semi-criminal'. The occupants may have been the former, but were they also the latter? A look at the trades of some of them suggests not. They included Henry Prollius, a forty-four-year-old cabinet-maker born in Germany, who lived with his twelve-year-old daughter Elizabeth; Isaac Newman, a thirty-five-year-old 'Hebrew book seller' born in Russia, who lived with his Russian wife and eight children; Barnet Cohen, a forty-five-year-old 'Boot finisher' from Germany, his Polish wife and three children; William Germantis, a thirty-year-old Polish-born 'Tailor's Presser', his wife, son and five Polish male lodgers – aged between eighteen and twenty-five – whose trades were tailors, table-makers and a 'skin dresser'; and Philip Swartzh, a twenty-year-old tailor from 'Russia Poland', his nineteen-year-old wife and their daughter.[21] It is hard to comprehend the manner in which the house was occupied but it is a distinct possibility that the Germantis family of three were obliged to occupy a single room together with their five male lodgers. Water would have been supplied to the basement and perhaps to a couple of landings, and the only lavatories – perhaps two – would have been in the back yard.

Number 17 'Princes Street', although extreme in its density of occupation, was not a completely exceptional case. Number 18 'Princes Street' (now number 19 Princelet Street) – which contained the synagogue in its basement, ground and first floor and former garden (see pages 355–6) – was occupied by thirteen people in three family groups in 1891. These people could have been obliged to cram themselves into the building's remaining three or four rooms. One family was formed by Harris Levy, the seventy-seven-year-old synagogue beadle, his wife and cousin, while another of the families comprised the widowed fifty-three-year-old Polish-born Leah Lichenstein and her five grown sons, working as tailors and bootmakers.

From Princelet Street Booth and French entered Brick Lane – 'Jews, shops mixture of good, bad and indifferent. At the SE end are brothels. The common lodging houses also have a bad name.' 'The best part of Brick Lane,' French told Booth, 'is the centre, both ends are bad.'[22] The pair walked south and then '. . . east into Flower & Dean Street, black on map, now purple. Tall 6 storied buildings on either side, belonging to the Rothschilds. Street 27 feet across, mess, bits of fish. The east end of this street narrows to 15 feet and has common lodging houses. "As black here as you like!"[23] said French.' In Thrawl Street ('Brick Lane end, on the south side') the hand of McCarthy was again apparent in the form of one of his lodging houses 'filled with thieves', while on the east side of 'Lolesworth Street, late George Street' Booth noted 'brothels, thieves, prostitutes, ponces . . . black'. In Wentworth Street, at the Brick Lane end, Booth saw 'one of the largest common lodging houses in London, called Wildermoth, built in 1893', which French told him 'holds about eight hundred persons'. The pair went south to Old Montague Street, the main shopping streets of the Jewish quarter, which Booth described as 'narrow, long, 3 storied houses, shops, owners living above, purple . . . many courts of the south side. All Jews.'[24] The main street he upgraded to pink from purple.

Evidently there had been some few improvements in the area since the 1880s. 'Black' areas in 'Flower and Dean Street' had been demolished[25] and 'betterment' was noticeable in some of the larger streets, such as Hanbury and Church Streets, owing to the coming of well-to-do Jewish families. The courts off Old Montague Street had also moved up in the world a little, owing to the 'displacement of rough English and Irish by poor but quiet Jews'. Racial tension, though, was never far away. Booth noted that in areas transformed by the 'invasion of Jews' with 'small English colonies dotted about', there was 'friction where the two live together on one street.'[26]

During the following week, in late March 1898, he and French continued their methodical survey of the outer environs of the Spitalfields area. Much of what they saw is now an utterly lost world. Not only have the communities he saw long gone but also all memory of them, along with virtually all the buildings, courts and alleys in which the late-Victorian inhabitants of the area lived and worked. Booth's telegrammatic descriptions nevertheless leave us with a powerful impression of what it must have been like. Again, Cooney was a constant lurking presence. One of his lodging houses – 'doubtless a brothel' – stood at the east end of Old Montague Street, while another two could be found at the east end of Chicksand Street, called 'Osborn Place'. 'Black' was Booth's unsurprising verdict. In 'George Court' he noted 'poor Jews' with '2 roomed houses letting at 5/- the house, no washrooms',[27] while Heneage Street, east of Brick Lane, was 'messy, Jews', and neighbouring Chicksand Street was also 'all Jews, principally tailors & machinists, building with workshops on the top & motto on the outside "Work, Wait, Win."' In this area bordering Whitechapel Booth noticed '. . . a greater mixture of well-to-do, poor & very poor in adjacent houses, or even in the same houses, among Jews than among Gentiles',[28] and observed that the heights of houses gradually increased towards Whitechapel, which, he thought, reflected 'a tendency of [the] Jewish district to increase accommodation . . .'

One or two aspects of the minutiae of street life also seized his attention: 'The children's games in vogue now', he recorded, 'are marbles and tip-cat [a game that involved 'tipping' a short tapering billet of wood into the air with a longer stick and, while it was in the air, hitting the billet a great distance]. Marbles coming in with much warmer weather.'[29]

On 22 March 1898 Booth continued his survey of the Spitalfields area with Sergeant French, by 'starting at the west end of Sclater Street, known in the locality as Club Row'. In the early eighteenth century this had been one of the main streets of Spitalfields' weaving district, with rows of terraced houses, furnished with wide upper windows, where journeymen weavers had toiled (see page 197). But by the 1890s it was dominated by a bird market: '3 and 4 storey houses, shops underneath', Booth noted; 'centre to bird fanciers, larks, thrushes, canaries, parrots, rabbits etc. in cages.' There were, he observed, 'small square cages wrapped up in pocket handkerchiefs outside windows'. These, French informed him, were 'for new birds to pick up the right note from their fellows.' He also noticed the 'long weavers' windows on top stories' but recorded 'no weavers now, nor prostitutes, simply rough class'. According to French the population of the street was 'all thieves or receivers of stolen goods; they go "dipping" [pick-pocketing] on Sunday morning, what we call larceny from the person'.[30]

At the east end of Sclater Street, at the corner with Brick Lane, Booth noticed 'an elaborate stone shield in a red brick niche. This is Sclater Street, 1778.' The date stone survives on 125 Brick Lane, and could just possibly read 1718 not 1778, a year that relates more closely to the origin of the street (see page 188) and the Baroque design of the niche. The pair then crossed Brick Lane and headed east into the old weaving quarter around Weaver Street. First they went down 'St John [S]treet (late King Street)' which by the 1890s had been all but obliterated by the ever-widening track lay-out of the railway viaducts and cuttings serving the Bishopsgate/Liverpool Street terminus and the Bishopsgate Goodsyard.[31] French described it as part of a typically rough English district. Booth observed that it was generally possible to tell where the Jews lived by which houses did not have broken windows.

The pair then walked east along 'Hare Street' (now Cheshire Street) – another street that for a long time had been home and workplace

Above: *among the last remaining open-fronted shops on Old Montague Street, which was one of the primary shopping streets – particularly for food – in Jewish Spitalfields and Whitechapel from the late nineteenth century. On the right is King Arms Court. This view was taken in 1961 before all was swept away for new housing and road widening.* Below: *the cartouche on the corner of Brick Lane and Sclater Street. It states that this is 'Sclater Street' and bears a date that can be read as 1778 – which is roughly the date of the house to which the plaque is affixed – or as 1718, which is when Sclater Street was laid out.*

to journeymen weavers (see page 196) – where Booth noticed 'some Jews, shops underneath, the rest rough, thieves.' He confirmed it dark blue as on his initial map. At 'Three Colt Corner', which was black on his map, Booth noted a factory on its south side and 'a bridge across the Great Eastern Railway train lines'. The bridge, for pedestrians only, survives – although the world around it has been transformed. The pair evidently crossed the bridge, passed through the cavernous vaulted arch of a viaduct and emerged amongst the two-storey former weavers' houses of Pedley Street (see page 374). This street Booth described as 'rather rough, poor drunken, some Irish but not so notoriously bad as Sclater Street.' He downgraded it from light blue to mostly dark blue. Then 'into Weaver Street, 2 storied houses, narrow, only fifteen feet between house and house, some Jews, others thieves. Poor.'[32] In 'Fleet Street' (which was to the west of Pedley Street and is now also called Pedley Street) Booth observed 'a child . . . with only one shoe, all children very dirty'. His surmise was that the ruinous buildings in the street now housed thieves and prostitutes forced from the Boundary Street area as it underwent demolition and redevelopment. Certainly, such people would not have been able to afford – and would very definitely not have been welcomed in – the Boundary Estate's new flats.[33]

Booth reflected on the manner of life he had observed in the 'triangle formed by Bethnal Green Road on the north, 'Fuller Street' on the east [and] Sclater Street on the south.' All appeared to be a 'rough class of costers, thieves, prostitutes, bird fanciers, mixed here and there [with] a chair or cabinet factory,' and he classed the area purple (as on the map). French told him that the denizens of this 'triangle' were known to the police as 'a sporting set of men "who bear no ill will to the police as long as we take [i.e. arrest] them fairly."'[34] Booth was perhaps a little less relaxed: 'streets look very rough,' he wrote, 'no Jews yet, much life in the street, several boys boxing with gloves on, only a few onlookers . . . children all looked sturdy ruffians, well fed.' The triangular area was, it seemed, 'a remnant of Old London with ante Board School traditions and habits. French said the majority of [the residents] would not know how to write their own names.' But, despite this, Booth noticed that the 'men have not the wastrel good for nothing look of the loafers of Commercial Street & the women more of the flower girl roughness, feathers & horseplay etc, than the absolute vicious depredation of the Dorset St. inhabitants.'[35] As far as he could tell, the people within the triangle lived together 'as a happy family' and when 'any of them gets into trouble there is at once a whip round for money for bail or defence.' This observation also gives an insight into the ramifications of the destruction of the Nichol area. As with Pedley Street, Booth supposed, or had been told, that 'a great part of the old Boundary St has come here', presumably bringing its tradition of self-support and its clannish loyalties with it.[36]

Brick Lane, at its north end, Booth thought full of life and 'good humour'. The market was very busy, including 'shops with stalls in front, strings of shoes & clothes over poles sticking out from shop wall, across side-walk, as in pictures of Old London.'[37]

But this atmosphere of conviviality and class loyalty among the poor did not seem to extend north of Bethnal Green Road, into the territory of the Nichol – in 1898 by now mostly a vast demolition and construction site as tall blocks of tenements rose on a new and generous street pattern. What was left of the Nichol seems to have remained desperate, dire and thoroughly criminalised – the haunt of East End gangs. Booth and French walked along 'Church Street' (which was the west end of Bethnal Green Road and is now Redchurch Street), where Booth noted 'thieves' and 'prostitutes' and shops on both sides known to be 'receivers' of stolen property. He downgraded the street from pink right down to black. On the corner with York Row he noted 'The Blue Anchor' public house, 'the most noted thieves' resort in London.' French told him that 'every Sunday they congregate here from all parts of London.' On the corner of Ebor Street (named York Street on the 1872/3 Ordnance Survey map), Booth saw 'a most sad looking man with a gray moustache, black bowler hat, brown coat, dark trousers, good boots, well brushed and gentlemanly looking'. This man, French told Booth, was 'a well-known thieves tutor.' As for Ebor Street itself, this was 'all thieves . . . black rather than the purple on the map.'[38]

On 24 March 1898 Booth and French penetrated into the heart of the old Nichol area. They walked east from Shoreditch High Street along Boundary Passage, the traditional entry into the Nichol slum where, to pass the bollards – the 'posties' – at the end of the passage was to cross a boundary into a lawless land. Virtually all was transformed, by recent demolition and construction. But the south side of Old Nichol's Street, virtually aligned with the passage, survived to mark the southern extent of the mass demolitions. The surviving buildings were, according to Booth, still light blue to dark blue.[39]

Booth observed the 'great changes here owing to County Council Boundary area improvement scheme' and mentioned the 'blocks of dwellings' that had been 'built up with an elevated pyramidal garden as a common centre, on the top of which a band plays in Summer.'[40] But the streets peripheral to the new blocks were, like Old Nichol's Street, still bad. Virginia Road to the north was still dark blue, as was Brick Lane north of Bethnal Green Road. As with the Pedley Street and the Sclater Street areas, Booth recorded that 'some of old Boundary street have come here, thieves, prostitutes, bullies . . .'[41] Gibraltar Walk, a little to the east, was, French said, 'the beginning of a hot bed of thieves'. Booth noted 'prostitutes, bullies' and 'mess in street . . . bird cages, dirt, ragged children, hatless . . .'[42] In fact, he concluded, the streets immediately to the east of the new Boundary Estate were worse than they used to be, 'by reason of the immigration of the worst characters from Boundary Street. Thieves, prostitutes and bullies, especially thieves.' While walking this peripheral area he observed 'here and there parties of three to six lads gossiping.' French described them 'Bethnal Green "nibs"' and said they were all thieves.'[43] French also told Booth that 'no Jews have their foot as yet in this district. They would not dare to, they would be so roughly handled.'

As he walked these streets – a few still old and crowded, others desolate from recent demolitions, and some new and lined with trees and tall blocks of apartments – Booth realised that in the transformed Nichol not only was he getting a glimpse of the future East End but he was also at the intersection of very different communities. To the south the streets were characterised by the 'whirr of the Jewish sewing machine' and activities of the rag trade and market stallholders. But in those streets that survived around the Boundary Estate, where the main industry was cabinet-making, his tour was accompanied by 'the scream of the circular saw' with 'legs of tables, unfinished chairs . . . much in evidence.' And slightly further to the north there was evidence of yet another, earlier and more traditional world. In the late seventeenth and eighteenth centuries Shoreditch had been a place of market gardens and nurseries, which was commemorated by the fact that 'in Spring and Summer . . . Columbia Road . . . is one of the great flower markets of London.' And the tradition of flower growing and selling – and appreciation – remained part of the daily life of the area. Flowers, observed Booth, are 'even now conspicuous in windows of poor streets . . . men & boys . . . of the poorest classes . . . are costers, flower sellers in Columbia Road & hawkers.'[44]

With the 'Flower and Dean Street' Rookery and the Nichol gone there was, at the beginning of the twentieth century, only one large and serious slum left in Spitalfields and its immediate environs – and that was 'Dorset Street', scene in 1888 of the murder of Mary Jane Kelly by Jack the Ripper. On 16 July 1901 it achieved national prominence again – also for all the wrong reasons. In an article in the *Daily Mail*, written by Frederick A. McKenzie and entitled 'The Worst Street in London', it was described as a street 'where our criminals are trained', a place 'which boasts of an attempt at murder on an average once a month, of a murder in every house, and one house at least, a murder in every room. Policemen go down it as a rule in pairs. Hunger walks prowling in its alleyways, and the criminals of to-morrow are being bred there to-day.'

This was sensational stuff. But was it true? Frederick Arthur McKenzie was not an East Ender; he was not even a Londoner. He was a Scots Canadian born in Quebec who had written much about politics in eastern Asia and in 1901 was a staff correspondent on the *Mail*, specialising in the Far East. So was he able to grasp what went on in 'Dorset Street' and put it in proper context? It is hard to be sure. Certainly, his main targets were familiar – the street's common lodging houses, which he claimed were 'the head centres of the shifting criminal population of London', a fraternity which in 'Dorset Street' was 'largely' represented by the 'common thief, the pickpocket, the area sneak, the man who robs with violence, and the unconvicted murderer.' He also argued that such people had a contaminating effect – that 'respectable people, whose main offence is their poverty' could be easily corrupted by being 'thrown in close contact with the agents of crime' and 'made familiar with law-breaking'. McKenzie asserted that 'thieves are trained as regularly and systematically around Dorset Street today as they were in the days of Oliver Twist'.

But if the lodging houses were bad, the 'furnished rooms' were, in McKenzie's view, very much worse. At least lodging houses were subject to 'certain official inspection'. Furnished rooms were not, and McKenzie pointed out that the 'farming' of furnished rooms was a very profitable business:

You take a seven- or eight-roomed house at a rent of 10s. or 11s. a week, you place on each door a padlock, and in each room you put a minimum amount of the oldest furniture to be found in the worst second-hand dealers' in the slums. The fittings of the average furnished room are not worth more than a few shillings. Then you let the rooms out to any comers for 10d. or 1s. a night. No questions asked. They pay the rent, you hand them the key. If by the next night they have not their 10d. or 1s. again ready, you go round and chuck them out and let a newcomer in.

Those who could not afford a room, who occupied the 'depths below the lowest deeps', could, McKenzie wrote, be seen on cold winter nights 'lying on the stones of the doorways, or crouched asleep by the half-dozen on the damp brick passage-ways of the furnished houses.'

The journalist did point to signs of recent improvement. 'I understand that the curate [he meant rector] of Christ Church, Spitalfields, has started in that neighbourhood a small home for respectable girls,' he wrote. But he added the caveat: 'he himself would probably be the first to admit that something very much more is wanted.' And for McKenzie 'more' had to come from outside the community – from the new London County Council, which, he argued, possessed the potential to alleviate human suffering and save public expenditure: 'The County Council showed what it could do in Boundary Street. Surely here, under such needs, it might make a special endeavour. For every pound spent in reforming this street would mean many pounds saved on our prisons and legal machinery to-morrow.'

The response from 'Dorset Street's' landlords, if not necessarily its humble occupants, was predictably hostile. The *Daily Mail* article had blackened their names and their working methods. The improvements it suggested could potentially be bad for business. One of their number therefore decided to take action. As Charles Booth had pointed out a few years previously, the dominant presence in 'Dorset Street' was Jack McCarthy, who owned three 'general shops' in the street, owned and operated two of its lodging houses, was a 'farmer' of rented accommodation, was probably a pimp living off immoral earnings and no doubt also a gangster and racketeer. He was not specifically named in the *Mail* article and could have scuttled off furtively into the shadows. But instead he decided to brazen it out, and to this end organised a public meeting at which the 'honour' of 'Dorset Street' would be defended, the *Daily Mail*'s accusations rebutted and the irritating 'do-gooders' of the area put to flight.

'Dorset Street' in about 1900. When Charles Booth walked its length in 1898 he described the women he saw as 'draggled' with 'torn skirts, unkempt, square jaws, standing about in the street or on doorsteps'. Lamps mark the locations of its many disreputable common lodging houses. A Daily Mail *article in 1901 described it as 'The Worst Street in London' – an accusation strongly resisted by 'Dorset Street's' dominant landlord, Jack McCarthy.*

The public meeting was duly held on 22 July in the Duke of Wellington public house in 'Shepherd Street' (now called Toynbee Street; the pub survives, although rebuilt) and seems to have been packed with McCarthy's supporters – probably his workmen, dependants of one kind or another – and by people in a similar line of business, who also felt themselves threatened by the *Mail*'s exposé. It had been organised and was chaired by Edwin Locock, one of the 'inhabitants' of 'Dorset Street' and most likely one of McCarthy's creatures. The man himself was billed to speak. And thanks to a pamphlet that purports to be a verbatim account of the meeting, we get a very clear sense of what the swaggering and supremely self-confident McCarthy was like.[45]

The meeting was attended by members of Spitalfields' 'swell mob' and various 'Dorset Street' businessmen and local residents including 'Mr W. Crossingham, who owned a considerable property in Dorset Street', the 'Rev. Mr Davies, Rector of Spitalfields', Mr Raymond of the Britannia public house in 'Dorset Street', various McCarthy relations and even – most courageously – Frederick McKenzie, author of the *Daily Mail* article. Locock got the evening started by calling the article a 'gross libel on everyone living in Dorset Street' and promptly gave the floor to Jack McCarthy.

Waving a copy of the *Daily Mail* in a most theatrical manner, he strode into position. This melodramatic entrance would not, perhaps, have surprised the audience since McCarthy had numerous associations with the local music hall and seems to have relished the role of public orator with all its opportunities for sardonic humour and strident self-expression. He told the audience that he intended to 'take this article, piece by piece, and prove to you there is not a particle of truth in it from beginning to end'. And for the next one hour and fifty minutes, with minimal interruption, that is precisely what he sought to do. McCarthy intoned:

> Gentlemen, the heading of this article is in very large type 'The Worst Street in London,' and under that, also in large type, 'Where our Criminals are Trained' (cries from the floor of 'lies, lies, lies'). Dorset Street, Spitalfields, has sprung into undesired notoriety; here we have a place which boasts of an attempt at murder once a month (a voice said, why, he ought to be smothered), of a murder in every house (lies, wicked lies), and in one house a murder in every room (what lies he tells . . .) . . . hunger walks prowling in its alleyways, and the criminals of to-morrow are being

bred there to-day. (Cries of lies, lies, where does he get his information from?) Now, gentlemen, is there an attempt at murder once a month? (No, no, that there a'nt, does he take us for cannibals?) Is there an attempt at murder in a year, or even two, three, four, five or ten years? (Cries of no, he knows there a'nt.) Does it not compare favourably with any street in the world? (Of course it does and is as good as any other place.) Has there been a murder in every house . . . and is there one house in the street in which a murder has been committed in every room? (He knows there a'nt . . .)

And so the meeting went on, with McCarthy attacking every point made by the article, and with the audience baying its support. Having spent many minutes mocking and traducing McKenzie, McCarthy brought his attack nearer to home. Evidently, over the years, he had been irked by the attention he had received from the reformers and philanthropists active in Spitalfields and so, referring to the *Mail*'s assertion that there was a 'great need' in Spitalfields for a lodging house for women, McCarthy said it was 'news to me' that the Rector of Spitalfields had – as the *Mail* claimed – 'started a home for respectable girls . . . where is it?' This was a fairly aggressive – certainly provocative – statement since the Rector was in the audience, as McCarthy probably well knew. The Rector – Mr Davies – stung into action and obliged to defend himself, therefore rose to speak on 'a point of order'. But the mob spirit was up and mischief was in the air. In one of their own pubs, on their own doorstep and surrounded by cronies, these 'Dorset Street' men were unstoppable. The chairman told the Rector to sit down as: 'Mr McCarthy was perfectly in order.' The delighted crowd cried 'Hear, hear' and howled, 'Sit down! Chuck him out . . .'

Emboldened by this display of popular support, McCarthy pressed home his attack: 'I don't see why I should spare those people . . . whenever the slightest little thing occurs in Dorset Street, the Rector of Spitalfields and the Toynbee Hall people pounce on it like a hungry man on a dinner.' McCarthy then compared Davies – unfavourably – to the previous rector, Mr Scott. He, apparently, had been accustomed to give tickets to the poor that they could exchange locally for food. But 'when Mr Davies came on the scene the poor had to do without their tickets altogether'. 'Why,' McCarthy went on, 'he cannot afford to clean or light the clock' (a reference to the large clock set in the tower of Christ Church). This jocular remark was met by peals of laughter. And McCarthy was not done yet: 'This is not the kind of man,' he declared, 'to open, at his own risk, a lodging house for single women ... possibly if he or Mr McKenzie received an anonymous thousand or two, one might be opened.' This barb was met with 'terrific applause'.

At this point, according to the clearly partisan author of the pamphlet, Davies – goaded beyond endurance and made a laughing stock in front of his own parishioners – 'got up, and, losing all control of himself, said, "I have not seen Mr McKenzie for two years ... I have nothing to do with him or Toynbee Hall, and don't wish to."' The chairman, however, cut him short again on a 'point of order', and as Davies stood, seemingly dumbfounded, the crowd cried 'chuck him out ... shut up!' It was the last that was heard that evening from the Rector. Evidently no one was going to get a word in but McCarthy. The tragic young prostitute Mary Jane Kelly had been disembowelled, mutilated and virtually flayed only a few years earlier in a room she'd rented from him off 'Dorset Street'; in 1898 Elizabeth Roberts had been murdered in a room above that formerly occupied by Kelly; and another young prostitute, Mary Ann Austin, had been stabbed to death in a room in Crossingham's lodging house at 35 'Dorset Street' only the previous May in an attack that had been so brutal that the press had called the case the 'Spitalfields Horror'. But in the Duke of Wellington, on this night and among his cronies, McCarthy got away with his claim that 'Dorset Street' was a decent place, that he was the 'hero' of East Enders beset by do-gooders, philanthropists, clergymen and West End newspapers and their reporters.

For McCarthy it was not the clergy or the 'people' from Toynbee Hall but the charitably minded 'sportsmen' of Spitalfields like himself – reluctant to 'boast of philanthropy' – who did 'more for the prevention of crime than any other class of people in the world.' These 'sportsmen', boasted McCarthy, went out of their way to employ 'the poor out-of-work' and 'handed out sixpences' to enable such men to set themselves up and go to 'the markets or docks to get a day's work.' With startling directness McCarthy revealed how his criminal system of almost feudal overlordship functioned; through a dole of sixpences he created a loyal power base and a docile and dependent coterie to do his bidding.

In fact Reverend W. N. Davies appears to have felt genuine concern for the welfare of the poor of Spitalfields, documenting their plight and agitating for their relief. Jack London's *The People of the Abyss*, published a couple of years after Davies' humiliation in the Duke of Wellington, describes how the clergyman carried out a 'census of some of the alleys in his parish' – he does not say when – to ascertain just how appallingly overcrowded they were. But on this occasion, in late July 1901, it seems the dark side prevailed. McCarthy basked in his triumph, and thereafter continued to preside unchallenged over his shops and pubs. It was to be over a quarter of a century before his fiefdom of 'Dorset Street' was forced to make way for a very different Spitalfields. As Fiona Rule explains, the 'combination of the [First World War] and the increasing prevalence of Eastern European Jews ... who, being enthusiastic proponents of the extended family saw little need for ... a single bed in a common lodging house ... effectively destroyed his trade in lodgings for the destitute.'[46] Then, in the late 1920s, the entire north side of 'Dorset Street' was demolished for the construction of the London Fruit and Wool Exchange (see page 598).

McCarthy died in June 1934, aged eighty-three. At his request, his funeral procession walked along what was left of 'Dorset Street' (by then renamed 'Duval Street' in an attempt to blot out its shame and hide its shady past). He was then buried at St Patrick's Roman Catholic cemetery in Leytonstone, next to his wife Elizabeth and near his one-time tenant and Ripper victim, Mary Jane Kelly.[47]

TWENTY

PEOPLE OF SPITALFIELDS

Jack London

When the twenty-six-year-old Jack London arrived in London from California via New York in August 1902 to write about conditions in the East End, he had led a full and adventurous life. Born in San Francisco in January 1876, he had already been an 'oyster pirate' poaching off the California coast, a seal hunter, a hobo who ended up serving a thirty-day sentence for vagrancy and, in 1897, a gold prospector during the Klondike gold rush. Here he had suffered terribly, developing scurvy, infection and swelling of the gums that led to the loss of his four front teeth, persistent muscle pain in his legs and hips, and facial scarring. Here, too, his experiences among the 'submerged tenth' had promoted within him strongly socialist leanings.

When London returned to California in 1898, a physically depleted and much worldlier man, he decided on a new career: he would be a writer. He soon gained a good reputation. His elemental short stories, often set in the Klondike and with animals as protagonists, were well received, as were his escapist adolescent adventure yarns, such as *The Cruise of the Dazzler*, published in 1902, featuring the escapades of the youthful 'Frisco Kid'. His first serious novel, however, was not a success. Published in the same year as *The Cruise of the Dazzler*, *A Daughter of the Snows* features an independent-minded and well-educated heroine named Frona Welse, 'Stanford graduate and physical Valkyrie', and tells how she goes to the Yukon, after upsetting her wealthy father and his friends, to resolve her conflicting passions for two men of opposing characters.[1] It's a long, somewhat limp novel, was delivered late to the increasingly exasperated publisher, and was not well received. After a brief spell of success, London was in trouble. As his biographer Alex Kershaw explains: 'By July 1902, aged just twenty-five [sic], Jack was burnt-out: $3,000 in debt and contemptuous of his work. If something did not come along soon, he told [his friend] Cloudesley Johns, he would turn to drink. Bess [his wife] had announced that she was pregnant again . . . Nor was his career matching his aspirations. Try as he might, he had not yet managed to dig himself out of the lucrative Klondike genre . . . '[2] What he wanted – what he needed – was a sensational project that he could complete quickly and profitably and that would reveal his diverse abilities.

In early 1902 a possible answer presented itself: the Anglo-Boer War. He would reinvent himself as a war correspondent.

London had a very particular attitude to the Boer War and it was not the one that might be expected from an American with socialist leanings. Britain had been roundly condemned for its imperial expansion in South Africa and for its brutal crushing of the Boer Republic that, against the odds, had given a very good account of itself (indeed so good an account that Britain, for a while, looked as though it might be forced to bow to the military prowess of the plucky Boers and acknowledge their republic). London, however, was not for the underdogs. He was for the might of the empire that had pitched itself against them. And his support for imperialism – be it British or American – was underpinned by deep-rooted racism. Frona Welse in *A Daughter of the Snows* proclaims that 'we are a race of doers and fighters, of globe-encirclers and zone-conquerors . . . All that the other races are not, the Anglo-Saxon, or Teuton if you please, is.' She was particularly enamoured of the 'sea-flung Northmen, great-muscled, deep-chested, sprung from the elements . . . A great race, half the earth its heritage and all the sea! In three score generations it rules the world!'[3] Her words could have been spoken by Jack London himself. He believed in the white American notion of 'Manifest Destiny' and maintained that it was the right of the 'superior' races to dominate the 'inferior'. And for him the master race was the Anglo-Saxon – certainly not the Boer.

London bared his soul to his friend Cloudesley Johns, and in so doing revealed an intoxication with the notion of the 'survival of the fittest' that Charles Darwin, and his disciple Herbert Spencer, had introduced to the world as a kind of objective, scientific dogma. On 23 June 1899, when war in South Africa seemed inevitable, London wrote to Johns:

If no race has the moral right to survive to the destruction of lesser races, where, in the whole animal kingdom are you going to draw the line? If the bastard races of one of the richest continents of the world, South Americans; if the niggers of Africa, the Indians of America, the Blackies of

Australia, should, for all their confessed inefficiency, continue to perpetu-
ate themselves to the dwarfing, to the shutting-out of the stronger, better
races, such as our own, where, I ask, are you to draw the line in the whole
animal kingdom?

And on 11 November 1899, a month after hostilities had broken out,
London told Johns, 'The day England goes under, that day sees sealed the
doom of the United States. It's the Anglo-Saxon people against the world.'[4]

The convictions London embraced – the 'claptrap' as his biographer
Alex Kershaw calls it[5] – notably the supposedly scientific basis for racial
'purity' and superiority, were common currency at the time, if now rightly
rejected as intellectually spurious, racist nonsense. And if they seem at
odds with his self-avowed socialism, he ultimately found a way to reconcile the two doctrines: he subscribed to a somewhat cynical and ethically
doubtful philosophy that viewed life as a survival game in which men of
enterprise and racial 'superiority', but also, unfortunately, of inadequate
funds, could develop and utilise their natural talents to beat the wealthy
capitalists at their own money-making manoeuvres. As he explained to
his friend Johns in a letter of 23 June 1899: 'Socialism is not an ideal system,
devised by man for the happiness of all life; nor for the happiness of all
man; but it is devised for the happiness of certain kindred races. It is
devised so as to give more strength to these certain kindred favoured races
so that they may survive and inherit the earth to the extinction of the
lesser, weaker races.'[6]

London's account of the final stages of the Boer War could have made
interesting reading – but he missed the boat. He had been commissioned
by the American Press Association to go to South Africa to cover the
peace negotiations, but by the time he reached New York from California
in late July 1902 the commission had been cancelled because events had
moved too fast and the story was cold. So London was left without a project. What he did have, though, was a ticket for England, which he had
planned to visit before going on to South Africa so that he could meet
publishers there and promote his work. He therefore decided to make the
trip anyway.

And it was at this moment that he hatched a plan to write a quick book
about the great imperial city he was about to visit. It would be a topical
book, for England's capital was shortly to witness the Coronation of
Edward VII in early August. But it would be a topical book with a

difference, for London decided to offer a worm's-eye view of life there. This was to be an account of the capital from the vantage point of its slums. Moreover, it would rely on information that London would himself gather while living in disguise among the slum dwellers. He had a distinct flair for the theatrical.

It was a strange plan to invent on the spur of the moment, but the circumstances were extraordinary, and London felt the need to push his writing career in a new direction. Although only recently established, he was increasingly fearful of being confined to one genre as a writer. As he wrote to Johns on 8 November 1901: 'A man does one thing in a passable manner and the dear public insists on his continuing to do it to the end of his days.'[7]

London's idea of gathering information and insights by living in disguise among slum dwellers was not novel. It is more than likely that, having to think rapidly on his feet, he took inspiration from Jacob Riis, who had lived among the poor of New York to produce *How the Other Half Lives: Studies Among the Tenements of New York*. Published in 1890, this was a compelling first-hand account of slum life – illustrated with atmospheric photographs taken by the author – and London seems rapidly to have perceived that he might be able to repeat Riis's success with a comparable book about the East End slums.[8] The fact that he had considerable experience of adventurous rough living meant that immersion in the slums of the East End probably held few terrors for London.

He equipped himself with a camera so that he could produce Riis-style photo reportage, but even while waiting to board his ship still seems to have been uncertain about this new enterprise. As late as 28 July 1902 he wrote to John Spargo, a member of the editorial board of the socialist magazine *The Comrade*, that: 'I may do some writing of the London slums, possibly a book, though as yet everything is vague & my main idea is to get a vacation.' London knew it was a daunting project. He must also have known he was hardly prepared for the task he was contemplating – the analysis of urban poverty was a life's work for many. Yet here he was, proposing to research and write a book about poverty in the world's largest city during a visit there lasting a matter of weeks. Ghastly failure was a distinct possibility, and with it humiliation and the probable eclipse of his nascent literary career. But whether success or failure would be the result, what was certain was that the job – if it were to be done – had to be done quickly. He must plunge into East End life, write up his experiences rapidly and then move on to other money-making ventures.

While on the ship from New York to England London wrote a letter that reveals his almost unfathomable and paradoxical nature and his brutal attitude to his subject matter. The letter was to Anna Strunsky, a strong-willed, highly intelligent Californian with strong socialist convictions, with whom the married London was conducting – or trying to conduct – an affair. On 31 July 1902 he wrote to her from the RMS *Majestic*:

> I am thinking of you today . . . It is 6.30 PM here . . . I sailed yesterday from New York, at noon. A week from today I shall be in London. I shall then have two days in which to make my arrangements and sink down out of sight in order to view the Coronation from the standpoint of the London beasts. That's all they are – beasts – if they are anything like the slum people of New York – beasts, shot through with stray flashes of divinity.[9]

The device London hit upon for the opening of his East End book, *The People of the Abyss*, was a conventional one: to cast East London as a dangerous no-go area, an 'Under-world' to which West Enders feared to travel and which London entered, as he explained in the book's preface, 'with the attitude of mind which I may best liken to that of an explorer.' To this end he seems to have concocted a tale which involved him being told by 'friends' in the capital that 'you can't do it, you know . . . there are places where a man's life isn't worth tu'pence . . .' Then, 'painfully endeavouring to adjust themselves to the psychological processes of a madman who had come to them with better credentials than brains', they suggested, 'you had better see the police for a guide'. London asked these 'friends' how to get to East London, and was told, 'It is over there, somewhere.' 'And they waved their hands vaguely in the direction where the sun on rare occasions may be seen to rise.'

These theatrics may seem absurd, but perceptions of East London as an exotic and alien – even dangerous – land survived into the 1930s (see page 589) and so London was probably doing no more than picking up on popular myth and hearsay. Certainly populist publications of the 1890s about life in the capital make it clear that many West Enders felt an irrational fear of the East End, a fear exaggerated, but to their minds confirmed, by the Ripper murders just a few years before. A caption to a photograph of the north-east side of Brick Lane in an 1896 book of

photographs entitled *Round London* nicely exemplifies the myth-making
that went on. The photograph shows a busy street market in progress. In
the doorway of one shuttered shop stands a local, casually surveying the
scene. He appears neutral and unexceptional. In the caption, though, he
has become 'a typical denizen of this district – a dangerous loafer in a
deerstalker cap, who was probably regarding our artist with amused contempt at the moment this view was taken'.[10]

Of course, anyone with even only a rudimentary knowledge of England's capital – or of any great city – would have known that East London
was a highly complex organism, full of light and shade and with no consistent all-embracing character. There were slum areas – indeed large and
famous ones – but there were also well-to-do merchant, manufacturing
and maritime areas, and the East End was the location of some of the
greatest and wealthiest commercial enterprises in Britain, including
manufactories and the great docks of Wapping, Shadwell and Limehouse.
Even a quick glance at Charles Booth's colour-coded map would have
shown Jack London that within whole swathes of the East End the majority of streets were coloured red and pink and so were very far from being
slums. And, as with all great cities at the time, the juxtaposition between
rich and poor streets was often dramatic with – typically – slum alleys
or mews set immediately behind prosperous main streets, making it
difficult to generalise even about small areas. But then Jack London's perceptions were shaped by a determination to find sensational material for a
best-seller.

London claims that in order to penetrate the dangerous region of London's East End he sought advice at Thomas Cook & Sons travel agency in
Cheapside in the City. But even Cook's, wrote London, 'the path-finders
and trail-clearers, living sign-post to all the world', which 'could send me
to Darkest Africa', could not get him to the 'East End of London, barely
a stone's throw distant from Ludgate.' Upon his enquiring for directions,
London claims that Cook's told him: '. . . you can't do it, you know . . . it
is so . . . unusual . . . we know nothing whatsoever about the place at
all . . . consult the police.'

So London writes that he took a cab. Predictably the cabbie proved reluctant to take any fare to such a dangerous location and grumbled until
London 'thundered . . . see here . . . drive me down to the East End, and at
once!' It is of course possible that he meant all this pantomime not to be
taken too seriously – indeed to be frightfully funny. The image created of a

The north end of Brick Lane, just south of its junction with Bethnal Green Road, in 1896. This was two years before Booth described this part of Brick Lane as full of life and 'good humour'. But the man who captioned this particular photograph for publication in Round London *saw all as sinister and described the man in a deerstalker cap (lower right-hand corner) as a 'dangerous loafer' and 'typical denizen' of the district.*

desolate outcast land, packed with potential and predatory 'beasts' – people dehumanised by want and poverty – is nevertheless pursued remorselessly, though in a far more serious manner, throughout the rest of the book.

As the cab moved through the East End, Jack London observed that:

> . . . the region my hansom was now penetrating was one unending slum. The streets were filled with a new and different race of people, short of stature, and of wretched or beer-sodden appearance. We rolled along through miles of bricks and squalor, and from each cross street and alley flashed long vistas of bricks and misery. Here and there lurched a drunken man or woman, and the air was obscene with sounds of jangling and squabbling. At a market, tottery old men and women were searching in the garbage thrown in the mud for rotten potatoes, beans, and vegetables, while little children clustered like flies around a festering mass of fruit, thrusting their arms to the shoulders into the liquid corruption, and drawing forth morsels but partially decayed, which they devoured on the spot . . . and as far as I could see were the solid walls of brick, the slimy pavements, and the screaming streets.

An 'unending slum . . . for miles'? One wonders what hell he was passing through. His eventual destination – 'Stepney Station' – was probably the now long-closed Stepney East Station, which means his cab would have travelled east along Commercial Road or, more possibly, the Ratcliffe Highway. Both these thoroughfares certainly had their slum sections, and the Ratcliffe Highway had a long-standing reputation as a place of garish entertainment for seamen from the nearby docks. But both also had long stretches of reasonable housing and prosperous shops and were home to profitable commercial enterprises, as Charles Booth's 'Poverty Maps' of the late 1880s and 1890s showed. London's mention of the 'cross streets' he passed is perhaps telling here: 'cross streets' are a piece of New York urban grid phraseology for what in England are called side streets, and London's use of the term suggests either a degree of linguistic casualness or more general laziness, as he imposed images gleaned from Riis's inspirational book about the New York slums on to the East End of London.

In the second chapter of *The People of the Abyss* Jack London, in rather melodramatic manner, tells his readers, 'I shall not give you the address of Johnny Upright. Let it suffice that he lives in the most respectable street in the East End – a street that would be considered very mean in America, but a veritable oasis in the desert of East London.' 'Johnny Upright' is a veteran police detective to whom London – by now in disguise as an unemployed American sailor down on his luck – confides his true identity, requesting help in finding a secure 'port of refuge'. He needs this, he explains, so he can store his goods and work on his book in between forays to workhouses, common lodgings and Salvation Army depots, and experiencing nights sleeping rough on the Embankment. Quite why London should have chosen to be coy about where the detective lived is not clear, but as it happens the address is not difficult to work out. The detective found London lodgings 'not half a dozen doors away', and we know from the flood of letters London then sent home that he was living at '89 Dempsey Street, Stepney, E.'

'Dempsey Street' has long been demolished. It stood near Whitechapel's Jubilee and Sidney Streets, on the edge of the area's large, vibrant and extremely politically active Jewish community. Some early-nineteenth-century terrace houses survive in Jubilee Street, however, and they are no doubt similar to those that lined 'Dempsey Street', which London describes as being eighteen feet wide and 'much like peas in a pod'. Charles Booth had them down as pink – meaning 'fairly comfortable, good ordinary earnings' – on his 1889 map. But nearby, to the south-west, were streets marked purple, and so home to quite poor inhabitants. As for number 89, we know from the 1901 census records that the household into which London moved had seven people in residence on the night of the census, seemingly in three family groups. Since it probably contained only about eight rooms, including the basement, it would have been quite crowded. There was a household headed by Richard Hedington, a thirty-six-year-old porter, who lived with his thirty-eight-year-old wife and a twenty-six-year-old lodger named Tom Preddy, a building labourer. The second household was headed by Walter Urquhart, a twenty-four-year-old insurance agent who lived with his twenty-three-year-old wife Emma; and the third contained only Jane Jones, a fifty-nine-year-old widow, who was a rare survival of Spitalfields' silk industry for her occupation was described as 'Jacquard (loom) machinist'. Presumably by the summer of 1902 Preddy had moved on and London occupied his room.

All Jack London tells us about his benevolent detective is that he had been given the name 'Johnny Upright' by 'a convicted felon in the dock' and that he was 'known far and wide'. But it's interesting to note that there was, indeed, a famous police detective living in 'Dempsey Street' in 1902 – at number 98, nearly opposite the house in which London lived. His name was Frederick Porter Wensley, he was a decorated officer, and although aged only thirty-seven in 1902, he had been involved not only in the Jack the Ripper hunt but also in several other high-profile police investigations, including the spectacular and dangerous arrest in 1896 of a murderer in Whitechapel named William Seaman, who had murdered a pawnbroker and his housekeeper. Wensley fought, subdued and arrested him in front of a goggling crowd. Possibly London combined Wensley with another retired policeman then living in Dempsey Street. This was Sergeant William Thick, who was indeed known as 'Johnny Upright'.[11]

From his room in 'Dempsey Street' London chronicled his life in the East End in letters home, written, it would seem, in his few spare moments between tramping the streets and working on the book. In these letters he stressed the toughness of the project, the speed of his work, and the horrors of his experiences. In a letter dated 16 August 1902 to Anna Strunsky he wrote that he was 'settled down & hard at work' and that 'the whole thing, all the conditions of life, the intensity of it, everything is overwhelming. I never conceived such a mass of misery in the world before.' He wrote to her again five days later, saying that the book was '1/5 written & typewritten. Expect to be done in five weeks from now', and that he was rushing because he was 'made sick by this human hell-hole called London Town. I find it almost impossible to believe that some of the horrible things I have seen are really so.' London signed this letter 'The Sahib'.[12]

This correspondence was part of London's long-distance courtship of Anna and so it is possible it contains exaggerations, calculated to impress her by emphasising his ability to produce copy at speed despite his physical and spiritual sufferings. But a day later – on 22 August – he wrote to George and Caroline Stirling in much the same vein:

> [T]his country is the Country God has forgotten he forgot. I've read of misery, and seen a bit; but this beats anything I could ever have imagined. Actually, I've seen things & looked the second time in order to convince myself that it really is so. This I know, the stuff I'm turning out will have to be expurgated or it will never see magazine publication . . . I am in the thick of it . . . have my book over one-quarter done and am bowling along in a rush to finish it & get out of here. I think I should die if I had to live two years in the East End of London . . . [13]

And on 9 September London informed Frederick I. Bamford that: 'Things are terrible here in London, & yet they tell me times are good and all are employed save the unemployable. If these are good times, I wonder what bad times are like?'[14]

London's contradictory attitude to the poor is one of the more baffling characteristics of *The People of the Abyss*. At times he looks beyond the outward signs of poverty, sees the spirits of the broken people he is documenting, perceives they are helpless victims of economic privation and not the cause of their own suffering, and shows great humanity and understanding, especially when he is writing about individuals with whom he seems to have forged personal contact. But at other times – as in the beginning of a chapter entitled 'A Vision of the Night' – he appears to be nothing more than a jittery foreigner in East London, way out of his depth as a social observer, and perceiving nothing but the dehumanising outward expressions of hunger, poverty and hopelessness. In such passages he appears to view brutality as the cause rather than the consequence of poverty, viewing those suffering privation as nothing more than base and predatory beasts. Perhaps, when he started writing 'A Vision of the Night' – it's Chapter XXIV and towards the end of the book – London was exhausted and jaded and his emotions too raw.

Writing this particular chapter, which takes the form of a sort of diabolical *Pilgrim's Progress*, provoked him to produce some of his bleakest – as well as most spirited – descriptions. He wrote:

> Late last night I walked along Commercial Street from Spitalfields to Whitechapel, and still continuing south, down Leman Street to the docks . . . It is rather hard to tell a tithe of what I saw. Much of it is untenable. But in a general way I may say that I saw a nightmare, a fearful slime that quickened the pavement with life, a mess of unmentionable obscenity . . . a menagerie of garmented bipeds that looked something like humans and more like beasts.

He was not, he says, wearing his 'seafaring' clothes but his middle-class attire and so was 'what is called a "mark" for the creatures of prey that prowled up and down.' He was glad the police were patrolling the street because the men:

> looked at me sharply, hungrily, gutter-wolves that they were, and I was afraid of their hands, of their naked hands, as one may be afraid of the paws of a gorilla. They reminded me of gorillas. Their bodies were small, ill-shaped, and squat. There were no swelling muscles, no abundant thews and wide-spreading shoulders. They exhibited, rather, an elemental

economy of nature, such as the cave-men must have exhibited. But there was strength in those meagre bodies, the ferocious, primordial strength to clutch and gripe and tear and rend . . . They possess neither conscience nor sentiment, and they will kill for a half-sovereign, without fear or favour, if they are given but half a chance. They are a new species, a breed of city savages. The streets and houses, alleys and courts, are their hunting grounds . . . The slum is their jungle, and they live and prey in the jungle.

After condemning the East End's male beggars, scavengers and thieves, London turned his attention to the women from whose 'rotten loins' the males had sprung:

They whined insolently, and in maudlin tones begged me for pennies, and worse. They held carouse in every boozing ken [a low drinking establishment], slatternly, unkempt, bleary-eyed, and towsled, leering and gibbering, overspilling with foulness and corruption, and, gone in debauch, sprawling across benches and bars, unspeakably repulsive, fearful to look upon.

And then there were the cripples to condemn, with their 'strange, weird faces and forms', whom London conceived of as:

twisted monstrosities . . . inconceivable types of sodden ugliness, the wrecks of society, the perambulating carcasses, the living deaths – women, blasted by disease and drink till their shame brought not tuppence in the open mart; and men, in fantastic rags, wrenched by hardship and exposure out of all semblance of men, their faces in a perpetual writhe of pain, grinning idiotically, shambling like apes, dying with every step they took and each breath they drew. And there were young girls, of eighteen and twenty, with trim bodies and faces yet untouched with twist and bloat, who had fetched the bottom of the Abyss plumb, in one swift fall.

But then, after all this pitilessness – and true to the weirdly contradictory nature of the book – the author felt moved to compassion and a little understanding. Many of these human beings were, he conceded, in this frightful condition through no direct fault of their own. They were suffering because they were deemed 'unfit' and 'unneeded' by the ruthless mechanisms of industry and capitalism. 'Miserable and despised and forgotten, dying in the social shambles', they were: 'the progeny of prostitution . . . the prostitution of labour.' Now, in high style and in uncompromising tones, London proclaims: 'if this is the best that civilisation can do for the human, then give us howling and naked savagery. Far better to be a people of the wilderness and desert, of the cave and the squatting-place, than to be a people of the machine and the Abyss.'

A good example of his less strident and more observational journalism is found in Chapter VI, entitled 'Frying Pan Alley and a Glimpse of the Inferno'. The writing here feels more as though it was inspired by engagement with actual people, and less of a polemic about stereotypical 'beasts'. It reads like an account of places, people and prospects actually seen by London, and of reflections stimulated by what he saw, rather than cobbled-together, third-hand opinions or appropriated facts. Even here, though, the narrative is not necessarily to be taken wholly at face value on every point.

London records that 'three of us' – himself and two East Enders he had met – walked down the Mile End Road. Nearing Leman Street, London asked to see the 'shop' in which one of the men worked. So they 'cut off . . . left into Spitalfields, and dived into Frying Pan Alley.' This narrow alley (see page 462) ran between Petticoat Lane/Sandys Row and Bell Lane, with its east end almost opposite the fearful slum houses of 'Dorset Street'; at the time of London's visit the narrow alley was lined with buildings, some late seventeenth century in origin. In a widened form, it survives today, operating largely as an entrance court to a residential high-rise building on its south side and as a location for tables served by upmarket cafes. Things were very different in 1902. When London entered the alley, presumably from its Bell Lane end, 'a spawn of children cluttered the slimy pavement' and 'in a narrow doorway, so narrow that perforce we stepped over her, sat a woman with a young babe, nursing at breasts grossly naked and libelling all the sacredness of motherhood.' In the 'black and narrow hall' the party 'waded through a mess of young life, and essayed an even narrower and fouler stairway', passing landings 'heaped with filth and refuse' as they climbed to the top floor. London noted that there were 'seven rooms in this abomination called a house. In six of the rooms, twenty-odd people, of both sexes and all ages, cooked, ate, slept, and worked. In size the rooms averaged 'eight feet by eight, or possibly nine.' And then they went into the seventh room, the 'den' in which five men 'sweated'.

It was seven feet wide by eight long, and the table at which the work was performed took up the major portion of the space. On this table were five lasts, and there was barely room for the men to stand to their work, for the rest of the space was heaped with cardboard, leather, bundles of shoe uppers, and a miscellaneous assortment of materials used in attaching the uppers of shoes to their soles. In the adjoining room lived a woman and six children. In another vile hole lived a widow, with an only son of sixteen who was dying of consumption. The woman hawked sweetmeats on the street, I was told, and more often failed than not to supply her son with the three quarts of milk he daily required. Further, this son, weak and dying, did not taste meat oftener than once a week; and the kind and quality of this meat cannot possibly be imagined by people who have never watched human swine eat.

London's companion told him that 'in good times', when there was a rush of work, he could 'earn as high as "thirty bob a week." – Thirty shillings! Seven dollars and a half!' London asked how long the 'rush season' lasted. '"Four months," was the answer; and for the rest of the year, he informed me, they average from "half a quid" to a "quid" a week ... and yet I was given to understand that this was one of the better grades of sweating.'

London then considered the prospect from the rear window of the workshop. It:

... should have commanded the back yards of the neighbouring buildings. But there were no back yards, or, rather, they were covered with one-storey hovels, cowsheds, in which people lived. The roofs of these hovels were covered with deposits of filth, in some places a couple of feet deep – the contributions from the back windows of the second and third storeys. I could make out fish and meat bones, garbage, pestilential rags, old boots, broken earthenware, and all the general refuse of a human sty.

The 1903 first edition of *The People of the Abyss* contains a photograph captioned 'Frying-Pan Alley'. It shows one side of a narrow alley, lined with houses. The ground-floor windows have external shutters but all traces of timber doorcases have gone, presumably rotted away through neglect or ripped off for firewood. A few children and women loiter in the alley, all watching a woman striding towards the camera. Presumably she is saying something of interest to the photographer.[15]

Other early photographs of Frying Pan Alley and the surrounding streets survive in the archives of the Bishopsgate Institute. They were taken in 1912. One confirms that Frying Pan Alley was very narrow, and the side that is shown is also lined with simple three-storey houses, some

The photograph of cramped and crowded Frying Pan Alley that Jack London
included in The People of the Abyss. *Most of the houses appear to date from the*
late seventeenth century, but lack their original timber doorcases, which were
presumably lost through neglect or to provide desperately needed firewood.

of which look to be late seventeenth century and others like utilitarian nineteenth-century reconstructions. The photograph shows the centre portion of the alley, where a crowd of children are bunched together, all of whom generally look well dressed, clean and well fed, with the exception of a ragged barefoot boy who just enters the frame.

The photos of adjoining streets are much the same: in each the children have boots, caps, coats or pinafores. All were taken by C. A. Mathew, a professional photographer, on Saturday, 20 April 1912.[16] Why he should have chosen to do so is not clear, although since many of the places recorded were soon to be demolished or transformed, it is possible he had an anti-quarian bent, or, more prosaically, was working for builders or speculators and producing a portfolio of images of potential development sites. The fact that the photographs were taken on a Saturday could be a clue to the smart appearance of the children, for in 1912 this was a largely Jewish area and Saturday is, of course, the Jewish Sabbath. Perhaps a tradition had been established that on Saturdays the children of the area, Jewish and non-Jewish, wore their 'Sunday best', even though it was Sunday not Saturday that was the day of promenade and conviviality in the Jewish East End. Whatever the reason, the smart appearance of the children of these streets is in stark and puzzling contrast to Jack London's descriptions of the area – and indeed to those made, only a few years earlier, by such observers as Israel Zangwill and Robert Blatchford.

As Jack London's party left the house in Frying Pan Alley the cobbler told London, 'I'll show you one of London's lungs.' They must then have walked down Dorset or Brushfield Street and so came to Christ Church and its churchyard. This, the cobbler said, was 'Spitalfields Garden', and here, intones London in solemn manner, 'in the shadow of Christ's Church, at three o'clock in the afternoon, I saw a sight I never wish to see again.' There were 'no flowers in this garden . . . grass only grows here, and it is surrounded by a sharp-spiked iron fencing . . . so that homeless men and women may not come in at night and sleep upon it'. The party entered this railed enclosure and, as they did, 'an old woman, between fifty and sixty, passed us, striding with sturdy intention if somewhat rickety action, with two bulky bundles, covered with sacking, slung fore and aft upon her. She was a woman tramp, a houseless soul, too independent to drag her failing carcass through the workhouse door. Like the snail, she carried her home with her. In the two sacking-covered bundles were her household goods, her wardrobe, linen, and dear feminine possessions.'

On the benches, to each side of a narrow gravelled walk in the garden, were ...

... arrayed a mass of miserable and distorted humanity, the sight of which would have impelled Doré to more diabolical flights of fancy than he ever succeeded in achieving. It was a welter of rags and filth, of all manner of loathsome skin diseases, open sores, bruises, grossness, indecency, leering monstrosities, and bestial faces. A chill, raw wind was blowing, and these creatures huddled there in their rags, sleeping for the most part, or trying to sleep. Here were a dozen women, ranging in age from twenty years to seventy. Next a babe, possibly of nine months, lying asleep, flat on the hard bench, with neither pillow nor covering, nor with any one looking after it. Next half-a-dozen men, sleeping bolt upright or leaning against one another in their sleep. In one place a family group, a child asleep in its sleeping mother's arms, and the husband (or male mate) clumsily mending a dilapidated shoe. On another bench a woman trimming the frayed strips of her rags with a knife, and another woman, with thread and needle, sewing up rents. Adjoining, a man holding a sleeping woman in his arms. Farther on, a man, his clothing caked with gutter mud, asleep, with head in the lap of a woman, not more than twenty-five years old, and also asleep ... On the pavement, by the portico of Christ's Church, where the stone pillars rise toward the sky in a stately row, were whole rows of men lying asleep or drowsing, and all too deep sunk in torpor to rouse or be made curious by our intrusion.

The party discussed the scene that confronted them. 'A lung of London,' said London, 'nay, an abscess, a great putrescent sore.' The cobbler confided, with 'a cheerful sneer', that, 'those women there ... will sell themselves for thru'pence, or tu'pence, or a loaf of stale bread.'

Now it so happens that London had his camera with him and so, in what is probably a pioneering moment in the history of observational writing in London, the author of such piercing words was able to take photographs of the images that provoked them. Only one of the photographs he took outside Christ Church that late-summer afternoon was included in *The People of the Abyss*. It is captioned 'Spitalfields Garden' and shows two pairs of women, shrouded in shawls, one with a straw boater on her head, sitting dozing on benches. Behind them is a pair of ornate eighteenth-century table or altar tombs, reminders of the affluent merchant community that once lived in the area.

The photographs in the book are of varied quality and interest. Some are by London, and these are the best – intimate, well composed, particular and closely related to the text. But others are general – even generic – and evidently bought in by the publisher. This seems strange given the high quality and quantity of the photographs London himself took. Presumably the publisher felt he had missed locations considered vital by them. Fortunately, the negatives of London's unused photographs were kept, catalogued and captioned by his stepsister Eliza London Shepard, and eventually published.[17] And they are stunning. The quality is crisp and brilliant and London appears to have had a lens that allowed him to create sweeping landscape panoramas. These include a view of the south side of the church's portico, looking towards the west end of Fournier Street. Just as London describes, men are lying huddled against the soot-blackened stone podium of the portico. Most sleep, one reads, a few others simply sit and stare. A woman leans against the railing in front of the portico. A straw boater is tipped over her eyes but she seems to be peering, bleakly and stony-faced, at London as he snaps the view. The images do not quite possess the dramatic quality of his words. But they certainly complement – rather than contradict – the atmosphere of hopeless gloom and despair conjured up by his text.

London does not appear to have explored 'Dorset Street', the east end of which was located opposite the churchyard. Certainly it is not described in his book, which is perhaps surprising given its fearsome reputation (see page 543). However the street does get a mention, almost in passing, in Chapter XXIII: 'The Children'. Here London writes of the bleak prospects of the street children of the poor:

> The boy, if he be lucky, can manage to make the common lodging-houses, and he may have any one of several ends. But the girl of fourteen or fifteen, forced . . . to leave the one room called home, and able to earn at the best a paltry five or six shillings per week, can have but one end. And the bitter end of that one end is such as that of the woman whose body the police found this morning in a doorway in Dorset Street . . . Homeless, shelterless, sick, with no one with her in her last hour, she had died in the night of exposure. She was sixty-two years old and a match vendor. She died as a wild animal dies.

Perhaps predictably the boisterous Jack London, a man in a hurry, intoxicated by action and adventure, took against the Whitechapel Art Gallery.

'Spitalfields Garden', with the tombs of Christ Church behind, as photographed by Jack London. Impoverished women doze on benches.

In *The People of the Abyss* he derides its aims and aspirations, although he does not mention it or its founder by name. It is, of course, obvious why a man like Jack McCarthy, the crime 'boss' of 'Dorset Street', should have had no time for the place, nor for Spitalfields' other enlightened institutions and the 'do-gooders' who ran them (see chapter 16). The reasons for London's animosity are more complex. He records going to 'an exhibition of Japanese art, got up for the poor of Whitechapel with the idea of elevating them, of begetting in them yearnings for the Beautiful and True and Good'. He then spells out his doubts:

> Granting (what is not so) that the poor folk are thus taught to know and yearn after the Beautiful and True and Good, the foul facts of their existence and the social law that dooms one in three to a public-charity death, demonstrate that this knowledge and yearning will be only so much of an added curse to them. They will have so much more to forget than if they had never known and yearned. Did Destiny to-day bind me down to the life of an East End slave for the rest of my years, and did Destiny grant me but one wish, I should ask that I might forget all about the Beautiful and True and Good … And if Destiny didn't grant it, I am pretty confident that I should get drunk and forget it as often as possible.

London clearly had no idea what the gallery was trying to do and held no truck with the somewhat abstract notions of enlightenment and inspiration. It was, of course, precisely because the lot of the East End poor was so grim that its founder Canon Barnett wanted to give them a taste for the 'Beautiful and True and Good'.

And it was not just the Whitechapel Art Gallery that, by implication, London attacked. He was also highly critical of the 'University Settlement' movement, exemplified by Toynbee Hall:

> These people who try to help! Their college settlements, missions, charities, and what not, are failures. In the nature of things they cannot but be failures. They are wrongly, though sincerely, conceived. They approach life through a misunderstanding of life, these good folk. They do not understand the West End, yet they come down to the East End as teachers and savants. They do not understand the simple sociology of Christ, yet they come to the miserable and the despised with the pomp of social redeemers. They have worked faithfully, but beyond relieving an infinitesimal fraction

of misery and collecting a certain amount of data which might otherwise have been more scientifically and less expensively collected, they have achieved nothing . . . They come from a race of successful and predatory bipeds who stand between the worker and his wages, and they try to tell the worker what he shall do with the pitiful balance left to him . . . As someone has said, they do everything for the poor except get off their backs.

One almost wonders whether London had been out drinking with Spital-fields' cynical 'sporting' men such as Jack McCarthy and John Cooney when he wrote this. Certainly, the views expressed here were would have struck a chord with the top dogs of the slums.

What London failed to notice while in the East End – and what he failed to understand – is as fascinating as what he saw and wrote about. In par-ticular he seems to have been wholly unaware of the extraordinary new world that was opening up right on his doorstep in 'Dempsey Street', a world that would play a key role in the creation of the greatest new polit-ical force of the twentieth century.

'Dempsey Street' stood on the eastern fringe of one of the key Russian and Russian-Polish Jewish East End communities. The 'Jewish East London' map of 1899 shows 'Dempsey Street' with between 25 and 50 per cent Jewish occupation, but parts of Jubilee Street immediately to its west were between 50 and 75 per cent and parts of Sidney Street and its imme-diate area were between 75 and 100 per cent Jewish occupancy. The Jewish population was largely low-profile and hard-working, but by 1902 parts of it had become politicised and included socialists, radicals, anarchists and groups that would become famous as Bolsheviks. It is hardly surprising that elements of Whitechapel's Jewish community should have yearned for a new world order that gave more power – and security – to the work-ing man. Many had, after all, been brutally driven into exile in Whitechapel from their homelands by the reactionary, oppressive and autocratic power of the Tsarist authorities.

In the streets just to the west of 'Dempsey Street' political activists met, debated and planned – some merely passing through on journeys around the globe dedicated to spreading their internationally applicable vision of a more just and egalitarian world order in which workers would grab decisive power for the first time from employers, landowners, aristocrats and royalty. In the New Alexandra Hall on Jubilee Street in March 1903, just months after London had left the East End, Lenin spoke at a meeting – in celebration of the thirty-second anniversary of the Paris Commune – that was to prove a key stepping stone in the rise of socialism. Four years later, in May 1907, he was in the area again, this time as a guest of the newly founded Anarchist Club and to attend the fifth Party Congress of the Russian Social Democratic Labour Party (RSDLP), held mostly at the Brotherhood Church in Southgate Road, Hackney. It was during this that a meeting of almost mythic significance took place in a modest house, which still survives, on the corner of Fulbourne Street and Whitechapel Road, and which, in the very early twentieth century, contained the headquarters of the Jewish Socialist Club. Here, and in an adjoining hall, in May 1907, during the fifth Congress, the RSDLP was 'mobilised' as the political supremacy of Lenin's Bolshevik faction was consolidated and delegates met to plan world-changing revolution. Present were 'all ... the founding fathers of the future Soviet Union',[18] including Lenin, Stalin, Trotsky, Maxim Gorky and Maxim Litvinov. By this time Jack London had, as far as it is possible to tell, given up all thoughts of East London and of campaigning for its poor and was cruising the Pacific in his purpose-built, forty-two-foot ketch-rigged sailboat, the *Snark*.

The political aspect of Whitechapel's Jewish community would have been evident – if less overtly so – in 1902. But London either blithely ignored it or simply failed to see it and so missed the big story right on his doorstep. In fact, and this is another oddity of *The People of the Abyss*, he writes hardly at all about the East End's Jewish community. At one point he reports an argument, overheard on the Mile End Waste, between East End working men, during which one said, 'But 'ow about this 'ere cheap immigration? ... The Jews of Whitechapel, say, a-cutting our throats right along?' In another passage London repeats the suggestion, when he writes that unemployed and homeless men he had encountered ascribed their condition 'to foreign immigration, especially of Polish and Russian Jews, who take their places at lower wages and establish the sweating system.' Of the Jews themselves, though, London has remarkably little to say. Even the chapter entitled 'The Ghetto' has more or less nothing to do with the Jewish community. London observed that 'at one time the nations of Europe confined the undesirable Jews

in city ghettos', but in 1902, he argued, the term simply meant the area
into which 'undesirable yet necessary workers' were confined: 'East
London is such a ghetto, where the rich and the powerful do not dwell,
and the traveller cometh not, and where two million workers swarm, pro-
create, and die.'

This observation provoked London to another of his strange, over-
simplified and overheated diatribes against the East End, one that reads
like the work of a writer who had toiled hard and unhappily through a
long night of labour:

> The City of Dreadful Monotony, the East End is often called [because] of
> the intolerable sameness and meanness of it all. If the East End is worthy
> of no worse title than The City of Dreadful Monotony, and if working
> people are unworthy of variety and beauty and surprise, it would not be
> such a bad place in which to live. But the East End does merit a worse
> title. It should be called The City of Degradation . . . it may well be said to
> be one gigantic slum . . . where . . . the obscenities and brute vulgarities of
> life are rampant. There is no privacy. The bad corrupts the good, and all
> fester together. Innocent childhood is sweet and beautiful: but in East
> London innocence is a fleeting thing, and you must catch them before they
> crawl out of the cradle, or you will find the very babes as unholily [sic] wise
> as you.

The anti-alien – particularly anti-Jewish – sentiment that London lightly
touches on here was, in point of fact, a growing and worrying issue in the
opening decade of the twentieth century. In 1900 the author and social
commentator George Haw, when discussing the complex causes and consequences of overcrowded homes in East London, had observed, rather
chillingly, that 'another element at work in driving out our people is found
in the Jews of East London. They inhabit nearly every house in
Whitechapel, and are now pouring in their thousands into St George's,
Mile End, Stepney, and Bethnal Green.' To support his assertion Haw
quoted a Vestry report which stated that 'foreign elements in St George'
were 'increasing at an alarming rate', with 'English families . . . being got
rid of to make room for Russian Jews . . .'[19] In 1902 Howard Angus
Kennedy, when describing in somewhat ironic manner the workings of
the East End's University Settlements, stated that one of the area's
problems was the 'alien', who was overcrowding the 'old and respectable
houses' of Spitalfields and encouraging sweated labour. In contrast to the

'Gentile', the Jewish population was, argued Kennedy, 'in the East End, not of it – strangers and sojourners in its midst.' The area was, he suggested, 'a test of assimilation between "devoted Jew and the English patriot"', with a reputation as 'the prowling ground of Jack the Ripper, as a labyrinth of reeking slums, or a Ghetto crowded with foreign Jews chattering in Yiddish over piles of old clothes.'[20] Even Charles Booth, in the section on 'Poverty' in the 1902 edition of *Life and Labour of the People in London*, observed: 'Just outside the old City walls, have always lived the Jews, and here they are now in thousands ... seeking their livelihood under conditions which seem to suit them on the middle ground between civilisation and barbarism.'[21]

Some retaliated against such attitudes. The radical anarchist Rudolf Rocker, for example – Roman Catholic and German-born – did much, mostly through his writing and publishing activities, to support the increasingly embattled East End Jewish community. By September 1902, after a spell in Leeds, he was back in the East End to relaunch the Jewish anarchist newspaper *Arbeter Fraynd* (*Worker's Friend* in Yiddish). Had he made an effort London could have arranged to meet him, or someone in his circle. It seems strange that he did not because London had indirect links with him via Anna Strunsky, who came from a Russian Jewish family that had escaped the pogroms in Russia and prided itself on its connections with the notorious Russian-born, American-based Jewish anarchist Emma Goldman (who had visited England in 1899 and was a supporter of Rudolf Rocker). But London was too hasty and, perhaps, too opinionated to engage with the subject.

On 28 September 1902 London wrote to Anna from 'Dempsey Street': 'Dear You:- The book is finished! I typed the last word of the last chapter ten minutes ago – 63,000 words. Now I shall have to move out of this room I have occupied seven weeks.' In this letter he transcribed the last paragraph of the book, which included the veiled attack on the Whitechapel Art Gallery, and the 'University Settlements'.[22]

But this is, in fact, not the last paragraph of the book as it was printed.

The day after writing to Anna, London wrote to George P. Brett, the man at Macmillan he hoped would publish *The People of the Abyss*. London was desperate to get business moving forward as rapidly as possible.

Dear Mr Brett,

... Concerning the East End book, I want you to have first chance at it for book publication. It is not a novel, by the way, but a dive by me into the Under-world and a narration of the people, things & conditions I encountered ... I have taken a number of photographs, which should make good illustrations for the book. The title I have chosen is *The People of the Abyss* ... the running of my household in California has been largely on the basis of credit, and will be for a couple of months or more to come. So I should like to know if you can find it compatible with your policy to advance another $150 to my wife should she require it ...?[23]

Brett advanced London the money he requested so that he could travel home to his wife and new baby daughter in Piedmont, California with some sense of financial security and achievement. By 4 November he was back in New York with what he believed to be the final draft of his book. He sent it to Brett who, however, was uneasy. He observed that the text showed 'signs of haste'. London's response was that this was because he had worked 'day and night, without taking rest',[24] and in a letter of 21 November justified the observational tone by stressing that it was 'simply the book of a correspondent writing from the field of industrial war', and that it 'proposed no remedies and devoted no space to theorising' because 'it is merely a narrative of things as they are.'[25]

These excuses masked a deeper problem with *The People of the Abyss*. The desperate speed with which London produced the book led to a fatal flaw that continues to compromise the authenticity and authority of the work. London was a plagiarist – and a serial offender at that. His perpetual haste when writing books, and no doubt his lack of experience as an academic writer, meant that he occasionally appropriated other people's facts and opinions – even language – without acknowledgement. One consequence is that it is sometimes hard to distinguish his direct and personal observations – which are usually of intense interest – from received, plagiarised, second-hand opinion.

London's record of plagiarism is catalogued by John Perry in *Jack London: An American Myth*, where he states of London that 'charges of plagiarism hounded his entire career.' As early as 1907 *Current Literature* remarked that: 'Of late [London] has even been charged with being in such a hurry to produce "copy" that he was forced to dip his pen into other people's ink', and it has been demonstrated that he copied sections from

Egerton R. Young's *My Dogs in the Northland* (1902) almost verbatim for *The Call of the Wild* (1903).[26] Frank Harris attacked London for plagiarism in *The Iron Heel* – London's dystopian novel, published in 1908, describing an oligarchic tyranny in the United States. Harris wrote: 'Mr Jack London began this controversy by showing himself to be not only light-fingered but heavy-handed as well. Being forced to admit that he had taken an article of mine and had incorporated it bodily and almost word for word'.[27] On occasion London defended himself by asserting that all 'fictionists' use factual material, but seems to have skirted the main issue: at what point and by what means does fair use become piracy?

There is unacknowledged copying and appropriation in *The People of the Abyss*. The process by which London researched the book, and manner in which he used his sources, is described by David Mike Hamilton in *The Tools of My Trade: The Annotated Books in Jack London's Library*. As Hamilton points out, London borrowed from a whole number of other works.[28] These ranged from Thomas Holmes's *Pictures and Problems from London Police Courts* (1900), to George Haw's *No Room to Live* (1900), to Oscar Wilde's 'The Soul of Man under Socialism' (1891).[29] Overall, London's reading list may seem impressive but the point is that the facts and opinions gleaned from these books are not fully or properly credited in *The People of the Abyss*, but mixed, usually without distinction, with London's own observations and rapidly gathered material. The consequence of this fusion is often not illumination but confusion and the dilution of the power of the narrative.

An analytical comparison of some material from Haw's *No Room to Live* with passages from *The People of the Abyss* is instructive. In Chapter XIX, 'The Ghetto', London quotes from a Professor Huxley at length, focusing on his recommendation that to live healthily each person requires 800 cubic feet of well-ventilated, pure air. In the capital, however, London points out, there are 900,000 people living with 'less than the 400 cubic feet prescribed by the law.' This is lifted straight from Haw, who quotes Professor Huxley, 'once himself a medical officer in East London'.[30] London quoting Haw was fair enough if the source had been acknowledged, but it was not. There are several other examples of such direct uncredited appropriations. It's as if London, in his naïvety, assumed it was all right to use Haw as a sort of unacknowledged research assistant or repository of public facts (Haw does get a credit in the text of *The People of the Abyss*, but only in the loosest possible way). More unsettling than the direct and uncredited lifting of facts is the lurking sense that London could also have taken emotive descriptive material from Haw and used it out of its original context. For example, Haw describes dwelling houses in West Ham that 'in some instances are not much better than donkey-sheds and hen-roosts . . . all over the place are mounds of decaying vegetables and solidified heaps of rubbish'.[31] London's description of the view of the back yards behind Frying Pan Alley, Spitalfields, is suspiciously similar.

The title he chose for his book is interesting. The word 'abyss' was common currency among authors of late-Victorian 'slum' literature. It formed part of the title of C. F. G. Masterman's first-hand account of tenement life in South-east London, *From the Abyss: Of Its Inhabitants by One of Them*, published in 1902 by R. B. Johnson. London could have picked up the word from such a work. Another source, however, is far more likely. In 1901 H. G. Wells published a sombre futuristic book entitled *Anticipations of the Reaction of Mechanical and Scientific Progress upon Human Life and Thought*. In this work Wells wrote of a possible new world order – the New Republic – in which the ruling authority, with a revised system of ethics and driven by eugenic policies, would terminate the existence of 'inferior' humans – those Wells termed 'people of the abyss'. As he put it:

> The men of the New Republic will not be squeamish . . . in facing or inflicting death, because they will have a fuller sense of the possibilities of life than we possess. They will have an ideal that will make killing worth the while . . . They will naturally regard the modest suicide of incurably melancholy, or diseased, or helpless persons as a high and courageous act of duty rather than a crime . . . People who cannot live happily and freely in the world without spoiling the lives of others are better out of it . . . the men of the New Republic will have the courage of their opinions.

And how, asks Wells:

> . . . will the New Republic treat the inferior races? How will it deal with the black? How will it deal with the yellow man? How will it tackle that alleged termite in the civilised woodwork, the Jew? . . . It will tolerate no dark corners where the people of the Abyss may fester, no vast diffused slums . . . no stagnant plague-preserves. Whatever men may come into its efficient citizenship it will let come – and the Jew also it will treat as any other man. It is said that the Jew is incurably a parasite on the apparatus of credit. If there are parasites on the apparatus of credit, that is a reason for the legislative cleaning of the apparatus of credit, but it is no reason for the

special treatment of the Jew. If the Jew has a certain incurable tendency to social parasitism, and we make social parasitism impossible, we shall abolish the Jew . . .

This was chilling stuff, and although presented in terms of science fiction, represented a recurring thread in Wells's (often self-contradictory) thinking: indeed he was later to describe *Anticipations* as 'the keystone of the main arch of my work'.[32] But it would seem that this was a ruthless future with which Jack London could identify, for why else would he choose to call the East End poor 'the People of the Abyss'? In a ghastly way it would appear that Wells's dark vision offered a programme and theory for London's book. And it perhaps helps to explain his extraordinary outbursts against the maimed and malnourished poor of East London and perhaps also suggests why he seems to have displayed no interest in, or perhaps chose to ignore, its large and very significant Jewish community.

Certainly London had an apocalyptic aspect to his character and would have been attracted by the radical notions toyed with by Wells. This tendency is expressed by a note he scribbled sometime after his return to America: '. . . if I were God one hour, I'd blot out all London and its 6,000,000 people, as Sodom and Gomorrah were blotted out, and look upon my work and call it good.'[33] It's almost as if London pictured himself as Kurtz in Joseph Conrad's 1899 novella *Heart of Darkness*, a story London knew by an author he much admired. Kurtz had gone out to work among primitive and savage people; they treated him as a god; but his personality was transformed by the experience, and he died whispering 'The horror! The horror!' In the novella the story-teller looks through Kurtz's notes – seemingly kindly and measured – but discovers a shattering and shocking statement 'that blazed . . . luminous and terrifying, like a flash of lightning in a serene sky: "Exterminate all the brutes!"'

George Brett at Macmillan continued to worry about the haste evident in *The People of the Abyss*. After some more brooding he wrote again to London on 17 December requesting a final chapter that was more 'optimistic', that pointed out 'the possibilities of amelioration of the terrible conditions that you set forth', and that would not imply any criticism of Edward VII or his government but 'focus' blame 'more pointedly on the criminal elements in London.'

The author seems not to have been in the least offended by this very significant editorial suggestion. He replied to Brett on 30 December stating that he thought the proposal 'excellent' and confirmed that he would write a 'final & hopeful chapter'. London also thanked Brett for earlier sending him a couple of books to read, presumably to furnish ideas and inspiration. One of these was Jacob Riis's latest effort, published in 1902, *The Battle with the Slum*. He was, he wrote, particularly pleased with this book because Riis pointed out the 'deadness & hopelessness that characterise the East-London slum' while there was 'life & promise in our American slum – "yeast" in our slum, as he called it.'[34]

This alleged difference between the London slums – where all seemed dead-end and hopeless – and the American slums where there was 'life and promise' and at least a chance for vagabonds (as London himself had been) to redeem themselves, gave him an argument for his new final chapter, which he simply tacked on to the end of the book, leaving his earlier rather gloomy and dyspeptic concluding observations intact in the penultimate chapter.

For the new end-thought London fashioned something fanciful and forceful that, in essence, compared the energy and opportunities offered in the New World with the decay and endemic enervation of the Old World. The new material also gave him a chance to return to the familiar topic of the Yukon and its Inuit population. Entitled 'The Management', the new chapter started by asking the question, 'Has civilisation bettered the lot of the average man?' To answer it London made comparison with the 'Innuit [sic] folk' of Alaska – 'a very primitive people' – who, although living in tents and subject to periods of want, were 'healthy, and strong, and happy' as well as entirely without debts. By contrast, 'the English folk . . . are a consummately civilised people' who 'gain their food, not by hunting and fishing, but by toil at colossal artifices'. Despite this, crowed the author, 'the greater number of them are vilely housed, do not have enough fuel to keep them warm, and are insufficiently clothed. A constant number never have any houses at all, and sleep shelterless under the stars. Many are to be found, winter and summer, shivering on the streets in their rags. They have good times and bad. In good times most of them manage to get enough to eat, in bad times they die of starvation.'

Almost triumphantly, he proclaimed:

> . . . they are dying now, they were dying yesterday and last year, they will die to-morrow and next year, of starvation; for they, unlike the Innuit, suffer from a chronic condition of starvation. There are 40,000,000 of the

English folk, and 939 out of every 1,000 of them die in poverty, while a constant army of 8,000,000 struggles on the ragged edge of starvation. Further, each babe that is born, is born in debt to the sum of £22. This is because of an artifice called the National Debt.

Several of these astonishing 'facts' were repeated from an earlier chapter, where London also stated 'one in every four in London dies on public charity' (elsewhere he gave the figure as 'one in three').

He probes the reasons for this shocking situation. Since 'civilisation' has increased general wealth by increasing the 'producing power' of the average man by 'a hundred-fold', why has it not 'bettered the lot of the average man?' There can only be one answer, he concludes: 'mismanagement'. And this becomes the dominant theme of the last chapter. It is not so much the system that is at fault – the same brand of capitalism was, after all, at work in both England and the United States – so much as the gross mismanagement of the British ruling elite. It is mismanagement, argues London, due to incompetence, to the hidebound class system of the Old World that stymies ambition and initiative, and to the gross selfishness and stupidity of the established managing class. It is, he observes, a mismanagement that not only causes misery to millions but which is also the undoing of Britain and its Empire.

What particularly irked London was that many of the ruling class were not merely incompetent and selfish but also – as members of society – grossly unproductive. 'If the 400,000 English gentlemen, "of no occupation", according to their own statement in the Census of 1881, are unprofitable, do away with them. Set them to work ploughing game preserves and planting potatoes. If they are profitable, continue them by all means, but let it be seen to that the average Englishman shares somewhat in the profits they produce by working at no occupation.' Much of this, of course, is in essence lifted from Wells's 'New Republic', but with 'English gentlemen' assuming the role of the 'inferior races', the people of the abyss. These were not, presumably, quite the 'criminal' class that Brett had in mind when he offered a brief for the new end chapter.

In short, according to London in this dashed-off last chapter, British society 'must be re-organised, and a capable management put at the head.'

That the present management is incapable there can be no discussion . . . It is inevitable that this management, which has grossly and criminally mismanaged, shall be swept away. Not only has it been wasteful and inefficient, but it has misappropriated the funds. Every worn-out, pasty-faced pauper, every blind man, every prison babe, every man, woman, and child whose belly is gnawing with hunger pangs, is hungry because the funds have been misappropriated by the management. It has drained the United Kingdom of its life-blood [so that it is] unable longer to struggle in the van of the competing nations. A vast empire is foundering on [sic] the hands of this incapable management. [It is] running down [and] in the hands of its management it is losing momentum every day.

London then writes of the 'blood empire' of the British as opposed to the 'political empire', and observes that 'the English of the New World and the Antipodes are strong and vigorous as ever.' This is the final lesson he seeks to teach in this concluding chapter. The decaying Old World must learn from the New.

At some point soon after his return from England to California, and before publication of *The People of the Abyss*, London started an affair with Charmian Kittredge. By June 1903 he was writing to her, 'I do not know whether I shall hear from you, whether or not you will come to me tonight; but this I do know – that I love you. And this also I know – that you will come to me. Some time, somewhere. It is inevitable . . .' So now London was cheating on his wife (who was nursing their new child), and on Anna. Do great artists have to be good men? Of course not – history teaches quite a different lesson. But an apparently documentary work like *The People of the Abyss* that purports to deal, to a degree, with moral and ethical issues – with life, death, truth – must be in some way undermined when the author reveals himself to be to a degree amoral, intent primarily on the gratification of his own immediate needs and desires. To respect such a book, one could argue, it is necessary to have some respect for the author's moral judgement and sense of integrity.

When published in the United States in 1903 *The People of the Abyss* was a surprise success, selling around 20,000 copies. It was reasonably well received by the critics, but the New York *Bookman* accused London of 'snobbishness because of his profound consciousness of the gulf fixed between the poor denizens of the Abyss and the favoured class of which he is the proud representative.'[35] The reception in Britain was, predictably, fairly hostile. A young American novelist panning the country by writing an emotive exposé of its slums – and all based on a stay there of a few weeks – was of course bound to irritate. The response of the London *Daily*

News was typical. Jack London, the paper's reviewer observed, 'has written of the East End of London as he wrote of the Klondike, with the same tortured phrase, vehemence of denunciation, splashes of colour, and ferocity of epithet. He has studied it "earnestly and dispassionately" – in two months! It is all very pleasant, very American, very young.'[36]

As can be imagined London's brutal and simplistic attack on the 'Settlement' movement offended many. R. H. Tawney, a Christian socialist, active supporter of adult education and resident of Toynbee Hall, reviewed the book in the *Toynbee Record* in a somewhat agonised but restrained manner. He observed that its bleak tone suggested that London had spent eight weeks in the East End with the sole intention of discovering 'painful things' to put into his book. 'No one', wrote Tawney, 'would paint Whitechapel as a paradise of good living . . . or even of good intentions. But behind both distress and the efforts to relieve it there is something which this author never touches – the humanity whose name he so often takes in vain.'[37]

Whatever others might have thought about *The People of the Abyss*, London himself rated it very highly and used it as a calling card. Three years after publication he wrote to Bailey Millard, editor of *The Cosmopolitan*: 'I have tremendous confidence, based on all kinds of work I have already done, that I can deliver the goods. Anybody doubting this has but to read *The People of the Abyss* to find the graphic, reportorial way I have of handling things . . . I gathered every bit of the material, read hundreds of books and thousands of pamphlets, newspapers and Parliamentary Reports, composed *The People of the Abyss*, and typed it all out, took two-thirds of the photographs with my own camera, took a vacation of one week off in the country – and did it all in two months. That's some going, isn't it?'[38] And years later London wrote: 'Of all my books, I love most *The People of the Abyss*. No other book of mine took so much of my young heart and tears as that study of the economic degradation of the poor.'[39]

But there were always, even among London's close supporters, suspicions about the book's authority, truthfulness and purpose. In her 1931 hagiography – *The Mystery of Jack London* – the author's old friend Georgia Loring Bamford felt compelled to observe of the book: 'years later, I visited London. I even went to the Whitechapel district and saw much misery in a small space, but none worse than could be found . . . in some of our own poorer districts. No, I cannot see why that book was written.'[40]

Despite its flaws London's book is important because the power – even the occasional magic – of his vehement prose captured, and has held, the popular imagination. The book is certainly not the whole truth – and it can lay few claims to being the objective truth – but it offers an impression of the East End at the turn of the twentieth century that to many has become the truth. It is now part of the undying legend of late-Victorian East London, a legend created not by those who actually lived there day to day but largely by writers who had lived there and had long ago moved on – such as Israel Zangwill and Arthur Morrison – or by arrant, arrogant and opinionated outsiders, like Jack London, blessed with the gift of words.

PART FOUR

AN EVER-CHANGING DISTRICT

Modern Spitalfields

TWENTY-ONE

WORLD WAR AND CIVIL CONFLICT

Spitalfields 1914–45

On 31 May 1915 the German Army Zeppelin LZ 38, 536 feet long and travelling at 50 m.p.h., crossed the coast near Margate and moved majestically towards London. It was sublime, but it was on a mission of destruction, though its targets were not primarily military or strategic. The First World War was just over ten months old, there was stalemate on the Western Front and this pioneering aerial attack on Britain's capital was designed as a propaganda coup. The intention was to demonstrate to the British Empire and the world the might of Germany's military technology and the ability of its aviators to penetrate, at will, the heart of London and drop bombs virtually unchallenged. It was, in other words, a coldly calculated terror raid aimed at sapping the will of the British people, already disheartened by casualties in Flanders and by the reverses of the bloody Gallipoli campaign, to continue the war.

Shortly after 11 p.m. the LZ 38 arrived over North London and then as it moved from north to south-east its crew – guided only by such landmarks as the glistening curve of the River Thames – dropped a series of unaimed bombs. The first fell on Stoke Newington, hitting a house in Alkham Road. A second fell on Cowper Road, causing the first fatality of the raid – three-year-old Elsie Leggett, who died as her home burnt (her eleven-year-old sister Elizabeth May died a few days later from injuries sustained in the fire). The Zeppelin then dropped bombs in Dalston, Hoxton, Shoreditch and Spitalfields – blasting glass out of the roofs of the Great Eastern Railway's Bishopsgate Goodsyard off Commercial Street – before heading back to the coast via Whitechapel and Stepney. Fifteen British aircraft took off to attack the raider but in vain. Operating at around 10,000 feet the LZ 38 was virtually impossible to see at night. One pilot caught a glimpse of it; another died as he attempted the difficult task of landing his aircraft in the dark. As the airship flew back over the North Sea, seven Londoners lay dead, thirty-five had been injured and forty-one fires were lighting up the night sky to the east and north-east. The modern age of total war – utilising the latest technology to achieve random carnage – had arrived in Spitalfields.

A few months later, on the night of 8/9 September 1915, the Germans returned to East London. This time the attacker was the German naval airship L 13. It droned, high and invisible, dropping unaimed bombs near Liverpool Street Station and in the streets of Spitalfields. By chance, one scored a direct hit on a number 8 bus as it passed along Norton Folgate at the junction with Folgate Street. Nine passengers died and ten were injured.

In the course of the war many other members of the Spitalfields community died, falling in battle in one of the various overseas theatres. The memorial cairn topped by a cross – an ungainly affair formed by rough-hewn blocks of granite – that stands in the burial ground of Christ Church bears eighty-two names wrought in lead. Inside Christ Church, another First World War memorial, carved on a marble tablet, carries the names of a further thirty-one men. This was originally housed in the Victorian church of St Stephen's Spitalfields, which stood at the north end of Commercial Street until 1930 when it was demolished to make way for a cinema.

The St Stephen's memorial is framed by pilasters and topped by a minuscule pilaster-framed and arched tablet, which in turn is emblazoned with a large Star of David. This would appear to be a very Jewish affair, rather like the elevation of a shrine within a synagogue in which the scrolls of the Torah are placed. But to judge by the names on the tablet most of the dead honoured by this memorial were not Jewish. St Stephen's stood, after all, in a part of Spitalfields that was by tradition Irish and English – certainly so in the late 1890s as Charles Booth made clear (see page 529). All are identified on the memorial as 'parishioners or relatives'; three were choristers of the church; one – Private F. J. Dittmer of the Royal Fusiliers – was the 'Organist and Choir Master'. Perhaps, then, the six-pointed star represents the Seal of Solomon and this is a memorial concocted by Spitalfields Freemasons.

Ironically, it is the more overtly Christian of the two memorials – the cairn outside Christ Church – that bears witness to the Jewish men of Spitalfields who fought and died between 1914 and 1918: among them

Private F. Goldstein, Rifleman A. Isaacs, Gunner H. Shatcofsky. Sir
Edwin Lutyens, when he designed the Cenotaph in Whitehall, made it
abstract and non-specific in religious imagery or form so that it could be a
fitting memorial to the soldiers of many faiths – Christians and Jews,
Muslims and Hindus – who had died for the British Empire. But the
designer of the Spitalfields memorial seems to have been either blissfully
unaware of the issue of religious symbolism, or simply not concerned.

By the time European hostilities ended in November 1918, a large and significant Jewish community had been a fixture of the East End for perhaps
a hundred years or so. For over fifty it had been firmly ensconced in the
streets of Whitechapel and central and south Spitalfields. Materially poor,
the community was incredibly rich in tradition and cultural inheritance –
and closely knit. Emanuel Litvinoff, born in Whitechapel the year of the
first Zeppelin raid and the son of Russian Jewish immigrant parents, in
later life vividly evoked the vibrant world of 'the ghetto of East London'
and, in particular, the life of his street, 'Fuller Street', now obliterated,
which ran off Cheshire Street in northern Spitalfields.[1]

His introduction to the area was not auspicious. 'Life began', he recalled,
'in bewilderment and terror at the age of three with my first coherent
memory, that of moving to our two-roomed flat and tiny kitchen in Fuller
Street Buildings, Bethnal Green . . . a tenement of sooty brick whose
squalor in retrospect seems unbelievable', and which possessed 'an evil-
smelling strangeness [that] permeated from rubbish bins and lavatories in
the yard.' But soon the new arrivals' neighbourhood had enveloped them.
The Litvinoffs arrived with 'our sewing machine and a cartload of
second-hand furniture' to be welcomed by 'the women of the tenement . . .
in a chatter of excited Yiddish . . . We had joined our tribal community.'[2]
Eastern Europe had been transplanted to the East End:

> The tenement was a village in miniature . . . we sang songs of the ghettos
> or folk-tunes of the old Russian Empire and ate the traditional dishes of its
> countryside . . . People spoke of Warsaw, Kishinev, Kiev, Kharkov, Odessa
> as if they were neighbouring suburbs. And the women kept the old folk
> ways alive; they shouted public gossip to one another over flapping laundry
> in the yard, screamed at unmanageable children, quarrelled, wept, cursed
> and laughed with exuberant immodesty.[3]

The boundaries of the 'Fuller Street' 'ghetto' were specific, its area small, and leaving it brought risks. Running into 'Fuller Street' was Bacon Street, which, recalls Litvinoff, was 'squalid even by our standards' and a place 'until I was big and fairly robust I could only walk through . . . by making myself invisible, crediting the simple folk down there with a malicious brutality that could only be circumvented by magic.' Bacon Street was home to another 'tribe' that – as in the days of Charles Booth's 1890s survey – consisted of poor English or Irish, 'whose wild children greeted us with the chant: "Abie, Abie my boy,"' and whose adults, when emerging drunk and violent from local corner pubs, would from time to time lurch into 'Fuller Street' and scream '"Christ-killers all of yer!" with a shrillness that pierced the dreams of sleeping children.'[4] No wonder the abstinent Jews, who might stand for ages on the streets speaking Yiddish, would 'avoid the corners occupied by pubs'.[5] To loiter by these was to ask for trouble from a drunken *goy*.

Litvinoff lived in a particularly rough part of early-twentieth-century Spitalfields, but his observation about street-corner pubs in Spitalfields probably holds true of most of the area. The environs of the Elder Tree in Elder Street and the Commercial tavern on the corner of Wheler and Commercial Streets were no doubt no-go areas for Jews on a Saturday night. Jews might drink, but generally with discretion and moderation, and were certainly not part of the rowdy drinking culture associated with Spitalfields' convivial but also – for Jews – downright dangerous pubs. These were the domain of the Irish and English working class of Spitalfields who, when drunk, could be violent and anti-Semitic.

The site of 'Fuller Street' is now covered by a sprawling and characterless housing estate that, in its suburban banality, attempts to give a sort of bland respectability to an area once notorious for its mean streets and poverty. The same cloak of banality has enveloped most of Cheshire Street, too. At its western end, on the north side, a splendid 1870s terrace survives, with handsome uniform shop frontages. Opposite this, until recent years, stood a disparate collection of early buildings that included a late-nineteenth-century synagogue, its galleried interior long derelict and abandoned. This was perhaps the Working Men's Synagogue whose Talmud Torah had once been attended – somewhat reluctantly, he admitted – by the young Emanuel Litvinoff.[6] Greatly reduced, too, is the vibrant Sunday street market that flowed through Brick Lane and Club Row, noted by Charles Booth in the late 1890s and which, no doubt, had its origins in the eighteenth century. Today Cheshire Street is an enclave defined by blocks of private flats, office buildings and specialist shops. Visitors now can have no idea that once, and for generations, the whole area was packed with life and that this street – with its Sunday street market – until only recently played a vital role in traditional East End life.

Those outsiders who ventured into the East End in the 1920s and 1930s were struck by its 'otherness'. 'Where is it?' the journalist and travel writer H. V. Morton asked in his 1925 book *The Heart of London*, based on a series of articles he had written for the *Daily Express*. 'It might be Cairo, Baghdad, Jerusalem, Aleppo, Tunis or Tangier, but, as a matter of fact, it is Petticoat Lane in Whitechapel – a penny ride from Ludgate Hill!' As he walked through Petticoat Lane Morton's attention was caught by 'a young girl with eyes like the fish-pools of Heshbon . . . her fingers . . . covered with rings' who sat 'outside a butcher's shop, on an upturned crate'. Morton thought her 'beautiful after her kind', but 'though her eyes are the eyes of Ruth among alien corn, her larynx is that of Bill Sykes[sic] . . . In five more years . . . her lithe grace . . . will be submerged in regrettable tissue . . . This is the burden of the Jewess.'[7] Morton used his eastern analogy again when exploring the Club Row Sunday market, noting breathlessly that '. . . thousands of things are happening at once in Oriental variety. This is what Baghdad was like in the days of the Caliph.'[8] Indeed for him the East End *was* the East, though without 'its lepers, without smallpox, without the flies, without the impertinent stinks.'

To us Morton's amused tone seems somewhat patronising. His humorous observations are a reminder that casual racism – based more on ignorance and shallow assumptions of superiority than the result of deep evil as in the case of the Nazis – remained common currency in the inter-war years, providing the prism through which Spitalfields was widely viewed. Foreigners and foreign communities and customs were regarded as sources of amusement, almost of childlike wonder, and Spitalfields as a place of apparently unlikely and ungainly juxtapositions. This was the shadow – often irritating and insulting – under which the large Jewish population of inter-war Spitalfields toiled as it endured poverty, overcrowding and poor amenities.

Unfortunately, once stereotypes are established, they can prove astonishingly difficult to shift. Writers and journalists who explored Spitalfields and the East End in the inter-war period constantly returned to the same clichés and lazy evocations of the exotic and the mysterious. 'East End!'

Thomas Burke wrote in *The Real East End*, published, with dramatic Expressionistic illustrations by Pearl Binder, in 1932:

> Visions in the public mind of slums, vice, crime, sin, and unnamable horrors ... Dregs of humanity. Beggars and thieves. Bare-footed waifs. Outcasts. Drunkards. Jack the Ripper. Crimping dens [cheap lodging houses]. Dangerous streets. Policemen walk in twos and threes. Opium dens ... Hooligans. Diseased harlots. Public-houses on every corner. Thugs lurking in every alley. Sudden death ...[9]

The Jews, Burke revealed, as if genuinely surprised by his discoveries:

> have made the streets of Whitechapel, Spitalfields and Bethnal Green very much their own. They have their special restaurants, about a score of synagogues ... four burial-grounds, their own Sunday markets, and their own theatre – the Pavilion, where drama and comedy are given in Yiddish by Jewish actors ... the main street of the Ghetto is Brick Lane ... It contains everything for the daily needs of the Jew, and there is scarcely a shop, a house or a stall that is not Jewish.[10]

Like Morton, Burke relished the 'oriental' character of much of the East End and its nature, which he was determined to see as solemn and even sinister. The East End was – to echo William Booth – still a place of 'darkness', with each district having its own brand of gloom: 'There is the darkness of the riverside, and the darkness of Stepney ... and the darkness of Spitalfields [where] you will hear the guttural Yiddish and old songs of Russia [and] feel the spirit that troubled the air around the waters of Babylon'. With Gentile surprise – perhaps even lurking disapproval – Burke observed that Saturday mornings in Spitalfields offered 'a scene of semi-desolation ... but on Sundays all the local Judea comes out ... all the shops open and all the restaurants busy ... Sunday morning in the markets – Wentworth Street, Middlesex Street, Old Montague Street and Brick Lane ... is a fashion-parade of youths and girls in smart clothes'.[11] Is this a factual or fanciful portrait of the East End in the early 1930s?

Burke's description is, at least in part, echoed by other more superficially sombre accounts. For example Ashley Smith, in his 1939 publication *A City Stirs*, included a 'Twilight Tour' of the capital that compared Trafalgar Square – represented as an international hub – with odd, alien and insular Spitalfields:

... the virtual ghetto of Hanbury Street and Old Montague Street where the flavours of un-English meals fill the air. Where the clansmen of some distant Polish or Russian town occupy whole lengths of a street, run in and out of each other's houses, and conduct their tiny synagogues – in the rear, perhaps, of some tailor's workshop. Jewish vitality and Jewish unhappiness and restlessness thrown like some bitter herb into the cooking-pot of mighty London. Aldgate, Whitechapel – so poor, so alien, so strange – beating on the gates of London.[12]

Together Smith and Burke evoked a place where legend had become more real than fact – Burke suggesting as much in his remark that while 'facts fade away and die ... legends are invulnerable and immortal.' The 'East End legend', Burke supposed, would 'last as long as there is any East End'.[13]

There was, however, a genuinely dark side to this legendary place, which Litvinoff hinted at when he described the tensions that existed between his community and the impoverished English and Irish inhabitants of neighbouring streets. Relations between these various groups had never been amicable. Hostility had often spilt over into verbal abuse – and sometimes worse. 'Christ-killers, all of yer!' can hardly have been the most bruising insult that local Jewish people had to endure.

In the 1930s this hostility grew more acute. The European fascism that had been taken up first in Italy, and then in Germany, had reached England in the form of Oswald Mosley's British Union of Fascists, and public rallies and meetings were being staged that aped the ugly, divisive and racist antics of the Nazis in Germany. And on 4 October 1936 the spectre of this continental fascism made itself felt in the East End as a body of about 3,000 members of Oswald Mosley's British Union of Fascists attempted to stage a march in their Italian Fascist-style black shirts. These fascists were not all from distant parts. One of Mosley's tactics had been to divide working-class East End areas by inflaming long-simmering and ignorant resentment of the Jews and, to a degree, he had succeeded. Emanuel Litvinoff, twenty-one at the time of the march and living in Spitalfields, recalls that when 'the day of Mosley and his fascists' arrived:

a frightening change came over the East End. Snotty-nosed kids with whom one had exchanged fairly harmless abuse suddenly appeared buckled and booted in black uniforms, looking anything but juvenile as they tramped through the district shouting 'We gotta get rid of the Yids, the Yids! We gotta get rid of the Yids!' And it was even difficult to laugh at the bespoke-tailored fascists who came from the suburbs to officer these eager troops.[14]

The march had been permitted by the authorities but a mixed collection of anti-fascists – including socialists, anarchists and communists – made it clear they would mobilise to block it. So although the fascists were given an escort of 6,000 police, they were confronted by an anti-fascist crowd of around 100,000, who brought them to a halt at Cable Street, about a quarter of a mile south of Aldgate, and then forced them to retreat, fighting running battles with the police as they did so.

The 'Battle of Cable Street' is now generally seen as a popular and resounding grass-roots defeat for the fascists, who, despite police protection, were prevented from strutting through Whitechapel and Spitalfields. But the full consequences of the affray were more complex. The Jewish population of Whitechapel and Spitalfields was – understandably and despite the fascists' undignified ejection – intimidated and frightened. For many Jewish families – familiar with the fascists' rapid rise to power in Italy and Germany and their increasingly ferocious anti-Semitic policies – Mosley's attempted invasion of their heartland was the writing on the wall, the sign of things to come. The deep-rooted nature of this alarm and fear – and the resigned and gloomy expectation of persecution – was revealed after the fall of France in June 1940 when, as if by some miraculous conjuring trick, a large part of the Jewish population of Spitalfields simply disappeared. Expecting an imminent Nazi invasion, and assuming that the invaders would know all about the East End 'ghetto', most Jewish residents did not choose to dawdle around to await their inevitable fate.

It was a decade when old demons were released and xenophobic and irrational fears stoked. Even observers who did not, as far as one can tell, harbour fascist tendencies, turned a jaundiced eye on what they perceived as alien or outsider communities, or seemed to display an unsavoury disregard for Jewish lives. Indeed it was what Litvinoff regarded as the often weak, conniving, complacent and compromising attitudes of his fellow countrymen to wartime Jewish suffering that ultimately made him such a bitter man. The touchstone of his brooding anger was the disaster that befell the *Struma* – a ship carrying nearly 800 Jews from Romania to the British Mandate of Palestine – which was destroyed as a direct consequence of a refusal on the part of British officials to intervene on her behalf.

Fascists march through the East End on 4 October 1936. Even though their chosen route was provocatively designed to take them through Jewish areas, it was sanctioned by the authorities, who supplied a 6,000-strong police escort. Violence was the inevitable result as the police and marchers clashed with 100,000 anti-fascist protesters in what became known as the 'Battle of Cable Street'.

In early 1942 the old ship with her failing engine limped into Istanbul where she was held while Turkish and British officials quibbled over what to do with her. The British were anxious not to upset the Palestinians by allowing more than the permitted quota of Jews to enter the Mandate, so while they allowed a few people to travel on and the Turks permitted a few people off (mostly children), the rest were forced to stay aboard. Then the ship – her engines now not working – was towed into the Black Sea by the Turkish Navy and set adrift. In circumstances that remain as contested as they are tragic a Soviet submarine – the *Shch-213* – torpedoed the helpless *Struma* on 24 February 1942. Around 790 people died. Litvinoff, who was then in the British Army, was devastated when he heard of the tragedy. Many years later, in 1966, he recalled hearing the 'desolating news' that 'blurred the frontiers of evil'. 'Those stony-hearted British and Turkish officials', he wrote, 'who could send people to their deaths because their papers were not in order were Hitler's accomplices. They were doing the Devil's work'.[15] Soon after the sinking of the *Struma* Litvinoff wrote a scathing poem of mourning and called the British uniform, of which he had been proud, a 'badge of shame'.[16]

If the 1930s saw Spitalfields' century-old Jewish community begin to disperse, it also witnessed its centuries-old silk industry finally disappear altogether. Its dying days were captured by A. K. Sabin in *The Silk Weavers of Spitalfields and Bethnal Green*, published in 1931. He noted that the last large weaving firm to leave the district was 'Warner & Sons, who acquired mills at Braintree in 1895, and shortly after transferred there sixty families of Bethnal Green silk weavers'. This left in 1931 'a scattered group of eleven [weavers] only, and these eleven all elderly persons, who will leave no successors to carry on the tradition of Spitalfields silk weaving, when at length they cease to toil at their looms.'[17] Increasingly taking the place of silk weaving was the 'rag trade', a quintessentially East End business that stretched back centuries and involved the repair and sale of old clothes and shoes and the production of new cheap garments and shoes through 'sweated' labour. Unlike the silk industry it required minimal capital investment and skill. What it demanded instead was much time and energy.

Meanwhile Truman's Brewery, the wholesale market and Great Eastern Railway continued to bring work to the area, and were joined in the inter-war years by such innovatory endeavours as the George Scammell &

*The splendid collection of Truman Brewery buildings on the east side of Brick Lane.
In the foreground, looking rather like a nonconformist chapel, is the ornamental
Vat House of 1803–5. Next to it is the brewery 'Engineer's House' of 1831–6, probably designed
by Robert Davison for his own occupation. To the left of that, in the distance,
with a sublime arcaded façade, are the brewery stables. Constructed in 1837, they housed
over 220 horses by the 1890s.*

Nephew engineering works. This was located in Fashion Street, in the shadow of Christ Church. Having started up in the late nineteenth century as coach builders, by 1920 Scammell's were pioneering a powerful, articulated six-wheeler lorry and went on to design and manufacture a wide range of tough vehicles, including the R100 artillery tractor for military use. In the late 1920s the company established its main factory in Watford but retained its Fashion Street works as a bodybuilding plant until as late as 1965. Another Spitalfields industry was the bell foundry of John Warner & Sons. The company had started in Cripplegate in 1763, moved to a site in Spelman Street, Spitalfields, in the late nineteenth century and continued to cast bells (including the clock chimes for the Palace of Westminster) for buildings around the world until 1924.

These local industries, in the process of conducting their businesses and expanding them, often exacted a heavy toll on the historic fabric and beauty of the area. The worst offender in this regard was Spitalfields Market. From 1885 to 1893 Robert Horner – the market's last private owner before it was acquired in 1920 by the Corporation of the City of London – had rebuilt the late-seventeenth-century core of the market and lined the east ends of Brushfield Street and Lamb Street and the west side of Commercial Street with new buildings, to form three sides of a large courtyard. These perimeter buildings were designed by George Sherrin in an Arts and Crafts manner, with flats above ground-floor shops and the courtyard covered by a roof of iron and glass. At virtually the same time, and in curious artistic contrast, Sherrin designed the nearby Roman Catholic St Mary Moorfields in a stone-faced Renaissance style (completed 1899).

In 1926, this market building was extended to the west, replacing late-seventeenth-century houses on Crispin Street, Gun Street and on the east side of Steward Street, north of Brushfield Street, with two-storey brick-built pavilions of neo-Georgian design. A little later – in 1927/8 – the palatial 1730s houses forming the south-east corner and north side of Spital Square/Lamb Street (22–27 Spital Square), along with much of 'Church'/Nantes Passage, were destroyed by the City of London to provide wider access roads to the market, along with loading areas and a covered flower market. Number 21 Spital Square was demolished in 1933.[18] Together, these reconstructions of the market, and the expansion of its operational area, destroyed much that survived of the heart of late-seventeenth- and early-eighteenth-century Spitalfields. In similar manner Truman's Brewery expanded to the west, devouring large portions of 'Little Pearl Street' and its

Above: *the central portion of the Fruit and Wool Exchange on Brushfield Street, soon after its completion in 1929. The architect, Sydney Perks, was inspired by nearby Christ Church and Spitalfields' early-Georgian domestic architecture.* Below: *a 1920s view of the interior of the Spitalfields fruit and vegetable market soon after it was extended.*

environs such as 'Crown Court'. At about the same time the Cambridge Music Hall and surrounding buildings on Commercial Street were replaced by faience-clad commercial constructions of diluted Art Deco design. These buildings, large and alien to their surroundings, were completed in 1936 for Messrs. Godfrey Phillips to serve as an extension to its tobacco factory. From the mid nineteenth century cigarette- and cigar-making had been one of the minor but staple trades of Spitalfields.

Arguably the most important Spitalfields building of these inter-war years was the Fruit and Wool Exchange on Brushfield Street. It was built in 1929 to the design of Sydney Perks, Surveyor to the City of London, to serve as offices and trading hall, operating under the control of the City Corporation. Perks utilised modern building materials – primarily steel for the structural frame and reinforced concrete for floor slabs – but for the external elevations took his lead from the existing architecture of the area, notably from the surrounding early-Georgian terrace houses and from the magnificent English Baroque masterpiece of Christ Church. Perks's problem, of course, was to adapt the architectural language of Spitalfields' early-Georgian domestic architecture to fit the scale and function of his modern commercial building. But he managed to do this with style and assurance and created a uniform and palatial elevation to Brushfield Street that does not detract from the heroic vista of Christ Church when viewed from Bishopsgate; indeed with his Fruit and Wool Exchange elevation – wrought of red brick and Portland stone – Perks created a fine setting for the portico of the church. This was no mean achievement. The Exchange was flanked by a bank at its east end and by a pub – The Gun – at its west, both designed in more humble permutations of Perks's neo-Georgian manner.

Nevertheless, despite its architectural good manners and deference to the area, the creation of the Exchange entailed the destruction of the entire north side of 'Dorset Street', and the network of courts and alleys running between it and Brushfield Street. Miller's Court, where Mary Jane Kelly was murdered in 1888 by Jack the Ripper, had been demolished earlier. It continued the remorseless obliteration of small buildings, alleys, yards and courts that had been the consequence of the earlier expansion of the market and of Truman's Brewery.

When the Second World War came in September 1939 the civilian population of Spitalfields was, as elsewhere, woefully unprepared for German attacks on home soil. Successive governments had accepted that any general European war was likely to involve aerial attacks on civilian targets, that these could prove difficult to counter (Stanley Baldwin's contention, voiced in the House of Commons as early as November 1932, that 'the bomber will always get through' was widely accepted),[19] and that they could well prove devastating. Yet by late 1939 no significant system of civilian defence had been implemented and no large or adequately strong public bomb shelters planned or executed by the National Government. This was partly – and disgracefully and insultingly – intentional. A number of key figures in the government and the civil service feared what they termed 'deep shelter mentality' among working people, who, they suggested, might be inclined to go to ground when bombing started and so fail to pursue their essential daytime occupations. They therefore instead promoted and pursued a policy to provide temporary, lightweight and uncomfortable shelters, often ad hoc, almost by definition inadequate. Initially these took the form of slit-trenches in parks, relatively flimsy brick-built surface shelters, hastily reinforced railway viaducts and other vaulted public places, or communal shelters constructed in the basements of tenements or terrace houses.

Such forms of civil defence were supplemented by the kit-of-parts Anderson shelter – an uncomfortable and chilly construction intended for 'emergency' outdoor use for those with access to a garden. Taking the form of corrugated steel sheets bolted together to form a semi-circular arched barrel vault that – in its basic form – was two metres long, 1.4 metres wide and 1.8 metres high, it was designed to be partly buried in the garden and partly covered with earth and sandbags. Anderson shelters started to be issued a few months before war broke out and distribution was means-tested. Anyone eligible and with an annual income of less than £250 got one free, otherwise it was necessary to pay £7 to protect oneself from aerial onslaught by His Majesty's enemies. By the end of the war 3.6 million of these shelters had been produced and – surprisingly, perhaps – proved robust and highly effective against all but a direct hit. In addition to these, in March 1941 – well after the first big German air raids on the City and the East End – the government introduced self-build shelters for those without access to gardens, or for people who preferred to shelter indoors rather than in a damp and cold steel vault half buried in the earth. This new addition to the self-defence armoury was called the Morrison shelter, essentially a two-metre-long, flat-topped steel cage (which doubled as a table) into which householders could crawl in order to have some protection against structural collapse. In reality, while these cages were possibly slightly more effective than simply taking shelter under the stairs or the dining table, they did little more than offer a sheltering family the opportunity to grill to death in their burning home. Distribution of Morrison shelters was also means-tested. Eventually around half a million were manufactured.

Taking shelter in London's underground railway system – which was to become one of the emblematic images of the London Blitz – was initially forbidden. The authorities argued that using the system's subterranean platforms and tunnels hampered potential troop movements and the functioning of the hard-pressed city and that it was hazardous and unhygienic. Unvoiced, of course, was the worry about morale-sapping 'deep shelter mentality'. But working people in East London were not inclined to be docile and simply do what they were told, and – mobilised by the Communist Party – they took action. From the beginning of September 1940 the East End started to bear the brunt of the Luftwaffe onslaught on London and on the night of 8 September 1940 – essentially the second night of the London Blitz – crowds surged towards the locked gates leading to Liverpool Street Station's deep Central Line platforms and tunnels, extended by 1940 to Bethnal Green but not operational. Most of the people who forced an entry must have come from Spitalfields and Shoreditch. The authorities had two options. To use force to repel the crowds of men, women and children – including soldiers seeking shelter for their families – or to bow to these circumstances. Wisely they chose the latter course.

By the end of September 1940 nearly eighty London underground stations had been opened to the public, giving shelter to around 177,000 a night – a total that included the 10,000 people who, each night by the end of September, were taking refuge on the platforms and unfinished tunnels of Bethnal Green Station.[20] According to the historian Angus Calder, because this particular station was not operational, some opted to stay for weeks, justifying 'to some extent the fears of a "deep shelter mentality"', but these were 'a minority within a small minority', including many homeless.[21]

Generally, at first, conditions in the tube shelters were chaotic and insanitary. People literally fought for places and, in the process, disrupted the operations of the underground service; there was also a distinct lack of facilities. But gradually order prevailed, bunks were installed – as were lavatories and rudimentary washing facilities – and shelterers and early-morning passengers found themselves able to co-exist. This order – brought about in part by access controls, time limits for use and even entry tickets – was imposed by an unlikely alliance of middle-class voluntary supervisors – often retired military men and bureaucrats – and the very active Communist Party Shelter Committee, whose slogan for working people was 'Stand Firm and Demand Bomb Proof Shelters'. The Communist Party also campaigned for the opening up to the public of strong and exclusive private shelters and demanded that empty houses and flats – particularly those owned by people who had absented themselves from the raging battle of London – be commandeered for the use of the bombed-out. Not without some justification, it sought to make political mileage out of a desperate situation, pointing out in strident manner that the middle and affluent classes could leave the capital for their country retreats or take shelter in the deep basements of modern upmarket steel- and reinforced-concrete-built West London hotels – places not generally welcoming to working-class visitors – while ordinary people had to make do with whatever was immediately to hand.

This simmering sense of injustice boiled over on 16 September 1940 – on the eighth night of the London Blitz – when about fifty people, mostly East Enders, invaded the grand Savoy Hotel off the Strand. Organised by the Communist Party and with press in attendance, it was essentially a political protest intended to highlight the proposition that workers were left exposed to the nightly battering of the Luftwaffe while the rich took shelter in safety and exclusive comfort. Quick on their toes, and anxious to avoid too much of a scene, the Savoy staff promptly invited the East Enders and their pets to stay the night and join its guests in the hotel's deep reinforced basements. The point had been made and the protest was not repeated, although relations between East Enders – particularly those with Communist sympathies – and the authorities remained strained. The people could take the bombing perhaps, but not the patronage of the pampered ruling elite. As Harold Nicolson, Minister for Information, recalled in his diary on 17 September: 'Everyone is worried about the feeling in the East End ... there is much bitterness. It is said that even the King and Queen were booed the other day when they visited the destroyed areas.'[22]

By contrast, when Frank Lewey, Mayor of Stepney during the Blitz, took King George VI on a tour of East London bombsites the morning after a heavy raid, he reported in his book *Cockney Campaign* that after the King had inspected the damage and asked heartfelt questions about the people's suffering, he was 'fairly mobbed': people 'beat him on the back and arms, shook hands with him, and yelled: "we can take it, only give it to 'em back!"'[23] It's a measure of the volatility of these discordant times that the Royal Family could meet with such different responses on different occasions.

Personal shelters in Spitalfields houses tended to be somewhat ad hoc affairs. After March 1941 people had access to Morrison shelters, of course, but Anderson shelters were of limited use in an area where only a few houses had gardens, and where such gardens as existed had generally been covered with random structures by 1939, or else were small paved yards. Generally speaking therefore the approach that appears to have been favoured in 1939 was to reinforce the basements of a few selected Spitalfields houses to serve as communal shelters for the occupants of those particular houses and other residents living nearby. Certainly, this is what happened at my house, 15 Elder Street, where works were carried out to the front basement room, probably by Stepney Borough Council. In the process the ceiling was strengthened with three reinforced steel joists – running from front façade to spine wall – each joist supported by four adjustable steel columns set in a concrete floor. These joists in turn supported a roofing 'sandwich' formed by sheets of corrugated steel, thick pine boards and sheets of asbestos. Blast shutters were fixed to the windows – essentially removable laminates of pine boards set within stout timber frames – and an escape hatch created through the party wall to 13 Elder Street. It is hard to know how many people would have occupied this space during the Blitz, but it must presumably have been the occupants of three or four houses – so perhaps between fifteen and twenty-five people. Several houses in Elder Street had similar reinforced basements. Many years later a 1939 halfpenny was found beneath a timber placed to hold a blast shutter. It had presumably been put there by builders in traditional manner to date the reinforcing works.[24]

So far as public shelters in the area were concerned, these were something of a mixed bag. Before the forced opening to shelterers of the Liverpool Street Station underground platforms, the only large public shelters in the area were in the crypt of Christ Church and beneath railway viaducts. Those seeking shelter in Christ Church – sleeping among the dust, debris and trimmings of Georgian death – were documented in memorable manner in November 1940 by Bill Brandt. He photographed an Indian Sikh family sitting, if not very happily at least resignedly, in a decaying alcove and a man sleeping soundly in an eighteenth-century stone sarcophagus. Those seeking security in local vaulted railway viaducts opted for the ones that crossed Wheler Street – mostly part of the Bishopsgate Goodsyard – which along with related tunnels and warehouse basements were strengthened for the purpose.

That they proved successful, though, was more to do with luck than inherent strength. Although viaducts appeared very sturdy, they offered little resistance to direct hits from even moderate-sized high-explosive bombs because the crown of the vault, including track and ballast, was neither very thick nor, of course, designed to resist such a violent assault. This was demonstrated with tragic clarity on 25 October 1940 when a nineteenth-century railway viaduct across the junction of Tanner Street and Druid Street, Bermondsey, was hit by a bomb which killed seventy-seven of the densely packed – and as it happens revelling – shelterers. A similar tragedy occurred nearby on 17 February 1941 when a couple of bombs hit a large viaduct in Stainer Street, adjoining London Bridge Station. Sixty-eight people were killed and 178 injured, many – ironically – by the large steel blast doors fitted within the viaduct that were blown off their hinges by the blast. That a similar disaster nearly befell the Wheler Street viaduct shelter is suggested by a dense spattering of bomb-splinter hits that still survive on a brick wall immediately to the south of the viaduct. A map tracing bomb strikes in Stepney confirms that a bomb did in fact fall near this location.[25]

The most successful of Spitalfields' public wartime shelters has a remarkable story. The large and robust City Corporation Fruit and Wool Exchange, on Brushfield Street, completed in 1929, had a modern and very robust steel-frame and reinforced-concrete construction behind its neo-Georgian façade of brick and stone. It also had a large basement with good head height. Inherently strong, the subterranean portion of the building became a bomb shelter as soon as the Blitz started, with part open to the public and part reserved for the occupants of the building.

Conditions initially were appalling. Soon, however, the shelter became an outstanding testimony to what East Londoners could do – in the face of terror and disgraceful public mismanagement – to organise and defend themselves. Key to this transformation was Mickey Davis – a thirty-year-old three-foot-three-inch-tall optician, of Russian Jewish decent (the

Mickey Davis, the inspirational force behind the creation of the 'model' air raid shelter in the basement of the Fruit and Wool Exchange in Brushfield Street, chatting to a happy shelterer, possibly his wife.

family changed its surname from Valpiensky to Davis), who lived nearby on Commercial Street. In his memoirs he describes his first experience at the start of the Blitz of the Brushfield Street shelter – crammed with over 10,000 people.

> Into this underground hell on the first night of September the 7th 1940 I fled out of an air raid that was making the streets untenable. I felt as if I had run headlong into a stinking wall of ammonial fumes of stagnant urine mingled with the sweat of almost putrefying humanity. Men and women were hysterical, the feeling of fear could be seen like a fog starting from their eyes . . . The heat . . . became literally hardly bearable [with] a steady stream of semi-conscious or unconscious people . . . passed towards the doorway.[26]

Davis and the democratically elected shelter committee of which he became marshal soon took control. They divided up the cavernous basement space. They installed lavatories, bunks and first-aid stations under the supervision of Vera Weizmann, the doctor wife of Chaim Weizmann, later the first president of Israel. They organised donations and practical support that permitted medical attention for shelterers and milk for children free of charge. Marks & Spencer's provided a canteen. The shelter, which in its reorganised form catered for 2,500 people a night, became a model of self-help initiative, visited by both the Soviet and US ambassadors and by Mrs Churchill. Wendell Wilkie, Roosevelt's former Republican rival for the presidency, who with Herbert Morrison visited the shelter on 29 January 1941, called it a showplace of British democracy. It also incurred a degree of official suspicion. The committee's Communist sympathies were well known and monitored (a large file on the shelter survives in the Home Office records in the National Archive). And the authorities weren't delighted at the poor reflection cast on their own inadequate efforts by a bunch of volunteers.

A fleeting glimpse of the Fruit and Wool Exchange shelter, and the shelter in the crypt of Christ Church, is offered by Peter Ritchie Calder in *Carry on London*, published in 1941. Calder met Davis at the Fruit and Wool Exchange during a raid and then made a dash to Christ Church. 'It was only the breadth of a broad road and a churchyard,' he wrote, 'but on this particular night it was like a sortie into No-Man's Land'. They reached the door to the crypt with 'the ice-cold light of incendiaries bursting not far away', pushed past the 'hanging draperies of the gas-curtains, damp and clammy, caressing one's face like a piece of wet fish', and entered

the bizarre world that had been so well visually documented by Bill
Brandt: 'In the vaults were sarcophagi . . . in them the bodies of the
centuries-old dead had mouldered away [and] now their heavy stone lids
had been levered off' so 'the last resting-place of the dead' could be
'claimed for the living.' Calder noted in 'one of them, as though he were
lying in state, a navvy was lying asleep.' Elsewhere he observed 'stretched
on the rough floor . . . the tall figure of an ex-Bengal Lancer, his magnificent shovel beard draped over a blanket, his head turbaned and looking, in
sleep, like a breathing monument of an ancient Crusader.'

Calder then recalled the terrible conditions that prevailed in the Fruit
and Wool Exchange shelter when the Blitz started in September 1940.
'Nothing like it, I am sure, could exist in the Western World . . . some of the
worst haunts on the water front at Marseilles which are a byword . . . were
mild compared with the cesspool of humanity which welled into that shelter
in those early days'. But then Mickey took over, order was imposed and the
'shelter ultimately became a model of organisation'. One day, Calder mused,
Mickey Davis 'may take his place with Gog and Magog [mythical guardians of the capital] among the traditional figures of London.'[27]

The Fruit and Wool Exchange and its exemplary shelter became, under
Mickey Davis, a monument to grass-roots East End initiative and spirited
self-help. It gave tangible and precise form to the notion of East London's
resilient, 'London can take it' spirit. Michael Foot, as a young journalist
working on the *Evening Standard*, wrote on Friday, 13 September 1940:
'The story of the East End of London is a terrible, tremendous story, a
story of anger, hate, love, defiance, a story of whole streets where you can
see women's eyes red with tears, but women's hearts overflowing with
kindness towards their neighbours . . . British courage rests on no system
of defence, not even on the seas. It is rooted in the hearts of the people.'
Quoting a long-suffering mother in John Steinbeck's 1939 novel *The Grapes
of Wrath*, Foot reminded his readers – and by extension the Germans –
that 'you can't lick the people'. The story of the Fruit and Wool Exchange
shelter does much to suggest that the spirited and stubborn resilience of
the East End in 1940 that Foot presented to his readers was no mere hyper-
bole but rooted in vivid fact.

Perhaps strangely, given Spitalfields' proximity to the City of London,
there were few very serious bomb incidents in the area. From late 1940
until mid 1941 forty-two high-explosive bombs are recorded as falling in
Spitalfields – that is, the area between Norton Folgate and Vallance Road

*A man taking shelter from the Blitz in the vaulted crypt of Christ Church,
as photographed by Bill Brandt in November 1940. At much the same time the socialist
writer and journalist Peter Ritchie Calder described how he had witnessed 'the last
resting-place of the dead' being 'claimed for the living' in Christ Church. In one
sarcophagus he observed a navvy asleep 'as though he were lying in state'.*

and Whitechapel High Street north to Bethnal Green Road.[28] These bombs fell in clusters around Bell Lane and along the south end of Commercial Street, with individual hits in the area east of Brick Lane. The most serious damage to the historic core was in White's Row where the handsome early-nineteenth-century Shepherd's Place arch leading into Tenter Street was destroyed; in Fournier Street at the junction with Brick Lane where four early-eighteenth-century houses on the south side were wiped out; and an area extending from Wilkes Street to Princelet Street where a cluster of bombs destroyed the large and ornate 4 Wilkes Street (formerly a Protestant Dissenting Charity School) and the once-famed Yiddish Theatre (numbered 3 Princelet Street).

Ironically, the theatre had previously been the setting for what must surely have been Spitalfields' worst peacetime disaster. It had been established in 1885, after a fund-raising appeal led by the Liberal MP for Whitechapel, Sir Samuel Montagu (who was also involved with the funding and construction of the Rothschild Buildings; see page 482). The impresario behind the project was the Odessa-born actor Jacob Pavlovich Adler who later did much to establish Yiddish theatre in New York and Chicago. Known as the Prince's Street Club, with its library and reading room for members (the subscription was one shilling per annum) it was initially a great success. But on the evening of 18 January 1887, during the performance of a light-hearted operetta called *The Gypsy Girl*, someone mistakenly or maliciously shouted 'Fire' (there was a simulated fire on stage at the time, so the former explanation is possible). A panic ensued, and in the rush to the exits seventeen people were crushed to death. Not surprisingly audiences avoided the theatre after the accident and it soon closed. Spitalfields was traumatised by the tragedy and a sense of darkness descended on Princelet Street that, in an uncanny way, seems to linger still.

TWENTY-TWO

DECAY AND RECOVERY
The Post-war Era

Spitalfields came through the war physically relatively unscathed. In most other respects, however, it was battered and unloved. Its Jewish community, largely dispersed at the beginning of hostilities, did not return in significant numbers; and although its institutions, shops and restaurants lingered on, their greatly reduced local clientele meant that they were on a downward curve. Most did not survive beyond the 1970s. In the immediate post-war years a Bangladeshi community did start to fill the vacuum – in many cases literally the buildings – left by the Jews, but it was decades before it was of sufficient strength to play an economically, culturally and socially significant role in Spitalfields.

There were ostensibly some signs of life: Truman's Brewery and the City of London-owned wholesale fruit, vegetable and flower market both expanded in the decades after the Second World War. But, ironically, their very growth was a reflection of the area's general decay. Spitalfields' run-down state, its declining population, its low status and its lack of friends in high or influential places, meant that as and when these two industries chose to expand or reshape themselves, few felt inclined to challenge or question what they had in mind, whatever impact they might have on the surrounding neighbourhood. The market extension of 1961, for example, saw the sweeping away by the City Corporation of the last surviving 1720s and 1730s 'merchant palaces' in Spital Square, including the large and stupendous 20 Spital Square (see page 189), without ceremony or any apparent regret. Also lost were the adjoining early-eighteenth-century 17, 18 and 19 Spital Square and a terrace of seven Georgian houses in Folgate Street and one house on Nantes Passage.[1] Most of these were listed by the government as buildings of historic or architectural interest. But in early 1960s Spitalfields nobody cared about such things. In an atmosphere of demoralisation and carelessness the City had its way and the terraces – a vital physical memorial of Spitalfields' noble past – were destroyed. They went for nothing more than a large and desolate parking place for market lorries.

At the same time Christ Church, too, came under threat. The church's extraordinary form, comprising 'a stack of Roman triumphal arches topped by a stark obelisk',[2] had no doubt been conceived by its creator to express Christian triumph over death, but in 1960 it seemed to signal no more than the mouldering and gloomy church's own imminent demise. It had virtually no parishioners and had been suffering from decades of physical neglect and mutilation. Its once fine plaster ceiling was in danger of collapse, demolition was mooted. Fortunately, on this occasion, there was a public outcry, the ceiling was repaired and the church saved and mothballed while its long-term future was debated. Even so, when I first got to know it well in the early 1970s it was still in limbo. I remember being struck by the extraordinary contrast between the church's immaculate-looking ceiling and its abandoned and derelict nave and aisles which were being used to store old newspapers, mattresses and other rubbish that the parish authorities presumably thought to be of some value.[3]

I gained a sense of what living in Spitalfields immediately after the war must have been like from Sid Grimsey, a member of the family that lived in the house I now occupy in Elder Street from the pre-war years until the late 1960s. During those years Sid ran a newsagent's shop in Commercial Street. In the 1970s he also ran a club for market workers, housed in the handsome Renaissance-style pavilion on the Commercial Street frontage of Spitalfields Market. It was called the Vesta Tilley Club because Sid claimed that the famous, cross-dressing Victorian and Edwardian music-hall artiste was a relative of his wife's parents.

In 1955 Grimsey had married the daughter of the head tenant of number 15, Mr Harris, who had had possession of two floors since before the Second World War. Grimsey and his wife slept in the first-floor rear room and his in-laws slept in the adjoining front room; the door connecting the two rooms had been sealed and its recess turned into a cupboard. The ground-floor front room was the 'best' sitting room or dining room, reserved for use on Sundays and when honoured guests visited. Here – insisted Grimsey – Tilley had been entertained. The ground-floor rear room was the kitchen, with a gas stove set against one panelled wall and a sink and water supply fitted in the south-east corner. Both second-floor rooms were used by the other tenant of the building: 'the spinster'. She slept in the front room, and had her dining room and kitchen in the rear room, with a small gas stove set next to the fireplace. Her sink and water supply were on the landing. The two top rooms had long been abandoned. Buckets had been placed to catch leaks in the roof, floorboards left to buckle gradually, undisturbed, in the damp. Evidently the landlords were happy to accept a low or reduced rent for the house in return for minimal maintenance work. The front basement room still contained the bomb shelter installed in 1939 (see page 602), while the rear basement room was derelict and abandoned. There was no bathroom, of course, but there were two lavatories – their doors facing each other – in the two rear corners of the yard.[4]

The darker side of Spitalfields in the 1950s is exemplified by the lives of local serial criminals Reggie and Ronnie Kray. Ironically they received more or less their first helping hand from the man who had done so much to see Spitalfields through the war: Mickey Davis. Councillor for the Spitalfields West Ward of Stepney Borough Council from 1949 until 1953 (the year before his death) and also deputy mayor, Davis started the Vallance Club for local boys immediately after the war and it was to this club that keen amateur boxers thirteen-year-old Reggie and Ronnie gravitated. Reggie Kray recalled Davis in his memoirs, describing him as 'a really nice Jewish fella who also happened to be a midget'. '[W]hat impressed me,' he went on, 'was how he was dressed. He might have been small but you never saw him in anything but a sharp tailored suit, shirt, tie and highly polished shoes. He had a reputation as a judo expert, which must have been an asset against potential piss-takers.' Kray clearly respected Davis, and seems to have been influenced by the steely determination that accompanied his sense of style. As for the club, Kray described it as 'rough and ready', but also said that it had 'a good atmosphere where everyone mixed in together'. It was, he remembered, initially 'based in the crypt of a well-known church'. That 'well-known church' was probably Christ Church, which stood virtually opposite Davis's home.[5] In another manifestation of Spitalfields' intricate spider's web of friendships and associations, Ronnie Kray was later to befriend novelist and poet Emanuel Litvinoff's half-brother David, a dubious figure whose gangland knowledge was to be put to cinematic use when he served as adviser on the 1970 film *Performance*, staring Mick Jagger and James Fox.

Reggie and Ronald Kray lived with their mother Violet at 178 Vallance Road – a thoroughfare that traditionally marks the unofficial eastern boundary of Spitalfields – and in the course of the later 1950s and 1960s sought, through cunning and brutality, to establish their own criminal 'firm'. The convivial centre of their gambling, extortion and pornography empire was the Carpenter's Arms on the corner of Cheshire Street and St Matthew's Row, just a few minutes' walk away from the twins' home in Vallance Road, immediately in front of Wood Close School which they had both attended, and the location for the Repton Boys' Club where they had first learnt to box. The Carpenter's Arms is a small and charming late-Victorian pub that once thrived on trade from the Sunday markets and today serves French-influenced food and good Burgundy. Quite what earlier customers would have made of its latest incarnation is hard to imagine, although Reggie and Ronnie, who aspired to smart West End life, would probably have approved. They bought the pub for their mother in 1967, and she would preside at the bar at weekends over a bevy of bejew-elled, buxom, peroxide blondes of a certain age. A favoured lunchtime tipple here, with men as well as women, was a double Courvoisier and lemonade.

Under the Krays' control the Carpenter's Arms became a gangster drinking paradise, its walls tricked out with Regency-style striped wallpaper – as in smart bars 'up West' – and, according to legend, with a bar made out of a large piece of wood acquired by the twins from a local coffin-maker. This imaginative touch was perhaps intended to stop any-one forgetting who the bosses were and to remind them of what could happen if they did. One man who failed to take warning from the coffin counter was Jack 'the Hat' McVitie, an East End hard man and crony of the Krays', but a crony who offered offence one time too many. A plan to 'straighten' him out was allegedly hatched over drinks in the Carpenter's Arms, and McVitie was subsequently murdered by Reggie in a most bru-tal and frenzied manner. His body was never found. It was his disappearance, however, that brought the lives of the twins 'tumbling down like a pack of cards' and led, ultimately, to life sentences for them.[6]

A murder rather closer to home was that of local villain 'Ginger' Marks. He was loitering between the Carpenter's Arms and the Repton Boys' Club one day, eating chips, with a safe-breaker called Jimmy Evans, when the Krays' friend and sometime hitman Freddie Foreman drove by. He had a score to settle with the pair, and while it's not entirely clear what

*The Carpenter's Arms on the corner of Cheshire Street and St Matthew's Row.
It was acquired in 1967 by Reggie and Ronnie Kray for their mother, Violet.
Local villain Tommy 'Ginger' Marks disappeared near it in 1965, and it is alleged
that in 1967, over drinks in the pub, the twins hatched the plan to murder Jack
'the Hat' McVitie. Behind is Wood Close School, where the twins – and
Emanuel Litvinoff – had been pupils.*

then happened, Evans escaped alive while Marks – like McVitie – was never seen again. The police found a morsel of chip embedded in a bullet hole in a nearby wall. Presumably the person dining on this Huguenot dish (see page 479) had been shot in the stomach.[7]

Spitalfields, of course, had acquired an unenviable reputation for crime – both petty and more serious – long before the Krays came on the scene, and one particular killing with which they were tangentially involved formed the final link in a local criminal chain stretching back to Victorian times. Since the 1880s – if not earlier – the Cooney clan had run pubs and common lodging houses of very dubious character in and around 'Flower and Dean Street'. Eight decades or so later, in 1960, their latest manifestation, Selwyn 'Jimmy' Cooney, was co-owner with Billy Ambrose of the Pen Club, on the south side of 'Dorset Street', just across Commercial Street from 'Flower and Dean Street'. According to Reggie Kray the club 'was a favourite East End haunt for many villains'.[8] In February 1960 it was the scene of an argument between Cooney and Ambrose and a group of men headed by Jimmy Nash that culminated in a shooting, leaving Ambrose wounded, Cooney dead, and Nash and his associates on the run. The Cooneys' long and active role in Spitalfields' underworld had come to an end.

According to Reggie Kray, Nash and his associates fled straight to the twins' Vallance Road house (he also claimed that it was Nash who had pulled the trigger). Kray knew and respected both Nash and Ambrose so, by his own account, he had the task of patching up a semblance of peace between the men and ensuring that 'our moral code' was adhered to – which is to say that no one should inform on anyone else to the police. And that, claims Kray, is what happened. Nash was tried but because Ambrose refused to testify against him, and other witnesses made themselves scarce, he was acquitted of murder, receiving instead a five-year sentence for manslaughter.[9] No doubt, so far as Kray was concerned, things turned out as they should have done: honour among criminals was upheld and the full retribution of the law avoided. And for him, this would have served as reinforcement of an attractive myth that the Krays were arbitrating guardians, peacemakers who 'improved' life in their 'manor' by making the streets safer; and that their murderous natures and criminal activities were redeemed because they loved their mother and showed protective respect towards women and children, even if they were quite happy to kill their husbands, brothers and fathers. In many respects the Krays were, of course, continuing the traditions of the gangland leaders of the Victorian

East End – such as Jack McCarthy – who portrayed themselves as the champions of local law and order and occasionally indulged in selective and self-serving acts of charity (see page 548). As one of the Krays' young admirers – 'John' Heibner – put it, the twins 'kept a sense of order where order was necessary. No informers and no muggings. The East End was a safe and exciting place to live'.[10] Heibner, incidentally, was convicted of murder in 1976, though he has always protested his innocence.

Reggie Kray's view of the world was a kill or be killed one. He and his like were tough, he argued, because they had no choice: 'living as they did in one of London's worst areas, East End men were tough, hard and took no nonsense from anyone, particularly authority. Ronnie and I grew up among such people. You either fought or you went under, and my family was no different.'[11] It was an exercise in self-justification that, of course, ignored the fact that in the 1940s many East Enders grew up in circumstances as desperate as the Krays' but did not then become predatory, exploitative, gangland murderers. Was it, as the Krays would no doubt have claimed, because such tame people lacked spirit? Or was it because they possessed the human decency and sense of morality and responsibility that the twins lacked? The Krays themselves came from a desperately marginal family. Both grandfathers gloried in being tough street fighters; their father was mostly absent – a petty criminal whose desire to profit from the black market during the war rendered him willing to risk prosecution as a deserter. But the twins' background – part Romany and possibly part Irish and Jewish through their grandmother – which might have made them sensitive to the sufferings of often persecuted minorities, seems simply to have hardened them. When they did come into money during the 1960s they did almost nothing to help the poor but honest majority that made up their 'manor'.

The depth of poverty in the East End during the late 1960s was revealed in startling manner by photographer Nicholas Hedges, who in the 1960s and 70s campaigned to improve living conditions for the nation's poor. Hedges worked for Shelter – a charity founded in 1966 to fight homelessness – and documented impoverished outcast communities in Liverpool and East London, revealing the appalling housing conditions many endured as part of Shelter's strategy to raise awareness and spur the nation into benevolent action.

In Spitalfields, Hedges focused on the Rothschild Buildings and the Nathaniel Dwellings, 'Flower and Dean Street' (see pages 482 and 490). Built in the 1880s these tenements had, for nearly a hundred years, done the job for which they were intended, but by the late 1960s were gaunt, grimy, gloomy and decaying, casting long shadows over the narrow courts that separated the tall blocks. Hedges' photographs revealed their squalor and atmosphere of neglect, heightened by the grudging architectural details on these aptly named Industrial Dwellings. His image of the flat occupied by the Rump family is particularly shocking, since it seems to hark back to the era of Victorian slums. One little girl bathes in a small stoneware kitchen sink. Her mother Peggy cooks in a filthy, decrepit and cramped kitchen. A large and crumpled double bed has to serve, or so it would seem, for all four children in the household.[12]

Jerry White, the historian of the Rothschild Buildings development, first saw the tenements in November 1971 when 'they were approaching the end of a long decline . . . were partly empty . . . oppressive . . . and starkly repulsive'. He believed they were 'without one redeeming feature', and recalls that 'the view from the inside of the courtyard gave me an almost physical sense of shock.'[13] I first explored them at much the same time. The architecture struck me as indeed utilitarian and grim, the scale was intimidating – but I was aware that these blocks had provided homes for many, and had done much to define life for several generations within a large portion of central Spitalfields. When demolition began in the early 1970s, these vast blocks of masonry and concrete died hard. They had been built to last. Perhaps, if fashions and requirements in housing had not changed, and if the tenements had been maintained and adapted to reflect new domestic aspirations, they could be there still. It is surely significant that the 1863 Peabody block on the corner of Commercial Street and Folgate Street escaped a similar fate. Abandoned by its tenants in the 1970s it stood derelict for years. But then it was repaired and converted into private apartments. The block is now called 'The Cloisters', is generally admired and is listed as a building of historic or architectural interest. The site of the Rothschild Buildings is now covered by new streets of low-rise public housing.

At the time the Rothschild Buildings were being demolished the social fabric of Spitalfields was undergoing great, and far-reaching, change, too. Since the 1880s, much of central and south Spitalfields and Whitechapel had been home to East European Jews. The 1899 map of 'Jewish East

Above: *the courtyard of the Rothschild Buildings c.1970.* Below: *the interior of one of the Rothschild Buildings flats showing the children of the Rump family in bed. (Photos taken by Nick Hedges.)*

London' shows the occupation of some streets as 95 to 100 per cent Jewish – notably 'Flower and Dean Street', Fashion Street, the west end of Wentworth Street and Old Montague Street – and in 1901 it was estimated that of the total population of Spitalfields of 28,000, 24 per cent was Jewish.[14] Even as late as 1962 Geoffrey Fletcher, a chronicler of the minutiae of London's changing life, could still characterise 'the full Whitechapel flavour' as being made up of streets 'rich in tottering old property and greasy doorways' with a population consisting largely of 'Jewish butchers and poulterers, often established in crazy old shops'. With these inhabitants, observed Fletcher, 'go the small one-man tailoring businesses and barbers, nearly all with foreign names above the door. Small, close-smelling shops sell Jewish candlesticks, Old Testaments, the Talmud, the Psalms of David and Songs of Zion'.

Seemingly entranced by the fact that Whitechapel still seemed a foreign land – much as it had to pre-war explorers – Fletcher noted that 'an entire alley opposite the Whitechapel Bell Foundry supports itself by the sale of Hebrew lucky charms and cheap gaudy jewellery', and that 'this part of Whitechapel abounds with shops for the sale of oily fish and crummy little eating-places. Above the shops, the property is invariably in an advanced state of decay.' Of Spitalfields to the north, Fletcher merely observed, fatalistically, that it was 'an area of fine decaying Georgian architecture'.[15]

But within a very few years much of the Jewish population that had survived the diaspora of the war years had moved on elsewhere, and by the early 1970s virtually all of Spitalfields' synagogues – once numbered in their scores – had closed. Only the one in Sandys Row (see page 495) still functioned on a regular basis. And by the mid 1970s a mere handful of Jewish businesses and shops survived. When I started to get to know Spitalfields intimately, from the early 1970s, there were various Jewish enterprises: Marks delicatessen in Middlesex Street; the Kosher Dining Club off Old Montague Street; Bloom's Restaurant in Aldgate; a couple of hardware shops and bakeries in Brick Lane, including the twenty-four-hour Beigel Bake; other bakeries on Quaker Street, Commercial Street and – since 1911 – Rinkoff's at 79 Vallance Road. Today, with the exception of the Brick Lane bakeries and Rinkoff's, all these remnants of the Jewish East End have gone – Bloom's in 1996, Marks soon after.

In place of the Jewish community a new one arose. Bangladeshis had started to arrive in Spitalfields in ever-growing numbers after the Second

World War. They first came in the wake of the turmoil of Indian Independence in 1947 and the partition of the subcontinent along religious lines that created, in north-east Bengal, the sovereign Muslim state of East Pakistan, part of, but physically separated from, the larger and more prosperous West Pakistan. When Geoffrey Fletcher published his 1962 book *The London Nobody Knows*, his focus was on Whitechapel's still-dominant Jewish population and on Spitalfields' 'fine decaying Georgian architecture'.[16] Just three years later, though, in *Pearly Kingdom*, writing of the splendid mid-eighteenth-century shopfront in Artillery Lane – 'without question the finest shop front in London still in situ' – he noted the presence of 'Pakistanis' alongside the 'evil-smelling white kids and derelict old men' in the midst of the street's poverty: 'Nuns stride past talking earnestly, rattling their beads, vacant girls walk about with transistors and old men roll up their trousers to apply ointment to scabby legs. Over all, a deafening noise from the betting shop in the odoriferous alley.'[17]

The second wave of immigration from the subcontinent followed the brutal War of Independence that broke out in 1971 and ended with the secession of East Pakistan and the birth of the new sovereign nation of Bangladesh. People fled not only the conflict but the uncertainty that followed and the rural poverty, particularly in the Sylhet region, that had so long prevailed. By 1991 Bangladeshis formed the majority of Spitalfields residents: 5,379 out of the area's population of 8,861 according to that year's census.[18] Symbolically, the synagogue that occupied the former Huguenot chapel on the corner of Fournier Street and Brick Lane now became a mosque to serve the growing Bangladeshi Muslim community.

In the winter of 1969, when I first saw the neglected shopfront in Artillery Lane that Fletcher had been so besotted with, Spitalfields hovered uncertainly between worlds. It was on the very edge of the commercially vibrant City of London and yet it was also strangely empty, desolate even, with streets of historic houses – notably Elder Street and Folgate Street – long empty, partly derelict, gloomily awaiting a fate that did not look promising. Other streets such as Fournier Street and Princelet Street were more alive, many of their buildings intensely occupied by Bangladeshi sweatshops, where machinists making cheap clothes toiled in old panelled rooms. It was an echo of the tenements and garment trade of the disappeared Jewish community.

The question was: what could be saved? Virtually all the area's older buildings had long been listed as being of architectural or historic interest – but listing meant very little in the apparent absence of any determination to save and reuse them. Tower Hamlets Council was evidently not particularly concerned with history, beauty and conservation. Owners were more interested in rebuilding that would – they hoped – turn abandoned and decaying Spitalfields into a potentially profitable adjunct to the City. Indeed recent events in Spitalfields confirmed that gloom about the prospects facing the area's historic buildings was the only reasonable response. On my first walk through the area I was already too late to see the last surviving significant and coherent part of Spital Square, where a magnificent group of early-Georgian houses had been demolished in 1961.

Mass demolition was very much on the agenda at the time with virtually no building – no matter how old or historically significant or whether it was listed – safe from complete obliteration or from insensitive and destructive alteration. This was made clear in the early 1970s by a string of demolitions that now seem incomprehensible. The first I witnessed, and the most distressing, was the complete demolition of the early houses on the north side of Hanbury Street. These, numbered from 21 to 43, dated from the early eighteenth century – some rebuilt around 1750 – and included number 29 where Annie Chapman had been murdered in 1888 by Jack the Ripper. The demolition was for the erection of a dreary single-storey bottle store for the adjoining Truman's Brewery. At about the same time the best-surviving – and virtually the last – of the 1680s houses adjoining the Old Artillery Ground was destroyed. It stood on Artillery Passage only a few metres west of the famed shopfront in Artillery Lane. Also lost in the early 1970s was a splendid merchant's mansion of c.1810 in Calvin Street (formerly 'Great Pearl Street') that had been occupied by James Lewis Desormeaux – a black-silk dyer – and the last Georgian house in this network of streets.[19]

Other individual or small groups of early houses fell victim in Brushfield Street, Fleur de Lis Street, Elder Street and Folgate Street. Perhaps the most serious loss, from the social and historical point of view, was the long group of largely early-eighteenth-century weavers' houses on Sclater Street. The humble homes and workshops of journeymen weavers have fared very poorly in Spitalfields and this was the last sustained terrace of houses with top-floor workshops – lit by long weavers' windows – placed

Above: *the splendid Calvin Street merchant's mansion of c.1810 shortly before its demolition in the early 1970s.* Below: *the remains of 78–88 Sclater Street photographed during demolition work in the early 1970s. Built in the 1720s this terrace was one of the last large groups of purpose-designed weavers' houses to survive in Spitalfields.*

over residential and commercial accommodation. I photographed these houses one Sunday in 1971. A few weeks later they were gone and the site levelled as if they had never existed.

But, with hindsight, it is possible to see that the tide was turning. This was expressed initially by a hardening of public opinion against demolition that moved from silent indignation and outrage to organised and open opposition and direct action. This popular reaction was – eventually – supported by local politicians, who could see the way the wind was blowing. The crucial year was 1975. This had been declared European Architectural Heritage Year by the Council of Europe, yet to many it seemed a cynical deception. Historic buildings continued to decay and be demolished. Active and mostly youthful conservationists therefore decided to ensure that the public should not be deluded into a sense of false security, and three of them – Marcus Binney, Simon Jenkins and John Harris – launched SAVE Britain's Heritage, a campaigning organisation that successfully harnessed the power of the press to alert the public to the continuing, even increasing, threat to Britain's architectural heritage. That same year – 1975 – I co-authored a book with Colin Amery entitled *The Rape of Britain*. Its aim – as with SAVE – was to publicise the dire threats that then hung over twenty-five of Britain's key historic towns and cities – places that most people believed were safe from devastation – as well as dozens of characterful historic quarters throughout the land. The threatened buildings listed included a number in Spitalfields.

The Rape of Britain was one of the inspirations behind the foundation in 1976 of the Spitalfields Historic Buildings Trust. In the spirit of SAVE, the Spitalfields Trust believed in bold and direct action – expressed not through press campaigns but through the acquisition and exemplary repair of threatened historic buildings, and by encouraging owners or purchasers of historic buildings to behave responsibly and to repair authentically and conserve rather than skimp or destroy. The Trust started business with £10,000 donated by Patrick Trevor-Roper, who had earlier been involved in the saving of Hawksmoor's Christ Church, and with this cash purchased its first Spitalfields house – the splendid and decaying 4–6 Fournier Street (see page 218). Works to this house initiated the Trust's rolling fund where money made on one conservation project was ploughed into the next.

The Trust was not operating alone in Spitalfields. Others had been moved by the plight of its dwindling stock of historic buildings and had taken action, but on a smaller and more personal scale. In the early 1970s Martin Lane had been instrumental in the purchase and repair of the long-derelict 30–36 Elder Street to provide a mixture of homes and offices, and also took on 34 as his own home. A trifle earlier Mariga Guinness and Hugh O'Neill had bought 23 Elder Street, repairing it to serve as a home, and helped to hold developers and demolition men at bay by demonstrating that the decaying houses of Spitalfields, long condemned as slums, could be restored and used. Mariga – who with then husband Desmond Guinness had helped found the Irish Georgian Society and save houses in Mountjoy Square, Dublin, as well as the palatial Castletown House – proved to be an inspiration in Spitalfields. With great style and aplomb she not only repaired her London home and furnished it with flair but also opened it to local and national politicians, even to local developers, who – regaled with Irish hospitality – could not fail to appreciate that historic Spitalfields still had a future and that its decaying early-Georgian houses still had prospects.

The crucial test for the Spitalfields Trust came in 1977 with the start of the demolition of 5 and 7 Elder Street by Napier Properties (a subsidiary of British Land) and the proposed 'conversion' of 9/11, 15, 17, and 21 Elder Street into offices and flats. All the houses date from the mid 1720s (see chapter 9), all were listed and all long empty and derelict, and some were badly damaged. By the summer of 1977 listed-building consent had been granted for the demolition of 5 and 7, with 7 also being the subject of a Dangerous Structures notice. This had prompted the removal of the house's roof structure. Nevertheless the Trust decided to take action.

As a newly founded conservation group, dedicated to the salvation of Spitalfields, it was intolerable to sit passively by while these two important houses were destroyed and the other houses subjected to works that would almost certainly result in the loss of their authentic interiors, character and interest. The Trust announced that it wanted to negotiate with Napier Properties and with the Newlon Housing Trust, which was, as part of a planning deal brokered by Tower Hamlets Council, to be the direct beneficiary of the demolition of 5 and 7 by being handed the cleared site for its own housing project. To lend weight to its negotiating hand the Trust decided – in accordance with the maxim that possession is nine-tenths of the law – to occupy numbers 5 and 7. This was a political squat, supported by many of the great and good including Sir John Betjeman, that had

The front and rear elevations of 5 and 7 Elder Street, photographed during the battle to save them in 1977. They were built in 1725. Note the wide weavers' window in the rear of number 5.

fascinating ramifications and led ultimately – with the unexpected but most welcome support of Tower Hamlets Council – to the saving of the houses. By the end of 1977 the Trust had agreed to purchase 5 and 7 Elder Street and at the same time the exasperated Napier Properties dumped the remainder of its Elder Street houses on the open market. All were eventually saved and sympathetically restored as single-family homes, which after a century or so of multi-occupation, returned them to their original use.

I still recall the first time I explored my future home at 15 Elder Street. By the mid 1970s it had been abandoned for a decade or so, but much of the last family's furniture remained, quietly rotting. Paint on the panelling was blistered where cookers had been located, and floorboards and joists rotted below leaking pipes and taps. Most evocative of all was the basement. Like the top floor, it too had been long abandoned, and both front and rear rooms were knee-deep in debris. The evidence for its last period of sustained use was a calendar pinned to the cupboard door in the front room. It was dated 1944.

This victory for conservation and homes over demolition and commerce changed the course of history in Spitalfields – at least temporarily. In the early 1980s it seemed that the battle had been fought and that conservation had won the day. The Spitalfields Trust became involved with houses throughout the area – by purchasing and selling on with covenants to sympathetic new owners, by helping to raise grant monies, or by offering advice to those wanting to move in and repair old buildings. The future of the essential historic fabric of Spitalfields seemed assured as much of the area returned to residential use, with new arrivals complementing the more established Bangladeshi community along, and east of, Brick Lane. Houses in Folgate Street, Fournier Street, Princelet Street, Spital Square, Artillery Lane, Gun Street, Brushfield Street and Heneage Street were acquired by the Trust and sold on to sympathetic occupants, or repaired with support and advice from the Trust.

Part of this new wave of occupation, either directly related to Trust activities or independent but sympathetic, was the widespread arrival of artists, architects, historians, writers and curators. Some had been attracted by the possibility of acquiring large, handsome but decaying buildings for modest sums, others were drawn by the history and surviving Georgian architecture of the area. The artists Gilbert and George were among the pioneers, moving into the area in the 1960s and into Fournier Street in the early 1970s. The historian Raphael Samuel was another. He lived in 19

Elder Street until his death in 1996. Others came slightly later, including the writer and decorator Jocasta Innes, and architects Richard MacCormac and Theo Crosby, who in the early 1980s all acquired parts of an early-nineteenth-century brewery complex in Heneage Street from the Trust. Soon afterwards artists Tracey Emin and Sarah Lucas moved into the area, briefly opening a 'shop' in Redchurch Street in the early 1990s that was more a gallery and an exercise in performance art than in humdrum retail. The novelist Jeanette Winterson also set up home in Spitalfields.

Part of the story of the transformation that overtook Spitalfields during the 1980s and 90s is told – in subtle and coded manner – in one of the area's great creations of that period: Dennis Severs' house at 18 Folgate Street. He bought this 1724 building from the Spitalfields Trust in 1979 and until his death twenty years later worked to turn it into a 'still-life drama' – or as he sometimes called it in contemporary art terms, 'an installation' – in which he sought to evoke the history of a mythic Huguenot family and of Spitalfields – indeed of London – from the date the house was built until the death of Queen Victoria. Severs would conduct tours, by candlelight, complete with sounds, smells and surprise events. In his hands, public tours became pieces of performance art. The 'installation' has survived the death of its inventor and lead actor, and the house – now once again owned by the Trust – remains one of London's more successful if strange cultural attractions. In the second-floor front room – which has been created as a rather grand mid-Georgian bedchamber – is an ornate fire surround with a dark and cavernous opening. Few peer inside. But they should because it is clad with blue and white Delft-style tiles made in expert and witty manner during the 1980s by the Spitalfields-based potter Simon Pettet. The tiles offer a gallery of Spitalfields characters at that time – mostly the people fighting to save it, to repair its historic fabric, to give it distinct life. Gilbert and George are there, as are the designer Marianna Kennedy, Jocasta Innes and her young daughter Daisy Goodwin (who has grown into a poet and novelist), and one woman – who must remain nameless – who acquired a rapid but transitory reputation in the area. She is shown within her favoured mount – a sports car – that is seen from the rear with the young woman's legs akimbo through the side windows.

But while the 1980s saw temporary victory for the conservationists, there was a sting in the tail. Preservation can bring stability and make an area attractive. These are beneficial qualities. But stability and attractiveness also – almost inevitably – lead to increased land and house values that can, in turn, fuel speculation and profiteering. And escalating land values can also be socially divisive. They undermine a community by creating great gulfs between rich and poor, between tenants and freeholders. The key problem when houses become extremely expensive is that they are accessible to only a few, and often these few tend to view their historic homes as investments or as second or occasional homes that – to realise their potential – need to be enlarged and modernised. Spitalfields' historic fabric – fragile and long neglected – is rare and important. The adding of rear extensions, the digging of basements, the insertion of state-of-the-art kitchens and bathrooms, can easily destroy what is special, replacing the unusual, ancient and authentic with the commonplace, bland and fake. Spending too much money on an historic house can be as destructive as spending too little – perhaps more so because money can destroy not only the body of an historic house but also its soul. The wise and sophisticated response to an old building is also the simplest. Do as little as is practicably possible. It is strange how few understand this.

The speculation and investment attracted by Spitalfields' stability and success have led not only to damage to individual houses but has also – ironically – proved potentially lethal to the very qualities that make the area attractive, stable and successful. In its most direct terms the problem lies with the creation of large development sites in the heart of the area and their arguably excessive exploitation, fuelled by the determination to maximise profits through the introduction of bulky new buildings and uses that are potentially valuable rather than desirable. The consequence is the proposal to construct – or the actual construction of – megastructures and high-rise buildings within and around Spitalfields.

The insertion of large commercial buildings into the heart of Spitalfields has happened before – for example with the creation of the Fruit and Wool Exchange in 1929 – and it is true that the history of Spitalfields is characterised by change: from Roman suburb and cemetery, to monastic enclave, merchant quarter, and nineteenth-century netherworld. But now the proposed changes are so vast in scale, so sustained and absolute in their nature, and so rapid in their proposed timescale, that surely little of the established and admired historic character of Spitalfields can survive. Indeed, as this book goes to press the identity of the area hangs in the balance.

When I first explored Spitalfields, nearly fifty years ago, its two main large industrial sites remained in traditional use. At least once a week the air of the neighbourhood was suffused by the pungent smell of hops drifting from Truman's Brewery on Brick Lane. By night the cobbled streets around the wholesale market off Commercial Street echoed to the sounds of porters carting fruits, vegetables and flowers to waiting trucks and vans, and in the morning the debris of the night before – crates of spurned fruit, abandoned timber pallets and diverse odds and ends of often curious origin – lay scattered and forgotten where hours earlier market workers had toiled. But all this has long gone. Truman's Brewery was closed in 1989 by Maxwell Joseph's Grand Metropolitan, which had owned it since 1972, and Spitalfields Market was closed in 1991 by its owners the City Corporation.

Each of these industries occupied about eleven acres (4.45 hectares) of Spitalfields' heartland. The market, still owned by the City Corporation but leased to commercial companies, has been transformed during the last two decades. The western half, reaching to the west side of Steward Street (see page 313) and comprising 1920s pavilions around an open-roofed court, was largely demolished from the 1990s. The works included a detailed excavation, conducted by Museum of London Archaeology, that has thrown much light on the life and architecture of medieval and post-medieval Spitalfields.[20] The western portion of the market has been replaced with eight- and twelve-storey minimalist commercial architecture of very little interest, while the late-nineteenth-century market buildings to the east remain as shops, restaurants and flats, with the court now housing varied market activities. The eventual fate of the Truman's Brewery site, acquired in 1995 by the locally based Zeloof Partnership, remains unresolved. Most of the brewery buildings that survived after brewing ceased in 1989 have been retained and adapted to house shops and restaurants, with the handsome eighteenth-century Directors' House on Brick Lane now in commercial use. The ultimate fate of this vital portion of Spitalfields, which also includes large amounts of open space and numerous small-scale buildings, is uncertain. But as land values in the area rise it must be assumed that high-density and high-rise commercial schemes will eventually be proposed.

The most efficient way to appreciate the forces now at work in Spitalfields that threaten huge and irredeemable change, and to discover the fates of many of the buildings, streets and places described in this book, is to draw up an inventory. And the simplest structure for this inventory is a walk, with the logical starting point being the site of the north precinct of the late-twelfth-century Augustinian priory or hospital of St Mary – the 'Spital' in the 'Fields'.

Nothing of the priory church or buildings appears to survive above ground and even the pattern formed by the existing streets and buildings on the site of the church and its related structures is confusing. Spital Yard, a small court and alley off Spital Square, has little to do with the historic Spital Yard that was from c.1700 enlarged and transformed into Spital Square. The existing Spital Yard roughly marks the western wall of the south transept of the priory church while the existing west–east arm of Spital Square stands, more or less, on the site of the church's nave, with the site of the altar now marked approximately by a manhole located at the eastern end of the road. The transformation of building into road was initiated by Stephen Vaughan when he acquired the priory buildings during the 1540s and gutted the nave, Lady Chapel and most of the transepts to form a series of yards and gardens serving buildings around the site of the former church, including his own mansion (see page 41). However, within the small stub of Spital Yard, there does survive the much altered and mutilated remains of what could be a seventeenth-century house that – perhaps – even incorporated fragments of the south transept of the priory church. This curious house, now with an early-twentieth-century brick façade, bears an old blue plaque set up by the Corporation of the City of London proclaiming it the birthplace on 20 January 1669 of Susanna Annesley, daughter of Samuel Annesley the Dissenting cleric (see page 108) and mother of John and Charles Wesley.

Susanna was a remarkable women. The youngest of twenty-five siblings, she had nineteen children herself, nine of whom died as infants, and a husband who, as an Anglican minister, proved unable to earn an adequate living and regularly absented himself from home, leaving his wife the material and moral responsibility for rearing the children. She did not fail. After a year-long separation caused by political differences – Susanna was a Jacobite while her husband as an Anglican minister was obliged to support and celebrate King William during his church services – the couple reunited in 1702. This was possible because in that year Queen Anne came to the throne and Susanna felt able to accept her as she was a daughter of the deposed James II. Nine months or so after this reconciliation of Susanna with her husband, John Wesley was born.

*The characterless Bishop's Square in the summer of 2016, looking north along
the site of Steward Street and across Fort Street on the Old Artillery Ground, past
the site of Spital Square, to the distant 1720s terrace that survives on Folgate Street.
See the photographs on page 641 for what this area once looked like.*

To the east of the site of the priory church is that of the early-seventeenth-century Brick House, inhabited from 1611 by Doña Luisa Carvajal and used by her as an illicit Roman Catholic nunnery. The site is now partly beneath a new residential and commercial block forming the east side of the rebuilt Spital Square. The garden, behind and to the east of the Brick House, where Doña Luisa's nuns would have taken their recreation and grown their vegetables, is once again a garden – now known as Elder Gardens – but with a ground level about two metres above the earlier one. The homes of the Venetian and Flemish ambassadors, who helped to sustain Doña Luisa, were probably on the land to the west of the site of the Brick House that now lies between Spital Square and Folgate Street, where Vaughan's mansion and his Principal Tenement were located from the 1540s. To the south of Doña Luisa's house, on a site now occupied by a wind-blown plaza and abutting pilotis supporting an eight-storey block of lawyers' offices, stood the Candle House, once part of the priory and from 1616 an occasional residence of Sir Francis Bacon's.

Walk south from Spital Square and you stand astride the substantial remains of the charnel house and chapel of St Mary Magdalene that from the early fourteenth century stood near the junction of the priory's inner or north precinct and its outer or south precinct. The south precinct was largely open land in monastic times while the north precinct was the location of the priory's major buildings. The south precinct was used for artillery practice after the Reformation and in 1682 was acquired and developed by a consortium of speculators working under Nicholas Barbon. None of the houses built during this 1680s speculation survive and even the street pattern laid out by Barbon and his collaborators has mostly gone, replaced by a pedestrian space called Bishop's Square that is framed by a cacophonous array of large-scale and arid early-twenty-first-century commercial buildings.

The south side of Bishop's Square is defined by Brushfield Street. Known until 1870 as Union Street, this portion of Brushfield Street was cut through the late-seventeenth-century fabric of the Old Artillery Ground from the early 1780s. The east end of Union Street incorporated the existing – but widened – Paternoster Row, which by the mid nineteenth century was known as Union Street East. The street was renamed in honour of Thomas Brushfield – a local worthy who earlier in the century had been a Justice of the Peace, a vestryman of Christ Church and trustee of the London Dispensary, based in Fournier Street (see pages 398–9).

This radical piece of street improvement was conceived as part of a grand highway that, connecting via Sun Street with Chiswell Street to the west, would form a route between Smithfield and Whitechapel by way of Spitalfields. This was to be a great commercial highway – much as Commercial Street was to be half a century later – intended to allow goods to flow more easily through the city and, in particular, ease the connection between Bishopsgate and Spitalfields Market. The works required an Act of Parliament – obtained in 1778 – that was supported by the City Corporation as well as the Vestry of Christ Church. In 1782 a second Act of Parliament was obtained to regulate the development of the new street and required that its architecture be uniform and its frontages unencumbered by porticoes, benches or deeply projecting bow windows. By 1786 the street had been constructed and named Union Street, presumably to celebrate the union of several key commercial locations that the new street helped to achieve.[21]

On the south side of what was Paternoster Row, now the south-east portion of Brushfield Street, stands the fine, neo-Georgian frontage of the London Fruit and Wool Exchange, constructed in 1929. In 2013 a property company named Exemplar announced plans to demolish it, leaving only its Brushfield Street façade standing, and to obliterate what traces remained of the late-seventeenth-century 'Dorset Street'. After due democratic process the scheme was rejected by the politicians of the Tower Hamlets planning committee. The new development Exemplar proposed was thought to be too dominant and destructive for its conservation-area site and too commercial in its content. But Boris Johnson, then Mayor of London, used the powers of his office to intervene. He declared that, since the proposal had London-wide implications, he had the power to call in the rejected scheme for his own determination. Johnson held a brief inquiry and then, acting as judge and jury in what to many appeared an audacious act of autocratic intervention, reversed the planning refusal and granted consent.

By the autumn of 2016 the basement shelter where in 1940 East Enders defied the Luftwaffe had been swept away and the theatrically retained façade of the Fruit and Wool Exchange presided over a vast excavation stretching south to White's Row. A deep pit, as far below ground as four-storey houses on White's Row rise above it, marked the site where 'Dorset Street' had stood for 350 years. The content of Exemplar's scheme – 260,000 square feet of offices and 40,000 square feet of largely retail use with no housing in an area that is significantly residential, and the replacement of independent buildings and the existing street pattern with monolithic architecture – illustrates only too well how Spitalfields' character, which has endured so much, is being assaulted, compromised and homogenised in the twenty-first century. The purely commercial nature of this transaction and transformation was revealed in March 2015 when Exemplar, once it had gained planning approval from Johnson, put the entire block and scheme on the market and sold it to M&G Real Estate for £55 million.[22] Concluding this deal leaves Exemplar free to move on, presumably to repeat the process elsewhere. Most people do not have to be reminded that places like Spitalfields, with rich and ancient histories, are far more than just real-estate opportunities. They are repositories of memory with their physical remains touchstones that act as portals to our past. To eradicate large swathes of the area is to deny us our heritage and our chance to remember extraordinary and heroic figures.

A five-minute walk north-west of the Fruit and Wool Exchange site, back across Bishops Square and Spital Square, will take you to yet another large potential building site. Its future – in the autumn of 2016 – remains contested and its fate could do much to determine the future of Spitalfields. The 0.9-hectare site lies within the old Liberty of Norton Folgate, with its southern portion being former monastic land that was used, until the Reformation, as the priory's service court. Most of the site – divided by roads and an alley into three portions – is currently covered by buildings. The largest of the sites, between Blossom Street and Norton Folgate, contains a rich mix of eighteenth-, nineteenth- and early-twentieth-century houses and warehouses that rise four storeys high. Located next to the Roman Ermine Street this site has been, it is reasonable to assume, inhabited by Londoners for around 2,000 years. All three sites are in a conservation area, with one fronting onto Elder Street, one of the best early-eighteenth-century streets to survive in London.

The current proposal for the site, put forward by British Land, is for the demolition of up to 70 per cent of the conservation area it controls, with only a few façades and two late-nineteenth-century warehouse interiors retained. The proposed architecture is generally commercial in use, large in scale and monolithic, ranging between eight and fourteen storeys high. A relatively small amount of residential building would be constructed off Elder Street. None of the threatened buildings is individually listed as being of national architectural or historic interest even though two date from the early eighteenth century. If the plan goes ahead, one of these would be completely demolished and the other gutted, only its façade retained.

Opponents of the scheme argue that it would do unacceptable harm to the conservation area, whose established architectural and social character ought to be respected and enhanced not diluted by new buildings. It has also been argued that, if built, this scheme would usher in physically destructive, high-density, high-rise, largely commercial architecture into a key and historic part of Spitalfields, where scale remains low and the grain is formed by a rich mix of individual buildings and uses. Opponents further point out that the site is a buffer zone between the high-rise and commercial City of London and the low-rise, largely residential Spitalfields, and that development consent provides an alarming precedent. The freeholder of the development site is the City Corporation, which it has been pointed out, might be expected to behave more sensitively when involved in a scheme in a conservation area in one of its neighboring local authorities.

In 2015, after much debate and representation, Tower Hamlets planning committee rejected the British Land scheme. Once again, however, the Mayor of London intervened and in January 2016 – to much public dismay and near disbelief – overturned the democratically reached decision to reject the scheme and used his planning powers to grant consent. Fortunately, the former Mayor's decision has not yet proved to be the last word. The Spitalfields Trust, having produced a conservation-orientated alternative scheme for the site, was granted a Judicial Review of the Mayor's conduct after the Trust's lawyers argued that this decision is unlawful. The Judicial Review duly took place at the Royal Courts of Justice and the Trust's case was not sustained. The Trust's request to appeal against this decision was refused, but it was allowed an oral hearing in front of a judge to argue the case for the request. This hearing took place in November 2016 and the Trust was not granted leave to appeal. As of February 2017 the planning approval has not been activated and the site continues to languish.

Elder Street also offers a perspective on another large and largely empty site whose future is crucial to the future of Spitalfields. The view north from Elder Street reveals a portion of the Bishopsgate Goodsyard – part of which was the original terminus of the Great Eastern Railway – that now comprises fragments of ruinous nineteenth-century railway architecture, including high-level sidings, viaducts, the stunted remains of warehouses and the concrete 'box' that encloses the Shoreditch High Street overground station.

It is on this 4.4-hectare site – where 'Anchor' and 'Phoenix' Streets once stood – that Hammerson and Ballymore propose a high-rise, mixed-use development including a series of residential towers that will mostly offer private apartments for sale. The pair of towers that would close the vista north from Elder Street would rise just over and just under forty storeys. The local battle to stop this scheme has been long, complex and bitter, with accusations levelled that the towers would not only visually dominate existing low-rise buildings and historic streets around the site – notably the recently much revived Redchurch Street – but also rob the existing community of its light and rights by condemning it to live within the shadows cast by this aspiring development. Naturally the developers have attempted to demonstrate that overshadowing would be minimal.

If the proposal were to go ahead the meagre remnants of the Nichol Rookery would be dominated by a mini-Manhattan with a glut of expensive and exclusive private high-rise apartments – an estimated 1,350 in number – lording it over a territory where journeymen weavers toiled through the eighteenth century and where some of the most desperate poor of late-Victorian London congregated within decaying terraces (see page 499). Hardly could a greater change take place.

The increasingly sceptical local authorities were preparing to confront this ambitious proposal when – yet again – Boris Johnson intervened. This time, rather than waiting for the local authorities to reach a decision, the Mayor in early 2016 called in the scheme for his own determination. But this time he failed to conduct a hearing before he left office and in the current atmosphere of uncertainty following the referendum decision for the UK to leave the EU, and with Johnson replaced by a less developer-friendly London Mayor, such an ambitious, high-value residential scheme appears too high-risk to pursue. The developers have announced that the current scheme is being revised, although at the time of going to press the nature of the revision remains unclear.

But if this architecturally and functionally audacious Goodsyard scheme, and that proposed by British Land for the Norton Folgate site, do go ahead then the historic core of Spitalfields will have been effectively outflanked. Already commercial towers spreading from the City of London mark Spitalfields' southern and south-western boundaries and high and dense developments – including a fifty-storey and 174-metre high

Foster and Partners-designed residential tower at Principal Place – are under way on the west side of Norton Folgate. And if the Goodsyard scheme receives consent tall residential and commercial towers would define its northern edge, dominating views from Spitalfields' streets and cutting the heart of the area off from Shoreditch and Hackney beyond. If these northern towers are built they can only be seen as harbingers of more to come. As God observed, in some dismay, when he contemplated the alarming bulk of the Tower of Babel rising from a throng of industrious humanity: '. . . now nothing will be restrained them, which they have imagined to do'.[23]

Spitalfields – a place characterised by change and which through those changes charts the history of 2,000 years of London life – is perhaps on the brink of its biggest change ever. Whether this change – if it happens – will reinvigorate or else dilute and ultimately destroy Spitalfields' special and distinct character is the key and dramatic question. The emerging pattern of new building, driven by a response to market forces and the quest for profit, involves the replacement of the small-scale, delicate, authentic and specific with the big, the bland and the universal. And, surely, to rob an area like Spitalfields of its special physical character and its memories, to deny current and future generations access to its history – and through its history to the broader history of London – is a serious cultural crime. I fear that after nearly 2,000 years Spitalfields' remarkable and individual identity – as a place of refuge, survival, revival and invention – is coming to an end. Future chroniclers of the area may prove me wrong. I hope they do.

FORT STREET AND THE GHOSTS OF SPITALFIELDS

Spitalfields is a haunted place – and the ghosts are many. Ghosts of people, of events, of long-lost buildings and of almost forgotten streets. Looking back on his family's time in a tenement in 'Fuller Street' near Brick Lane, the poet and writer Emanuel Litvinoff, born in Whitechapel in 1915, recalled in his biography the intensity of life in his new home, which he described as 'a village in miniature' within the 'Ghetto of East London'.[1] The once vibrant 'Fuller Street' has since then been wiped from the map and its surrounding neighbourhood utterly transformed. Such radical, often rapid and even brutal change made Litvinoff ponder. In a poem, he considered his early life in the street and reflected on its fate and that of the Spitalfields he had known. Now, he lamented, there was 'only sometimes a ghost shuffling by, talking to the wind and lonely.'[2] I feel much the same as Litvinoff's ghost.

In many ways I find the streets of Spitalfields the most moving and melancholic mementos of its past. They formed the area; they were the warp and weft around which the fabric of its life was woven, and now many of the oldest and once most important streets are long gone or altered out of all recognition. Wheler Street – for a while in the late seventeenth century the premier new address in Spitalfields – has been reduced to a mere stub, and even that remnant has recently been renamed as if to consign this once great street to complete oblivion. The formerly important Crispin Street is a truncated shadow of its former self, almost lost and forgotten. 'Anchor Street' has completely gone, as have 'King Street' and Phoenix Street, while 'Great' and 'Little Pearl' Streets and 'Corbet's Court' have been eradicated or else relegated to mere, or near, anonymous and characterless backwaters. Even Spital Square, the architectural jewel of Spitalfields from the 1730s and the location of the area's merchant palaces, has been mostly destroyed or sadly disfigured, and Old Montague

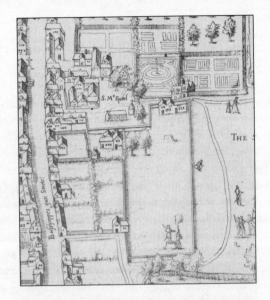

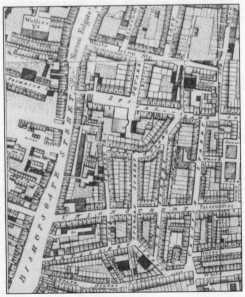

Above: *the site of the former north precinct of St Mary's Priory and, to its south,*
the Artillery Ground, as shown on the 'Copperplate' map of c.1553.
Below: *the same portion of Spitalfields shown on Richard Horwood's map of 1799–1819.*

Street, the once narrow and bewitching high street of late-nineteenth-century Jewish Spitalfields, has been widened and straightened into a busy traffic route lined with arid modern buildings.

This process of eroding and coarsening the urban grain of Spitalfields continues. In 2015 the late-seventeenth-century 'Dorset Street' was, despite much public protest, totally erased – a victim of the quest for profits on the part of a private developer and of the exercise of public power on the part of the Mayor of London, who, in autocratic manner, reversed a planning refusal by Tower Hamlets Council that had rejected its destruction. In such depressing ways history and memory are lost and obscured.

But perhaps the most wholesale loss has been the gradual destruction of the Old Artillery Ground development. Dating from the early 1680s, and masterminded by Nicholas Barbon, this speculative building project represented one of the earliest and most architecturally ambitious and coherent developments in Spitalfields and was key to the transformation of the area from its status as a semi-rural suburb to a close-built adjunct of the City (see pages 129–30). Today only the barest of fragments survive.

In this epilogue I want to tell the story of two of the houses that once stood in Fort Street, a thoroughfare on the Old Artillery Ground that is now so completely lost it's as if it had never existed. All that now survive are references in scattered documents, and – more substantially – the information gleaned during a series of intricate archaeological digs that took place on the site from 1991 to 2007. So expertly was the excavation handled (as is clear from the Museum of London's splendid publication *The Spitalfields Suburb, 1539–c.1880* describing it) that, paradoxically, it is on occasion possible to know more about the history of lost streets and houses – about life within them and about what was eaten, drunk, used and discarded there – than about those that still exist.[3]

⋯

If today you stand above the truncated south wall of the early-fourteenth-century charnel house on Bishop's Square you are standing in what were once the rear yards of 24 and 25 Fort Street. Apart from the charnel house beneath your feet there are no physical clues, in this bustling, modern commercial plaza, that terraces of late-seventeenth-century homes once stood here. All that has been retained is the ground level that was raised when the terraces were built, burying the remains of the charnel house completely. If, when astride the wall, you look south then you are looking towards the site where – five metres distant – the rear elevations of 24 and 25 Fort Street once stood. The front elevations of these houses stood about fourteen and a half metres south of the charnel-house wall. By bizarre chance the depth of the lost houses and their yards is illustrated by the spacing of the steel structural columns or pilotis that adjoin the site of the houses and form part of the modern office building nearby. These columns start a few metres south of the charnel-house wall and the span between their centres is ten and a half metres so they mark approximately the location of the frontage of this pair of houses. In such strange and haunting ways do the echoes of the past make themselves felt in the present, with modern construction unintentionally illuminating lost buildings.

The 1680s development involved the construction of long narrow streets consisting of small and generally similar houses. Judging from a watercolour of c.1914 by E. A. Phipson that shows the junction of Fort Street and Steward Street, Fort Street was no exception, its width in front of number 25 being just under five and a half metres (or eighteen feet).[4] The vistas along these long yet constricted streets must have been extraordinary. The longest, Gun Street, was 175 metres long, and also no more than 5.5 metres wide. The south side of Fort Street is also shown in a watercolour of 1884, which has in the foreground a picturesque wedge-shaped tavern that formed the junction of Fort Street with Gun Street.[5] Building leases for the north side of Fort Street were granted by Nicholas Barbon and his partners to Thomas Denning in January 1683. By 1710, when John Shorter sold on the plots, the whole of the north and north-west side of Fort Street, at least ten houses – probably numbers 21 to 30 – had been built.[6]

Number 24, built by Thomas Denning in or soon after 1683,[7] had a frontage thirty feet wide. This made it one of the largest houses built on the Old Artillery Ground – probably five windows wide at first-floor level.[8] The archaeologists who excavated the site suggested that it had a basement divided into at least two rooms, a central doorway on the ground floor, and then two further storeys (if the watercolour of c.1914 showing neighbouring houses is anything to go by), but a fourth floor was possible too, either a full storey or a weaving garret.[9]

In the yard behind the house, the archaeologists unearthed 'a moderately sized but massively built brick ice house' and a 'brick-lined ice pit', both possibly dating from the early days of the house; both, of course, designed to keep perishable food cool in hot weather. A nearby brick-lined

Above: *the east side of the north end of Steward Street at its junction with Fort Street in 1925. The houses on the corner of Steward Street date from c.1683 to c.1710. A fragment of 24 Fort Street can be seen on the left; its front was rebuilt soon after 1825.*
Below: *the splendid mid-eighteenth-century 28 Steward Street. The house was already in decay when photographed by architect Marshall Sisson in c.1925 but survived until about 1960.*

circular pit that had once served as a soakaway for a drain from the house had accumulated some sheep and fish bones. And another pit lined with horncoreage (see page 118),[10] which in the mid eighteenth century had been used for household rubbish, contained 'a well-preserved group of wine bottles together with ceramics . . . which indicate formal dining and tea drinking'. At the back of the yard lay the house's privy, with brick-lined cesspit beneath.[11] This, of course, would have had to be emptied from time to time by night-soil men – by no means a pleasant task for either the workmen or the householder.

Cesspits often ended up with more than human waste in them, and because they were difficult to clean some items could remain lodged there. Dating the deposits can sometimes be tricky. Many cesspits were sealed in the 1850s as the newly formed Metropolitan Board of Works assumed responsibility for London's sewers (a move taken in the wake of the great cholera epidemic of the late 1840s when it was confirmed that the disease was spread by tainted water). The remainder were closed in the 1880s, as landlords became required to provide connections from outhouses to the Board of Works' main sewers. The 'primary fill' of the privy in the yard of 24 Fort Street was found to contain a large number of clay tobacco-pipe fragments, many dating from 1730–70. An upper layer of later waste contained more clay tobacco pipes, fragments of pottery, hearth sweepings, food refuse and, of course, night soil, along with a 'refined whiteware teacup decorated with a mother and child playing' which dates from the early nineteenth century and suggests that the privy was being used in 1812.[12]

Until well into the early nineteenth century 24 Fort Street remained in domestic use. According to *The Spitalfields Suburb*, and Land Tax records, a James Cox lived there in 1809[13] and a Robert Howitt the following year,[14] though a Sun Life insurance record for July 1810 shows that the cabinet-maker John Morris was also in residence at that time.[15] From 1811 until 1825 it was home to the Grahams, a family of silk manufacturers comprising initially Joseph and Ann Graham, and their sons Mark and James.[16] The Grahams leased the house from the Trustees of the Cripplegate School, who – as was then common practice – had acquired an interest in it as an investment so that the rent would contribute to the school's annual income.[17] The Land Tax shows that it was one of the most expensive properties in Fort Street at the time – unsurprising, given that it was one of the largest – costing £30 per annum to rent in 1822.[18]

It was during the Grahams' time in occupation that the privy cesspit was finally abandoned, but before that happened the family seem to have taken the opportunity to fill it with a whole range of damaged or unwanted items. Perhaps, as the Museum of London archaeologists speculate, they did so as they prepared to move out of Fort Street altogether in 1825. Certainly the number and range of things they abandoned is extraordinary: 'up to 448 ceramic vessels ... many of which were around 10–20 years old at the time of discard.' There were also 'dress accessories and sewing equipment relating to the textile business' and 'two finds of unidentified textile [and] flax seeds [which] are common to the cesspit fills'. The archaeologists explained their possible usage: 'In addition to pressing the seeds for linseed oil for cooking or fuel for lanterns, the flax seed could be utilised as one of the raw materials for making linen, with coarser grades used for rope and twine.'[19]

Much that was abandoned suggests that those at 24 Fort Street in Regency times had an eye for the fashionable, and that they lived very comfortably. For example, the archaeologists uncovered 'chimney ornaments' of the 1780s and 1790s, including 'a creamware spill holder with applied neo-classical sprigged portrait decoration' used to hold twisted paper or wood shavings for lighting candles, lamps or pipes from the fireplace. They unearthed a painted creamware whistle in the shape of a bird – perhaps a child's toy. They discovered the figure of a young shepherdess that no doubt originally had a sheep and a shepherd companion pieces. There were portions of a miniature Caughley jug with a 'hand-painted ... Chinese-type island design', numerous fragments of blue, transfer-printed pearlware tea bowls and saucers decorated with chinoiserie designs, and relatively expensive fluted saucers and tea bowls with scalloped rims.[20]

And then there was a somewhat enigmatic find: parts of a large armorial Chinese-made rounded porcelain bowl with, on both sides, the gold-enamelled monogrammed initials E & L, set within a crest framed by a garland of flowers and flanked by images showing two doves perched upon a garland above a love heart.[21] The archaeologists speculated that the bowl celebrated a wedding and that the initials commemorated the names of the husband and wife: 'such vessels', they pointed out, 'were specially commissioned, with the design specifications sent to an agent for production in China. Special orders of this type were often decorated with overglaze colour and gilt in Guangzhou (Canton) on glazed porcelain blanks from Jingdezhen, although the underglaze blue decoration was added at Jingdezhen'.[22] It was an exercise that would have involved careful planning, since it would have taken at least six months for the specification to be sent to China for manufacture and for the completed item then to arrive – hopefully in good time for the wedding. Various other Chinese porcelain items found with the bowl – 'two larger rounded bowls (perhaps used as punch bowls . . .) and up to 12 tea bowls and saucers' – appear to be associated with it, suggesting that together they formed a treasured family heirloom, perhaps displayed in the dining parlour. The service is certainly later than 1760 but predates the Grahams' arrival in 24 Fort Street in 1811. Did they inherit or otherwise acquire it? Why was it thrown away? And who were E and L? Sadly, we don't know.

Other fragmentary items confirm the Grahams' comparative affluence. The remains of over forty wine bottles were excavated, including one made of clear blue-green glass 'probably from southern France or Italy'.[23] There were also pieces of up to fourteen matching or similar-looking conical-shaped and faceted wine glasses. Wine appears to have been consumed in quantity and with style. A small number of spirit bottles were found, too, including one, complete with its cork, that probably once contained imported gin. There were also numerous fragments of clay pipes. So, in the Graham household, it would seem that, together with the consumption of wine, smoking was a popular pastime. And as well as drinking in style, the ceramic and food fragments found suggest the Grahams also liked to dine in style. They had matching dining crockery, and, judging from the animal bones found in the cesspit, served good-quality food on it. The archaeologists identified bones from 'more expensive cuts' including 'a significant proportion of veal and occasional lamb remains among a majority of prime beef and mutton.'[24] Remains were also found of pork, young chicken, fish and rabbit – and head and foot bones from cattle that would have been boiled to produce aspic and fillings for pies and savoury puddings.

It's worth recalling that the Grahams' time here coincided with the end of Spitalfields' second Golden Age. Perhaps it is no coincidence that this apparently successful weaving family left its home in Fort Street – and probably the industry – the year after the Spitalfields Acts were repealed in 1824 and just before the consequences of the repeal hit the industry (see chapter 13). Perhaps they saw the writing on the wall and so decided to close their business and the place of work that had also been their home for over ten years. From 1818 to 1824 Ann Graham's name appeared on commercial and street directories for 24 Fort Street as A. Graham & Sons, silk manufacturers.[25] Her son Mark served in the office of headborough for the Liberty of the Old Artillery Ground in November 1819[26] and is mentioned in January 1822 as the lessee in the minutes of the Trustees of the Cripplegate School.[27] But after 1824, when they prepared to leave their Spitalfields house behind them, the Grahams disappeared from the trade directories for Spitalfields.

Fort Street nevertheless retained its contacts with the silk trade. Judging from the 1841 census and a selection of commercial and street directories published between 1817 and 1841, about half of the houses on this street were consistently occupied by businesses, nearly all of which 'comprised male individuals listed as silk manufacturers with English rather than French [i.e. Huguenot] surnames.'[28] The national census of 1841 records that 'most of the silk manufacturers' premises were inhabited by a single family . . . many of whom employed one female servant. The remaining houses on Fort Street can be characterised as dwellings in multiple occupancy and usually lived in by those of lower-class artisan status with the male occupants . . . employed as shoemakers, labourers and carpenters, with females working as straw hat- and dressmakers or in domestic service.'[29]

The record of one event that occurred during the Grahams' occupation of the house throws a little further light both on the life they led and also on the darker side of Spitalfields at that time. On 15 January 1817 a sixteen-year-old boy named John Moore was put on trial at the Old Bailey.[30] The charge was burglary. The alleged victims were his employers: Ann Graham and her son Mark.

The account of the trial records the charge that Moore, at 'about seven in the night . . . being in the dwelling-house of Ann Graham and Mark Graham, did steal therein one gown, value 30s.; two cloaks, value 7s.; two handkerchiefs, value 4s.; one set of bed furniture, value 15s.; one counterpane, value 2s.; and one pair of stockings, value 1s., the property of the said Ann Graham; and one coat, value 20s.; two pair of pantaloons, value 2s.; and one pair of trowsers, value 3s., the property of Mark Graham; and having committed the said felony, about seven in the night of the same day, burglariously did break and get out of the said dwelling-house.'

Ann Graham, in her evidence, explained that her husband Joseph had died (presumably only recently), that John Moore worked in a workshop on the same floor as her bedroom (suggesting, since it would appear that Ann Graham slept on the first floor, that the workrooms were dispersed around the house), and that on the day in question Moore had been at work for only an hour before he left the house (even though 'there was work for him all day if he had come to do it'). Her son Mark, who slept on the floor above, testified that Moore had taken things from his room, too, and that he had later spotted them in a pawnbroker's shop in Brick Lane owned by William Sowerby. Her other son James said that he was the one who had let Moore into the house 'while my mother was at tea'.

Moore was clearly a pretty inept criminal, and his arrest was distinctly unheroic. John Brown – presumably a parish constable – explained the circumstances:

> I am an officer. On Friday, the 20th of January, I stopped the prisoner, at eleven o'clock in the morning, in White Horse-lane, Mile-end, he had a bag with him; I told him that I was an officer, and asked him what was in the bag; he said, he was my prisoner, and surrendered. The bag contained the skirt of a gown, one cloak, one sheet, and two pair of pantaloons, Mr and Mrs Graham afterwards claimed them. He said that he had stolen them, and begged me to let him go. I found the duplicate [pawnbroker's ticket] of a coat, pledged on the 17th of January at Sowerby's, on him, I went there and found the coat.

Moore's defence was feeble and unconvincing: 'I picked the bag up two or three doors from my master's house, and got a young woman to pledge them.' Not surprisingly he was found guilty by the jury and sentenced by the Common Sergeant to be whipped and confined for one year. The goods he had stolen were valued at £4.4.0 – perhaps around six to eight weeks' wages for a skilled but underpaid young weaver in the early years of the nineteenth century.

Moore lost his job, his character and in all likelihood his trade. And during his year in confinement he would have been exposed to the company of professional criminals. This probably explains what appears to have happened next, for the Old Bailey archives contain the records of another prosecution in Spitalfields, barely two years later on 21 April 1819, in which the defendant is named as John Moore, and his age is said to be seventeen. This time he was 'indicted for stealing, on the 1st of March, 10 lbs. of iron, value 1s., and 30 lbs. of rope, value 2s., the goods of John Edmeads.'

Edmeads explained the circumstances: 'I am a broker, and live in White Lion-street, Spitalfields. On the 1st of March, I saw the prisoner climbing over my gates; I secured him. He had my iron and rope in a bag.' Moore was found guilty but this time only whipped and not imprisoned.[31] After that he disappears from the historical record. Perhaps he learnt his lesson and stopped his life of crime or perhaps he simply learnt how not to get caught.

As for 24 Fort Street, it stood empty for a year and then in around 1825/6 was converted into the Rose and Crown public house, which had previously occupied the smaller 26 Fort Street.[32] At this time, it seems, 24 was given a new, fashionable façade. The Ordnance Survey map for 1872/3 shows that it was still in business nearly half a century later

The Grahams' near neighbours, the Vernells, lived at number 25 Fort Street, one of a pair of houses (the other being number 26) built probably by Robert Harris in or soon after 1683.[33] Both had frontages of eighteen feet (five and a half metres) and the archaeologists excavating the site of number 25 in the 1990s established that it was – at basement level at least – one room wide and two rooms deep, and that the front room was fitted with a fireplace while the rear room apparently was not. It thus followed the usual arrangement of having a front room for cooking food and a 'wet' kitchen in the rear where food was stored in cool conditions and water was kept in a lead cistern, fed by a pump or by an occasional piped water supply (see page 212). The house probably rose four storeys – including a garret – above the basement.

We know nothing about the early tenants of the house, beyond the fragmentary detritus they left behind them that was unearthed by archaeologists three hundred years later: pottery and four wine bottles dating to the period between c.1680 and 1710.[34] The upper part of the privy was filled with household waste of the early nineteenth century and appears to have been sealed soon after 1821.[35] This coincides with the period when the Vernells decided to move on.

James Vernell was – unsurprisingly – a silk manufacturer. He rented the house from 1813/14 to 1824 and was joined by his wife Elizabeth Ive Vernell upon their marriage in 1815.[36] In March 1824 he served notice to his landlord, the Trustees of the Cripplegate School, having issued notice to pay £30 per annum rent on Lady Day 1824 before leaving the house.[37]

But if this decision to leave the house suggests that the Vernells, like so many others, might have been struggling to keep their heads above water in an industry now in terminal decline, the opposite was actually the case. This may have been an ominous year for the silk trade as a whole, but when the Vernells left 25 Fort Street in 1824 they did not leave the area or the trade. Instead they moved into the far more expensive and fashionable Spital Square. How they were able to do this is a mystery. Vernell's father had died in 1819 in the poorhouse of St Matthew, Bethnal Green, so James's rise in the world could scarcely be down to the fact that he had recently come into money.[38] And yet over the next few years the family's star continued to rise. Perhaps the simplest explanation is also the most likely one: that Vernell was a very able businessman. Certainly that is the picture that seems to emerge from the facts painstakingly compiled by Museum of London archaeologists in *The Spitalfields Suburb*.

As with the Grahams, we know a little more about the Vernells thanks to the criminal records of the Old Bailey. For their part, the Grahams seem to have fallen victim to a distinctly amateur thief. The Vernells, by contrast, appear to have suffered at the hands of a professional. William Lee was a hardened petty criminal – an opportunist whose 'lay' was to win the confidence of a shopkeeper by posing as a customer, usually seeking or apparently acting for an acquaintance, and then to make off with an item of merchandise. On 5 December 1810 he had been indicted 'for feloniously stealing, on the 25th of October, a counterpane, value 14s. two remnants of ticking, value 3s. two yards of cotton, value 2s. and four yards of velveteen, value 10s. the property of John Strachan and John Thomas Thompson.' He had pleaded guilty and been confined for six months in the House of Correction and fined one shilling (he was lucky not to have been whipped or – if he had been older and the value of the stolen goods greater – transported).[39]

Six years later, on 18 September 1816, William Lee – presumably the same person – was indicted 'for stealing, on the 10th of August, a pair of shoes, value 1s. a shawl, 6d. a knife, value 2d. and three farthings, the property of Joseph James Evans, from his person'. Apparently, he had come across Evans asleep 'down by Wapping Dock' and relieved him of his possessions; a watchman, Charles Cox, had seen Lee – shoes in hand – acting suspiciously, challenged him as to where he had obtained the shoes, and been understandably unconvinced by the answer: 'he said, he had pulled them off his feet to ease his feet; but I found he had shoes on besides.' Not surprisingly, the jury found Lee guilty and he was confined for three months and fined one shilling.[40]

And yet, remarkably, while he was actually awaiting trial for the alleged theft from Evans, he managed to get himself accused of yet another theft – this time from the premises of James Vernell. The trial was held on 30 October 1816.[41] Lee was 'indicted for stealing, on the 10th of September, a piece of silk, value 17l [£17] the property of James Vernell, in his dwelling-house.' Vernell himself seems to have known little about the circumstances of the crime, testifying: 'I only know a preceding fact to the robbery, which is, that at the latter end of August, or beginning of September last, the prisoner came into my shop, and enquired for a person of the name of Brown. I told him I had no such person in my employ. That is all I know.' Vernell's foreman John Barclay, by contrast, was witness to the alleged crime. 'I know the person of the man at the bar,' he stated in court:

> On the 10th of September last he came into Mr Vernell's warehouse, and asked me if Mr Vernell was at home. I told him he was not. There was a piece of Mazarene sarsnet and a piece of drab lustring on the counter. They were within his reach. He told me to look into the back warehouse, and look for the name of Brown. I went into the back warehouse, and just turned over a leaf or two of the weaver's book, and came back again. I am sure it was the name of Brown he made use of. I then returned to the front warehouse again. The prisoner was still there. I told him I could find no such name. He said yes, he was sure there was, and I must go and look again. I went again, for I thought it was of consequence. He appeared respectably dressed. I was not gone the second time more than ten minutes at farthest. I could see no such name. I then returned, and the prisoner was gone. The lustring was there still, but the sarsnet gone. There were sixty-seven yards of it. I ran out of doors directly, but could not see the prisoner. I am quite sure he is the man.

From Barclay's testimony it is clear that the ground-floor front room of 25 Fort Street was a shop, or at least a room in which fabrics were displayed on a counter, customers received and business conducted. It is also clear that the ground-floor rear room was a warehouse in which fabrics were stored and the 'weaver's book' kept. Museum of London archaeologists speculate that this book was 'probably a list of Vernell's journeymen employees'.[42] It could well have been that, but perhaps it was also a list of the customers whose orders had been placed with the journeymen. Sarsnet, incidentally, was a fine silk used for lining.

Lee's line of defence was a simple one. He denied everything: 'My Lord,' he declared, 'all the defence I have got to make is to say that I am as innocent as a new born baby.' One might have thought that the jury would have found this hard to swallow. Vernell's evidence made it clear that Lee had tried the same ploy a little earlier and had presumably only abandoned the attempt because he could not think of a way to get Vernell to leave the shop or didn't have the nerve to order the master of the business to go off and root around in the weaver's book. Moreover, the fact that Lee could be arrested even though the silk was not found in his possession suggests that he was well known in Spitalfields as a fraudulent customer. But clearly, the jury thought such evidence merely circumstantial. Lee was acquitted.

That this was almost certainly the wrong decision is suggested by the fact that virtually the moment he was found innocent of this charge he was 'indicted for a like offence' – in fact, an almost identical crime. This time the victim was John Weaver, a silk manufacturer who lived in 'Chapel Yard, Christchurch'. His employee James Allan explained the circumstances:

> The prisoner came into my master's warehouse, and enquired for a strange name, and asked me if we manufactured figured sarsnets. I told him, no, that we only manufactured plain goods. He then asked to see a piece. I put a piece on the counter before him, and he asked what was the net price of it, as he was going into the country, and he would pay money for it. I went to the desk to see what was the net price; that was about three yards from me; and he walked over to the press where the goods were kept. That was opposite the counter, and he remarked what long lengths they were; and he said he had got a friend waiting at the door, and he would go and ask him to come up. He then left the warehouse, but did not return. I was not alarmed. It was four or five minutes before I suspected any thing. We had only one piece of sarsnet in the house. I do not know when I had seen it before, but I know I did not sell it. I did not look for that, as there was only one piece, and I did not miss any of the others. I did not miss that plain piece until two or three days afterwards. I cannot swear it was taken that day. I have never seen it again.

Again Lee was found not guilty, presumably because the missing sarsnet was not found in his possession, he was not actually seen taking it nor was it missed immediately after he left the warehouse and there was no one to corroborate Allan's account. Of course, it was just conceivable that Allan himself had purloined the silk and sought to blame its loss on Lee. Such a possibility would have been sufficient to acquit Lee.[43]

Some months later, on 14 January 1818, a William Lee, along with one John Wingate, was indicted at the Old Bailey 'for stealing, on the 29th of December, one bag, value 6d., and 12 quarts of hemp-seed, value 7s., the goods of John Keer', removed from a wagon as it entered Windmill Yard, St John Street, Clerkenwell. This William Lee gave his age as twenty, so he may not have been the same man as the one who visited Vernell's shop. Then again, the serial suspect William Lee would have known enough by now about the operation of the law to hope that if he lied about his age he might get a more lenient sentence if found guilty. If so, then his luck had just run out. Both prisoners were found guilty by the jury, and sentenced to be transported for seven years.[44] Lee was probably sent to New South Wales, where in due course, no doubt, he picked up his criminal career again.

The Vernells, meanwhile, continued to thrive. An article in *The Times* for 21 March 1833 records that in May 1833 James Vernell would be acting as Steward for the annual dinner of the London Orphan Asylum.[45] He was also a member of the Spitalfields Mathematical Society (see pages 334–8).[46] By the time he died in 1839, he was renting a fashionable house in the recently completed Tavistock Square in Bloomsbury. His will confirms that he had made a considerable fortune in the silk industry, 'leaving £20,000 alone to his brother John (of Steward Street, Spitalfields) and to his business partner John Townend'.[47] To his widow Elizabeth – who did not die until 1856 – he left household goods valued at £1,000. No children are mentioned so presumably the couple died childless.

———

After the Grahams and Vernells had left Fort Street it continued in residential and commercial use. Charles Booth in his re-survey of 1898 (see page 527) noted it as 'fairly well-to-do' with a 'few middlemen' residing in it. Steward Street, running south from Fort Street, was similar. He upgraded both to pink from purple. In its guise as the Rose and Crown, however, 24 Fort Street ceased trading in 1899, and may have been demolished around then to expand the open area, for loading and unloading, at the north-west corner of the Spitalfields wholesale fruit and vegetable market.

Bit by bit, the market intruded further on the old residential streets around it. Gun Street, north of Brushfield Street, and the east side of Steward Street, also north of Brushfield Street, were swept away – mostly before the Second World War – to allow the market to expand further. Houses changed from largely residential use to largely commercial and warehouse use. Usage was rough, maintenance poor, and houses were rebuilt and demolished in piecemeal manner. Bomb damage during the Second World War added to the sense of decay. A photograph taken in 1941 looking north up a ruinous Duke Street (by then confusingly renamed Fort Street) shows that the nineteenth-century warehouses on the sites of 30 and 31 Fort Street still stood, as did 25, 26 and 27 Duke/Fort Street from the 1680s,[48] while a dilapidated portion of the north side of Fort Street survived into 1944 – a photograph of numbers 27, 28, 29 is in the London Metropolitan Archives.[49] Virtually all had been cleared by the time the *Survey of London* was published in 1957. What then survived were a few buildings on the west side of Steward Street – including the spectacular mid-eighteenth-century number 28 – and a small group of buildings forming the north-west corner of Fort Street with Duke Street.[50]

By the end of the 1960s, when I first explored the Old Artillery Ground, all these sad but fascinating fragments had been destroyed. In many ways the loss of virtually all of the streets of the Old Artillery Ground, and all its late-seventeenth-century buildings, is one of the greatest urban and historic tragedies to overtake the area – perhaps worse than the almost complete destruction of the early-Georgian merchant palaces of Spital Square. In its large-scale and architectural coherence the Old Artillery Ground development did much to establish Spitalfields' distinct architectural character as a merchant quarter and adjunct to the City, and it was one of London's pioneer developments that led the way for the much admired Georgian transformation of the capital into a world-class city.

Now, walking the architecturally characterless commercial plaza that has replaced the late-seventeenth-century streets is a tremendous challenge to the imagination. But if you try very hard you might fancy the presence of a few 'shuffling . . . ghosts' in the wind-blown Bishop's Square, and if you look closely you'll find a few evocative details that seem to unlock memories of another age, another Spitalfields. On 42 Brushfield Street and 9 Artillery Passage, for instance, there are 'Broad Arrows', a sign inspired by archery and since the 1580s used to denote government property (particularly pieces of ordnance of the type tested on the Artillery Ground), and which here signifies that these houses stand on land

Above: a 'Broad Arrow' boundary marker of land ownership on 42 Brushfield Street, and a parish boundary marker of 1871. Below: detail of a Christ Church parish cast-iron bollard of 1819 on the corner of Hanbury and Wilkes streets. Its beautiful and bold design was inspired by cannon; its gnarled appearance commemorates nearly two hundred years of hard, useful life in the streets of Spitalfields.

once owned by the Crown and used by the Gunners of the Tower and the 'Guylde of Artyllary of longbows, Crossebowes and handegonnes'. There are also two dates accompanying the arrows – one obscured and the other clearly 1682. The first date could be 1535, which was roughly when the Crown acquired the land from St Mary's Priory and a few years before it leased it to the gunners, and the other is the year the Crown sold the land to Nicholas Barbon and his associates. So these signs are not just badges of land ownership or site boundaries but ancient commemorations of an important period, and important events, in the history of Spitalfields.

And then there are the handsome cast-iron bollards, many of which still stand sentinel in the streets of Spitalfields after nearly 200 years. The best are around Christ Church, marked 'Cht. Ch Middx 1819' (although one alone is dated 1818). The pair on the corner of Wilkes and Hanbury Streets tilt at a rakish angle, suggesting their years of hard labour guarding the kerb and protecting pedestrians from wayward carriages and drays, while their domed and polished pinnacles reveal the happy perches they have provided for generations of Spitalfields dwellers, be they shiftless loafers observing the world or exhausted working men grabbing a moment's rest. The fact that these bollards exist at all – and the lettering they bear – says much. Evidently the parish of Christ Church Spitalfields – located in the county of Middlesex – undertook a major repaving scheme in 1819, as part of a policy to beautify itself. This chimes with the history of 15 Princelet Street, which was also remodelled in fashionable manner at roughly the same time (see pages 362–4). The bollards, like the house, are probably monuments to the optimism of Spitalfields' short-lived second 'Golden Age', when for a brief spell many believed – falsely as it turned out – that the long-ailing silk industry had been revived.

Visually these objects do not, perhaps, seem to signify much, and are certainly ignored by most. But they do conjure up memories of significant moments in the story of Spitalfields and are reminders that a few telling details, a few stories and some pertinent facts can bring the dead to life and make a lost world tangible, if only for a fleeting moment.

THE OCCUPANTS OF ELDER STREET 1841–1911

T he history of the construction and early occupation of Elder Street has been outlined in chapter 9 and a limited number of sample houses described. The story of the street from the mid nineteenth century onwards can be traced, and the houses 'peopled', by examination of increasingly extensive and consistent official documentation. The broad picture that emerges for this particular street is typical of Spitalfields as a whole: the houses became more crowded, the ethnic mix of the community changed, and the trades of the occupants became more varied and humble as the silk-weaving industry gradually decayed and disappeared.

What did not change was the ownership of the houses. The Tillard Estate, which developed Elder Street in the early eighteenth century, remained the landlord, and appears to have been happy to accept relatively low rents – or the level of rents the residents of Spitalfields could afford – as a quid pro quo for minimal expenditure on the maintenance of the fabric of the houses. One consequence of this policy was that little or no upgrading or updating was undertaken to reflect rising expectations of comfort and convenience or any change in fashion. For example, virtually none of the houses in Elder Street acquired inside water-closets until the 1970s when a wave of conservation-based repair engulfed the long-languishing street. This general absence of major works until recent times, when the houses' historical significance was recognised, means that those that remain have remarkably intact early-eighteenth-century exteriors and interiors.

The key documents that chart the houses' changing fortunes are the census returns that from 1841, in ever-increasing detail, record the domestic circumstances of London's ordinary working people.

1841 CENSUS

The 1841 census is an often scanty and hasty affair, with minimal information rendered in a sometimes almost illegible hand. Nevertheless it
captures a moment of transition in Spitalfields, from the old world of the
traditional weaving community to the emerging one of industry and
ignoble squalor. The houses built for single families – some with weaving
workshops on the upper floors – became multi-occupied, which, given
their relatively flimsy construction, cannot have been easy. Floors and
stairs must have creaked under the comings and goings of so many people,
the fabric of the structures must have frayed rapidly, and privacy must
have been limited, as former room doors became front doors and landings
communal, almost public, areas. All the tenants must have made use of
the lavatory in the yard and, presumably, had access to the water supplied
to the basement kitchen, which perhaps was a communal room where
food could be prepared and washing done. Certainly in houses with two
basement rooms it is likely that one would have contained a 'copper' –
incorporating a large pot that could be heated and used for washing
clothes. It is probable that the basement contained water-storage tanks
and perhaps a pump to deliver water to upper-level cisterns.

By 1841 life in the street would have been relatively recently transformed by
the replacement of oil lamps – as described in the 1759 draft Act of Parliament
for Watching, Cleansing and Lighting the Liberty of Norton Folgate – with
gas lights, that offered brighter and more reliable illumination.

Number 5 (in 1841 numbered 14) was occupied by six people on the day of
the census, apparently organised as two households. The dominant occupants were the Symonds or Symons family, who had been in the house since
at least 1812, according to Land Tax assessments (see page 230). The head of
the household appears to have been Mary Symons, aged fifty-five, a 'Silk
Weaver' born in Middlesex, along with William Symons, twenty-five, a
'Silk Weaver', Susannah Symons, twenty, William Symons, eleven months.
Also in residence were Ann Thorn, sixty-five, who was 'employed', and
Ann Fowler, forty-five, a 'Silk Warper' (a warper set the silk threads on the
warp loom). So the house remained in the occupation of a long-established
Spitalfields family that was still engaged in the area's traditional industry.

Number 15 (formerly 18) contained twelve people on the day of the
census, probably organised in two separate households. One comprised

Richard Jones, aged thirty-five, a grocer, his wife Mary, the same age, and their four-month-old daughter, also named Mary. They perhaps occupied the two rooms of one floor. Head of the second family in occupation was Ebenezer Swain, fifty, a painter. His wife, Harriet, was forty-five years old, and the couple shared their accommodation with five children. The oldest, twenty-year-old son Joseph (shown erroneously as aged fifteen), was an engraver (see page 255), who as manager at the engraving department at *Punch* magazine would later engrave the works of many leading artists and illustrators, including Sir John Tenniel. Then there were fifteen-year-old daughter Hipzibath and three other daughters, the youngest aged ten. It would be reasonable to assume that this seven-strong family occupied four rooms on two of the floors. Also in occupation were Elizabeth Avery, fifteen, a milliner, and Alfred White, fifteen, who was 'employed'. This pair probably lodged with one or other of the families and could have occupied the two rooms on the third floor, which would have left the basement rooms to act as a kitchen for one or other – or both – of the families. Twelve people in ten rooms was a reasonable density of occupation for the time in Spitalfields. None of the occupants was in the silk industry.

Number 17 (formerly 19) tells a very different story. Although built as a pair with 15 it possessed only one room per floor. The volumes could have been subdivided with timber partitions or screens, so the house would have contained between five and eight rooms (if eight, some of the rooms would have measured little more than seventeen by eight feet and would have been unheated). Despite its relatively small size, 17 Elder Street nevertheless contained sixteen people, in four family units, on the day of the census.

The head of the first household listed was William Forgason, aged twenty, a 'Farrier' or 'Furrier', his wife Eliza, also aged twenty, and their daughter Elizabeth, aged one month. The head of the neighbouring family, the Warings, seems to have been Susannah Waring (though it's possible that she had a husband who happened to be absent on the day of the census). She was sixty-five, 'employed', and shared rooms with her unmarried children Elizabeth, thirty-five, a 'machinist', Henry, thirty, a porter, and Josiah, twenty-five, a labourer. Mary Ann Freeman, aged forty and a dressmaker, seems to have been the head of her family, comprised of two daughters. The final family was formed by Benjamin Brackman, a twenty-five-year-old butcher, his wife and their three young children. Finally there was Harriet Plumpton, fifteen, presumably a lodger or relative attached to one of the families, most likely the Brackmans.

The number of people and family units means that there must essentially have been one family per one-room floor, with three to six people per room. Some privacy would have been achieved by the use of fabric screens and curtains. None of the occupants worked in the silk industry although two, possibly three, were in the garment industry or semi-skilled 'rag trade' that was its replacement.

Number 19 (formerly 20) appears to have been occupied by only two family units. Susanna Kilburn, thirty-five, a 'silk winder', seems to have been the head of her family, which on the day of the census included five children, of whom Susanna, fifteen, was also a silk winder, Rachel, ten, a 'Rug Weaver', and Charlotte, ten, a 'silk washer'. The other family was headed by Christopher Mote, twenty-five, a porter, who lived with his wife Hannah and four-year-old son Christopher. So nine people occupied the five, six or possibly seven rooms of 19 Elder Street.

Number 21 (formerly also 21) contained five or six households and sixteen people on the day of the census. These included Anne Grover, seventy, a lodging house-keeper, and Mary Church, seventy, of like occupation (however, the lodging house they kept was evidently not 21 Elder Street for the other occupants were not single men or women but generally organised in family groups). Among other occupants were Thomas Barker, a sixty-year-old painter; Margaret Tharata, sixty-five, a perfumier, and thirty-five-year-old Mary Ann, a 'Straw Bonnet maker'. The two-storey and two-room rear extension was probably in existence by 1841, although perhaps then only one storey high. The census entry is very faint, so much has to be left to surmise and all ages seen approximate.

To take these five houses as representative of the density of occupation in Spitalfields in the early 1840s is probably not wise, since Elder Street was one of the better streets in the area. Nevertheless it can be seen as presenting a median between the best and worst of the area. In total, in a minimum of thirty-six rooms (seven of which were at basement level), lived forty-four people – on average just over one person per room. For the time and place this was very reasonable.

1851 CENSUS

The census of 1851 suggests that the density of population had, during the past decade, remained fairly stable in Elder Street. But things were to get worse.

Number 5 was occupied by five households and thirteen people on the day of the census. Mary Symons, now said to be sixty-nine and confirmed as a native of Bethnal Green, was still in residence, but lived alone, the 'Head' of her own household. She was still listed as being employed as a 'Weaver of Silk' – and as such was among the declining number of silk weavers still working in Spitalfields. She probably worked in the house's upper rooms fitted with wide weavers' windows.[1] Other 'households' in 5 Elder Street included Mary Helpin, a fifty-year-old married 'house keeper' from Manchester, and her twenty-five-year-old unmarried son W. Helpin, a 'Confectioner', born in London; William Mills, a thirty-year-old journeyman tailor born in Cornwall, his wife Mary, and their four children aged from twelve years to two months; and Matthew Morris, a seventy-nine-year-old 'Looking glass maker', born in Shoreditch.

Number 15 was occupied by just two households, with eight people occupying its ten rooms. One household consisted of George Ellis, a fifty-eight-year-old coal merchant, born in Surrey, and his forty-nine-year-old wife Maria, born in Suffolk. The other household is more intriguing. It was formed by Harriet Glessing, a thirty-seven-year-old widow and 'Musical string maker' from Blackfriars, her four daughters aged six to thirteen years, and a servant – Mary Self aged thirty-five – who came from Norwich. The three eldest Glessing daughters were all 'scholars'. Harriet, with her connection to musical instruments, might have been involved with the neighbouring house to the north (now 13 and then 17 Elder Street). The 'Head' here was Mary Boulton, a forty-year-old spinster described as a 'school mistress', who lived with her thirty-year-old unmarried sister Caroline, listed rather grandly as a 'Professor of Music'. Also present on the day of the census was the sisters' ten-year-old niece Mary, and a fifteen-year-old 'House Servant' named Hannah Staples. This was evidently a Dame School with which it's tempting to imagine Harriet Glessing and her daughters were involved.

Number 17 contained four households and fourteen people – with its six or seven rooms this meant an average of two or more people per room. The occupants included Robert Langman, a fifty-eight-year old 'Colour maker' from Westminster, his thirty-four-year-old wife Mary, who was a laundress born in Buckinghamshire, and two young children, both born in Norton Folgate. There was also James Nowlon, a thirty-two-year-old sailor born in the City, his twenty-seven-year-old wife Maria from Hornsey, their four small children, and Mary Nowlon, James's twenty-seven-year-old unmarried sister, who had been born in Tower Hamlets. Her trade was given as 'warper' – presumably of silk – which suggests that the Nowlons might have been an old Spitalfields weaving family. In addition there was forty-year-old Charlotte Ashley, married and a 'Warper of silk', who had been born in Bethnal Green, her thirteen-year-old son Edward, and – listed as a separate household – Sarah Hill, a forty-two-year-old widow, born in Essex, who was by trade a 'warper of silk' but currently 'out of employment'.

Number 19 contained three households and eleven people. These included Richard Prior, a forty-four-year-old pianoforte maker from Cornwall, who formed one single-member household, and Mary Wade, a thirty-three-year-old widowed 'Mantle maker' from Shoreditch and her thirteen-year-old daughter, who formed a second. The largest household was headed by Anthony Cantram, a fifty-five-year-old 'stable servant' from Essex and comprised his forty-three-year-old wife Sarah, also from Essex, his eighteen-year-old unmarried son Robert, a 'Groom and porter', his sixteen-year-old daughter Sarah, a needlewoman, his fourteen-year-old son Frederick, an errand boy, and two other children aged nine and twelve.

Number 21 contained five households and thirteen people. One household comprised Essex-born Marian Hassell, a fifty-nine-year-old 'Servant out of situation', her forty-one-year-old unmarried daughter Marian, and thirty-five-year-old son J. N. Hassell. Both children were also servants by occupation and also both out of 'situations'. It was clearly a most unfortunate family. Other households were headed by Ann Tipper, a forty-five-year-old widowed charwoman whose origins are marked as 'not known', Frances Eddensill, a seventy-four-year-old widow and upholsterer, born in Wiltshire, Valentine Potts, a twenty-seven-year-old basket-maker from Bethnal Green, and Elizabeth Waring, a forty-five-year-old, unmarried silk winder from the City of London, and thirty-six-year-old unmarried brother Josiah, a 'Labourer at machine'. (A Waring family is listed in the 1841 census as residing in number 17; presumably they were related.)

1861 CENSUS

The census of 1861 confirms that the high-density occupation and increasing poverty in Elder Street, suggested by the 1851 survey, had become an established pattern. It also shows that affiliations to the silk industry lingered on in Elder Street and surrounding streets, although the numbers of weavers and silk warpers had decreased significantly since 1851.

Number 5 with its eight rooms (including two in the basement) was occupied by four households comprising eleven people on the day of the census. Residents included Robert Rayner, thirty-three, a carpenter and joiner; Mary Elizabeth Can, a sixty-five-year-old married 'needlewoman'; Ann Smith, a seventy-six-year-old former laundress and her forty-three-year-old unmarried son James, who was a railway porter; and Abraham Gunter, a thirty-five-year-old cabinet-maker, and his wife Susannah, the same age – a milliner and dressmaker.

The origins and trades of this group of residents are revealing. Rayner and his wife and Gunter, all of whom came from Ely in Cambridgeshire, are representative of the many rural families who were now moving to London to seek a new life and whose path to the capital was made easier by the arrival of the railways (by 1861 trains were running from Cambridgeshire into the Shoreditch terminus). The railways themselves, of course, offered employment opportunities – as James Smith's occupation demonstrates. Older trades were represented by Abraham Gunter and his wife, though it's interesting to note that no one in the house was involved with silk weaving.

Number 15 was occupied by five households and nineteen people on the day of the census – so on average nearly two people per room. The Broadway family was the largest. The fact that it is mentioned first suggests it occupied the lower portion of the house – perhaps the six rooms of the basement, ground floor and first floor. The family consisted, on the day of the census, of Southwark-born Jonathan Broadway, thirty-five, a 'Foreman St Katherine [sic] Dock Company' (a twenty-five-minute walk from Elder Street), his thirty-three-year-old wife Jane Rebecca, and their five children, aged from two years to eleven. In addition there was Mary Costello, a sixteen-year-old unmarried servant from Battle, Sussex, Robert Bass, sixty-two, and Elizabeth Bass, fifty-seven. They are described as the father-in-law and mother-in-law of Jonathan Broadway, both born in Ireland and both silk weavers by trade. They had evidently been in the area some time because their daughter Jane Rebecca is listed as having been born in Whitechapel. How these ten people were packed into six or so rooms is hard to say, but they were evidently the prominent family in the house, with their own servant and with Jonathan holding the responsible job of foreman for a major East End company. He must have been a man of considerable prestige in Elder Street. Presumably, he, his wife and their younger children slept in one room, the older children in another, the in-laws in a third and the servant on a landing, which would leave three rooms free for living, cooking and storage.

Another household in residence, the Anger family, consisted of John, thirty-three, a warehouseman, his thirty-year-old wife Eliza Ann, and their daughter, less than a year old. It is reasonable to assume that they occupied one second-floor room – perhaps the smaller rear room. Then there was the Holden family, consisting of Robert, twenty-three, a warehouseman in St Katherine's (sic) Dock (and presumably a beneficiary of Jonathan Broadway's patronage), his twenty-two-year-old wife Eliza, and their son and daughter, aged two and less than a year. Perhaps they occupied the two third-floor rooms. Finally there were Samuel Noble, twenty-eight, a 'Gentleman's Servant', and his wife Charlotte, aged twenty, described as a 'drawer'. They could have occupied the second-floor front room.

Number 17 contained three households or families and fourteen people on the day of the census. The Jacobs family consisted of John, fifty-one, a 'Traveller in glass' born in 'Muscovy', his forty-two-year-old wife Louisa, born in Newington, Surrey (now the Elephant and Castle area), and their four children aged from two to eleven. John Jacobs was, presumably, Jewish and so was a forerunner of the waves of Jewish immigrants who settled in East London in large numbers after 1881 to escape pogroms in Russia and Russian-controlled Poland. There had been a pogrom in Odessa in 1859 but Jacobs was evidently in London by at least 1850 because his eldest child – Dinah – was born in Middlesex. Perhaps, like Karl Marx, Jacobs came to London in the late 1840s to escape a wave of reactionary oppression in Europe following the series of revolutions and popular uprisings in 1848. A widow, Martha Ashley, fifty, a 'Silk warper', and her son Edward, a twenty-three-year-old, unmarried 'Commercial Traveller', formed another, small household. The third household was the largest and perhaps possessed the highest social status. It was headed by John Pendleton, fifty-seven, a 'Relieving officer', who had been born in the grand West End parish of St George's Hanover Square. He was an officer of the workhouse (presumably the Spitalfields and Whitechapel Union workhouse), and so responsible for administering relief to the destitute of the Liberty. With him were his fifty-two-year-old wife Caroline, also born in St George's parish, two unmarried daughters aged fifteen and seventeen, and two sons aged twelve and ten.

Number 19 was, with its six rooms or so, occupied by three family groups comprising twelve people on the night of the census. These included Charles Widdowson, twenty-four, a tailor from Leicestershire; Catherine Wilkinson, a Stepney-born fifty-seven-year-old widow and book stitcher, her twenty-seven-year-old unmarried son Richard, a coach painter, her twenty-year-old unmarried 'tailoress' daughter Kate, and fifteen-year-old son Herbert, who was a 'light porter'; and Willian Neve, a fifty-eight-year-old bricklayer's labourer from Norfolk, his fifty-eight-year-old wife Elizabeth Ann, a 'Silk Warpress', and two unmarried daughters – aged twenty-eight and thirty-one – with the surname of Holmes, and so presumably Elizabeth Ann's children by a previous marriage. Both daughters were 'Silk Warpresses' like their mother.

Number 21 contained five households and eighteen people on the day of the census, so on average just over two and a half inhabitants per room. The first household was headed by Ann Tippett, a fifty-three-year-old widow from Poplar who worked as a 'Machinest'. It is probable that she was related in some way to the Tipper family in residence in the house in 1851 and that her name is a misspelling. She had a lodger, the forty-year-old, unmarried Mary Bates, 'a silk weaver' born in Shoreditch. The 'Head' of the second household was Joseph Weston, a thirty-seven-year-old confectioner. The third household comprised Jas. Speary, a sixty-two-year-old widower from Wiltshire, and his thirty-year-old son James, a cabinet-maker, and eighteen-year-old William, a wood turner. The fourth household had Emma Penney as its 'Head', a forty-year-old widow from Limehouse who worked as a needlewoman, and her unmarried daughters Sarah, Emma and Mary Anne, who lived with her. Her twenty-one-year-old son Thomas was a 'porter at optician'. The fifth household was headed by Frederick Parker, a thirty-one-year-old basket-maker from Wiltshire. Finally there was Miriam Conner, a sixty-nine-year-old widow, who had been born in Shoreditch and by occupation was a 'Silk Winder'. She was presumably a lodger, but of which household is not specified.

1871 CENSUS

Number 5 was occupied by three households and ten people. The families were headed by Joseph Wilson, thirty, a 'Book Machinist', Charles Paston, twenty-six, a clerk, and thirty-two-year-old John Shirt, who appears to have made parts of carriages. All the adults had been born outside

Spitalfields – three in Yarmouth, Norfolk. None was in the weaving industry.

Number 15 was occupied by only one family and five people on the day of the census. The family was headed by Ann Jackson, a fifty-year-old widow. Her twenty-year-old son Charles W. Jackson was a carpenter (the 1871 *Post Office Directory* lists Charles Jackson, carpenter, at this address).

Number 17 had been crowded in 1861 but was much more so now – with on average around four people per room. Four families and twenty-two people lived there in 1871, most of them in fairly humble trades. There were Cyrus Lloyd, forty-four, a 'tin plate worker', his wife Lydia, also forty-four – both from Birmingham – and their six daughters and two sons; George Mitchell, twenty-seven, a 'turncock for water works', his wife Annie and two sons; George Wright, twenty-three, an upholsterer, his wife Esther, also an upholsterer, and two sons aged one and two; James Cantle, a sixty-year-old 'Basket Maker', his sixty-two-year-old wife Elizabeth, a 'needle woman', and their two unmarried daughters, both of whom gave their occupations as 'envelope folders'. Most of the adults had been born outside Spitalfields. As with some other houses in Elder Street there seems to have been a tendency for people from the same area to end up congregating in the same house. In number 5 in 1861 several occupants came from Cambridgeshire; at number 17 in 1871 George Mitchell and his son Joseph, and James Cantle, all came from Lancashire.

Number 19 was occupied by three families and nine people. One household was headed by Maria Bloom, forty-five, a 'straw bonnet maker' from Bedfordshire, who lived with her eighteen-year-old son Frederick, a 'sugar refiner'. Catherine Wilkinson was still in occupation, now listed as 'without any' trade or profession, along with her still unmarried 'tailoress' daughter Kate, and sons Richard (still a 'coach painter') and Herbert (now a 'warehouseman'). Also living with the family was a five-year-old niece, Mary Richardson. Finally there was the household of William Spens, a fifty-four-year-old 'wholesaler', who lived with his fifty-eight-year-old wife Eliza.

The intriguing occupant here is Maria Bloom – the 'straw bonnet maker'. Was she related to John Troake or did she buy the straw bonnet business he had established in the house in the early nineteenth century? Or had Troake installed straw bonnet-making machinery that made the house a natural residence and workshop for any in the trade?

Number 21 contained three households and fourteen people. Occupants included twenty-eight-year-old William Speary, who appeared in the 1861 census and was still a wood turner by trade. He lived with his twenty-nine-year-old wife Ann, their two young children, and Mary Bates, the widowed 'silk weaveress', who was now this family's lodger. Emma Penney, the widowed needlewoman, was also still in residence, now living only with her unmarried son Thomas, who seems to have had the unusual job of being an 'assistant ship's compass adjustor' – the fruits presumably of starting working life as a porter at an optician's. The Penney household also had a lodger – Mary Devens, a thirty-eight-year-old silk winder born in Spitalfields. Fanny Murray was the 'Head' of the third family, a married thirty-three-year-old laundress from Colchester. She lived with her three children, aged nine, eleven and thirteen, and a sixty-nine-year-old widowed lodger named Lucy Hamblin, who had been born in London and worked as a laundress.

1881 CENSUS

By the time of the 1881 census the house numbers in Elder Street had changed to their current arrangement, with number 1 being on the north-east corner with Fleur de Lis Street and then progressing south, with odd numbers on the east side and even on the west, starting with 2 on the corner with Commercial Street and culminating with 36 on the south-west corner with 'White Lion Street'/Folgate Street. The east side of Elder Street north of Fleur de Lis Street, was occupied by the cell block of the police station, built in 1874–5 and fronting onto Commercial Street.

Other changes had also taken place in Elder Street since the 1871 census. By the 1880s gas had arrived in most of the houses, which would have been candle-, oil- or paraffin-/kerosene-lit in the 1860s and 70s, and a more thorough system of drainage had gradually been installed since the late 1840s, so that by the 1880s in most houses the cesspits in the rear yards were connected, via ceramic pipes set below the house's basement floors, to the sewer running below Elder Street. The sewer, brick-built, egg-shaped in section and about a yard in height, had been constructed in the early eighteenth century to carry away surface water and, to a limited degree, liquid waste from the houses and cesspits in Elder Street, but certainly not solid wastes, so the lavatories being discharged into it from the late 1840s must have caused some concern. But the flow of water, emptied into the sewer with each flush of the cisterns in the modern water closets, appears to have been adequate to prevent the solid waste from congealing and blocking the sewer. Bathing within the Elder Street houses would have been limited to the use of tin baths filled with heated water. But more likely those tenants who wished to bathe would have used one of the local bath houses – for example, that in the yard between Blossom Street and Norton Folgate, mentioned by Charles Booth in 1898, and which survives, derelict and threatened with demolition, in the autumn of 2016.

Number 5 contained three families and eleven people on the day of the census, including George Oram, forty-one, a plumber from Lancashire, his forty-year-old East End-born wife Emma, their sixteen-year-old son George, also a plumber, and two other children; and Selina Solomons, a fifty-two-year-old widow, born in Whitechapel and a 'Boy's cap maker' by trade, and her unmarried daughter Matilda, twenty-two, a 'cigar maker'.

Number 15 was occupied by four families, with fifteen people present on the day of the census, so on average one and a half people per room. These included Benjamin Liegenberg, a thirty-three-year-old furrier/leather dresser born in London, his twenty-nine-year-old wife Esther, a 'Tailoress', also born in London, and their nineteen-month-old daughter Elizabeth; Hugh Windrum, a thirty-three-year-old tailor, his fifty-year-old wife Josephine, born in Brighton, and their sixteen-year-old daughter Isabell – a 'Tailoress' by trade – and twelve-year-old son Charles; John William Stowe, a 'cordwainer' or shoemaker by trade, his sixty-four-year-old wife Lucy from Suffolk, and two 'Boarders' and two 'Lodgers'. The distinction between 'Boarders' and 'Lodgers' must have been subtle. Lodgers, presumably, had a slightly more permanent status than boarders. All were unmarried. The boarders were Charles Squire, a twenty-three-year-old jeweller's apprentice, born in Middlesex, and George E. Mash, a twenty-six-year-old 'Traveller' – presumably a travelling salesman – born in the City of London. The lodgers were Ma. (Matilda or Martha) Hill, a fifty-six-year-old dressmaker born in the City of London and Helen Hill, fifty-three, also a dressmaker and also born in the City. Presumably they were sisters.

Number 17 housed five families with twenty-five people in residence on the day of the census, including eleven children, aged fourteen or less, suggesting a density of perhaps five people per room. This was high for Elder Street but not exceptional for the area. A government survey of 1885 describes a house in Brick Lane that had nine rooms with on average seven people in each, and only one bed per room. The inhabitants, noted the report, 'were all respectable people'.[2]

The community within 17 Elder Street in 1881 consisted of Elijah Bigmore, a forty-three-year-old 'Carman' or railway or tram worker, born in Shoreditch, his wife and their eight children, aged from five to twenty-one, including the eldest Sophia, an unmarried 'bookfolder' and nineteen-year-old Emily, a 'Flower mounter'. Also in residence were Richard Harris, a twenty-eight-year-old 'pianoforte maker', and family; Edward Woodroof, a sixty-two-year-old 'invalid' wood turner, and family; and James J. Wood, a thirty-five-year-old 'journeyman tailor', and his wife and three children.

Number 19 housed only one family – still headed by Catherine Wilkinson, now seventy-seven, and once again listed as a 'Book stitcher' by trade. Her family had occupied part of the house in 1861 and 1871 but now it appears to have occupied the entire property. (It is possible, of course, that a portion of the house was empty in 1881, awaiting the arrival of new tenants.)

Number 21 contained three households (including one with a servant) and eleven people. Elizabeth Beck, a seventy-two-year-old widow from Ripon, kept forty-two-year-old, Bishopsgate-born Richd. Dicks as a 'General servant' and had William Bridges as her lodger. Bridges was seventy years old and a 'Naval Pensioner', born in Portsmouth. He was a veteran of the early Victorian Royal Navy, when ships were largely still wind-powered and made of timber. James Theobald – a sixty-one-year-old 'Stableman/groom' from Essex – was the 'Head' of the second family listed. He lived with his wife, his fifteen-year-old granddaughter, a 'waistcoatmaker/tailor', and had two lodgers – Lewis Weiner, an unmarried twenty-six-year-old cabinet-maker from Russia and Saul Levy, aged twenty-three and also unmarried, a cabinet-maker from Russia. The final household was still headed by Emma Penney, now termed a 'seamstress', who lived with her now forty-one-year-old son Thomas, who remained an 'Assistant' to a ship compass regulator. This pair had a lodger – twenty-one-year-old Job Levy, a boot-finisher born in Middlesex.

The urban and industrial context of Elder Street in the 1880s is suggested by the fire insurance maps produced by Charles E. Goad Ltd. from c.1885 and colour-coded to indicate combustibility of structure (see illustration on page 524). The base maps were updated on a regular basis, with revised patches added, and often not dated, so individual editions can vary. But broadly speaking they create a vivid image of the activities taking place in late-Victorian Spitalfields. To the east of Elder Street are shown stables, and a 'card. box. pack.' establishment. Also shown are the locations of lavatories in the rear yards of the Elder Street houses. To the west of Elder Street were a dairyman's yard – entered off Folgate Street and behind 34 and 36 Elder Street – and a clothing factory in the yard entered through the carriageway beneath.

1891 CENSUS

By the 1890s Spitalfields was becoming more cosmopolitan, as ever more East European Jews arrived in the area. But the arrival of this new community was evidently gradual. Some Russian and Polish Jews are listed as living in 21 Elder Street in 1881, but even in 1891 most of the residents in the sample houses in Elder Street had been born in Britain.

Number 5 contained three families and thirteen people on the day of the census. These included John Thomas O'Connell, a twenty-two-year-old tailor, born in London, and his family; Frederick Walker, a twenty-three-year-old 'Porter of Buildings' born in Surrey, and his wife; Arthur Sumnett, a forty-eight-year-old 'Paperbag maker' from Staffordshire, his wife Mary, born in Ireland, and their five unmarried children, including Arthur John and Frederick James, twenty-one and fifteen respectively, both hotel waiters, and Mary Ann, nineteen, a 'feather cutter'.

Number 15 contained two families and six people: head of the first was Morris Michaels, a thirty-nine-year-old tailor, who lived with his forty-one-year-old wife Rachel – both born in 'Poland Russia' – and their eighteen-year-old son Jacob, a tailor. He had been born in Mile End New Town, demonstrating that the family had been in the area for nearly twenty years, if not longer. The second household consisted of George Woolf, a thirty-three-year-old fruit salesman, and his thirty-two-year-old wife Sarah – both of whom had been born in the Netherlands. The Woolfs also had a seventeen-year-old 'domestic servant', Martha Gibbons, born in London.

Number 17 contained two households and seven people: Julius Otto, a thirty-two-year-old butcher, and his thirty-one-year-old wife Heloise, both born in Germany; Clara Walker, a fifty-nine-year-old widow born in Surrey, her nineteen-year old unmarried daughter Emma, a milliner's assistant, and seventeen-year-old son Herbert, a merchant's clerk, both also born in Surrey. There was also a nine-year-old granddaughter, named Rachel, born in Cambridge, and an eighty-year-old lodger, Charlotte Clark, 'living on her own means'.

Number 19 contained three families and nine people, with the trades of the 'Heads' of the families being 'printer's compositor', 'carpenter' and 'Labourer (waterside)'. The 'Heads' came from Exeter, Winchester and Kent.

Number 21 contained ten people in two households. These were seemingly connected because both were named Caplin and both 'Heads' came originally from Minsk in Russia. Morris Caplin, twenty, was a 'Bootmaker finisher' and Nick. Caplin, thirty-two, a wholesale furrier who, with his wife Rose, had four children. The eldest, Mary, was aged nine and all had been born in Spitalfields, showing that the family had been in the area for at least a decade. Nick. Caplin's family also had a fifteen-year-old 'domestic servant' named Annie Rogers, from Kingsland, Hackney, and on the day of the census a visitor was present – Nathan Eliphant, twenty – also born in Russia.

The walk the philanthropist and social reformer Charles Booth took through Spitalfields on 17 March 1898 with Sergeant French of the Metropolitan Police provides the social and physical context for the 1891 census (see page 525). As their exploration makes clear, during the preceding hundred years or so the urban grain of the area had been transformed, becoming far more dense, with gardens, and once-generous yards built upon to create an often labyrinthine network of courts and alleys containing hundreds of small and mean cottages, often with no outlook since other buildings would be only a few yards distant. These cottages and courts became the dark places of Victorian Spitalfields, haunts of crime, poverty and squalor – usually marked light blue, dark blue or black on Booth's map. Such were the cottages between Blossom Street and Elder Street, including Loom Court. The cramped condition of these buildings is best revealed by scrutiny of the 1873 Ordnance Survey map of Spitalfields or the fire insurance maps of Charles E. Goad Ltd. from c.1885.

1901 CENSUS

Number 5 was occupied by three households and nine people on the day of the census. They included Leah Billingsby, a sixty-five-year-old widow of 'no occupation', whose place of origin was 'not known', and her unmarried forty-five-year-old son Joseph, who worked as a 'carman' on the railway or trams. Arthur Sumnett was still in residence (he was now a 'foreman' paperbag maker), with his wife Mary. The couple's daughter, 'Mary A.', remained at home, unmarried and still a 'feather cutter' making quilts. Number 5 was also home to Richard Milton, the 'Head' and sole member of his household – a fifty-eight-year-old widower of 'no occupation'.

Number 15 contained four families and twelve people. Maurice (or Morris) Michaels was still in residence, and still working as a tailor, and this census, slightly more detailed than its predecessors, explains that he 'worked at home' – so in 1901 15 Elder Street contained a tailor's workshop, perhaps on the top floor. The other members of the household were Rachel Michaels, Maurice's wife, and son Jacob, also a tailor; Elias Solomons, a thirty-four-year-old 'Boot fastener', born in Whitechapel, his thirty-three-year-old wife Leah, born in 'Holland', and their three children – aged four to 'under 1 month' – who had all been born in London; Israel Burner, a twenty-four-year-old 'costume Presser' born in Russia, and his twenty-five-year-old, London-born wife Rose; and finally Betsy Simmo, a thirty-year-old 'Tent-maker' born in London and her twelve-year-old son Henry. It would appear that by 1901 number 15 had become an entirely Jewish household.

Number 17 contained three households and eight people: Thomas H. Walker, a forty-one-year-old bank messenger from Surrey, his thirty-one-year-old wife Ellen from Norwich and their two young daughters; Louise Duncome, a seventy-one-year-old spinster, the sole member of her household, who had been born in Spitalfields and lived 'on own means'; Mary Benson, a forty-four-year-old widow and charwoman born in Whitechapel, her twenty-year-old unmarried daughter Elizabeth, a 'shoe-trimmer', and a seventy-five-year-old widowed boarder, Amelia Kiddle, who lived 'on own means' and came from Essex.

Number 19 was occupied by three families and seven people. Henry Sturgeon, a twenty-two-year-old carman from London and his twenty-year-old wife Sophie, born in Spitalfields; Thomas Neill, a seventy-one-year-old 'journeyman tailor' from Soho, his sixty-five-year-old Irish-born wife Alice and thirty-four-year-old unmarried daughter Ann. Both mother and daughter were tailoresses, and both worked 'at home'. Finally there was Fanny L. Chambers, a sixty-six-year-old widow, born in Bishopsgate, who worked as an office cleaner, and her twenty-five-year-old unmarried niece Fanny L. Linsdale, born in Stepney, who worked as a servant.

Number 21, in the composition and number of its residents, was in striking contrast to its neighbours. It contained five families and no fewer than nineteen people in residence on the day of the census, squeezed within its seven or so rooms – two of them being basement rooms and one a garret. But more striking than the number of residents are their origins. Like number 15 this house had become an almost exclusively Jewish home, with virtually all its residents foreign-born, and with only their younger children being born in London. There was Deborah Dewilde, a sixty-one-year-old widow born in Amsterdam and her seventeen-year-old, London-born unmarried daughter Sarah, who was a cigar maker; Miriam Cupinski, a fifty-year-old widow, born in Russia, and her two unmarried daughters, Rachel and Leah, aged nineteen and seventeen respectively, who had been born in Russia, worked as tailoresses and 'supported' their mother; Ruben Cohen, a twenty-two-year-old cabinet-maker and his twenty-one-year-old wife Ann – both of whom had been born in Poland – their two-month-old daughter Betsy, and forty-two-year-old Louise Borgas, listed as 'Father' (presumably Ann's), who worked as a milkman and had been born in Poland; Annie Levy, twenty-two and married but whose husband was absent on the day of the census, who worked 'at home' as a tailoress, had been born in Poland and had two daughters (one, Rachel, aged four, had been born in Poland while Sarah, ten months, had been born in England – so clearly the family had arrived in London relatively recently). Also living in this household was Abraham Caplan, 'brother', aged twenty, single, born in Poland and a tailor, and Woolf Maroski, a forty-five-year-old uncle, married but with no wife listed in the census, a tailor born in Poland. Finally there was Philip Reuben, a thirty-year-old cabinet-maker born in Poland, his thirty-year-old wife Minnie, and their three children aged five years to two months.

The ethnic profile of Elder Street at the end of the nineteenth century is perhaps surprising considering Spitalfields had been a centre of Jewish immigration, mostly from Poland and Russia, for forty years or so. In 1891 the twelve houses on the west side of the street – 14 to 36 – contained eighty-three people on the day night of the census. Of these, most were London-born and with English surnames, a large number were born elsewhere in England and Wales, a very few came from Ireland, two from Morocco, one from Malta, one from Portugal, one from the West Indies and only one from Russia (thirty-seven-year-old Jacob Kesler), and one from Poland (forty-two-year old Lewis Solomon, a 'skin merchant').

In 1901 the same twelve houses contained 104 people on the day of the census and once again the overwhelming majority were London-born, with a fair scattering from other parts of Britain. In addition, there was one person from the Netherlands, one from Germany and four from Palestine. From Russia there were only Marx Saltzman, a thirty-one-year-old tailor and his twenty-four-year old wife Annie; Sarah Barnet, a fifty-four-year-old merchant; Abraham Cohen, a twenty-four-year-old merchant; and Isaac Mazec, a twenty-five-year-old furrier whose twenty-three-year-old wife Dora was described as 'Palestinian' (it is evident that 'Palestinian' was used to denote European Jews who had emigrated to Palestine – then under Ottoman control – or been born there of Jewish émigré parents, and subsequently returned to Europe). From Poland came Samuel Levy, a thirty-six-year-old tailor whose wife and seven children were London-born; and Mark Clement, a seventy-one-year-old master tailor.

In the general context of Elder Street's pattern of occupation around 1900 it would seem that 15 and 21 Elder Street were unusual for their largely Jewish occupation.

1911 CENSUS

The 1911 census contains considerably more information than previous census returns about individuals and individual households – notably the numbers of rooms in a house that each family occupied.

Number 5 was occupied by two families and seven people. William John Jones Moore, a forty-nine-year-old Kent-born lift attendant in a 'block of chambers', lived there with his forty-four-year-old wife Sarah Elizabeth, born in Spitalfields, two grown-up children, and his wife's mother Sarah Anne Trimworth, a seventy-one-year-old widow born in Spitalfields, by trade a 'Pew opener, church' and the beneficiary of a government 'Old Age Pension'. (The Old Age Pensions Act had been introduced in 1908 and provided five shillings a week to eligible people over the age of seventy whose annual income did not exceed £31.10.0.) This family occupied seven rooms. Richard Milton was still in occupation, the 'Head' of his own household, aged sixty-nine and now described as being of 'private means'. He occupied two rooms. The house contains eight rooms, so apparently one had been subdivided.

Number 15 was occupied by four separate households and sixteen people on the day of the census. There was Alexander Laskoffesky, a thirty-six-year-old cabinet-maker, born in 'Russia Poland', his thirty-six-year-old wife Rebecca, also born in 'Russia Poland', his eighteen-year-old unmarried daughter Jessy, who worked 'at home', and his twenty-eight-year-old unmarried sister Rose, who was a tailoress. Both these women had also been born in 'Russia Poland'. This family of four occupied two rooms, presumably one floor in the house, probably the ground floor with husband and wife in one room and the daughter and sister in the other. Then there was Barnett Laskoffesky, 'Head' of a separate household, although presumably related to Alexander. He was twenty-nine, also a cabinet-maker and also born in 'Russia Poland'. With him were his twenty-four-year-old wife Esther, born in 'Russia Poland', and their four children, ranging in age from one to five. All had been born in Spitalfields. This family occupied three rooms – so one entire floor and a room on another floor; it would be reasonable to assume the first floor and one room on the floor above. The third family consisted of Jacob Levin, a thirty-one-year-old tailor born in 'Russia Poland', his thirty-year-old wife Annie and six-year-old daughter Jessy – also both born in 'Russia Poland' – and two younger sons, aged two and five, born in the Parish of St George-in-the-East, between Whitechapel and Wapping. This family occupied two rooms, perhaps the top floor of the house. The final resident was twenty-four-year-old, unmarried Sarah Ginsberg, the 'Head' of her own household, who was an embroideress by trade and was listed as a Russian 'resident' in Britain. She occupied a single room, perhaps the one on the second floor not occupied by the Laskoffeskys. This makes a total of eight occupied rooms. Presumably the two basement rooms – the kitchen and washroom – were in communal use.

Number 17 was occupied by two families and seven people. Thomas Harvey Walker was still in residence, and still a bank messenger. He lived with his wife Elizabeth, two young children, and his seventy-nine-year-old widowed mother who, for whatever reason, was not in receipt of an old age pension. This family occupied seven rooms. Also living there was Margaret Bowman, a seventy-two-year-old widow 'kept by her daughter', and Mary, the forty-three-year-old unmarried daughter, who worked as a 'manufacturing chemist'. This pair, both born in the 'City', occupied two rooms. Nine rooms is an interesting total. Number 17 contains one room per floor and is five storeys high – including a basement kitchen. Goad's insurance map confirms there was no rear extension. So the basement must have been in the sole occupation of one family and most of the upper rooms divided in two by partitions.

Number 19 was occupied by three families and nine people. Alfred Holloway, a fifty-nine-year-old 'Army Pensioner', born in Hertfordshire, working as a commissionaire at a solicitor's office, and his London-born, fifty-nine-year-old wife Amy, occupied one room. William Carter, a thirty-year-old French polisher from Hoxton, his twenty-nine-year-old wife Jane, also from Hoxton, and their three children also occupied just one room. Finally, there was James McCarthy, a fifty-year-old widower and 'Fruit hawker' from Whitechapel, and his nineteen-year-old unmarried daughter Mary, a 'Boxmaker' born in Spitalfields. This pair occupied three rooms – so once again, given that the house contains just five rooms, it would seem that the basement kitchen was occupied by a single family. However, one of the upper rooms could have been subdivided – giving the house a total of six rooms – leaving the kitchen for communal use.

Number 21 was occupied by two families and seventeen people, and most – if not all – of these residents were Jewish. This suggests that a form of segregation had taken place in Elder Street with some houses becoming homes to Jewish families while others tended to house 'gentiles'. But to interpret this as a deliberate expression of religious, cultural or ethnic separation is probably a mistake. More likely houses took on a particular character because resident families tended to encourage relatives to settle with them when the opportunity arose. Other houses – such as 15 Elder Street – had a history of Jewish and gentile co-habitation, although admittedly becoming from the 1890s a largely Jewish household.

One of the families living in number 21 comprised Philip Reuben, a forty-year-old cabinet-maker born in Russia, his forty-year-old wife Minnie, a 'general dealer', also born in Russia, and their nine children, aged from one to fifteen. All had been born in Spitalfields. The eldest, Rebecca, worked as an embroideress, her fourteen-year-old younger brother David worked as an errand boy. Also part of the family were Miriam Capinsky, Minnie's sixty-year-old mother, a widow with 'no occupation', who had been born in Russia, and Leah, Minnie's twenty-four-year-old, unmarried sister, who had been born in Russia and who worked as a tailoress. This large and extended family occupied six rooms in the house.

The other family in the house consisted of Jacob Bosman, a thirty-three-year-old street hawker, born in Spitalfields, his forty-one-year-old wife Mary Anna, of 'no occupation' and born in Amsterdam, his thirty-one-year-old brother Louis, a 'Market Porter (fruit)', born in Whitechapel, and Mary Anna's seventeen-year-old brother, Alexander Ossendreiwer, a bootmaker, born in Amsterdam. This family occupied four rooms. The house contained seven so presumably the basement was inhabited and most of the upper rooms subdivided.[3]

The relatively large scale and dignity of Elder Street's houses (as noted by Charles Booth), its proximity to Spital Square, which in the early twentieth century remained reasonably well occupied, and to the City ensured that the street did not descend to the squalid and criminal level of nearby Quaker Street, 'Flower and Dean Street' and 'Dorset Street'. That said, Arthur Harding (see page 510) suggests that the area wasn't always tranquil. 'A lot of garotting went on,' he recorded in his flamboyant autobiography. 'Five years and a bashing you got for it – eighteen strokes with the cat. This was the penalty. But a lot of it still went on, by Flowery Dean Street, and in the pubs at the back of Leman Street, and all down the Highway. Even at the "Fleur de Lis" in Elder Street . . . [Y]ou had to be tall to do it. You would come up to a man from behind, put your arms around his throat, with your fists on his throttle. If it went on for more than a few seconds he would choke, so you had to be skilled. Some of them had a girl working for them – she would get a man well boozed, mix his drinks for him and they'd get him while he was drunk . . .'[4] Harding is presumably referring to the pub called the Elder Tree, which stood on the north-east corner of Elder Street and Fleur de Lis Street. The Valuation Office records from 1912 show that the freehold was owned by Arthur George Tillard, whose family had owned the land since the very early eighteenth century. The pub closed some time after the Second World War. It was demolished in the early 1970s.

Introduction

1   Samuel Smiles, speech: 'Educating the working classes', 1845.

2   *Survey of London*, vol. XXVII: Spitalfields and Mile End New Town, ed. F. H. W. Sheppard, LCC, 1957, p. 265.

3   Victoria County History, *Middlesex*, vol. XI: Stepney and Bethnal Green, ed. T. F. T. Baker, 1998, pp. 87, 212–17.

4   *Survey of London*, vol. XXVII, p. 265.

5   Charles Knight, ed., *London*, vol. II, Charles Knight & Co., 1842, pp. 356–7.

Prologue: The Golden Heart of Spitalfields

1   *Survey of London*, vol. XXVII: Spitalfields and Mile End New Town, ed. F. H. W. Sheppard, LCC, 1957, pp. 190, 256–7. A property conveyance of 1712/13 refers to 'a small piece of ground heretofore a Bowling Alley' near to or on the site of the Golden Heart. This was a convivial use associated with taverns, suggesting there was a tavern on the site at the time.

2   Historic England list description; Geoff Brandwood and Jane Jephcote, *London Heritage Pubs: An Inside Story*, CAMRA, 2008, p. 119; Emily Cole, *The Urban and Suburban Public House in Inter-war England*, HE research report series, no. 4/2015, The Golden Heart, Luke Jacob; London Metropolitan Archives, LCC Building Case File. GLC/AR/BR/17/076700 – original drawings dated November 1934.

1: The Land of the Dead

1   See Chris Thomas, *Life and Death in London's East End: 200 Years at Spitalfields*, Museum of London Archaeology Services, 2004, pp. 15–19.

2   Ibid., p. 19.

3   John Stow, *A Survey of London*. Reprint from text of 1603, introduction and notes by Charles Lethbridge Kingsford, Clarendon Press, 1908, vol. 1, pp. 163–70.

4   *The Exeter Book*, Exeter Cathedral library MS 3501; *The Anglo-Saxon World: An Anthology*, ed. Kevin Crossley-Holland, Oxford University Press, 1984, pp. 59–60.

5   Chris Thomas, of Museum of London Archaeology, in conversation with the author.

6   St Augustine, *Confessions*, book X, ch. 27; *Sermons*, 336, 1Pl 38 1472. This is the popular interpretation of 'Cantare amantis est' ('singing belongs to one that loves').

7   Thomas, *Life and Death in London's East End*, p. 33.

8   Chiz Harward et al., *The Spitalfields Suburb, 1539–c.1880: Excavations at Spitalfields Market, London E1, 1991–2007*, Museum of London Archaeology, Monograph 61, 2015, p. 252.

9   Information from Lee Hollingsworth, a local water diviner.

10 Chiz Harward, one of the Museum of London archaeologists who dug the site during the 1990s, confirms that the priory had at least one well in the outer precinct for a supply of local, non-plumbed water, but points out that its use of the Snecocke spring suggests that was 'the nearest natural large-scale supply to the monastic core, although there was of course the Bishop of London's supply running down Bishopsgate.' (Communication between author and Nigel Jeffries of MOLA.)

11 In conversation with the author.

12 Thomas, *Life and Death in London's East End*, pp. 42–3.

13 Ibid., p. 36.

14 Stow, *A Survey of London*, reprint of 1908, vol. I, pp. 163–70.

15 Ibid., p. 119.

16 *Book of Revelation*, 4:4.

17 Nigel Saul, *For Honour and Fame: Chivalry in England, 1066–1500*, Random House, 2011, p. 208.

18 Harward et al., *The Spitalfields Suburb*, pp. 24–5.

19 Thomas, *Life and Death in London's East End*, pp. 30–1.

2: Reformation and Rebirth

1   Chiz Harward et al., *The Spitalfields Suburb, 1539–c.1880: Excavations at Spitalfields Market, London E1, 1991–2007*, Museum of London Archaeology, Monograph 61, 2015, p. 34.

2   G. W. Bernard, 'The Dissolution of the Monasteries', *History*, The Journal of the Historical Association, Blackwell Publishing Ltd., vol. 96, issue 324, October 2011, pp. 399–409.

3   Harward et al., *The Spitalfields Suburb*, p. 23.

4   *Survey of London*, vol. XXVII, Spitalfields and Mile End New Town, ed. F. H. W. Sheppard, LCC, 1957, p. 24.

5 National Archives, E 326/8106.

6 *Survey of London*, vol. XXVII, pp. 39–40.

7 *Survey of London*, vol. VIII, Shoreditch, Sir James Bird, LCC, 1922, pp. 178 and 188.

8 *Calendar of Letters and Papers, Foreign and Domestic, Henry VIII*, eds. James Gairdner and R. H. Brodie, HMSO, 1895, vol. 14, part 2, no. 433, p. 154.

9 *Survey of London*, vol. XXVII, p. 22–3.

10 Ibid., p. 24.

11 John Stow, *A Survey of London*. Reprint from text of 1603, introduction and notes by Charles Lethbridge Kingsford, Clarendon Press, 1908, vol. I, pp. 163–70.

12 *Survey of London*, vol. XXVII, p. 28.

13 Ibid., p. 39.

14 Ibid., p. 23.

15 Ibid., p. 39; Chris Thomas, B. Sloane and C. Phillpotts, *Excavations at the Priory and Hospital of St Mary Spital, London*, Museum of London Archaeology, Monograph 1, 1997, p. 77.

16 See Harward et al., *The Spitalfields Suburb*, figure 15, p. 34.

17 Ibid., p. 34; and Thomas, Sloane and Phillpotts, *Excavations at the Priory and Hospital of St Mary Spital*, p. 77.

18 *Survey of London*, vol. XXVII, pp. 40–1.

19 Bodleian MS. Charters, Middlesex 59; *Survey of London*, vol. XXVII, pp. 47–8.

20 *Survey of London*, vol. XXVII, p. 49; and Harward et al., *The Spitalfields Suburb*, pp. 32, 34, 38.

21 Chris Thomas, *Life and Death in London's East End: 2000 Years at Spitalfields*, Museum of London Archaeology, 2004, pp. 80–1.

22 Harward et al., *The Spitalfields Suburb*, p. 37.

23 Ibid., pp. 36–8; copies of the print are in the Bishopsgate Institute and the London Metropolitan Archive.

24 *Survey of London*, vol. XXVII, p. 46.

25 The identification of 'le Posterne' as the 'Brick House' seems to have occurred by 1573, and is confirmed in 1586 in the assignment of the 1536 lease by Raffe Bott 'of London, gentleman', who in 1589 claimed an interest in the forty-three acres of Lolesworth Fields (*Survey of London*, vol. XXVII, p. 46).

26 *Survey of London*, vol. XXVII, illustration 6a.

27 Thomas, Sloane and Phillpotts, *Excavations at the Priory and Hospital of St Mary Spital*, p. 133.

[28] Harward et al., *The Spitalfields Suburb*, pp. 46–51.

[29] Stow, *A Survey of London*, reprint of 1908, vol. I, pp. 163–70.

[30] Ibid.

[31] The information conveyed by the most evocative 'Copperplate' map is complemented, and to a degree confirmed, by the enigmatic print that purports to show Norton Folgate in late-Tudor times but which is preserved only in a late-nineteenth-century version. This offers a view from the west, looking east across what would appear to be a winding 'Hog Lane' towards a row of large buildings on Norton Folgate, including perhaps the Principal Tenement within the former site of St Mary's Priory. The view is dominated by a massive tree, which rises in the foreground and in the centre of the composition, dwarfing all else. To the north of the extraordinary tree is a diminutive windmill, roughly located where a windmill is shown on the 'Copperplate' map. MOLA archaeologists date this view to around 1600 (Thomas, *Life and Death in London's East End*, p. 80).

[32] The 'Agas' map can be fairly precisely dated because the spire on St Paul's Cathedral is not shown (it was destroyed in 1561) and because one of the woodblocks from which the map was printed has been altered to show the Royal Exchange, completed in 1570.

[33] *Survey of London*, vol. XXVII, p. 123.

[34] The map produced by G. Braun and F. Hogenberg in 1572, like the 'Agas' map is evidently based on the 'Copperplate' map of around twenty years earlier. Bishopsgate, Spitalfields and Shoreditch appear much the same but, since the scale of the map is larger, the detail is far less. People, cattle and drying fabric have completely disappeared from the landscape, but the charnel house is still there, the large field to the east of 'Busshoppes gate Strete' is still named 'The Spitel Fields'. The map extends north, beyond 'Hog Lane', stopping just short of St Leonard's Church Shoreditch.

[35] John Stow, *A Survey of London*, reprint of 1908, vol. I, p. 167.

[36] *Survey of London*, vol. XXVII, p. 41.

[37] Harward et al., *The Spitalfields Suburb*, p. 38.

[38] *Survey of London*, vol. XXVII, pp. 69–70.

[39] Harward et al., *The Spitalfields Suburb*, pp. 78–9.

[40] Richard W. Stewart, *The English Ordnance Office: A Case-study in Bureaucracy*, Royal Historical Society, Boydell Press, 1996.

[41] Harward et al., *The Spitalfields Suburb*, pp. 79–82; Will of Valentine Pyne, Captain and Master Gunner of England, lying in the Old Artillery Garden, London: dated 3 May 1677, National Archive, PROB. 11/354/12.

[42] Several early-seventeenth-century documents and records of expenditure have been found by MOLA that can be interpreted as referring to the construction of the fort.

[43] Thomas, *Life and Death in London's East End*, p. 73.

[44] Pietro Contarini is recorded as being in occupation in 1617 – see Victoria & Albert Museum notes on Sir Paul Pindar's House, the façade of which is in its collection.

[45] Calendar of State Papers, Venice, 1642–3, p. 257, quoted in Benjamin Woolley, *The Herbalist: Nicholas Culpeper and the Fight for Medical Freedom*, Harper-Collins, 2004, p. 206.

[46] Harward et al., *The Spitalfields Suburb*, pp. 86–7.

[47] Sarah Tarlow, *Ritual, Belief and the Dead in Early Modern Britain and Ireland*, Cambridge University Press, 2010, pp. 56–7.

[48] See V. Smith and P. Kelsey, *The Lines of Communication: The Civil War Defences of London*, Palgrave Macmillan, 1996, p. 81.

3: On the Fringes of Society

[1] The boundary between the two was marked by the north elevation of the charnel house, and so echoed the boundary of the City Ward of Bishopsgate-without. The Liberty of Norton Folgate is particularly intriguing because the origin of its boundaries remains strangely 'obscure' (*Survey of London*, vol. XXVII, Spitalfields and Mile End New Town, ed. F. H. W. Sheppard, LCC, 1957, p. 15). Its formation was evidently more complex than simply redefining the priory's northern precinct as a Liberty, because its boundaries not only embraced the heartland of the priory's northern precinct but also roughly coincided with the boundaries of the ancient Manor of Norton Folgate – or Norton Folyot – that was from the eleventh century owned by, or connected with, the Dean and Chapter of St Paul's Cathedral. This connection is revealed by the fact that the land that became the Liberty of Norton Folgate – 8.7 acres in extent – did not conform exactly with the boundary of the former northern precinct but extended to the west of Bishopsgate, while the precinct did not. On the other hand the Manor of Norton Folyot did extend to the west of Bishopsgate, seemingly confirming that its ancient boundaries influenced those of the Liberty. One of the earliest references to the former monastic land being a Liberty in its own right comes from John Stow's *Survey of London* of 1598 where he describes 'Norton fall gate' as a 'liberty so called, belonging to the Deane of Powles'. (*Survey of London*, vol. XXVII, p. 16.)

[2] *Survey of London*, vol. XXVII, p. 49; Prerogative Court of Canterbury, 5 Coode. Chiz Harward et al., *The Spitalfields Suburb, 1539–c.1880: Excavations at Spitalfields Market, London E1, 1991–2007*, Museum of London Archaeology, Monograph 61, 2015, pp. 37–8, take a slightly broader view and speculate that Wyatt could have occupied Vaughan's Principal Tenement although this is not 'absolutely certain'.

[3] As the *Survey of London* puts it: 'Proximity to the City together with immunity from parochial authority made the former [monastic] precinct attractive to Roman Catholic recusants' (vol. XXVII, pp. 1–2).

[4] That Spitalfields, and in particular the former northern precinct of the priory in the Liberty of Norton Folgate, became a favourite abode of Roman Catholics is made clear by the Calendar of State Papers Domestic, Addenda, 1566–79, p. 550, which lists the Catholics living in Spitalfields a few years after Rugg's death (*Survey of London*, vol. XXVII, pp. 49–50).

[5] Harward et al., *The Spitalfields Suburb*, pp. 32, 310–12.

[6] John Stow, *A Survey of London*. Reprint from text of 1603, introduction and notes by Charles Lethbridge Kingsford, Clarendon Press, 1908, p. 167.

[7] Nancy Pollard Brown, 'Howard [Dacre], Anne, Countess of Arundel (1557–1630), *Oxford Dictionary of National Biography*, Oxford University Press, 2004; online edn, Jan 2008.

[8] Harward et al., *The Spitalfields Suburb*, pp. 29 and 31.

[9] *Survey of London*, vol. XXVII, p. 50.

[10] Harward et al., *The Spitalfields Suburb*, p. 29.

[11] *Survey of London*, vol. XXVII, p. 50.

[12] Thomas Fairman Ordish, *Early London Theatres: In the Fields*, Elliot Stock, 1899, p. 30.

[13] *I Kings*, 7:13–22, 41–2; *Jeremiah*, 52:20–2.

[14] Frances Yates, *The Occult Philosophy in the Elizabethan Age*, Routledge, 2001 edn, p. 190.

[15] George B. Williams, *A Guide to Literary London*, HarperCollins, 1988, p. 59.

[16] As argued in detail by Park Honan in *Christopher Marlowe: Poet and Spy*, Oxford University Press, 2005.

[17] Yates, *The Occult Philosophy in the Elizabethan Age*, pp. 136–142.

4: People of Spitalfields

[1] Chiz Harward et al., *The Spitalfields Suburb, 1539–c.1880, Excavations at the Priory and Hospital of St Mary Spital, London*, Museum of London Archaeology, Monograph 61, 2015, pp. 51–2.

2   Ibid., p. 328.

3   Ibid., pp. 53–4.

4   Margaret A. Rees, *The Writings of Doña Luisa de Carvajal y Mendoza*, Edwin Mellen Press, 2002, p. 2.

5   Evelyn Waugh, *Edmund Campion*, Penguin, 1957, p. 73.

6   Ibid., p. 87.

7   Ibid., p. 88.

8   Ibid.

9   Ibid., p. 89.

10 Glyn Redworth, *The She-Apostle: The Extraordinary Life and Death of Luisa de Carvajal*, Oxford University Press, 2008, p. 115.

11 Ibid., p. 198; Harward et al., *The Spitalfields Suburb*, p. 52. See also Christopher Thomas, Barney Sloane and Christopher Phillpotts, *Excavations at the Priory and Hospital of St Mary Spital, London*, Museum of London Archaeology, Monograph 1, 1997, p. 133.

12 These have recently been analysed in detail by Glyn Redworth and published in 'Letters of Luisa de Carvajal y Mendoza', *English Historical Review*, vol. 129, number 536, 2014, pp. 203–4; and his *She-Apostle*.

13 Redworth, *She-Apostle*, p. 202; Redworth, 'Letters', 139, p. 347.

14 Redworth, *She-Apostle*, p. 202; Redworth, 'Letters', 130, p. 330.

15 Redworth, *She-Apostle*, p. 202.

16 Ibid., p. 218.

17 Harward et al., *The Spitalfields Suburb*, p. 311.

18 Rees, *Writings of Doña Luisa*, pp. 27–8.

19 Ibid., p. 26.

20 Ibid., p. 27.

21 Redworth, *She-Apostle*, p. 203.

22 Ibid., p. 215.

23 Ibid., p. 203.

24 Ibid., p. 204.

25 Ibid.

26 Ibid., p. 211.

27 Ibid.

28 Ibid., pp. 211–12; Redworth, 'Letters', 151, p. 369.

29 Redworth, *She-Apostle*, p. 212.

30 Ibid., p. 217.

31 Ibid.

32 Rees, *Writings of Doña Luisa*, p. 1.

33 Redworth, *She-Apostle*, p. 219.

34 Ibid., p. 220.

35 Rees, *The Writings of Doña Luisa*; Lisa McClain, *Lest We Be Damned: Practical Innovation and Lived Experience among Catholics in Protestant England, 1559–1642*, Routledge, 2004, pp. 167–9.

36 Redworth, *She-Apostle*, pp. 226–8.

37 *Survey of London*. vol. XXVII, Spitalfields and Mile End New Town, ed. F. H. W. Sheppard, LCC, 1957, p. 53.

38 Thomas, Sloane and Philpotts, *Excavations at the Priory and Hospital of St Mary Spital*, p. 133; GL, MS 4524/1 ff. 123v,138; 4526/1; Charity Comm., 1897, I, 300-1; Harward et al., *The Spitalfields Suburb*, p.46.

39 Lisa Jardine and Alan Stewart, *Hostage to Fortune: The Troubled Life of Francis Bacon*, Victor Gollancz, 1998, p. 464; John Aubrey, *Brief Lives*, II. Oliver Lawson Dick editing *Aubrey's Brief Lives*, Secker & Warburg, 1958, spells '*paiderastos*' in Greek, p. 11, which presumably was Aubrey's code for recording such delicate subjects.

40 See essay 'Of Simulation and Dissimulation' in *Lord Bacon's Essays or Counsels, Civil and Moral*, 1625.

41 Frances Yates, *The Rosicrucian Enlightenment*, Routledge, 2003, pp. 164-9.

42 Harward et al., *The Spitalfields Suburb*, pp. 46–51.

43 From Sir Simonds D'Ewes, *Autobiography and Correspondence*, quoted by Rictor Norton on website Sir Francis Bacon; and Jardine and Stewart, *Hostage to Fortune*, pp. 464–5.

44 *Dictionary of National Biography*, vol. V, eds. L. Stephen and S. Lee, Oxford University Press, 1917, p. 286.

45 Newton E. Key: 'Annesley, Samuel', *Oxford Dictionary of National Biography*, Oxford University Press, 2004; online edn, May 2013.

5: Building on Rubble

1 *The Diary of Samuel Pepys*, Robert Latham and William Matthews eds., Bell & Hyman, 1983, vol. III, pp. 57–8.

2 Chiz Harward et al., *The Spitalfields Suburb, 1539–c.1880: Excavations at Spitalfields Market, London E1, 1991–2007*, Museum of London Archaeology, Monograph 61, 2015, figure 41, p. 61; figure 47, p. 65, and figure 68, p. 86.

3 In 1631 Sir Edmund vested the freehold in his relative, Richard Wheler of Westminster, who in the same year leased it for ninety-nine years, 'under certain trusts', to a John Wheler of Datchet, 'gentleman'. The reversion of this lease devolved upon Sir Edmund's son, William Wheler of Datchet,

while the lease itself 'and trusts devolved upon his kinsman, William Wheler of Westbury, Wiltshire', in whom the estate was vested in 1654. The precise relationship between these Whelers is now difficult to determine, but it is likely that the father of William Wheler of Westbury was the John Wheler who acquired the ninety-nine-year lease in 1631. (*Survey of London*, vol. XXVII, Spitalfields and Mile End New Town, ed. F. H. W. Sheppard, LCC, 1957, pp. 96–7.)

4   The Reverend Sir George was the son of Charles Wheler of Charing, Kent, who acquired part of the estate in 1670.

5   *Survey of London*, vol. XXVII, pp. 100-4.

6   Harward et al., The *Spitalfields Suburb*, p. 116.

7   *Survey of London*, vol. XXVII, p. 46; *Endowed Charities*, London, vol. V, 1903, p. 642; Harward et al., *The Spitalfields Suburb*, p. 52.

8   *Survey of London*, vol. XXVII, pp. 97–8.

9   Ibid., p. 98.

10 Norman G. Brett-James, *The Growth of Stuart London*, George Allen & Unwin, 1935, pp. 105–6, 120–4, 297–8, 498.

11 Ibid., p. 297.

12 Information from communications between the author and Nigel Jeffries, Chris Thomas and Chiz Harward, all of whom were part of the MOLA Spitalfields team in the 1990s. The extent of the raising and the levelling of the land in the eastern parts of Spitalfields, and the boundary of the manipulation of the terrain, remains uncertain. Perhaps it extended as far as Brick Lane: certainly in recent years vaults, arches and cobbled and paved surfaces have been found below the mid-1720s basements and gardens of 11, 12, 15 and 27 Fournier Street, suggesting the land here was also raised in this part of Spitalfields before coherent development (information from James Howett and Gilbert and George). If land-raising around Fournier Street did occur then it must have been completed by 1714 when Christ Church was started, for the church – as it was designed and built – was clearly intended to rise from the existing street level. Land-raising could have been made necessary by the excavation of brick earth in the Lolesworth Field area in the late sixteenth century – as noted by John Stow in his *Survey* – or have been associated with the construction and subsequent removal of the large earth-built Civil War ramparts along the line of Brick Lane.

13 *Pepys' Diary*, Latham and Matthews eds., vol. IX, pp. 517–18.

14 Harward et al.,*The Spitalfields Suburb*, fig. 51, p. 70.

15 Browns Lane may have been part of the system of lanes or tracks that linked

Roman Ermine Street (Bishopsgate/Norton Folgate/Shoreditch High Street) to the Roman road leading to Colchester (Whitechapel Road/High Street/Mile End Road/Bow Road). Its existence is implied by the 'Copperplate' map of c.1553 and in March 1648/9 it was described as 'newly named or known by the name of Lolesworth Lane or Street' (*Survey of London*, vol. XXVII, p. 189).

[16] *Survey of London*, vol. XXVII, pp. 189–90.

[17] Ibid., pp. 136–7.

[18] Ibid., p. 127; PRO PC2/63, p. 265.

[19] See John Timbs, *Curiosities of London*, David Bogue, 1868 edn, p. 744.

[20] *Survey of London*, vol. XXVII, p. 127.

[21] *Survey of London*, vol. XXVIII, p. 178. PRO. C5/64/75, and Dr Nick Barratt research notes of 4 June 2000 for the BBC2 series *House Detectives*, in author's possession, p. 1.

[22] *Survey of London*, vol. XXVII, p. 144.

[23] Ibid.

[24] Ibid., p. 128.

[25] Brett-James, *Growth of Stuart London*, p. 490.

[26] *Autobiography of the Hon. Roger North*, A. Jessop ed., D. Nutt, 1887, pp. 54–5. See also Harward et al., *The Spitalfields Suburb*, p.155.

[27] Harward et al., *The Spitalfields Suburb*, pp. 157–8.

[28] Ibid., p.155.

[29] Ibid.

[30] Brett-James, *Growth of Stuart London*, pp. 85–6.

[31] Entry for 20 October 1660. Pepys at this time was living in Seething Lane, in the City. *Pepys' Diary*, Latham and Matthews eds., vol. I, p. 269.

[32] Daniel Defoe, *A Journal of the Plague Year* [1722], Falcon Press, 1950, p. 25. Pepys doesn't specifically mention Spitalfields in his diary account of the Great Plague, although his entry for 15 June 1665 does touch on areas nearby: 'The town grows very sickly, and people to be afeared of it – there dying this last week of the plague 112, from 43 the week before – whereof, one in Fanchurch-street and one in Broadstreete by the Treasurer's office.' His entry for 31 August 1665 gives an idea just how high mortality rates rose during the outbreak: 'In the city died this week 7,496; and of them, 6,102 of the plague. But it is feared that the true number of dead this week is near 10,000 – partly from the poor that cannot be taken notice of through the greatness of the number, and partly from the Quakers and others that will not have any bell ring for them.' *Pepys' Diary*, Latham and Matthews eds., vol. VI, p. 208.

33   Defoe, *A Journal of the Plague Year*, pp. 246–8.

34   *Poysoning in Nortonfolgate*, Bishopsgate Institute, QD8 TRU, pp. 1–3, quoted in part in *Survey of London*, vol. XXVII, p. 73.

35   Brett-James, *Growth of Stuart London*, p. 490; J. Trevers, *An Essay to the Restoring of our decayed Trade . . . 1675*, p. 36, quoted in M. Dorothy George, *London Life in the Eighteenth Century*, Kegan Paul, Trench, Trubner & Co., 1925; Defoe, *A Journal of the Plague Year*, p. 25.

36   M. Dorothy George, *London Life in the Eighteenth Century*, pp. 187–8.

37   PRO. SP/29/274, no. 205, f. 397r; quoted by Robin D. Gwynn, *Huguenot Heritage: The History and Contribution of the Huguenots in Britain* (1984), Sussex Academic Press, 2000, p. 140.

38   *Survey of London*, vol. XXVII, p. 128.

39   Ibid., pp. 128-9.

40   In eastern Spitalfields these included the large and well-organised Hambletons Garden and Clarks Land, in the northern part of what was known as 'The Hamlet of Mile End Newtowne'.

41   *Survey of London*, vol. XXVII, p. 129.

42   The initial layout is shown clearly on Joel Gascoyne's 1703 map of the parish of St Dunstan Stepney. Robert Seymour, in his 1734–5 updating of John Stow, *A Survey of the cities of London and Westminster*, explains the fate of the market house. Among the 'remarkable Places and Things' of London was 'Spittle-fields-market, wherein there was a Market-house, but having been consumed a few Years since by Fire, Stalls have been built all round the Market, and in the Middle are sold Greens, Roots, etc.' (Robert Seymour, *Survey of the Cities of London and Westminster, Borough of Southwark*, 1734–5, vol. II, book VI, p. 729; *New Remarks of London*, Worshipful Company of Parish Clerks, E. Midwinter, 1732, p. 190.)

43   According to Historic England, 'a brewhouse was built on the land west of Brick Lane by Thomas Bucknall – citizen and Merchant Taylor – in c.1666', which 'was purchased by Joseph Truman in 1679'. (See List Description of the Directors' House, number 1252152.) Truman was certainly in possession of the brewery by August 1683 for he is mentioned as a brewer 'of Brick Lane' in St Dunstan's Stepney Register of Christenings for that month. (*Survey of London*, vol. XXVII, p. 116.)

44   John Burnett, *Liquid Pleasures: A Social History of Drinks in Modern Britain*, Routledge, 1999, p.114.

45   Information from Lee Hollingworth to the author.

46   *Survey of London*, vol. XXVII, p. 189.

47 His will is dated 15 March 1720 (National Archives, Prob. 11/573/116).

48 *Survey of London*, vol. XXVII, p. 185.

49 The uneven spacing of windows on the Brick Lane elevation of the Directors'
House and a vertical straight joint in the brickwork suggest that the building
evolved over a period of time. The architect for works to the house in the
1740s – from which much of the interior still dates – could have been John
Price, who at the time was working on other brewery buildings.

50 As the *Survey of London* points out, it is known that in 1697 and 1704 the 3rd
Earl of Bolingbroke granted leases to builders on the neighbouring south side
of 'White Lion Yard'/Folgate Street, so it is highly likely he granted the Spital
Square building leases at roughly the same time (vol. XXVII, p. 58).

51 The eastern edge of the new square is marked on the 1712/13 survey by an 'Old
Building' and its garden wall. This must be the remains of the Candle House.
To its north is another 'Old Building' that must be the Brick House of c.1600,
but considerably extended to the west. The south side of the new square was
formed by the garden wall of the Bolingbroke family mansion. The mansion
itself, offering one flank to the square, was placed at the west end of the garden, over which its major elevation enjoyed views to the east. West of
Bolingbroke House and its garden were a pair of houses (later numbered 36
and 37) helping to form the re-entrant angle to the square, with the pair on its
west side.

52 Harward et al., *The Spitalfields Suburb*, p. 212; *Survey of London*, vol. XXVII,
pp. 69–70.

53 Robert Seymour, in his 1734/5 updating of John Stow's *Survey*, notes that
where the priory stood 'are now built many handsome houses for merchants
and others' (*Survey of London*, vol. XXVII, p. 55).

54 *Survey of London*, vol. XXVII, pp. 58–66.

6: 'Distressed Strangers'

1 M. Power, 'East London Housing in the Seventeenth Century', in Peter Clark
and Paul Slack eds., *Crisis and Order in English Towns, 1500–1700*, Routledge
& Kegan Paul, 1972, pp. 237–62; and Catherine Swindlehurst, 'An Unruly and
Presumptuous Rabble: The Reaction of the Spitalfields Weaving Community
to the Settlement of the Huguenots, 1660–90' in Randolph Vigne and Charles
Littleton eds., *From Strangers to Citizens: The Integration of Immigrant Com-
munities in Britain, Ireland and Colonial America, 1550–1750*, Sussex Academic/
Huguenot Society, 2001, p. 366.

2 The Jews represented a parallel migration with merchant families arriving –

largely from Amsterdam – during the Commonwealth of the 1650s and settling around Dukes Place, Aldgate, where the Great Synagogue was built in c.1690.

3   Victoria County History, *Middlesex*, vol. II, General, ed. W. Page, 1911, pp. 132–7.

4   Robin D. Gwynn, 'The Number of Huguenot Immigrants in the Late Seventeenth Century', *Journal of Historical Geography*, vol. 9, no. 4, 1983, pp. 384–98.

5   Lindsey German and John Rees, *A People's History of London*, Verso, 2012, pp. 71–2.

6   Swindlehurst, 'An Unruly and Presumptuous Rabble', p. 368.

7   J. Trevers estimated the native force as 'an hundred thousand people small and great' in *An Essay to the Restoring of our decayed Trade*, 1675, p. 36. In *Review*, 20 March 1705, Daniel Defoe, writing against the engine-loom riots of 1675 (not 'in and about 1679 and 80' as Defoe states), suggested 50,000, but in his *A Journal of the Plague Year*, 1722, appears to go for Trevers' estimate of 100,000 ('the chiefest number of whom lived . . . about Spitalfields'). Estimates of 40,000 seem more likely. See M. Dorothy George, *London Life in the Eighteenth Century*, Penguin, 1976, p.178; Norman G. Brett-James, *The Growth of Stuart London*, George Allen & Unwin, 1935, p. 490.

8   See Anne J. Kershen, *Strangers, Aliens and Asians: Huguenots, Jews and Bangladeshis in Spitalfields 1660–2000*, Routledge, 2005, p. 171; and M. Weber, *The Protestant Work Ethic and the Spirit of Capitalism*, Unwin, 1938.

9   Huguenot Society Publication XI, 1898, p. iii; Victoria County History, *Middlesex*, vol. II, General, pp. 132–77; *Survey of London*, vol. XXVII, p. 143.

10 Robin D. Gwynn, *Huguenot Heritage: The History and Contribution of the Huguenots in Britain*, Sussex Academic Press, 2000, p.166.

11 Ibid., p. 170.

12 Ibid., pp. 167–8; BL Add. MSS 34,502, ff, 61r and 52,279, 30 Oct. 1685; Robin D. Gwynn, 'James II in the Light of his Treatment of Huguenot Refugees in England, 1685–9', *English Historical Review*, XCII, 1977, pp. 820–33.

13 Gwynn, *Huguenot Heritage*, p. 169.

14 Ibid., p. 168.

15 Ibid.

16 *The Entering Book of Roger Morrice: A Journal of Late-seventeenth-century London*, ed. Mark Goldie, Boydell Press, 2007.

17 *The Entering Book of Roger Morrice*, vol. III, p. 54.

18 Gwynn, *Huguenot Heritage*, p. 169.

19 *Diary of John Evelyn*, IV, ed. E. S. de Beer, Oxford University Press, Oxford,

2000 edition, pp. 508, 509. Evelyn merely states in his entry for 25 April 1686: 'this day was the Briefe for a collection of reliefe to the Persecuted French protestants (so cruely, barbarously & inhumanely oppressed) read in our churches; but which had ben [sic] so long expected ... The interest of the French Ambassador & cruel papists obstructing it.'

20 Gwynn, *Huguenot Heritage*, p. 169; quoting *Letters of Lady Rachel Russell*, 7th edn, 1809, p. 87, 15 January 1686.

21 Gwynn, *Huguenot Heritage*, p. 171.

22 Ibid., pp. 168–9.

23 Ibid., p. 170.

24 Ibid.

25 Ibid., p. 171.

26 Ibid.

27 Victoria County History, *Middlesex*, vol. II, General, pp. 132–7.

28 *The Entering Book of Roger Morrice*, vol. III, pp. 62–3.

29 Ibid., p. 114.

30 Gwynn, *Huguenot Heritage*, p. 172.

31 Ibid., p. 169.

32 Ibid.

33 Ibid.

34 *The Entering Book of Roger Morrice*, vol. III, p. 388.

35 Ibid., vol. IV, p. 61.

36 Ibid., pp. 60–1.

37 PRO. SP29/431/20; Swindlehurst, 'An Unruly and Presumptuous Rabble', pp. 370–1. See also L. Catherine Swindlehurst, *Trade Expansion, Social Conflict and Popular Politics in the Spitalfields Silk Weaving Community, c.1670–1770*, Cambridge University Press, 1999.

38 Swindlehurst, 'An Unruly and Presumptuous Rabble', p. 368.

39 Alfred Plummer, *The London Weavers' Company, 1600–1970*, Routledge & Kegan Paul, 1972, 2006, p. 461. In her contribution to *From Strangers to Citizens*, eds. Vigne and Littleton, 2001, p. 370, Swindlehurst observes of the Weavers' Company: '... as the seventeenth century progressed [it] became less able to deal effectively with the weavers' concerns; especially as the Huguenots tended to settle in areas like Spitalfields, which were beyond the legal jurisdiction of the Weavers' Company.' She is referring to the situation in 1683 and presumably it was to resolve this that the 1685 charter was granted.

40 Guildhall Library, MS 4655/9, fos. 12, pp. 37–8; and Swindlehurst, 'An Unruly and Presumptuous Mob', pp. 368–9.

41 *The Valiant Weaver*, London, 1681; Swindlehurst, 'An Unruly and Presumptuous Mob', pp. 369–70.

42 PRO. SP 29/431/21; Swindlehurst, 'An Unruly and Presumptuous Mob', p. 366.

43 PRO. SP29/431/21–20; Swindlehurst, 'An Unruly and Presumptuous Mob', pp. 370–1.

44 PRO. SP29/430/79; Swindlehurst, 'An Unruly and Presumptuous Mob', p. 371.

45 Ibid.; PRO. SP29/431/3.

46 Francis Blomefield, *An Essay Towards a Topographical History . . . of Norfolk*, 5 vols, Smith, Elder & Co., 1739–75, vol. II, p. 294. Blomefield says 1682, but he is wrong. See John Miller, *Cities Divided: Politics and Religion in English Provincial Towns, 1660–1722*, Oxford University Press, 2007, pp. 44–6.

47 Miller, *Cities Divided*, p. 213; and Calendar of State Papers Domestic, Charles II January to June 1683, p. 363, 4 September 1683: 'Journeymen and apprentice weavers in London'.

48 *The Entering Book of Roger Morrice*, vol. II, p. 360.

49 John Strype, *Survey of London and Westminster*, 1720, vol. II, book 1, p. 48 includes a *Map of Spittlefields and Places Adjacent*.

50 *A Brief State of the Question Between the Printed and Painted Callicoes and the Woollen and Silk Manufacture, As far as it relates to the Wearing and Using of Printed and Painted Callicoes in Great Britain*, Boreham, 1719, p. 5.

51 Thanks to Robin Gwynn who directed my attention to Denis's pamphlet.

52 *Survey of London*, vol. XXVII, pp. 184, 189.

53 Victoria County History, *Middlesex*, vol. II, General, p. 309.

54 Ibid., pp. 132–7.

7: God's Chosen People

1 *Survey of London*, vol. XXVII, Spitalfields and Mile End New Town, ed. F. H. W. Sheppard, LCC, 1957, p. 176.

2 Robin D. Gwynn in *Huguenot Heritage: The History and Contribution of the Huguenots in Britain*, Sussex Academic Press, 2000, has produced a map showing the location of these temples: 1. St Jean, which was located in St John's Street, which, in 1700, was the most northerly built-up street to the east of Brick Lane; 2. L'Église de L'Hôpital in Black Eagle Street, which was north of and parallel with Browns Lane; 3. La Patente, 'Paternoster Row', near the junction with Crispin Street, and from 1740 to 1786 in Browns Lane; 4. L'Artillerie (II), Artillery Lane/Old Artillery Ground, as named on Rocque's map of 1746, looking

north up Steward Street; 5. Crispin Street – in the middle, roughly where cut by 'Paternoster Row'/Brushfield Street; 6. Quaker Street (site now under Commercial Street); 7. in Great Pearl Street, halfway between Commercial Street and Brick Lane; 8. Wheler Street, on a site just to the west of the Peabody block on Commercial Street; 9. DuMarché, in Spitalfields Market.

3   Taken from Horace, *Odes*, book IV, ode VII, line 16: *Pulvis et Umbra Sumus* – we are but dust and shadow.

4   *Survey of London*, vol. XXVII, plates 41a and b.

5   *Register of the Church of Saint Jean Spitalfields 1687–1827*, edited for the Huguenot Society by Susan Minet, Publications of the Huguenot Society of London, 1938. The church had been established by the Ministers Benjamin de Joux and Lean (sic) Lions on the north side of the street and occupied a building used previously by nonconformists. Most of the congregation of St Jean came from Pays de Caux in Haute Normandie and from Picardy. In 1765 a new church was built on the site, on land leased from John Cooper. Samuel Beuzeville was its minister.

6   *Register of the Church of Saint Jean Spitalfields*, p. xv.

7   *From Strangers to Citizens: The Integration of Immigrant Communities in Britain, Ireland and Colonial America, 1550–1750*, eds. Randolph Vigne and Charles Littleton, Sussex Academic Press/Huguenot Society, 2001: see especially Eileen Barrett, 'Huguenot Integration in Late Seventeenth and Eighteenth Century London: Insights from Records of the French Church and Some Relief Agencies', p. 380.

8   See Stephen Macfarlane, 'Studies in Poverty and Poor Relief in London at the End of the Seventeenth Century', D. Phil Oxford University, 1982; Dorothy Marshall, *The English Poor in the Eighteenth Century*, Routledge, 1926, p. 103; Vigne and Littleton eds., *From Strangers to Citizens*, p. 380.

9   John Calvin, *Institutes of the Christian Religion*, 1536, book III, chapter 21.

10 *Deuteronomy*, 7:16.

11 Ibid., 7:10.

12 A critique of the potentially paradoxical nature of Calvinist belief and its conundrums is offered in a most original manner by James Hogg in his 1824 novel *The Private Memoirs and Confessions of a Justified Sinner*.

13 Guildhall Library, MS 4655/9, fos. 12, pp. 37–8; Catherine Swindlehurst, 'An Unruly and Presumptuous Rabble', in Vigne and Littleton eds., *From Strangers to Citizens*, pp. 368–9.

14 George, *London Life in the Eighteenth Century*, Kegan Paul, Trench, 1925, pp. 184–5.

[15] See *Money, Power and Print: Interdisciplinary Studies on the Financial Revolution in the British Isles*, eds. Charles Ivar McGrath and Christopher J. Fauske, Associated University Press, 2008, p. 169; *The Gentleman's Magazine*, vol. 29, June 1759, p. 6; *The London Magazine, Or Gentleman's Monthly Intelligencer*, vol. 28, 1759, p. 416.

[16] Natalie Rothstein, *Spitalfields Silk*, V&A, HMSO, 1975, p. 2.

[17] *Survey of London*, vol. XXVII, pp. 186, 217.

[18] Daniel Defoe, *A Brief State of the Question Between the Printed and Painted Callicoes and the Woollen and Silk Manufacture, As far as it relates to the Wearing and Using of Printed and Painted Callicoes in Great Britain*, Boreham, 1719, pp. 42–3.

[19] Much information from George, *London Life in the Eighteenth Century*, pp. 177–8. See also: Anne J. Kershen, *Strangers, Aliens and Asians: Huguenots, Jews and Bangladeshis in Spitalfields, 1660-2000*, Routledge, 2005, Chapter 7, for a very good description of the working of the eighteenth-century silk industry and on the Ogiers, pp. 168–72; Natalie Rothstein, 'Silk in the Early Modern Period' in David Jenkins ed., *The Cambridge History of Western Textiles*, 2003, pp. 554–5.

[20] In the National Art Library at the Victoria and Albert Museum, London.

[21] Susan Hare, *Paul de Lamerie: At the Sign of the Golden Ball*, 1990, p. 9. Exhibition catalogue, Goldsmiths' Hall.

[22] Lucy Inglis, *Georgian London: Into the Streets*, Viking, 2013, p. 171.

[23] V&A M.9–1956. From 1723 to 1728 de Lamerie was in partnership with Ellis Gamble, the silver engraver who had been Hogarth's master.

[24] In the case de Lamerie is referred to as Delamirie: Armory v Delamirie [1722] EWHC KB J 94, 31 July 1722.

8: 'Built New from the Ground'

[1] In *A Journal of the Plague Year*, published in 1722, Defoe states that 'the upper end of Hand Alley, in Bishopsgate street . . . was then a green field.' See F. Bastian, *Defoe's Early Life*, Palgrave Macmillan, 1981, and Ogilby and Morgan's map of 1676 for the location of 'Hand Alley'. The 'long streets' were Duke, Steward and Gun Streets and the 'Spittle-yard-back-Gate' was where Spital Square – an expansion of Spital Yard – had been in gradual course of creation from c.1700.

[2] If its floral name is anything to go by 'Primrose Street', on the west side of Bishopsgate and now entirely lost, could also have been built by the Tillard family, although the ground on which it stood was not part of its estate nor part of the Liberty of Norton Folgate. To judge from Rocque's map 'Primrose

Street' was a visually exciting space. Accessed at each end by narrow streets, it was exceptionally broad and so must have felt like a square – indeed rather like a western counterpart to Spital Square, which stood opposite, on the east side of Bishopsgate.

3   *Survey of London*, vol. XXVII, Spitalfields and Mile End New Town, ed. F. H. W. Sheppard, LCC, 1957, pp. 54–5.

4   Daniel Defoe, *A Brief State of the Question Between the Printed and Painted Callicoes and the Woollen and Silk Manufacture . . .*, Boreham, 1719, p. 5; *The Complete English Tradesman* [1726], Alan Sutton, 1987, p. 224.

5   Isaac Tillard also made minor purchases later, such as the former monastic Candle House and the Brick House in Spital Yard in 1719: see *Survey of London*, vol. XXVII, p. 47.

6   *Survey of London*, vol. XXVII, p. 54.

7   National Archives, Prob. 11/609.

8   *A Survey of the Cities of London and Westminster, Borough of Southwark and parts adjacent*: 'The whole being an improvement of Mr Stow's and others surveys by adding whatever alterations have happened in the said cities . . .' (vol. II, book VI, J. Read, 1735, pp. 729–30).

9   *Survey of London*, vol. XXVII, pp. 59–60.

10   Ibid., pp. 215–16.

11   Clare Browne, 'Lekeux, Peter (1648–1723), Peter Lekeux (*bap.* 1684, *d.* 1743); Peter Lekeux (1716–1768)': *Oxford Dictionary of National Biography*, Oxford University Press, 2004; online edn, Jan 2008 (pp. 295–6 in published edn).

12   *From Strangers to Citizens: The Integration of Immigrant Communities in Britain, Ireland and Colonial America, 1550–1750*, eds. Randolph Vigne and Charles Littleton, Sussex Academic Press/Huguenot Society, 2001. See chapter 'Huguenot Master Weavers: Exemplary Englishmen, 1700–1750', Natalie Rothstein, p. 165.

13   *Survey of London*, vol. XXVII, p. 217.

14   Victoria County History, *Middlesex*, vol. XI, Stepney and Bethnal Green, ed. T. F. T. Baker, 1998, pp. 103–9.

15   Peter Guillery, *The Small House in Eighteenth-Century London: A Social and Architectural History*, Yale University Press, 2004, pp. 83, 90, 92–3.

16   Victoria County History, *Middlesex*, vol. XI, Stepney and Bethnal Green, pp. 103–9.

17   Guillery, *The Small House*, pp. 102–3.

18   Ibid., p. 100; National Archives, Kew, Prob. 3/34/36.

19   Other early houses, most incorporating weavers' workshops, to survive on the

Red Cow Estate are: 97–9 Sclater Street; 149 Brick Lane; and 122, 130–8 Bethnal Green Road. See Guillery, *The Small House*, pp. 98–107.

20 Ibid., pp. 78, 107, 113.

21 Ibid., p. 108.

22 Ibid., p. 106.

23 Ibid., p. 103.

24 Victoria County History, *Middlesex*, vol. XI, Stepney and Bethnal Green, pp. 103–9.

25 Peter Guillery, *The Small House*, pp. 96, 112.

26 *The Carpenters' Company Broadsheet and Report to the Livery*, no. 52, July 2015, p. 11.

27 Victoria County History, *Middlesex*, vol. XI, Stepney and Bethnal Green, pp. 103–9.

28 Victoria County History, *Middlesex*, vol. XI, Stepney and Bethnal Green, pp. 155–68.

29 Ibid., pp. 103–9. (See Horwood's map of 1799 where Mount Street is not shown and the edition of 1819 where it is.)

30 Peter Guillery, *The Small House*, pp. 92, 238.

31 Perhaps some early fabric remains in a few Byde Estate buildings on Redchurch Street. For example number 34, the Owl and Pussy Cat public house, retains some early panelling and one perhaps late-seventeenth-century corbelled fire surround.

32 Peter Guillery, *The Small House*, pp. 92, 99.

33 *Survey of London*, vol. XXVII, pp. 238–9, 277–80.

34 Ibid., pp. 237–9.

35 Victoria County History, *Middlesex*, vol. XI, pp. 103–9.

36 Peter Guillery, *The Small House*, p. 112.

37 *Survey of London*, vol. XXVII, pp. 145–7, 243.

38 *Records of the Honourable Society of Lincoln's Inn*, vol. I, 1896, p. 358. He lodged in 1712 'at one Mr Brawnes . . . a Haberdashers in Chancery Lane' (Lambeth Palace Library, *Records of the Commissioners for Building 50 New Churches, Papers*, Christ Church, box II, no. 10).

39 London Metropolitan Archives (LMA), *Tower Hamlets Commissioners of Sewers Minutes 1729–32*.

40 *Register of Admissions to the Middle Temple*, vol. I, 1949, p.257.

41 Thomas Cromwell, *History and Description of the Parish of Clerkenwell*, Longman, 1828, p. 144.

42 *Survey of London*, vol. XXVII, p. 178.

43 *London Gazette*, 5 October 1745.

44 Hertfordshire County Record Office, deed of Mr Hugh Crallan, 10–11 September 1718.

45 *Survey of London*, vol. XXVII, pp. 182–3, 186; Howard Colvin, *A Biographical Dictionary of British Architects, 1600–1840*, John Murray, 1978, p. 917.

46 *Survey of London*, vol. XXVII, p. 152.

47 Ibid., p. 190.

48 Middlesex Land Register, 1719/3/36-7; *Survey of London*, vol. XXVII, p. 191.

49 *Survey of London*, vol. XXVII, p. 184.

50 Colvin, *Biographical Dictionary of British Architects*, pp. 661–2.

51 Phipps seems to have been working under the design control of Worrall, who acquired from Wood and Michell the freehold of the land rather than, as was then usual, the leasehold.

52 *Survey of London*, vol. XXVII, p. 79. A slightly earlier example of the use of segmental arched windows is the pair of houses, now numbered 19–21 Folgate Street, which were built on the Tillard Estate under a lease dated February 1722/3 by Daniel Le Seur of Spitalfields, a goldsmith.

53 *Survey of London*, vol. XXVII, pp. 205, 208.

54 As expressed by Sir John Vanbrugh, one of the 1711 Commissioners for the Fifty New Churches. See 'Introduction' in *The Commissions For Building Fifty New Churches: The Minute Books, 1711–27, A Calendar*, ed. M. H. Port, London Record Society, 1986, pp. ix–xxxiii.

55 Robert Seymour, *Survey of London*, vol. II, book VI, J. Read, 1735, p. 729.

56 James Ralph, *Critical Review of the Public Buildings . . . in and about London and Westminster*, C. Ackers, 1734, p. 115.

9: Houses and People

1 See Ogilby and Morgan's maps of 1676 and 1681–2.

2 Book of Numbers, 21:7–9.

3 This seems to have been a vernacular detail on the Tillard Estate. The front doors of the lost houses in Spital Square were also reached via flights of steps, as is the case with the surviving 1740s house at 37 Spital Square. The most dramatic external staircase leading to a front door survived until recently, set parallel to the front elevation of the 1730s number 5 White's Row. Very unfortunately this staircase – an important and unique survival in Spitalfields – was, despite numerous protests, destroyed in 2012.

4 *Survey of London*, vol. XXVII: Spitalfields and Mile End New Town, ed.

F. H. W. Sheppard, LCC, 1957, p. 81; Middlesex Land Registry [London Metropolitan Archive], 1724/5/67.

5   *Survey of London*, vol. XXVII, p. 82. The second block to be built comprised what became 14–22 Elder Street on a site granted by the Tillard Estate to Thomas Bunce in May 1724. Number 16 was remarkable, with wide weavers' windows on its second and third floors, suggesting that Elder Street was at this time envisioned as a more humble street, rather than as a street for master weavers' houses as it soon became. This group was demolished in the early 1970s.

6   Ibid., pp. 78–9, 82.

7   Ibid., p. 79.

8   Andrew Saint, 'Street-Mews-Street', *The Georgian Group Journal*, vol. XXIV, 2016, pp. 23–34.

9   The correlation of sill heights between 19, 21 and 23 Elder Street is particularly striking.

10   Conversations with the author in mid 2015.

11   *Survey of London*, vol. XXVII, p. 81; Guildhall Library, MS 2087.

12   For 1767 see MR/PLT/5578.

13   This became 29 Folgate Street, which was demolished at some time in the 1960s, but is illustrated in *Survey of London*, plate 61b.

14   *Proceedings of the Old Bailey*, t17650522-2.

15   London Metropolitan Archives, MJ/SP/1760/05/028.

16   London Metropolitan Archives, MJ/SP/1771/02/004.

17   *Proceedings of the Old Bailey*, t17710220-27.

18   Norton Folgate minute books, record of 1759 Act (191), Tower Hamlets Bancroft Road History Library. See Mark Girouard, in *The Saving of Spitalfields*, Spitalfields Trust, 1989, pp. 35–48, for a detailed account of local government in the parish of Christ Church during the eighteenth century.

19   *Survey of London*, vol. XXVII, p. 84; Middlesex Land Registry, 1725/5/464; 1727/5/404; 1727/2/132.

20   Dan Cruickshank and Neil Burton, *Life in the Georgian City*, Viking, 1990, p. 210.

21   The 1759 Land Tax makes it clear that Thomas Taylor was head tenant of what is now 28 Elder Street and Miles Burkitt of what is now 30 Elder Street; LMA BPS450150439.

22   RSA. B. 57. *Kent's Directory* of 1777 lists 'Isaac Martell, Weaver' in Elder Street, but confusingly places him in number 16 (modern 9/11) rather than in the Martell family home of 5 (originally 14) Elder Street. But this might have been a mistake because the Land Tax assessment of 1780 suggests that he

occupied 5 Elder Street, and he was still in residence in 1785, according to the assessment of that year.

23 Middlesex Land Registry, 1741/2/341. The 1767 Land Tax returns confirm that James Payton and his brother John were still paying tax – £1.4.0 – on two houses in Elder Street. Other contemporary documents make it clear the Paytons were in Elder Street well before 1759. *The Universal Director . . . by Mr Mortimer* suggests that John Payton was in Elder Street by 1741.

24 Middlesex Land Registry, 1745/1/91. Although almost certainly in Elder Street in 1741, John Payton was seemingly not in number 17 because this house, according to the 1743 Land Tax returns, appears to have been occupied by a William Flemming. However the Middlesex Land Register of 1745 confirms that John Payton was by then living in what is now 17 Elder Street.

25 *Survey of London*, vol. XXVII, p. 85.

26 *London Gazette*, 5 October 1745.

27 In the Prerogative Court of Canterbury, 1770 2531509.

28 During repairs in the late 1970s an early – probably original – decorative paint scheme on the panelling was discovered. It was painted with trompe l'oeil representations of more conventional early-eighteenth-century panelling, showing a lower plinth panel and dado rail, with tall panelling above: a trifle naive perhaps, but playful and executed with relaxed charm. The scheme has since been overpainted. See Cruickshank and Burton, *Life in the Georgian City*, p. 156.

29 Or did before the current cycle of adaptation and extension of Spitalfields houses got under way in the 1980s.

30 Cruickshank and Burton, *Life in the Georgian City*, pp. 218–19.

31 Ibid., p. 219.

32 The wages are specified in the *Gazetteer and Daily Advertiser*, 14 March 1765. *The Parents Director* of 1761 states that 'the best hands among the journeymen' were 'seldom able to get above 15s. a week'. As M. Dorothy George observes of the early 1760s, 'even highly skilled brocade weavers could not expect to earn above 20s a week. And this was at a time of great prosperity.' (*London Life in the Eighteenth Century*, Kegan Paul, Trench, 1925, p. 179.)

33 See Kirstin Olsen, *Daily Life in Eighteenth-Century England*, Greenwood, 1999, pp. 140–50.

34 Tower Hamlets Local History Library and Archives, L/ASP/E/1/62; 5605.

35 *Proceedings of the Old Bailey*, t18090412-43.

36 London Metropolitan Archives, WACW16652390675.

37 London Metropolitan Archives, CLC/B/192/F/001/MS 11936/444/816112 5/5.

38 London Metropolitan Archives, CLC/B/192/F/001/MS11936/467/9088/16.

39 London Metropolitan Archives, CLC/B/192/F/001/MS 11936/427/743605.

40 *Survey of London*, vol. XXVII, p. 85: '13 was occupied in 1812–13 by John Wallen . . . and in 1836 and 1851 was used as a girls' school.'

41 Howard Colvin, *A Biographical Dictionary of British Architects, 1600–1840*, John Murray, 1978, pp. 862–3.

42 *Survey of London*, vol. XXVII, p. 84.

43 As suggested by the 1812 Land Tax assessment. Steel's occupation of 18 and trade are confirmed by *Pigot and Co.'s London & Provincial Commercial Directory for 1828–29*, which lists among Painters, Plumbers and Glaziers . . . 'Jos. Steel, 18 Elder Street, Norton falgate'.

44 The Land Tax assessment for 1828 records that Troake in 19/20 and Steel in 15/18 were still in occupation, along with the Symonds family in 5/14 – suggesting a continuity of occupation for a number of the houses in the street, in which families were probably living in fairly comfortable circumstances. Jos. Steel's occupation of 15/18 Elder Street is confirmed by *Robson's London Street Key, or District Register* of 1831, but by 1836 it seems that Steel had left 18 (or was no longer working as a painter) for he is not listed in *Pigot and Co.'s . . . Commercial Directory*.

10: Spitalfields' Dark Underbelly

1 Lindsey German and John Rees, *A People's History of London*, Verso, 2012, pp. 70–1.

2 Calendar of State Papers, Venice 1673–5, p. 449, 30 August, 1675. See also Tim Harris, *London Crowds in the Reign of Charles II: Propaganda and Politics from the Restoration until the Exclusion Crisis*, Cambridge University Press, 1987, pp. 138, 201.

3 Part of the worry was due to the large, violent and religiously motivated 'Bawdy House Riots' of 1668. Dissenters – outraged that in 1664 the king and government had outlawed Conventicles (nonconformist places of worship) while taking no action against the huge number of brothels in the City – ransacked and destroyed 'bawdy houses' and assaulted prostitutes. The rioters were regimented, marching behind colours, and the authorities were exposed as virtually powerless. 'Bawdy Houses' in Moorfields and one in Shoreditch – near St Leonard's Church – fell victims to the godly mob. Samuel Pepys in a diary entry for 25 March 1668 noted that 'the guards and militia of the town have been in armes all this night . . . and the 'prentices [as Pepys termed the rioters] have made fools of them . . . Some blood hath been spilt, but a great many houses pulled down.'

Pepys also recorded that many rioters, perhaps led by Puritan former soldiers of Cromwell's army, claimed they 'did ill in contenting themselves in pulling down the little bawdy-houses, and didn't go and pull down the great bawdy-house at White Hall.' The authorities saw the riots as at least anti-monarchical and so their eventual response was ferocious. Fifteen 'ringleaders' were tried for high treason, of whom four were hanged, drawn and quartered. See Tim Harris, *The Historical Journal*, Cambridge University Press, vol. 29, 3 September 1986, pp. 537–56.

4　M. Dorothy George, *London Life in the Eighteenth Century*, Kegan Paul, Trench, 1925, p. 187.

5　Peter Linebaugh, *The London Hanged: Crime and Civil Society in the Eighteenth Century*, Allen Lane, 1991, pp. 19–20.

6　Robert O. Bucholz and Joseph P. Ward, *London: A Social and Cultural History, 1550–1750*, Cambridge University Press, 2012, p. 276, and *The Weekly Journal or Saturday Post*, 7 May 1720; Linebaugh, *The London Hanged*, p. 20.

7　See the *Weekly Journal*, 20 June 1719, and Victoria County History, *Middlesex*, vol. II, General, ed. W. Page, 1911, pp. 132–7.

8　*A Further examination of the Weavers' Pretences . . .*, 1719, p. 13; George, *London Life in the Eighteenth Century*, p. 180.

9　London, 1721 British Library: 164. 1. 31.

10　7 Geo. I, c.7.

11　Bucholz and Ward, *London: A Social and Cultural History*, p. 276.

12　Daniel Defoe, *A Brief State of the Question Between the Printed and Painted Callicoes and the Woollen and Silk Manufacture, As far as it relates to the Wearing and Using of Printed and Painted Callicoes in Great Britain*, Boreham, 1719, pp. 3, 4, 6, 9–13, 42–3.

13　Bucholz and Ward, *London: A Social and Cultural History*, p. 276.

14　Jonathan Bardon, *A History of Ulster*, Blackstaff Press, 1997, pp. 167–8.

15　Ibid., p. 168.

16　Ibid.

17　Ibid., pp. 168–9.

18　Ibid., p. 169.

19　Ibid., p. 170.

20　Ibid.

21　Ibid.

22　Quoted in George, *London Life in the Eighteenth Century*, p. 111.

23　*Survey of London*, vol. XXVII: Spitalfields and Mile End New Town, ed. F. H. W. Sheppard, LCC, 1957, pp. 270–1.

[24] In *Colonel Jack*, a novel of 1722 by Daniel Defoe, the pauper hero 'went to a boyling house . . . and got a Mess of Broth, and a piece of Bread. Price a Half penny.'

[25] George, *London Life in the Eighteenth Century*, pp. 113–14.

[26] Printed for C. Peterson, 'Near St James's, London', 1736. British Library: 515.I.2. (236).

[27] A report in the *Daily Journal* for Monday 2 August 1736 (issue 5753) records that a mob of Englishmen assembled to attack Irish pubs and houses in Whitechapel on 'Friday night last' (30 July) and were eventually put down by a party of Grenadiers. I am grateful to Jo Maddocks at the British Library for this reference.

[28] George, *London Life in the Eighteenth Century*, p. 117.

[29] The violent anti-Catholic feelings in London revealed by the Gordon Riots of 1780 were, arguably, an expression of a long-held prejudice against the Catholic Irish in particular. George concludes, in *London Life in the Eighteenth Century*, that the 'Irish were a disturbing element in London life [whose] low standards of life and their increasing numbers lowered the wages of casual and unskilled labour' and whose 'customs . . . were peculiarly unfortunate . . . from a sanitary point of view', pp. 118–19, 123–4.

[30] Cutting in Bishopsgate Institute, in Spital Square file 515.i. [236].

[31] Derek Morris, *Whitechapel, 1600–1800*, the East London History Society, 2011, p. 69; and George, *London Life in the Eighteenth Century*, p. 179.

[32] Dan Cruickshank and Neil Burton, *Life in the Georgian City*, Viking, 1990, pp. 121–2.

[33] George, *London Life in the Eighteenth Century*, p. 188.

[34] Peter Guillery, *The Small House in Eighteenth-Century London*, Yale University Press, 2004, p. 87.

[35] See *Gentleman's Magazine*, xxxiii, pp. 514–15; Victoria County History, *Middlesex*, vol. II, pp. 132–7. The house attached probably belonged to master weaver Lewis Chauvet.

[36] Roland Thorne, 'Ellis, Welbore, 1st Baron Mendip (1713–1802)', *Oxford Dictionary of National Biography*, Oxford University Press, 2004; online edn Jan. 2008.

[37] *A Letter from A Spitalfields Weaver, to a Noble Duke*, 1765, British Library, 8276 cc 12.

[38] Ibid., pp. 6–9.

[39] Ibid., pp. 11–12.

[40] *Institute of Historical Research, Journal of the Board of Trade*, vol. XII, January 1764 to December 1767, ed. H. Ledward, 1936, pp. 132–44.

41 Victoria County History, *Middlesex*, vol. II, pp. 132–7.
42 G. Rudé, *The Crowd in History, 1730–1848*, Lawrence & Wishart, 1981, p. 76; German and Rees, *A People's History of London*, pp. 70–1.
43 Linebaugh, *The London Hanged*, p. 271.
44 Dan Cruickshank, *The Secret History of Georgian London*, Random House, 2010, p. 529; and Bucholz and Ward, *London: A Social and Cultural History*, p. 276.
45 The Shelburne Papers, University of Michigan, quoted Guillery, *The Small House*, pp. 87–8, and Linebaugh, *The London Hanged*, p. 274.
46 Linebaugh, *The London Hanged*, pp. 19–20.
47 *Proceedings of the Old Bailey*, t17691018-22.
48 Ibid., t17691018-38.
49 Ibid., t17691018-31.
50 Ibid., s17691018-1.
51 *The Gentleman's Magazine*, vol. 39, 1769, p. 611; *The Oxford Magazine, or Universal Museum*, vol. 3, 1769, pp. 241–5.
52 Linebaugh, *The London Hanged*, pp. 280–1; German and Rees, *A People's History of London*, pp. 71–3.
53 'Eyre, Sir James, 1734–99', *Oxford Dictionary of National Biography*.
54 Ibid.
55 Michael T. Davis, 'Tooke, John Horne (1736–1812)', *Oxford Dictionary of National Biography*, Oxford University Press, 2004; online edn Oct. 2009.
56 *Proceedings of the Old Bailey*, t17691206-34.
57 Ibid., t17691206-31.
58 Ibid.
59 Ibid., t17710703-59.
60 Linebaugh, *The London Hanged*, pp. 280–3.
61 *Proceedings of the Old Bailey*, t17710703-59.
62 Ibid., t17501205-60.
63 Ibid., t17710703-59.
64 Victoria County History, *Middlesex*, vol. XI, Stepney and Bethnal Green, ed. T. F. T. Baker, 1998, p. 178; G. F. Vale, *Old Bethnal Green*, Blythenhale Press, 1934, pp. 36–7.
65 *Proceedings of the Old Bailey*, t17710703-2.
66 German and Rees, *A People's History of London*, pp. 71–3.

11: Radicals and Enthusiasts

1 Joseph Priestley, *Letters to the Right Honourable Edmund Burke occasioned by*

Reflections on the Revolution in France etc.,Thomas Pearson, 1791. Letter XIII: 'Of the Prospect of the General Enlargement of Liberty, civil and religious, opened by the Revolution in France'. Priestley's stirring letters were in response to Burke's *Reflections on the Revolution in France*, published in November 1790, which was a conservative text highly critical of the revolution and its consequences.

2 Book VI, lines 681–5.

3 *The Dispatches and Letters of Vice Admiral Lord Viscount Nelson (1774–1794)*, ed. Nicholas Harris Nicolas, vol. 1, Henry Colburn, 1844, pp. 292–5.

4 *The Autobiography of Francis Place*, ed. Mary Thale, Cambridge University Press, 1972.

5 Tom Pocock, *Horatio Nelson*, Bodley Head, 1987, pp. 137–8.

6 See 'Committee of Secrecy', House of Commons Reports of 1794 and 1799; *Journal of the House of Commons*, 1 January 1803, vol. 49, p. 64. And see Arthur E. Sutherland Jr., 'British Trials for Disloyal Association During the French Revolution', *Cornell Law Review*, vol. 34, issue 3, 1949, pp. 303–30, for additional information about the LCS, the circumstances in which the toasts were given and comparable political associations including the aristocratic and learned Society for Promoting Constitutional Information, founded in 1780; the Whig Society of Friends of the People; the London Revolutionary Society organised by Dissenters; and the British Convention of the Delegates of the Friends of the People Associated to obtain Universal Suffrage and Annual Parliaments, founded in Edinburgh in autumn 1793.

7 National Archives, Kew, PC1/44/158.

8 *Selections from the Papers of the London Corresponding Society, 1792–99*, ed. Mary Thale, Cambridge University Press, 1983.

9 National Archives, Kew, PC1/23/28, PC1/41/138, PC1/21/35A, TS11/993, KB33/6/1.

10 Sutherland, 'British Trials for Disloyal Association', pp. 328–9.

11 See also Joseph Gurney, *The Trial of James O'Coigly*, M. Gurney, 1798.

12 PRO/PC1/23/38: Names and addresses of members of LCS's 25th Division as of 20 February 1794: Geo. Bowden, 49 Wheeler Street; John Bowden, King Street; Edward Jones, Ball Alley; Jn. Davenport, 170 Brick Lane; Tho. May, Wheeler Street; John Pierce, Brick Lane; Wm. Jervis, 26 Great Pearl Street; Wm. Moody, Phoenix Street; Jn. Jervis, Great Pearl Street; Jos. Butler, 6 Fleur de Lis Ct.; Wm. Cooper, 150 Brick Lane; Tho. Sanders, 14 Elder Street, Shoreditch; George Vapeur, 130 Brick Lane; Sam. Breilet, 2 Maidenhead Ct.; Elias Fletcher, Maidenhead Court; Rob. Winter, Brick Lane; Dan. Reynolds,

7 Quaker Street; Peter Bayley, 12 White's Row; Andrew Lanker, 7 Grey Eagle Street; Joshua Price, 28 Norton Falgate; Thomas Mackey, 3 Smock Alley; Jn. Wyllie, 7 Smock Alley; David Daniel, Duke's Head, Norton Falgate.

13 Certain French traditions seem to have lingered into the early nineteenth century. The antiquarian John Williams, giving evidence in the late 1830s to the Parliamentary Commission on Hand-loom Weavers, stated that: '... within the memory of persons now living ... religious rites were performed' in French, and recalled that 'I have heard French sung in the streets, [t]here might be half a dozen French public houses [and] conversation in the street was often in French.' He also said that 'The church in Church-street [Fournier Street] ceased to be French in 1809, and in St. John-street Bethnal Green, some few years later, and that was the last.' (Vol. 23, pp. 215–16.)

14 *The Trial of Thomas Breillat for Seditious Words. Before Mr Mainwaring, at the Sessions-house, Clerkenwell-Green, December 6, 1793. Taken in short-hand by Mr Ramsay.* Printed for the defendant, 1794. Copy in the National Archives, Kew.

15 See *The Genuine Trial of Thomas Hardy for High Treason, at the Sessions House in the Old Bailey from October 28 to November 5 1794*, Jordan, 2nd edn, 1795.

16 'Eyre, Sir James', *Oxford Dictionary of National Biography*, Oxford University Press, 2004; online edn Jan. 2008.

17 See Robin Veder, 'Flowers in the Slums: Weavers' Floristry in the Age of Spitalfields' Decline', *Journal of Victorian Culture*, 14, 2, 2009, pp. 261–81.

18 John Thelwall, 'On the Causes of the Late Disturbances', *Tribune*, 30, 23 September 1795, pp. 317–18, a 'periodical publication consisting chiefly of the political writings of John Thelwall'; Veder, 'Flowers in the Slums'.

19 See Veder, 'Flowers in the Slums'; Claudius Loudon, *Encyclopaedia of Gardening*, Longman & etc., 1822, p. 95.

20 Veder, 'Flowers in the Slums', pp. 261–81.

21 Edward Church interviewed by James Mitchell in 'Report of J. Mitchell, Esq., LL.D., on "The East of England"', House of Commons Parliamentary Commission on Hand-loom Weavers, Parliamentary Sessional Paper, 43 (1), 1840, vol. XXIII, part 2, p. 216. Mitchell writes: 'There was a Floricultural Society ... they passed their leisure hours, and generally the whole family dined on Sundays at the little gardens in the environs of London, now mostly built upon, in small rooms ... with a fire-place at the end.' The Commission was set up in 1837 to inquire into unemployment and poverty in Britain's weaving industry. A number of reports were produced by 1841.

22 William Tallack, *Peter Bedford: The Spitalfields Philanthropist*, Partridge, 1865, p. 13.

23 'Dwellings of the Poor in Bethnal-Green', *Illustrated London News*, 24 October 1863.

24 Mitchell, 'Report . . . on "The East of England"', p. 218.

25 Ibid.

26 Veder, 'Flowers in the Slums', quoting John Gray in 1839 from Theodore Compton, *Recollections of Spitalfields: An Honest Man and his Employers, being an extension of the Memoir of John Gray, originally published in 1839*, Edward Hicks, Jr., 1894, pp. 8–90.

27 Veder, 'Flowers in the Slums'; House of Commons Parliamentary Commission on Hand-loom Weavers, vol. XXIV, appendix to report, p. 69: William Bresson examined by Mr Hickson, 14 July 1838.

28 Henry Mayhew, 'The Spitalfields Silk-Weavers, Letter II, 23 October 1849' (1889), republished in *The Unknown Mayhew: Selections from the Morning Chronicle, 1849–1850*, eds E. P. Thompson and Eileen Yeo, Penguin, 1984, pp. 127, 128.

29 Dr Hector Gavin, *Sanitary Ramblings*, 1848, pp. 11–12.

30 Isaac Taylor, 'Memorials of the Huguenot Colony in Spitalfields and Bethnal Green', *Golden Hours*, 1 April 1869, p. 264.

31 Veder, 'Flowers in the Slums'; F. H. S., 'Hints for the Improvement of Florists' Flowers', *The Annals of Horticulture*, 1, 4, April 1846, p. 180; 'Culture of the Auricula', *Paxton's Magazine of Botany and Register of Flowering Plants*, 1, 1, January 1834, pp. 9–12.

32 House of Commons Parliamentary Commission on Hand-loom Weavers, notes and observations made during a tour through the weaving districts by W. E. Hickson, vol. XXIV, 1840, p. 10.

33 Veder, 'Flowers in the Slums'; Charles Knight, ed., *London*, Virtue & Co., 1841–4.

34 Henry Mayhew, *London Labour and the London Poor*, vol. I, Griffin, Bohn & Co., 1861, pp. 132, 138.

35 Veder, 'Flowers in the Slums'; E. P. Thompson, *The Making of the English Working Class*, Pantheon Books, 1963, pp. 143, 291–2.

36 Victoria County History, *Middlesex*, vol. II, General, ed. W. Page, 1911, pp. 132–7.

37 Augustus Hare, *Walks in London*, vol. I, Dalby, Isbister & Co., 1878, pp. 315–16.

38 See Deborah Kraak, 'Eighteenth-Century English Floral Silks', *The Magazine Antiques*, 153, 6 June 1998, pp. 847, 843–9, quoted in Veder, 'Flowers in the Slums'. See also Robin D. Gwynn, *Huguenot Heritage: The History and*

Contribution of the Huguenots in Britain, Sussex Academic Press, 2000, pp. 60–71; Nathalie Rothstein, *Silk Designs of the Eighteenth Century in the Collection of the Victoria and Albert Museum*, Bullfinch Press, 1990, pp. 18–20; J. F. Flanagan, *Spitalfields Silks of the Eighteenth and Nineteenth Centuries*, F. Lewis, 1954, pp. 19–20; Margaret Cox, *Life and Death in Spitalfields, 1700–1850*, Council for British Archaeology, 1996, pp. 62–6.

39   British Museum, MS 3999.

40   Mitchell, 'Report . . . on "The East of England"'.

41   Peter Guillery, *The Small House in Eighteenth-Century London*, Yale University Press, 2004, p. 86; N. K. A. Rothstein, 'Huguenots in the English Silk Industry in the Eighteenth Century', in Irene Scouloudi, ed., *Huguenots in Britain and their French Background, 1550–1800*, Macmillan, 1987, p. 136.

42   British Library, Tracts, B. 733 (3), pp. 3–11.

43   J. W. S. Cassels, 'The Spitalfields Mathematical Society', *The Bulletin of the London Mathematical Society*, vol. XI, 1979, pp. 241–58, and Addendum, vol. XII, 1980, p. 343.

44   L. Stewart and P. Weindling, 'Philosophical Threads: Natural Philosophy and Public Experiment among the Weavers of Spitalfields', *British Journal for History and Science*, 28, 1995, pp. 37–62.

45   *Survey of London*, vol. XXVII: Spitalfields and Mile End New Town, ed. F. H. W. Sheppard, LCC, 1957, pp. 269–70.

46   R. A. Sampson, 'The Decade 1840 to 1850', in J. L. E. Dreyer and H. H. Turner, eds, *History of the Royal Astronomical Society*, Royal Astronomical Society, 1923, pp. 83–109.

47   Mitchell, 'Report . . . on "The East of England"', p. 216.

12: People of Spitalfields

1   The Ogier genealogy, from Pierre and Jeanne to William born in 1812, is published as figure 8.4 on p. 127 in Theya Molleson and Margaret Cox, with A. H. Waldron and D. K. Whittaker, *The Spitalfields Project, vol. 2: The Anthropology – The Middling Sort*, Council for British Archaeology, 1993. This family tree plots the issue from the marriages of eldest sons and selected members of the family and so follows the result of the marriage in 1710 of Pierre Ogier's son Pierre or Peter II (1680–1740) to Catherine Rabaud. This couple had nine children and the 'tree' follows two of them. It shows the issue of the marriage of their son Peter III (1711–75) to Elizabeth Gatineau, which resulted in the birth of eight children, and of Peter III's younger brother, Thomas Abraham (1716–70), who in 1740 married Magdeleine Barnard. They had seven children.

Peter III's body was found in the crypt of Christ Church during archaeological explorations in the mid 1980s. His skeleton is catalogued as number 2863.

2   See extracts from the Court Book of the Weavers' Company of London, HSQS XXXIII, p. 77.

3   *The Spitalfields Manufacturers and the Young Pretender, Proceedings of the Huguenot Society*, vol. II, pp. 453–6; *The London Gazette*, 5 October 1745.

4   *Survey of London*, vol. XXVII: Spitalfields and Mile End New Town, ed. F. H. W. Sheppard, LCC, 1957, p. 188.

5   Jonathan Swift, *A Panegyric of the Reverend Dean Swift*, J. Roberts & N. Blandford, 1729–30.

6   The Land Tax returns of 1743 for Christ Church Middlesex (MS/6008/1. [736/8]).

7   The 1719 conveyance of 19 Princelet Street to Worrrall included 30 Hanbury Street, which Worrall had also built. Presumably the joint ownership of these houses continued into Ogier's time (*Survey of London*, vol. XXVII, p. 188).

8   Pilon's will was proved in Essex on 4 May 1762 (Prob11/876 sig. 211).

9   15 Princelet Street had been built in 1718–19 by Samuel Worrall for John Vunmandine, a glazier, who held a lease from the Wood–Michell Estate. In 1720 the lease was assigned to Peter Bourdon. Bourdon's acquisition of the new house might have been an investment but by 1724 it was occupied by Pilon, then married to Bourdon's daughter. London Metropolitan Archive (MLR 1718/2/190-1); (MLR 1720/2/174); (MLR 1719/2/103); *Survey of London*, vol. XXVII, p. 188.

10   Sabatier occupied 16 Princelet Street in 1736 and 16 and 14 in 1750, *Survey of London*, vol. XXVII, p. 186. For details of his business, see *Spitalfields Silks of the Eighteenth and Nineteenth Centuries*, ed. J. F. Flanagan, F. Lewis, 1954, p. 17, and *Survey of London*, vol. XXVII, pp. 186, 216–17.

11   24 Hanbury Street was built in 1717 by Worrall and was one of the first houses constructed on the Wood–Michell Estate.

12   *Survey of London*, vol. XXVII, p. 191.

13   Molleson and Cox, *The Spitalfields Project*, figure 8.4, p. 127.

14   Natalie Rothstein, 'Huguenot Master Weavers: Exemplary Englishmen, 1700–1750', in R. Vigne and C. Littleton, eds, *From Strangers to Citizens: The Integration of Immigrant Communities in Britain, Ireland and Colonial America, 1550–1750*, Sussex Academic Press/Huguenot Society, 2001, p. 167.

15   PROB11/649 sig, 5. The total value of his bequests was £6,880.

16   Dan Cruickshank and Neil Burton, *Life in the Georgian City*, Viking, 1990, pp. 180–9.

17 Analysis of the surviving early paint on the surround suggests that it was originally painted a pale stone, almost cream, and coated with a clear shellac glaze. This lacquer-like finish would have been most fashionable in the 1750s, emphasising the surround's playful Rococo and chinoiserie character. Paint analysis thanks to James Howett.

18 Molleson and Cox, *The Spitalfields Project*, pp. 40–1.

19 Ibid., pp. 98, 127, figure 8.4 showing genealogy of the Ogier family.

20 Rothstein, 'Huguenot Master Weavers', p. 165.

21 Ibid., p. 167.

22 Ibid., p. 162.

23 Bernard de Mandeville, *Fable of the Bees*, 1714 and 1723, p. 208, quoted by Sarah Jordan in *The Anxieties of Idleness: Idleness in Eighteenth-Century British Literature and Culture*, Bucknell University Press, 2003, p. 37.

24 Mary Bayliss, 'The Unsuccessful Andrew and Other Ogiers: A Study of Failure in the Huguenot Community', in R. Vigne and G. Gibbs, eds, *The Strangers' Progress: Integration and Disintegration of the Huguenot and Walloon Refugee Community, 1567–1889*, Proceedings of the Huguenot Society, 26, 1995, pp. 230–40.

25 For background information see Tessa Murdoch, *The Quiet Conquest: Huguenots, 1685–1985*, Museum of London catalogue, 1985.

26 Molleson and Cox, *The Spitalfields Project*, p. 100; Marie Louise Sander, *Traces of our Heritage*, 1986, p. 28; Natalie Rothstein, 'Huguenots in the English Silk Industry in the Eighteenth Century', in Irene Scouloudi, ed., *Huguenots in Britain and their French Background, 1550–1800*, Macmillan, London, 1987.

27 Mary Bayliss, 'The Unsuccessful Andrew'.

28 Information from Mary Bayliss of the Huguenot Society in conversation with the author and from notes on 37 Spital Square by the Society for the Protection of Ancient Buildings, which now occupies the building. These notes are the source for the George Courtauld quote.

29 Much of the information for the story of the Ogiers comes from notes given to the author in the 1980s by Mary Bayliss of the Huguenot Society; from Mary Cox, *Life and Death in Spitalfields, 1700–1850*, Council for British Archaeology, 1996; Molleson and Cox, *The Spitalfields Project*; Ogier family tree by Margaret Cox ibid (Mary Bayliss said of the Cox Ogier family tree, based on pedigrees in the Huguenot Library, that it's 'gappy'); Natalie Rothstein, *Silk Designs in the Eighteenth Century*, Thames & Hudson, 1980, pp. 330–2; Natalie Rothstein, unpublished thesis, 'The Silk Industry in London, 1702–66', University of London, 1961; W. M. Jordan, unpublished thesis, 'The

Silk Industry in London, 1760–1880', University of London, 1931; Henry Kent, *The Directory of Merchants and Other Eminent Traders*, 1736; Mary Bayliss, 'Poor Journeymen: Prevosts and Provosts in London and Leek', *Proceedings of the Huguenot Society*, vol. XXV, no. 4, 1992; Murdoch, *The Quiet Conquest*, Museum of London catalogue with entries by Natalie Rothstein.

30 *Proceedings of the Old Bailey*, t17860426-15.

31 National Archives, HO 107 1542 district 12.

32 *Survey of London*, vol. XXVII, pp. 188–9.

33 Rodinksy's belongings were discovered by the Spitalfields Trust and documented when it bought the house. See Rachel Lichtenstein and Iain Sinclair, *Rodinsky's Room*, Granta, 1999.

13: Spitalfields in Peril

1 Victoria County History, *Middlesex*, vol. II: General, ed. W. Page, 1911, pp. 132–7.

2 Published in the *European Magazine*, 1802, quoted in M. Dorothy George, *London Life in the Eighteenth Century*, Kegan Paul, Trench, 1925, p. 186.

3 George, *London Life in the Eighteenth Century*, p. 187.

4 Ibid.

5 Guildhall Library, ref. MS6008, and thanks to Dr Nick Barratt who worked on the programme in the BBC2 series *House Detectives* that focused on 15 Princelet Street.

6 An Abraham Dupree is listed in the Land Tax assessment of 1743 as being in residence at the north-east end of the street. James Dupree is described in his will of 1829 (FRC, PROB11/1760) as a 'Gentleman' living at Stamford Hill with numerous freehold and leasehold properties near Finsbury Square; in the parish of St Leonard's Shoreditch; in Fort Street, Spitalfields; in Stamford Hill; and in Tottenham High Cross.

7 Edger was certainly resident in the house in 1816 because in that year he is listed in the *Post Office Annual Directory* as trading from or living in 15 Princelet Street, and is also listed in *Johnstone's* directory of 1817 and in *Robson's* directory of 1820, where he appears as 'John Edger, silk manufacturer, at 20 Princes Street'. He appears still to have been in the house in 1822 because he's listed in *Underhill's Triennial* of that year, but to have left by 1823 because he is not listed in that year's edition of *Robson's*.

8 Alfred, Lord Tennyson, *In Memoriam*, written 1833–49, canto 56.

9 Willam Hale, *An Appeal to the Public in Defence of the Spitalfields Act*, E. Justins, 1822.

10 J. H. Clapham, 'The Spitalfields Act, 1773–1824', *Economic Journal*, 20, 1916, p. 470.

11 The letter from 4 Wood Street is now in the Senate House Library, University of London.

12 Noel W. Thompson, *The People's Science: The Popular Economy of Exploitation and Crisis, 1816–1834*, Cambridge University Press, 2002, p. 38.

13 Ibid., p. 11.

14 Hale, *An Appeal to the Public*, p. 13.

15 Ibid., p. 15.

16 Ibid., p. 16.

17 Ibid., p. 22.

18 Ibid., p. 33.

19 Ibid., p. 35.

20 Ibid., p. 42

21 *Observations on the Ruinous tendency of the Spitalfields Act to the silk manufacture of London*, J. & A. Arch, 1822.

22 Ibid., pp. 1–2.

23 Ibid., pp. 5–6.

24 Ibid., p. 2.

25 Ibid., p. 3.

26 Ibid., p. 4.

27 Robin Veder, 'Flowers in the Slums: Weavers, Floristry and the Age of Spitalfields' Decline', *Journal of Victorian Culture*, 2009, pp. 261–81, quotes J. F. Flanagan, introduction, *Spitalfields Silks of the 18th and 19th Centuries*, F. Lewis, 1954, pp. 20–3.

28 Marc W. Steinberg, *Fighting Words: Working-class Formation, Collective Actions and Discourse in Early Nineteenth Century England*, Cornell University Press, 1999, p. 102.

29 See Chapter 12 on the Ogier family.

30 Joseph Merceron was born in about 1764, probably in his family home in Brick Lane, and by 1787 was embroiled in local politics. He realised that crime could pay, and even seem legal, if one appeared to be operating within the system, and accordingly managed to get himself elected (presumably by bribery) to the vestry of Bethnal Green parish (essentially the centre of local government in Bethnal Green), to the post of local tax commissioner and as a Justice of the Peace. It seems he systematically and corruptly abused his powers by rewarding supports with advantageous tax assessments and renewals of public house licences – no doubt for a fee. He then invested his illicit fortune in pubs and

property, which, of course, increased and seemingly legitimised (in modern parlance, 'laundered') his income, and gave him increased power over the Bethnal Green population as employer and landlord. As treasurer of the parish funds, then Merceron was in a position to steal – including those raised to help the poor. This brought him into a bitter confrontation in 1809 with a new and canny rector who eventually persuaded the vestry clerk to give evidence against him. In 1818 Merceron was finally convicted of appropriating £925 of parish funds and imprisoned for eighteen months. Unfortunately, the rector then left the parish (he was possibly threatened by Merceron's out-of-pocket henchmen) and a new and accommodating regime took his place, so business returned pretty much to usual for Merceron after his release: he did not regain his position as a JP, but his supporters did vote him back on to the vestry. When he died in 1839, leaving a staggering fortune of £300,000, he was given a lavish funeral at St Matthew's Bethnal Green. Merceron was the model for later nineteenth- and twentieth-century East End gangsters, including the Kray twins. See W. B. Gurney, *Merceron's Trial for Fraud and Corruption*, W. Wright, 1819, Ian Doolittle, 'Merceron, Joseph (c.1764–1839)', *Oxford Dictionary of National Biography*, Oxford University Press, 2004, and George F. Vale, *Old Bethnal Green*, Blythenhale Press, 1934, pp. 31–4.

[31] Ibid., p. 194.

[32] Report from Assistant Hand-loom Weavers' Commissioner W. Bresson, quoted in the House of Commons Parliamentary Commission on Hand-loom Weavers, appendix to vol. XXIV, 1840, p. 216; George, *London Life in the Eighteenth Century*, p. 192.

[33] 'Report of J. Mitchell, Esq., LL.D., on "The East of England"' for the House of Commons Parliamentary Commission on Hand-loom Weavers, vol. XXIII, p. 216.

[34] Veder, 'Flowers in the Slums', quotes House of Commons Commission on Hand-loom Weavers, vol. XXIII, pp. 219–27, vol. XXIV, pp. 10–11.

[35] Thomas Archer, *The Pauper, the Thief and the Convict*, Groombridge & Sons, 1865, pp. 9–10.

[36] A. K. Sabin, *The Silk Weavers of Spitalfields and Bethnal Green*, Board of Education, 1931, pp. 17–18.

[37] Orange Street ran north from Bethnal Green Road and the smaller Daniel Street ran parallel and to the east of Orange Street, near Florida Street. Bresson's house must have been relatively new in 1838 because Daniel and Orange Streets were not built when Richard Horwood's map of 1819 was published.

[38] Mitchell, 'Report ... on "The East of England"', House of Commons

Parliamentary Commission on Hand-loom Weavers, Parliamentary Sessional Paper, 43 (1), 1840, vol. XXIV, part 2, p. 716, quoted in George, *London Life in the Eighteenth Century*, p. 190; *The Unknown Mayhew: Selections from the Morning Chronicle, 1849–1850*, ed. E. P. Thompson and Eileen Yeo, Penguin, 1984, pp. 125, 127.

39 George, *London Life in the Eighteenth Century*, p. 192.

40 Hale, *An Appeal to the Public*, p. 17.

41 *Unknown Mayhew*, ed. Thompson and Yeo, pp. 125–7.

42 Ibid., pp. 126–7.

43 RG12, piece 265, folio 20, p. 35.

44 *Unknown Mayhew*, ed. Thompson and Yeo, pp. 128–9.

45 Ibid., p. 131.

46 *Unknown Mayhew*, ed. Thompson and Yeo, pp. 132–5.

47 Mayhew got this information from Mitchell, 'Report . . . on "The East of England"', House of Commons Parliamentary Commission on Hand-loom Weavers, Parliamentary Sessional Paper, vol. XXIII, p. 216.

48 The 'depreciation' of the value of wages in the Spitalfields silk industry in the second quarter of the nineteenth century is revealed by Mayhew, who states that the 'average weekly earnings of the operative silk weaver in 1824' at the time of the repeal of the Spitalfields Acts was fourteen shillings and sixpence, but by 1849 only five shillings and sixpence. *The Unknown Mayhew*, ed. Thompson and Yeo, pp. 125–6.

49 Houses then numbered 10, 11, 12, 15, 17, 28, 33, 35 and 41.

50 HO 107, pieces 1542, folio 324, pages 106–13.

51 Peter Guillery, *The Small House in Eighteenth-Century London*, Yale University Press, 2004, p. 98.

52 *Proceedings of the Old Bailey*, t18360509-1137.

53 PROB 11/2122/358.

54 *Johnstone's* trade directory of 1817 notes M. Meadows & Son, Black & Col. Dyers at 12 Princes Street. The house had been built in 1706 when it was occupied by Henry Coates, dyer. See *Survey of London*, vol. XXVII: Spitalfields and Mile End New Town, ed. F. H. W. Sheppard, LCC, 1957, pp. 186–7.

55 *Proceedings of the Old Bailey*, t18160214-39.

56 Kellow Chesney, *Victorian Underworld*, Pelican, 1972, p. 138.

57 Hector Gavin, *Sanitary Ramblings: Being Sketches and Illustrations of Bethnal Green*, Churchill, 1848, pp. 36–9.

58 HO1077, piece 1542, folio 209, p. 10.

59 In the late nineteenth century, number 79 became 74 'Hare Street' and then the

pair became 74 and 76 Cheshire Street. Peter Guillery in *The Small House in Eighteenth-Century London*, p. 83, suggests that 74 had been 57 Hare Street. This is not supported by Horwood's map, while the 1872 OS shows number 57 already obliterated by a massive 'Engine Shed'.

60 *Proceedings of the Old Bailey*, t18501216-245.

61 B351, one, pp. 160–1.

62 'Dwellings of the Poor in Bethnal Green', *Illustrated London News*, 24 October 1863. Anonymous but perhaps written by Thomas Archer.

63 G. Dodd, 'Spitalfields' in Charles Knight, ed., *London*, vol. II, Charles Knight & Co., 1842, pp. 385–400.

64 Archer, *The Pauper, the Thief and the Convict*, pp. 9–10, 17.

65 Ibid., p. 17.

66 Ibid., pp. 18–21.

67 *Household Words*, no. 54, April 1851, p. 30.

14: Soup Kitchens and Body-snatchers

1 The Poor Law authorities in 1834 calculated the total population of Spitalfields and related Liberties and parishes as 64,141, but this can have been no more than an informed estimate; see House of Commons Parliamentary Commission on Hand-loom Weavers, 1840, vol. XXIII, p. 214; William Hale, *A Letter to Samuel Whitbread Esq. containing Observations on the Distresses Peculiar to the Poor of Spitalfields arising from their Local Situation*, Williams & Smith, 1806, n.p.; Anne J. Kershen, *Strangers, Aliens and Asians: Huguenots, Jews and Bangladeshis in Spitalfields, 1660–2000*, Routledge, 2005, pp. 72–3.

2 http://www.workhouses.org.uk/Whitechapel/

3 J. Fayle, *The Spitalfields Genius: The Story of William Allen*, Hodder & Stoughton, 1884.

4 Ibid., pp. 18–19.

5 *Oxford Dictionary of National Biography* states Allen was born in 'Stewart' – meaning Steward – Street, the Old Artillery Ground, Spitalfields, and worked in Plough Court for J. G. Bevan's 'chemical establishment'; 'Allen, William (1770–1843)', Rev. G. F. Bartle, *Oxford Dictionary of National Biography*, Oxford University Press, 2004 [http://www.oxforddnb.com/view/article/392].

6 Fayle, *The Spitalfields Genius*, p. 19.

7 Ibid., pp. 64–5.

8 *Survey of London*, vol. XXVII: Spitalfields and Mile End New Town, ed. F. H. W. Sheppard, LCC, 1957, p. 126.

9 Fayle, *The Spitalfields Genius*, pp. 61–2.

¹⁰ *Survey of London*, vol. XXVII, p. 126.

¹¹ *Illustrated London News*, 9 March 1867, p. 225.

¹² See in the Bishopsgate Institute: Thomas Bernard, *Extract from an Account of a Charity in Spitalfields, for supplying the poor with soup and potatoes*, 1798; *Report of the Committee of the Spitalfields Soup Society for 1811-12*; *The Report of the Spitalfields Association*, 1816.

¹³ *The Philanthropist, or Repository for Hints and Suggestions calculated to Promote the Comfort and Happiness of Man*, vol. II, W. Allen, 1812, pp. 173-97.

¹⁴ Brewing was a significant Spitalfields industry during the eighteenth and early nineteenth centuries. The best surviving set of buildings from one of the smaller breweries are at 3-9 Heneage Street; they include the brewer's house, the brewery 'tap' (now the 'Pride of Spitalfields') and the brewhouse and warehouse. The buildings, arranged around a small courtyard, appear to date from the early nineteenth century. *The London Directory* of 1839 records John Turner, brewer, at what was then 2 Heneage Street, while the 1841 census states that he was a 'brewer employing 6 men', that he was located between 3 and 4 Heneage Street, and that he was aged 63. His house seems to have been that now numbered 5. Turner is not mentioned in *Johnson's Commercial Directory* of 1818 nor is his brewery shown on Horwood's map of 1819, when Heneage Street itself had not been fully laid out. So presumably Turner started his business, and constructed his brewery buildings, between c.1820 and 1839.

¹⁵ M. Dorothy George, *London Life in the Eighteenth Century*, Kegan Paul, Trench, 1925, p. 187.

¹⁶ William Tallack, *Peter Bedford: The Spitalfields Philanthropist*, S. W. Partridge, 1865, p. 26.

¹⁷ Thanks to Philip Carstairs, at pjc46@student.lse.ac.uk, for information on the Ladling Society.

¹⁸ Elizabeth Ray, *Alexis Soyer: Cook Extraordinary*, Southover Press, 1991.

¹⁹ This is identified in the *Survey of London* records as 'an interesting two-storeyed building of uncertain date, timber-framed and weather-boarded', which stood until 1955 and which the *Survey* speculates perhaps originally served 'for a factory or warehouse' (vol. XXVII, p. 219). In fact a survey of the rear structure, dated to March 1951 and now lodged in the London Metropolitan Archives, states that the structure was 'possibly formerly a Stable, Harness Room and Loft over.' (LMA, letters between Secretary of London Dispensary and lawyers, LMA 1951. A/LD/01-02/02/001). Information courtesy of James Howett.

²⁰ National Archives PROB11/649 sig. 5.

21 *Survey of London*, vol. XXVII, p. 219.

22 Minutes of London Dispensary reference number: A/LD/01/01/01.

23 See plans in *Survey of London*, vol. XXVII, p. 219.

24 Bill Luckin, 'Aldis, Charles James Berridge (1808–1872)', *Oxford Dictionary of National Biography*, Oxford University Press, 2004 [http://www.oxforddnb.com/view/article/311].

25 H.O. 107/710/8.

26 R.G. 10/507.

27 Sarah Wise, *The Italian Boy: Murder and Grave-Robbery in 1830s London*, Pimlico, 2005, p. 36.

28 Ibid., p. 31.

29 Ibid.

30 Ibid., pp. 34–6.

31 *Proceedings of the Old Bailey*, t18311201-17.

32 National Archives, HO 12/46 Gq 70; Bodleian Library, Oxford, Ox. Harding, B.9 (III).

33 Wise, *The Italian Boy*, p. 156.

34 Hector Gavin, *Sanitary Rambles*, Leicester University Press, 1971, pp. 9–10.

35 George Godwin, *Town Swamps and Social Change*, 1859, p. 23; Wise, *The Italian Boy*, pp. 280–1.

36 Interview with Baroness Burdett-Coutts, *Strand Magazine*, vol. 7, 1894, p. 248.

37 HRH Princess Mary Adelaide, Duchess of Teck, 'Baroness Burdett-Coutts: A Sketch of Her Public Life and Work', 1893, quoted in Wise, *The Italian Boy*, pp. 281–2.

15: 'A Dismal Squalid District'

1 Old Testament, Psalm 74:19–20.

2 'When we first gazed at the destitution and horrible wretchedness of Spital-fields, our blood ran cold at the sight . . . You traverse street after street . . . and see nothing but the most disgusting, the most beseeching poverty. There are thousands of men and women there who never have known what plenty is, what pure joy is, but are herded together, thieves, prostitutes, robbers and working men, in frightful masses. You meet beggars at every step . . . the streets are crowded by a filthy set of vagabonds [and at night] with wretched women, called in mockery, "women of pleasure" . . . the streets were very low and dirty [and] the odours that greeted us at every step were nauseating.' David W. Bartlett, *What I Saw in London: or, Men and Things in the Great Metropolis*, Derby & Miller, 1852, pp. 19, 39, 111–12, 116.

3   Friedrich Engels, *The Condition of the Working Class in England*, Oxford University Press, 1993, p. 45.

4   Ibid., pp. 41–4.

5   G. Dodd, 'Spitalfields' in Charles Knight, ed., *London*, vol. II, Charles Knight & Co., 1842, pp. 385–400.

6   Gustave Doré and Blanchard Jerrold, *London: A Pilgrimage*, Grant & Co., 1872, pp. 124, 150.

7   Charles Dickens, *Oliver Twist: or, The Parish Boy's Progress*, published in serial form 1837–9, Chapter 19.

8   Charles Dickens, 'Spitalfields', *Household Words*, no. 54, 5 April 1851, pp. 25–30.

9   W. Gasprey, *Tallis's Illustrated London in Commemoration of the Great Exhibition of 1851*, Tallis & Co., 1851, p. 306.

10   *Household Words*, 14 June 1851, pp. 269–70.

11   A fourth volume, written in collaboration with other researchers – Bracebridge Hemyng, John Binny and Andrew Halliday – appeared in 1861. This was more sensational in its approach. It abandoned the interview format, relied more heavily on the use of impressive statistics and dealt with the seemingly exotic lives of 'streetwalkers' (prostitutes), thieves and beggars.

12   *The Unknown Mayhew*, ed. E. P. Thompson and Eileen Yeo, Penguin, 1984, p. 123.

13   Quoted in Alex Atkinson and Ronald Searle's *The Big City, or The New Mayhew*, Perpetua, 1958, pp. 11–12.

14   *Proceedings of the Old Bailey*, t18261026-34.

15   See Sarah Wise, *The Blackest Streets: Life and Death of a Victorian Slum*, Bodley Head, 2008.

16   Old Nichol Street was the first of the east–west streets and is shown on Gascoyne's survey of 1703, when it was called 'Nicolls Street'.

17   Orientation is now confusing because only the north portion of Club Row now survives, the rest having been obliterated in the late nineteenth century for the realignment of Bethnal Green Road.

18   By the time of Horwood's map – 1799–1819 – all the streets in the neighbourhood were spelt Nicols.

19   Victoria County History, *Middlesex*, vol. XI: Stepney, Bethnal Green, ed. T. F. T Baker, 1998, pp. 155–68. Even by the time the Nichol Estate was acquired by Chandos something had already gone seriously wrong with the area. In 1750/1 Henry Fielding, in his capacity as magistrate, visited the streets near Shoreditch church and noted that 'two little houses [that] were emptied' contained 'near seventy Men and Women' whose total funds 'did not amount

to one shilling.' *An Enquiry into the Causes of the Late Increase of Robbers*, A. Miller, 1751, pp. 70–1.

[20] 'Dwellings of the Poor in Bethnal Green', *Illustrated London News*, 24 October 1863.

[21] *Medical Times & Gazette*, 22 September 1866, vol. II, p. 322.

[22] Thomas Archer, *The Pauper, the Thief and the Convict*, Groombridge & Sons, 1865, pp. 21–2.

[23] Ibid., pp. 22–3.

[24] Ibid., pp. 26–7.

[25] *The Builder*, vol. xxi, no. 1082, 31 October 1863.

[26] RG. 9/250.

16: Doing the Lord's Work

[1] Gillian Wagner, *Barnardo*, Weidenfeld & Nicolson, 1979, p. 94.

[2] Created under Acts of Parliament of 1839 and 1840.

[3] Following Acts of Parliament in 1846, 1850 and 1853.

[4] *Survey of London*, vol. XXVII: Spitalfields and Mile End New Town, ed. F. H. W. Sheppard, LCC, 1957, pp. 256–7.

[5] Ibid., pp. 256, 321.

[6] *Household Words*, 14 June 1851, p. 267.

[7] The architects were the City-based Tillot and Chamberlain.

[8] Wesker then went 'to Christ Church Primary [in Brick Lane], where the majority of the children were Jewish . . .' and from which he could see his tenement home in Fashion Street. 'Then the war broke out. My sister went to a good school in Spitalfields, the Central Foundation Girls' School [in Spital Square], which was evacuated to Ely'. London Metropolitan Archives ACC/2712/AJE/03/022-024; interview with Jonathan Sale, *The Independent*, 23 July 2008.

[9] *Survey of London*, vol. XXVII, p. 262.

[10] Wagner, *Barnardo*, p. 53.

[11] Ibid., pp. 49–50.

[12] Ibid., p. 51.

[13] Ibid., p. 45.

[14] Ibid., p. 44.

[15] Ibid., p. 30.

[16] Ibid., p. 44.

[17] Ibid., p, 144.

[18] Ibid., pp. 144–5.

[19] Ibid., p. 112.

[20] Ibid., p. 164.

[21] Ibid., pp. 162–3.

[22] Ibid., p. 168.

[23] Charles Booth, *Life and Labour of the People in London*, Macmillan, 1892, p. 127.

[24] Jack London, *The People of the Abyss*, Macmillan, 1903, Chapter 26.

[25] Wagner, *Barnardo*, pp. 159–60.

[26] Warner's father ran a renowned wallpaper printers in North London, working for William Morris and other Arts and Crafts artists. Until very recently the relationship between Warner and the Bedford Institute was little more than surmise, as was the estimated date of around 1905–12 for the photographs. What was certain was that the Bedford Institute had possession of a number of Warner's photographs of East End street children – originally purchased for a 1912 annual report – twenty-four of which it republished in 1975 in a small book entitled *Spitalfields Nippers*. In 2013 *Spitalfields Life*, a website chronicling past and present life in Spitalfields, investigated *Spitalfields Nippers* and Horace Warner and discovered additional caches of his photographs, including some of Finsbury, seemingly unpublished and lodged in the archives of the Quaker Friends House on Euston Road and in the possession of the Warner family, now living in Norfolk. These photos, taken mostly in 1902, are remarkable. They include not only portraits but also places and a few are captioned to identify location. Crucially they show the wider context in which the *Spitalfields Nippers* portraits were made and the few with captions on them confirm that they were taken in the network of courts and alleys south from Quaker Street to 'Great Pearl Street' and then south of 'Great Pearl Street' to Corbet's Court. The locations south of 'Great Pearl Street' include the claustrophobic Crown Court and Vine Yard – both opening off 'Little Pearl Street'. All these were shown as dark blue or black in Booth's system of street classification.

[27] See Horace Warner, *Spitalfields Nippers*, Spitalfields Life Books, 2014.

[28] Clara M. S. Lowe, *God's Answers: A Record of Miss Annie MacPherson's Work at the Home of Industry, Spitalfields, London, and in Canada* [1882], Echo Library, 2007, pp. 16–17.

[29] Ibid., pp. 18–19.

[30] Ibid., pp. 19–20.

[31] Kenneth Bagnell, *The Little Immigrants: The Orphans Who Came to Canada*, Dundurn Group, 2001, p. 44.

[32] Margaret Humphreys, *Empty Cradles*, Doubleday, 1994.

33　Booth, *Life and Labour of the People in London*, p. 122.

34　Sir Arthur Conan Doyle, 'The Adventure of the Naval Treaty', *Chambers's Edinburgh Journal*, 1893.

35　See William Tallack, *Peter Bedford: The Spitalfields Philanthropist*, S. W. Partridge, 1865.

36　Howard Angus Kennedy, 'London Social Settlements', in *Living London*, ed. George R. Sims, Cassell and Co., 1902.

37　J. A. R. Pimlott, *Toynbee Hall, Fifty Years of Social Progress, 1883–1934*, J. M. Dent, 1935, p. 168; and Asa Briggs and Anne McCartney, *Toynbee Hall: The First Hundred Years*, Routledge & Kegan Paul, 1984, p. 57.

38　Briggs and McCartney, *Toynbee Hall*, p. 59.

39　Warner, *Spitalfields Nippers*, pp. 104–11.

40　*Survey of London*, vol. XXVII, p. 262.

41　Ibid., p. 263.

42　*The Builder*, 23 January 1864, p. 67; *Survey of London*, vol. XXVII, pp. 262–3. Sources for wages: Henry Mayhew, *London Labour and the London Poor*, 1851; *The Unknown Mayhew*, ed. E. P. Thompson and Eileen Yeo, Penguin, 1984, pp. 125–6; A. L. Bowley, *Wages in the United Kingdom in the Nineteenth Century*, Cambridge University Press, 1900; John Burnett, *A History of the Cost of Living*, Penguin, 1969; Lee Jackson, *Dirty Old London: The Victorian Fight Against Filth*, Yale University Press, 2014.

43　James Greenwood, *In Strange Company: Being the experiences of a roving correspondent*, Vizetelly & Co., 1883, p. 158.

44　Jerry White, *Rothschild Buildings: Life in an East End Tenement Block, 1887–1920*, Routledge & Kegan Paul, 1980, p. 7.

45　Mayhew, Binny, et al., *London Labour and the London Poor*, vol. IV, Charles Griffin & Co., 1861, pp. 311–16.

46　Andrew Mearns, *The Bitter Cry of Outcast London*, James Clarke & Co., 1883, pp. 7–11.

47　George R. Sims, *How the Poor Live; and, Horrible London*, Chatto & Windus, 1889, pp. 61–3. Further examples of Wrack discovering the living being compelled to co-exist with the decaying dead are recorded by Sims: at 28 'Church Street', Spitalfields (probably what is now Redchurch Street rather than Fournier Street), Wrack 'found in the second floor front room the dead body of a child which had died of scarlet fever on the 1st of the month. The body was not coffined, and it lay exposed on a table in one corner of the room. The room was occupied as a living and sleeping room by five persons.' The 'smell on entering the room was', noted Wrack, 'most sickening.' The occupants of the room were all members of the dead child's family – all 'engaged in tailors work' – and when questioned about the circumstances could only explain that they were 'waiting . . . to raise the means of burying' the child. Wrack had similar experiences with the bodies of long-dead children in 17 Hope Street, Spitalfields (where the child had been decomposing for fifteen days) and in 28 King Street, Spitalfields.

48 White, *Rothschild Buildings*, pp. 6–7 (quoting James Greenwood, *Undercurrents*, p. 54).

49 Ibid., p. 11.

50 Whitechapel Board of Guardians, *Minutes*, 21 December 1875 and 25 January 1876; Whitechapel District Board of Works, *Minutes*, 10 April 1876, quoted in White, *Rothschild Buildings*, p. 11.

51 White, *Rothschild Buildings*, p. 11.

52 *Report of the Medical Officer of Health for Whitechapel District*, quarter ended 1 April 1876, quoted in White, *Rothschild Buildings*, p. 12.

53 White, *Rothschild Buildings*, p. 13.

17: The Children of the Ghetto

1 Edgar Samuel, 'London's Portuguese Jewish Community, 1540–1753', in *From Strangers to Citizens: The Integration of Immigrant Communities in Britain, Ireland and Colonial America, 1550–1750*, ed. Randolph Vigne and Charles Littleton, Sussex Academic Press/Huguenot Society, 2001, p. 240.

2 Ibid.

3 Ibid., p. 241.

4 Ibid.

5 Ibid.

6 Ibid., p. 244.

7 'Report of J. Mitchell, Esq., LL.D., on "The East of England"' for the House of Commons Parliamentary Commission on Hand-loom Weavers, vol. XXIII, 1840, p. 272.

8 Henry Mayhew, *London Labour and the London Poor*, vol. II, Dover Publications, 1968, p. 117.

9 Ibid.

10 Ibid., pp. 117–18.

11 Ibid., p. 124.

12 Ibid., p. 27.

13 William J. Fishman, *East End Jewish Radicals, 1875–1914* [1975], Five Leaves, 2004, p. 67. The *Jewish Chronicle* – described by Fishman as the 'mouthpiece'

of established Anglo-Jewry – had as early as March 1877 noted 'the very pleasing fact that there is a very material decrease in the number of poor foreign Jewish immigrants, and a very material increase in the poor Jews who have left this country to seek subsistence elsewhere' (pp. 64–5).

14 Jerry White, *Rothschild Buildings: Life in an East End Tenement Block, 1887–1920*, Routledge & Kegan Paul, 1980, pp. 17–18.

15 Ibid., p. 19.

16 See J. N. Tarn, *Five Per Cent Philanthropy: An Account of Housing in Urban Areas Between 1840 and 1914*, Cambridge University Press, 1973.

17 White, *Rothschild Buildings*, p. 21.

18 George Haw, *No Room to Live: The Plaint of Overcrowded London*, W. Gardner, Darton & Co., 1900, p. 9.

19 White, *Rothschild Buildings*, p. 24.

20 *The Times*, 1 September 1888.

21 Martin Fido, *The Crimes, Detection and Death of Jack the Ripper*, Weidenfeld & Nicolson, 1987, pp. 46–7; medical report in Coroner's Inquests, No. 135, Corporation of London Records.

22 Gillian Wagner, *Barnardo*, Weidenfeld & Nicolson, 1979, pp. 212–14.

23 Philip Sugden, *The Complete History of Jack the Ripper*, Robinson Publishing, 1994.

24 See for example Ivor Edwards, *Jack the Ripper's Black Magic Ritual*, John Blake, 2002, and Spiro Dimolianis, *Jack the Ripper and Black Magic*, McFarland & Company, 2011.

25 White, *Rothschild Buildings*, p. 27.

26 Ibid., pp. 29–30.

27 Israel Zangwill, *Children of the Ghetto*, 3 vols, Heinemann, 1892, vol. I, p. 1.

28 Ibid., pp. 2, 3.

29 Ibid., p. 14.

30 Ibid.

31 Ibid., pp. 19–20.

32 Ibid., p. 258.

33 Mayhew, *London Labour and the London Poor*, vol. II, p. 119.

34 Zangwill, *Children of the Ghetto*, vol. I, p. 7.

35 Ibid., pp. 258–9.

36 Robert Blatchford, *Dismal England*, Clarion Press, 1899. Henry Walker, *East London: Sketches of Christian Work and Workers*, the Religious Tract Society, London, 1896, pp. 62–5, quoted in Jerry White, *London in the Nineteenth Century*, Jonathan Cape, 2007, p. 129.

[37] Ibid., p. 130.

[38] Ibid.

18: Demolishing the 'Fever Dens'

[1] RG12, piece 256, folios 61-2, pp. 30-2.

[2] In the London Metropolitan Archives there is a map of the Nichol area, col-our-coded to indicate the condition of the existing houses, proposed demolitions and proposed uses for some of the land. Evidently the map was drawn up immediately prior to the clearance of the area, which started in 1893. House numbers are hand-written on house plans in 'Half Nichol's Street' and – if these are accurate – number 40 was on the south-east corner with 'Nichol's Row'. The house does not appear to be larger than its neighbours, although the two buildings to its south on 'Nichol's Row' (including a large rear structure) are not numbered and so perhaps also formed part of number 40. The house was not colour-coded for demolition. This map appears as an endpaper in the hardback edition of *The Blackest Streets* by Sarah Wise.

[3] Sarah Wise, *The Blackest Streets: The Life and Death of a Victorian Slum*, Bodley Head, 2008, p. 10.

[4] Henry Lazarus, *Landlordism: an illustration of the rise and spread of Slumland as evinced on the great estates of the great ground landlords of London*, General Publishing Company, 1892, p. 6; Wise, *The Blackest Streets*, p. 10. Lazarus goes on to say: '. . . there are none more hated (and well deserving to be hated) than the landlords of properties in the Slums. Landlords? Land-devils were an apter title for them. Without a care but to suck as fat a rental as the helpless dwellers can be made to yield, these curses of the poor batten upon the over-crowded hovels, neglect them, even *cultivate* their dilapidation' (pp. 43–4). Lazarus's particular targets were the aristocratic and institutional owners of London's slums – the Marquis of Camden, Lady Somerset, the Ecclesiastical Commissioners, the Skinners' Company (p. 6).

[5] *Pall Mall Gazette*, 16 October 1883; Wise, *The Blackest Streets*, p. 10.

[6] Wise, *The Blackest Streets*, p. 10.

[7] Ibid., p. 285.

[8] P. J. Keating, *The Working Classes in Victorian Fiction*, Routledge & Kegan Paul, 1971, p. 167.

[9] Robert Blatchford, 'On Realism', *My Favourite Books*, Clarion Press, 1900. See introduction and biographical note by Anita Miller in Arthur Morrison, *A Child of the Jago*, Academy Chicago, 1995, p. 163.

[10] H. G. Wells, 'A Slum Novel', *Saturday Review*, LXXXII, 28 November 1896;

Wise, *The Blackest Streets*, pp. 234, 310. It is interesting to contrast Wells's conclusion with other of his writings that are seemingly contradictory and in which he appears to support the controversial theories of eugenics and the benefits of good breeding and 'superior' races. See for example *Anticipations of the Reaction of Mechanical and Scientific Progress upon Human Life and Thought* of 1901. See also an admiring but anonymous review, 'How Realistic Fiction is Written: The Origin of The Child of the Jago', in the *St James's Gazette*, XXXIII, 2 December 1896.

11 Keating in *The Working Classes in Victorian Fiction* confirms that 'very little . . . is known about his early life [and] it seems reasonable to assume that at least some of his childhood was spent in the East End, but it is impossible to draw any definite conclusions about this period of his life', p. 167.

12 Diana Maltz, 'Arthur Morrison, Criminality, and Late-Victorian Maritime Subculture', 19: Interdisciplinary Studies in the Long Nineteenth Century, 2011 (13). DOI: http://doi.org/10.16995/ntn.624.

13 Quoted by P. J. Keating in his biographical study and introduction to *A Child of the Jago*, Panther, 1971, pp. 12–13.

14 Ibid., pp. 11–22.

15 Miller, introduction to *A Child of the Jago*, p. v.

16 Ibid., p. vi.

17 For Morrison's 1897 preface see *A Child of the Jago*, ed. Miller, pp. ix–xiv.

18 Keating, introduction and biographical study in *A Child of the Jago*, p. 24.

19 *Daily News*, 12 December 1896, and in 'The Methods of Mr Morrison', *Academy*, L, 12 December 1896, p. 531.

20 Sarah Wise in *London Fictions*, ed. Andrew Whitehead and Jerry White, Five Leaves, 2013, pp. 59–60.

21 Ibid., p. 61.

22 *New Review*, 16 March 1897, p. 332.

23 Wise in *London Fictions*, p. 60.

24 Sarah Wise, *The Blackest Streets*, pp. 99–100.

25 Miller, *A Child of the Jago*, ed. Miller, p. 80.

26 Ibid.

27 Ibid., p. 26.

28 Ibid., p. 31.

29 Raphael Samuel, *East End Underworld: Chapters in the Life of Arthur Harding*, Routledge & Kegan Paul, History Workshop Series, 1981, pp. 5–6.

30 Ibid., p. 17.

31 RG11, piece 433, folio 54–5, pp. 1–16.

32 RG09, piece 263, folio 54, p. 18.

33 'In 1899, the Chinese Ambassador was asked his opinion of Victorian London. He replied ... "too dirty". He was only stating the obvious. Thoroughfares were swamped with black mud, composed principally of horse dung, forming a tenacious glutinous paste; the air was peppered with soot, flakes of filth tumbling to the ground "in black Plutonian show'rs".' Lee Jackson, *Dirty Old London: The Victorian Fight Against Filth*, Yale University Press, 2014, p. 1; *Punch*, 30 December 1882.

34 Samuel, *East End Underworld*, p. 8.

35 The only parts of the Nichol to survive the mass clearance were the south side of Old Nichol's Street and to its south Redchurch Street, along with the connecting stub of 'Cross Street'/Chance Street and, to its west, York Street/Ebor Street. To the west of the Nichol area, the west side of Boundary Street also survived along with Boundary Passage, better known as the 'Posties'. To the east, the east side of 'Nichol's Row' survived, along with Club Row to the south of Redchurch Street. To the north destruction of the Nichol was complete, as far as Virginia Road/Row.

36 George Haw, *No Room to Live: The Plaint of Overcrowded London*, W. Gardner, Darton & Co., 1900, p. 49.

37 Jack London, *The People of the Abyss*, Macmillan, 1903, Chapter VI.

38 Preface in *A Child of the Jago*, ed. Miller, p. xiv.

19: Under the Microscope

1 The first fruit of Booth's toil was volume I, *Life and Labour of the People*, published in 1889; it was followed by volume II, *Labour and Life of the People*, in 1891. Booth realised the need for frequent updates, covering larger areas of the capital and responding to its rapid growth and change. So re-surveys were constant, leading to the nine-volume second edition *Life and Labour of the People in London* of 1892–7, with a seventeen-volume third edition appearing in 1902–3.

2 LSE reference: B351, pp. 94–5.

3 Ibid., pp. 96–7.

4 Ibid., pp. 98–9.

5 Ibid., pp. 100–1.

6 Ibid., pp. 102–3.

7 Ibid., pp. 104–5.

8 Ibid., pp. 106–7.

9 Ibid., pp. 108–9.

10 Ibid., pp. 110–11 plus 113a.

11 Ibid., pp. 118–19.

12 *Proceedings of the Old Bailey*, t18050702-42.

13 The photograph of 'Poole's Square' is published in Horace Warner, *Spitalfields Nippers*, Spitalfields Life Books, 2014, p. 59. The original photograph, probably taken in 1902, is inscribed on its back, in an old-fashioned hand, 'An open-air concert group. Poole's Sq. Quaker st.'

14 B351, pp. 122–3.

15 *Survey of London*, vol. XXVII: Spitalfields and Mile End New Town, ed. F. H. W. Sheppard, LCC, 1957, p. 75.

16 Fiona Rule, *The Worst Street in London*, Ian Allen, 2008, p. 93.

17 B351, pp. 124–5.

18 Three surviving houses are contenders for the location of Cooney's lodging houses – 25 and 27 Princelet Street along with the adjoining 65 Brick Lane.

19 Rule, *The Worst Street in London*, p. 150; a Mrs Elizabeth Cooney was licensee of the Weaver's Arms in 1910–11, according to the *London Post Office Directory*.

20 RG 12, piece 273, folio 137, p. 4.

21 RG12/273, district 4.

22 B351, pp. 126–7.

23 Ibid., pp. 128–9.

24 Ibid., pp. 130–1.

25 Ibid., pp. 134–5.

26 Ibid., pp. 136–7.

27 Ibid., pp. 148–9.

28 Ibid., pp. 154–5.

29 Ibid., pp. 156–7.

30 Ibid., pp. 158–9.

31 There is a 'King Street' shown on the 1872/3 Ordnance Survey map, running west of Brick Lane and roughly aligned with the site of the by then lost St John Street to the east of Brick Lane. 'King Street', located immediately south of Sclater Street, was narrow and looked on to the railway viaduct. By the time of the 1893 Ordnance Survey map 'King Street' had been demolished for widening of the railway tracks, and a short new version of St John's Street (now called Grimsby Street) had been constructed east of Brick Lane where it was crossed by the railway viaduct. It was presumably this street, truncated by railway development, which Booth walked down.

32 B351, pp. 160–1.

33 Ibid., pp. 162–3.

34 Ibid., pp. 168–9.

35 Ibid., pp. 176–7.

36 Ibid., pp. 170–1.

37 Ibid., pp, 172–3.

38 Ibid., pp. 174–5.

39 Ibid., pp. 178–9.

40 Ibid., pp. 180–1, 182, 183.

41 Ibid., pp. 182–3.

42 Ibid., pp. 184–5.

43 Ibid., pp. 196–7.

44 Ibid., pp. 198–9.

45 A copy is in Tower Hamlets Bancroft Road History Library.

46 Rule, *The Worst Street in London*, p. 197.

47 Ibid., pp. 197–8. McCarthy's two eldest daughters and their husbands continued to run lodging houses in Spitalfields.

20: People of Spitalfields

1 Clarice Stasz, *Jack London's Women*, University of Massachusetts Press, 2001, and Alex Kershaw, *Jack London: A Life*, HarperCollins, 1997, pp. 100–1.

2 Kershaw, *Jack London*, p. 114.

3 Ibid., p. 101.

4 *The Letters of Jack London*, vol. I: 1896–1905, ed. Earle Labor, Robert C. Leitz, and I. Milo Shepard, Stanford University Press, 1988, pp. 88, 123.

5 Kershaw, *Jack London*, p. 101.

6 *The Letters of Jack London*, ed. Labor, Leitz and Shepard, p. 89; and Kershaw, *Jack London*, p. 102, where a slightly differently worded version of the letter is given.

7 *The Letters of Jack London*, ed. Labor, Leitz and Shepard, p. 258.

8 Ibid., p. 302.

9 Ibid. pp. 303–4. The Coronation of Edward VII was scheduled to take place on 9 August so London knew he was on an unforgiving schedule.

10 *Round London*, George Newnes Ltd, 1896, p. 125.

11 The Wensley family archives at the Bishopsgate Institute. Information on William Thick (or Thicke) thanks to Gregg Morgan. Thick had been involved in the hunt for the Ripper and acquired his nickname for being an 'upright witness' and for 'fair and square dealing' with criminals. See *The Pall Mall Gazette*, 29th October 1891, 'London Night by Night' column, in which Thick was granted anonymity by being 'rechristened' Sergeant 'Quick'.

12 *The Letters of Jack London*, ed. Labor, Leitz and Shepard, pp. 305–9. The letter of 21 August is addressed from '89, Dempsey Street, Stepney, E., London'.

13 Ibid., p. 306.

14 Ibid., p. 310.

15 *The People of the Abyss*, Isbister & Co., 1903, opposite text on p. 54.

16 *The Eastern Fringe of the City: A Photographic Tour of the Bishopsgate Area in 1912*, Bishopsgate Institute, 1974.

17 *Jack London: Photographer*, ed. Jeanne Campbell Reesman, Sara S. Hodson and Philip Adam, University of Georgia Press, 2010. This book makes clear which of the photographs published in *The People of the Abyss* are by London, and shows his unpublished East London photographs. See also http://spital-fieldslife.com/2014/11/25/jack-london-photographer/

18 William J. Fishman and Nicholas Breach, *The Streets of East London*, Duckworth, 1987, pp. 124–5.

19 George Haw, *No Room to Live: The Plaint of Overcrowded London*, W. Gardner, Darton & Co., 1900, p. 62.

20 Howard Angus Kennedy, 'London's Social Settlements', in *From Strangers to Citizens: The Integration of Immigrant Communities in Britain, Ireland and Colonial America, 1550–1750*, ed. Randolph Vigne and Charles Littleton, Sussex Academic Press/Huguenot Society, 2001; in George R. Sims, ed., *Living London*, Cassell & Co., 1902, p. 267.

21 Charles Booth, *Life and Labour of the People in London*, vol. I: Poverty, Macmillan, 1902, pp. 66–7.

22 *The Letters of Jack London*, ed. Labor, Leitz and Shepard, p. 313.

23 Ibid., pp. 314–15.

24 Kershaw, *Jack London*, p. 122.

25 *The Letters of Jack London*, ed. Labor, Leitz and Shepard, pp. 317–22.

26 John Perry, *Jack London: An American Myth*, Nelson-Hall, 1981, pp. 195–7.

27 Ibid., p. 199.

28 David Mike Hamilton, *The Tools of My Trade: The Annotated Books in Jack London's Library*, University of Washington Press, 1986, pp. 17–18.

29 Other books London drew on, according to Hamilton, included Peter Kropotkin's *Fields, Factories and Workshops* (1898); Robert Blatchford's *Dismal England* (1899), and Edward Bowmaker's *The Housing of the Working Class* (1895). Other reading included Henry Salt's *Cruelties of Civilisation: A Programme of Human Reform* (1894–7).

30 Haw, *No Room to Live*, p. 18.

31 Ibid., p. 91.

32 Norman and Jeanne Mackenzie, *H. G. Wells: A Biography*, Simon and Schuster, 1973, p. 161.

33 Kershaw, *Jack London*, p. 120.

34 *The Letters of Jack London*, ed. Labor, Leitz and Shepard, pp. 330–1.

35 Kershaw, *Jack London*, p. 120.

36 Ibid.

37 'The Call of the Wild', *Toynbee Record*, July–September 1904, quoted in Asa Briggs and Anne McCartney, *Toynbee Hall: The First Hundred Years*, Routledge & Kegan Paul, 1984, p. 71.

38 Hamilton, *The Tools of My Trade*, pp. 17–18.

39 Kershaw, *Jack London*, p. 119. By the time *The People of the Abyss* was published in 1903 the paradoxical London had come up with an alternative origin for the book. It is a curious account that appears in some 1903 editions and brazenly contradicts London's own earlier letters. A brief introductory 'note' – seemingly based on an account that appeared in *T. P.'s Weekly* of 14 November 1902 – informs the reader that London's English publishers 'wrote and advised him to come to Europe and see something of the Old World, especially of the East End of London . . . this was sometime last Spring. He wrote from his home in California saying that he hoped to do it – some day. About five weeks ago he walked into the publishers' offices. They were delighted to see him, and asked him when he arrived in London. "About two months ago," was the reply. "But where have you been all the time?" "In the East End – down by the docks. This is the first call I have made." And it was a fact.'

40 Georgia Loring Bamford, *The Mystery of Jack London*, Holmes Book Company, 1931, pp. 130–1. On reading *The People of the Abyss*, Bamford recalls: '. . . it fell flat, I was disappointed not only in the book but in Jack London; it served no purpose and was not literature . . . it [was] simply "yellow journalism", an effort to pander to the sensational with nothing accomplished in the way of alleviating the distressing conditions depicted.'

21: World War and Civil Conflict

1 Emanuel Litvinoff, *Journey Through a Small Planet*, Penguin, 2008, p. 175; the book is edited by Patrick Wright and includes the 1966 essay 'A Jew in Britain'.

2 Ibid., pp. 20–1, 170.

3 Ibid., pp. 21–2.

4 Ibid., p. 22.

5 Ibid., p. 170.

6 Ibid., p. 28.

7 H. V. Morton, *The Heart of London*, Methuen, 1943, pp. 11–12.

8 Essay entitled 'Oriental' in *The Heart of London*, p. 58.

9 Thomas Burke and Pearl Binder, *The Real East End*, Constable & Co., 1932, p. 2.

10 Ibid., p. 16.

11 Ibid., p. 51.

12 Ashley Smith, *A City Stirs*, Chapman & Hall, 1939, p. 114.

13 Ibid., pp. 2–3.

14 Litvinoff, *Journey Through a Small Planet*, p. 173.

15 Ibid., pp. 181–3.

16 Ibid.

17 A. K. Sabin, *The Silk Weavers of Spitalfields and Bethnal Green*, Board of Education, 1931, pp. 18–19.

18 *Survey of London*, vol. XXVII, Spitalfields and Mile End New Town, ed. F. H. W. Sheppard, LCC, 1957, p. 68.

19 *The Times*, 11 November 1932.

20 Angus Calder, *The People's War, 1939–45*, Jonathan Cape, 1969, p. 184.

21 Ibid., pp. 184–5.

22 See Calder, *The People's War*; Harold Nicolson, *Diaries and Letters, 1939–45*, William Collins, 1967, p. 114. The entry is omitted in *The Harold Nicolson Diaries, 1907–1963*, Weidenfeld & Nicolson, 2004, edited by Nigel Nicolson.

23 Frank R. Lewey, *Cockney Campaign*, Stanley Paul & Co., c.1944, p. 46.

24 Author's observations and discoveries.

25 'Bombs in Stepney', bomb-damage map of Stepney, Tower Hamlets Archive, Local History Library, Bancroft Road.

26 Mickey Davis, *The Shelter of London*, 1944, quoted by Calder in *The People's War*, p. 183.

27 Peter Ritchie Calder, *Carry on London*, English Universities Press Ltd, 1941, pp. 36–43. See Calder, *The People's War*, p. 183; Angus Calder, *The Myth of the Blitz*, Jonathan Cape, London, 1991; Lewey, *Cockney Campaign*, foreword by Clement Atlee.

28 'Bombs in Stepney', bomb-damage map, Tower Hamlets Archives.

22: Decay and Recovery

1 *Survey of London*, vol. XXVII: Spitalfields and Mile End New Town, ed. F. H. W. Sheppard, LCC, 1957, pp. 55–72.

2 Edwin Heathcote, *Financial Times*, 4 January 2016.

3 The ceiling was repaired and reconstructed thanks to the campaign of the Hawksmoor Committee, founded 1962, using money from the sale of St John's, Smith Square. In 1976 the Friends of Christ Church initiated a repair and restoration programme that was not finally completed until 2004, with the organ not repaired until 2014.

4   Information from Sid Grimsey, in conversation with the author in the early 1980s, and John Grimsey in July 2014.

5   *Reggie Kray's East End Stories: The Lost Memoirs of the Gangland Legend*, Reggie Kray and Peter Gerrard, R. W. F. Howes Ltd, 2010, p. 84.

6   *Reggie Kray's East End Stories*, pp. 214–17.

7   Ed Glinert, *East End Chronicles*, Allen Lane, 2005, p. 281; Fergus Linnane, *London's Underworld: Three Centuries of Vice and Crime*, Robson Books, 2000. p. 175.

8   *Reggie Kray's East End Stories*, p. 175.

9   Ibid., p 117.

10 Ibid., p. 230.

11 Ibid., p. 190.

12 Information to author from Nick Hedges.

13 Jerry White, *Rothschild Buildings: Life in an East End Tenement Block, 1887–1920*, Routledge & Kegan Paul, 1980, p. xii.

14 Census of 1901, HMSO, 1902, pp. 10, 20, 34, quoted in Michael Keating, *The History of Spitalfields and its Communities*, University of East London, 1999.

15 Geoffrey Fletcher, *The London Nobody Knows*, Hutchinson, 1962, p. 84.

16 A DVD of the short 1969 film based on the book is available. Narrated by James Mason, it includes footage of Hanbury Street and the yard where Annie Chapman was murdered by Jack the Ripper.

17 Geoffrey Fletcher, *Pearly Kingdom*, Hutchinson, 1965, p. 86.

18 1991 Census County Report, HMSO, 1993, quoted in Keating, *The History of Spitalfields and its Communities*, p. 18.

19 *Survey of London*, vol. XXVII, pp. 110–11.

20 Detailed in Chiz Harward et al., *The Spitalfields Suburb, 1539–c.1880: Excavations at Spitalfields Market, London E1, 1991–2007*, Museum of London Archaeology, Monograph 61, 2015.

21 *Survey of London*, vol. XXVII, pp. 141–3.

22 *Evening Standard*, 4 March 2015. An M&G press release of 4 March 2015 states that 'following the completion of the acquisition M&G Real Estate and Exemplar will work in partnership to develop the site'.

23 Genesis 11:6.

Epilogue: Fort Street and the Ghosts of Spitalfields

1   Emanuel Litvinoff, *Journey Through a Small Planet*, Penguin, 2008, pp. 21, 175. This edition, edited by Patrick Wright, includes the 1966 essay 'A Jew in England'.

2   Ibid., 'A Long Look Back', pp. 192–3.

3   Chiz Harward et al., *The Spitalfields Suburb, 1539–c.1880: Excavations at*

Spitalfields Market, London E1, 1991–2007, Museum of London Archaeology, Monograph 61, 2015, p. 252.

4 The view is looking towards 22 Steward Street (c.1683) and 4 Fort Street (also c.1683) with 5 Fort Street, dating from c.1710, on the left – the view was made from the street outside 22/23 Fort Street. Number 24 Fort Street, a large house looking south down Steward Street, is just out of view on the right. London Metropolitan Archives SC/PZ/ST/01/89.

5 View by John Crowther in the London Metropolitan Archives, COLLAGE record number 18000.

6 These fronted south onto Fort Street and closed the prospect north along Duke Street (the surviving fragment of Duke Street south of Brushfield Street is now, most confusingly, named Fort Street). *Survey of London*, vol. XXVII: Spitalfields and Mile End New Town, ed. F. H. W. Sheppard, LCC, 1957, pp. 27, 32; Harward et al., *The Spitalfields Suburb*, p. 157.

7 MDR 1709/1/110.

8 Its rear yard, although short, was wider still because it extended slightly behind 25 Fort Street. The depth of the yard was limited because the boundary of the Old Artillery Yard was defined by the south elevation of the largely demolished and partly buried charnel house.

9 Harward et al., *The Spitalfields Suburb*, p. 164.

10 Ibid.

11 Ibid., pp. 164–5.

12 Harward et al., *The Spitalfields Suburb*, p. 166.

13 Guildhall Library MS 6005/45.

14 Guildhall Library MS 6005/46.

15 Guildhall Library MS 11936/449/846699.

16 Harward et al., *The Spitalfields Suburb*, p. 164.

17 Guildhall Library MS 6005/47–51.

18 Guildhall Library MS 6005/55.

19 Harward et al., *The Spitalfields Suburb*, p. 166.

20 Ibid.

21 Ibid.

22 Ibid.

23 Ibid., p. 167.

24 Ibid., pp. 170–1.

25 *Johnstone's* 1817: Guildhall Library MIC 96917.

26 TH L/OAG/1/2.

27 Guildhall Library MS 6473/4.

28 Census: NA HO/107/659/1 fos 25–27, 32–35, 41v. Directories: *Johnstone's London Commercial Guide and Street Directory* of 1817; *Robson's London Commercial Directory* of 1830; and *Robson's London Directory* of 1835, 1841. See also Harward et al., *The Spitalfields Suburb*, pp. 159–60.

29 Ibid., p. 160.

30 *Proceedings of the Old Bailey*, t18170115-106.

31 Ibid., t18190421-201.

32 See *Robson's London Commercial Directory* for 1825/6; Harward et al., *The Spitalfields Suburb*, p. 164.

33 London Metropolitan Archives, Middlesex Deed Register, 1709/1/110; Harward et al., *The Spitalfields Suburb*, p. 171.

34 Ibid.

35 The cesspit serving the privy was brick-lined, roughly square in section, about 1.7 metres across, 2 metres deep, and located to the rear yard of the house, descending in the angle formed by the wall and south-west buttress of the early-fourteenth-century charnel house. The wall and buttress survive so it is now possible to pinpoint the precise location of number 25's cesspit.

36 Harward et al., *The Spitalfields Suburb*, pp. 171–2.

37 Guildhall Library MS 6473/3 13 November 1823; Harward et al., *The Spitalfields Suburb*, p. 172.

38 This is known from an obituary placed in *The Times* by '. . . James Vernell, of Fort Street . . .' on 12 April 1819, p. 3, issue 10645, col. E; Harward et al., *The Spitalfields Suburb*, p. 172.

39 *Proceedings of the Old Bailey*, t18101205-28.

40 Ibid., t18160918-108.

41 Ibid., t18161030-21.

42 Harward et al., *The Spitalfields Suburb*, p. 172.

43 *Proceedings of the Old Bailey*, t18161030-22.

44 Ibid., t18180114-170.

45 *The Times*, 21 March 1833, p. 3, issue 15118, col. A.

46 L. Stewart and P. Weindling, 'Philosophical Threads', *British Journal of Historical Science*, 28, 1995, pp. 37–62.

47 TNA PROB 11/1911; Harward et al., *The Spitalfields Suburb*, p. 172.

48 THLHLA, P08074; *The Spitalfields Suburb*, p. 188.

49 SC/PHL/01/338(F2344); *The Spitalfields Suburb*, p. 178.

50 *Survey of London*, vol. XXVII, pp. 35–6, records 28 Steward Street. This was a fine, double-fronted house built under a seventy-one-year building lease granted in May 1755 by J. B. Parson and Charles Lanoe to Jacob and John

Delamare, silk merchants. This house, on the west side of the street, was described as 'dilapidated' in 1957 and had been demolished by c.1960. A detail of its ground floor with doorcase, taken c.1925, is published in *The Saving of Spitalfields*, Spitalfields Trust, London, 1989. This photograph reveals the high architectural quality of the building and its then state of neglect.

Appendix

1 Although silk-weaving was certainly in serious decline by the 1850s, the 1851 census reveals there were still quite a few exponents in Norton Folgate. For example, fifty-nine-year-old George Pickard, in 1 Elder Court off Elder Street, was a weaver, along with his wife and three older children, as were thirty-one-year-old Sarah Jones of 3 Blossom Street, fifty-one-year-old Mary Bay and her daughter in 2 Fleur de Lis Street (both of whom are listed as 'hand loom Silk weaveresses'), forty-five-year-old William Webb and his wife and two daughters at 8 Elder Street, and thirty-two-year-old William Gorbould, of 11 Elder Street, who was of Huguenot descent. Of considerable interest are sixty-five-year-old James Gammon and his son-in-law William Endersby at 1 Elder Street (now 36), both of whom were listed as 'silk weavers', who no doubt used the weaving garret that still survives. James Gammon was already established at 1 Elder Street as a silk weaver by 1841, when he appears in the first census. Interestingly, the area's remaining working weavers tended to occupy the more humble buildings or locations in Spitalfields and – perhaps predictably and sensibly – used those old houses furnished with wide-windowed weaving workshops or garrets. The 1861 census records James Gammon, aged seventy-five, still weaving at 1 Elder Street. Other silk weavers included Michael Gouldon, aged forty-five, with his wife and daughter at 8 Elder Street; Ann Grey, aged fifty-two at 9 Elder Street; Thomas Kendall, aged sixty-six, his wife and two daughters at 3 Fleur de Lis Street, and Eliza Spear, aged forty-six, at 10 Blossom Street. Sophie Hyams, a sixty-nine-year-old 'Silk Winder', had rooms in 22 Elder Street, on the corner with White Lion Street. By 1871 virtually all trace of the silk industry had disappeared, with weaving and silk-winding being replaced by the humbler, far less skilled and more mechanised occupations of laundress and 'machinist'. Even so there were a few poignant survivals. Michael Gouldeau (or Gouldon), aged fifty-five, still worked in 'Silk Manufacture' in 8 Elder Street; Susannah Taylor, aged forty-eight, still wound silk in 3 Elder Street (now 32). And James Gammond (or Gammon), aged eighty-five, still lived in part of 1 Elder Street, although he was now a widower and, according to the census, a 'Retired silk

weaver'. Gammon, as might be expected, does not appear in the 1881 census. And in the 1881 census the silk trade is conspicuous by its absence. The very few references are to veteran residents of the Liberty, who appear almost as ghosts from a bygone age. Hannah (or Susannah) Taylor, aged sixty, still lived at 32 Elder Street (formerly 3) and still described her occupation as a 'silk winder', but who in Spitalfields can she have wound silk for in 1881? At 36 Elder Street (formerly 1) William Endersley, James Gammon's son-in-law and now aged sixty-eight, remained in residence and continued to describe himself as a silk-weaver. But he must have been living in very straightened and curtailed circumstances, for the house, which numbered about twelve rooms including basement, small closets and garret, contained sixteen people on the day of the census. No doubt Endersley was supported by his sixty-nine-year-old wife Elizabeth and his thirty-year-old unmarried daughter Ann who toiled as seamstresses. Such was the sad fate that befell the weaving families who lingered in Spitalfields.

2 Quoted in Ian McAuley, *Guide to Ethnic London*, Immel Publishing, 1993, p. 124.

3 The Valuation Office records from 1912, compiled by the Inland Revenue and now in the National Archives, shed a little further light on the houses of Elder Street. The 'Gross value Land and buildings' of number 5 was £12 and its 'Rateable value land and buildings' was £9. The 'Gross Value land and building' of number 15 was £40 and its 'Rateable Value land and building' £35, the owner of the 'Freehold interest' being Winifred A. Tillard and the 'Subordinate Interest' being a lease of forty-two years in 1886' with 'g.r.' (the 'ground rent') being £32. Number 15 is described as an 'Old Building, 3 floors [in fact, four floors] & Basement, Front sound but back only weatherboarded.' Its 'Market Value of Fee Simple . . . in present condition' was estimated at £525 (IR 58 N9035 84558). Number 17 had a 'Gross Value' of £32, a 'Rateable Value' of £26, was occupied on a weekly tenancy of eighteen shillings rent and was described as an 'Old plain house, 3 stories [again, incorrect] & basement. Good Order.' It was valued in its 'present condition' at £400. Number 19 had four separate entries, presumably reflecting a division into four households. The 'Gross Value' of 19 Elder Street sub-divisions ranged from £0 to £7 and 'Rateable Value' from £4; the rents paid for the weekly tenancies included two at five shillings and sixpence, one at five shillings and one at three. The house was described as an 'Old Building, 3 floors & basement similar to 17 . . .' and valued in its 'present condition' at £400.

4 Raphael Samuel, *East End Underworld: Chapters in the Life of Arthur Harding*, Routledge & Kegan Paul, History Workshop Series, 1981, pp. 111–12.

BIBLIOGRAPHY

——◆·◆——

Below is a list of books, grouped by subject, that have been essential reading. Additional books, newspaper and periodical articles, manuscripts and archives are listed in the notes.

Archaeology

Cox, Margaret, *Life and Death in Spitalfields, 1700–1850*, Council for British Archaeology, 1996.

Harward, Chiz et al., *The Spitalfields Suburb, 1539–c.1880: Excavations at Spitalfields Market, London E1, 1991–7*, Museum of London Archaeology, Monograph 61, 2015.

Molleson, Theya, and Cox, Margaret, with Waldron, A. H., and Whittaker, D. K., *The Spitalfields Project, Vol. 2: The Anthropology – The Middling Sort*, Council for British Archaeology, 1993.

Reeve, Jez, and Adams, Max, *The Spitalfields Project, Vol. 1: The Archaeology – Across the Styx*, Council for British Archaeology, 1993.

Thomas, Chris, *Life and Death in London's East End: 2000 Years at Spitalfields*, Museum of London Archaeology, 2004.

Thomas, Chris, Sloane, B., and Phillpotts, C., *Excavations at the Priory and Hospital of St Mary Spital, London*, Museum of London Archaeology, Monograph 1, 1997.

Architecture, Urban History and Local Government

Brett-James, Norman G., *The Growth of Stuart London*, George Allen & Unwin, 1935.

Girouard, Mark, 'Local Government in Spitalfields in the Eighteenth Century' in Girouard et al., *The Saving of Spitalfields*, Spitalfields Trust, 1989.

Guillery, Peter, *The Small House in Eighteenth-Century London: A Social and Architectural History*, Yale University Press, 2004.

White, Jerry, *Rothschild Buildings: Life in an East End Tenement Block, 1887–1920*, Routledge & Kegan Paul, 1980.

East End Poverty, Crime and Philanthropy

Bartlett, David W., *What I Saw in London: or, Men and Things in the Great Metropolis*, Derby & Miller, 1852.

Blatchford, Robert, *Dismal England*, Clarion Press, 1899.

Booth, Charles, *Life and Labour of the People*, vol. I, Macmillan, 1889; *Labour and Life of the People*, vol. II, Macmillan, 1891; *Life and Labour of the People in London*, 9 vols, Macmillan, 1892–7.

Fayle, J., *The Spitalfields Genius: The Story of William Allen*, Hodder & Stoughton, 1884.

Fido, Martin, *The Crimes, Detection and Death of Jack the Ripper*, Weidenfeld & Nicolson, 1987.

Gavin, Hector, *Sanitary Ramblings: Being Sketches and Illustrations of Bethnal Green*, Churchill, 1848.

Greenwood, James, *In Strange Company: Being the experiences of a roving correspondent*, Vizetelly & Co., 1883.

Haw, George, *No Room to Live: The Plaint of Overcrowded London*, W. Gardner, Darton & Co., 1900.

Lazarus, Henry, *Landlordism: an illustration of the rise and spread of Slumland as evinced on the great estates of the great ground landlords of London*, General Publishing Company, 1892.

Lichtenstein, Rachel, and Sinclair, Iain, *Rodinsky's Room*, Granta, 1999.

London, Jack, *The People of the Abyss*, 1903. Several editions published by Macmillan and Isbister & Co., some without illustrations. Illustrations vary between US and UK editions.

Mearns, Andrew, *The Bitter Cry of Outcast London: An Inquiry into the Condition of the Abject Poor*, James Clarke & Co., 1883.

Rule, Fiona, *The Worst Street in London*, Ian Allen, 2008.

Samuel, Raphael, *East End Underworld: Chapters in the Life of Arthur Harding*, Routledge & Kegan Paul, History Workshop Series, 1981.

Sims, George, *How the Poor Live; and, Horrible London*, Chatto & Windus, 1883.

Veder, Robin, 'Flowers in the Slums: Weavers' Floristry in the Age of Spitalfields' Decline', *Journal of Victorian Culture*, 14, 2, 2009.

Warner, Horace, *Spitalfields Nippers*, Bedford Institute Association, 1975.

Warner, Horace, *Spitalfields Nippers*, Spitalfields Life Books, 2014.

Wise, Sarah, *The Blackest Streets: The Life and Death of a Victorian Slum*, Bodley Head, 2008.

Wise, Sarah, *The Italian Boy: Murder and Grave-Robbery in 1830s London*, Jonathan Cape, 2004.

Histories

Archer, Thomas, *The Pauper, the Thief and the Convict*, Groombridge & Sons, 1865.

Bucholz, Robert O., and Ward, Joseph P., *London: A Social and Cultural History, 1550–1750*, Cambridge University Press, 2012.

Burke, Thomas, and Binder, Pearl, *The Real East End*, Constable & Co., 1932.

Calder, Angus, *The People's War: Britain, 1939–45*, Jonathan Cape, 1969.

Dyos, H. J., and Wolff, Michael, eds, *The Victorian City: Images and Realities*, 2 vols, Routledge & Kegan Paul, 1973.

F. H. W. Sheppard, ed., *Survey of London*, vol. XXVII: Spitalfields and Mile End New Town, LCC, 1957.

Fishman, William J. and Breach, Nicholas, *The Streets of East London*, Duckworth, 1987.

Fishman, William J., *East End Jewish Radicals, 1875–1914* [1975], Five Leaves, 2004.

Fletcher, Geoffrey, *Pearly Kingdom*, Hutchinson, 1965.

Fletcher, Geoffrey, *The London Nobody Knows*, Hutchinson, 1962.

George, M. Dorothy, *London Life in the Eighteenth Century*, Kegan Paul, 1925.

German, Lindsey, and Rees, John, *A People's History of London*, Verso, 2012.

House of Commons Parliamentary Commission on Hand-loom Weavers, Parliamentary Sessional Paper, 43 (1), vols XXIII and XXIV, 1840.

Jackson, Lee, *Dirty Old London: The Victorian Fight Against Filth*, Yale University Press, 2014.

Keating, Michael, *The History of Spitalfields and its Communities*, University of East London, 1999.

Keating, P. J., *The Working Classes in Victorian Fiction*, Routledge & Kegan Paul, 1971.

Knight, Charles, ed., *London*, vol. XI, Charles Knight & Co. 1842.

Lewey, Frank R., *Cockney Campaign*, Stanley Paul & Co., c.1944.

Linebaugh, Peter, *The London Hanged: Crime and Civil Society in the Eighteenth Century*, Allen Lane, 1991.

Litvinoff, Emanuel, *Journey Through a Small Planet*, Penguin, 2008, with introduction by Patrick Wright.

Mayhew, Henry, *London Labour and the London Poor*, vols I, II and III, Frank Cass & Co., 1851; vol. IV, Charles Griffin & Co., 1861.

Morton, H. V., *The Heart of London*, Methuen, 1943.

Ritchie Calder, Peter, *Carry on London*, English Universities Press Ltd., 1941

Seymour, Robert, *Survey of the cities of London and Westminster, Borough of Southwark*, 1734–5, vol. II, book VI.

Stow, John, *A Survey of London*. Reprint of text of 1603 edition, introduction and notes by Charles Lethbridge, Clarendon Press, 1908.

Strype, John, *Survey of London and Westminster*, 1720.

Thompson, E. P., and Yeo, Eileen, eds, *The Unknown Mayhew: Selections from the Morning Chronicle*, Penguin, 1984.

Victoria County History, *A History of the County of Middlesex*, vol. II: General, ed. W. Page, 1911; vol. XI: Stepney and Bethnal Green, ed. T. F. T. Baker, 1998.

Vigne, Randolph, and Littleton, Charles, eds, *From Strangers to Citizens: The Integration of Immigrant Communities in Britain, Ireland and Colonial America, 1550–1750*, Sussex Academic Press/Huguenot Society, 2001.

Whitehead, Andrew, and White, Jerry, eds, *London Fictions*, Five Leaves, 2013.

Huguenots and Silk Weaving

Flanagan, J. F., *Spitalfields Silks in the Eighteenth and Nineteenth Centuries*, F. Lewis, 1954.

Gwynn, Robin D., *Huguenot Heritage: The History and Contribution of the Huguenots in Britain*, Sussex Academic Press [1984], 2000.

Hale, William, *An Appeal to the Public in Defence of the Spitalfields Act*, E. Justins, 1822.

Irene Scouloudi, ed., *Huguenots in Britain and their French Background, 1550–1800*, Macmillan, 1987.

Kershen, Anne J., *Strangers, Aliens and Asians: Huguenots, Jews and Bangladeshis in Spitalfields, 1660–2000*, Routledge, 2005.

Murdoch, Tessa, *The Quiet Conquest: Huguenots, 1685–1985*, Museum of London catalogue, 1985.

Observations on the Ruinous tendency of the Spitalfields Act to the silk manufacture of London, J. & A. Arch, 1822, British Library, 8245 D 43.

Rothstein, Natalie, *Spitalfields Silk*, V&A, HMSO, 1975.

Sabin, A. K., *The Silk Weavers of Spitalfields and Bethnal Green*, Board of Education, 1931.

Novels

Defoe, Daniel, *A Journal of the Plague Year* [1722], Falcon Press, 1950.

Morrison, Arthur, *A Child of the Jago* [1896], ed. Anita Miller, Academy Chicago, 1995.

Zangwill, Israel, *Children of the Ghetto*, 3 vols, Heinemann, 1892.

Tudor and Jacobean 'Outsiders'

Jardine, Lisa, and Stewart, Alan, *Hostage to Fortune: The Troubled Life of Francis Bacon*, Victor Gollancz, 1998.

Ordish, Thomas Fairman, *Early London Theatres: In the Fields*, Elliot Stock, 1899.

Redworth, Glyn, *The She-Apostle: The Extraordinary Life and Death of Luisa de Carvajal*, Oxford University Press, 2008.

Rees, Margaret A., *The Writings of Doña Luisa de Carvajal y Mendoza*, Edwin Mellen Press, 2002.

Yates, Frances, *The Occult Philosophy in the Elizabethan Age*, Routledge, 2001 edn.

INDEX

◆ ◆ ◆

Page numbers in *italics* denote illustrations.

Dan Cruickshank

The Secret History of Georgian London: How the Wages of Sin Shaped the Capital

'This is a colossal melting pot of a book: ambitious, rigorously
researched, vigorously narrated and marvellously illustrated.
All of life is here, but not as we know it'
SUNDAY TIMES

Georgian London evokes images of elegant buildings and fine
art, but it was also a city where prostitution was rife, houses of
ill repute widespread, and many tens of thousands of people
dependent in some way or other on the wages of sin. The sex
industry was, in fact, a very powerful force indeed, and in The
Secret History of Georgian London, Dan Cruickshank compellingly
shows how it came to affect almost every aspect of life and
culture in the capital.

Examining the nature of the sex trade, he offers a tantalising
insight into the impact of prostitution to give us vivid portraits
of some of the women who became involved in its world. And
he discusses the very varied attitudes of contemporaries –
those who sympathised, those who indulged, and those who
condemned. As he powerfully argues, these women, and many
thousands like them, not only shaped eighteenth-century
London, they also helped determine its future development.

'Fascinating'
DAILY MAIL

'I heartily recommend this scholarly romp'
A.N. WILSON, READER'S DIGEST

'Belle de Jour for the 18th century. Funny, fantastical, full of impossible facts
and scandalous stories. Scholarly, but also the ideal stocking
(and suspender) filler'
JEANETTE WINTERSON, GUARDIAN

Newport Community
Learning & Libraries